AUSTRALIAN DICTIONARY

OF BIOGRAPHY

General Editor
JOHN RITCHIE

AUSTRALIAN DICTIONARY OF BIOGRAPHY

INDEX: VOLUMES 1 to 12

1788-1939

General Editor
JOHN RITCHIE

Deputy General Editor
CHRISTOPHER CUNNEEN

Index Editor
HILARY KENT

MELBOURNE UNIVERSITY PRESS

First published 1991

Typeset by Abb-typesetting Pty Ltd
Printed in Australia by Brown Prior Anderson Pty Ltd,
Burwood, Victoria, for
Melbourne University Press, Carlton, Victoria 3053
U.S.A. and Canada: International Specialized Book Services, Inc.,
5602 NE Hassalo Street, Portland, Oregon 97213-3640
United Kingdom, Ireland and Europe: Europa Publications Limited
18 Bedford Square, London WC1B 3JN

© Melbourne University Press   1991

National Library of Australia Cataloguing-in-Publication entry

Australian dictionary of biography. Index. Volumes 1 to 12 (1788–
1939).

Bibliography.
ISBN 0 522 84459 6.
ISBN 0 522 84236 4 (set).

1. Australian dictionary of biography—Indexes. 2. Australia—
Biography—Dictionaries—Indexes. 3. Australia—History—
1788–1900—Indexes. 4. Australia—History—1901–1945—Indexes.
I. Ritchie, John, 1941-   . II. Cunneen, Christopher, 1940-   .
III. Kent, Hilary.

920.094

PREFACE

To compile an index to a single book is arduous; to compile an index to twelve volumes is herculean. The *Australian Dictionary of Biography* published its first volume in 1966 and its twelfth in 1990. Volumes 1 and 2 deal with people prominent between 1788 and 1850, Volumes 3 to 6 with persons who flourished in the period 1851-1890, and Volumes 7 to 12 with those whose careers reached a peak in the years 1891 to 1939. In total, the twelve volumes run to 7104 pages of text with two columns per page. This index contains references to the names of 10 442 individuals, including the 7211 major entries in the *A.D.B.*, as well as every minor (small-capped) entry and many lesser ones. It also divides these people into 379 separate occupational categories. It further sets out the 61 different countries in which they were born, subdividing these places into states or counties, cities or towns, villages or pastoral stations. The index is by no means all-encompassing, but concentrates on who the people were, where they came from and the work they did. It took Hilary Kent eighteen months (part time) of dedicated effort to complete her index. In so doing, she had to read and analyse each volume, to differentiate between every name (there are no fewer than eighty-seven Smiths, and eleven of them are William), to re-check all birthplaces and to examine a host of occupations. Hers is a monumental achievement.

Included in this volume is a consolidated corrigenda. In compiling it, Darryl Bennet —with assistance from Suzanne Edgar—had to re-examine every correction to the *A.D.B.* published between 1967 and 1990, together with some previously unpublished, to integrate them by name and volume, and even on occasion to make corrections to the corrections. His part-time work took months of care and effort; the result is a tribute to his scholarship, and to his patience.

J.R.

CONTENTS

Preface   v

Committees   ix

Introduction   xi

Select Bibliography   xv

Names   1

Places of Birth   87

Occupations   166

Consolidated Corrigenda   287

COMMITTEES

EDITORIAL BOARD

D. W. A. Baker; G. C. Bolton; P. F. Bourke; K. J. Cable; C. M. H. Clark; C. Cunneen; Ann Curthoys; C. Hazlehurst; K. S. Inglis (chair); W. R. Johnston; Lenore Layman; N. B. Nairn; G. M. Neutze; R. J. O'Neill; J. D. Playford; C. Plowman; J. R. Poynter; Heather Radi; J. D. Ritchie; Jill Roe; O. M. Roe; A. G. Serle; A. G. L. Shaw; G. Souter; R. B. Ward; D. J. Whalan.

SECTION EDITORS

G. C. Bolton; C. Hazlehurst; W. R. Johnston; R. J. O'Neill; J. D. Playford; Heather Radi; Jill Roe; O. M. Roe; A. G. Serle.

ADB STAFF

D. T. Bennet; Wendy Birman; Helen Boxall; F. H. Brown; G. R. Browne; Martha Campbell; Suzanne Edgar; Anne-Marie Gaudry; Joyce Gibberd; Emma Grahame; Helga Griffin; Jennifer Harrison; Edna Kauffman; Hilary Kent; Diane Langmore; Ivy Meere; Sally O'Neill; Anne Rand; Margaret Steven; Sheila Tilse and S. J. Trigellis-Smith.

WORKING PARTIES

Armed Services
F. H. Brown; P. Burness; C. D. Coulthard-Clark; P. Dennis; B. Eaton; P. G. Edwards; W. D. H. Graham; A. J. Hill (chair); D. M. Horner; J. McCarthy; Perditta McCarthy; A. L. Morrison; A. J. Sweeting.

Commonwealth
C. Hazlehurst (chair); J. Ann Hone; C. Hughes; Anthea Hyslop; Margot Kerley; C. J. Lloyd; G. Powell; J. Zubrzycki.

New South Wales
J. M. Bennett; K. J. Cable; J. J. Carmody; Alison Crook (chair); C. Cunneen; R. Curnow; Ann Curthoys; F. Farrell; S. Garton; E. M. Goot; Beverley Kingston; Ann Moyal; N. B. Nairn; Heather Radi; Jill Roe; G. Souter; G. P. Walsh.

Queensland
Nancy Bonnin; M. D. Cross; Helen Gregory; I. F. Jobling; W. R. Johnston (chair); G. N. Logan; R. I. Longhurst; Lorna McDonald; Margaret O'Hagan; S. J. Routh; C. G. Sheehan; V. T. Vallis.

South Australia
Joyce Gibberd; R. M. Gibbs; P. A. Howell; Helen Jones; J. H. Love; Susan Marsden; J. D. Playford (chair); Patricia Stretton; R. E. Thornton; J. M. Tregenza.

INTRODUCTION

The need for an index to the *Australian Dictionary of Biography* has long been apparent. Reviewers and librarians have frequently suggested that an index would overcome the difficulties created for readers, especially more casual users, by the *A.D.B.*'s use of periods and by its arrangement of biographies on the *floruit* principle. In addition, researchers have drawn attention to a range of untapped information contained in the biographies, some of which can cast light on people's jobs and origins. Successive *A.D.B.* editorial boards decided that the original project's twelve volumes should be completed before an integrated index was produced.

Following a seminar at the Australian National University's Research School of Social Sciences in July 1988, a proposal was submitted to the *A.D.B.*'s editorial board for the preparation of an index containing three separate elements: names, places of birth and occupations. The proposal took into account the frequency and content of requests addressed to the *A.D.B.*; the views expressed at the seminar and by other interested parties; and pragmatic considerations, such as the likely levels of use, the wish to produce a volume of comparable quality and appearance to the regular volumes, a publishing deadline and resource constraints. The board gave its agreement and detailed work began in July 1989.

NAMES

The index to names is designed to remove any confusion arising from periodization and the *floruit* principle. It lists in one consolidated, alphabetical compilation all major and minor (small-capped) entries appearing in Volumes 1 to 12 of the *Australian Dictionary of Biography*, together with the names of other persons about whom information is contained in the text. The index is not, however, a concordance, and the lesser names were subject to selection criteria: three lines of text and two pieces of data were the basic requirements for their inclusion.

Where more than one reference to an individual is listed, the principal entry appears in bold type. Life dates have been used to distinguish between identical or largely similar names. Where full life dates were not available, identifying qualifiers have followed a hierarchy of abbreviated life dates, *floruit*, arrival dates, departure dates and occupations. Cross-references have been used to help the reader with pseudonyms, aliases and commonly-used names. Space precluded the cross-referencing of all married women to their maiden names, except in those cases where information in the text related to activities carried out under more than one name.

PLACES OF BIRTH

The places of birth index lists the birthplaces, where known, of all major and small-capped entries in Volumes 1 to 12, omitting those for whom place-of-birth information is unclear, or simply unavailable. Entries in the index have been affected by the changes in political geography during the period (1788-1939) covered by Volumes 1 to 12. As a result, it was necessary to devise a scheme which allowed, as far as possible, the retention of historical accuracy for the date of birth, while providing ease of access for contemporary readers. Arrangement of this section of the index is therefore by country, corrected to the date of birth. Those countries which comprise the largest number of entries (for example, Australia and England) are further broken down where possible by State or county and by town. The geographical areas which now form part of the modern states of Italy and Germany have been grouped under those umbrella headings, but are qualified by sub-headings which denote past provinces, states or political entities (such as Papal States).

OCCUPATIONS

Each year our office receives a large number of requests for information about the occupations of people whose biographies appear in the *A.D.B.* Research students, in particular, often frame their topics around some type of occupational grouping. The preparation of a consolidated occupational listing which covers almost two centuries of social and technological change presented some difficulties. Even at the most basic level there were problems associated with changes in the meaning and usage of language—both the language of the worlds of commerce and work, and the language used by historians over some twenty-five years of writing. Such problems were exacerbated by the tension between the underlying aims of the *A.D.B.* and those of the index. The *A.D.B.* celebrates and emphasizes the individuality and difference of its biographical subjects, whereas an index is concerned with similarities and the need to categorize individual efforts and achievements as parts of larger wholes.

The indexing practices of other national biographical dictionaries were examined, as were previous collations of the occupational information in the *A.D.B.* None of them provided a framework or model suitable for a comprehensive index. Nor was it possible to adopt the categories used in the standard classification of occupations developed by Australian statisticians: such categories are concerned with occupations at one fixed point and are not designed to cover two centuries of change, or the whole work experience of one individual's lifetime.

The occupations index attempts to standardize and categorize jobs, professions, and social and cultural activities to a degree that makes the listing useful as a tool for historical research. It therefore includes entries such as 'Women's rights activist' and 'Community leader, Chinese', though strictly speaking neither is an occupation. It also attempts to tease out the full range of occupational experience to be found in the *A.D.B.* For example, every individual who served as a soldier during the Great War is listed as 'Soldier, World War I', rather than limiting the list only to those who appear in the *A.D.B.* because of their achievement in that war. Accordingly, it follows that an individual may be, and usually is, listed under more than one category. On average, each individual has two listings, but there are a few special cases with as many as five.

In general terms the occupations index is arranged alphabetically, with names rather than page numbers as reference points. Cross-references are provided to guide the user through alternative nomenclature and to indicate related occupations. Where possible, very large groups have been qualified in some way: pastoralists and politicians are divided by State, clergy by denomination, manufacturers by product, and soldiers by conflict. A complete list of categories appears at the front of the occupations index. An asterisk after an individual's name indicates that he or she was also an elected politician after the introduction of responsible government.

DATABASE

Additional material not published in this index is held in the *A.D.B.*'s computer database and is available to researchers. It already contains information on religious observance, militia involvement, freemasonry and gender. Eventually it is planned to expand the database to include business firms, schools, universities, clubs, societies and other organizations.

No enterprise on this scale is a solo effort and thanks are due to many people. Barry Howarth generously shared the results of his earlier work on birthplaces for Volumes 1 to 6. Helen Boxall did most of the research on European place names and, together with Darryl Bennet and Sheila Tilse, helped with additional research and keyboarding. The general editor, John Ritchie, was always available to discuss problems; he gave helpful advice and assisted with proof-reading. Mac Boot, Martha Campbell, Chris Coulthard-Clark, Chris Cunneen, Ann Curthoys, Robert Hyslop, Bruce Kent, Gino Moliterno, John Merritt, John Molony, John Mulvaney, Peter Read, Geoffrey Serle, Barry Smith and Margaret Steven also provided expert advice. Suzanne Edgar, Anne-Marie Gaudry, Helga Griffin, Edna Kauffman, Diane Langmore and Ivy Meere helped with proof-reading. The indomitable Daniel Fritsch kept the computer alive, a crucial and, at times, demanding task.

HILARY KENT

SELECT BIBLIOGRAPHY

APAIS Thesaurus: A list of subject terms used in the Australian Public Affairs Information Service, 4th edition, Canberra, 1990.

Australian Bicentennial Historic Records Search, *Thesaurus*, Canberra, 1988.

Australian Bureau of Statistics, *Australian Standard Classification of Occupations*, Canberra, 1986.

Les Blake, *Place Names of Victoria*, Adelaide, 1976.

G. G. Chisholm, *The Times Gazetteer of the World*, London, 1899.

H. C. Darby and H. Fullard, *The New Cambridge Modern History Atlas*, London, 1970.

E. C. Gleeson, *List of Localities in New South Wales*, Sydney, 1954.

N. E. S. A. Hamilton, *The National Gazetteer of Great Britain and Ireland*, 12 vols, London, 1864.

Index to the Townland, and Towns, Parishes and Baronies of Ireland, 1851, Dublin, 1984.

Department of Interior, *Gazetteer No 40: Australia*, Washington, 1957.

B. and B. Kennedy, *Australian Place Names*, Sydney, 1988.

Library of Congress Subject Cataloguing Division, *Library of Congress Subject Headings*, 11th edition, Washington, 1988.

J. G. Marshall and R. C. S. Trahair, *Occupational Index to the Australian Dictionary of Biography (1788-1890)*, La Trobe Working Papers in Sociology No 43, Bundoora, 1979.

J. G. Marshall and R. C. S. Trahair, *Occupational Index to the Australian Dictionary of Biography (1891-1939) Volumes VII-IX A-Las*, Latrobe Working Papers in Sociology No 71, Bundoora, 1985.

A. E. Martin, *Place Names in Victoria and Tasmania*, Sydney, 1944.

R. W. Munro, *Johnston's Gazetteer of Scotland*, Edinburgh, 1937.

Department of Minerals and Energy, *Australia 1:250,000 Map Series Gazetteer*, Canberra, 1975.

W. H. Oliver (ed.), *The Dictionary of New Zealand Biography*, Volume One, 1769-1869, Department of Internal Affairs, Wellington, 1990.

Penguin Atlas of World History, London, 1978.

K. S. Pinson, *Modern Germany*, New York, 1966.

R. Praite and J. C. Tolley, *Place Names of South Australia*, Adelaide, 1970.

Reader's Digest Atlas of Australia, Sydney, 1977.

G. Grant Robertson and J. G. Bartholomew, *An Historical Atlas of Modern Europe from 1789 to 1922*, London, 1924.

Royal Geographical Society, *A Gazetteer of the World*, Edinburgh, 1853.

Surveyor-General's Office, *Register of Place Names in Victoria*, Melbourne, 1983.

The Times Index–Gazetteer, London, 1965.

The Times Atlas of the World, London, 1988.

R. P. Whitworth, *Bailliere's Gazetteer of New South Wales*, Melbourne, 1866.

R. P. Whitworth, *Bailliere's Tasmanian Gazetteer and Road Guide*, Melbourne, 1877.

Names

Aaron, Isaac, 1.1
Aarons, Joseph, 3.1
Abbott, Arthur Edgar, 3.4
Abbott, Charles, 3.3
Abbott, Edward, 2.436
Abbott, Edward (1766-1832), 1.2
Abbott, Edward (1801-1869), 1.2
Abbott, Edward (1828-1877), 3.3
Abbott, Elizabeth Matilda, 7.2
Abbott, Francis (1799-1883), 3.2
Abbott, Francis (1834-1903), 3.3
Abbott, George Henry, 3.4
Abbott, Gertrude, 7.1
Abbott, J. P., 12.206
Abbott, John, 1.2
Abbott, John Henry (Macartney), 7.1
Abbott, Joseph, 3.3
Abbott, Joseph Henry, 3.4
Abbott, Sir Joseph Palmer, 3.5
Abbott, Percy Phipps, 7.2
Abbott, Robert Palmer, 3.7
Abbott, William, 3.3
Abbott, William Edward, 7.3
à Beckett, Ada Mary, 7.4
à Beckett, Arthur Martin, 3.9
à Beckett, Emma Minnie, 3.12
à Beckett, Sir Thomas, 3.7
à Beckett, Thomas Turner, 3.9
à Beckett, Sir William, 3.10
à Beckett, William Arthur Callander, 3.11
Abel, Charles William, 7.5
Abigail, Ernest Robert, 7.6
Abigail, Francis, 3.12
Abrahams, Barnett, 7.7
Abrahams, Joseph, 7.7
A'Court, Alan Worsley Holmes, see Holmes
à Court
Adam, David Stow, 7.8
Adam, George Rothwell Wilson, 7.8
Adams, Agnes Eliza Fraser, 10.529
Adams, Arthur Henry, 7.9
Adams, Francis William Lauderdale, 3.13
Adams, George, 3.15
Adams, Sir Hamilton John Goold, see
Goold-Adams
Adams, John, 2.288
Adams, Nancy, see Adams, Agnes Eliza
Fraser
Adams, Philip Francis, 3.16
Adams, Robert Patten, 3.16
Adams, Walter, 3.17
Adamson, John, 7.10
Adamson, Lawrence Arthur, 7.11
Adamson, Travers, 3.18
Adcock, William Eddrup, 7.13
Addis, Edward, see Addis, William
Addis, William, 7.14
Adey, Stephen, 1.3
Adey, William James, 7.15

Agar, Edward Larpent, 7.16
Agar, Wilfred Eade, 7.16
Agnew, Charles Stewart, 3.19
Agnew, Sir James Willson, 3.18
Agnew, Roy (Robert) Ewing, 7.17
Ahern, Elizabeth, 7.18
Ahern, Thomas, 7.19
Ah Kaw, see Chin Kaw
Ah Ket, 7.19
Ah Ket, William, 7.19
Ah Mouy, Louis, 3.19
Ahuia Ova, 7.20
Aikenhead, James, 1.3
Ainsworth, Alfred Bower, 7.21
Ainsworth, George Frederick, 7.21
Ainsworth, Thomas Hargreaves, 7.21
Ainsworth, William, 7.22
Airey, Henry Parke, 7.22
Airey, Peter, 7.23
Aitken, George Lewis, 7.24
Aitken, James, 7.24
Aitken, John, 1.4
Akhurst, Daphne Jessie, 7.25
Alanson, Alfred Godwin, 7.26
Alanson, Roger Godwin, 7.26
Alanson-Winn, Rowland George, see
Headley, Baron
Albert, Frank, see Albert, Michel François
Albert, Jacques, 7.27
Albert, Michel François, 7.27
Albiston, Arthur Edward, 7.28
Albiston, Elizabeth Barbara, 7.28
Albiston, Joseph, 7.29
Albiston, Walter, 7.29
Alcock, Alfred Upton, 7.30
Alcock, Henry, 7.30
Alcock, Randal James, 7.31
Alderman, Walter William, 7.32
Alderson, William Maddison, 3.20
Alexander, Frederick Matthias, 7.32
Alexander, Matthias, 7.32
Alexander, Maurice, 3.20
Alexander, Samuel, 7.33
Allan, Andrew (clerk), 1.358
Allan, Andrew (farmer), 7.34
Allan, David, 1.5
Allan, Edwin Frank, 7.39
Allan, George Clark, 3.22
Allan, George Leavis, 3.21
Allan, James Thomas, 3.22
Allan, John, 7.34
Allan, Percy, 7.36
Allan, Robert Marshall, 7.37
Allan, Stella May, 7.39
Allan, William, 3.23
Allard, Sir George Mason, 7.40
Allardyce, Sir William Lamond, 7.40
Allen, Ada Rosalie Elizabeth, Lady, 7.42-3
Allen, Alfred, 3.26

Allen, Sir Carleton Kemp, 7.44
Allen, Edith Margaret, 7.42
Allen, George, 1.5
Allen, George Boyce, 3.25
Allen, George Thomas, 7.41
Allen, Sir George Wigram, 1.6, **3.24**
Allen, Sir Harry Brookes, 7.42
Allen, Horace William, 7.45
Allen, James, 3.98
Allen, Joseph Francis, 7.44
Allen, Leslie Holdsworth, 7.44
Allen, Marian, Lady, 3.25
Allen, Mary Cecil, 7.46
Allen, Richard, 1.5
Allen, William (1790?-1856), 1.7
Allen, William (1847-1919), 7.44
Allen, William Bell, 3.25
Allen, William Johnston, 3.26
Alleyne, Haynes Gibbes, 3.26
Allingham, Christopher, 3.27
Allison, Francis, 1.7
Allison, Nathaniel Paul, 1.7
Allison, William Race, 1.7
Allman, Francis, 1.8
Allport, Cecil, 3.28
Allport, Joseph, 1.9
Allport, Morton, 3.28
Allum, Mahomet, 7.47
Allwood, Robert, 1.10
Alsop, Rodney Howard, 7.47
Alston, James, 7.48
Alston, Mary, 7.49
Alt, Augustus Theodore Henry, 1.11
Alwyn, Phyllis Ethel von, 9.100
Amadio, John (Bell), 7.49
Ambrose, Ethel, 7.50
Ambrose, Theodore, 7.50
Amess, Samuel, 3.29
Amos, Adam, 1.12
Amos, John, 1.12
Ampt, Gustav Adolph, 7.51
Anderson, Alexander, 7.56
Anderson, Charles, 7.51
Anderson, Sir David Murray, 7.52
Anderson, Ernest Augustus, 7.53
Anderson, Sir Francis, 7.53
Anderson, Henry Charles Lennox, 7.55
Anderson, Hugh, 1.14
Anderson, James (1773-1845), 3.29
Anderson, James (arr.1842), 3.31
Anderson, Jean Cairns, Lady, 7.63
Anderson, John (1790-1858), 1.13
Anderson, John (1893-1962), 7.56
Anderson, John Gerard, 3.29
Anderson, John Wilson, 3.30
Anderson, Joseph, 1.13
Anderson, Maybanke Susannah, 7.59
Anderson, Peter Corsar, 7.60
Anderson, Phyllis Margery, 7.61
Anderson, Sir Robert Murray McCheyne, 7.62
Anderson, Robert Stirling Hore, 3.30
Anderson, Samuel, 1.14
Anderson, Thomas, 1.14

Anderson, Valentine George, 7.63
Anderson, William (1828-1909), 3.31
Anderson, William (arr.1840), 4.62
Anderson, William (1868-1940), 7.63
Anderson, William Acland Douglas, 1.14, **3.32**
Andrade, David Alfred, 7.64
Andrade, William Charles, 7.64
Andrew, Henry Martyn, 3.33
Andrew, Matthew, 3.33
Andrews, Arthur, 7.65
Andrews, Cecil Rollo Payton, 7.66
Andrews, Edward, 3.34
Andrews, Edward William, 3.34
Andrews, Ernest Clayton, 7.67
Andrews, John Arthur, 7.69
Andrews, Richard Bullock, 3.35
Angas, George Fife, **1.15**, 3.36
Angas, George French, 1.18
Angas, John Howard, 3.36
Angel, Henry, 3.38
Angel, Mary, 3.38
Angelo, Edward Fox, 7.70
Angelo, Edward Houghton, 7.70
Angliss, Sir William Charles, 7.60
Angus, David Mackenzie, 7.71
Angus, James, 7.72
Angus, John Henry Smith, 7.72
Angus, Samuel, 7.73
Angus, William, 7.74
Angwin, William Charles, 7.75
Anivitti, Giulio, 3.38
Annand, Frederick William Gadsby, 7.76
Annand, James Douglas, 7.76
Annear, Harold Desbrowe, 7.77
Anselm, Sister Mary, see O'Brien, Catherine Cecily
Anstey, Arthur Oliphant, 1.21
Anstey, Edward Alfred, 7.78
Anstey, Francis George, 7.79
Anstey, George Alexander, 1.20
Anstey, Henry Frampton, 1.21
Anstey, Julia Capper, 1.20
Anstey, Thomas, 1.19
Anstey, Thomas Chisholm, 1.20
Anthon, Daniel Herbert, 7.81
Antill, Henry Colden, 1.21
Antill, John Macquarie, 7.81
Antonieff, Valentin Andreevich, 7.82
Aplin, John, 3.40
Aplin, William, 3.39
Appel, George, 3.40
Appel, John George, 7.83
Appleford, Alice Ross, see Ross-King
Appleton, William Thomas, 7.84
Aquin, Mother, see Leehy, Mary Agnes
Arabanoo, 1.22
Archdall, Henry Kingsley, 7.86
Archdall, Mervyn (1846-1917), 7.85
Archdall, Mervyn (1884-1957), 7.86
Archer, Archibald, 1.22
Archer, Charles, 1.22
Archer, Colin, 1.22
Archer, David, **1.22**, 2.566

Archer, Edward Walker, 1.23, **7.87**
Archer, Francis Henry Joseph, 7.86
Archer, John, 1.22
Archer, John Lee, 1.23
Archer, Joseph, 1.24
Archer, Robert Stubbs, 7.87
Archer, Thomas (1790-1850), 1.25
Archer, Thomas (1823-1905), 1.22
Archer, William (1818-1896), 1.22
Archer, William (1820-1874), 3.40
Archer, William (1856-1924), 1.23
Archer, William Henry, 3.41
Archibald, Charlotte Jane, 3.43
Archibald, John, 7.88
Archibald, Joseph, 3.43
Archibald, Jules François, 3.43
Archibald, Robert John, 7.88
Archibald, William Oliver, 7.89
Arden, George, 1.26
Ardill, George Edward (1857-1945), 7.90
Ardill, George Edward (1889-1964), 7.91
Ardill, Katie Louisa, *see* Brice, Katie Louisa
Ardill, Louisa, 7.90
Argyle, Edward, 7.92
Argyle, Sir Stanley Seymour, **7.92**, 10.55
Armfield, Lillian May, 7.94
Armit, Henry William, 7.95
Armit, William Edington, 3.48
Armitage, Allan Leathley, 3.49
Armitage, Frederick, 3.49
Armitage, Frederick Lionel, 3.49
Armstrong, Edmund la Touche, 7.95
Armstrong, James, 3.51
Armstrong, John (1837-1899), 3.50
Armstrong, John (arr.1839), 3.50
Armstrong, Joseph, 12.395
Armstrong, Richard Ramsay, 3.50
Armstrong, Robert Grieve, 3.50
Armstrong, Thomas, 3.50
Armstrong, Thomas Henry, 7.96
Armstrong, Warwick Windridge, 7.96
Armstrong, William, 3.50
Armstrong, William George, 7.97
Armytage, Charles Henry, 3.51
Armytage, Frederick William, 3.51
Armytage, George, 1.27
Armytage, Thomas, 1.27
Arndell, Thomas, 1.27
Arnold, Ellen, 7.98
Arnold, Joseph, 1.29
Arnold, Richard Aldous, 7.99
Arnold, Samuel, 1.172
Arnold, Thomas, 1.29
Arnold, Thomas Francis, 7.99
Arnold, William Munnings, 3.52
Arnot, Arthur James, 7.100
Arnott, William, 3.53
Aronson, Frederick, 7.101
Aronson, Zara, 7.101
Arscott, John, 1.31
Artem, *see* Sergeyev, Fedor Andreyevich
Arthur, Charles, 1.32
Arthur, Sir George, **1.32**, 2.219, 2.249
Arthur, Henry, 1.38

Arthur, John Andrew, 7.102
Arthur, Richard, 7.103
Arundale, George Sydney, 7.104
Asche, Thomas, 7.105
Asche, Thomas Stange(r) Heiss Oscar, 7.105
Ascough, James, 2.284
Ash, George, 7.106
Ashbolt, Sir Alfred Henry, 7.107
Ashby, Edwin, 7.108
Ashcroft, Edgar Arthur, 7.109
Asher, Morris, 3.54
Ashton, Eliza, 7.114
Ashton, Frederick, 7.111
Ashton, George Rossi, 7.115
Ashton, Helen, 7.111
Ashton, James (1859-1935), 7.109
Ashton, James (1861-1918), 7.111
Ashton, James (1864-1939), 7.110
Ashton, James Henry, 7.111
Ashton, Sir John William, 7.112
Ashton, Julian Howard, 7.113
Ashton Julian Rossi, 7.114
Ashworth, Thomas Ramsden (1864-1935), 7.115
Ashworth, Thomas Ramsden (d.1876), 7.115
Aslatt, Harold Francis, 7.116
Aspinall, Arthur Ashworth, 7.117
Aspinall, Butler Cole (1830-1875), 3.55
Aspinall, Butler Cole (1861-1935), 3.55
Aspinall, Clara, 3.55
Aspinall, James, 3.55
Aspinall, Jessie Strahorn, 7.118
Astley, William, 3.56
Aston, Matilda Ann, 7.118
Atherton, John, 3.57
Atkin, Robert Travers, 3.58
Atkins, John Ringrose, 3.59
Atkins, Richard, 1.38
Atkins, Thomas, 1.40
Atkinson, Caroline Louisa Waring, **3.59**, 3.333
Atkinson, Charles, 1.41
Atkinson, Evelyn John Rupert, 7.119
Atkinson, Evelyn Leigh, 7.119
Atkinson, Harry Leigh, 7.119
Atkinson, Henry Brune, 7.120
Atkinson, James, 1.42
Atkinson, Meredith, 7.121
Attiwill, Ethel, *see* Richardson, Ethel Tracy
Auld, James Muir, 7.122
Auld, Patrick, 3.60
Auld, William Patrick, 3.60
Auricht, Christian, 3.61
Auricht, Johann Christian, 3.61
Auricht, Louisa, 3.61
Austin, Albert (1834-1916), 3.61
Austin, Albert (1855-1925), 7.122
Austin, Edward Arthur, 7.122
Austin, Edwin Henry, 7.122
Austin, Baron Herbert, **3.62**, 6.431
Austin, James (1776-1831), 1.42
Austin, James (1810-1896), 1.43

Austin, Sidney, 7.122
Austin, Thomas, 1.43
Austral, Florence Mary, 7.49, **7.124**
Australian Silverpen, *see* Glenny, Henry
Australie, *see* Manning, Emily Matilda
Avery, David, 7.125
Ayers, Sir Henry, 3.63
Babbage, Benjamin Herschel, 3.65
Babbage, Charles, 3.65
Babbidge, Benjamin Harris, 3.66
Baccarini, Antonio, 7.127
Backhaus, George Henry, 3.66
Backhouse, Alfred Paxton, 7.127
Backhouse, Benjamin, 7.127
Backhouse, James, **1.45**, 2.562
Bacon, Anthony, 1.46
Baddeley, John Marcus, 7.128
Badger, Joseph Stillman, 7.129
Badgery, Henry Septimus, 3.67
Badgery, James, 3.67
Badham, Charles (1813-1884), **3.68**, 7.130
Badham, Charles (snr), 3.68
Badham, Edith Annesley, 3.70, **7.130**
Baffen, John, *see* Baughan, John
Bage, Anna Frederika, 7.131
Bage, Edward Frederic Robert, 7.132
Bage, Ethel Mary, 7.132
Bagot, Charles, 1.48
Bagot, Charles Hervey, 1.47
Bagot, Edward Daniel Alexander, 7.132
Bagot, Edward Meade, 3.71
Bagot, Robert Cooper, 3.71
Bagot, Walter Hervey, 7.133
Bagshaw, John Augustus, 3.72
Bagshaw, John Stokes, 3.72
Bailey, Albert Edward, 7.133
Bailey, Arthur Rudolph, 7.134
Bailey, Frederick Manson, 3.73
Bailey, Henry Stephen, 7.135
Bailey, John (1800-1864), 3.73
Bailey, John (1871-1947), 7.136
Bailey, John (journalist), 11.381
Bailey, John Frederick, 7.137
Bailey, Margaret Ann Montgomery, 7.138
Bailey, Mary, 1.48
Bailey, William, 1.48
Baillie, Charles Wallace Alexander
  Cochrane, *see* Lamington
Baillieu, Arthur Sydney, 7.139
Baillieu, Clive Latham, **7.142**, 7.144
Baillieu, Edward Lloyd, 7.139
Baillieu, James George, 7.138
Baillieu, Richard Percy Clive, 7.139
Baillieu, William Latham, 7.145
Baillieu, William Lawrence, 5.68, **7.138**
Bain, J. A., 9.208
Bain, James, 1.49
Baines, Jennie, *see* Baines, Sarah Jane
Baines, Sarah Jane, 7.145
Bainton, Edgar Leslie, 7.146
Bainton, John Richard, 7.147
Baird, Adam, 7.148
Baird, William, 7.148
Baker, Alice, 7.156

Baker, Bridget, 7.155
Baker, Catherine, 7.149
Baker, Ezekiel Alexander, 3.74
Baker, Frank, 7.150
Baker, Henry Herbert, 7.150
Baker, John, 3.75
Baker, Reginald Leslie, 7.150
Baker, Sir Richard Chaffey, 3.76, **7.152**
Baker, Richard Thomas, 7.154
Baker, Shirley Waldemar, 3.76
Baker, Snowy, *see* Baker, Reginald Leslie
Baker, Thomas (1840-1923), 7.155
Baker, Thomas (1854-1928), 7.156
Baker, Thomas Charles Richmond, 7.157
Baker, William Harold, 7.151
Bakewell, Samuel, 11.22
Balcombe, Alexander Beatson, 3.77
Balcombe, Emma Juana, 6.19
Balcombe, Lucia Elizabeth (Betsy), 3.77
Balcombe, Thomas Tyrwhitt, 3.78
Balcombe, William (1779-1829), 3.77
Balcombe, William (d.1852), 3.78
Baldwin, Charles, 3.79
Baldwin, Henry, 3.79
Baldwin, Joseph Mason, 7.157
Baldwin, Otto, 3.79
Bale, Alice Marian Ellen, 7.158
Bale, William Mountier, 7.158
Balfe, John Donnellan, 3.79
Balfour, James, 3.80
Balfour, James Lawson, 7.159
Balfour, William, 1.49
Ball, George, 7.160
Ball, Henry Lidgbird, 1.50
Ball, Percival, 7.160
Ball, Richard Thomas, 7.161
Ballard, Robert, 3.82
Ballentine, Maria Anne, 9.32
Ballow, David Keith, 1.51
Balls-Headley, Walter, 3.83
Balmain, William, 1.51
Balsillie, John Graeme, 7.162
Bamford, Frederick William, 7.162
Bancks, James Charles, 7.163
Bancroft, Joseph, 3.84
Bancroft, Thomas Lane, 7.164
Banfield, Edmund James, 7.165
Banfield, Jabez Walter, 7.165
Banks, Elizabeth Lindsay, 3.85
Banks, Sir Joseph, 1.52
Banks, Mary Macleod, 5.134
Bannerman, Alexander Chalmers, 3.86
Bannerman, Charles, 3.86
Bannister, Saxe, 1.55
Baptista, Mother Mary, *see* Bell, Mary
  Bridget
Baracchi, Pietro Paolo Giovanni Ernesto,
  7.166
Baragwanath, William, 7.167
Barak, William, 3.87
Barber, Alice, 10.331
Barber, George Walter, 7.168
Barber, John Andrew, 7.169
Barber, William Henry, 1.220, 2.393

Barbour, Eric Pitty, 7.170
Barbour, George Pitty, 7.170
Barbour, Peter, 7.171
Barbour, Robert, 3.88
Barbour, Robert Roy Pitty, 7.170
Barclay, Andrew, 1.56
Barclay, Charles James, 3.89
Barclay, David, 7.171
Bardolph, Douglas Henry, 7.171
Bardolph, Kenneth Edward Joseph, 7.171
Bardsley, Warren, 7.172
Barff, Charles, 2.599
Barff, Henry Ebenezer, 2.600, **7.173**
Barff, Jane, 7.173
Barker, Collet, 1.57
Barker, Edward, 3.89
Barker, Frederic, 3.90
Barker, George Robert, 3.250
Barker, Jane Sophia, 3.91
Barker, John (1815-1891), 3.90, **3.94**
Barker, Mary Anne, Lady, see Broome, Mary Anne
Barker, Stephen, 7.174
Barker, Thomas, 1.57
Barker, Tom, 7.174
Barker, William, 3.89
Barkly, Sir Henry, 3.95
Barlee, Charles, 3.98
Barlee, Ellen, 3.98
Barlee, Sir Frederick Palgrave, 3.96
Barlee, Jane, 3.96, 3.98
Barlee, Louisa, 3.98
Barling, Joseph, 3.99
Barlow, Andrew Henry, 7.175
Barlow, Christopher George, 7.176
Barlow, Mary Kate, 7.177
Barlow, William, 7.178
Barnard, James, 1.58
Barnard, Olive, 11.437
Barnes, George Powell, 7.178
Barnes, Gustave Adrian, 7.179
Barnes, Henry, 3.99
Barnes, John, 7.180
Barnes, Walter Henry, 7.178
Barnes, William (1791?-1848), 1.59
Barnes, William (1832-1898), 1.59
Barnet, James Johnstone, 3.100
Barnett, Frederick Oswald, 7.181
Barnett, Henry Walter, 7.182
Barnett, Neville George, **3.102**, 7.183
Barnett, Percy Neville, 3.102, **7.183**
Barney, George, 1.60
Baroni, see Bignold, Hugh Baron
Barr, John Mitchell, 3.102
Barr Smith, Tom Elder, see Smith, Tom Elder Barr
Barraclough, Sir Samuel Henry Egerton, 7.184
Barrallier, Francis Luis, 1.61
Barrett, Charles Leslie, 7.185
Barrett, Edith Helen, 7.185
Barrett, George, 7.189
Barrett, Sir James William, 7.186
Barrett, John George, 7.189

Barrett, John Joseph, 3.103
Barrett, Walter Franklyn, 7.190
Barrington, George, 1.62
Barron, Ellen, 7.622
Barron, Sir Harry, 7.190
Barron, Johanna, 7.191
Barrow, John Henry, 3.104
Barrow, Louisa, 3.110
Barry, Alfred, 3.105
Barry, Dan, see Atkins, John Ringrose
Barry, John, 7.192
Barry, John Arthur, 7.192
Barry, Mary Gonzaga, 3.107
Barry, Sir Redmond, 3.108
Barry, Zachary, 3.111
Bartlett, Charles Henry Falkner Hope, 7.193
Bartley, Nehemiah, 3.112
Bartley, Theodore Bryant, 1.63
Barton, Alan Sinclair Darvall, 7.193
Barton, Sir Edmund, 7.194
Barton, George Burnett, 3.113
Barton, Russell, 3.115
Barton, Wilfred, 7.200
Barton, William, 7.194
Barwell, Sir Henry Newman, 7.200
Basedow, Herbert, 7.202
Basedow, Martin Peter Friedrich, 7.203
Basham, Maude Harris, 8.526
Baskerville, Margaret Francis Ellen, 7.204
Bass, George, **1.64**, 1.107
Bassett, Samuel Symons, 7.205
Bassett, William Augustus, 7.206
Bassett, William Frederick, 3.116
Bassett, William Frederick Prichard, 3.116
Batchelor, Egerton Lee, 7.206
Bate, Allen, see Taylor, Sir Allen Arthur
Bate, Samuel, 1.66
Bateman, Edward La Trobe, 3.117
Bateman, John, 1.66
Bateman, Walter, 1.66
Bates, Daisy May, 7.208
Bath, Henry, 3.118
Bath, Thomas Henry, 7.209
Bathurst, Earl, see Bathurst, Henry
Bathurst, Henry, 1.67
Batman, Henry, 1.68
Batman, John, 1.67
Batman, William, 1.67
Battler, see Pattison, James Grant
Batty, Francis de Witt, 7.210
Battye, James Sykes, 7.212
Baudin, Nicolas Thomas, 1.71
Bauer, Ferdinand Lukas, 1.73
Baughan, John, 1.74
Bavin, Sir Thomas Rainsford, 7.214
Bavister, Thomas, 7.216
Baxter, Alexander Macduff, 1.74
Baxter, Annie Maria, see Dawbin, Annie Maria
Baxter, Maria del Rosaria Anna, 1.75
Bayldon, Arthur Albert Dawson, 7.217
Bayldon, Francis Joseph, 7.217
Baylebridge, William, 7.218

Baylee, Pery, 1.75
Bayles, Norman, 7.219
Bayles, William, 3.119
Bayley, Arthur Wellesley, 7.220
Bayley, George, 1.49
Bayley, James Garfield, 10.140
Bayley, Sir Lyttleton Holyoake, 3.119
Bayley, Percy Molineux, 10.139
Baylis, Henry, 3.120
Bayly, Nicholas, 1.76
Bayly, Nicholas Paget, 3.121
Baynes, Ernest, 7.221
Baynes, George, 7.221
Baynes, Harry, 7.221
Baynes, William Henry, 7.221
Baynton, Barbara Jane (Janet Ainsleigh), 7.222
Beach, William, 3.122
Beadle, Jane, 7.223
Beal, George Lansley, 7.224
Beale, Octavius Charles, 7.225
Beamont, John, 1.76
Bean, Charles Edwin Woodrow, 7.226
Bean, Edwin, **3.123**, 7.226
Bean, Isabelle, 7.229
Bean, John Willoughby Butler, 7.230
Beaney, James George, 3.124
Bear, Annette Ellen, 7.230
Bear, John Pinney, 7.230
Bear-Crawford, *see* Bear
Beardsmore, Robert Henry, 7.231
Beasley, John Albert, 9.664-5
Beatham, Robert Matthew, 7.232
Beattie, John Watt, 7.232
Beattie, Joseph Aloysius, 7.233
Beatty, Raymond Wesley, 7.234
Beauchamp, Earl, 7.235
Beaumont, Edward Armes, 3.126
Beaurepaire, Sir Francis Joseph Edmund, 7.236
Beazley, William David, 7.237
Becke, George Lewis (Louis), 7.238
Becker, Ludwig, 3.127
Beckett, Clarice Marjoribanks, 7.239
Beckett, William James, 7.239
Bedford, Alfred, 7.241
Bedford, Edward, 1.78
Bedford, Edward Samuel Pickard, 3.128
Bedford, Sir Frederick George Denham, 7.240
Bedford, George Randolph, 7.241
Bedford, Robert, *see* Buddicom, Robert Arthur
Bedford, William (1781?-1852), 1.77
Bedford, William (jnr), 1.78
Bedggood, Daniel, 3.129
Bedggood, John Charles, 3.129
Bee, James, 7.242
Beeby, Doris Isabel, 7.246
Beeby, Sir George Stephenson, 7.243
Beg, Wazir, 3.130
Beggs, Amy, 7.247
Beggs, Francis, 7.246
Beggs, Hugh Norman, 7.246

Beggs, Robert Gottlieb, 7.246
Beggs, Theodore, 7.246
Behan, Sir John Clifford Valentine, 7.247
Beirne, Thomas Charles, 7.248
Beit, John Nicholas, 3.130
Beit, William, 3.130
Bejah, Dervish, 7.250
Belbin, James, 1.78
Belcher, George Frederick, 3.131
Belisario, John, 3.132
Bell, Alexander Foulis, 7.250
Bell, Archibald (1773-1837), 1.78
Bell, Archibald (1804-1883), 1.80
Bell, Barbara (1870-1957), 3.107, **7.251**
Bell, Barbara (d.1898), 1.82
Bell, Bertram Charles, 7.252
Bell, Ella, *see* Hickson, Ella Violet
Bell, Ernest Thomas, 7.256
Bell, Frederick William, 7.253
Bell, George Frederick Henry, 7.253
Bell, Sir George John, 7.254
Bell, Gertrude Augusta, 7.256
Bell, Henrie, 1.82
Bell, James, 3.133
Bell, James Thomas Marsh, 7.256
Bell, Jane, **7.257**, 8.93
Bell, John (1790-1841), 1.80
Bell, John (1821-1876), 1.81
Bell, Sir Joshua Peter, 3.134
Bell, Joshua Thomas, 7.258
Bell, Mary Bridget, 7.252
Bell, Peter Albany, 7.259
Bell, Thomas, 1.81
Bell, Victor Douglas, 7.253
Bell, William Montgomerie, 1.82
Bellasis, George Bridges, 1.83
Bellerive, *see* Tishler, Joseph
Bellew, Harold Kyrle Money, 7.259
Bellingshausen, Fabian, *see* Bellingshausen, Faddei Faddeevich
Bellingshausen, Faddei Faddeevich, 1.83
Belmore, Earl of, 3.135
Belstead, Charles Torrens, 3.138
Belstead, Francis, 3.138
Belstead, Henry, 3.138
Belt, Francis Walter, 7.260
Benham, Ellen Ida, 7.261
Benham, Frederic Charles Courtenay, 7.261
Benigna, Mother, *see* Desmond, Anna Maria
Benjamin, Arthur Leslie, 7.262
Benjamin, Sir Benjamin, 3.139
Benjamin, David Samuel, 7.263
Benjamin, Louis Reginald Samuel, 7.264
Benjamin, Samuel, 1.84
Benjamin, Sophia, 7.264
Benjamin, Zoe, *see* Benjamin, Sophia
Benn, John, 3.140
Bennelong, 1.84
Bennet, David, 3.141
Bennett, Agnes Elizabeth Lloyd, 7.265
Bennett, Alfred Edward, 7.266
Bennett, Alfred Joshua, 7.267

Bennett, George, 1.85
Bennett, George Henry, 7.268
Bennett, Harry Scott, *see* Bennett, Henry Gilbert
Bennett, Henry Gilbert, 7.268
Bennett, James Mallett, 7.269
Bennett, Mary Montgomerie, 7.270
Bennett, Samuel, 3.142
Bennett, Suzanne, 12.489
Bennett, William Christopher, 3.142
Benny, Benjamin, 7.271-2
Benny, Susan Grace, 7.271
Benson, John Robinson, 3.144
Benson, Louisa, 7.272
Benson, Lucy Charlotte, 7.272
Benstead, Thomas Arthur, 7.273
Bent, Andrew, 1.86
Bent, Ellis, 1.87
Bent, James, 3.144
Bent, Jeffery Hart, 1.87
Bent, Sir Thomas, 3.144
Bentham, George, 3.146
Bentham, Neales, *see* Neales, John Bentham
Beor, Henry Rogers, 3.147
Berchmans, Mother Mary, *see* Daly, Anne; *and see also* McLaughlin, Clara Jane
Bergin, Michael, 7.274
Bermingham, Patrick, 3.148
Bernacchi, Angelo Giulio Diego, 7.274
Bernacchi, Louis Charles, 7.275
Bernays, Charles Arrowsmith, 3.149
Bernays, Claude Lewis, 3.149
Bernays, Geoffrey Charles Arrowsmith, 3.149
Bernays, Lewis Adolphus, 3.149
Bernays, Roy Marr, 3.149
Berry, Alexander, **1.92**, 2.620
Berry, David, 3.149
Berry, Sir Graham, **3.151**, 3.359
Berry, Henry, 3.156
Berry, John, 3.150
Berry, Richard James Arthur, 7.276
Berry, William, 7.277
Bertie, Charles Henry, 7.278
Beruk, *see* Barak, William
Bessell-Browne, Alfred Joseph, 7.279
Best, Amy Jane, 3.156
Best, Charles, 1.95
Best, Dudley Robert William, 7.280
Best, Henry (1809-1878), 1.95
Best, Henry (1832-1913), 3.157
Best, Henry (banker), 1.95
Best, Joseph (1830-1887), 3.157
Best, Joseph (1880-1965), 3.157
Best, Sir Robert Wallace, 7.280
Betche, Ernst, 3.158
Bethune, Frank Pogson, 7.281
Bethune, John Walter, 7.281
Bethune, Walter Angus, 1.95
Bettington, Albemarle Brindley, 3.159
Bettington, James Brindley (1796-1857), 3.158
Bettington, James Brindley (1837-1915), 3.159

Bettington, James Brindley (d.1893), 3.159
Bettington, William John Henshall, 3.159
Betts, Selwyn Frederic, 7.283
Beuzeville, James, 3.159
Bevan, David John Davies, 7.285
Bevan, Hopkin Llewelyn Willett, 7.285
Bevan, Llewelyn David, 7.283
Bevan, Louis Rhys Oxley, 7.285
Bevan, Louisa Jane, 7.284
Bevan, Penry Vaughan, 7.285
Bevan, Sibyl, 7.285
Bevan, Theodore Francis, 3.160
Beveridge, Andrew, 3.161
Beveridge, Peter, 3.161
Bew, George, *see* Kwok Bew
Bibb, John, 1.96
Bice, Sir John George, 7.285
Bicheno, James, 1.97
Bicheno, James Ebenezer, 1.97
Bickersteth, Kenneth Julian Faithfull, 7.286
Bickford, James, 3.162
Biddell, Walter (Vivian Harcourt), 7.286
Biddlecombe, Janet, 2.409
Bidmead, Martha Sarah, 7.287
Bidwill, John Carne, 1.98
Bigge, John Thomas, 1.99
Biggs, Leonard Vivian, 7.288
Bignold, Esme, 7.289
Bignold, Hugh Baron, 7.289
Billardière, *see* La Billardière
Billson, Alfred Arthur, 7.289
Billson, George, 7.289
Billson, John William, 7.290
Billy, 10.665
Bindon, Samuel Henry, 3.163
Bingham, Edward, 4.231
Bingham, John, *see* Baughan, John
Bingle, John, 1.101
Bingle, Walter David, 7.291
Binney, Thomas, 3.164
Binns, Kenneth, 7.292
Binns, Kenneth Johnstone, 7.293
Biraban, 1.102
Birch, Thomas William, 1.104
Bird, Bolton Stafford, 3.165
Bird, Frederic Dougan, 7.293
Bird, Samuel Dougan, 3.166
Birdwood of Anzac and Totnes, Baron, *see* Birdwood, William Riddell
Birdwood, William Riddell, 7.293
Birkbeck, Gilbert Samuel Colin Latona, 7.296
Birkbeck, Morris, 5.428
Birks, Frederick, 7.296
Birnie, James, 1.104
Birnie, Richard (1760-1832), 3.166
Birnie, Richard (1808-1888), 3.166
Birrell, Frederick William, 7.297
Birtles, Francis Edwin, 7.297
Biscoe, John, 1.105
Bisdee, Edward, 1.106
Bisdee, John, 1.106
Bisdee, John Hutton, 1.107, **7.298**
Bishop, Charles, 1.65, **1.107**

Bishop, Charles George, 7.299
Bishop, Peter, 1.108
Bjelke-Petersen, Hans Christian, 7.300
Bjelke-Petersen, Marie Caroline, 7.300
Black, Alexander, 3.167
Black, Archibald MacGregor, 3.168
Black, Dorothea Foster, 7.301
Black, George, 3.168
Black, George Mure, 7.302
Black, George Murray, 3.168
Black, Helen, 7.304
Black, John, 3.168
Black, John McConnell, 7.304
Black, Maurice Hume, 3.169
Black, Morrice Alexander, 3.170
Black, Niel, 3.171
Black, Percy Charles Herbert, 7.305
Black, Reginald James, 7.305
Black, William Robert, 7.306
Blackall, Samuel Wensley, 3.172
Blackall, William Edward, 7.307
Blackburn, Arthur Seaforth, 7.307
Blackburn, Sir Charles Bickerton, 7.308
Blackburn, Doris, 7.312
Blackburn, James, 1.109
Blackburn, Maurice McCrae, 7.310
Blacket, Arthur, 3.173
Blacket, Cyril, 3.173
Blacket, Edmund Thomas, 3.173
Blacket, John, 7.312
Blacket, Wilfred, 7.313
Blackett, Charles Edward, 7.314
Blackett, Cuthbert Robert, 3.175
Blackett, William Arthur Mordey, 7.314
Blackham, John McCarthy, 3.176
Blacklock, Walter, 7.314
Blacklow, Archibald Clifford, 7.315
Blackman, James (1762?-1842), 1.110
Blackman, James (1792?-1868), 1.110
Blackman, Meredith George, 7.316
Blackmore, Edwin Gordon, 3.176
Blackmore, James Newnham, 3.176
Blackwood, Arthur Ranken, 7.317
Blackwood, Francis Price, 1.111
Blackwood, James, 3.177
Blackwood, John Hutchison, 3.178
Blackwood, Lady Helen, see Munro
 Ferguson, Helen Hermione, Lady
Blackwood, Robert Officer, 7.316
Blair, David, 3.179
Blair, James, 1.111
Blair, Sir James William, 7.317
Blair, John, 7.321
Blakeley, Arthur, 7.322
Blakeley, Frederick, 7.322
Blakeney, Charles John, 3.181
Blakeney, Charles William, 3.180
Blakeney, William Theophilus, 3.181
Blakey, Othman Frank, 7.323
Blanc, Francis (François) Edward, 7.323
Blanc, Gustave, 7.323
Blanch, George Ernest, 7.324
Bland, Revett Henry, 3.181
Bland, Sarah, 1.112

Bland, William, 1.112
Blandowski, William, 3.182
Blashki, Myer, see Evergood, Miles
Blaxcell, Garnham, 1.115
Blaxland, Gregory, 1.115
Blaxland, John, 1.117
Bleakley, John William, 7.325
Bleasdale, John Ignatius, 3.183
Bligh, William, **1.118**, 2.156, 2.231
Blocksidge, Charles William, see
 Baylebridge, William
Bloodsworth, James, 1.122
Bloodworth, James, see Bloodsworth, James
Blosseville, Jules Poret de, 1.122
Bluegum, Trooper, see Hogue, Oliver
Blundell, Reginald Pole, 7.326
Blyth, Sir Arthur, 3.184
Blyth, Ernest Frederick Burns, 9.240
Blyth, John, 3.185
Blyth, Neville, 3.184
Boake, Barcroft Henry Thomas, 3.186
Boan, Henry, 7.327
Board, Peter, 7.327
Board, Ruby Willmet, 7.330
Board, William, 7.327
Boas, Abraham Tobias, 7.331
Boas, Harold, 7.332
Boas, Isaac Herbert, 7.332
Boas, Lionel Tobias, 7.332
Boase, Hannah Elliot, 6.14
Bochsa, Robert Nicholas Charles, 3.187
Bock, Alfred, 1.124
Bock, Thomas, 1.123
Bock, William, 1.124
Bodley, George Frederick, 3.240
Body, Eliel Edmund Irving, 7.333
Body, Frederick Edmund, 7.333
Body, Ted, see Body, Eliel Edmund Irving
Boehm, Traugott Wilhelm, 7.333
Bogue Luffman, see Luffman, Charles
 (Bogue)
Boismenu, Alain Marie Guynot de, 7.334
Bold, William Ernest, 7.335
Bolden, Armyne, 1.124
Bolden, John Satterthwaite, 1.124
Bolden, Lemuel, 1.124
Bolden, Samuel Edward, 1.124
Bolden, Sandford George, 1.124
Boldrewood, Rolf, see Browne, Thomas
 Alexander
Bolton, William Kinsey, 7.337
Bon, Ann Fraser, 7.338
Bon, John, 7.338
Bon, William, 7.339
Bond, Ensign, 1.76
Bond, George Alan, 7.339
Bond, John, 9.656
Bongaree, see Bungaree
Bonney, Charles, 3.188
Bonney, Thomas, 3.188
Bonnor, George John, 3.190
Bonwick, James, 3.190
Bonwick, Walter, 3.192
Bonython, Constance Jean, Lady, 7.342

Bonython, Sir John Langdon, 7.339
Bonython, Sir John Lavington, 7.341
Boote, Henry Ernest, 7.342
Booth, Charles, 7.343
Booth, Charles O'Hara, 1.125
Booth, Doris Regina, 7.343
Booth, Edwin Thomas, 3.192
Booth, Ellen, 7.347
Booth, Henry Herbert, 7.344
Booth, John, 3.193
Booth, Mary, 7.345
Booth, Norman Parr, 7.346
Booth, William, 7.344
Boothby, Benjamin (1803-1868), 3.194
Boothby, Benjamin (1831-1883), 3.196
Boothby, Guy Newell, 7.347
Boothby, Josiah, 3.196
Boothby, Thomas Wilde, 3.196
Boothby, William Robinson, 3.196
Boothman, John Broadhurst, 1.126
Borchgrevink, Carsten Egeberg, 7.348
Boreham, Frank William, 7.349
Borella, Albert Chalmers, 7.349
Borthwick, Thomas, 7.350
Bosanquet, Sir Day Hort, 7.351
Bosch, George Henry, 7.352
Bosisto, Joseph, 3.197
Boston, John, 1.126
Boswell, Annabella, 2.4
Boswell, William Walter, 7.352
Botham, Mary, see Howitt, Mary
Bothroyd, Margaret Grace Stuart, 12.91
Bottrill, David Hughes, 7.353
Bottrill, Frank, 7.354
Boucaut, Sir James Penn, 3.199
Boucher, Charles, 1.127
Boucher, Frederick, 1.127
Boucicault, Dionysius George, 3.200
Boulger, Edward Vaughan, 3.202
Boungaree, see Bungaree
Bourchier, Sir Murray William James, 7.354
Bourcicault, Dionysius Lardner, 3.200
Bourke, John Philip, 7.356
Bourke, Mary, 5.437
Bourke, Sir Richard (1777-1855), 1.128
Bourke, Richard (1812-1904), 1.133
Bourke, William David, 7.356
Bourne, Eleanor Elizabeth, 7.356
Bourne, George Herbert, 7.357
Bourne, Joseph Orton, 3.202
Bourne, Robert, 2.599, 3.202
Bourne, Una Mabel, 7.358
Bouton, Wilbur Knibloe, 7.359
Bowden, Edmund, 1.134
Bowden, Eric Kendall, 7.360
Bowden, Matthew, 1.134
Bowden, Philippa Bull, 1.134
Bowden, Thomas, 1.135
Bowen, Esther Gwendolyn, 7.360
Bowen, Sir George Ferguson, 3.203
Bowen, George Meares Countess, 1.135
Bowen, John, 1.136
Bowen, Rowland Griffiths, 7.361

Bowen, Stella, see Bowen, Esther Gwendolyn
Bowes, Euphemia Bridges, 7.362
Bowes, Evangeline Grace, 7.362
Bowes, John, 7.362
Bowes, John Wesley, 7.362
Bowes Smyth, see Smyth, Arthur Bowes
Bowker, Richard Ryther Steer, 3.207
Bowles, William Leslie, 7.363
Bowling, Peter, 7.363
Bowman, Alexander, 3.208
Bowman, David, 7.364
Bowman, Edward, 3.209
Bowman, George, 1.139, 3.208
Bowman, George Pearce, 3.208
Bowman, James, 1.137
Bowman, John, 1.138
Bowman, Robert, 3.208
Bowman, William (1799-1874), 1.139
Bowman, William (of Muswellbrook), 3.209
Bowser, Sir John, 7.365
Bowyer, Richard, see Atkins, Richard
Boxall, Arthur d'Auvergne, 7.366
Boxer, Walter Henry, 7.367
Boyce, Charles, 3.209
Boyce, Francis Bertie, 7.368
Boyce, Francis Stewart, 7.369
Boyce, Sir Harold Leslie, 3.210, **7.369**
Boyce, Thomas Burnham, 3.209
Boyce, William Binnington, 3.210
Boyd, Adam Alexander, 7.370
Boyd, Alva, 7.374
Boyd, Archibald, 1.139
Boyd, Arthur Merric, 7.371
Boyd, Benjamin, 1.140
Boyd, Edith Susan, 7.373
Boyd, Edward, 1.142
Boyd, Emma Minnie, 7.372
Boyd, Esna, 7.374
Boyd, James Arthur, 7.373
Boyd, Theodore Penleigh, 7.371
Boyd, William Alexander Jenyns, 7.374
Boyd, William Merric, 7.371
Boyes, George Lukin, 1.143
Boyes, George Thomas William Blamey, 1.143
Boyland, John, 7.375
Boyle, Henry Frederick, 3.212
Boyle, Ignatius George, 7.375
Brabyn, John, 1.144
Brabyn, Mary, 1.144
Bracefell, see Bracewell, David
Bracefield, David, see Bracewell, David
Bracegirdle, Sir Leighton Seymour, 7.376
Bracewell, David, 1.144
Brache, Jacob, 3.212
Bracker, Frederick John Henry, 3.213
Bracy, Henry, 7.377
Braddon, Sir Edward Nicholas Coventry, 7.378
Braddon, Sir Henry Yule, 7.380
Bradfield, John Job Crew, 7.381
Bradfield, Keith, 7.383
Bradley, Henry Burton, 3.214

Bradley, Jonas, 3.215
Bradley, Joseph, 7.384
Bradley, Luther, 7.385
Bradley, William (1757-1833), 1.145
Bradley, William (1800-1868), 3.215
Brady, Alfred Barton, 7.385
Brady, Edward John, 7.386
Brady, Edwin James, 7.386
Brady, John, 1.146
Brady, Joseph, 3.216
Brady, Lyndon Francis, 3.217
Brady, Matthew, 1.147
Bragg, Sir William Henry, 7.387
Bragg, Sir William Lawrence, 7.387
Brahe, Mary Hannah, 7.389
Brahe, May, see Brahe, Mary Hannah
Braim, Thomas Henry, 3.217
Bramston, Sir John, 3.219
Brand, Charles Henry, 7.390
Brand, Henry Robert, see Hampden, Sir
 Henry Robert Brand, Viscount
Brassey, Earl, see Brassey, Thomas
Brassey, Thomas, 7.391
Braund, George Frederick, 7.392
Bray, Sir John Cox, 3.220
Brayton, Lily, 7.105
Brazenor, John Alexander Smyth, 7.394
Brazenor, William, 7.393
Brazier, John, 3.221
Brazier, John William, 3.221
Bready, see Brady, Matthew
Bredt, Bertha, see McNamara, Matilda
 Emilie Bertha
Breillat, Charles, 3.223
Breillat, Robert Graham, 3.223
Breillat, Thomas Chaplin, 3.222
Breinl, Anton, 7.394
Bremer, Sir James John Gordon, 1.148
Brenan, Jennie Frances, 7.395
Brenan, John O'Neill, 1.149
Brenan, John Ryan, 1.149
Brennan, Anna Teresa, 7.395
Brennan, Christopher, 7.397
Brennan, Christopher John, 7.397
Brennan, Edward Thomas, 7.399
Brennan, Ellen, 7.400
Brennan, Francis, 7.400
Brennan, Frank Tennison, 7.402
Brennan, Louis, 3.223
Brennan, Martin, 7.403
Brennan, Mary, 7.400
Brennan, Mary Catherine (May), 7.396,
 7.400
Brennan, Michael, 7.400
Brennan, Michael Austin, 7.400
Brennan, Peter Joseph, 3.224
Brennan, Richard, 7.400
Brennan, Sarah Octavia, 7.403
Brennan, Thomas Cornelius, 7.402
Brennan, William Adrian, 7.402
Brent of Bin Bin, see Franklin, Stella
 Maria(n) Sarah Miles
Brentnall, Elizabeth, 3.227
Brentnall, Frederick Thomas, 3.226

Brentnall, Thomas, 7.404
Brereton, Ernest Le Gay, 7.405
Brereton, John Le Gay (1827-1886), 3.227,
 7.405
Brereton, John Le Gay (1871-1933), 3.228,
 7.405
Brewer, Henry, 1.149
Brewis, Charles Richard Wynn, 7.406
Brewis, Corry Jeannette, 7.406
Brewster, John Gray, 3.228
Brewster-Jones, Hooper, see Jones, Hooper
 Josse Brewster
Brice, Katie Louisa, 7.91
Bride, Thomas Francis, 3.228
Bridges, Frederick, 3.229
Bridges, Sir (George) Tom Molesworth,
 7.406
Bridges, Hilda Maggie, 7.408
Bridges, Royal Tasman, 7.407
Bridges, Sir William Throsby, 7.408
Brient, Albert Lachlan, 7.411
Brient, Lachlan John, 7.411
Brier, Percy, 7.412
Brierly, Sir Oswald Walters, 3.230
Brigden, James Bristock, 7.412
Briggs, Sir Henry, 7.414
Bright, Charles, 3.231
Bright, Charles Edward, 3.232
Bright, Robert, 3.232
Brigstocke, Charles Ferdinand, 1.150
Brinsmead, Horace Clowes, 7.415
Brisbane, Sir Thomas Makdougall, 1.151
Brisbane, William Peter, 7.416
Britton, Fred, 12.257
Broadbent, George Robert, 7.416
Broadbent, Joseph Edward, 7.417
Broadbent, Kendall, 7.417
Broadbent, Robert Arthur, 7.417
Broadhurst, Charles Edward, 3.233
Broadhurst, Edward, 3.234
Broadhurst, Eliza, 3.234
Broadhurst, Florance Constantine,
 3.234
Brock, Harold James, 7.418
Brock, Henry Eric, 7.418
Brock, Henry James, 7.418
Brockman, Edmund Ralph, 3.236
Brockman, Elizabeth Deborah, 3.236
Brockman, Frederick Slade Drake-, see
 Drake-Brockman
Brockman, Henry, 3.236
Brockman, William Locke, 1.155
Brodie, Ellen, see Nicholson, Ellen
Brodney, Alfred Tennyson, 7.420
Brodney, Spencer, see Brodzky, Leon
 Herbert Spencer
Brodribb, Thomas, 3.237
Brodribb, William Adams (1789-1861),
 3.237
Brodribb, William Adams (1809-1886),
 3.237
Brodribb, William Kennedy, 3.239
Brodsky, Julius, 7.420
Brodzky, Horace Ascher, 7.420

Brodzky, Leon Herbert Spencer, 7.420
Brodzky, Maurice, 7.419
Brodzky, Vivian, 7.420
Broinowski, Gracius Joseph, 3.239
Broinowski, Leopold Thomas, 7.420
Broinowski, Robert Arthur, 7.421
Bromby, Charles Hamilton, 3.241
Bromby, Charles Henry, 3.240
Bromby, Elizabeth, 3.242
Bromby, Henry Bodley, 3.240
Bromby, John Edward, 3.241
Bromham, Ada, 7.421
Bromilow, Harriet Lilly, 7.423
Bromilow, William Edward, 7.422
Bromley, Edward Foord, 1.155
Bromley, Frederick Hadkinson, 7.423
Brooke, Gustavus Vaughan, 3.243
Brooke, John, 3.245
Brooke, John Henry, 3.245
Brooker, Thomas Henry, 7.424
Brookes, Herbert Robinson, 7.425
Brookes, Ivy, 7.426
Brookes, Dame Mabel, 7.428
Brookes, Sir Norman Everard, 7.427
Brookes, William (1825-1898), 3.245
Brookes, William (d.1910), 7.425
Brookfield, Percival Stanley, 7.428
Brookman, Sir George, 7.429
Brookman, William Gordon, 7.430
Brooks, George Vickery, 7.431
Brooks, Joseph, 7.432
Brooks, Richard, 1.156
Brooks, Samuel Wood, 3.247
Brooks, William, 7.433
Broome, Sir Frederick Napier, **3.248**, 3.250-1
Broome, George Herbert, 7.434
Broome, Mary Anne, 3.248, **3.250**
Broomfield, Frederick John, 7.435
Brophy, Daniel, 3.251
Brophy, William, 3.251
Brough, Florence Trevelyn, 3.252
Brough, Lionel Robert, 3.252
Broughton, Bartholomew, 1.156
Broughton, Thomas Stafford, 3.253
Broughton, William, 1.157
Broughton, William Grant, **1.158**, 1.255
Broun, Peter Nicholas, 1.164
Brown, Alexander (1827-1877), 3.259
Brown, Alexander (1851-1926), 7.443
Brown, Alfred Reginald Radcliffe, see Radcliffe-Brown
Brown, David Laughland, 3.254
Brown, David Michael, 7.436
Brown, Francis Ernest, 7.436
Brown, Frederick, 3.255
Brown, George, 3.256
Brown, Gilbert Wilson, 3.257
Brown, Harry, 1.103
Brown, Sir Harry Percy, 7.437
Brown, Henry Yorke Lyell, 7.439
Brown, Herbert Basil, 7.440
Brown, James (1816-1894), 3.259
Brown, James (1820-1895), 3.258

Brown, James Drysdale, 7.440
Brown, Janet le Brun, 9.543
Brown, John (1801?-1879), 1.165
Brown, John (1850-1930), 7.441
Brown, John (builder), 7.239
Brown, John Ednie, 3.261
Brown, John Hunter, 3.255
Brown, John Vigor, 7.441
Brown, Joseph Tilley, 7.443
Brown, Maitland, 3.262
Brown, Mamie, see Brown, Mary Home
Brown, Margaret Hamilton, 7.444
Brown, Mary Home, 7.444
Brown, Nicholas John, 3.263
Brown, Peter, see Broun, Peter Nicholas
Brown, Robert, 1.166
Brown, Stephen Campbell, 3.264
Brown, Sylvester John, 3.267
Brown, Thomas (1861-1934), 7.445
Brown, Thomas (d.1863), 3.262
Brown, Thomas (d.1912), 3.255
Brown, Thomas Herbert, 3.255
Brown, Thomas Stubbs, 9.571
Brown, Vera Scantlebury, see Scantlebury Brown
Brown, Walter, see Barrett, Walter Franklyn
Brown, Walter Ernest, 7.446
Brown, William Jethro, 7.447
Browne, Alfred Joseph Bessell-, see Bessell-Browne
Browne, Anna, 3.270
Browne, Archibald, 3.266
Browne, Sir Denis John, 11.611
Browne, Eyles Irwin Caulfield, 3.265
Browne, Fielding, 1.168
Browne, Hugh Junor, 3.266
Browne, John Harris, 3.270
Browne, Reginald Spencer, 7.448
Browne, Thomas Alexander, 3.267
Browne, Sir Thomas Gore, 3.269
Browne, William, 2.292
Browne, William Henry (1800-1877), 1.168
Browne, William Henry (1846-1904), 7.449
Browne, William James, 3.270
Browne, William James Merrick Shawe, 7.448
Browning, Colin Arrott, 1.169
Brownlee, John Donald Mackenzie, 7.450
Brownless, Sir Anthony Colling, 3.271
Brownlow, Frederick Hugh Cust, 7.451
Brownlow, Mary Ann, 6.183
Brownlow, Richard (1832-1873), 3.272
Brownlow, Richard (d.1845), 3.272
Brown-Potter, Cora, 7.259
Brownrigg, Marcus Blake, 3.273
Brownrigg, Marcus Freeman, 3.273
Bruce, Alexander, 3.274
Bruce, Eyre Lewis, 7.452
Bruce, George, 1.170
Bruce, John, 3.275
Bruce, John Leck, 7.451
Bruce, John Munro, **3.276**, 7.453
Bruce, John Vans Agnew, 3.277

Bruce of Melbourne, Viscount, *see* Bruce, Stanley Melbourne
Bruce, Minnie (Mary) Grant, 7.452
Bruce, Stanley Melbourne, 3.277, **7.453**
Bruce, Theodore, 7.461
Bruce, Sir Wallace, 7.461
Bruche, Sir Julius Henry, 7.462
Brudenell-Bruce, Lady Mabel Emily Louisa, 11.605
Brumby, James, 1.171
Brunker, James Nixon, 3.278
Brünnich, Johannes Christian, 7.463
Brunning, Frederick Hamilton, 3.279
Brunning, George, 3.279
Brunning, George Edward, 3.279
Brunning, Herbert John, 3.279
Brunning, William, 3.279
Brunskill, Anthony, 7.464
Brunskill, George, 7.464
Bruntnell, Albert, 7.465
Brunton, Thomas, 3.280
Brunton, Sir William, 7.466
Bruny D'Entrecasteaux, Joseph-Antoine Raymond, 1.171
Bruton, Dorothy Josephine, 7.467
Bruton, Mary Catherine, 7.467
Bruxner, Sir Michael Frederick, 7.468
Bryan, Samuel, 1.172
Bryan, William, 1.172
Bryant, Charles David Jones, 7.469
Bryant, Mary, 1.173
Bryant, William, 1.173
Bryce, Lucy Meredith, 7.470
Buchanan, Benjamin, 3.280
Buchanan, Charles Henry, 3.285
Buchanan, David, 3.281
Buchanan, Florence Griffiths, 7.471
Buchanan, Gwynneth Vaughan, 7.471
Buchanan, James, 3.283
Buchanan, Nathaniel, 3.284
Buchanan, William, 3.285
Buchanan, William Frederick, 3.285
Buck, Ettie, 7.472
Buck, Robert Henry, 7.472
Buckinghamshire, Earl of, *see* Hobart, Robert
Buckland, Fanny, 3.288
Buckland, John Richard, 3.287
Buckland, John Vansittart, 3.287
Buckland, Katherine, 3.288
Buckland, Thomas, 3.288
Buckland, Sir Thomas, 7.473
Buckland, William Harvey, 3.288
Buckle, Edward Barlee, 3.96
Buckley, Alexander Henry, 7.474
Buckley, Henry, 3.289
Buckley, Mars, 3.290
Buckley, Maurice Vincent, 7.475
Buckley, William, 1.174
Budd, Henry Hale, 3.291
Budd, Richard Hale, 3.290
Buddicom, Robert Arthur, 7.475
Bugden, Patrick Joseph, 7.476
Buggy, Edward Hugh, 7.477

Bugnion, François Louis, 3.291
Buhôt, John, 3.292
Bulcock, Emily Hemans, 7.478
Bulcock, Robert, 3.293
Bull, Hilda Wager, 8.192, 8.440
Bull, John Edward Newell, 3.294
Bull, John Wrathall, 1.175
Buller Murphy, Deborah, *see* Hackett, Deborah Vernon, Lady
Bullmore, Ursula Mary, 9.366
Bunbury, Henry William St Pierre, 1.175
Bunbury, William St Pierre, 1.176
Bunce, Daniel, 1.176
Buncle, John, 3.295
Bundey, Sir William Henry, 3.296
Bungaree, 1.177
Bunker, Eber, 1.178
Bunn, Anna Maria, 2.274
Bunning, Robert, 7.478
Bunny, Brice Frederick, 3.297
Bunny, Rupert Charles Wulsten, 7.479
Buntine, Walter Murray, 7.480
Buntine, William Odell Raymond, *see* Ordell, Talone
Bunton, Haydn William, 7.481
Burbury, Thomas, 1.178
Burdekin, Marshall, 3.297
Burdekin, Sydney, 3.297
Burdekin, Thomas, 3.297
Burdett, Basil, 7.482
Burfitt, Walter Charles Fitzmaurice, 7.482
Burford, William Henville, 1.179
Burges, Lockier Clere, 12.98
Burges, William, 1.180
Burgess, Amelia, 1.181
Burgess, Edward James, 3.300
Burgess, Francis, 1.180
Burgess, Gordon Walter Haines, 1.181
Burgess, Henry Thomas, 7.483
Burgess, Murray, 1.181
Burgess, William Henry (1821-1878), 3.299
Burgess, William Henry (1847-1917), 3.299
Burgess, William Henry (1870-1933), 3.299
Burgoyne, Thomas, 7.484
Buring, Adolph Wilhelm Rudolph, 3.300
Buring, Hermann Paul Leopold, 3.301
Buring, Leo, *see* Buring, Hermann Paul Leopold
Buring, Rudi, *see* Buring, Adolph Wilhelm Rudolph
Buring, Theodor Gustav Hermann, 3.300
Burke, James Lester, 1.214
Burke, John, 7.484
Burke, John Augustine, 7.485
Burke, John Edward, 7.484
Burke, Peter Patrick, 7.485
Burke, Robert O'Hara, 3.301
Burke, Thomas Michael, 7.486
Burke, William Joseph, 7.485
Burley, Johnston, 7.487

Burley Griffin, Walter, *see* Griffin, Walter Burley
Burn, Alan, 7.487
Burn, David, 1.181
Burn, Jacobina, 1.181
Burnage, Granville John, 7.488
Burnett, James Charles, 3.303
Burnett, John, 1.182
Burnett, William, 3.303
Burns, George Mason, 10.128
Burns, Sir James, 7.489
Burns, John Fitzgerald, 3.304
Burnside, Robert Bruce, 7.491
Burrell, Henry James, 7.492
Burrell, Susan, 7.493
Burrow, James, *see* Reibey, Mary
Burrowes, John, 3.305
Burrowes, Robert, 3.306
Burrows, John, 3.307
Burston, James, 7.493
Burston, Samuel, 7.493
Burt, Sir Archibald Paull, 3.307
Burt, Octavius, 7.496
Burt, Septimus, 7.494
Burton, Alexander Stewart, 7.496
Burton, David, 1.183
Burton, Henry, 3.308
Burton, John Wear, 7.497
Burton, Sir William Westbrooke, **1.184**, 3.214
Burwell, Lilian, *see* Turner, Lilian Wattnall
Bury, Thomas, 3.309
Busby, George, 1.189
Busby, James, 1.186
Busby, John, 1.188
Busby, William, 3.310
Bushell, Alfred Thomas, 7.498
Bushell, Alfred Walter, 7.498
Bushell, Philip Howard, 7.498
Buss, Frederic William, 7.499
Buss, Garnet Leslie, 7.499
Bussau, Sir Albert Louis, 7.500
Bussell, Alfred Pickmore, 3.310
Bussell, Charlotte, 1.190
Bussell, Ellen, 3.311
Bussell, Grace Vernon, 3.311, 8.340
Bussell, John Garrett, 1.189
Bussell, William John, 7.501
Bustard William, 7.501
Butler, Arthur Graham, 7.502
Butler, Charles Philip, 7.503
Butler, Edward, 3.312
Butler, Francis, 1.191
Butler, Gamaliel, 1.190
Butler, Gamaliel Henry, 3.315
Butler, Henry, 1.191, **3.315**
Butler, Henry John, 7.504
Butler, James, 1.191
Butler, Sir Richard, 7.505
Butler, Sir Richard Layton, 7.506
Butler, Robert John Cuthbert, 7.508
Butler, Thomas John, 7.509
Butler, Walter Richmond, 7.510
Butler, William Frederick Dennis, 7.511

Buttenshaw, Ernest Albert, 7.511
Butters, James Stewart, 3.316
Butters, Sir John Henry, 7.512
Butters, William, 3.317
Buttfield, Herbert, 12.556
Button, Henry, 2.493, **3.318**
Buvelot, Abram-Louis, 3.319
Buxton, Sir Thomas Fowell, 7.514
Buxton, Lady Victoria, 7.514-5
Buzacott, Charles Hardie, 3.320
Buzacott, William, 3.320
Buzacott, William James, 3.321
Byatt, John, 7.516
Byrne, Frederick, 7.516
Byrne, Joseph Patrick, 3.321
Byrnes, Charles Joseph, 3.323
Byrnes, James (1806-1886), 3.322
Byrnes, James (arr.1808), 3.322
Byrnes, Thomas Joseph, 7.517
Byrnes, William, 3.323
Byron, John Joseph, 7.519
Cabena, William Whyte, 7.521
Cadell, Francis, 3.324
Cadman, John, 1.192
Cadogan, Muriel, 8.349
Caffyn, Kathleen Mannington, 3.325-7
Caffyn, Stephen Mannington, 3.325
Caffyn, William, 3.86
Cahill, Patrick, 7.521
Cahill, William Geoffrey, 7.522
Cain, Sir Jonathon Robert, 7.523
Cain, William, 3.327
Caird, Colin Young, 3.328
Caird, Edward, 3.328
Caird, George Sutherland, 3.328
Caird, John, 3.328
Caire, Nicholas John, 3.328
Cairnduff, Alexander, 1.192
Cairns, Adam, 3.329
Cairns, Hugh McCalmont, 3.330
Cairns, Sir Hugh William Bell, 7.524
Cairns, Sir William Wellington, 3.330
Calder, George, 7.525
Calder, James Erskine, 1.193
Calder, William, 7.526
Caley, George, 1.194
Callaghan, Elizabeth, *see* Thompson, Eliza
Callaghan, James Joseph, 7.527
Callaghan, Thomas, 1.195
Callister, Cyril Percy, **7.527**, 12.358
Calvert, Albert Frederick, 7.528
Calvert, Cecil Harnett Hamilton, 3.334
Calvert, James, 3.331
Calvert, James Snowden, 3.333
Calvert, John (1807-1869), 1.81
Calvert, John (1814-1897), 7.528
Calvert, John Jackson, 3.333
Calvert, Louisa, *see* Atkinson, Caroline Louisa Waring
Cambage, John (Fisher), 7.529
Cambage, Richard Hind, 7.529
Cambridge, Ada, 3.334
Camden, Charles, *see* Rowe, Richard
Camden, Earl, 1.196

Cameron, Alexander (arr.1854), 7.536
Cameron, Alexander (1864-1940), 7.530
Cameron, Angus, 3.335
Cameron, Archibald Preston, 3.338
Cameron, Charles, 1.196
Cameron, Cyril St Clair, 7.535
Cameron, Donald (1780-1857), 3.336
Cameron, Donald (1814-1890), 3.337
Cameron, Donald (arr.1838), 9.14
Cameron, Donald (1838-1916), 3.337
Cameron, Donald (1877-1950), 7.531
Cameron, Donald Allan, 3.338
Cameron, Donald Charles (arr.1852), 7.537
Cameron, Sir Donald Charles (1879-1960), 7.532
Cameron, Donald James, 7.533
Cameron, Donald Norman, 7.535
Cameron, Ewen Hugh, 3.338
Cameron, Ewen Wallace, 1.197, **3.339**
Cameron, James (1827-1905), 3.340
Cameron, James (1846-1922), 7.536
Cameron, John (1847-1914), 7.537
Cameron, John Alexander, 3.338
Cameron, Mary Isabella, 3.337
Cameron, Robert, 3.337
Cameron, Samuel Sherwen, 7.539
Cameron, Walter Evan, 3.338
Camfield, Julius Henry, 7.539
Camidge, Charles Edward, 7.540
Campbell, Alexander (1805-1890), 1.197
Campbell, Alexander (1812-1891), 3.341
Campbell, Alexander James, 3.342
Campbell, Alfred Walter, 7.541
Campbell, Allan, 7.542
Campbell, Archibald George, 7.543
Campbell, Archibald James, 7.543
Campbell, Bessie, see Campbell, Elizabeth
Campbell, Charles, 1.198
Campbell, Charles William, 7.550
Campbell, Colin, 3.343
Campbell, Donald (d.1860), 7.551
Campbell, Donald (1886-1945), 7.544
Campbell, Edward (1883-1944), 7.544
Campbell, Edward (d.1931), 7.544
Campbell, Elizabeth, 7.545
Campbell, Envidale Savage Norman, 3.344
Campbell, Eric, 7.546
Campbell, Ethel, 8.127
Campbell, Francis Rawdon Hastings, 3.345
Campbell, Frederick Alexander, 7.547
Campbell, Gerald Ross, 7.548
Campbell, James, 7.549
Campbell, James Lang, 7.550
Campbell, John (1802-1886), 1.199
Campbell, John (d.1876), 1.201
Campbell, John Alan, 7.551
Campbell, John Archibald, 7.551
Campbell, John Dunmore, 7.549
Campbell, John Edwin, 1.201
Campbell, John Fauna, 7.552
Campbell, John Thomas, 1.199
Campbell, Lindsay, 8.196
Campbell, Malcolm Alexander, 3.347
Campbell, Oswald Rose, 3.346

Campbell, Pieter Laurentz, 1.201
Campbell, Robert (1769-1846), 1.202
Campbell, Robert (1789-1851), 1.206
Campbell, Robert (1804-1859), 1.206
Campbell, Roland, 7.544
Campbell, Sir Thomas Cockburn, see
  Cockburn-Campbell
Campbell, Thomas Irving, 7.552
Campbell, Tinker, see Campbell, John
  (d.1876)
Campbell, Walter Scott, 7.553
Campbell, William, 3.347
Campbell, William Douglas, 1.208
Campbell Praed, Mrs, see Praed, Rosa
  Caroline
Campion, Frederick Henry, 7.554
Campion, Sir William Robert, 7.555
Cani, John, 3.348
Canice, Mother, see Bruton, Mary
  Catherine
Cann, George, 7.555
Cann, John Henry, 7.555
Cann, William Henry, 7.556
Cannan, Kearsey, 3.349
Canning, Alfred Wernam, 7.557
Canterbury, Viscount, 3.350
Cape, William, 1.209
Cape, William Timothy, 1.209
Carandini, Cristofero Palmerston, see
  Palmerston, Christie
Carandini, Jerome, 3.351
Carandini, Marie, **3.351**, 5.393
Carandini, Rosina, see Palmer, Rosina
  Martha Hosanah
Carboni, Raffaello, 3.352
Card, Mary, 7.558
Cardigan, see Wolfe, Herbert Austin
Cardwell, Viscount Edward, 3.354
Carew-Smyth, Ponsonby May, 7.558
Carey, George Jackson, 3.354
Carey, John Randal, 7.559
Carington, Rupert Clement George, 7.560
Carleton, Caroline, 5.91
Carlile, Sir Edward, 7.561
Carlton, James Andrew, 7.561
Carmichael, Ambrose Campbell, 7.562
Carmichael, Grace Elizabeth Jennings,
  7.564
Carmichael, Henry, 1.210
Carmichael, Mary, Lady, 7.565
Carmichael, Sir Thomas David Gibson,
  7.564
Carmichael of Skirling, Baron, see
  Carmichael, Sir Thomas David Gibson
Carnarvon, Earl of, 3.355
Carne, Joseph Edmund, 7.565
Carne, Thomas, 7.565
Carne, Walter Mervyn, 7.566
Carnegie, David Wynford, 7.566
Caroline, Sister, 8.140
Caron, Leon Francis Victor, 3.356
Carpenter, John Bolton, 7.567
Carpenter, Sir Walter Randolph, 7.567
Carr, Maria Theresa, 5.58

Carr, Thomas Joseph, 7.569
Carr, William James, 7.570
Carr-Boyd, William Henry James, 3.357
Carrick, Ethel, see Fox, Ethel Carrick
Carrington, Baron, see Carington, Rupert
  Clement George
Carrington, Cecilia Margaret, Lady, 3.358
Carrington, Charles Robert, 3.358
Carrington, Francis Thomas Dean, 3.359
Carroll, Daniel Joseph, 7.571
Carroll, Edward John, 7.571
Carroll, Jack, see Hardwick, Arthur Ernest
Carroll, John, 7.572
Carroll, Robert Joseph, 7.573
Carron, William, 3.360
Carruthers, George Simpson, 7.574
Carruthers, J. E., 12.342
Carruthers, Sir Joseph Hector McNeil,
  7.574
Carslaw, Horatio Scott, 7.578
Carson, Alfred, 7.579
Carson, David, 3.361
Carson, Duncan, 7.580
Carson, John, 3.361
Carter, Arthur John, 7.581
Carter, Bryce Morrow, 7.581
Carter, Charles, 3.362
Carter, Francis Mowat, 7.581
Carter, Godfrey Downes, 3.363
Carter, Herbert Gordon, 7.582
Carter, Herbert James, 7.583
Carter, Hubert Reginald, 7.581
Carter, Norman St Clair, 7.584
Carter, Samuel, 3.362
Carter, Thomas, 7.585
Cartwright, Robert, 1.211
Carvosso, Benjamin, 1.212
Cary, Henry, 3.363
Cary, Henry Francis, 3.363
Case, James Thomas, 7.585
Casey, Cornelius Gavin, 1.213
Casey, Ethel Marian Sumner, 11.492
Casey, Gilbert Stephen, 7.586
Casey, James Joseph, 3.365
Casey, Maie, see Casey, Ethel Marian
  Sumner
Casey, Richard Gardiner, 3.366
Cash, Martin, 1.214
Cass, Walter Edmund Hutchinson, 7.587
Cassell, James Horatio Nelson, 3.367
Castella, Charles Hubert de, 3.367
Castella, François Robert de, 3.368
Castella, Paul Frédéric de, 3.367
Castelnau, Comte de, see Laporte, François
  Louis Nompar de Caumont
Castles, Amy Eliza, 7.588
Castles, Eileen, 7.588
Castles, Ethel (Dolly), 7.588
Castles, George, 7.588
Castleton, Claud Charles, 7.589
Catani, Carlo Giorgio Domenico Enrico,
  7.589
Catchpole, Margaret, 1.215
Cathcart, James Faucitt, 3.369

Cathcart, Mary Fanny, 3.369
Cato, Frederick John, 7.590
Catt, Alfred, 3.371
Cattanach, William, 7.591
Catts, Dorothy Marguerite, 7.592
Catts, James Howard, 7.591
Cavenagh, George, 1.216
Cavill, Arthur, 7.593
Cavill, Charles, 7.593
Cavill, Ernest, 7.593
Cavill, Frederick, 7.593
Cavill, Percy, 7.593
Cavill, Richmond Theophilus, 7.593
Cawker, Thomas, 3.371
Cawood, Dorothy Gwendolen, 7.594
Cawthorne, Charles Wittowitto, 7.594
Cawthorne, William Anderson, 7.594
Cayley, Henry Priaulx, 7.595
Cayley, Neville William, 7.596
Cazaly, James, 7.596
Cazaly, Roy, 7.596
Cazneaux, Harold Pierce, 7.597
Cecil, Robert Arthur Talbot Gascoyne,
  3.372
Chabrillan, Céleste de, 3.373
Chace, Samuel Rodman, 2.31
Chaffey, Ben, 7.601
Chaffey, Charles, 7.600
Chaffey, Frank Augustus, 7.598
Chaffey, George, 7.599
Chaffey, William Benjamin, 7.599
Challinor, Henry, 3.373
Challinor, Richard Westman, 7.601
Challis, John Henry, 3.374
Chalmers, Frederick Royden, 7.602
Chalmers, James, 3.375
Chalmers, William, 3.376
Chambers, Charles Haddon Spurgeon,
  7.603
Chambers, James, 3.377
Chambers, John, 3.377
Chambers, Thomas, 3.378
Champ, William Thomas Napier, 3.379
Champion, Henry Hyde, 7.603
Champion, Herbert William, 7.605
Champion de Crespigny, Sir Constantine
  Trent, 7.606
Champion de Crespigny, Philip, 7.606
Chandler, Alfred Elliott, 7.607
Chandler, Gilbert, 7.608
Chandler, Thomas Charles, 7.608
Chandler, William, 7.607
Chanter, John Courtenay, 7.610
Chanter, John Moore, 7.609
Chapman, Alfred Godwin, see Alanson,
  Alfred Godwin
Chapman, Arthur, 3.380
Chapman, Sir Austin, 7.610
Chapman, Edgar, 3.380
Chapman, Edward Shirley, 7.611
Chapman, Ernest, see Hatfield, William
Chapman, Frederick, 7.612
Chapman, Henry George, 7.612
Chapman, Henry Samuel, 3.380

Chapman, Israel, 1.217
Chapman, Mary, see Cooper, Mary
Chapman, Richard, see Alanson, Roger
  Godwin
Chapman, Sir Robert William, 7.613
Chapman, Samuel, 3.382
Chapman, Thomas Daniel, 3.383
Chapman, Thomas Evans, 1.217
Chapman, Wilfred, 7.612
Chapman, William Neate, 1.218
Chapple, Frederic, 7.615
Chapple, Phoebe, 7.615
Charles, Amy, 8.107
Charles, Samuel, 3.384
Charleston, David Morley, 7.616
Charlton, Andrew Murray, 7.617
Charlton, Matthew, 7.617
Charteris, Archibald Hamilton, 7.619
Charteris, Francis James, 7.619
Charteris, Matthew, 7.619
Chartres, George, 1.218
Chase, Ernest Edward, 7.620
Chase, Muriel Jean Eliot, 7.620
Chataway, James Vincent, 7.621
Chataway, Thomas Drinkwater, 7.621
Chatfield, Florence, 7.622
Chauvel, Charles Edward, 7.623
Chauvel, Sir Henry George, 7.624
Chauvel, James Allan, 7.623
Checchi, Ettore, 7.628
Cheeke, Alfred, 3.384
Cheel, Edwin, 7.628
Cheeseman, William Joseph Robert, 7.629
Chelmsford, Baron, 7.630
Cheney, Sydney Albert, 7.631
Cheong Cheok Hong, 3.385
Chermside, Sir Herbert Charles, 7.631
Cherry, Edward, 7.633
Cherry, Frances, 7.620
Cherry, Percy Herbert, 7.632
Cherry, Thomas, 7.633
Chester, Henry Marjoribanks, 3.386
Chevalier, Louis, 3.387
Chevalier, Nicholas, 3.387
Chewings, Charles, 7.634
Cheyne, Alexander, 1.219
Chidley, John James, 7.635
Chidley, William James, 7.635
Child, Coles, 3.388
Child, William Knox, 2.38, 3.389
Childe, Vere Gordon, 7.636
Childers, Hugh Culling Eardley, 3.390
Childs, Joseph, 1.220
Chin Kaw, 7.637
Chiniquy, Charles Pasqual, 3.299
Chinn, Henry, 7.638
Chinnery, Ernest William Pearson, 7.639
Chipper, Alicia, see Kelly, Alicia Mary
Chipper, Donald John, 7.640
Chipper, John, 7.640
Chirnside, Andrew Spencer, 3.391
Chirnside, John Percy, 7.640
Chirnside, Thomas, 3.391
Chisholm, Alexander, 7.641

Chisholm, Dame Alice Isabel, 7.642
Chisholm, Archibald, 1.221-2
Chisholm, Caroline, 1.221
Chomley, Arthur Wolfe, 3.392
Chomley, Charles Henry, 7.642
Chomley, Hussey Malone, 3.393
Chomley, Mary Elizabeth, 3.392
Christian, Sydney Ernest, 7.643
Christie, Alexander, 7.644
Christie, Francis, see Gardiner, Francis
Christie, James, 7.644
Christie, John Mitchell, 7.644
Christie, Robert, 7.645
Christie, William Harvie, 2.609-10, **3.393**
Christison, Alexander, 3.395
Christison, Robert, 3.394
Christison, Willie, 3.395
Christmas, Harold Percival, 7.646
Chubb, Charles Edward, 3.395
Chubb, Charles Frederick, 3.396
Chumleigh, Harold Vere, 7.646
Chumleigh, Harry, see Ransom, Henry
  Alfred David
Chute, Sir Trevor, 3.396
Cimitiere, Gilbert, 1.223
Clamp, John Burcham, 8.1
Clapp, Francis Boardman, 3.397
Clapp, Sir Harold Winthrop, 8.1
Clare, Chapman James, 8.3
Clark, Alexander Russell, 1.224
Clark, Alfred Thomas, 3.398
Clark, Alister, 8.4
Clark, Andrew Inglis, 3.399
Clark, Caroline Emily, 3.401
Clark, Charles, 3.402
Clark, Charles George Henry Carr, 3.403
Clark, Donald, 8.5
Clark, Sir Ernest, 8.6
Clark, George Carr, 1.224
Clark, George Daniel, 8.7
Clark, George John Edwin, 3.403
Clark, Hannah Maria, 1.225
Clark, Henry, 3.496
Clark, Henry Marcus, 8.11
Clark, Hubert Lyman, 8.8
Clark, James, 8.9
Clark, James Purcell, 8.10
Clark, James William, 8.11
Clark, John, 1.224
Clark, John Howard, 3.404
Clark, John James, 3.406
Clark, Mary, Lady, 8.7
Clark, Ralph, 1.225
Clark, Sir Reginald Marcus, 8.11
Clark, Robert, 3.407
Clark, Thomas (1756?-1828), 1.226
Clark, Thomas (1814?-1883), 3.408
Clark, Walter, 8.4
Clark, William Nairne, 1.227
Clarke, Andrew (1793-1847), 1.228
Clarke, Sir Andrew (1824-1902), 3.409
Clarke, Charles James, 8.12
Clarke, Ernest Edward Dowling, 8.18
Clarke, Evan, 12.372

Clarke, Sir Francis Grenville, 8.16
Clarke, Frank, *see* Gardiner, Francis
Clarke, George (arr.1822), 3.411
Clarke, George (1823-1913), 3.411
Clarke, George O'Malley, 3.412
Clarke, Sir George Sydenham, 8.13
Clarke, Henry, 3.414
Clarke, Henry Lowther, 8.14
Clarke, Jacob Richard, 3.414
Clarke, Janet Marion, Lady, 3.415
Clarke, John (1846?-1867), 3.418
Clarke, John (d.1866), 3.418
Clarke, Joseph, 3.424
Clarke, Marcus Andrew Hislop, 3.416
Clarke, Margaret Turner, 3.413
Clarke, Maria Galatea, 8.515
Clarke, Marian, 8.15
Clarke, Mary Ann, 2.87
Clarke, Sir Rupert Turner Havelock, 8.16
Clarke, Thomas (1756?-1828), *see* Clark
Clarke, Thomas (1840?-1867), 3.418
Clarke, William, 3.419
Clarke, William Branwhite, 3.420
Clarke, William Hislop, 3.416
Clarke, Sir William John, 3.422
Clarke, William John Turner, 1.228
Clarke, William Lionel Russell, 8.16
Clarkson, Sir William, 8.18
Claxton, Marshall, 3.424
Claxton, Norman, 8.19
Clay, Charles, 3.425
Clay, Henry Ebenezer, 3.425
Clayton, Arthur Ross, 8.20
Cleary, Patrick Scott, 8.20
Cleary, William James, 8.21
Cleburne, Richard, 1.229
Cleland, Edward Erskine, 8.22
Cleland, George Fullerton, 3.426
Cleland, Sir John Burton, 8.23
Cleland, John Fullerton, 3.426
Clemens, Sir William James, 8.25
Clement, Dixie Paumier, 8.25
Clements, Frederick Moore, 8.26
Clemes, Samuel, 8.27
Clendinnen, Frederick John, 8.28
Clendinnen, Leslie John, 8.28
Clibborn, George, 3.427
Clibborn, Thomas Strettel, 3.426
Clifton, Marshall Waller, 3.427
Climpson, Joseph, 8.29
Clint, Mary Ann, 1.230
Clint, Raphael, 1.230
Clinton, Henry, *see* Newcastle-under-Lyme
Clisby, George, 3.430
Clisby, Harriet Jemima Winifred, 3.430
Clode, Samuel High, 1.252
Clogstoun, Henry Oliver, 8.30
Close, Edward Charles (1790-1866), 1.231
Close, Edward Charles (1825-1877), 1.231
Clow, James, 1.232
Clowes, Evelyn, *see* Mordaunt, Evelyn May
Clubbe, Sir Charles Percy Barlee, 8.30
Clubbe, Phyllis, 8.31, 12.447
Clucas, Robert John Miller, 8.31

Clune, Patrick Joseph, 8.32
Clunie, James Oliphant, 1.233
Clunies Ross, Robert, 8.33
Clunies Ross, William John, 8.33
Clutterbuck, Katherine Mary, 8.34
Coalby, *see* Colebe
Coane, Henry Edward, 8.35
Coane, John Montgomery (1848-1923), 8.35
Coane, John Montgomery (1884-1910), 8.35
Coates, George James, 8.36
Coates, James, 8.37
Coates, Joseph, 3.431
Coates, Joseph Farrar, 8.37
Coath, John William, 3.246
Cobb, Chester Francis, 8.38
Cobb, Freeman, 3.432
Cobb, Nathan Augustus, 8.39
Cobb, Victor Ernest, 8.40
Cobbett, Norah, 2.27
Cobbett, William Pitt, 8.40
Cobby, Arthur Henry, 8.41
Coburn, Isaac, 3.433
Cochrane, George Henry, *see* Hervey, Grant
Cochrane-Baillie, Charles Wallace Alexander Napier, *see* Lamington, Baron
Cock, John, 1.252
Cockburn, Sir John Alexander, 8.42
Cockburn-Campbell, Sir Thomas, 3.434
Cockerill, George, 8.44
Cockle, Sir James, 3.435
Cockram, Thomas (1831-1912), 8.45
Cockram, Thomas (1860-1920), 8.45
Cocks, Sir Arthur Alfred Clement, 8.45
Cocks, Fanny Kate Boadicea, 8.46
Cocks, Nicholas John, 8.47
Cocks, Thomas, 8.45
Code, Edward Percival, 8.48
Code, Edward Thomas, 8.48
Coghlan, Sir Timothy Augustine, 8.48
Cohen, Annie, 8.58
Cohen, Cedric Keith, 8.56
Cohen, Colyn Keith, 8.56
Cohen, Edward, 3.436
Cohen, Fanny, 8.51
Cohen, Francis Lyon, 8.52
Cohen, George Judah, 8.52
Cohen, Harold Edward, 8.53
Cohen, Henry Emanuel, 3.437
Cohen, Isaac Henry, 8.54
Cohen, John Jacob, 8.55
Cohen, Laurence, 8.56
Cohen, Sir Lewis, 8.57
Cohen, Montague, 8.57
Cohen, Samuel, 8.52
Cohen, Sir Samuel Sydney, 8.58
Cohn, Carola, 8.59
Cohn, Ola, *see* Cohn, Carola
Coldham, Walter Timon, 8.60
Cole, Edward William, 3.438
Cole, Frank Hobill, 8.61

Cole, George Henry, 8.61
Cole, George Ward, 1.233
Cole, Joseph Stear Carlyon, 8.62
Cole, Percival Richard, 8.63
Colebatch, Sir Harry (Hal) Pateshall, 8.64
Colebe, 1.234
Coleman, Percy Edmund Creed, 8.65
Coles, Sir Jenkin, 8.66
Collett, Herbert Brayley, 8.67
Collick, Edward (Henry) Mallan, 8.68
Collicott, John Thomas, 1.234
Collicott, Thomas, 1.5
Collie, Alexander, 1.235
Collier, Elsie Louise, 8.69
Collier, Frederick Redmond, 8.68
Collier, James, 8.69
Collier, Jenkin, 3.440
Collier, Phillip, 8.70
Collin, William, 3.441
Collingridge de Tourcey, Arthur, 8.72
Collingridge de Tourcey, George Alphonse, 8.72
Collings, Joseph Silver, 8.73
Collings, Rhoda Florence, 12.129
Collins, Charles, 3.441
Collins, Cuthbert Quinlan Dale, 8.74
Collins, David, 1.236
Collins, George, 1.239
Collins, George Thomas, 8.75
Collins, Henrietta Wyse, *see* Greville, Henrietta
Collins, Henry Michael, 8.75
Collins, Herbert Leslie, 8.76
Collins, James Richard, 8.77
Collins, John William Fitzclarence, 8.78
Collins, Maria Stuart, 1.237-40
Collins, Sir Robert Henry Muirhead, 8.79
Collins, Robert Martin, 3.442
Collins, Tom, *see* Furphy, Joseph
Collins, William (1760?-1819), 1.240
Collins, William (1846-1909), 3.442
Collits, Mary, 1.240
Collits, Pierce, 1.240
Colls, Thomas, 3.443
Colp, Ann, 1.252
Colquhoun, Alexander, 8.80
Colquhoun, George, 8.81
Colquhoun, Percy Brereton, 8.81
Colton, Sir John, 3.444
Colton, William, 3.444
Colvin, Sir Ragnar Musgrave, 8.81
Combes, Edward, 3.445
Comino, Athanassio, 8.82
Comino, John, 8.82
Conacher, Charles William Davy, 8.83
Condamine, *see* De La Condamine
Condell, Henry, 2.442
Conder, Charles Edward, 3.446
Conder, Walter Tasman, 8.84
Coneybeer, Frederick William, 8.85
Coningham, Arthur, 8.85
Connah, Thomas William, 8.86
Connell, Cornelius Myles, 8.87
Connell, Hugh John, 8.87

Connibere, Sir Charles Wellington, 8.88
Connibere, Ernest William Richards, 8.88
Connibere, Frederick George, 8.88
Connolly, Eric Alfred, 8.89
Connolly, Henry James, 8.89
Connolly, Sir James Daniel, 8.90
Connor, Daniel, 8.90
Connor, Francis, 8.384
Connor, Dame Jean, *see* Macnamara, Dame Annie Jean
Conolly, Philip, 1.241
Conrick, Horatio Victor Patrick, 8.91
Considen, Dennis, 1.242
Considine, Michael Patrick, 8.92
Conyers, Evelyn Augusta, 8.93
Cooch, Alexander, 8.93
Coode, Sir John, 3.447
Cook, Bertie Stuart Baxter, 8.94
Cook, James, 1.243
Cook, James Newton Haxton Hume, 8.95
Cook, Sir Joseph, 8.96
Cook, Robert, 8.99
Cook, Solomon, 3.449
Cooke, Arbella, 3.450, 6.425
Cooke, Cecil Pybus, 3.450
Cooke, Ebenezer, 3.450
Cooke, John (1852-1917), **8.100**, 8.424
Cooke, John (1867-1943), 3.451
Cooke, Samuel Winter, 8.101
Cooke, Thomas, 8.102
Cooke, William, 3.451
Cooke, William Ernest, 8.102
Cookworthy, Charlotte, *see* Bussell, Charlotte
Cooley, Sarah, 2.171
Coombe, Ephraim Henry, 8.103
Coombes, Richard, 8.104
Cooper, Amy, *see* Charles, Amy
Cooper, Sir Charles, 1.244
Cooper, Daniel (1785-1853), 1.245
Cooper, Sir Daniel (1821-1902), 3.452
Cooper, Emma, 3.453
Cooper, Frederick Augustus, 1.246
Cooper, George Henry, 8.107
Cooper, Harry, *see* Cooper, George Henry
Cooper, James, 1.253
Cooper, Joe, *see* Cooper, Robert Joel
Cooper, John Henry, 7.620
Cooper, Lilian Violet, 8.105
Cooper, Lynch, 8.108
Cooper, Mary, 1.575
Cooper, Sir Pope Alexander, 8.105
Cooper, Reuben 8.107
Cooper, Robert, 1.246
Cooper, Robert Joel, 8.106
Cooper, Thomas, 3.453
Cooper, Walter Hampson, 3.453
Cooper, William, 8.107
Coote, Audley, 3.455
Coote, William, 3.456
Cope, Thomas Spencer, 3.457
Cope, William, 8.108
Copeland, Henry, 3.458
Copley, S. L., 7.620

Copley, William, 8.109
Coppin, George Selth, 3.459
Coppleson, Albert Abram, 8.109
Coppleson, Sir Victor Marcus, 8.109
Corbasse, Louise, see Lovely, Louise Nellie
Corbett, Claude Gordon, 8.112
Corbett, James Francis, 8.111
Corbett, William Francis, 8.112
Corbould, William Henry, 8.113
Corby, John McKenzie, 8.113
Cordeaux, William, 1.246
Cordner, William John, 3.462
Cordula, Sister Mary, see Rowland, Caroline Ann
Corey, Ernest Albert, 8.114
Corfield, H. C., 3.463
Corfield, William Henry, 3.463
Corin, William, 8.115
Corlette, James Montagu Christian, 8.116
Corlette, Ruby, 8.116
Cornish, William Crocker, 3.464
Corrigan, James, 3.464
Corrigan, Tom, 3.465
Cory, Edward Gostwyck, 1.247
Cosh, James, 3.466
Costello, James Jasper, 8.117
Costello, John, 3.467
Costello, Michael, 3.467
Cottee, William Alfred, 3.468
Cotter, Albert, 8.118
Cotter, Thomas Young, 1.248
Cotton, Alfred John, 8.118
Cotton, Catherine Drummond 8.120
Cotton, Francis (1801-1883), 1.248
Cotton, Francis (1857-1942), 8.119
Cotton, Frank Stanley, 8.119
Cotton, Frederick Sidney, 8.119
Cotton, George Witherage, 3.469
Cotton, Hugh Calveley, 1.250
Cotton, John, 1.249
Cotton, Leo Arthur, 8.119
Cotton, Sir Sidney John, 1.250
Cottrell, Ida Dorothy Ottley, 8.121
Coulter, William, 12.372
Counsel, Edward Albert, 8.121
Couppé, Louis, 8.122
Couvreur, Auguste, 3.470
Couvreur, Jessie Catherine, 3.470
Coveny, Christopher, 3.472
Coveny, Robert, 3.471
Coveny, Robert de Courcy, 3.471
Coveny, Thomas Bossuet, 3.471
Cover, James Fleet, 1.251
Coverdale, John, 1.253
Cowan, Edith Dircksey, 8.123
Cowan, John (arr.1852), 8.124
Cowan, Sir John (1866-1953), 8.124
Cowan, John Lancelot, 8.125
Cowan, Theodora Esther, 8.125
Coward, Harry Keith, 8.126
Cowen, Sir Frederick Hymen, 3.472
Cowen, Louise, see Lovely, Louise Nellie
Cowie, Bessie Lee, see Lee, Betsy
Cowie, James, 3.473

Cowles, Charles, 3.474
Cowley, Sir Alfred Sandlings, **3.474, 8.127**
Cowley, Isaac, 3.474
Cowlishaw, James, 3.475
Cowlishaw, Leslie, 8.127
Cowper, Charles, 3.479
Cowper, Sir Charles, 3.475
Cowper, William, 1.254
Cowper, William Macquarie, 3.480
Cox, Arthur Brooks, 3.484
Cox, Charles Frederick, 8.128
Cox, Sir Edward John Owen, 8.129
Cox, Edward King, 3.482
Cox, Erle, 8.130
Cox, Erle Harold, 8.131
Cox, Francis William, 3.484
Cox, Frederick Holdship, 1.256
Cox, George Henry, 3.486
Cox, James, 1.256
Cox, James Charles, 3.482
Cox, John Edward, 1.257
Cox, Lois, 3.485
Cox, Mary Ann, 1.257
Cox, Samuel Emanuel, 1.258
Cox, William (1764-1837), 1.258
Cox, William (hatter), 3.484
Coxen, Charles, 3.487
Coxen, Elizabeth Frances, 3.488
Coxen, Henry, 1.465
Coxen, Henry William, 3.488
Coxen, Stephen, 3.488
Coxen, Walter Adams, 8.131
Coyne, David Emmet, 8.132
Coyne, John Harry, 8.132
Cozens, Daphne, see Akhurst, Daphne Jessie
Cracknell, Edward Charles, 3.488
Craig, Robert, 8.133
Craig, Robert Gordon, 8.133
Craigie, Edward John, 8.134
Craigie, Tom, 8.134
Cramp, Karl Reginald, 8.135
Crampton, Walter Russell, 8.135
Cramsie, John, 8.136
Cramsie, John Boyd, 8.136
Cran, James, 8.137
Cran, John, 8.137
Cran, Robert (1821-1894), 8.137
Cran, Robert (1856-1940), 8.137
Crane, Martin, 3.489
Craven, Richard, 8.138
Crawford, Alexander, 8.139
Crawford, Andrew, 3.490
Crawford, Emma, 8.140
Crawford, George John, 3.491
Crawford, Thomas Simpson, 8.140
Crawford, Thomas William, 8.141
Crawford, William Hugh, 8.142
Creal, Rose Ann, 8.142
Creed, John Mildred, 3.492
Creed, Louise, see Mack, Marie Louise Hamilton
Creer, Herbert Victor, 8.143
Creer, Reginald Charles (Ferrers), 8.143

Cressy, Charles, 2.223
Creswell, John, 8.144
Creswell, Sir William Rooke, 8.145
Creswick, Alexander Thomson, 8.147
Crews, John Branscombe, 3.493
Cribb, Benjamin, 3.493
Cribb, Henry Smart, 8.148
Cribb, James Clarke, 8.148
Cribb, Robert, 3.493
Cribb, Thomas Bridson, 8.148
Crick, Stanley Sadler, 8.149
Crick, William Patrick, 8.150
Crisp, Christopher, 3.495
Crisp, Sir Harold, 8.152
Crofts, Charles Alfred, 8.152
Croll, Robert Henderson, 8.154
Crombie, James, 8.155
Crombie, William, 8.155
Crommelin, George Whiting, 3.496
Crommelin, Minard Fannie, 3.496, **8.155**
Crompton, Henry Woodhouse, 3.497
Crompton, Joseph, 3.496
Crompton, Owen, 3.497
Crompton, Robert, 3.497
Crompton, Susan Mary, 3.497
Cronin, Bernard Charles, 8.156
Crook, William Pascoe, 1.259
Crooke, Edward, 3.497
Crooke, Edward Jolley, 3.498
Crookes, John, 1.261
Cropper, Charles William, 8.157
Crosby, Charles, 3.499
Crosby, William (1805-1885), 3.498
Crosby, William (1832-1910), 3.498
Cross, Ada, see Cambridge, Ada
Cross, George Frederick, 3.335
Cross, John, 1.261
Cross, Zora Bernice May, 8.158
Crossley, Ada Jemima, 8.159
Crossley, George, 1.262
Crotty, James, 8.160
Crouch, George Stanton, 3.501
Crouch, James Joseph, 3.499
Crouch, Richard Armstrong, 8.160
Crouch, Sarah, 3.500
Crouch, Thomas James (1805-1890), 3.500
Crouch, Thomas James (d.1889), 3.501
Crowder, Frederick Thomas, 8.161
Crowder, Thomas Ristol, 1.264
Crowe, Robert, 8.162
Crowe, William, 8.163
Crowley, Catherine, 2.582
Crowley, Grace, 8.518
Crowther, Edward Lodewyk, 3.503
Crowther, George Henry, 8.163
Crowther, George O'Dell, 8.163
Crowther, Henry Arnold, 8.163
Crowther, William, 3.501
Crowther, William Lodewyk, 3.501
Crummer, Henry Samuel Walker, 1.265
Crummer, James Henry, 1.264
Crump, Sylverius, 2.260
Cudmore, Sir Collier Robert, 8.165
Cudmore, Daniel Henry, 8.164

Cudmore, Daniel Michael Paul, 8.164
Cudmore, James Francis, 8.164
Cullen, Edward Alexander Ernest, 8.165
Cullen, John Hugh, 8.166
Cullen, Paul, 3.504
Cullen, Sir William Portus, 8.167
Culley, Charles Ernest, 8.169
Cumberlege, Claude Lionel, 8.169
Cumbrae-Stewart, Francis William Sutton, 8.170
Cumbrae Stewart, Janet Agnes, 8.171
Cumbrae-Stewart, Zina Beatrice Selwyn, 8.172
Cuming, James (1835-1911), 8.172
Cuming, James (1861-1920), 8.172
Cuming, Robert Burns, 8.172
Cumming, John (1830-1883), 3.504
Cumming, John (arr.1833), 3.505
Cumming, Thomas Forrest, 3.504
Cummins, John, 8.173
Cumpston, John Howard Lidgett, 8.174
Cuningham, Hastings, 3.506
Cunneen, James Augustine, 3.506
Cunning, Alice, see Sewell, Alice Maud, Lady
Cunningham, Allan, 1.265
Cunningham, Arthur Henry Wickham, 8.176
Cunningham, Sir Edward Sheldon, 8.177
Cunningham, James, 8.178
Cunningham, Peter Miller, 1.267
Cunningham, Richard, **1.268**, 2.239
Curlewis, Ethel Jean Sophia, 12.291
Curlewis, Herbert Raine, 12.290
Curley, James, 3.507
Curnow, James Henry, 8.178
Curnow, William, 8.179
Curr, Edward, 1.269
Curr, Edward Micklethwaite, 3.508
Curran, John (Michael) Milne, 3.322, **3.508**
Currey, William Matthew, 8.180
Currie, Archibald, 3.509
Currie, Sir (Henry) Alan, 8.180
Currie, John Lang (1818-1898), 3.510
Currie, John Lang (1856-1935), 8.180
Currie, Neal Lincoln, 8.182
Currie, Patrick, 8.181
Curtin, John, 8.22, 8.616, 9.422, 9.665
Curtis, Anthony, 1.272
Curtis, George Silas, 8.182
Cusack, John Joseph, 8.183
Cussen, Sir Leo Finn Bernard, 8.184
Cussen, Maurice, 8.184
Cussen, Patrick Edward, 1.272
Custance, John Daniel, 3.511
Cuthbert, Sir Henry, 3.513
Cuthbert, John, 3.514
Cuthbertson, James Lister, 3.514
Cuthbertson, John, 1.273
Cuthbertson, Margaret Gardiner, 8.186
Cutlack, Frederic Morley, 8.186
Cutts, William Henry, 3.515
Dacey, John Rowland, 8.188
Dacre, Ranulph, 1.275

Dadson, Leslie, 8.188
Daglish, Henry, 8.189
Daintree, Richard, 4.1
Dakin, William John, 8.190
D'Albertis, Luigi Maria, 4.2
Dale, John, 8.191
Dale, Robert William, 4.2
Daley, Charles, 8.192
Daley, Charles Studdy, 8.192
Daley, Jane, 8.193
Daley, Jean, see Daley, Jane
Daley, Victor James William Patrick, 8.194
Dalgarno, Isabella, 4.3
Dalgarno, Joseph, 4.3-4
Dalgety, Frederick Gonnerman, 4.4
Dalgleish, Daniel Cameron, 4.5
Dallachy, John, 4.6
Dallas, Roderic Stanley, 8.195
Dalley, Ianthe Pauline Lamonerie, 8.197
Dalley, John Bede, 8.196
Dalley, William, 8.197
Dalley, William Bede, **4.6**, 4.18
Dalley-Scarlett, Robert, 8.197
Dalrymple, Alexander, 1.275
Dalrymple, David Hay, 8.199
Dalrymple, Ernest George Beck Elphinstone, 1.276
Dalrymple, George Augustus Frederick Elphinstone, 4.9
Dalton, James, 4.10
Dalton, Joseph, 4.11
Dalton, Thomas, 4.11
Daly, Anne, 8.199
Daly, Clarence Wells, 8.200
Daly, Sir Dominick, 4.12
Daly, Harriet, 4.93
Daly, John Joseph, 8.201
Dalyell, Elsie Jean, 8.201
Dalziel, Henry, 8.202
Dampier, Alfred, 4.13
Dampier, Katherine Alice, 4.13
Dampier, William, 1.277
Dana, Henry Edward Pulteney, 1.278
Dana, James Dwight, 1.278
Dana, William Augustus Pulteney, 1.278
Daneš, Jiří Václav, 8.203
Dangar, Albert Augustus, 4.14
Dangar, Charles Cary, 1.281
Dangar, Francis Richard, 4.14
Dangar, Frederick Holkham, 4.14
Dangar, Henry, 1.280
Dangar, Henry Cary, 4.14
Dangar, Richard Cary, 1.281
Dangar, Thomas, 1.281
Dangar, Thomas Gordon Gibbons, 4.13
Dangar, William, 1.281
Dangar, William John, 4.14
Danglow, Jacob, 8.204
Danks, John, 4.15
Dannevig, Annie, 8.205
Dannevig, Gunder Mathisen, 8.205
Dannevig, Harald Kristian, 8.204
Daplyn, Alfred James, 4.16
D'Arcy, Dame Constance Elizabeth, 8.205

Darcy, James Leslie, 8.206
D'Arcy, William Knox, 8.207
D'Arcy-Irvine, Gerard Addington, 8.209
D'Arcy-Irvine, Malcolm Mervyn, 8.210
Darke, John Charles, 1.282
Darley, Benjamin, 4.17
Darley, Sir Frederick Matthew, 4.17
Darley, Lucy Forest, Lady, 4.19
Darling, Sir Charles Henry, 4.19
Darling, David, 2.599
Darling, Harold Gordon, 8.210
Darling, John (1831-1905), 4.21
Darling, John (1852-1914), 4.22
Darling, Joseph, 8.211
Darling, Sir Ralph, **1.282**, 1.394-6, 2.169, 2.238
Darnell-Smith, George Percy, 8.212
Darrell, George Frederick Price, 3.370, **4.22**
Darrell, Mary Fanny, see Cathcart, Mary Fanny
Darrell, Rupert, 4.23
Dartnell, Wilbur Taylor, see Dartnell, William Thomas
Dartnell, William Thomas, 8.213
Darvall, Sir John Bayley, 4.23
Darwin, Charles Robert, 1.286
Dash, John, 8.213
Dashwood, Charles James, 8.214
Dashwood, George Frederick, 1.287
Dattilo-Rubbo, Anthony, see Rubbo, Antonio Salvatore Dattilo
Davenport, Francis, 4.25
Davenport, George, 4.25
Davenport, Robert, 4.25
Davenport, Sir Samuel, 4.25
Davey, Arnold Edwin, 8.215
Davey, Constance Muriel, 8.216
Davey, Edwin, 8.215
Davey, Margaret, 1.289
Davey, Phillip, 8.217
Davey, Thomas, **1.288**, 2.87
Davice, Hannah, see Clark, Hannah Maria
David, Caroline Martha, Lady, 8.218, 8.221
David, Charles St John, 8.217
David, Sir Tannatt William Edgeworth, 8.218
Davidson, Sir Alfred Charles, 8.221
Davidson, (Charles) Mark Anthony, 8.228
Davidson, Sir Colin George Watt, 8.223
Davidson, Daniel Sutherland, 8.224
Davidson, Ethel Sarah, 8.225
Davidson, James (1865-1936), 8.226
Davidson, James (1885-1945), 8.226
Davidson, James Edward, 8.227
Davidson, John, 4.26
Davidson, John Ewen, 8.228
Davidson, Lydia, 4.26
Davidson, Margaret Agnes, Lady, 8.229
Davidson, Sir Walter Edward, 8.229
Davidson, Walter Stevenson, 1.290
Davidson, William, 8.230
Davidson, William St John Stevens, 8.231

Davies, Arthur, 1.290
Davies, Charles Ellis, 8.233
Davies, David Mortimer, **4.26**, 8.232
Davies, Ebenezer, 4.29
Davies, Edward Harold, 8.232
Davies, George Schoen, 4.29
Davies, John (1772-1855), 1.353
Davies, John (1813-1872), 4.27
Davies, John (1839-1896), 4.28
Davies, Sir John George, 8.233
Davies, Sir John Mark, 4.29
Davies, Joseph, 4.31
Davies, Joseph Bartlett, 4.29
Davies, Sir Matthew Henry, 4.29
Davies, Maurice Coleman, 4.32
Davies, Michael John, 4.27
Davies, Robert Rowland, 1.291
Davies, Sarah, *see* Davis, Sarah (d.1794)
Davies, Walter David, 4.33
Davies, William (1824-1890), 4.33
Davies, William (1882?-1956), 8.235
Davis, Alexander Barnard, 4.34
Davis, Alfred, 8.237
Davis, Arthur Hoey, 8.235
Davis, Charles (1824?-1914), 8.236
Davis, Charles (b.1865), 8.237
Davis, Charles Henry, 1.292
Davis, Charles Herbert, 8.237
Davis, Edward (1816-1841), **1.293**, 1.300
Davis, James, 1.294
Davis, John King, 8.238
Davis, Joseph, 8.239
Davis, Sarah (d.1794), 1.264
Davis, Sarah (d.1849), 2.600
Davis, Thomas Martin, 8.240
Davis, Violet Christina, 8.235
Davis, William Walter, 8.241
Davitt, Arthur, 4.34
Davitt, Marie Antoinette Hélène Léontine, 4.35
Davoren, Laurence, 2.388
Davy, Edward, 1.295
Davy, Ruby Claudia Emily, 8.242
Davy, Thomas Arthur Lewis, 8.242
Davy, Thomas George, 8.242
Dawbin, Annie Maria, 1.296
Dawbin, Robert, 1.296-7
Dawes, Nathaniel, 8.243
Dawes, William, 1.297
Dawson, Anderson, *see* Dawson, Andrew
Dawson, Andrew, 8.244
Dawson, Frances Emily, 3.496
Dawson, James, 4.35
Dawson, Peter Smith, 8.245
Dawson, Robert, 1.298
Dawson, Robert Barrington, 4.36
Day, Edward Denny, 1.300
Day, Ernest Charles, 8.246
Day, George, 4.37
Day, Robert Alexander, 8.246
Day, Theodore Ernest, 8.247
Deacon, Clare, 8.248
Deakin, Alfred, 3.241, 6.234, 7.599, 8.98, **8.248**, 11.40

Deakin, Elizabeth Martha Ann, 3.266, 8.255
Deakin, Kate, 8.255
Deakin, Pattie, *see* Deakin, Elizabeth Martha Ann
Deakin, William, 8.248
Deamer, Mary Elizabeth Kathleen Dulcie, 8.256
Dean, Edwin Theyer, 8.258
Dean, George, 6.82, **8.257**, 10.470
Dean, George Henry, 8.258
Dean, Horace, 4.37
Deane, Henry, 8.259
Deane, Henry James, 8.260
Deane, John Horace, 8.260
Deane, John Philip, 1.301
Deane, Percival Edgar, 8.261
Deas Thomson, *see* Thomson, Sir Edward Deas
De Bavay, Auguste Joseph François, 8.262
De Bernales, Claude Albo, 8.264
De Beuzeville, Wilfred Alexander Watt, 8.265
De Blosseville, *see* Blosseville
De Boos, Charles Edward Augustus, 4.38
De Burgh, Ernest Macartney, 8.266
De Caen, General, 1.390
De Castella, *see* Castella
Dechaineux, Emile, 8.267
Dechaineux, Florent Vincent Emile Lucien, 8.266
Dechaineux, François Prosper, 8.266
Dechaineux, Josephine Leopold Leontine, 8.266
De Chair, Sir Dudley Rawson Stratford, 8.267
De Crespigny, *see* Champion de Crespigny
Deeming, Frederick (Bailey), 8.268
Deeming, Marie, 8.268
De Eredia, *see* Eredia
Deffell, George Hibbert, 4.39
De Garis, Clement John, 8.269
De Garis, Elisha (Elizee) Clement, 8.270
De Garis, Mary Clementina, 8.271
De Gillern, William, 1.301
Degotardi, John, 4.40
Degraves, Peter, 1.302
Degraves, William, 4.40
De Hamel, Lancel Victor, 8.271
De La Condamine, Thomas, 1.303
Delany, John Albert, 4.41
Delany, Patrick, 8.272
De Largie, Hugh, 8.272
De Lissa, Alfred, 4.42
De Lissa, Lillian Daphne, 8.273
De Lissa, Solomon Aaron, 4.42
De Little, Robert, 1.304
De Loitte, *see* Loitte
Delprat, Guillaume Daniel, 8.274
Demaine, William Halliwell, 8.276
De Maistre, LeRoy Leveson Laurent Joseph, 4.43, **8.277**
De Mestre, Edward McKenzie, 4.43
De Mestre, Etienne George, 4.43

De Mestre, Etienne Livingstone, 1.305, **4.42**
De Mestre, Hurtle Edwin, 4.43
De Mestre, Prosper, **1.305**, 4.42
De Mole, Lancelot Eldin, 8.278
Dempsey, E. J., 12.542
Dempster, Andrew, 4.44
Dempster, Charles Edward, 4.44
Dempster, James McLean, 4.43
Dendy, Arthur, 8.279
Denehy, Charles Aloysius, 8.280
Denham, Digby Frank, 8.281
Denham, Howard Kynaston, 8.282
Deniehy, Daniel Henry, 4.44
Deniehy, Henry, 4.44
Denison, Sir Hugh Robert, 8.283
Denison, Sir William Thomas, 4.46
Denman, Gertrude Mary, Lady, 8.285
Denman, Thomas, Baron, 8.285
Dennis, Alexander, 4.53
Dennis, Clarence Michael James, 8.286
Dennis, James, 8.286
Denny, William Joseph, 8.287
Dennys, Charles John, 4.54
De Noskowski, Ladislas, *see* Noskowski, Ladislas Adam de
Denovan, William Dixon Campbell, 4.55
Denton, James Samuel, 8.288
De Pury, Frédéric Guillaume, 4.56
Derby, Earl, *see* Stanley, Edward George Geoffrey Smith
Derham, Charles Alfred Melbourne, 4.57
Derham, Enid, 8.289
Derham, Frederick John, 4.57
Derham, Frederick Thomas, 4.56
De Rougemont, Louis, 8.290
Derrington, Edwin Henry, 4.58
Derry, John Dickson, 4.58
Desailly, Francis William Wisdom, 4.59
Desailly, George Peter, 4.59
De Salis, Leopold Fabius Dietegan Fane, 4.60
De Satgé de St Jean, Ernest Valentine, 4.61
De Satgé, Oscar John, **4.61**, 4.301
Desbrowe-Annear, *see* Annear
Desmond, Anna Maria, 8.290
Desmond, Arthur, 8.291
Desmond, Varney, *see* Peterson, Isabel Varney Desmond
Despeissis, Jean Marie Adrian, 8.292
De Strzelecki, *see* Strzelecki
Dethridge, George James, 8.293
Dethridge, John Stewart, 8.293
De Torres, *see* Torres
De Tourcey,, *see* Collingridge de Tourcey
Dettmann, Herbert Stanley, 8.294
Deuchar, John, 4.62
Devanny, Jane, 8.295
Devenish-Meares, *see* Meares
Devine, Edward, 4.62
Devine, Sir Hugh Berchmans, 8.296
Devine, James Edward Joseph, 8.297
Devine, Matilda (Mary), 8.297

Devine, William, 8.298
De Vis, Charles Walter, 4.63
De Vlamingh, *see* Vlamingh
De Wesselow, *see* Simpkinson de Wesselow
Dexter, Caroline, 3.430, **4.64**
Dexter, Walter Ernest, 8.298
Dexter, William, 4.64
D'Hage, Ludwig, 8.299
Dibbs, Sir George Richard, 4.65
Dibbs, John, 4.65
Dibbs, Sir Thomas Allwright, 4.69
Dibdin, Edward John, 8.300
Dick, James Adam, 8.301
Dick, Robert, 8.301
Dickens, Alfred D'Orsay Tennyson, 4.71
Dickens, Charles, 1.222, **4.70**
Dickens, Edward Bulwer Lytton, 4.71
Dickinson, Mrs, 8.302
Dickinson, Edward Alexander, 8.302
Dickinson, Sir John Nodes, 4.71
Dickinson, Sidney, 8.302
Dickson, Frederick, 8.305
Dickson, James (1813-1863), 4.72
Dickson, James (1859-1949), 8.303
Dickson, Sir James Robert, 8.304
Dickson, James (snr), 8.303
Dickson, John, 1.306
Dietrich, Amalie, 4.73
Dietrich, Wilhelm August Salomo, 4.73
Diggles, Silvester, 4.73
Dilke, Sir Charles Wentworth, 4.74
Dill Macky, William Marcus, 8.305
Dillon, Peter, 1.306
Disney, Thomas Robert, 4.75
Divine, Nicholas, 1.308
Dixon, Francis Burdett, 4.75
Dixon, Graham Patrick, 8.306
Dixon, Horace Henry, 8.307
Dixon, James, 1.309
Dixon, Robert, 1.309
Dixson, Emma Elizabeth, Lady, 8.308
Dixson, Hugh (1810-1880), 4.77
Dixson, Sir Hugh (1841-1926), 4.77, **8.308**
Dixson, Hugh Robert, *see* Denison, Sir Hugh Robert
Dixson, Robert, 4.77
Dixson, Thomas Storie, 8.308
Dixson, Sir William, 8.309
Dobbie, Edward David, 8.310
Dobie, John, 1.310
Dobson, Alfred, 4.79
Dobson, Emily, 8.310
Dobson, Frank Stanley, 4.77
Dobson, Henry, 8.311
Dobson, Sir William Lambert, 4.78
Docker, Ernest Brougham, 8.312
Docker, Joseph (1793-1865), 1.311
Docker, Joseph (1802-1884), 4.79
Dodd, Arthur William, 8.313
Dodd, Henry Edward, 1.311
Dodd, Josiah Eustace, 8.314
Dodds, Sir John Stokell, 4.80
Dodds, Thomas Henry, 8.314
Dodery, George, 4.81

Dodery, William, 4.81
Dods, Robert Smith, 8.316
Dods, Robin, see Dods, Robert Smith
Doherty, Denis J., 8.384
Dollmann, Mrs, 4.186
Don, Charles Jardine, 4.82
Don, William, 4.82
Donaghy, John, 4.82
Donald, George McGarvie, 8.317
Donald, William Henry, 8.317
Donaldson, John (1841-1896), 4.83
Donaldson, John (1886-1933), 8.318
Donaldson, Robert Thomas, 8.319
Donaldson, St Clair George Alfred, 8.319
Donaldson, Sir Stuart Alexander, 4.84
Donaldson, Stuart Alexander, 4.84
Donnelly, John Francis, 8.320
Donnithorne, Eliza Emily, 4.86
Donnithorne, James, 4.86
Donohoe, Charles Joseph, 8.322
Donohoe, Francis Patrick, 8.322
Donohoe, James, 8.322
Donohoe, James Joseph, 8.321
Donohoe, John, 1.312
Donohoe, William Patrick, 8.322
Donovan, Thomas Joseph, 8.322
Doolette, Dorham Longford, 8.323
Doolette, Sir George Philip, 8.323
Dooley, James Thomas, 8.324
Dooley, John Braidwood, 8.325
Doorly, James Gerald Stokely, 8.326
Dore, Richard, 1.313, 2.388
Dorrington, Albert, 8.327
Dorsey, William McTaggart, 4.86
Dougherty, Constantine, 5.61
Douglas, Sir Adye, 4.87
Douglas, Alexander Douglas, 4.88
Douglas, John, 4.89
Douglas, Kathleen, 4.181
Douglas, Roger, 8.328
Douglas, William Bloomfield, 4.92
Douglass, Benjamin, 4.93
Douglass, Henry Grattan, 1.314
Dove, Frederick Allan, 8.328
Dow, David Hill, 4.93
Dow, David McKenzie, 4.95
Dow, John Lamont, 4.93
Dow, Thomas Kirkland, 4.95
Dowie, John Alexander, 4.95
Dowling, Christopher Vincent, 4.96
Dowling, Edward, 8.329
Dowling, Henry (1780-1869), 1.316
Dowling, Henry (1810-1885), 1.316
Dowling, Sir James, 1.317, 4.97
Dowling, James Arthur, 4.98
Dowling, James Sheen, 4.97
Dowling, Robert, 2.493
Dowling, Robert Hawker, 4.98
Dowling, Thomas, 4.98
Dowling, Vincent James, 4.99
Downer, Henry, 8.332
Downer, Sir John William, 8.330
Downes, Major Francis, 4.100
Downes, Rupert Major, 4.101, 8.332

Downey, Michael Henry, 8.334
Dowse, Richard, 8.335
Dowse, Thomas, 4.101
Doyle, Andrew (1774-1841), 1.320
Doyle, Andrew (1815-1878), 1.321
Doyle, Cyrus Matthew, 1.320
Doyle, Jeremiah Joseph, 8.336
Doyle, Mary, 1.514
Doyle, Stuart Frank, 8.337
Doyne, William Thomas, 4.102
Drake, Alice Maud, 12.542
Drake, F. L., 2.80
Drake, James George, 8.338
Drake-Brockman, Edmund, see Brockman,
    Edmund Ralph
Drake-Brockman, Edmund Alfred, 8.339
Drake-Brockman, Frederick Slade, 8.340
Drake-Brockman, Geoffrey, 8.341
Drake-Brockman, Karl Edgar, 8.341
Draper, Alexander Frederick John, 8.341
Draper, Daniel James, 1.321
Draper, Thomas Percy, 8.342
Drayman, John, see Woods, Walter Alan
Drennan, Frederick, 1.322
Drew, John Michael, 8.343
Driscoll, Cornelius, 1.323
Driver, Elizabeth, see Paterson
Driver, Richard, 4.102
Druce, Joseph, see Bruce, George
Druce, William, see Bruce, George
Druitt, George, 1.324
Druitt, Robert, 4.103
Druitt, Thomas, 4.103
Drummond, David Henry, 8.344
Drummond, James (1784-1863), 1.325
Drummond, James (1814-1873), 1.326
Drummond, James (saddler), 8.345
Drummond, John (fl.1796-1812), 1.327
Drummond, John (fl.1808-1823), 1.327
Drummond, John Nicol, 1.326
Drummond, Johnston, 1.325
Drummond, Ralph, 1.327
Drummond, Stanley Gillick, 8.345
Drury, Albert Victor, 4.104
Drury, Edward Robert, 4.104
Dry, Richard (1771-1843), 1.328
Dry, Sir Richard (1815-1869), 1.329
Dryblower, see Murphy, Edwin Greenslade
Dryer, Albert Thomas, 8.346
Drysdale, Alexander Leslie, 4.105
Drysdale, Anne, 1.330
Drysdale, George Russell, 4.105
Drysdale, John, 4.105
Drysdale, William, 4.105
Du Cane, Sir Charles, 4.106
Ducharme, Léon, 2.353
Duckworth, Arthur, 8.347
Du Croz, Frederick Augustus, 4.107
Dudley, Rachel, Lady, 8.348, 8.400
Dudley, William Humble Ward, Earl, 8.347
Duesbury, Frank Wentworth, 8.348
Duesbury, John William, 8.348
Du Faur, Emmeline Freda, 8.349
Du Faur, Frederick Eccleston, 4.108

Duff, Sir Robert William, 8.350
Duffield, Walter, 4.109
Duffield, Walter Geoffrey, 8.351
Duffy, Sir Charles Gavan (1816-1903), 4.109
Duffy, Charles Gavan (1855-1932), 4.113, **8.352**
Duffy, Sir Charles Leonard Gavan, 8.351
Duffy, Sir Frank Gavan, 8.352
Duffy, John Gavan, 4.113
Duffy, Maurice Boyce, 8.353
Duffy, Philip, 4.113
Dugdale, Henrietta Augusta, 4.114
Duggan, Bernard Oscar Charles, 8.354
Duggan, Edmund, 8.355
Duggan, Eugenie Marian, 7.64
Duggan, Georgina, 7.302
Duggan, William Joseph, 8.356
Duhig, Sir James, 8.356
Duhig, James Vincent, 8.359
Duigan, John Robertson, 8.360
Dulhunty, Alfred, 1.332
Dulhunty, John (d.1828), 1.331
Dulhunty, John (b.1841), 1.332
Dulhunty, Lawrence (arr.1824), 1.331
Dulhunty, Lawrence (b.1844), 1.332
Dulhunty, Robert Venour, 1.331
Dumaresq, Edward, 1.332
Dumaresq, Henry, 1.333
Dumaresq, John Saumarez, 1.334, **8.361**
Dumaresq, William John, 1.333
Dumolo, Elsie, 8.363
Dumolo, Harriet Alice, 8.362
Dumolo, Nona, 8.362
Dun, Percy Muir, 8.363
Dun, William Sutherland, 8.364
Dunbabin, Robert Leslie, 8.364
Dunbabin, Thomas Charles, 8.365
Dunbabin, Thomas James, 8.366
Duncan, Andrew Henry, 1.335
Duncan, Annie Jane, 1.335, **8.366**
Duncan, George Smith, 4.115
Duncan, Handasyde, 1.335
Duncan, John, 4.115
Duncan, Sir John James, 4.115
Duncan, Walter John Clare, 8.367
Duncan, Walter Leslie, 8.367
Duncan, William Augustine, 1.335
Dundas, Henry, 1.337
Dunhill, Mary Elizabeth, 8.368
Dunhill, Sir Thomas Peel, 8.368
Dunkley, Louisa Margaret, 8.369
Dunlop, Eliza Hamilton, 1.337
Dunlop, James, 1.338
Dunlop, James Matthew, 8.370
Dunlop, William Philip (d.1906), 8.370
Dunlop, William Philip (1877-1954), 8.370
Dunmore, Mary, 2.76
Dunn, Andrew (1854-1934), 8.371
Dunn, Andrew (1880-1956), 8.371
Dunn, Edward John, 8.372
Dunn, James Alfred, 1.339
Dunn, James Patrick Digger, 8.373
Dunn, John (1790-1861), 1.338

Dunn, John (1802-1894), 4.116
Dunn, John (1830-1892), 4.117
Dunn, Katharine, 8.371
Dunn, William Fraser, 8.374
Dunn, William Henry, 4.117
Dunn, William Herbert Alan, 8.371
Dunne, John, 8.375
Dunne, Patrick, 4.117
Dunne, Sarah, see Allen, Edith Margaret
Dunne, William John, 4.118
Dunningham, Sir John Montgomery, 8.375
Dunstan, Sir Albert Arthur, 8.376
Dunstan, Benjamin, 8.379
Dunstan, Edward Tremayne, 8.380
Dunstan, Thomas, 8.381
Dunstan, William, 8.381
Dunstan, William John, 8.382
Durack, Ernest, 8.383
Durack, Fanny, see Durack, Sarah
Durack, Michael Patrick, 8.384
Durack, Patrick, **4.119**, 5.459
Durack, Sarah, 8.385
Duramboi, see Davis, James
Duriault, François, 2.371
Duriault, Winifred, see Redmond, Winifred
Duryea, Townsend, 4.120
Duterrau, Benjamin, 1.339
Dutton, Charles Boydell, 4.120
Dutton, Francis Stacker, 1.341
Dutton, Frederick Hansborough, 1.341
Dutton, Pelham John Richard, 1.341
Dutton, William, 1.340
Dutton, William Hampden, 1.341
Dwight, Henry Tolman, 4.121
Dwyer, Catherine Winifred, 8.386
Dwyer, James Francis, 8.387
Dwyer, Joseph Wilfrid, 8.387
Dwyer, Michael, 8.386
Dwyer, Patrick Vincent, 8.387
Dwyer, Sir Walter, 8.389
Dwyer-Gray, Edmund John Chisholm, 8.390
Dyason, Edward Clarence Evelyn, 8.391
Dyer, James, 8.392
Dyer, Louise Berta Mosson Hanson, 8.392
Dyett, Sir Gilbert Joseph Cullen, 8.393
Dymock, David Lindsay, 4.122
Dymock, William, 8.394
Dyson, Ambrose Arthur, 8.398
Dyson, Edward George, 8.395
Dyson, George Arthur, 8.395
Dyson, Jane, 8.395
Dyson, William Henry, 8.396
Eade, Joel, 4.124
Eades, Richard, 4.124
Eady, Charles John, 8.399
Eagar, Edward, 1.343
Eagar, Geoffrey, 4.125
Eales, John (1799-1871), 1.344
Eales, John (1831-1894), 1.345
Eames, William L'Estrange, 8.399
Eardley-Wilmot, Sir John Eardley, 1.345
Earle, Augustus, 1.348
Earle, John, **8.401**, 11.67
Earp, George Frederick, 8.402

Earsman, William Paisley, 8.403
East, Hubert, 8.404
East, Hubert Fraser, 8.404
Easterbrook, Claude Cadman, 8.404
Easterbrook, Elijah, 8.404
Easty, John, 1.349
Eather, Richmond Cornwallis, 8.405
Ebden, Charles Hotson, 1.349
Ebsworth, Frederick Louis, 4.127
Ebsworth, Octavius Bayliffe, 4.127
Ebsworth, Thomas, 4.127
Edden, Alfred, 8.406
Eddy, Edward Miller Gard, 8.407
Edelfelt, Erik Gustaf, 7.229
Edelfelt, Isabelle, see Bean, Isabelle
Eden, Charles Henry, 4.127
Eden, Guy Ernest Morton, 4.128
Edgar, Alexander Robert, 8.408
Edgar, William Haslam, 8.409
Edge, Fane, 1.351
Edgell, Maxwell, 8.410
Edgell, Robert Gordon, 8.409
Edgerton, Clive, 8.410
Edgerton, Eric Henry Drummond, 8.410
Edgerton, James, 8.410
Edgerton, William, 8.410
Edinburgh, Alfred Ernest Albert, Duke, 4.128
Edkins, Boyd Robertson Huey, 8.411
Edkins, Edward Rowland, 4.129
Edkins, Edward Rowland Huey, 8.411
Edments, Alfred, 8.412
Edmond, James, 8.413
Edmondstone, George, 4.129
Edmunds, Richard, 12.250
Edmunds, Walter, 8.414
Edwards, Agnes Ann, 2.276
Edwards, Albert Augustine, 8.415
Edwards, Edward, 2.151
Edwards, Frederick Lewis, 8.370
Edwards, George, 8.416
Edwards, Sir James Bevan, 4.130
Edwards, John Harold McKenzie, 8.417
Edwards, Lewis David, 8.418
Edwards, Percy Malcolm, 8.418
Edwards, William Burton, 8.419
Edye, Sir Benjamin Thomas, 8.420
Egan, Daniel, 4.130
Eggers, Carl Friedrich Wilhelm (1854-1944), 4.131
Eggers, Julius Friedrich Carl, 4.131
Eggers, Karl Friedrich Wilhelm (1815-1882), 4.131
Eggleston, Sir Frederic William, 8.421
Eggleston, John, 4.132
Eggleston, Louisa (Lulu) Augusta, 8.421
Eipper, Christopher, 1.351
Elau, 1.85
Elder, Alexander Lang, 4.133
Elder, David, 4.132
Elder, Douglas, 4.132
Elder, George, 4.133
Elder, James, 1.352

Elder, Sir James Alexander Mackenzie, 8.424
Elder, Sir Thomas, 4.133
Elder, William, 4.133
Eliott, Gilbert, 4.135
Elizabeth, Sister Mary, see Brennan, Sarah Octavia
Elizabeth, Mother Mary, see Forbes, Catherine Ellen
Elkington, John Simeon, 8.425
Elkington, John Simeon Colebrook, 8.425
Ellery, Robert Lewis John, 4.135
Ellington, Sir Edward, 9.34
Elliot, Thomas Frederick, 1.353
Elliott, Charles Hazell, 8.426
Elliott, Frederick, 8.431
Elliott, George Robinson, 8.431
Elliott, Gilbert Charles Edward, 8.427
Elliott, Harold Edward, 8.428
Elliott, Helena Sumner Locke, see Locke
Elliott, James, 8.431
Elliott, James Frederick, 8.431
Elliott, Robert Charles Dunlop, 8.431
Elliott, Sizar, 4.137
Elliott, Sumner Locke, 10.127
Elliott, (William) Edward, 1.354
Ellis, Constance, 8.433
Ellis, Harold Wilfred, 11.253
Ellis, Henry Augustus, 8.433
Ellis, Henry Havelock, 4.137
Ellis, William, 2.599
Elliston, William Gore, 1.355
Elmslie, George Alexander, 8.434
Elphinstone, Augustus Cecil, 8.435
Elsasser, Carl Gottlieb, 4.138
Elsey, Joseph Ravenscroft, 4.139
Elyard, Samuel, 4.139
Elyard, William (1804-1865), 4.139
Elyard, William (arr.1821), 4.139
Emanuel, Isadore Samuel, 8.436
Emanuel, Samuel, 8.436
Emanuel, Sydney Phillip, 8.436
Embley, Edward Henry, 8.436
Embling, Thomas, 4.140
Emery, George Edwin, 8.437
Emmett, Evelyn Temple, 8.438
Emmett, Henry James, 1.356
Enderby, Samuel, 1.357
Enright, Walter John, 8.439
Eredia, Manuel Godinho de, 1.357
Erskine, James, 1.358
Erskine, James Elphinstone, 4.141
Erskine, John Elphinstone, 4.141
Esmond, James William, 4.142
Essex Evans, George, see Evans, George Essex
Esson, Hilda, see Bull, Hilda Wager
Esson, Thomas Louis Buvelot, 8.440
Estell, John, 8.441
Esther, Mother, see Silcock, Emma Caroline
Etheridge, Robert, 8.442
Evans, Ada Emily, 8.443
Evans, Alexander Arthur, 8.444

Evans, Daniel Edward, 8.445
Evans, George Essex, 8.446
Evans, George Samuel, 4.142
Evans, George William, 1.359
Evans, Henry Congreve, 4.143
Evans, Sir John William, 8.447
Evans, Lindley, 9.413
Evans, Mary, 2.224
Evans, Matilda Jane, 4.143
Evans, William James, 4.143
Evatt, Herbert Vere, 8.22
Eve, Richard, 7.593
Everard, John, 4.143
Everett, Edwin, 4.144
Everett, George, 4.144
Everett, John, 4.144
Evergood, Miles, 8.447
Everingham, Matthew James, 1.360
Ewan, James, 4.145
Ewart, Alfred James, 8.448
Ewart, David, 4.146
Ewart, Edmund Brown, 8.448
Ewart, Florence Maud, 8.450
Ewen, John Carr, 8.451
Ewing, John, 8.452
Ewing, Norman Kirkwood, 8.452
Ewing, Robert, 8.453
Ewing, Thomas James, 1.361
Ewing, Sir Thomas Thomson, 8.455
Eyre, Alfred John, 1.365
Eyre, Edward John, **1.362**, 2.629
Eyre, John (1768-1854), 1.365
Eyre, John (b.1771), 1.365
Facy, Peter (1822-1890), 4.147
Facy, Peter (d.1832), 4.147
Fahey, John, 8.456
Fairbairn, Charles, 8.456
Fairbairn, Frederick William, 8.456
Fairbairn, Geoffrey Forrester, 8.458
Fairbairn, George (1816-1895), 4.147
Fairbairn, Sir George (1855-1943), 8.456
Fairbairn, James Valentine, 8.458
Fairbairn, Stephen, 8.459
Fairbridge, James William, 8.460
Fairbridge, Kingsley Ogilvie, 8.460
Fairfax, Sir James Oswald, 8.460
Fairfax, Sir James Reading, 8.460
Fairfax, John, 2.41, 2.591, **4.148**
Fairfax, John Hubert Fraser, 8.462
Fairfax, Mabel Alice Emmeline, Lady,
   8.461
Fairfax, Ruth Beatrice, 8.462
Fairley, Sir Andrew Walker, 8.463
Fairley, James, 8.463
Faithful, George, 1.367
Faithful, William, 1.367
Faithful, William Pitt (1774-1847), 1.367
Faithfull, William Pitt (1806-1896), 4.149
Falconer, William Rose, 4.149
Falder, see Kaleski, Robert Lucian
   Stanislaus
Falk, Leib Aisack, 8.464
Falkiner, Franc Brereton Sadleir, 8.464
Falkiner, Franc Sadlier, 4.150

Falkiner, Otway Rothwell, 8.464
Fallon, Cyril Joseph, 8.466
Fallon, James Thomas, 4.151
Fanning, Edward, 4.151
Fanning, Frederick, 4.152
Fanning, William, 4.152
Farber, Henry Christian, 8.467
Farleigh, John, 8.467
Farleigh, John Gibson, 8.467
Farmer, Joseph, 4.153
Farmer, Sir William, 4.153
Farnell, Frank, 4.154, **8.468**
Farnell, James Squire, 4.154
Farquhar, Sir Walter, 1.290
Farr, George Henry, 4.155
Farrar, Ernest Henry, 8.469
Farrell, John (1851-1904), 4.156
Farrell, John (1883-1955), 8.470
Farrelly, Mary Martha, 8.470
Farrer, William James, 8.471
Farthing, William Armstrong, 4.157
Fatnowna, John Kwailiu Abelfai, 8.473
Fatnowna, Orrani, 8.474
Faucett, Peter, 4.157
Fauchery, Antoine Julien, 4.158
Faulding, Francis Hardey, 4.159
Faunce, Alured Dodsworth, 1.368
Faunce, Alured Tasker, 1.367
Faunce, Thomas, 1.367
Favenc, Ernest, 4.160
Fawkner, John Pascoe, 1.368
Fawsitt, Charles Edward, 8.474
Feakes, Henry James, 8.475
Feetham, John Oliver, 8.476
Feez, Adolph Frederick Milford, 8.477
Feez, Arthur Herman Henry Milford, 8.477
Fegan, Donald, 8.479
Fegan, John Lionel, 8.478
Fehon, William Meeke, 8.479
Fell, David, 8.480
Fell, William Scott, 8.480
Fellows, Thomas Howard, 4.160
Felton, Alfred, 4.161
Fenner, Charles Albert Edward, 8.481
Fenton, Charles Benjamin Monds, 4.163
Fenton, Elizabeth, 1.371
Fenton, James, 4.162
Fenton, James Edward, 8.482
Fenton, Michael, 1.371
Fereday, Dudley, 1.371
Ferguson, Charles William, 4.163
Ferguson, Sir David Gilbert, 8.484
Ferguson, Emily, 8.487
Ferguson, Eustace William, 8.484
Ferguson, John (1802-1883), 1.372
Ferguson, John (1830-1906), 8.485
Ferguson, John (1852-1925), 8.486
Ferguson, Mephan, 4.163
Ferguson, Sir Ronald Craufurd Munro, see
   Munro Ferguson
Ferguson, William, 8.487
Fergusson, Sir James, 4.164
Ferres, John, 4.165
Ferrier, Jim, 12.501

Ferry, Michael Augustus, 8.488
Ferry, Thomas Arthur, 8.488
Fetherston, Gerald Henry, 8.489
Fetherston, Richard Herbert Joseph, 8.489
Fetherstonhaugh, Cuthbert, 4.166
Fewings, Eliza Ann, 8.490
Fiaschi, Carlo Ferruchio, 8.491
Fiaschi, Piero Francis Bruno, 8.491
Fiaschi, Thomas Henry, 8.491
Fidler, Isabel Margaret, 8.492
Fidler, Mabel Maude, 8.492
Fidler, William, 8.492
Field, Barron, 1.373
Field, Edward Percy, 8.493
Field, Ernest, 8.494
Field, Henry, 11.10, 12.113
Fihelly, John Arthur, 8.495
Fincham, George, 4.167
Finch-Hatton, Harold Heneage, 4.168
Findley, Edward, 8.496
Fink, Benjamin Josman, 4.168
Fink, Theodore, 7.140, **8.497**
Finlay, Mary McKenzie, 8.498
Finlayson, John Harvey, 4.169
Finn, Edmund, 1.376
Finn, Henry, 8.499
Finnerty, John Michael, 8.501
Finney, Thomas, 4.170
Finnis, John, 1.376
Finniss, Boyle Travers, 1.377
Finsch, Otto, 4.170
Fishbourne, John William Yorke, 8.501
Fisher, Andrew, 8.502
Fisher, Charles Brown, 4.171
Fisher, James Cowley Morgan, 4.172
Fisher, Sir James Hurtle, 1.379
Fisher, Jemima, 4.173
Fisher, John, 4.173
Fisher, Joseph, 4.172
Fisher, Joshua, 4.172
Fisher, Lala, see Fisher, Mary Lucy
Fisher, Mary Lucy, 8.507
Fisher, Robert, 8.502
Fisher, Thomas, 4.173
Fisk, Sir Ernest Thomas, 8.508
Fisken, Archibald, 4.174
Fison, Lorimer, 4.175
Fitch, Algernon Sydney, 8.510
Fitchett, William, 8.511
Fitchett, William Henry, 8.511
Fitts, Frederick A., 6.244
Fitz, Robert, 1.157, **1.380**
Fitz, William John, 1.381
FitzGerald, Charles, **1.381**, 3.428
Fitzgerald, Charles Borromeo, 4.179
FitzGerald, Eleanora Caroline, 1.382
Fitzgerald, George Parker, 4.176
Fitzgerald, Sir Gerald, 4.176
Fitzgerald, John Daniel, 8.513
Fitzgerald, Nicholas, 4.176
Fitzgerald, Richard, 1.383
Fitzgerald, Robert, 4.177
FitzGerald, Robert David, 4.178
Fitzgerald, Thomas Henry, 4.179

FitzGerald, Sir Thomas Naghten, 4.180
FitzGibbon, Edmund Gerald, 4.181
Fitzhardinge, William, 4.183
Fitzhardinge, William George Augustus,
   4.182
Fitzmaurice, R., 3.463
Fitzpatrick, Columbus, 4.183
Fitzpatrick, John, 4.184
Fitzpatrick, John Charles Lucas, 8.515
Fitzpatrick, Kathleen, 11.238
Fitzpatrick, Michael, 4.184
FitzRoy, Sir Charles Augustus, 1.384
FitzRoy, Mary, Lady, 1.385
Fitzsimmons, Robert, 8.516
Fitzsimons, Herbert Paton, 8.517
Fitzsimons, William Robert, 8.517
Fiveash, Rosa Catherine, 8.517
Fizelle, Rah, see Fizelle, Reginald Cecil
   Grahame
Fizelle, Reginald Cecil Grahame, 8.518
Flack, Edwin Harold, 8.519
Flanagan, Mervyn, 12.421
Flanagan, Roderick, 4.185
Flanagan, Thomas, 9.188
Flannery, George Ernest, 8.520
Flaxman, Charles, 1.16
Flegg, Henry (d.1894) 8.52l
Flegg, Henry (1878-1960), 8.521
Flegg, Jersey, see Flegg, Henry
   (1878-1960)
Fleming, John William, 8.521
Fleming, Joseph, 4.186
Fleming, Sir Valentine, 4.187
Fleming, William Montgomerie, 8.522
Fletcher, Charles Brunsdon, 8.523
Fletcher, James, 4.188
Fletcher, James Lionel, 8.524
Fletcher, John William, 8.524
Fletcher, Joseph Horner, 4.189
Fletcher, Joseph James, 8.525
Fletcher, Lionel Bale, 8.526
Fletcher, Michael Scott, 8.526
Fletcher, Richard, 5.450
Fletcher, William Roby, 4.189
Flierl, Johann, 8.527
Flinders, Matthew, 1.389
Flood, Edward, 4.190
Florance, Thomas, 1.391
Flower, Horace, 4.191
Flower, Willoughby, 8.528
Flowers, Fred, 8.528
Floyd, Alfred Ernest, 8.530
Flynn, Errol Leslie, 8.534
Flynn, Jeremiah Francis, see O'Flynn
Flynn, John, 8.531
Flynn, Julia Teresa, 8.534
Flynn, Theodore Thomson, 8.534
Foelsche, Paul Heinrich Matthias, 4.192
Foley, James Joseph, see Griffen-Foley
Foley, Laurence, 4.193
Folingsby, George Frederick, 4.193
Follett, Frank William, 8.536
Foott, Cecil Henry, 8.536
Foott, Mary Hannay, 4.194

Foran, Martin Henry (Harry), 8.537
Forbes, Arthur Edward, 8.538
Forbes, Catherine Ellen, 8.539
Forbes, Sir Francis, 1.392
Forbes, Francis Ewen, 4.195
Forbes, Frederick Augustus, 4.195
Forbes, George, 1.392
Forbes, Henry Ogg, 4.195
Forbes, James, 1.399
Forbes, William Anderson, 4.196
Ford, Mary, 1.383
Ford, Richard, 4.197
Forgan Smith, see Smith, William Forgan
Forlong, Eliza, 1.400
Forlong, John, 1.400
Forlong, William, see Forlonge
Forlonge, Andrew, 1.401
Forlonge, William, 1.400
Forrest, Alexander, **8.540**, 11.449
Forrest of Bunbury, Baron, see Forrest, Sir
  John (1847-1918)
Forrest, David, 8.542
Forrest, Edward Barrow, 8.543
Forrest, Haughton, 8.543
Forrest, John (1820-1883), 4.198
Forrest, Sir John (1847-1918), 8.544
Forrest, John (1848-1911), 8.552
Forrest, John (1887-1960), 8.543
Forrest, Margaret, 8.544
Forrest, Margaret Elvire, Lady, 8.545
Forrest, Matthew, 8.540
Forrest, Robert, 1.401
Forrest, William (arr.1842), 8.544
Forrest, William (1835-1903), 8.551
Forster, Anthony, 4.198
Forster, Baron, see Forster, Sir Henry
  William
Forster, Frederick, 8.554
Forster, Sir Henry William, 8.552
Forster, Johann Georg(e) Adam, 1.402
Forster, Johann Reinhold, 1.403
Forster, Matthew, 1.404
Forster, Norman Lachlan, 8.554
Forster, Thomas Richmond, 8.553
Forster, William, 4.199
Forster, William Mark, 4.201
Forsyth, Archibald, 4.202
Forsyth, George, 4.203
Forsyth, James, 8.554
Forsyth, John Keatly, 8.555
Forsyth, Marjory, 8.395
Forsyth, Samuel, 8.556
Forth, Nowell Barnard de Lancey, 8.556
Forwood, Walter Weech, 4.204
Fosbery, Edmund Walcott, 4.204
Fosbrook, Leonard, 1.405
Fossey, Joseph, 1.406
Foster, Alfred William, 8.557
Foster, Hubert John, 8.559
Foster, John, 1.407
Foster, John Leslie Fitzgerald Vesey, 4.205
Foster, Richard Witty, 8.560
Foster, Roland, 8.560
Foster, William, 1.407

Foster, William James, 8.561
Foster, William John, 4.206
Foveaux, Joseph, 1.407
Fowler, David, 4.207
Fowler, Elizabeth Lilian Maud, 8.562
Fowler, Enoch, 4.209
Fowler, Francis Edmund Town, 4.208
Fowler, George Swan, 4.207
Fowler, Hugh Lionel, 8.563
Fowler, James, 4.207
Fowler, James Mackinnon, 8.564
Fowler, James Richard, 4.208
Fowler, Laura Margaret, 4.208
Fowler, Margaret, 4.207-8
Fowler, Robert, 4.209
Fowler, Thomas Walker, 8.565
Fowler, W. Warde, 12.34
Fowles, Edwin Wesley Howard, 8.565
Fowles, Herbert James, 8.566
Fowles, Joseph, 1.409
Fox, Emanuel Phillips, 8.567
Fox, Ethel Carrick, 8.568
Fox, Sir Frank Ignatius, 8.568
Fox, Henry Thomas, 4.210
Foxton, John Greenlaw, 8.569
Foxton, Justin Fox Greenlaw, 8.569
Foy, Francis, 8.570
Foy, Mark (1830-1884), 4.211
Foy, Mark (1865-1950), 8.570
Franc, Maud Jeanne, see Evans, Matilda
  Jane
Francis, Alice Ellen, 10.129
Francis, James Goodall, 4.211
Francis, Leonard, 8.571
Francis, Maurice, 8.416
Frankenstein, Rosa, 3.45
Franki, James Peter, 8.572
Frankland, George, 1.410
Franklin, Jane, Lady, **1.411**, 1.415
Franklin, Sir John, **1.412**, 2.38, 2.249
Franklin, Miles, see Franklin, Stella
  Maria(n) Sarah Miles
Franklin, Richard Penrose, 8.573
Franklin, Stella Maria(n) Sarah Miles,
  8.574
Franklyn, Henry Mortimer, 4.213
Fraser, Alexander, 4.214
Fraser, Archibald Colquhoun (1832-1896),
  4.214
Fraser, Archibald Colquhoun (b.1868),
  4.215
Fraser, Charles, see Frazer
Fraser, Charles Forbes, 3.470
Fraser, Sir Colin, 8.576
Fraser, Eliza Ann, 1.468
Fraser, Hugh, 8.578
Fraser, John Edward, 8.577
Fraser, Sir Malcolm, 4.215
Fraser, Peter Gordon, 1.415
Fraser, Simon (1824?-1889), 4.216
Fraser, Sir Simon (1832-1919), 4.216
Fraser, Simon Alexander, 8.578
Frater, Robert Guy, 7.223
Frater, William, **8.579**, 11.244

Frayne, Clara, see Frayne, Ursula
Frayne, Ursula, 4.217
Frazer, Charles, 1.416
Frazer, Charles Edward, 8.580
Frazer, John, 4.218
Frazier, Charles, see Frazer
Freame, Wykeham Henry Koba, 8.581
Freedman, David Isaac, 8.581
Freehill, Eileen Marie, 4.219
Freehill, Francis Bede, 4.219
Freehill, Patrick, 4.219
Freeleagus, Christy Kosmas, 8.582
Freeling, Sir Arthur Henry, 4.220
Freeling, Sir Francis, 4.220
Freeman, Ambrose William, 8.583
Freeman, James, 4.220
Freeman, Jessie, see Aspinall, Jessie
  Strahorn
Freeman, Paul, 8.584
Freeman, Samuel, 10.68
Freeman, William Addison, 8.583
Freeman, William Glover Webb, 4.220
French, Charles, 8.585
French, Charles Hamilton, 8.585
French, Sir George Arthur, 8.586
French, John, 8.587
French, Sir John Russell, 8.587
Frencham, Henry, 4.221
Frewin, Kenneth Moreton, 8.588
Freycinet, Louis-Claude Desaulses de, 1.71
Friend, Matthew Curling, 1.417
Friström, Carl Magnus Oscar, 8.589
Fritzsche, Gotthard Daniel, 2.33
Frodsham, George Horsfall, 8.590
Froggatt, Walter Wilson, 8.591
Frome, Edward Charles, 1.418
Frost, Frederick Charlesworth, 8.592
Frost, John, 1.419
Froude, James Anthony, 4.221
Fry, Henry Phibbs, 1.420
Fry, James, 4.222
Fryar, William, 4.223
Fryberg, Abraham, 9.571
Fryett, Richard William, 1.421
Fuhrman, Osmond Charles William, 8.592
Fullarton, Robert Russell, 4.223
Fuller, Sir Benjamin John, 8.593
Fuller, Colin Dunmore, 8.594
Fuller, Sir George Warburton, 8.595
Fuller, John (1879-1959), 8.593
Fuller, John (d.1923), 8.593
Fuller, Sir John Michael Fleetwood, 8.597
Fullerton, George, 4.224
Fullerton, James, 4.224
Fullerton, Mary Eliza, 8.598
Fullerton, Robert, 8.598
Fullwood, Albert Henry, 8.598
Fulton, Henry, 1.421
Fulton, Thomas, 2.84, **4.225**
Furber, Thomas Frederick, 8.599
Furphy, John, 4.225
Furphy, Joseph, 8.600
Fyans, Foster, 1.422
Fysh, Sir Philip Oakley, 8.602

Fysh, Sir Wilmot Hudson, 8.603
Gabriel, Charles John, 8.606
Gabriel, Charles Louis (1857-1927), 8.606
Gabriel, Charles Louis (snr), 8.606
Gabriel, Joseph, 8.606
Gaby, Alfred Edward, 8.607
Gadsden, Jabez, 8.607
Gainford, Thomas, 4.227
Gairdner, Gordon, 1.425
Gale, Charles Frederick, 8.608
Gale, John, 4.227
Gale, Walter Augustus, 8.608
Gale, Walter Frederick, 8.609
Gall, William, 8.610
Galway, Sir Henry Lionel, 8.611
Galway, Marie Carola Franciska Roselyne,
  Lady, 8.611
Game, Sir Philip Woolcott, **8.612**, 9.665
Gamman, Andrew, see Garran, Andrew
  (1825-1901)
Gannon, James, 4.228
Gannon, Michael, 4.228
Gant, Tetley, 8.613
Garden, James, 8.614
Garden, John Smith, 8.614
Gardener, Alfred Henry, 4.229
Gardiner, Albert, 8.617
Gardiner, Francis, 4.229
Gardiner, James, 8.618
Gardiner, John, 1.425
Gardiner, John A., 3.1
Gardner, John, 4.230
Gardner, Robert, 8.619
Gardner, William, 1.425
Garland, David John, 8.619
Garland, James, 4.230
Garland, John, 8.620
Garlick, Daniel, 4.231
Garlick, Moses, 4.231
Garling, Frederick (1775-1848), 1.426
Garling, Frederick (1806-1873), 1.427
Garling, Frederick Augustus, 1.428
Garnsey, Arthur Henry, 8.621
Garnsey, Charles Frederick, 4.232
Garnsey, Thomas Rock, 4.232
Garran, Andrew (1825-1901), 4.233
Garran, Andrew (1906-1965), 8.625
Garran, Sir Isham Peter, 8.625
Garran, John Cheyne, 8.625
Garran, Richard Randolph, 8.625
Garran, Sir Robert Randolph, 4.233, **8.622**
Garrard, Jacob, 4.234
Garratt, Charles Clement, 8.625
Garrett, James, 1.428
Garrett, Thomas, 4.235
Garrett, Thomas William, 8.625
Garrick, Sir James Francis, 4.235
Garsia, Rupert Clare, 8.626
Garvan, James Patrick, 4.236
Garvan, Sir John Joseph, 8.627
Garvin, Lucy Arabella Stocks, 8.628
Gascoigne, Stephen Harold, 8.629
Gatehouse, George, 1.428
Gatehouse, Silas, 1.429

Gatenby, Andrew, 1.429
Gates, William, 1.430
Gatliff, John Henry, 8.629
Gatty, Harold Charles, 8.630
Gaunson, David, 4.238
Gaunson, William, 4.238
Gaunt, Cecil Robert, 8.631
Gaunt, Sir Ernest Frederick Augustus, 8.631
Gaunt, Sir Guy Reginald Archer, 8.631
Gaunt, Mary Eliza Bakewell, 8.632
Gaunt, William Henry, 4.238
Gavan Duffy, see Duffy, Charles Gavan (1855-1932)
Gawler, George, 1.431
Gawler, Henry, 1.435
Gay, William, 8.633
Geach, Portia Swanston, 8.634
Geake, William Henry Gregory, 8.635
Geikie, Archibald Constable, 4.239
Geils, Andrew, 1.435
Gell, John Philip, 1.436
Gellatly, Francis Mephan, 8.635
Gellibrand, Isabella, 8.636
Gellibrand, Sir John, 8.636
Gellibrand, Joseph Tice, 1.437-8
Gellibrand, Mary Selina, 1.438
Gellibrand, Thomas Lloyd, 1.437
Gellibrand, Walter Angus Bethune, 1.437
Gellibrand, William St Paul, 1.438
Geoghegan, Patrick Bonaventure, 4.240
George, Henry, 4.241
George, Madeline Rees, 8.639
George, William James, 8.639
Gepp, Sir Herbert William, 8.640
Gerard, Alfred Edward, 8.642
Gerard, Edwin Field, 8.643
Gerard, John, 3.29
Gericke, Johann Wilhelm, 2.422-3
Gerler, Carl Friedrich, 2.422-3
Gerrald, Joseph, 1.438
Gerstaecker, Friedrich, 4.242
Gess, George, see Guest
Gibb, William, 8.644
Gibbes, John George Nathaniel, 1.439
Gibbons, Geraldine Scholastica, 4.242
Gibbs, Cecilia May, 8.644
Gibbs, Herbert William, 8.644
Gibbs, Sibyl Enid Vera Munro, see Morrison
Giblin, Lyndhurst Falkiner, 4.244, **8.646**
Giblin, Ronald Worthy, 8.648
Giblin, William Robert, 4.243
Gibney, Matthew, 8.649
Gibson, Alexander, 8.660
Gibson, Alexander James, 8.651
Gibson, Angus, 4.244
Gibson, Bessie, see Gibson, Elizabeth Dickson
Gibson, Colin, 8.660
Gibson, David (1780?-1858), 1.439
Gibson, David (arr.1860), 8.658
Gibson, David Havelock, 8.658
Gibson, Elizabeth Dickson, 8.651

Gibson, Grace, 8.658
Gibson, James Alexander (1772-1841), 1.440
Gibson, James Alexander (1814-1860), 1.440
Gibson, John Edward, 8.654
Gibson, John Lockhart, 8.652
Gibson, Keith, 8.660
Gibson, Quentin, 8.660
Gibson, Ralph, 8.660
Gibson, Robert (1855-1936), 8.653
Gibson, Sir Robert (1863-1934), 8.654
Gibson, William, 8.656
Gibson, William Alfred, 8.657
Gibson, William Gerrand, 8.658
Gibson, William Ralph Boyce, 8.659
Giffen, George, 4.244
Gilbert, Charles Marsh (Nash) Web, 9.1
Gilbert, David John, 9.2
Gilbert, Edward, 9.3
Gilbert, John (1810?-1845), 1.441
Gilbert, John (1842?-1865), 4.245
Gilbert, Joseph, 4.245
Gilbert, Maggie Jane, 9.482
Gilbert, William, 4.246
Gilchrist, John, 1.442
Gilchrist, William Oswald, 1.442
Giles, Clement, 9.4
Giles, Ernest, 4.246
Giles, William, 1.443
Gilfillan, Robert, 4.247
Gill, Harry Pelling, 9.4
Gill, Henry Horatio, 4.247
Gill, James Howard, 4.248
Gill, Myra, see Kemble
Gill, Richard, 4.248
Gill, Samuel Thomas, 1.444
Gill, Thomas, 9.5
Gill, William Henry, 4.247
Gill, William Wyatt, 4.249
Gillbee, Sarah, 4.249-50
Gillbee, William, 4.249
Gillen, Francis James, 9.6
Gillen, Peter Paul, 9.7
Gilles, Osmond, 1.445
Gillespie, Sir Robert Winton, 9.8
Gillies, Dougald, 9.11
Gillies, Duncan, 4.250
Gillies, Harriett Turquand, 4.252
Gillies, James Hynds, 9.9
Gillies, John, 9.10
Gillies, Robert Towers, 9.11
Gillies, William Neil (Neal), 9.11
Gillison, Andrew, 9.12
Gillison, Douglas Napier, 9.12
Gillott, Sir Samuel, 9.12
Gilmore, Hugh, 4.252
Gilmore, Dame Mary Jean, 9.14
Gilmore, William Alexander, 9.14
Gilpin, Oliver, 9.16
Gilruth, Andrew, 9.17
Gilruth, Ann, 9.17
Gilruth, John Anderson, 9.17
Gipps, Sir George, 1.446

Girdlestone, Henry, 9.19
Gisborne, Henry Fyshe (Fysche), 1.453
Givens, Thomas, 9.20
Gladman, Frederick John, 4.253
Gladman, Philip Howard, 4.254
Glasfurd, Alexander, 9.20
Glasfurd, Charles Eric, 9.21
Glasfurd, Divie Colin Peter, 9.21
Glasfurd, Duncan John, 9.20
Glasgow, Sir Thomas William, 9.21
Glass, Barnet, 9.24
Glass, Hugh, 4.254
Glassey, Thomas, 9.24
Glauert, Ludwig, 9.25
Gleadow, John Ward, 1.454
Gledson, David Alexander, 9.26
Glencross, Eleanor, 9.27
Glenelg, Baron, 1.455
Glennie, Benjamin, 4.255
Glenny, Henry, 4.256
Glossop, John Collings Taswell, 9.28
Glover, Charles Peter, 9.29
Glover, Charles Richmond John, 9.29
Glover, John, 1.455
Glowery, Mary, 11.50
Glyde, Lavington, 4.257
Glynn, Eugene, 9.32
Glynn, Sir Joseph, 9.32
Glynn, Patrick McMahon, 9.30
Glynn, Robert, 9.32
Goble, Joseph, 9.32
Goble, Joseph Hunter, 9.32
Goble, Stanley James, 9.33
Gocher, William Henry, 9.35
Goddard, Benjamin, 9.35
Goddard, Ernest James, 9.36
Goddard, Henry Arthur, 9.37
Goderich, Viscount, 1.456
Godfrey, Frederick Race, 4.257
Godfrey, Sidney George, 9.38
Goe, Field Flowers, 9.39
Goethe, Matthias, 4.258
Goldberg, Albert, 8.256
Goldberg, Dulcie, see Deamer, Mary
  Elizabeth Kathleen Dulcie
Goldfinch, Sir Philip Henry Macarthur,
  9.39
Goldhar, Pinchas, 9.40
Goldie, Alexander, 1.457
Goldie, Andrew, 4.259
Golding, Annie Mackenzie, 9.41
Golding, Isabella Theresa, 9.41
Golding, Kate, see Dwyer, Catherine
  Winifred
Goldsbrough, Richard, 4.260
Goldsmith, Frederick William, 9.42
Goldstein, Isabella, 9.43
Goldstein, Jacob Robert Yannasch, 9.43
Goldstein, Vida Jane Mary, **9.43**, 9.490
Goll, Edward, 9.45
Gooch, Walter, 9.46
Goodchap, Charles Augustus, 4.261
Goode, Agnes Knight, 9.47
Goode, Sir Charles Henry, 4.262

Goodenough, James Graham, 4.262
Goodenough, Victoria, 4.263
Goodisson, Albert Elliot, 9.47
Goodisson, Lillie Elizabeth, 9.47
Goodlet, John Hay, 4.263
Goodman, George, 4.264
Goodman, Margaret Elizabeth, 4.265
Goodman, Sir William George Toop, 9.48
Goodwin, Sir Thomas Herbert John
  Chapman, 9.49
Goodwin, William Lushington, 1.457
Goold, James Alipius, 4.265
Goold, Stephen Styles, 4.267
Goold-Adams, Sir Hamilton John, 9.50
Gordon, Adam Lindsay, 4.267
Gordon, Alexander (1815-1903), 4.269
Gordon, Sir Alexander (1858-1942), 4.269,
  9.55
Gordon, Alexander (dep.1859), 4.276
Gordon, Bernard Sidney, 9.50
Gordon, Sir David John, 9.51
Gordon, Douglas Peel, 9.52
Gordon, George, 4.270
Gordon, George William, 1.364
Gordon, Grosvenor George Stuart, 9.52
Gordon, James (1779-1842), 1.458
Gordon, James (arr. 1859), 9.53
Gordon, Sir John Hannah, **9.53**, 12.419
Gordon, John Rutherford, 9.52
Gordon, Joseph Maria, 9.54
Gordon, Margaret Jane, 9.55
Gordon, Patrick Robertson, 4.270
Gordon, Samuel Deane, 4.271
Gordon, Sandy, 5.287
Gordon, Sir Thomas Stewart, 9.56
Gordon, William Beattie, 9.53
Gore, Elizabeth, 4.272
Gore, John, 4.271
Gore, Robert, 4.272
Gore, St George Ralph, 4.273
Gore, St George Richard, 4.272
Gore, St John Thomas, 4.272
Gore, Thomas, 4.272
Gore, Thomas Jefferson, 4.273
Gore, William, 1.459
Gore, William Francis, 4.272
Gorman, John Thomas, 9.57
Gormanston, Jenico William Joseph
  Preston, Viscount, 9.57
Gormly, James, 4.273
Gorton, Margaret, 2.482
Gorumbaru, Stephen, 12.288
Gosling, John William, 1.460
Gosman, Alexander, 4.274
Gosman, John, 4.275
Gosman, William, 4.275
Gosse, William, 4.276
Gosse, William Christie, 4.276
Gotch, John Speechly, 4.276
Goudie, Sir George Louis, 9.58
Gouger, Henry, 1.461
Gouger, Robert, 1.461
Gough, Doris Lucy Eleanor Bloomfield,
  7.372

Goulburn, Frederick, 1.200, **1.463**
Goulburn, Henry, 1.464
Gould, Sir Albert John, 9.59
Gould, Charles, 4.277
Gould, Elizabeth, 1.465
Gould, Ellen Julia, 9.59
Gould, John, **1.465**, 4.139
Gould, Nathaniel, 9.61
Gould, William Buelow, 1.467
Governor, Jimmy, 9.62
Govett, William Romaine, 1.467
Gow, Robert Milne, 9.62
Gowlland, John Thomas Ewing, 4.278
Gowrie, Sir Alexander Gore Arkwright
  Hore-Ruthven, Earl, 9.63
Gowrie, Zara Eileen, Lady, 9.63, **9.64**
Goyder, George Woodroffe, 4.278
Grace, Joseph Neal, 9.65
Graebner, Carl Friedrich, 9.65
Graham, Arthur Ernest James Charles
  King, 9.66
Graham, Charles James, 4.280
Graham, George, 9.67
Graham, James (1819-1898), 4.282
Graham, Sir James (1856-1913), 4.281
Graham, John, 1.468
Graham, Margaret, 9.68
Graham, Peter, 8.349
Grahame, William Calman, 9.69
Grainger, George Percy, 9.69
Grainger, Henry William Allerdale, 9.72
Grainger, John Harry, 9.69
Grainger, Rosa (Rose) Annie, 9.71
Gramp, Gustav, 4.283
Gramp, Johann, 4.283
Gramp, Louis Hugo, 4.283
Grano, Paul Langton, 9.73
Grant, Alexander Charles, 9.74
Grant, Charles see Glenelg, Baron
Grant, Charles Henry, 9.74
Grant, Charles William, 9.75
Grant, Donald McLennan, 9.75
Grant, Douglas, 9.76
Grant, James, 1.468
Grant, James Macpherson, 4.283
Grant, John (b.1776), **1.469**, 2.111
Grant, John (arr.1794), 1.126
Grant, Kenneth McDonald, 9.77
Grant, Sir Kerr, 9.77
Grant, Mrs P. G., 11.492
Grant, Robert, 9.76
Grant, William, 9.79
Granville, Cecil Horace Plantagenet, 9.80
Grasby, William Catton, 9.81
Gratton, Norman Murray Gladstone, 9.82
Graves, James Abraham Howlin, 4.284
Graves, James Joseph, 9.83
Graves, John Woodcock, 4.285
Gray, Edmund Dwyer, see Dwyer-Gray,
  Edmund John Chisholm
Gray, Ethel, 9.84
Gray, George Wilkie, 9.84
Gray, Herbert Victor, 9.86
Gray, Isabel, 9.85
Gray, James, 4.286
Gray, John Edward, 1.470
Gray, Moses Wilson, 4.287
Grayndler, Edward, 9.86
Grayson, Henry Joseph, 9.87
Greaves, Edwin, 9.88
Greaves, William Clement, 9.88
Green, Albert Ernest, 9.89
Green, Alfred, 4.288
Green, Alfred Lawrence, 4.289
Green, Arthur Vincent, 9.90
Green, Daniel Cooper, 9.91
Green, Florence Emily, 9.90
Green, James, 9.92
Green, Percy Gordon, 9.93
Green, Richard, 4.288
Green, Samuel, 4.289
Green, Solomon, 9.94
Green, William Herbert, 9.94
Greene, George Henry, 9.95
Greene, Molesworth Richard, 4.289
Greene, Sir Walter Massy, see
  Massy-Greene
Greene, William Pomeroy, 9.95
Greene, William Pomeroy Crawford, 9.96
Greenfield, Alexander Mackay, 9.96
Greenfield, Angus, 9.97
Greenup, Jane, 4.291
Greenup, Richard, 4.290
Greenway, Charles Capel, 1.472, **4.291**
Greenway, Francis, 1.470
Greenway, Mary, 1.472
Greenwell, Sybil, see Morrison, Sibyl Enid
  Vera Munro
Greenwood, James, 4.292
Greeves, Augustus Frederick Adolphus,
  4.292
Greeves, Carji, see Greeves, Edward
  Goderich
Greeves, Edward Goderich, 9.97
Gregor, John, 1.472
Gregory, Sir Augustus Charles, 4.293
Gregory, David William, 4.295
Gregory, Edward James, 4.296
Gregory, Edward William, 4.295
Gregory, Francis Thomas, 4.295
Gregory, Henry, 9.98
Gregory, Henry Gregory, 1.473
Gregory, Jack Morrison, 9.99
Gregory, John, 1.474
Gregory, John Walter, 9.100
Gregory, Sydney Edward, 4.296
Gregson, Jesse, 4.296
Gregson, John Compton, 1.476
Gregson, Thomas George, 1.475
Greig, Clara Puella, 9.101
Greig, Grata Flos Matilda, 9.101
Greig, Jane Stocks, 9.101
Greig, Janet Lindsay, 9.101
Greig, Robert Lindsay, 9.101
Greig, Stella Fida, 9.101
Gresham, Ada, 4.298
Gresham, William Hutchison, 4.297
Gresswell, Dan, 9.103

Gresswell, Dan Astley, 9.103
Greville, Edward, 4.298
Greville, Hector, 9.104
Greville, Henrietta, 9.104
Grey, Earl, *see* Grey, Henry George
Grey, Sir George, **1.476**, 3.428
Grey, Henry George, 1.480
Grey-Smith, Sir Ross, 6.144
Gribble, Ernest Richard Bulmer, 4.299
Gribble, John Brown, 4.299
Grice, Elsa, 9.106
Grice, Sir John, 9.105
Grice, Richard, 4.300
Grieve, Robert Cuthbert, 9.106
Griffen Foley, James Joseph, 9.107
Griffen Foley, John Raymond, 9.107
Griffin, Marion Lucy Mahony, 9.108
Griffin, Thomas John Augustus, 4.300
Griffin, Walter Burley, 9.107
Griffith, Arthur Hill, 9.110
Griffith, Charles James, 4.301
Griffith, Edward, 9.112
Griffith, Sir Samuel Walker, 3.246, **9.112**
Griffiths, Albert, 9.119
Griffiths, Alfred Atherton, 9.121
Griffiths, George Herbert, 9.121
Griffiths, George Richard, 1.485
Griffiths, George Washington, 9.120
Griffiths, Herbert Tyrrell, 1.485
Griffiths, John, 1.197, 1.340, **1.486**
Griffiths, John Alfred, 9.121
Griffiths, Jonathan, 1.485
Griffiths, Philip Lewis, 9.122
Griffiths, Thomas (1865-1947), 9.123
Griffiths, Thomas (cotton merchant), 9.120
Griffiths, William Russell, 1.485
Grimes, Charles, 1.487
Grimley, Frank, 9.124
Grimley, Sarah Anne, 6.71
Grimm, Arthur Hetherington, 4.302
Grimm, George, 4.302
Grimmett, Clarence Victor, 9.125
Grimshaw, Beatrice Ethel, 9.125
Grimwade, Alfred Sheppard, 4.303, 9.127
Grimwade, Edward Norton, 4.303, **9.126**
Grimwade, Frederick Sheppard, 4.302
Grimwade, Harold William, 4.303, **9.126**
Grimwade, Sir Wilfrid Russell, 4.303,
 9.126
Grin, Henri Louis, *see* De Rougement,
 Louis
Griver, Martin, 4.303
Groom, Arthur, 9.128
Groom, Arthur Champion, 9.129
Groom, Dolly, *see* Groom, Marion Flora
Groom, Henry Littleton, 9.130
Groom, James, *see* Pamphlett, Thomas
Groom, Sir Littleton Ernest, 9.130
Groom, Marion Flora, 9.130
Groom, William, 9.130
Groom, William Henry, **4.304**, 9.131
Groom, William Henry George, 9.130
Grose, Francis, 1.488
Grose, Joseph Hickey, 1.490

Gross, Christiane Alicia, 9.646
Grove, James, 1.490
Grover, Montague MacGregor, 9.133
Grubb, Frederick William, 4.305
Grubb, William Dawson, 4.305
Gruner, Elioth (Elliott) Lauritz Leganyer,
 9.134
Gsell, Francis Xavier, 9.135
Guerard, Johann Joseph Eugen von, 4.306
Guerin, Bella, *see* Guerin, Julia Margaret
Guerin, Julia Margaret, 4.327, **9.136**
Guest, George, 1.491
Guilfoyle, John, 4.307
Guilfoyle, William Robert, 4.307
Gullett, Henry, 9.136
Gullett, Henry Baynton, 9.139
Gullett, Sir Henry Somer, 9.137
Gullett, Lucy Edith, 9.139
Gullett, Minnie, 9.139
Gunn, Aeneas, 9.140
Gunn, James Arndell, 1.494
Gunn, Jeannie, 9.140
Gunn, John, 9.141
Gunn, John Alexander, 11.653
Gunn, Ronald Campbell, 1.492
Gunn, William, 1.493
Gunning, George Weston, 1.494
Gunson, John Michael, 4.308
Gunson, William Henry, 4.308
Gunter, Howel, 9.142
Gunther, William James, 4.308
Guo Biao, *see* Kwok Bew
Gurner, Henry Field, 1.495, **4.309**
Gurner, John, 1.494
Gurney, Johanna Cornelia, 4.310
Gurney, Louisa Jane, 12.19
Gurney, Theodore Thomas, 4.309
Gurney, Thomas William Henry, 4.309
Guthrie, Frederick Bickell, 9.143
Guthrie, James Francis, 9.144
Guthrie, Robert Storrie, 9.145
Guthrie, Thomas, 4.310
Gwynn, Sir Charles William, 9.146
Gwynne, Edward Castres, 4.311
Gye, Harold Frederick Neville, 9.147
Gye, Walter Neville, 9.147
Gyles, John, 1.495
Habberlin, William, 5.246
Hack, John Barton, 1.497
Hack, Stephen, 4.313
Hack, Theodore, 1.497
Hack, Wilton, 4.313
Hackenschmidt, George, 12.430
Hackett, Deborah Vernon, Lady, 9.149
Hackett, Sir John, 9.149
Hackett, Sir John Winthrop, 9.150
Hackett, William Philip, 9.153
Hacking, Henry, 1.497
Haddon, Frederick William, 4.313
Haddon, Robert Joseph, 9.154
Hagelthorn, Frederick William, 9.155
Hagen, Jacob, 1.498
Hagenauer, Friedrich August, 4.314
Hague, James, 9.156

Hague, William, 9.156
Hailes, William Allan, 9.157
Hain, Gladys Adeline, 9.158
Hain, Reginald (Rex) Edric, 9.158
Haines, William Clark, 4.315
Haining, Robert, 1.499
Hake, Dora, *see* Serle, Dora Beatrice
Halcomb, Frederick, 9.159
Hale, Horatio, 1.279
Hale, Matthew Blagden, 4.317
Hales, Alfred Arthur Greenwood, 9.159
Hales, Francis, 4.319
Hales, Thomas, 4.320
Halfey, John, 4.320
Halford, George Britton, 4.321
Halford, George Dowglass, 8.243
Hall, Arthur Charles, 9.160
Hall, Benjamin, 4.322
Hall, David Robert, 9.161
Hall, Edward Smith, 1.500
Hall, Edward Swarbreck, 1.502
Hall, Eliza Rowdon, 9.168
Hall, Elsie Maude Stanley, 9.162
Hall, Francis Richard, 9.163
Hall, George, 4.324
Hall, George William Louis Marshall, *see* Marshall-Hall
Hall, George Wilson, 4.323
Hall, Hayden Hezekiah, 4.323
Hall, Henry Edward, 4.325
Hall, James, 1.503
Hall, John Joseph, 9.164
Hall, Lindsay Bernard, 9.164
Hall, Robert, 9.166
Hall, Susannah, 8.27
Hall, Thomas Ramsay, 9.163
Hall, Thomas Sergeant, 9.166
Hall, Thomas Simpson, 4.324
Hall, Walter Russell, 9.168
Hall, William, 1.503
Hall, William Shakespeare, 4.325
Hall, William Stanley, 9.162
Hallahan, Walter Rewi, 9.169
Hallen, Ambrose, 1.504
Hallen, Edward, 1.504
Haller, John Friederick, 1.505
Halley, Ida Gertrude Margaret, 9.170
Halley, Jacob John, 4.326
Halley, Robert, 4.326
Halliday, William, 4.326
Halligan, Gerald Harnett, 9.171
Halloran, Henry, 1.507, **4.327**
Halloran, Henry Ferdinand, 9.171
Halloran, Laurence Hynes, 1.506
Haly, Charles Robert, 4.327
Ham, Cornelius Job, 4.328
Ham, Theophilus Job, 4.328
Ham, Thomas, 4.328
Ham, Wilbur Lincoln, 9.172
Hamilton, Agnes, 8.107
Hamilton, Alexander Greenlaw, 9.173
Hamilton, Edward William Terrick, 4.329
Hamilton, Frank, 9.174
Hamilton, Henry, 9.174

Hamilton, Hugh Montgomerie, 9.175
Hamilton, Jean, 12.35
Hamilton, John (1834-1924), 4.330
Hamilton, John (1841-1916), 4.330
Hamilton, John (1896-1961), 9.176
Hamilton, Sir Robert George Crookshank, 4.331
Hamilton, Thomas Ferrier, **4.332**, 6.28
Hamilton, William (arr.1832), 4.330
Hamilton, William (1858?-1920), 9.176
Hamilton, William Henry, 1.507
Hamilton, Winifred, 8.236
Hamlyn-Harris, Ronald, 9.177
Hammond, George Meysey, 9.178
Hammond, John, 8.223
Hammond, Mark John, 4.332
Hammond, Robert Brodribb Stewart, 9.179
Hampden, Sir Henry Robert Brand, Viscount, 9.180
Hampton, Henry George, 1.509
Hampton, John Stephen, 1.508
Hampton, Mary, 1.509
Hancock, Henry Richard, 4.333
Hancock, John, 9.181
Hancock, Josias Henry, 9.182
Hancock, William, 9.182
Hancock, William John, 9.183
Handcock, Peter Joseph, 9.184
Handfield, Henry Hewett Paulet, 4.334
Handt, Johann Christian Simon, 1.509
Handy, John, 3.219
Hankinson, Robert Henry, 9.185
Hann, Frank Hugh, 4.335
Hann, Joseph, 4.335
Hann, William, 4.335
Hanna, George Patrick, 9.186
Hanna, Pat, *see* Hanna, George Patrick
Hannaford, Ernest Hayler, 9.186
Hannaford, George, 9.186
Hannan, Joseph Francis, 9.187
Hannan, Patrick, 9.188
Hannaway, Ann, 2.279
Hannell, James, 4.336
Hanrahan, Francis, *see* Hanran, Francis
Hanran, Francis, 9.189
Hanran, John, 9.189
Hanran, Patrick Francis, 9.189
Hansen, Martin Peter, 9.189
Hanson, Sir Richard Davies, 4.336
Hanson-Dyer, Louise, *see* Dyer, Louise Berta Mosson Hanson
Harbottle, Olive Grant, 7.488
Harcus, William, 4.340
Hardacre, Herbert Freemont, 9.190
Hardcastle, William, 6.20
Harden, Arthur, 12.601
Hardey, Joseph, 1.510
Hardie, Sir David, 9.191
Hardie, John Jackson, 9.192
Hardie, John Leslie, 9.192
Harding, Elizabeth, 1.43
Harding, George Rogers, 4.341
Hardman, Edward Townley, 4.342
Hardwick, Arthur Ernest, 9.193

Hardwick, Thomas, 9.193
Hardwicke, Charles Browne, 1.511
Hardy, Alfred, 4.343
Hardy, Arthur, 4.342
Hardy, Charles (arr.1862), 9.194
Hardy, Charles (d.l934), 9.194
Hardy, Charles Downey, 9.194
Hardy, John Richard, 4.343
Hardy, Thomas, 4.344
Hare, Charles Simeon, 4.345
Harford, Lesbia Venner, 9.195
Hargrave, Ann, 9.196
Hargrave, John Fletcher, **4.345**, 9.196
Hargrave, Lawrence, 9.196
Hargrave, Margaret, 9.198
Hargraves, Edward Hammond, 4.346
Hargreaves, William Arthur, 9.198
Harington, Thomas Cudbert, 1.511
Harker, Constance Elizabeth, 9.199
Harker, George, 4.347
Harmer, John Reginald, 9.199
Harold, James, 1.512
Harper, Andrew, **9.200**, 9.207
Harper, Charles, 4.348
Harper, Charles Walter, 9.202
Harper, George, 1.513
Harper, Herbert Reah, 9.203
Harper, Jane, 9.206
Harper, John, 9.206
Harper, Margaret Hilda, 9.204
Harper, Nathaniel White, 9.205
Harper, Robert, 9.206
Harper, Robert Rainy, 9.207
Harper, William, 9.206
Harpur, Charles, 1.514
Harpur, Joseph, 1.514
Harpur, Joseph Jehoshaphat, 1.515
Harpur, Sarah, 1.514
Harrap, Alfred, 4.349
Harrap, George Edward, 4.349, **9.207**
Harricks, Dudley Francis John, 9.208
Harriman, Benjamin Cosway, 4.350
Harrington, William Frederick, 9.209
Harris, Alexander, 1.515
Harris, Alfred, 9.209
Harris, Flora Macdonald, 5.278
Harris, George, 4.350
Harris, George Prideaux Robert, 1.516
Harris, John (1754-1819), 1.518
Harris, John (1754-1838), 1.519
Harris, John (fl.1783-1803), 1.517
Harris, John (1819-1895), 4.350
Harris, John (1838-1911), 4.351
Harris, John (d.1844), 4.350
Harris, Sir John Richards, 9.210
Harris, Lawrence Herschel Levi, 9.211
Harris, Sir Matthew, 9.212
Harris, Norman Cleaver, 9.214
Harris, Richard Deodatus Poulett, 4.352
Harris, Samuel Henry, 9.212
Harris, Thistle, 12.58
Harris, Vida, see Jones, Nina Eva Vida
Harris, William, 9.213
Harrison, Alastair Brian, 9.216

Harrison, Amy, see Mack, Amy Eleanor
Harrison, Eric, 9.214
Harrison, Eric Fairweather, 9.215
Harrison, Henry Colden Antill, 4.353
Harrison, James, 1.520
Harrison, John, 4.353
Harrison, Sir John, 9.216
Harrison, Launcelot, **9.217**, 10.288
Harry, Gilbert, 9.218
Hart, Alfred, 9.218
Hart, Fritz Bennicke, 9.219
Hart, John, 4.355
Hart, John Stephen, 9.220
Hart, Thomas Stephen, 9.221
Hart, William, 4.356
Hart, William Ewart, 9.222
Hartigan, Patrick Joseph, 9.223
Hartley, John Anderson, 4.356
Harvey, Sir John Musgrave, 9.224
Harvey, Lewis Jarvis, 9.225
Harvey, Madison, see Hervey, Grant
Harvey, William Henry, 4.357
Hassall, Elizabeth, 1.522
Hassall, James Samuel, 1.523
Hassall, Rowland, 1.521
Hassall, Samuel, 1.522
Hassall, Thomas, 1.522
Hassell, Albert Young, 4.358
Hassell, George Frederick, 9.225
Hassell, John, 4.358
Hassell, John Frederick Tasman, 4.358
Haswell, William Aitcheson, 9.226
Hatfield, William, 9.227
Haugh, Denis Robert, 9.228
Haussmann, Johann Gottfried, 2.422
Havelock, Sir Arthur Elibank, 9.228
Haverfield, Robert Ross, 4.359
Hawdon, Joseph, 1.524
Hawes, John Cyril, 9.229
Hawke, Jessica, 12.306
Hawken, Roger William Hercules, 9.230
Hawker, Charles Allan Seymour, 9.231
Hawker, Edward, 4.360
Hawker, Edward William, 9.232
Hawker, George Charles, 4.360
Hawker, Godfrey Carew, 9.235
Hawker, Harry George, 9.233
Hawker, James Clarence, 9.234
Hawkins, Herbert Middleton, 9.235
Hawkins, Thomas Fitzherbert, 1.524
Hawkins, Thomas Jarman, 1.525
Hawthorn, Arthur George Clarence, 9.236
Hay, Alexander, 1.525
Hay, Clifford Henderson, 9.236
Hay, James, 9.237
Hay, Sir John, 4.361
Hay, Robert Snowdon, 9.238
Hay, Robert William, 1.525
Hay, William Gosse, 9.239
Haydon, Edward, 4.362
Haydon, George Henry, 4.362
Haydon, Samuel James Bouverie, 4.362
Hayes, Bully, see Hayes, William Henry
Hayes, Catherine, 4.363

Hayes, Sir Henry Browne, 1.526
Hayes, Sir John, 1.527
Hayes, John Blyth, 9.239
Hayes, Michael, 1.527
Hayes, William Henry, 4.364
Hayes-Williams, William Gordon, 9.240
Haynes, John, 3.44, **4.365**
Haynes, Richard Septimus, 9.241
Haynes, Thomas Watson, 9.242
Hayter, Henry Heylyn, 4.366
Hayward, Charles Wiltens Andrée, 9.242
Hayward, James, 1.353
Hayward, Johnson Frederick, 9.242
Hayward, Thomas, 4.367
Hazon, Roberto, 9.243
Head, Frederick Waldegrave, 9.244
Head, Walter Alan, see Woods, Walter Alan
Headlam, Charles, 4.368
Headley, Baron, 7.223
Headley, Lady, see Baynton, Barbara Jane
  (Janet Ainsleigh)
Heagney, Muriel Agnes, 9.245
Heagney, Patrick Reginald, 9.245
Heales, Richard (1801-1882), 4.368
Heales, Richard (1821-1864), 4.368
Healy, Cecil Patrick, 9.246
Healy, George Daniel, 9.247
Heane, James, 9.248
Hearn, William Edward (1826-1888), 4.370
Hearn, William Edward (d.1855), 4.370
Hearn, William Edward Le Fanu, 4.372
Heath, Albert Edward, 9.249
Heath, George Poynter, 4.372
Heathershaw, Henry Robilliard, 9.250
Heathershaw, James Thomas, 9.250
Heathershaw, Sydney Arthur, 9.250
Heathershaw, William Philip, 9.250
Heaton, Herbert, 9.250
Heaton, Sir John Henniker, 4.372
Hebblethwaite, James, 9.251
Hedley, Charles, 9.252
Heidenreich, Franz Theodor Paul, 4.373
Heidenreich, Georg Adam, 4.373
Heidenreich, Johannes Heinrich Siegfried,
  4.374
Heinicke, August Moritz Hermann, 9.253
Heir, Fanny, see Cathcart, Mary Fanny
Heir, Robert James, 3.370
Hellyer, Henry, 1.528
Helms, Richard, 4.374
Helpman, Benjamin Franklin, 1.529
Hely, Frederick Augustus, 1.529
Hely, Hovenden, 4.374
Hemmant, William, 4.375
Henderson, Anketell Matthew, 9.257
Henderson, Sir Edmund Yeamans Walcott,
  4.376
Henderson, George Cockburn, 9.254
Henderson, Isabella Thomson, 9.255
Henderson, Jessie Isabel, 9.256
Henderson, John Baillie, 4.377
Henderson, John Brownlie, 9.256
Henderson, Kenneth Thorne, 9.256
Henderson, Kingsley Anketell, 9.257

Henderson, William, 4.377
Heney, Thomas William, 9.258
Henley, Frank Le Leu, 9.259
Henley, Sir Thomas, 9.260
Henn, Percy Umfreville, 9.261
Hennessy, Arthur Stephen, 9.262
Hennessy, Sir David Valentine, 9.262
Hennessy, John Francis, 9.263
Hennessy, Mary (Minnie) Quinlan, 9.263
Henning, Biddulph, 4.378
Henning, Rachel Biddulph, 4.378
Henry, Alfred, 4.379
Henry, Alice, 9.264
Henry, Charles Ferguson, 9.264
Henry, Ernest, 4.379
Henry, Frederick Ormiston, 9.266
Henry, Henry Goya, 9.265
Henry, James Henderson, 9.266
Henry, John, 9.266
Henry, John Henderson, 9.266
Henry, Juliette, 4.380
Henry, Lucien Felix, 4.379
Henry, Robert, 9.266
Henry, Samuel Pinder, 1.252
Henry, William, 1.251
Henslowe, Francis Hartwell, 1.530
Hensman, Alfred Peach, 4.380
Henty, Charles Shum, 1.531
Henty, Edward, 1.531
Henty, Francis, 1.531
Henty, Henry, 4.381
Henty, Herbert James, 4.381
Henty, James, **1.531**, 4.381
Henty, Jane, 1.531
Henty, John, 1.531
Henty, Stephen George, 1.531
Henty, Thomas (1775-1839), 1.531
Henty, Thomas (1836-1887), 4.381
Henty, William, 1.531
Henty-Creer, Henty, 8.144
Hentze, Margaret Edith, 9.267
Herbert, Algernon, 4.382
Herbert, Charles Edward, 9.268
Herbert, Harold Brocklebank, 9.268
Herbert, Sir Robert George Wyndham,
  4.382
Heritage, Francis Bede, 9.269
Herlitz, Hermann, 4.385
Herman, Hyman, 9.270
Hernsheim, Eduard, 4.385
Heron, Alexander Robert, 9.272
Heron, Robert, 9.273
Herring, Sydney Charles Edgar, 9.273
Herrod, Ernest Edward, 9.274
Hervey, Grant, 9.275
Herz, Julius, 4.386
Herz, Max Markus, 9.275
Hetherington, Irving, 4.387
Hewlett, Herbert Maunsell, 9.276
Heydon, Charles Gilbert, 1.536, **9.277**
Heydon, George, 9.278
Heydon, Jabez King, 1.534
Heydon, Louis Francis, 1.536, **9.277**
Heydon, Sophia, 1.534

Heyer, Johannes, 9.278
Heyne, Carl, 4.388
Heyne, Ernst Bernhard, 4.388
Heysen, Hans, see Heysen, Sir Wilhelm
  Ernst Hans Franz
Heysen, Louis Heinrich Wilhelm, 9.279
Heysen, Nora, 9.280
Heysen, Sir Wilhelm Ernst Hans Franz,
  9.279
Hibbins, Thomas, 1.536
Hickey, Simon, 9.281
Hickman, Frances May, 9.303
Hicks-Beach, Sir Michael, 3.206
Hickson, Ella Violet, 9.282
Hickson, Robert Newburgh, 9.282
Hickson, Robert Rowan Purdon, 4.389
Hides, Jack Gordon, 9.282
Higgins, Arthur Embery, 9.283
Higgins, Ernest Henry, 9.283
Higgins, Henry Bournes, 9.285
Higgins, John, 9.285
Higgins, Sir John Michael, 9.289
Higgins, Joseph, 9.290
Higgins, Mary Alice, 9.285
Higgins, Mervyn Bournes, 9.285, 9.288
Higgins, Patrick, 4.389
Higgins, Tasman George, 9.283
Higgs, William Guy, 9.291
Highett, John, 4.390
Highett, William, 4.390
Higinbotham, George, 4.391
Higinbotham, Thomas, 4.397
Hilda, Mother Mary, see Benson, Louisa
Hilder, Jesse Jewhurst, 9.292
Hill, Alfred Francis, 9.293
Hill, Charles, 9.293
Hill, Charles Lumley, 4.398
Hill, Clement, 9.295
Hill, George, 4.398
Hill, Henry John, 4.399
Hill, James Peter, 9.296
Hill, James Richard, 4.399
Hill, Joshua, 2.288
Hill, Kate, 9.296
Hill, Lionel Laughton, 9.297
Hill, Richard (1782-1836), 1.537
Hill, Richard (1810-1895), 4.400
Hill, Samuel Prout, 1.538
Hill, Thomas, 9.299
Hill, William, 4.398
Hill, William Caldwell, 9.299
Hill, William Duguid, 9.300
Hillary, Michael James, 9.301
Hillary, Richard, 9.301
Hills, Alice, 9.302
Hills, John Francis, 9.302
Hinchcliffe, Albert, 9.302
Hinder, Eleanor Mary, 9.304
Hindley, William George, 9.304
Hindmarsh, Sir John (1785-1860), **1.538**,
  2.116
Hindmarsh, John (d.1903), 1.541
Hinkler, Herbert John Louis, 9.305
Hinton, Howard, 9.307

Hipkiss, Richard, 1.541
Hirsch, Maximilian, 9.308
Hirschfeld, Eugen, 9.309
Hirst, Godfrey, 9.309
Hitchcock, George Michelmore, 4.401
Hitchcock, Howard, 9.310
Hitchcock, Walter Michelmore, 4.401
Hitchcock, William, 4.401
Hixson, Francis, 4.402
Hoad, Sir John Charles, 9.311
Hoad, Oswald Vick, 9.312
Hoadley, Abel, 9.312
Hoadley, Albert, 9.313
Hoadley, Charles Archibald Brookes, 9.313
Hoadley, Gordon, 9.313
Hoare, Benjamin, 9.314
Hobart, Robert, 1.542
Hobbs, Howard Frederick, 9.316
Hobbs, James, 1.542
Hobbs, John Mervyn, 9.316
Hobbs, Sir Joseph John Talbot, 9.315
Hobbs, William, 4.402
Hobler, George, 1.543
Hobler, George Alexander, 9.317
Hobson, Edmund Charles, 1.544
Hobson, Edward William, 1.544
Hobson, Marie, 1.545
Hobson, William, 1.412
Hobson, William (1793-1842), 1.545
Hocking, Percy, 9.318
Hocking, Sidney Edwin, 9.318
Hoddle, Robert, 1.547
Hodel, Joseph, 9.319
Hodge, Charles Reynolds, 9.319
Hodges, Henry, 9.320
Hodges, Sir Henry Edward Agincourt,
  9.320
Hodges, Peter, 1.252
Hodgkinson, Clement, 4.403
Hodgkinson, William Oswald, 4.404
Hodgson, Sir Arthur, 4.405
Hodgson, Christopher Pemberton, 4.406
Hodgson, Richard, 4.406
Hodgson, William, 4.408
Hodgson, William Roy, 9.321
Hoesch, Fanny Amalia, 12.587
Hoff, George Rayner, 9.322
Hoffnung, Sigmond, 4.408
Hogan, Edmond John, 9.323
Hogan, James Francis, 4.409
Hogan, Michael, 1.548
Hogan, Patrick Gould, 1.548
Hogan, Percival James Nelson, 9.325
Hogan, Sarah Maria, 1.549
Hogan, Teresa Elizabeth, 1.549
Hogan, William, 1.548
Hogue, James Alexander, 9.325
Hogue, Jessie, 9.326
Hogue, Oliver, 9.326
Hokor, see Rusden, Henry Keylock
Holden, Albert Thomas, 9.327
Holden, Sir Edward Wheewall, 9.330
Holden, Frances Gillam, 9.328
Holden, George Frederick, 9.329

Holden, George Kenyon, 4.410
Holden, Henry James, 9.330
Holden, James Alexander, 9.330
Holden, John Rose, 1.549
Holden, Leslie Hubert, 9.332
Holden, William, 5.446
Holder, Sir Frederick William, 9.333
Holder, James Morecott, 9.333
Holder, Julia Maria, 9.333
Holdsworth, Albert Armytage, 9.335
Holdsworth, Philip Joseph, 4.411
Holdsworth, Philip Risby, 4.411
Holland, Henry Edmund, 9.336
Hollis, Robert, 9.337
Holloway, William James, 4.476
Holman, Ada Augusta, 9.337
Holman, John Barkell, 9.338
Holman, Katherine Mary, 9.338
Holman, Mary Alice, 9.338
Holman, May, see Holman, Mary Alice
Holman, Richard Charles Frederick, 9.339
Holman, Richard Dudley, 9.340
Holman, William Arthur, 9.340
Holme, Ernest Rudolph, 9.347
Holme, John Barton, 9.348
Holme, Thomas, 9.348
Holmes, Albina Emma, 9.349
Holmes, Henry Diggens, 9.349
Holmes, Marion Louisa, 9.349
Holmes, Marion Phoebe, 9.349
Holmes, William, 9.349
Holmes à Court, Alan Worsley, 9.351
Holroyd, Arthur Todd, 4.411
Holroyd, Sir Edward Dundas, 4.412
Holt, Bland, see Holt, Joseph Thomas
Holt, Jack, see Holt, Michael
Holt, Joseph, 1.258, 1.550
Holt, Joseph Frederick, 4.413
Holt, Joseph Thomas, 4.413
Holt, Michael, 9.352
Holt, Thomas, 4.414
Holt, Tom, 12.221
Holtermann, Bernhardt Otto, 4.415
Holtze, Maurice William, 9.353
Holyman, James, 9.354
Holyman, Thomas Henry, 9.354
Holyman, William (1833-1919), 4.416
Holyman, William (1858-1921), 9.354
Homburg, Gerta, 9.514
Homburg, Hermann Robert, 9.355
Homburg, Robert (1848-1912), 9.355
Homburg, Robert (1875-1948), 9.356
Homburg, Wilhelm, 9.355
Hone, Frank Sandland, 9.357
Hone, Joseph, 1.551
Hood, Sir Alexander Jarvie, 9.358
Hood, Sir Joseph Henry, 9.358
Hood, Margaret, 9.358
Hood, Robert, 9.359
Hood, Robert Alexander David, 9.359
Hood, Thomas Hood, 4.89
Hook, Alfred, 12.493
Hook, Charles, 1.551
Hooker, Sir Joseph Dalton, 4.416

Hooker, Sir William Jackson, 4.416
Hoolan, John, 9.360
Hooley, Daniel, 4.417
Hooley, Edward Timothy, 4.417
Hooper, Richard, 9.361
Hoover, Herbert Clark, 9.361
Hooworth, Ann, see Roseby, Ann
Hop, see Hopkins, Livingston (Yourtee)
  York
Hope, Louis, 4.418, 6.5
Hope, Robert Culbertson, 4.419
Hopetoun, Hersey Alice, Lady, 9.362
Hopetoun, John Adrian Louis Hope, Earl,
  9.362
Hopkins, Felicia, 9.363
Hopkins, Francis, 9.363
Hopkins, Francis Rawdon Chesney, 4.420
Hopkins, Henry, 1.552
Hopkins, John Rout, 4.420
Hopkins, Livingston (Yourtee) York, 4.421
Hopley, William, 1.553
Hopwood, Henry, 4.422
Horder, Clarence, 9.364
Horder, Harold Norman, 9.364
Hordern, Ann, 4.423
Hordern, Anthony (1819-1876), 4.423
Hordern, Anthony (1842-1886), 4.423
Hordern, Anthony (d.1869), 4.423
Hordern, Anthony (1889-1970), 9.365
Hordern, Charlotte Isabel Annie, Lady,
  9.365
Hordern, Samuel (1849-1909), 4.423
Hordern, Sir Samuel (1876-1956), 4.423,
  9.365
Hore-Ruthven, Alexander Gore Arkwright,
  see Gowrie
Horgan, John, 9.367
Horn, William Austin, 9.367
Horne, Richard Henry, 4.424
Horne, Thomas, 4.424
Horniman, Robert John, 9.369
Horniman, Vicary, 9.369
Hornung, Ernest William, 9.369
Horrocks, Joseph Lucas, 4.425
Horsfall, Alfred Herbert, 9.370
Horsfall, John Sutcliffe, 4.426
Horsley, Charles Edward, 4.427
Horton, Sir Robert Wilmot, 1.554
Hose, Henry Judge, 4.428
Hosie, Constable, 5.248
Hosking, John (1806-1882), 1.554
Hosking, John (d.1850), 1.554
Hosking, Peter Mann, 1.555
Hoskins, Arthur Sidney, 9.373
Hoskins, Sir Cecil Harold, 9.371
Hoskins, Charles Henry, 9.371
Hoskins, George, 9.371
Hoskins, James, 4.428
Hoskins, John R., 4.428
Hotham, Sir Charles, 4.429
Houghton, Sydney Robert, 9.373
Houghton, Thomas John, 9.374
Houlding, John Richard, 4.430
Houston, William, 4.431

Houtman, Frederik de, 1.555
Hovell, William Hilton, 1.556
Howard, Amos William, 9.374
Howard, Arthur Clifford, 9.375
Howard, Charles Beaumont, 1.557
Howard, Charles Stanley Allan, 4.432
Howard, Henry, 9.376
Howard, Stanley, 4.431
Howchin, Walter, 9.377
Howe, Edward, see Rowe, Richard
Howe, George, 1.557, 2.605
Howe, George Terry, 1.559
Howe, Jackie, see Howe, John Robert
Howe, James Henderson, 9.378
Howe, John, 1.560
Howe, John Robert, 9.379
Howe, Michael, 1.560
Howe, Robert, 1.558, 2.605
Howe, Sarah, 2.605
Howe, William, 1.561
Howell, Cedric Ernest, 9.379
Howell, George Julian, 9.380
Howell-Price, David Clayton Winchcombe, 9.382
Howell-Price, Frederick Phillimore, 9.381
Howell-Price, John, 9.381
Howell-Price, Owen Glendower, 9.381
Howell-Price, Philip Llewellyn, 9.381
Howell-Price, Richmond Gordon, 9.381
Howick, Viscount, see Grey, Henry George
Howie, Sir Archibald, 9.382
Howie, Clara Jane, 9.383
Howie, Laurence Hotham, 9.383
Howitt, Alfred William, 4.432
Howitt, Anna Mary, 3.117
Howitt, Godfrey, 4.435
Howitt, Mary, 4.435
Howitt, Richard, 4.435
Howitt, William (1792-1879), 4.435
Howitt, William (1846?-1928), 9.384
Howse, Sir Neville Reginald, 9.384
Hübbe, Ulrich, 4.436
Hudd, Sir Herbert Sydney, 9.386
Huddart, James, 4.437
Hudson, Henry, 4.438
Hudson, William Henry, 4.438
Huffer, John, 4.439
Hughes, Agnes Eva, 9.387
Hughes, Ernest Selwyn, 9.388
Hughes, Francis Augustus, 9.389
Hughes, Fred William, 9.390
Hughes, Frederic Godfrey, 9.387
Hughes, Geoffrey Forrest, 9.391
Hughes, George, 1.562
Hughes, Herbert Bristow, 4.439
Hughes, John Bristow, 4.439
Hughes, John Francis, 9.392
Hughes, Louisa, Lady, 9.393
Hughes, Dame Mary Ethel, 9.400
Hughes, Sir Thomas, 9.392
Hughes, Sir Walter Watson, 4.440
Hughes, William Morris, 8.623, 9.393
Huie, Alexander Gordon, 9.400
Hull, Arthur Francis Basset, 9.401

Hull, George, 1.562, 4.441
Hull, Hugh Munro, 4.441
Hullock, William Henry, 3.434
Humble, George Bland, 4.442
Humble, William, 4.443
Hume, Andrew Hamilton, 1.563, 2.10
Hume, Elizabeth, 1.564
Hume, Ernest, 9.402
Hume, Fergusson (Fergus) Wright, 4.443
Hume, Francis Rawdon, 1.565
Hume, Hamilton, 1.564, 1.556
Hume, Walter Reginald, 9.402
Hume Cook, see Cook, James Newton Haxton Hume
Humffray, John Basson, 4.444
Humphery, Frederick Thomas, 4.445
Humphrey, Adolarius William Henry, 1.565
Hungerford, Emanuel, 4.445
Hungerford, Richard Colin Campbell, 9.403
Hungerford, Thomas, 4.445
Hunt, Alfred Edgar, 9.405
Hunt, Atlee Arthur, 9.403
Hunt, Charles Cooke, 4.446
Hunt, Henry Ambrose, 9.405
Hunt, John Charles, 9.405
Hunt, John Horbury, 4.447
Hunt, Percy, 9.184
Hunt, Philip Charles Holmes, 9.406
Hunt, Thomas, 4.447
Hunt, William, 4.447
Hunter, Alexander Maclean, 1.572
Hunter, Andrew Francis, 1.572
Hunter, George, 4.448
Hunter, Henry, 4.448
Hunter, James Aitchison Johnston, 9.407
Hunter, James Arthur Carr, 1.572
Hunter, John (1737-1821), 1.566, 2.573
Hunter, John (1820-1868), 1.572
Hunter, John Irvine, 9.408
Hunter, John McEwan, 9.409
Hunter, Robert, 4.448
Hunter, William Fergusson, 1.572
Hunter-Watts, Frediswyde, 12.486
Huntingfield, William Charles Arcedeckne Vanneck, Baron, 9.410
Huon de Kerilleau, Charles, 5.261
Huon de Kerilleau, Gabriel Louis Marie, 1.573
Huon de Kerilleau, Paul, 1.573
Hurley, James Francis, 9.411
Hurley, John (1796-1882), 4.450
Hurley, John (1844-1911), 4.450
Hurst, George, 4.451
Hurst, John Herbert, 9.412
Hussey, Henry, 4.452
Hutchens, Francis, 9.413
Hutchins, William, 1.573
Hutchinson, John, 2.291
Hutchinson, Mary, 2.291
Hutchinson, William (1772-1846), 1.574
Hutchinson, William (1864-1924), 9.414
Hutchinson, William Alston, 4.453
Hutchison, James, 9.414
Hutt, John, 1.575, 3.428

Hutt, William, 1.575
Hutton, Sir Edward Thomas Henry, 9.415
Hutton, George Samuel, 9.418
Huxham, John Saunders, 9.419
Huxley, Thomas Henry, 1.577
Hyam, Solomon Herbert, 4.454
Hyde, Sir George Francis, 9.420
Hyeronimus, Nicholas, 6.104
Hyett, Francis William, 9.422
Hyman, Arthur Wellesley, 9.423
Hynes, Maurice Patrick, 9.424
Icely, Thomas, 2.1
Idriess, Ion Llewellyn, 9.426
Ievers, George Hawkins, 4.456
Ievers, Robert Lancelot, 4.456
Ievers, William (1818-1901), 4.455
Ievers, William (1839-1895), 4.455
Ifould, William Herbert, 9.426
Iliffe, John, 9.427
Illingworth, Frederick, 9.428
Illingworth, Nelson William, 9.429
Imlay, Alexander, 2.2
Imlay, Alexander Peter, 9.430
Imlay, Alexander William, 9.430
Imlay, Ellen Jeanie, 9.430
Imlay, George, 2.2
Imlay, Norman George, 9.430
Imlay, Peter, 2.2
Ingham, William Bairstow, 4.456
Ingle, John, 2.3
Inglis, James, 4.457
Ingram, George Mawby (Morby), 9.431
Innes, Archibald Clunes, 2.3
Innes, Frederick Maitland, 4.458
Innes, George, 2.4
Innes, Gustavus Archibald Clunes, 2.4
Innes, Sir Joseph George Long, 4.459
Innes, Reginald Heath Long, 9.432
Innes-Noad, Sidney Reginald, 9.433
Inwood, Reginald Roy, 9.434
Iota, see Caffyn, Kathleen Mannington
Iredale, Francis Adams, 9.434
Iredale, Lilian, see Medland, Lilian
  Marguerite
Iredale, Tom, 9.435
Ireland, Horace, 9.436
Ireland, Jesse, 9.436
Ireland, Richard Davies, 4.460
Irenaios, Archimandrite (Kasimatis), 9.620
Ironside, Adelaide Eliza, 4.461
Irvine, Gerald Addington D'Arcy, see
  D'Arcy-Irvine
Irvine, Hans William Henry, 9.437
Irvine, Malcolm Mervyn D'Arcy, see
  D'Arcy-Irvine
Irvine, Margaret, 9.439
Irvine, Robert Francis, 9.438
Irvine, Sir William Hill, 9.439
Irving, Clark, 4.462
Irving, Edward, 4.462
Irving, Godfrey George Howy, 4.463,
  9.441
Irving, James, 9.443
Irving, James Washington, 9.443

Irving, John, 2.4
Irving, Martin Howy, 4.462
Irwin, Frederick Chidley, 2.5
Irwin, James, 2.5
Irwin, Leighton Major Francis, 9.443
Isaac, Elizabeth, see Coxen, Elizabeth
  Frances
Isaac, Sam, 3.311
Isaacs, Alfred, 9.444
Isaacs, Sir Isaac Alfred, 9.444
Isaacs, John Alfred, 9.446
Isaacs, Rebecca, 9.444
Isaacs, Robert Macintosh, 4.464
Israel, John Cashmore, 9.450
Israel, John William, 9.450
Ives, Joshua, 9.450
Ivory, Francis Jeffrey, 4.465
Ivory, James, 4.464
Ixia, see Pelloe, Emily Harriet
Jack, Robert Lockhart, 4.466
Jack, Robert Logan, 4.466
Jacka, Albert, 9.452
Jackey Jackey, **2.7**, 2.44
Jackson, Alexander, 9.453
Jackson, Archibald, 9.453
Jackson, Clements Frederick Vivian, 9.454
Jackson, Sir Cyril, 9.455
Jackson, Ernest Sandford, 9.457
Jackson, John Alexander, 2.7
Jackson, John Serocold, 2.7
Jackson, John William Alexander, 9.458
Jackson, Peter, 9.458
Jackson, Samuel, 2.9
Jackson, Sidney Ann, 4.170
Jackson, Sidney William, **9.459**, 12.469
Jacob, Archibald Hamilton, 4.466
Jacob, Caroline, **9.460**, 12.218
Jacobs, Edward, 9.214
Jacobs, Isaac, 9.445
Jacobs, Joseph, 9.460
Jacobs, Sir Roland, 9.462
Jacobs, Samuel Joshua, 9.461
Jageurs, Morgan Peter, 9.462
James, Alice Mary, 9.463
James, Charles, 9.464
James, Charles Henry, 4.467
James, Sir Claude Ernest Weymouth, 9.462
James, David, 9.463
James, Eleanora Marie Gwenyfred, Lady,
  9.468
James, Frederick Alexander, 9.464
James, Henry Kerrison, 4.468
James, Isaac, 9.469
James, John Charles Horsey, 4.468
James, John Stanley, 4.469
James, Meyrick Edward Clifton, 4.469
James, Thomas (lieut.), 5.271
James, Thomas (merchant), 9.464
James, Tristram Bernard Wordsworth,
  9.466
James, Sir Walter Hartwell, 9.466
James, William Edward, 9.469
James, Winifred Llewellyn, 9.470
Jamieson, John, 2.10

Jamieson, William, 9.470
Jamison, Sir John, 2.10
Jamison, Robert Thomas, 2.12
Jamison, Thomas, 2.12
Janssen, Willem, 2.13
Jansz, Willem, see Janssen
Jaques, Theodore James, 4.470
Jardine, Alexander William, 4.471
Jardine, Francis Lascelles, 4.471
Jardine, John, 4.470
Jarrett, Marjorie Kate, 9.199
Jarvis, Eric Roy, 9.471
Jasprizza, Nicholas, 4.471
Jauncey, Leslie Cyril, 9.472
Jeanneret, Charles Edward, 4.472
Jeanneret, Henry, 4.472
Jeffcott, Sir John William, 2.14
Jeffcott, Sir William, 2.15
Jefferies, Richard Thomas, 9.472
Jefferis, James, 4.473
Jefferis, Marian, 4.475
Jefferson, Joseph, 4.475
Jeffery, Walter James, 9.473
Jeffreys, Charles, 2.15
Jeffries, Clarence Smith, 9.474
Jeffries, Elsie, 9.476
Jeffries, Jim, 9.459
Jeffries, Lewis Wibmer, 9.475
Jeffries, Maud Evelyn Craven, 9.476
Jeffries, Shirley Williams, 9.475
Jenkin, John Grenfell, 9.476
Jenkins, Sir George Frederick, 9.477
Jenkins, John Greeley, 9.478
Jenkins, Robert, 2.16
Jenks, Edward, 9.479
Jenner, Caleb Joshua, 4.476
Jenner, Isaac Walter, 9.480
Jennings, Elizabeth Esther Ellen, 4.476
Jennings, Sir Patrick Alfred, 4.477
Jensen, Harald Ingemann, 9.480
Jensen, Jens August, 9.481
Jensen, Joergen Christian, 9.482
Jenyns, Essie, see Jennings, Elizabeth
  Esther Ellen
Jephcott, Sydney Wheeler, 9.483
Jerger, Charles Adolph, 9.484
Jersey, Margaret Elizabeth, Countess of,
  9.485
Jersey, Sir Victor Albert George
  Child-Villiers, Earl of, 9.484
Jervis, Samuel Emanuel, see Cox, Samuel
  Emanuel
Jervois, Sir William Francis Drummond,
  4.479
Jess, Sir Carl Herman, 9.485
Jess, Carl McGibbon, 9.487
Jess, John David, 9.487
Jessep, Thomas, 9.487
Jevons, Harriet Winefrid, 4.481
Jevons, William Stanley, 4.480
Jewell, Richard Roach, 4.481
Joachim, William, 5.381
Jobson, Alexander, 9.488
Jobson, Nancy, 9.489

John, Bevan, 9.491
John, Cecilia Annie, 9.490
John, Isabelle, see Bean, Isabelle
John, Morgan Bevan, 9.491
Johns, Alfred, 4.483
Johns, Frank, 6.343
Johns, Frederick, 9.491
Johns, Joseph Bolitho, 4.482
Johns, Peter, 4.482
Johnson, Edward Angas, 9.492
Johnson, Edwin, 4.483
Johnson, Florence Ethel, 9.493
Johnson, George, 9.493
Johnson, George French, 1.227
Johnson, John Andrew, 9.494
Johnson, Joseph Colin Francis, 9.495
Johnson, Richard, 2.17
Johnson, Robert Ebenezer, 4.484
Johnson, Thomas Revel, 4.484
Johnson, William Dartnell, 9.496
Johnson, Sir William Elliot, 9.497
Johnston, Charles Melbourne, 9.498
Johnston, Edward Bertram, 9.499
Johnston, Esther, 2.19
Johnston, Frederick Marshall, 9.500
Johnston, George (1764-1823), 2.20, 2.156
Johnston, George (1790-1820), 2.22
Johnston, George Jameson, 9.500
Johnston, Harry Frederick, 9.499
Johnston, James Stewart, 4.485
Johnston, Joseph, 4.486
Johnston, Langloh, 11.167
Johnston, Robert Mackenzie, 9.501
Johnston, Thomas Harvey, 9.501
Johnstone, John Lorimer Gibson, 9.503
Johnstone, Robert, see Johnston, Robert
  Mackenzie
Johnstone, Robert Arthur, 4.486
Johnstone, Thomas, 4.487
Jollie-Smith, see Smith, Christian Brynhild
  Ochiltree Jollie
Jolly, Norman William, 9.504
Jolly, William Alfred, 9.504
Jones, Alfred James, 9.505
Jones, Allan Murray, 9.506
Jones, Auber George, 4.488
Jones, Charles, 12.331
Jones, Charles Edwin, 4.488
Jones, Sir Charles Lloyd, 9.507
Jones, David, 2.23
Jones, David Mander, 2.24
Jones, Doris Egerton, 9.508
Jones, Ernest, 9.509
Jones, Frederic Wood, 9.510
Jones, Gertrude, 9.510
Jones, Harold Edward, 9.512
Jones, Harriet, see Knowles
Jones, Sir Henry, 9.513
Jones, Hooper Josse Brewster, 9.514
Jones, Inigo Owen, 9.515
Jones, John, 12.394
Jones, John Alexander Stammers, 9.518
Jones, John Percy, 9.516
Jones, Joseph, 4.489

Jones, Kathleen Annie Gilman, 9.517
Jones, Leslie John Roberts, 9.518
Jones, Mabel Mary Trevor, 11.442
Jones, Mary, *see* Morgan, Molly
Jones, Nina Eva Vida, 9.518
Jones, Owen, 3.117
Jones, Sir Philip Sydney, 2.24, **4.490**
Jones, Rees Rutland, 9.519
Jones, Richard (1786-1852), 2.24
Jones, Richard (1816-1892), 2.25
Jones, William (arr.1840), 1.419
Jones, William (1842-1907), 9.520
Jones, William Ernest, 9.520
Jonsson, Nils Josef, 9.521
Jordan, Sir Frederick Richard, 9.522
Jordan, Henry, 4.491
Jorgenson, Jorgen, 2.26
Jose, Arthur Wilberforce, 9.523
Jose, George Herbert, 9.524
Jose, William Wilberforce, 9.523
Joseland, Richard George Howard, 9.524
Joseph, Samuel Aaron, 4.492
Josephson, Jacob, 4.492
Josephson, Joshua Frey, 4.492
Joubert, Didier Numa, 4.493
Joubert, Jules François de Sales, 4.493
Jowett, Edmund, 9.525
Joyce, Alfred, 2.28
Joyce, Edmund Michael, 9.526
Joyce, George, 2.28
Joyce, Thomas, 2.28
Joynton-Smith, James John, *see* Smith, Sir
  James John Joynton
Judkins, George Alfred, 9.527
Judkins, William Henry, 9.527
Jukes, Joseph Beete, 2.29
Julius, Sir George Alfred, 9.528
Jull, Martin Edward, 9.529
Jull, Roberta Henrietta Margaritta, 9.530
Jupiter, 5.303
Kabat, Leopold, 5.40
Kable, Henry (1763-1846), 2.31
Kable, Henry (jnr), 2.32
Kable, James, 2.32
Kable, John, 2.32
Kaeppel, Carl Henry, 9.532
Kaleski, Robert Lucian Stanislaus, 9.532
Kane, Benjamin Francis, 5.1
Kane, Henry Plow, 2.32
Kashiwagi, Taira, 9.533
Kater, Henry Edward, 5.1
Kater, Henry Herman, 5.1
Kater, Mary Eliza, 5.1
Kater, Sir Norman William, 9.534
Kates, Francis Benjamin, 5.2
Kauffmann, John, 9.535
Kauper, Henry Alexis, 9.536
Kavanagh, Edward John, 9.537
Kavel, August Ludwig Christian, 2.33
Kay, Alick Dudley, 9.538
Kay, Joseph Henry, 2.34
Kay, William Elphinstone, 9.538
Kay, William Porden, 2.34
Kayser, Heinrich Wilhelm Ferdinand, 5.3

Kean, Charles John, 5.4
Kean, Ellen, 5.4
Keane, Edward Vivien Harvey, 5.4
Keaney, Paul Francis, 9.540
Kearney, Catherine, 2.36
Kearney, Thomas, 2.36
Kearney, William, 2.36
Keartland, George Arthur, 9.540
Keating, John Henry, 9.541
Keating, Sarah Alice, 9.542
Keatinge, Maurice Barber Bevan, 9.542
Keats, Horace Stanley, 9.543
Keegan, John Walter, 9.544
Keegan, Thomas Michael, 9.544
Keenan, Sir Norbert Michael, 9.545
Keene, William, 5.5
Kefford, Rhoda Harriet, 4.172
Kellaway, Cecil Lauriston, 9.545
Kellaway, Charles Halliley, 9.546
Kellermann, Annette Marie Sarah, 9.548
Kellett, Adelaide Maud, 9.549
Kellow, Charles, *see* Kellow, Henry Brown
Kellow, Henry Arthur, 9.550
Kellow, Henry Brown, 9.550
Kelly, Alicia Mary, 9.551
Kelly, Anthony Edwin Bowes, 9.552
Kelly, Cecilia, *see* Gibbs, Cecilia May
Kelly, Charles, 9.555
Kelly, Dan, 5.7
Kelly, David Frederick, 5.6
Kelly, Edward, 5.6
Kelly, Ethel Knight, 9.553
Kelly, Frederick Septimus, 9.554
Kelly, Sir George Dalziel, 9.555
Kelly, James (1791-1859), 2.36
Kelly, James (b.1858), 5.7
Kelly, John, 5.6
Kelly, John Edward, 5.9
Kelly, Michael, 9.556
Kelly, Nicholas William, 9.558
Kelly, Robert, 9.559
Kelly, Robert Hume Vandeleur, 9.560
Kelly, Robert Vandeleur, 9.560
Kelly, Thomas Herbert, 9.560
Kelly, Thomas Hussey, 5.9
Kelly, William (1813?-1872), 5.10
Kelly, William (1823-1909), 5.10
Kelly, William Henry, 9.561
Kelly, William Stanley, 9.559
Kelsall, Roger, 2.37
Kelynack, William, 5.11
Kemble, Francis, 2.38
Kemble, Myra, 5.12
Kemp, Anthony Fenn, 2.39
Kemp, Charles, 2.40
Kemp, Henry Hardie, 9.562
Kempt, John Francis, 5.12
Kendall, Basil, 5.13
Kendall, Eleanor Jane, 9.564
Kendall, Ernest Arthur, 9.563
Kendall, Hector, 9.564
Kendall, John, 9.564
Kendall, Thomas, 2.42
Kendall, Thomas Henry, 5.13

Kendall, William Augustus, 9.564
Kendall, William Tyson, 9.563
Kenneally, James Joseph, 9.564
Kennedy, Alexander, 5.14
Kennedy, Sir Arthur Edward, 3.429, **5.15**
Kennedy, Colin, 9.566
Kennedy, Edmund Besley Court, 2.7, **2.43**
Kennedy, Hugh, 5.15
Kennedy, John, 9.566
Kennedy, John Joseph, 9.565
Kennedy, Malcolm, 9.566
Kennedy, Michael, 5.7
Kennedy, Thomas, 9.567
Kennedy, Thomas James, 9.568
Kennerley, Alfred, 5.16
Kenniff, James, 9.568
Kenniff, Patrick, 9.568
Kennion, George Wyndham, 5.17
Kenny, Augustus Leo, 9.569
Kenny, Elizabeth, 9.570
Kenny, John, 2.44
Kenny, Thomas James Bede, 9.571
Kent, Thomas, 2.44
Kent, William (1751-1812), 1.572, **2.46**
Kent, William (1799-1870), 2.47
Kent, William George Carlile, 2.47
Kentish, Nathaniel Lipscomb, 2.48
Kenyon, Alfred Henderson, 9.572
Kenyon, Alfred Stephen, 9.572
Kerferd, George Briscoe, 5.17
Kerillac, see Huon de Kerilleau
Kerilleau, see Huon de Kerilleau
Kermode, Robert Quayle, 2.50
Kermode, William, 2.49
Kernot, Charles, 5.19
Kernot, Charles Home, 9.574
Kernot, Frederick Archer, 9.574
Kernot, Maurice Edwin, 9.573
Kernot, Wilfred Noyce, 9.573
Kernot, William Charles, 5.20
Kerr, Andy, see Kerr, David McFarlane
  McLachlan
Kerr, David McFarlane McLachlan,
  9.574
Kerr, George, 9.575
Kerr, James Semple, 9.576
Kerr, Peter, 5.22
Kerr, William, 2.50
Kerr, William Warren, 9.577
Kerry, Charles Henry, 9.577
Kershaw, James Andrew, 9.578
Kerz, Helen Josephine, 9.62
Kesteven, Hereward Leighton, 9.579
Kethel, Alexander, 9.580
Keynes, Ellen, 9.581
Keynes, Joseph, 9.581
Keynes, Richard Robinson, 9.581
Keys, Constance Mabel, 9.581
Keysor, Leonard Maurice, 9.582
Khull, Edward, 5.23
Kibble, Nita Bernice, 9.583
Kickett, Arthur, 9.214
Kidd, John, 5.24
Kidman, Sir Sidney, 9.583

Kidston, William, 8.281, **9.585**
Kiek, Edward Sidney, 9.587
Kiek, Winifred, 9.587
Kieran, Bernard Bede, 9.588
Kiernan, Esmond Laurence, 9.589
Kilburn, John George, 9.590
Kilgour, Alexander James, 9.591
Killian, Andrew, 9.591
Kimpton, Edward, 5.24
Kimpton, William Stephen, 5.24
Kinchela, John (1774?-1845), 2.51
Kinchela, John (jnr), 2.52, 2.266
King, Alice Ross, see Ross-King
King, Anna Josepha, 2.52
King, Arthur Septimus, 5.27
King, Catherine, 10.631
King, Copland, 9.592
King, George (1813-1899), 5.25
King, George (1814-1894), 5.26
King, Sir George Eccles Kelso, 9.593
King, George Raymond, 9.594
King, Georgina, 9.594
King, Henry, 9.595
King, Henry Edward, 5.27
King, James, (snr) 2.54
King, James (1800-1857), 2.54
King, James Harold, 9.596
King, John (1820-1895), 5.27
King, John (1841-1872), 5.28
King, John Charles, 2.55
King, Joseph, 9.596
King, Norfolk, 2.52, 2.61
King, Olive May, 9.597
King, Philip Gidley (1758-1808), 2.55
King, Philip Gidley (1817-1904), 2.63, **5.29**
King, Phillip Parker, 2.61
King, Reginald Macdonnell, 9.598
King, Robert Lethbridge, 2.63, **5.30**
King, Sydney, 2.61
King, Thomas Mulhall, 9.598
King, William Essington, 5.27
King, William Francis, 5.31
Kingsford, Richard Ash, 5.31
Kingsford Smith, Sir Charles Edward,
  9.599
Kingsley, Henry, 5.32
Kingsmill, Sir Walter, 9.601
Kingston, Charles Cameron, 9.602
Kingston, Sir George Strickland, 2.64
Kingston-McCloughry, see McCloughry,
  Edgar James
Kinnear, Edward Hore, 9.605
Kinnear, George, 9.605
Kinnear, Henry Humphrey, 9.605
Kinross, John, 5.33
Kintore, Algernon Hawkins Thomond
  Keith-Falconer, Earl, 5.34
Kippax, Alan Falconer, 9.606
Kirby, Herbert, 11.36
Kirby, Joseph Coles, 5.35
Kirk, George, 9.168
Kirk, Maria Elizabeth, 9.607
Kirkby, Sydney James, 9.608
Kirkcaldie, David, 9.609

Kirkcaldie, Katherine Vida, 9.610
Kirkcaldie, Rosa Angela, 9.609
Kirkland, John Drummond, 5.118
Kirkland, Katherine, 2.65
Kirkland, Kenneth William, 2.65
Kirkpatrick, Andrew Alexander, 9.610
Kirkpatrick, John, 9.611
Kirkpatrick, John Simpson, 9.612
Kirkpatrick, Mary, 9.613
Kirton, Alfred James, 9.614
Kirton, Joseph William, 9.613
Kirwan, Sir John Waters, 9.614
Kirwan, Michael Joseph, 9.616
Kitamura, Toranosuke, 9.616
Kitson, Sir Albert Ernest, 9.617
Kitson, John, 9.617
Kitson, Margaret Wishart, 9.617
Kitson, Mary, see Tenison Woods, Mary
  Cecil
Klevesahl, Friedricke Charlotte, 9.493
Klotz, George, 11.304
Knaggs, Samuel Thomas, 5.36
Knatchbull, Sir Edward, 2.65
Knatchbull, John, 2.65
Kneebone, Elizabeth Ann, 9.618
Kneebone, Henry, 9.618
Kneeshaw, Frederick Percival, 9.619
Kneeshaw, John, 9.619
Knetes, Christophoros, 9.620
Knibbs, Sir George Handley, 9.620
Knight, Albert, 9.621
Knight, Bill, 9.621
Knight, Hattie Martha, 10.44
Knight, Joe, 9.621
Knight, John George, 5.37
Knight, John James, 9.622
Knipe, John Hanlon, 5.37
Knopwood, Robert, 2.66
Knowles, Conrad Theodore, 2.67
Knowles, Sir George Shaw, 9.623
Knowles, Harriet, 2.67-8
Knowles, Marion, 9.623
Knox, Ada Victoria, Lady, 9.629
Knox, Sir Adrian, 9.624
Knox, Sir Edward, 5.38
Knox, Edward William, 9.626
Knox, Sir Errol Galbraith, 9.628
Knox, Sir George Hodges, 9.629
Knox, MacPherson, 9.629
Knox, Sir Robert Wilson, 9.630
Knox, William, 9.631
Knox, William Johnstone, 9.629
Koch, John Augustus Bernard, 9.632
Kodak, see O'Ferrall, Ernest Francis
Koerstz, Christian Christiansen, 9.633
Kolp, Ann, see Colp
Komine, Isokichi, 9.633
Kong Meng, see Lowe Kong Meng
Kopsen, William, 9.634
Korff, John, 5.40
Korff, Mary, 5.40
Kossak, Ladislaus Sylvester, 5.40
Kraegen, Edward Charles, 9.635
Kranewitter, Aloysius, 5.41

Krausé, Ferdinand Moritz, 5.42
Krefft, Johann Ludwig (Louis) Gerard, 5.42
Krichauff, Friedrich Eduard Heinrich Wulf,
  5.44
Krome, Eleanor Victoria, 9.636
Krome, Otto Georg Hermann Dittmar,
  9.636
Kruse, Johann Secundus, 5.44
Kruttschnitt, Julius, 9.636
Kubary, John Stanislaw, 5.45
Kum How, 3.19
Kwailiu, John, see Fatnowna, John Kwailiu
  Abelfai
Kwok Bew, 9.637
Kyngdon, Leslie Herbert, 9.638
La Billardière, Jacques-Julien Houtou de,
  2.69
Labilliere, Charles Edgar de, 5.47
Labilliere, Francis Peter, 5.47
Laboureyas, Pierre, 5.47
Laby, Thomas Howell, 9.640
Laby, Thomas James, 9.640
Lacey, Andrew William, 9.641
Lackey, Sir John, 5.48
Lackey, William, 5.48
Lade, Frank, 9.642
Laffer, George Richards, 9.643
Laffer, Philip Frederick, 9.643
Lahey, Frances Vida, 9.643
Lahey, Romeo Watkins, 9.644
Laidlaw, Thomas, 5.49
Laidler, Thomas Percival, 9.645
Laidley, James, 2.69
Laing, Charles, 2.70
Laing, Henry, 2.71
Lake, George Hingston, 9.646
Lakeland, John, 2.71
Laker, Jane, see Muskett, Alice Jane
Lalor, James Fintan, 5.50
Lalor, Patrick, 5.50
Lalor, Peter, 5.50
Lalor, Vivian William, 9.647
Lamaro, Joseph, 9.648
Lamartiniere, Alexander Henry, 9.577
Lamb, Alfred, 2.73
Lamb, Edward William, 2.73, **5.54**
Lamb, Ernest, 5.55
Lamb, Helen, 5.55
Lamb, Henry, 5.55
Lamb, Sir Horace, 5.54
Lamb, John, 2.72
Lamb, John de Villiers, 5.55
Lamb, Sir Walter, 5.55
Lamb, Walter, 2.73, **5.56**
Lambe, David, 2.73
Lambert, Ada, see à Beckett, Ada Mary
Lambert, George Washington Thomas,
  9.649
Lambert, William Henry, 9.651
Lambie, Charles George, 9.651
Lamble, George Edwin, 9.652
Lamington, Baron, 9.653
Lamond, Hector, 9.654
Lancaster, G. B., see Lyttleton, Edith Joan

Lancaster, Samuel, 9.655
Landale, Thomas, 2.74
Landor, Edward Willson, 2.74
Landsborough, William, 3.284, **5.56**
Landseer, Albert Henry, 9.655
Lane, Ernest Henry, 9.656
Lane, Frederick Claude Vivian, 9.657
Lane, Hannah Elliot, *see* Boase
Lane, Laura, *see* Luffman, Lauretta
 Caroline Maria
Lane, Timothy, 7.268
Lane, William, 9.658
Lane, Zebina, 9.659
Lane, Zebina Bartholomew, 9.659
Lane-Poole, Charles Edward, 9.660
Lane-Poole, Sir Richard Hayden Owen,
 9.661
Lang, George, 2.80
Lang, Gideon Scott, 2.75
Lang, John, 5.58
Lang, John Dunmore, 2.76
Lang, John Thomas, 9.661
Lang, Matthew, 5.59
Lang, Wilhelmina, 2.82
Langdon, Thomas, 9.667
Langdon, William, 2.83
Langham, Frederick, 5.60
Langlands, George, 5.60
Langlands, Henry, 2.84
Langlands, Robert, 2.84
Langler, Sir Alfred, 9.667
Langley, George Furner, 9.668
Langley, Hudson John Watson, 9.669
Langridge, George David, 5.61
Langton, Edward, 5.62
Langwell, Hugh, 9.670
Lanigan, William, 5.63
Lansell, George, 5.63
Lansell, Sir George Victor, 9.671
Lansell, William, 5.63
La Pérouse, Jean-François de Galaup, 2.85
Laporte, François Louis Nompar de
 Caumont, 5.64
Lapsley, James McFarlane, 9.671
Lara, James, *see* Larra
Larcombe, James, 9.672
Lardner, John, 5.65
Larkin, Edward Rennix, 9.673
Larkin, Herbert Benjamin George, 9.674
Larkin, Herbert Joseph, 9.674
Larnach, Donald, 5.65
Larnach, John, 2.86
Larra, James, 2.86
Larsen, Niels Hertzberg, 10.18, 10.23
Larsen, Peter, *see* Larsen, Niels Hertzberg
Lascelles, Edward Harewood, 5.66
Lascelles, Thomas Allen, 2.87
Laseron, Charles Francis, 9.675
Lasseter, Lewis Hubert (Harold Bell),
 9.676
Lassetter, Frederic, 5.67
Lassetter, Henry Beauchamp, 5.68
Lassetter, Matthew, 5.67
Latham, Alan Thomas, 10.6

Latham, Sir Charles George, 10.1
Latham, Edward, 5.68
Latham, Eleanor Mary (Ella), 10.5
Latham, John, 2.88
Latham, Sir John Greig, 10.2
Latham, Leslie Scott, 10.6
Latham, Richard Thomas Edwin, 10.6
Latham, Thomas, 10.2
Latimer, Hugh, 10.6
Latimer, William Fleming, 10.6
La Trobe, Charles Joseph, **2.89**, 2.125
Laurens, John, 5.69
Laurie, Henry, 10.7
Lavater, Louis Isidore, 10.8
Laver, Alfred Edmund, 10.10
Laver, Charles William, 10.9
Laver, Frank Jonas, 10.9
Laver, Ralph Herbert, 10.10
Laver, William Adolphus, 10.10
Law, Sydney James, 10.11
Lawes, Frank, 5.70
Lawes, Sir John, 8.228
Lawes, William George, 5.69
Lawless, Clement Francis, 2.93
Lawless, John Paul, 2.93
Lawless, Paul, 2.93
Lawley, Annie Allen, Lady, 10.12
Lawley, Sir Arthur, 10.12
Lawlor, Adrian, 10.12
Lawrence, Charles Edward, 10.13
Lawrence, Gordon Ord, 10.14
Lawrence, Marjorie Florence, 10.14
Lawrence, Robert William, 2.95
Lawrence, William Effingham, 2.93
Lawrie, John, 1.486
Lawry, Walter, 2.95
Lawson, Abercrombie Anstruther, 10.15
Lawson, Sir Harry Sutherland Wightman,
 10.16
Lawson, Henry, 4.438, **10.18**
Lawson, James (1884-1965), 10.22
Lawson, James (publican), 10.22
Lawson, James Robert, 10.22
Lawson, Louisa, 10.19, **10.23**
Lawson, William (1774-1850), 2.96
Lawson, William (1876-1957), 10.25
Lawton, John Thomas, 10.26
Lawton, Thomas, 10.26
Lay, Percy, 10.27
Laybourne-Smith, Louis, *see* Smith, Louis
 Laybourne
Laycock, Burdett, 10.28
Laycock, Frederick, 10.28
Laycock, Hannah, 2.97
Laycock, Thomas (1756?-1809), 2.97
Laycock, Thomas (1786?-1823), 2.97
Layh, Herbert Thomas Christoph, 10.29
Lazar, John, 2.98
Lazar, Rachel, 2.98
Lazarev, Mikhail Petrovich, 2.99
Lazarus, Daniel Barnet, 10.30
Lazzarini, Carlo Camillo, 10.30
Lea, Arthur Mills, 10.31
Leach, John Albert, 10.32

Leadbeater, Charles Webster, 10.33
Leaf, Charles John, 6.317
Leahy, John, 10.34
Leahy, Michael James, 10.34
Leahy, Patrick James, 10.34
Leahy, Thomas Joseph, 10.36
Leak, John, 10.37
Leake, George (1786-1849), 2.99
Leake, George (1856-1902), 5.71, **10.37**
Leake, George Walpole, 5.70
Leake, John, 2.100
Leake, Sir Luke Samuel, 5.70
Leakey, Caroline Woolmer, 5.71
Leane, Allan William, 10.39
Leane, Edwin Thomas, 10.39
Leane, Ernest Albert, 10.40
Leane, Sir Raymond Lionel, 10.39
Leane, Thomas John, 10.39
Learmonth, Andrew James, 2.100
Learmonth, Frederick Valiant Cotton, *see*
  Livingstone-Learmonth
Learmonth, John, 2.100
Learmonth, John Ralston, 5.73
Learmonth, Peter, 5.72
Learmonth, Somerville, 2.100
Learmonth, Thomas (1783-1869), 2.100
Learmonth, Thomas (1818-1903), 2.100
Learmonth, William, 5.72
Leary, Joseph, 5.73
Leason, Percy Alexander, 10.41
Leckie, Alexander Joseph, 10.42
Leckie, Hattie, *see* Knight, Hattie Martha
Leckie, John William, 10.43
Le Couteur, Philip Ridgeway, 10.44
Le Couteur, Wilson, 7.199
Ledger, Charles, 5.73
Lee, Alfred, 10.45
Lee, Benjamin (1825-1917), 5.74
Lee, Benjamin (d.1879), 5.74
Lee, Betsy (Bessie), 10.46
Lee, Charles Alfred, 10.46
Lee, David, 5.75
Lee, Dick, *see* Lee, Walter Henry
  (1889-1968)
Lee, Frederick Norman, 10.45
Lee, George, 5.76
Lee, George Leonard, 10.47
Lee, Ida Louisa, 10.48
Lee, John Henry Alexander, 10.49
Lee, John Robert, 10.49
Lee, Mary, 10.50
Lee, Minnie, 10.45
Lee, Sir Walter Henry (1874-1963), 10.52
Lee, Walter Henry (fl.1882-1942) l0.53
Lee, Walter Henry (1889-1968), 10.53
Lee, William, 2.101
Leehy, Mary Agnes, 10.54
Lee On, *see* Leon, Andrew
Leeper, Alexander, 10.54
Leeper, Alexander Wigram Allen, 10.56
Leeper, Sir Reginald (Rex) Wildig Allen,
  10.57
Lees, Harrington Clare, 10.57
Lees, Samuel Edward, 10.58

Leeson, Ida Emily, 10.58
Lee Steere, Sir Ernest Augustus, 10.59
Leete, Benjamin, *see* Rickards, Harry
Le Fanu, Henry Frewen, 10.60
Lefroy, Anthony O'Grady, 5.77
Lefroy, Gerald de Courcy, 5.77
Lefroy, Sir Henry Bruce, 10.62
Lefroy, Sir John Henry, 5.77
Legge, James Gordon, 10.63
Legge, Robert Vincent, 5.78
Legge, William Vincent, 5.78
Leggo, Arthur Victor, 10.65
Leggo, Henry Madren, 10.65
Le Hunte, Sir George Ruthven, 10.66
Leibius, Charles (Carl) Adolph, 5.79
Leibius, Gustav Hugo, 5.79
Leichhardt, Friedrich Wilhelm Ludwig,
  2.102, 5.338
Leidig, Georg Friedrich, 10.67
Leigh, Kathleen Mary Josephine, 10.68
Leigh, Samuel, 2.105
Leighton, Arthur Edgar, 10.69
Leist, Frederick William, 10.70
Leitch, Emily Bertha, Lady, 10.71
Leitch, Sir Walter, 10.71
Leitch, William, 9.514
Lemmon, John, 10.72
Lemmone, John, 10.73
Lempriere, Thomas, 2.105
Lempriere, Thomas James, 2.105
Lenehan, Henry Alfred, 10.73
Lenehan, Robert William, 10.74
Lennon, Hugh, 5.79
Lennon, William, 10.75
Lennox, David, 2.106
Leon, Andrew, 5.80
Le Rennetel, Pierre François, 10.76
Lesina, Vincent Bernard (Joseph), 10.77
Leslie, Patrick, 2.107
Leslie, William Durham, 10.78
Le Souef, Albert Alexander Cochrane, 5.80
Le Souef, Albert Sherbourne, 10.78
Le Souef, Ernest Albert, 10.78
Le Souef, Lance, 10.80
Le Souef, William Henry Dudley, 10.78
Leverrier, Francis Hewitt, 10.80
Levey, Barnett (Bernard), 2.108
Levey, George Collins, 5.81
Levey, James Alfred, 10.81
Levey, Solomon, **2.110**, 2.321
Levi, Nathaniel, 5.82
Levien, Cecil John, 10.82
Levien, Jonas Felix Australia, 5.83
Levien, Robert Henry, 10.83
Levy, Sir Daniel, 10.84
Levy, Lewis Wolfe, 5.83
Lewin, Anna Maria, 2.112
Lewin, John William, 2.111
Lewis, Arndell Neil, 10.85
Lewis, Charles Ferris, 5.84
Lewis, David (Dafydd) Edward, 10.86
Lewis, Edward Powell, 10.86
Lewis, Eliza, 10.93
Lewis, Essington, 10.87

Lewis, Fred, 10.92
Lewis, George, 10.92
Lewis, Hubert Charles, 10.86
Lewis, James, 10.93
Lewis, John, 10.93
Lewis, Mortimer William, 2.112
Lewis, Sir Neil Elliott, 10.94
Lewis, Richard, 2.113
Lewis, Robert, 10.95
Lewis, Thomas, 1.173
Lewis, William Howard Horatio, 10.96
Ley, Thomas John, 10.97
Lhotsky, John, 2.114
Liardet, Frank, 2.115
Liardet, Hector, 2.115
Liardet, Wilbraham Frederick Evelyn, 2.115
Liebe, Friederich Wilhelm Gustav, 10.98
Ligar, Charles Whybrow, 5.85
Light, Francis, 2.116
Light, Mary, 2.117
Light, William, 2.64, **2.116**
Lightfoot, Gerald, 10.99
Liguori, Sister Mary, see Partridge, Bridget
Lihou, James Victor, 10.100
Lilley, Sir Charles, 3.246, **5.86**
Lilley, Charles Mitford, 10.100
Lilley, Edwyn, 5.87
Lilley, Kathleen Mitford, 10.101
Lillico, Sir Alexander, 10.102
Lillico, Alexander Elliot, 10.102
Lillie, John, 2.118
Lilly, James, 5.88
Lincolnshire, Marquis of, see Carrington, Charles Robert
Lind, Sir Albert Eli, 10.102
Lind, Edmund Frank, 10.103
Lindeman, Henry John, 5.89
Lindesay, Sir Patrick, 2.119
Lindrum, Frederick William (1865-1943), 10.104
Lindrum, Frederick William (d.1880), 10.104
Lindrum, Frederick William (1888-1958), 10.104
Lindrum, Horace Norman William, 10.105
Lindrum, Walter Albert, 10.104
Lindsay, David, 10.105
Lindsay, Sir Ernest Daryl, 10.106
Lindsay, Jack, 10.111
Lindsay, Sir Lionel Arthur, 10.106
Lindsay, Norman Alfred Williams, 10.106
Lindsay, Percival Charles, 10.106
Lindsay, Philip, 10.110, **10.113**
Lindsay, Raymond, 10.110, **10.112**
Lindsay, Ruby, 10.106
Lindt, John William, 5.89
Linger, Carl Ferdinand August, 5.90
Linlithgow, Countess of, see Hopetoun, Hersey Alice, Lady
Linlithgow, Marquess, see Hopetoun, John Adrian Louis Hope, Earl
Linton, James Alexander Barrow, 10.115
Linton, James Walter Robert, 10.115

Linton, Sir Richard, 10.116
Linton, Sydney, 5.91
Lisgar, Baron, see Young, Sir John (1807-1876)
Lister, Meryl, see O'Hara Wood, Meryl Aitken
Lister, William Lister, 10.117
Liston, John James, 10.117
Litchfield, James, 5.92
Litchfield, Jessie Sinclair, 10.118
Lithgow, Alexander Frame, 10.119
Lithgow, William, 2.119
Little, Robert, 5.92
Little, Robert Alexander, 10.120
Little, Robert de, see De Little
Littlejohn, Emma Linda Palmer, 10.121
Littlejohn, Robert, 2.120
Littlejohn, William Still, 10.122
Littler, Charles Augustus Murray, 10.123
Littler, Frank Mervyn, 10.124
Liversidge, Archibald, 5.93
Livingston, John, 10.124
Livingston, Thomas, 10.125
Livingstone-Learmonth, Frederick Valiant Cotton, 10.126
Lloyd, Charles William, 5.94
Lloyd, Edward Henry, 5.94
Lloyd, George Alfred (1815-1897), 5.95
Lloyd, George Alfred (d.1921), 5.97
Lloyd, Henry, 5.96
Lloyd, Henry Grant, 5.96
Lloyd, Jessie Georgina, 5.97
Lloyd, John Charles, 5.94
Lloyd-Jones, Sir Charles, see Jones, Sir Charles Lloyd
Loader, Thomas, 5.97
Loane, Ro(w)land Walpole, 2.120
Loch of Drylaw, Baron, see Loch, Henry Brougham
Loch, Elizabeth, Lady, 5.99
Loch, Henry Brougham, 5.98
Lochée, Francis, 2.121
Locke, Helena Sumner, 10.127
Locke, Lilian Sophia, 10.127
Lockington, William Joseph, 10.128
Lockwood, Alfred Wright, 10.129
Lockwood, Joseph, 10.129
Lockwood, Lionel, 10.129
Lockwood, Rupert, 10.129
Lockyer, Edmund, 2.123
Lockyer, Sir Nicholas Colston, 10.130
Lodewyckx, Augustin, 10.131
Loftus, Lord Augustus William Frederick Spencer, 5.99
Loftus-Hills, Clive, 10.132
Logan, John, 2.442
Logan, Patrick, 2.124
Logan, Robert Abraham, 2.124
Loitte, Lavinia Florence de, 12.320
Lonergan, John Joseph, 10.132
Long, Charles Richard, 10.133
Long, Clarence, see Milerum
Long, George Merrick, 2.29, **10.134**
Long, Henry Samuel, 10.133

Long, Richard Hooppell, 10.135
Long, Sydney, 10.136
Long, William, 5.100
Long, William Alexander, 5.100
Longford, Raymond John Walter Hollis, 10.137
Long-Innes, see Innes, Sir Joseph George Long
Longman, Albert Heber, 10.138
Longman, Irene Maud, 10.139
Longmore, Francis, 5.101
Longmore, Lydia, 10.140
Longmore, Mary Jane McFarlane, 8.406
Longstaff, Sir John Campbell, 10.141
Longstaff, William Frederick, 10.142
Longworth, Thomas (1857-1927), 10.143
Longworth, Thomas (d.1884), 10.143
Longworth, William (1846-1928), 10.143
Longworth, William (1892-1969), 10.144
Lonigan, Thomas, 5.7
Lonsdale, William, 2.124
Lord, Clive Errol, 10.144
Lord, David, 2.126
Lord, Edward (1781-1859), 2.127
Lord, Edward (1814-1884), 2.131
Lord, Francis, 2.131
Lord, George William, 2.131, **5.102**
Lord, James, 2.126
Lord, John Ernest Cecil, 10.145
Lord, Simeon (1771-1840), 2.128
Lord, Simeon (1800-1892), 2.131
Lord, Thomas Daunt, 2.131
Lording, Rowland Edward, 10.146
Lorimer, Charlotte, 5.103
Lorimer, Sir James, 5.102
Lorimer, Philip Durham, 5.103
Lothian, Thomas Carlyle, 10.147
Loton, Sir William Thorley, 10.147
Loughlin, Martin, 5.103
Loughlin, Peter Ffrench, 10.148
Loughnane, M. J., 6.329
Loureiro, Artur José, 5.104
Love, Ernest Frederick John, 10.149
Love, George Clarke, 10.150
Love, Harriet, see Knowles, Harriet
Love, James, 10.153
Love, James Robert Beattie, 10.150
Love, James Robinson, 5.105
Love, James Simpson, 4.466, **10.151**
Love, Sir Joseph Clifton, 10.152
Love, Nigel Borland, 10.152
Love, William, 5.105
Love, Wilton Wood Russell, 10.153
Lovekin, Arthur, 10.154
Loveless, George, 2.132
Lovell, Esh, 2.133
Lovell, Henry Tasman, 10.155
Lovely, Louise Nellie, 10.156
Lovett, Mildred Esther, 10.157
Low, Sir David Alexander Cecil, 10.158
Lowe Kong Meng, 5.106
Lowe, Robert (1783-1832), 2.134
Lowe, Robert (1811-1892), **2.134**, 3.235
Lowe, William, 2.137

Lower, Leonard Waldemere, 10.159
Lowerson, Albert David, 10.160
Lowes, Thomas Yardley, 2.137
Lowrie, William, 10.160
Lowry-Corry, Somerset Richard, see Belmore, Earl of
Loyau, George Ettienne, 5.107
Loynes, James, 10.161
Lucas, Antony John Jereos, 10.162
Lucas, Arthur Henry Shakespeare, 10.163
Lucas, Sir Edward, 10.164
Lucas, James, 2.138
Lucas, John, 5.107
Lucas, Nathaniel, 2.139
Lucas, Samuel, 10.163
Lucas, Walter Henry, 10.165
Lucas-Tooth, Sir Robert Lucas, see Tooth
Ludovic, Brother, see Laboureyas, Pierre
Luffman, Charles (Bogue), 10.166
Luffman, Lauretta Caroline Maria, 10.167
Luftig, P., see Airey, Peter
Lukin, Gresley, 5.108
Lukin, Lionel Oscar, 10.167
Lumholtz, Carl Sophus, 5.109
Lumsdaine, John Sinclair, 10.168
Lundie, Francis Walter, 10.169
Luttrell, Edward, 2.139
Lutwyche, Alfred James Peter, 5.109
Luxton, Sir Harold Daniel, 10.170
Luxton, James, 5.113
Luxton, Thomas, 5.113
Lyall, David, 9.283
Lyall, James, 5.113
Lyall, John, 5.114
Lyall, William, 5.114
Lycett, Joseph, 2.140
Lyell, Andrew, 5.115
Lyell, George, 10.171
Lyell, Lottie Edith, 10.171
Lygon, Sir William, see Beauchamp
Lyle, Sir Thomas Ranken, 10.172
Lynas, William James Dalton, 10.174
Lynch, Annie, 10.175
Lynch, Arthur Alfred, 10.176
Lynch, John (1828-1906), 10.176
Lynch, John (fl.1841-1848), 2.141
Lynch, Patrick Joseph, 10.177
Lynch, Thomas (Joseph), 10.178
Lynch, William, 4.64
Lyne, Charles Emanuel, 10.178
Lyne, Sir William John, 7.198, **10.179**
Lynn, Robert John, 10.182
Lyon, John Lamb, 10.182
Lyon, Robert, 2.632
Lyons, Charles, 10.183
Lyons, Herbert William, 10.183
Lyons, Joseph Aloysius, 9.665, **10.184**
Lyons, Samuel (1791-1851), 2.141
Lyons, Samuel (b.1826), 2.143
Lyons, Thomas, 10.189
Lysaght, Andrew, 10.190
Lysaght, Andrew Augustus, 10.190
Lysaght, Herbert Royse, 10.190
Lysaght, John, 10.191

Lyster, John Sanderson, 10.191
Lyster, William Saurin, 5.116
Lyttle, Margaret, 10.26
Lyttleton, Edith Joan, 2.143
Lyttleton, William Thomas, 1.173, **2.143**
Macadam, John, 5.118
Macalister, Arthur, 5.118
Macalister, Lachlan, 2.183
McAlpine, Daniel, 10.193
McAlroy, Michael, 5.120
Macandie, George Lionel, 10.194
Macansh, John Donald, 5.121
McArthur, Alexander, 5.121
Macarthur, Archibald, 2.144
McArthur, David Charteris, 5.122
Macarthur, Sir Edward, 5.122
Macarthur, Elizabeth, 2.144
Macarthur, George Fairfowl, 2.149, **5.123**
Macarthur, Hannibal Hawkins, 2.147
Macarthur, James, **2.149**, 5.124
Macarthur, John (1767-1834), 2.147,
   2.153, 2.318
McArthur, John (1875-1947), 10.194
McArthur, John Neil, 10.196
Macarthur, Sir William, 2.149, **5.124**
McArthur, Sir William Gilbert Stewart,
   10.195
Macarthur-Onslow, Elizabeth, 5.370,
   10.198
Macarthur-Onslow, Francis Arthur, 10.196
Macarthur-Onslow, George Macleay,
   10.196
Macarthur-Onslow, James William, 10.196
Macarthur Onslow, Rosa Sibella, 10.198
Macartney, Charles George, 10.199
Macartney, Sir Edward Henry, 10.200
Macartney, Henry Dundas Keith, 10.201
Macartney, Hussey Burgh, 5.125
Macartney, John Arthur, 5.126
Macartney, Sir William Grey Ellison,
   10.202
McAulay, Alexander, 10.202
McAulay, Alexander Leicester, 10.202
McAulay, Ida Mary, 10.203
MacBain, Sir James, 5.127
McBeath, Sir William George, 10.204
McBride, Sir Peter, 10.205
McBryde, Duncan Elphinstone, 10.206
McBurney, Mona Margaret, 10.207
McBurney, Samuel, 5.128
McCabe, Stanley Joseph, 10.208
McCall, Sir John, 10.208
McCall, John Hare, 10.208
McCallum, Alexander, 10.209
MacCallum, Dorette Margarethe, Lady,
   10.213
McCallum, Francis McNeiss McNiel, *see*
   Melville, Francis
MacCallum, Sir Mungo William, 10.211
McCann, Arthur Francis, 10.215
McCann, Bernard Aloysius, 10.215
McCann, Sir Charles Francis Gerald,
   10.213
McCann, Edward John, 10.214

McCann, Frank, *see* McCann, Arthur
   Francis
McCann, Nicholas, 10.215
McCann, Peter, 10.215
McCann, Wesley Burrett, 10.215
McCann, William Francis James, 10.216
McCarron, John Francis, 5.129
McCarthy, Charles, 5.129
MacCarthy, Charles William, 10.217
McCarthy, Denis, *see* McCarty
McCarthy, Dame Emma Maud, 10.218
McCarthy, Lawrence Dominic, 10.219
McCarty, Denis, 2.159
McCash, John McDonald, 10.220
McCathie, Harriette Adelaide, 7.133,
   10.220
McCaughey, Sir Samuel, 5.130
McCawley, Thomas William, 10.221
McCay, Adam Cairns, 10.222
McCay, Andrew Ross, 10.223
McCay, Andrew Ross Boyd, 10.224
McCay, Campbell Ernest, 10.223
McCay, Delamore William, 10.222
McCay, Hugh Douglas, 10.223
McCay, Sir James Whiteside, 10.224
McCay, Walton, 10.223
McClelland, David John, 10.227
McClelland, Hugh, 10.228
McClelland, William Caldwell, 10.228
McClintock, Albert Scott, 10.228
McCloughry, Edgar James, 10.229
McCloughry, Kingston, *see* McCloughry,
   Edgar James
McCloughry, Wilfred Ashton, 10.229
McColl, Hugh, 5.131
McColl, James Hiers, 5.132, **10.230**
McComas, Jane Isabella, 10.232
McComas, John Wesley, 10.231
McComas, Robert Bond Wesley, 10.231
McCombie, Thomas, 5.132
McConnel, David Cannon, 5.133
McConnel, Mary, 5.133
McCorkindale, Isabella, 10.232
McCormack, William, 10.233
McCormack, William Thomas
   Bartholomew, 10.235
MacCormick, Sir Alexander, 10.236
McCormick, Peter Dodds, 10.237
McCourt, William Joseph, 10.238
McCoy, Sir Frederick, 3.183, **5.134**
McCoy, William Taylor, 10.238
McCracken, Alexander, 10.240
McCracken, Robert, 5.136
McCrae, Andrew Murison, 2.160
McCrae, George Gordon, 5.136
McCrae, Georgiana Huntly, **2.160**, 5.136
McCrae, Hugh Raymond, 10.240
McCrea, William, 5.138
McCrone, Francis Nesbitt, 2.161
McCubbin, Frederick, 10.242
McCubbin, Louis Frederick, 10.243
MacCullagh, John Christian, 5.138
McCulloch, Allan Riverstone, 10.244
McCulloch, George, 5.139

McCulloch, Sir James (1819-1893), 5.140
McCulloch, James (1841-1904), 5.142
McCulloch, William, 5.143
McCutcheon, Robert George, 10.245
Macdermott, Henry, 2.161
MacDevitt, Edward O'Donnell, 5.144
McDonagh, Isabella Mercia, 10.245
McDonagh, Paulette de Vere, 10.245
McDonagh, Phyllis Glory, 10.245
Macdonald, Alexander Cameron, 5.144
Macdonald, Alexander Rose, 5.146
McDonald, Arthur Stephen, 10.247
Macdonald, Benjamin Wickham, 10.247
Macdonald, Charles (1851-1903), 5.146
McDonald, Charles (1860-1925), 10.248
Macdonald, Donald Alaster, 10.249
McDonald, Edgar Arthur, 10.249
McDonald, Edith Roseina Ethell, 10.247
McDonald, Eleanor, 1.485
McDonald, George Roy William, 10.250
McDonald, Hugh, 2.162
MacDonald, James Stuart, 10.251
McDonald, Lewis, 10.252
Macdonald, Louisa, 10.253
Macdonald, Malcolm Melville, 2.81
MacDonald, May, 12.454
McDonald, Sydney Fancourt, 10.254
Macdonald, William Neil, 5.146
Macdonell, Donald, 10.255
McDonnell, Francis, 10.256
McDonnell, Morgan Augustus, 5.147
McDonnell, Percy Stanislaus, 5.147
MacDonnell, Randal, 5.147
MacDonnell, Sir Richard Graves, 1.381,
   5.148
McDougall, Archibald Campbell, 5.149
McDougall, Charles Edward, 10.257
McDougall, Dugald Gordon, 10.257
McDougall, Frank Lidgett, 10.258
MacDougall, James, 10.259
Macdougall, John, 2.163
Macdougall, John Campbell, 2.163
McDougall, John Keith, 10.260
Macdougall, Mary Ann, 2.163
McDougall, Robert, 5.150
McDougall, Stanley Robert, 10.261
McDowall, Archibald, 10.261
McDowall, Valentine, 10.262
Macdowell, Edward, 2.164
Macdowell, Thomas, 2.164
McEacharn, Sir Malcolm Donald, 10.263
McEachern, Walter Malcolm Neil, 10.264
McElhone, John, 5.150
McEncroe, John, 2.165
McEvilly, Walter O'Malley, 5.152
Macfarlan, Sir James Ross, 10.265
McFarland, Alfred, 5.152
MacFarland, Sir John Henry, 10.266
Macfarlane, Samuel, 5.153
McGarvie, John, 2.166
McGarvie, William, 2.166
McGavin, Matthew, 5.154
McGaw, Andrew Kidd, 10.268
McGee, Lewis, 10.268

Macgeorge, Norman, 10.269
McGibbon, John, 5.154
McGill, Alec Douglas, 10.270
McGill, John, see Biraban
MacGillivray, John, 2.167
MacGillivray, Paul Howard, 5.155
McGirr, James, 10.271
McGirr, John Joseph Gregory, 10.270
McGirr, Patrick Michael, 10.271
McGlinn, John Patrick, 10.272
McGowan, Samuel Walker, 5.156
McGowen, James Sinclair Taylor, 10.273
McGrath, Ada, 11.42
McGrath, David Charles, 10.275
McGrath, Edward, 11.54
McGregor, Alexander, 5.157
MacGregor, Duncan, 5.157
McGregor, Gregor, 10.275
McGregor, John Gibson, 5.157
Macgregor, Lewis Richard, 10.276
McGregor, Martin Robert, 10.277
MacGregor, Sir William, 5.158
Macgroarty, Neil Francis, 10.278
McGuigan, Brigid, 10.279
McGuinness, Arthur, 10.279
McHale, James Francis, 10.280
McIlrath, Hugh, 10.281
McIlrath, Sir Martin, 10.281
McIlrath, William, 10.281
McIlwraith, Andrew, 10.282
McIlwraith, John, 5.160
McIlwraith, Sir Thomas, 5.161
McInnes, William Beckwith, 10.283
McIntosh, Harold, 10.283
McIntosh, Hugh Donald, 10.284
Macintosh, John, 5.164
McIntosh, John Cowe, 11.133
McIntyre, Donald, 5.165
McIntyre, Duncan, 5.165
McIntyre, Sir John, 5.165
McIntyre, Peter, 2.168, 2.195
Macintyre, Ronald George, 10.286
McIntyre, Thomas, 5.7
McIntyre, William (1805-1870), 5.166
McIntyre, William (1830-1911), 5.167
Mack, Amy Eleanor, 10.287
Mack, Marie Louise Hamilton, 10.287
Mackaness, George, 10.288
Mackaness, John, 2.169
McKay, Alexander, 2.170
Mackay, Angus, 5.168
Mackay, Donald George, 10.289
McKay, George, 10.291
Mackay, George Hugh Alexander, 10.290
McKay, Hugh Victor, 10.291
Mackay, James Alexander Kenneth, 10.294
Mackay, John (1839-1914), 5.169
McKay, John (1861-1936), 10.291
Mackay, John Hilton, 10.295
Mackay, Murdoch, 5.168
McKay, Nathaniel Breakey 10.291
McKay, Samuel, 10.291, 10.294
MacKay, William John, 10.296
Mackellar, Sir Charles Kinnaird, 10.297

MacKellar, Duncan, 2.171
Mackellar, Isobel Marion Dorothea, 10.298
McKellar, John Alexander Ross, 10.299
McKellar, Lilias, 1.327
MacKellar, Neil, 2.170
McKelvey, Sir John Lawrance, 10.300
McKenna, Bernard (Joseph), 10.300
McKenna, Martin, 5.170
Mackennal, Sir Edgar Bertram, 10.301
McKenny, John, 2.171
McKenzie, Alexander Kenneth, 2.172
Mackenzie, David, 2.172
Mackenzie, Sir Evan, 5.170
McKenzie, Hugh, 10.302
Mackenzie, Sir Robert Ramsay, 5.171
Mackenzie, Roderick, 10.303
MacKenzie, Seaforth Simpson, 10.304
McKenzie, William, 10.305
MacKenzie, Sir William Colin, 10.306
Mackenzie, William Kenneth Seaforth, 10.308
McKeown, Keith Collingwood, 10.309
Mackersey, John, 2.173
Mackey, Sir John Emanuel, 10.309
Mackie, Alexander, 10.311
Mackie, George, 5.172
Mackie, William Henry, 2.174
McKillop, Donald, 5.173
McKillop, Mary Helen, 5.174
McKinlay, John, 5.174
McKinley, Alexander, 5.176
Mackinnon, Daniel, 5.176
Mackinnon, Donald (1859-1932), 10.312
Mackinnon, Donald (1892-1965), 10.314
MacKinnon, Eleanor Vokes Irby, 10.315
Mackinnon, Ewen Daniel, 10.314
Mackinnon, James Curdie, 10.315
Mackinnon, Kenneth Wulsten, 10.314
Mackinnon, Lauchlan (1817-1888), 5.177
Mackinnon, Lauchlan (1877-1934), 10.316
Mackinnon, Sir Lauchlan Charles, 10.316
Mackinnon, Lauchlan Kenneth Scobie, 10.316
McKinnon, Thomas Firmin, 10.316
McKivat, Christopher Hobart, 10.317
Mackness, Constance, 10.318
Macknight, Charles Hamilton, 5.178
Mackrell, Edwin Joseph, 10.319
Macky, William Marcus Dill, see Dill Macky
McLachlan, Alexander John, 10.320
McLachlan, Charles, 2.175
McLachlan, Duncan Clark, 10.321
McLachlan, Hugh, 10.322
McLachlan, Lachlan, 5.179
Maclagan, see Sinclair-Maclagan
Maclanachan, James, 5.181
McLaren, Alexander, 2.177
McLaren, Charles Inglis, 10.323
McLaren, David, 2.176
McLaren, John (Jack), 10.324
McLaren, Sir John Gilbert, 10.324
McLaren, Samuel Bruce, 10.325
McLaren, Samuel Gilfillan, 10.326

McLaughlin, Clara Jane, 10.326
MacLaurin, Charles, 10.329
MacLaurin, Sir Henry Normand (1835-1914), 10.327
MacLaurin, Henry Normand (1878-1915), 10.329
McLaurin, James, 5.181
Maclay, Nicholas, see Mikluho-Maklai, Nicholai Nicholaievich
Mclean, Alexander Grant, 5.182
McLean, Allan, 10.329
McLean, Donald, 5.184
Maclean, Harold, 5.183
McLean, John Donald, 5.184
McLean, Margaret, 10.331
McLean, William, 5.184
McLeay, Alexander, 2.177
Maclay, Sir George, 2.180
Macleay, Sir William John, 5.185
Macleay, William Sharp, 2.182
McLeish, Duncan, 10.331
McLellan, William, 5.187
McLeod, Donald, 10.332
McLeod, Donald Norman, 10.333
McLeod, John Norman, 10.333
Macleod, Thomas, 10.334
Macleod, William, 10.335
McLerie, John, 5.188
MacMahon, Sir Charles (1824-1891), 5.189
MacMahon, Charles (1861?-1917), 10.337
McMahon, Gregan, 10.336
MacMahon, James, 10.337
McMaster, Sir Fergus, 10.338
McMaster, Sir Frederick Duncan, 10.339
McMaster, Thelma, 10.340
McMeckan, James, 5.190
McMillan, Angus, 2.183
McMillan, Robert, 10.340
McMillan, Sir Robert Furse, 10.341
McMillan, Samuel, 10.342
McMillan, Sir William, 10.342
McMinn, Gilbert Rotherdale, 5.191
McMinn, William, 5.191
McNab, Duncan, 5.192
Macnaghten, Charles Melville, 10.344
Macnamara, Dame Annie Jean, 10.345
McNamara, Daniel Laurence, 10.347
McNamara, David John, 10.347
McNamara, Frank (Francis) Hubert, 10.348
McNamara, Matilda Emilie Bertha, 10.349
McNamara, William Henry Thomas, 10.350
McNaughtan, Alexander, 5.193
McNeil, Neil, 5.193
MacNeil, Neil Harcourt, 10.351
McNeill, John James, 10.352
McNess, Sir Charles, 10.353
McNicoll, Sir Walter Ramsay, 10.354
Maconochie, Alexander, 2.184
McPhee, Sir John Cameron, 10.355
McPherson, Sir Clive, 10.356
McPherson, David, 11.283
McPherson, Dugald, 6.249
McPherson, James Alpin, 5.194

McPherson, John Abel, 9.415, **10.357**
MacPherson, John Alexander, 5.195
MacPherson, Margaret, 10.358
MacPherson, Peter, 5.195
McPherson, Sir William Murray, 10.359
McPhillamy, John Smith, 5.196
McPhillamy, Verania, 7.642, **10.360**
McPhillamy, William, 5.196
Macquarie, Charles, 2.187
Macquarie, Donald, 2.187
Macquarie, Elizabeth Henrietta, 2.186
Macquarie, Hector, 2.187
Macquarie, Lachlan (1762-1824), 1.99,
  2.186, **2.187**
Macquarie, Lachlan (d.pre-1785), 2.187
Macquarie, Margaret, 2.187
McQueen, E. Neil, 10.408
Macqueen, Thomas Potter, 2.195
McRae, Christopher John, 10.361
McRae, James, 10.362
Macredie, Andrew, 5.197
Macredie, George, 5.198
Macredie, John, 5.198
Macredie, Robert Reid, 5.197
Macredie, William, 5.197
MacRory, Margaret, 10.363
Macrossan, Hugh Denis, 10.363
Macrossan, John Murtagh, 5.198
McSharry, Terence Patrick, 10.364
Mactier, Robert, 10.365
McVicars, John, 10.366
McVilly, Cecil Leventhorpe, 10.367
Macvitie, Thomas, 2.196
McWhae, Sir John, 10.367
Macwhirter, Frances Elliott, 3.344
McWilliam, John James, 10.368
McWilliam, Samuel, 10.368
McWilliams, Thomas Cole, 10.369
McWilliams, William James, 10.369
Madden, Sir Frank, 10.370
Madden, Sir John (1844-1918), 10.371
Madden, John (d.1902), 10.371
Madden, Walter, 10.370
Maddock, Sarah, 10.373
Madigan, Cecil Thomas, 10.374
Madsen, Sir John Percival Vaissing
  (Vissing), 10.376
Magarey, Silvanus James, 2.197
Magarey, Thomas, 2.197
Magrath, Edward Crawford, 10.377
Maguire, James Bernard, 10.378
Mahomet, Faiz, 10.378
Mahon, Hugh, 10.379
Mahony, Daniel James, 10.380
Mahony, Francis, 10.381
Mahony, William Henry, 10.381
Maiden, Joseph Henry, 10.381
Mailey, Alfred Arthur, 10.383
Main, Edward, 1.252
Main, Hugh, 10.384
Mair, Alexander, 10.385
Mair, William, 5.199
Mais, Henry Coathupe, 5.200
Maitland, Andrew Gibb, 10.386

Maitland, Charles, 5.202
Maitland, Edward, 5.201
Maitland, George Brumfitt Gibb, 10.387
Maitland, Sir Herbert Lethington, 10.387
Makinson, Thomas Cooper, 2.198
Makutz, Bela, 5.202
Male, Arthur, 10.388
Maley, John Stephen, 5.202
Mallalieu, Henrietta, *see* Willmore
Mallett, Cara, *see* David, Caroline Martha,
  Lady
Malmgrom, Helen Dorothy, *see* Stirling,
  Nell
Maloney, William Robert (Nuttall), 10.389
Manifold, Edward, 10.391
Manifold, James Chester, 10.391
Manifold, John, 2.199
Manifold, Peter, 2.199
Manifold, Thomas, 2.199
Manifold, Sir Walter Synnot, 10.390
Manifold, William Thomson, 10.391
Mann, Charles (1799-1860), 2.200
Mann, Charles (1838-1889), 2.201
Mann, David Dickenson, 2.201
Mann, Edward Alexander, 10.392
Mann, Sir Frederick Wollaston, 10.393
Mann, Gother Victor Fyers, 10.394
Mann, James Gilbert, 10.394
Mann, John Frederick, 5.202
Mann, Thomas, 10.395
Manners-Sutton, John Henry Thomas, *see*
  Canterbury, Viscount
Manning, Charles James, 5.203
Manning, Edye, 2.202
Manning, Emily Matilda, 5.204
Manning, Frederic, 10.396
Manning, Frederic Norton, 5.204
Manning, Sir Henry Edward, 10.397
Manning, James, 5.205
Manning, James Alexander Louis, 5.206
Manning, John Edye, 2.202
Manning, Sir William Montagu, 5.207
Manning, Sir William Patrick, 10.397
Mannix, Daniel, 10.398
Mansergh, James, 5.209
Mansfield, Ralph, 2.204
Mansour, Sylwanos, 10.405
Manton, John Allen, 2.205
Marceau, Joseph, 2.353
March, Frederick Hamilton, 10.405
Marchant, George, 10.406
Marconi, Joseph Cornelius, 10.407
Marden, John, 10.407
Margarot, Maurice, 2.206
Margolin, Eliezer, 10.408
Margolin, Lazar, *see* Margolin, Eliezer
Marin la Meslée, Edmond Marie, 5.210
Marina, Camillo, 5.211
Marina, Carlo, 5.210
Marks, Alexander Hammett, 10.409
Marks, Charles Ferdinand, 10.410
Marks, Douglas Gray, 10.410
Marks, Ernest Samuel, 10.413
Marks, Gladys Hope, 10.411

Marks, James, 5.212
Marks, John, 5.211
Marks, Percy, 10.412
Marks, Percy Joseph, 10.413
Marks, Theodore John, 5.212, **10.414**
Marks, Walter Moffitt, 10.415
Marlowe, Margaret Mary, 10.415
Marmion, William Edward, 10.416
Marquet, Claude Arthur, 10.417
Marr, Sir Charles William Clanan, 10.418
Marriott, Charles John Bruce, 10.48
Marriott, Fitzherbert Adams, 2.207
Marriott, Ida, see Lee, Ida Louisa
Marryat, Charles, 10.419
Marsden, Eliza, 1.523
Marsden, Samuel, 1.314, **2.207**
Marsden, Samuel Edward, 5.212
Marsh, Matthew Henry, 5.213
Marsh, Rosetta, see Terry, Rosetta
Marsh, Stephen Hale Alonzo, 5.213
Marshall, James Waddell, 5.214
Marshall, Mary, 2.444
Marshall, Norman, 10.419
Marshall, William Henry George, 5.215
Marshall-Hall, George William Louis,
    10.420
Martens, Conrad, 2.212
Martin, Arthur Patchett, 5.215
Martin, Catherine Edith Macauley, 10.423
Martin, Sir Charles James, 4.322, **10.423**
Martin, David, 10.425
Martin, Edward Fowell, 10.426
Martin, Florence, 10.427
Martin, Isabella, Lady, 5.219
Martin, Sir James (1820-1886), 5.216
Martin, James (1821-1899), 5.219
Martin, John, 5.216
Martin, Lewis Ormsby, 10.428
Martin, William Clarence, 10.428
Martindale, Ben Hay, 5.220
Martyn, Athelstan Markham, 10.429
Martyn, James, 10.430
Martyn, Nellie Constance, 10.430
Mary of the Cross, Mother, see McKillop,
    Mary Helen
Mashman, Ernest James Theodore, 10.430
Mashman, Henry, 10.431
Mashman, William, 10.430
Mason, Francis Conway, 5.221
Mason, Horatio William, 1.270
Mason, Martin, 2.213
Mason, Thomas (1800-1888), 2.214
Mason, Thomas (b.c1851), 6.353
Mason, Thomas (snr), 2.214
Massey, Thomas, 2.215
Massie, Robert John Allwright, 10.431
Massina, Alfred Henry, 5.222
Masson, Sir David Orme, 10.432
Masson, Sir James Irvine Orme, 10.435
Masson, Mary, Lady, 10.434
Massy-Greene, Sir Walter, 10.435
Masters, George, 5.223
Mate, Thomas Hodges, 5.224
Mather, Emily Lydia, 8.268

Mather, John, 10.438
Mather, Joseph Francis, 10.439
Mather, Robert, 1.552, **2.216**
Matheson, Sir Alexander Perceval, 10.440
Matheson, John, 5.224
Mathew, John, 10.440
Mathews, Gregory Macalister, 10.441
Mathews, Hamilton Bartlett, 10.442
Mathews, Julia, see Matthews
Mathews, Robert Hamilton, 5.225
Mathews, Robert Henry, 10.443
Mathias, Louis John, 10.444
Matson, Henry Manifold, 2.200
Matson, Phillip Henry, 10.445
Matters, Muriel Lilah, 10.445
Matthews, Charles Henry Selfe, 10.446
Matthews, Daniel, 5.226
Matthews, Harley, 10.447
Matthews, Julia, 3.301, **5.227**
Matthews, Susan May, 10.448
Matthews, William, 5.227
Matthias, Elizabeth, 10.449
Mattingley, Arthur Herbert Evelyn, 10.449
Maudsley, Sir Henry Carr, 10.450
Maudsley, Henry Fitzgerald, 10.451
Mauger, Samuel, 10.451
Maugham, William James, see Maum
Maughan, Sir David, 10.453
Maughan, James, 5.228
Mault, Alfred, 5.229
Maum, William James, 2.216
Maund, Benjamin, 5.230
Maund, John, 5.230
Maurice, Furnley, see Wilmot, Frank Leslie
    Thompson
Maurice, Price, 5.231
Mawson, Sir Douglas, 10.454
Mawson, Francisca Adriana (Paquita),
    Lady, 10.457
Maxted, Edward, 10.457
Maxted, George, 10.457
Maxted, Sydney, 10.457
Maxwell, George Arnot, 10.459
Maxwell, Joseph, 10.459
Maxwell, Walter, 10.460
Maxwell, William, see Maxwell-Mahon
Maxwell-Mahon, William Ion, 10.461
May, Frederick, 5.231
May, Philip William, 5.232
May, Sydney Lionel, 10.462
May, William Lewis, 10.463
May Day, see Hickman, Frances May
Maygar, Leslie Cecil, 10.463
Mayne, James O'Neil, 10.464
Mayne, Mary Emelia, 10.464
Mayne, William Colburn, 5.233
Mayo, George Elton, 10.465
Mayo, Helen Mary, 10.466
Mayo, Sir Herbert, 10.466
Mayo, John Christian, 10.466
Mayo, Mary Penelope, 10.466
Mead, Cecil Silas, 5.234
Mead, Elwood, 10.467
Mead, Gertrude Ella, 10.468

Mead, Silas, 5.234
Meagher, John, 10.469
Meagher, Richard Denis, 10.470
Meagher, Richard James, 8.370, **10.472**
Meagher, Thomas Francis, 2.217
Mealmaker, George, 2.218
Meares, Charles Edward Devenish, 10.473
Meares, Richard Goldsmith, 2.218
Medland, Lilian Marguerite, 9.435
Meehan, James, 1.564, **2.219**
Meeks, Sir Alfred William, 10.474
Meeson, Dora, 8.36
Mehaffey, Maurice William, 10.474
Mei Quong Tart, 5.234
Mein, Charles Stuart, 5.235
Mein, James, 2.220
Melba, Dame Nellie, 9.220, 10.73, **10.475**
Melbourne, Alexander Clifford Vernon, 10.479
Meldrum, Duncan Max, 10.480
Melhuish, Mary, 11.478
Melhuish, William, 11.478
Melrose, Alexander John, 10.483
Melrose, Charles James, 10.482
Melrose, Sir John, 10.482
Melville, Francis, 5.236
Melville, Henry, 2.221
Melville, Ninian, 5.237
Melville, Viscount, *see* Dundas, Henry
Melvin, John, 10.483
Melvin, Joseph Dalgarno, 10.483
Mendes da Costa, Benjamin, 5.238
Menge, Johann, 2.222
Menkens, Frederick Burnhardt, 5.239
Mennell, Philip Dearman, 10.484
Menzies, Sir Charles, 2.222
Mercer, George, 2.223
Mercer, George Duncan, 2.223
Mercer, John Edward, 10.484
Mercer, John Henry, 2.223
Mercer, William Drummond, 2.223
Meredith, Charles, 2.225, **5.239**
Meredith, George, 2.224
Meredith, John, 2.224
Meredith, John Baldwin Hoystead, 10.485
Meredith, Louisa Ann, 5.239
Merewether, Edward Christopher, 5.240
Merewether, Francis Lewis Shaw, 5.241
Merrett, Sir Charles Edward, 10.486
Merrett, Samuel Headen, 10.486
Merriman, George, 10.487
Merriman, James, 5.242
Merriman, Sir Walter Thomas, 10.487
Merritt, Walter Lancelot, *see* Schwarz, Walter Leslie
Mesley, Martha, 9.327
Messenger, Herbert Henry, 10.488
Meston, Archibald, 5.243
Meston, Archibald Lawrence, 10.489
Metcalfe, Michael, 5.244
Meudell, George Dick, 10.490
Meudell, William, 10.490
Meyer, Felix Henry, 10.491
Meyer, Mary Fisher, 10.491

Meynell, Clyde, 8.16
Michael, James Lionel, 5.244
Michaelis, Moritz, 5.245
Michel, Louis John, 5.246
Michelides, Peter Spero, 10.492
Michell, Anthony George Maldon, 10.492
Michell, John Henry, 10.494
Michie, Sir Archibald, 5.246
Michie, John Lundie, 10.495
Micklem, Philip Arthur, 10.496
Middleton, George Augustus, 2.226
Middleton, John, 5.248
Miethke, Adelaide Laetitia, 10.497
Mikluho-Maklai, Nicholai Nicholaievich, 5.248
Mileham, James, 2.227
Milerum, 10.498
Miles, Beatrice, 10.499
Miles, Edward, 8.574
Miles, Edward Thomas, 10.500
Miles, John Campbell, 10.501
Miles, William, 5.250
Miles, William Augustus (1753?-1817), 2.228
Miles, William Augustus (1798-1851), 2.228
Miles, William John, 10.501
Milford, Charles Sussex, 5.252
Milford, Frederick, 5.252
Milford, Henry John Bede, 5.252
Milford, Herman, 5.252
Milford, Samuel Frederick, 5.251
Millen, Edward Davis, 10.502
Millen, John Dunlop, 10.503
Miller, Alexander, 10.504
Miller, Andrew, 2.229
Miller, David, 10.505
Miller, Sir Denison Samuel King, 10.506
Miller, Edmund Morris, 10.507
Miller, Sir Edward, 5.253, **10.509**
Miller, Emma, 10.509
Miller, Everard Studley, 10.510
Miller, Frederick, 2.229
Miller, George, 2.230
Miller, Granville George, 5.253
Miller, Gustave Thomas Carlisle, 10.511
Miller, Henry (1809-1888), 5.252
Miller, Henry (d.1866), 5.252
Miller, Horatio Clive, 10.511
Miller, Marion, *see* Knowles, Marion
Miller, Maxwell, 5.253
Miller, Montague David, 10.512
Miller, Robert (d.1876), 5.253
Miller, Robert Byron, 5.253
Miller, Robert William, 10.513
Miller, Roderick, 10.513
Miller, William, 5.254
Milligan, Joseph, 2.230
Milligan, Stanley Lyndall, 10.514
Mills, Arthur Edward, 10.515
Mills, Arthur James, 10.515
Mills, Charles (1832-1916), 5.255
Mills, Charles (1877-1963), 10.516

Mills, Charles Frederick, 2.231
Mills, John Brabyn, 2.231
Mills, Peter, 2.231
Mills, Richard Charles, 10.517
Mills, Stephen, 10.519
Mills, William George James, 10.519
Milne, Edmund Osborn, 10.520
Milne, John Alexander, 10.521
Milne, Sir William, 5.255
Milson, James (1783-1872), 2.232
Milson, James (1814-1903), 2.232
Minahan, James Mark, 10.523
Minahan, Patrick Joseph, 10.522
Minchin, Alfred Corker, 5.258, **10.523**
Minchin, Alfred Keith, 10.524
Minchin, Henry Paul, 5.257
Minchin, Richard Ernest, 5.256
Minchin, Ronald Richard Luther, 10.523
Minchin, William, 2.233
Minifie, Richard Pearman, 10.524
Minns, Benjamin Edwin, 10.525
Minogue, Henry, 10.525
Minogue, Michael Andrew, 10.525
Mirams, James, 5.258
Mitchel, John, 2.234
Mitchell, David, 5.259
Mitchell, David Scott, 2.237, **5.260**
Mitchell, Sir Edward Fancourt, 10.526
Mitchell, Eliza Fraser, Lady, 10.527
Mitchell, Ernest Meyer, 10.528
Mitchell, Isabel Mary, 10.528
Mitchell, James (1792-1869), 2.235
Mitchell, James (d.1827), 1.353
Mitchell, James (1835-1914), 5.261
Mitchell, Sir James (1866-1951), 10.530
Mitchell, Janet Charlotte, 10.528
Mitchell, John, 10.532
Mitchell, Joseph Earl Cherry, 5.261
Mitchell, Sir Mark, 10.536
Mitchell, Nancy, see Adams, Agnes Eliza
  Fraser
Mitchell, Robert, 10.533
Mitchell, Samuel James, 10.533
Mitchell, Thomas (1844?-1908), 10.534
Mitchell, Thomas (d.1887), 5.261
Mitchell, Thomas (d.1917), 12.431
Mitchell, Sir Thomas Livingstone, 2.238
Mitchell, William (1786-1837), 1.573
Mitchell, William (1834-1915), 5.262
Mitchell, Sir William (1861-1962), 10.535
Mitchell, Sir William Henry Fancourt,
  5.262
Mo, see Rene, Roy
Mocatta, George Gershon, 5.263
Moffat, John, 10.537
Moffatt, Thomas de Lacy, 5.263
Moffitt, Ernest Edward, 10.538
Moffitt, William, 2.242
Mogador, Céleste, see Chabrillan,
  Céleste de
Molesworth, Henrietta, 5.264
Molesworth, Hickman, 10.539
Molesworth, Sir Robert, 5.264
Molesworth, Voltaire, 10.539

Molineux, Albert, 5.265
Molineux, Edward, 5.265
Molle, George James, 2.243
Molle, William Macquarie, 2.243
Mollison, Alexander Fullerton, 2.243
Mollison, Crawford Henry, 10.540
Mollison, Ethel, see Kelly, Ethel Knight
Mollison, William Thomas, 2.243
Molloy, Georgiana, 2.244
Molloy, John, 2.245
Molloy, Thomas George Anstruther,
  10.541
Moloney, Parker John, 10.542
Moloney, Patrick, 5.266
Molyneux, Henry Howard, see Carnarvon,
  Earl of
Monahan, Thomas, 5.266
Monash, Sir John, 9.485, **10.543**
Monckton, Charles Arthur Whitmore,
  10.549
Monckton, William, 6.353
Moncrieff, Alexander Bain, 10.550
Moncrieff, Gladys Lillian, 10.551
Mondalmi, 10.553
Monds, Albert William, 10.553
Monds, Thomas, 2.245
Monds, Thomas Wilkes, 2.245
Monger, Alexander Joseph, 10.554
Monger, Frederick Charles, 10.554
Monger, John Henry (1831-1892), 5.267
Monger, John Henry (d.1867), 5.267
Monk, Cyril Farnsworth, 10.555
Monks, Lallie, see Keating, Sarah Alice
Monnier, Joseph, 5.268
Montagu, Algernon Sidney, 2.246
Montagu, John (1718-1792), 1.52
Montagu, John (1797-1853), 2.248
Montague, Alexander, 5.268
Montefiore, Dorothy Frances, 10.556
Montefiore, Eliezer Levi, 5.269
Montefiore, Jacob, 2.251
Montefiore, Jacob Levi, 5.270
Montefiore, Joseph Barrow, 2.250
Montez, Lola, 5.271
Montford, Paul Raphael, 10.557
Montgomery, Christina Smith, 10.558
Montgomery, Henry Hutchinson, 10.558
Montgomery, Sydney Hamilton Rowan,
  10.559
Montgomery, Walter, 5.272
Monty, Mrs, see Cohen, Annie
Moody, Ella, 11.51
Moondyne Joe, see Johns, Joseph Bolitho
Moonlite, Captain, see Scott, Andrew
  George
Moor, Henry, 2.251
Moore, Annie May, 10.560
Moore, Arthur Edward, 10.561
Moore, Caroline Ellen, 10.562
Moore, Charles (1820-1895), 5.273
Moore, Charles (1820-1905), 5.274
Moore, David, 5.275
Moore, Donald Ticehurst, 10.563
Moore, Eleanor May, 10.564

Moore, George, 5.276
Moore, George Fletcher, 2.252
Moore, Gladys, see Owen, Gladys Mary
Moore, Henry Byron, 5.275
Moore, James (1807-1895), 5.276
Moore, James (1834-1904), 5.277
Moore, James Lorenzo, 10.565
Moore, John Charles, 10.566
Moore, John Drummond Macpherson, 10.566
Moore, Joseph Sheridan, 5.278
Moore, Joshua John, 2.254
Moore, Maggie, **5.279**, 6.406
Moore, Minnie Louise, 10.560
Moore, Sir Newton James, 10.567
Moore, Nicholas, 10.569
Moore, Samuel Joseph Fortescue, 5.281
Moore, Samuel Wilkinson, 10.570
Moore, Thomas, 2.254
Moore, Thomas Bather, 10.571
Moore, William (1821-1893), 5.280
Moore, William (1859-1927), 10.571
Moore, William Dalgety, 5.280
Moore, William George, 10.572
Moore, Sir William Harrison, 10.573
Moore, William Henry, 2.255
Moorhouse, James, 5.281
Moorhouse, Matthew, 5.283
Moran, Charles John, 10.575
Moran, Herbert Michael, 10.576
Moran, Patrick Francis, 10.577
Morant, Harry Harbord, 9.184, **10.581**
Mordaunt, Evelyn May, 10.582
Morehead, Boyd Dunlop, 5.284
Morehead, Robert Archibald Alison, 2.257
Morell, Sir Stephen Joseph, 10.583
Moresby, John, 5.285
Moreton, Berkeley Basil, 5.286
Moreton, Matthew Henry, 5.286
Morey, Edward, 5.286
Morgan, Sir Arthur, 10.584
Morgan, Frederick Augustus, 5.287
Morgan, Godfrey, 10.585
Morgan, James, 5.288
Morgan, John, 2.258
Morgan, Molly, 2.259
Morgan, Sir William, 5.288
Morgans, Alfred Edward, 10.586
Moriarty, Abram Orpen, 5.289
Moriarty, Daniel, 10.586
Moriarty, Edward Orpen, 5.291
Moriarty, Ellen, 2.260
Moriarty, Merion Marshall, 5.290
Moriarty, William, 2.259
Morice, James Percy, 10.587, **10.588**
Morice, Louise (Lucy), 10.587
Morison, Alexander, 5.291
Morisset, Edric Norfolk Vaux, 2.261, 6.339
Morisset, James Thomas, 2.260
Morley, William, 10.588
Moroney, Timothy, 10.589
Morphett, Sir John, 2.261
Morphett, Nathaniel, 2.261
Morres, Elsie Frances, 10.590

Morrill, James, 2.262
Morris, Albert, 10.591
Morris, Augustus (1820?-1895), 5.292
Morris, Augustus (convict), 5.292
Morris, Edward Ellis, 5.293
Morris, Ellen Margaret, 10.591
Morris, George Francis, 5.294
Morris, Sir John Newman, see Newman-Morris
Morris, Myra Evelyn, 10.591
Morris, Robert Newton, 5.295
Morrison, Alexander, 5.295
Morrison, Askin, 5.297
Morrison, Charles Norman, 10.592
Morrison, Edward Charles, 10.593
Morrison, Eliza Fraser, see Mitchell, Eliza Fraser, Lady
Morrison, George, **5.298**, 5.296
Morrison, George Ernest, 10.593
Morrison, Robert, 5.296
Morrison, Sibyl Enid Vera Munro, 10.596
Morrow, James, 5.298
Mort, Eirene, 10.596
Mort, Henry, 5.301
Mort, Thomas Sutcliffe, **5.299**, 6.138
Mort, William, 5.299
Mortlock, William Ranson, 5.301
Mortlock, William Tennant, 5.302
Morton, Alexander, 10.597
Morton, Frank, 10.598
Morton, William Lockhart, 5.302
Moseley, H. N., 12.33
Mosman, Archibald, 2.263
Mosman, George, 2.263
Mosman, Hugh, 2.264, **5.303**
Moss, Alice Frances Mabel (May), 10.599
Moss, William, 5.303
Mott, George Henry, 10.599
Mott, Hamilton Charnock, 10.599
Moubray, Thomas, 5.304
Moulden, Beaumont Arnold, 10.600
Moulden, Deborah, see Hackett, Deborah Vernon, Lady
Moulden, Sir Frank Beaumont, 10.600
Moulds, Constance, 10.601
Moulds, George Francis, 10.601
Moulton, James Egan, 5.305
Mountgarrett, Jacob, 2.264
Mouton, Jean Baptiste Octave, 10.602
Mowton, George, 3.432
Moyes, Morton Henry, 10.602
Moyle, Edward, see Miles, Edward
Mudie, James, 2.264
Mudie, John McBain, 10.98
Muecke, Carl Wilhelm Ludwig, 5.306
Muecke, Hugo Carl Emil, 10.604
Mueller, Baron Sir Ferdinand Jakob Heinrich von, 5.306
Muir, Thomas, 2.266
Muirden, William, 10.604
Mulgrave, Peter Archer, 2.267
Mullagh, Johnny, 5.308
Mullaly, John Charles, 10.605
Mullan, John, 10.606

Mullen, Leslie Miltiades, 10.607
Mullen, Samuel, 5.309
Müller, C. W. Chateau, 8.262
Muller, Frederick, 10.607
Mulligan, James Venture, 5.310
Mullins, John Lane, 10.608
Mulquin, Katherine, 10.609
Mulvany, Edward Joseph, 10.610
Mummery, Joseph Browning, 10.610
Mundy, Godfrey Charles, 2.268
Munro, Andrew Watson, 10.611
Munro, David, 5.311
Munro, David Hugh, 10.614
Munro, Edward Joy, 10.612
Munro, Grace Emily, 10.613
Munro, Hugh Robert, 10.614
Munro, James, 5.312
Munro, James Leslie, 10.614
Munro, John, 5.311
Munro Ferguson, Helen Hermione, Lady,
  10.616
Munro Ferguson, Sir Ronald Craufurd,
  10.615
Munton, Ellen, 3.462
Muramats, Jirō, 10.618
Murdoch, James (1785-1848), 2.268
Murdoch, James (1852-1925), 2.268
Murdoch, James (1856-1921), 10.618
Murdoch, Sir James Anderson, 10.620
Murdoch, John, 2.268
Murdoch, John Smith, 10.621
Murdoch, Sir Keith Arthur, 10.622
Murdoch, Lesley Elizabeth, 10.629
Murdoch, Madoline, 10.627
Murdoch, Nina, see Murdoch, Madoline
Murdoch, Patrick John, 10.628
Murdoch, Peter, 2.269
Murdoch, Thomas (1868-1946), 10.628
Murdoch, Thomas (1876-1961), 10.629
Murdoch, Sir Walter Logie Forbes, 10.630
Murdoch, William David, 10.632
Murdoch, William Lloyd, 5.314
Murnin, Michael Egan, 5.315
Murphy, Agnes Cruickshank, 6.19
Murphy, Arthur William, 10.633
Murphy, Bennett Francis, 10.633
Murphy, Bernard, see Murphy, Bennett
  Francis
Murphy, Daniel, 5.316
Murphy, Dryblower, see Murphy, Edwin
  Greenslade
Murphy, Edmund Francis, 12.556
Murphy, Edwin Greenslade, 10.634
Murphy, Francis (1795-1858), 2.269
Murphy, Sir Francis (1809-1891), 5.316
Murphy, George Francis, 10.635
Murphy, George Read, 10.636
Murphy, Herbert Dyce, 10.637
Murphy, Jeremiah Matthias, 10.638
Murphy, Peter, 10.639
Murphy, William Emmett, 5.318
Murray, Agnes Ann, Lady, 10.646
Murray, Andrew, 5.318
Murray, David (1829-1907), 5.319

Murray, David (d.1837), 2.271
Murray, Sir George, 2.270
Murray, George Gilbert Aimé, 10.645
Murray, Sir George John Robert, 10.640
Murray, Henry William, 10.641
Murray, Hugh, 2.271
Murray, James, 5.320
Murray, James Fitzgerald, 2.274
Murray, John (b.1775?), 2.272
Murray, John (1837-1917), 10.643
Murray, John (1851-1916), 10.644
Murray, Sir John Hubert Plunkett, 10.645
Murray, Pembroke Lathrop, 10.649
Murray, Reginald Augustus Frederick,
  5.321
Murray, Robert William Felton Lathrop,
  2.272
Murray, Russell Mervyn, 10.649
Murray, Stuart, **5.322**, 7.600
Murray, Terence, 2.274
Murray, Sir Terence Aubrey, **2.274**,
  10.645
Murray, Virginius, 5.321
Murray, William Gilmour, 6.316
Murray-Prior, Thomas Lodge, 5.323
Murray-Smith, Robert, see Smith, Robert
  Murray
Murrell, 2.617
Murrills, James, see Morrill
Muscio, Bernard, 10.650
Muscio, Florence Mildred, 10.651
Musgrave, Sir Anthony (1828-1888), 5.324
Musgrave, Anthony (1895-1959), 10.651
Musgrove, George, **5.324**, 6.406
Muskett, Alice Jane, 10.652
Muskett, Philip, 10.652
Mussen, Sir Gerald, 10.653
Mustar (Mustard), Ernest Andrew, 10.655
Mutch, Thomas Davies, 10.655
Myer, Elcon Baevski, 10.657
Myer, Sidney, see Myer, Simcha Baevski
Myer, Simcha Baevski, 10.657
Nairn, William, 2.278
Nairn, William Edward, 5.326
Nangle, James, 7.329, **10.661**
Nanson, Edward John, 10.663
Nanson, Janet, 10.664
Nanson, John Leighton, 10.663
Nanya, 10.664
Nash, Clifford Harris, 10.665
Nash, James, 5.326
Nash, Richard West, 2.278
Nash, Robert, 2.278
Nathan, Charles, 5.327
Nathan, Sir Charles Samuel, 10.666
Nathan, Isaac, 2.279
Nathan, Sir Matthew, 10.667
Naylor, Henry Darnley, 10.668
Naylor, Rupert (Rufus) Theodore, 10.668
Neale, William Lewis, 10.669
Neales, John Bentham, 2.280
Neave, Stacey, 12.532
Ned, Cabbage Tree, see Devine, Edward
Neighbour, George Henry, 10.670

Neil, Edwin Lee, 10.658, **10.671**
Neild, James Edward, 5.327
Neild, John Cash, 10.672
Neild, Joseph, 5.329
Neilson, John, 10.673
Neilson, John Shaw, 10.673
Neitenstein, Frederick William, 10.674
Nelson, Charles, 10.675
Nelson, Harold George, 9.18, **10.676**
Nelson, Sir Hugh Muir, 10.677
Nelson, Wallace Alexander, 10.678
Nepean, Evan, 2.281
Nepean, Nicholas, 2.281
Nerli, Girolamo Pieri Ballati, 10.679
Nesbit, (Edward) Paris(s), 11.1
Nesbitt, Francis, *see* McCrone, Francis
  Nesbitt
Nesbitt, Thomas Huggins, 11.2
Ness, John Thomas, 11.3
Nettlefold, Alfred John, 11.3
Nettlefold, Isaac Robert, 11.3
Nettlefold, Sir Thomas Sydney Richard,
  11.3
Nettleton, Charles, 5.329
Neumayer, Georg Balthasar von, 5.329
Neville, Auber Octavius, 11.5
Neville, Dalton Thomas Walker, 11.6
Newbery, James Cosmo, 5.331
Newbigin, William Johnstone, 11.6
Newcastle-under-Lyme, Henry Pelham
  Fiennes Pelham Clinton, Duke, 5.332
Newcomb, Caroline Elizabeth, 1.330
Newdegate, Sir Francis Alexander
  Newdigate, 11.7
Newell, Hugh Hamilton, 11.8
Newell, John, 5.333
Newland, Sir Henry Simpson, 11.8
Newland, James Ernest, 11.9
Newland(s), Sir John, 11.12
Newland, Ridgway William, 2.281
Newland, Simpson, 11.10
Newland, Victor Marra, 11.11
Newling, Cecil Bede, 11.12
Newman, Leslie John William, 11.14
Newman-Morris, Sir Geoffrey, 11.15
Newman-Morris, Sir John, 11.14
Newton, Frank Graham, 11.15
Newton, Frederick Robert, 5.333
Newton, Henry, 5.333
Newton, Sir Hibbert Alan Stephen, 11.16
Ngunaitponi, James, 12.303
Niall, James Mansfield, 11.17
Niall, Kenneth Mansfield, 11.18
Nicholas, Alfred Michael, 11.18
Nicholas, Emily Hilda, 11.20
Nicholas, George Richard Rich, 11.18
Nicholas, Harold Sprent, 11.21
Nicholas, John Liddiard, 2.282
Nicholls, Charles Frederick, 5.334
Nicholls, Elizabeth Webb, 11.22
Nicholls, Henry Richard, 5.334
Nicholls, Sir Herbert, 5.335, **11.22**
Nicholls, William Henry, 11.23
Nichols, George Robert, 5.335

Nichols, Hubert Allan, 11.24
Nichols, Isaac, 2.283
Nichols, Reginald Gordon Clement, 11.24
Nicholson, Sir Charles, 2.283
Nicholson, Charles Archibald, 2.285
Nicholson, Edmund James Houghton, 11.25
Nicholson, Ellen, 11.28
Nicholson, Euphemia Scott, 11.26
Nicholson, George Gibb, 11.26
Nicholson, Germain, 5.336
Nicholson, John Barnes, 11.27
Nicholson, John Henry, 5.337
Nicholson, Mark, 5.337
Nicholson, Reginald Chapman, 11.28
Nicholson, Sydney, 2.285
Nicholson, William (1816-1865), 5.338
Nicholson, William (scientist), 2.102
Nickel, Theodor August Friedrich Wilhelm,
  11.29
Nickle, Sir Robert, 5.339
Nicolas, Augustus, 6.21
Nicolay, Charles Grenfell, 5.340
Nicoll, Bruce Baird, 5.341
Nicoll, George, 5.341
Nicoll, George Wallace, 5.342
Nicolle, Eugéne Dominique, 5.342
Nielsen, Niels Peter, 11.29
Nielsen, Niels Rasmus Wilson, 11.29
Nimmo, John, 5.342
Niqué, Johann Peter, *see* Niquet, Peter
Niquet, Peter, 2.423
Nisbet, James Hume, 11.30
Nixon, Anna Maria, 2.287
Nixon, Francis Russell, 2.285
Nobbs, Charles Chase Ray, 11.31
Nobbs, George Hunn, 2.288
Nobbs, John (1845-1921), 11.32
Nobbs, John (gardener), 11.32
Nobelius, Carl Axel, 5.343
Noble, Angelina, 11.33
Noble, James, 11.32
Noble, Montague Alfred, 11.33
Noblet, Charles Constant, 11.34
Noblet, Marie Thérèse Augustine, 11.34
Nock, Horace Keyworth, 11.35
Nock, Sir Norman, 11.36
Nock, Thomas, 11.36
Nolan, Sara Susan, 11.37
Norman, Sir Henry Wylie, 11.37
Normanby, George Augustus Constantine
  Phipps, Marquess, 5.344
Norriss, Elizabeth May, 12.160
North, Alexander, 11.38
North, Charles Frederic, 11.39
North, Frederic Dudley, 11.39
North, John Britty, 5.345
Northcote, Alice, Lady, 11.40
Northcote of Exeter, Baron, *see* Northcote,
  Sir Henry Stafford
Northcote, Sir Henry Stafford, 11.39
Northmore, Sir John Alfred, 11.40
Norton, Albert, 5.346
Norton, James (1795-1862), 2.289
Norton, James (1824-1906), 5.346

Norton, John, 11.41
Noskowski, Ladislas Adam de, 11.42
Novar of Raith, Viscount, *see* Munro
  Ferguson, Sir Ronald Craufurd
Nowland, Horace Henry, 11.43
Nunn, Crumpton John, 3.290
Oakden, Percy, 2.290, **5.348**
Oakden, Philip, 2.290
Oakes, Charles William, 11.45
Oakes, Elizabeth Mary, 11.45
Oakes, Francis, 2.290
Oakes, George, 5.349
Oakes, George Spencer, 11.45
Oakes, John Leigh, 11.45
Oakley, Robert McKeeman, 11.46
Oatley, James (1770-1839), 2.291
Oatley, James (1817-1878), 2.292
O'Brien, Catherine Cecily, 11.47
O'Brien, Cornelius, 2.292
O'Brien, Henry, 2.292
O'Brien, James Thomas, 11.47
O'Brien, John Patrick, 11.48
O'Brien, Mary Jane, *see* Abbott, Gertrude
O'Brien, Thomas, 7.1
O'Brien, William Smith, 2.293
O'Callaghan, Thomas, 11.49
O'Connell, Cecily Maude Mary, 11.49
O'Connell, Mary, 2.295
O'Connell, Sir Maurice Charles, 5.350
O'Connell, Sir Maurice Charles Philip,
  2.294
O'Connell, Michael William, 11.50
O'Connell, Patrick Martin, 11.49
O'Connor, Charles Yelverton, 11.51
O'Connor, Daniel, 5.351
O'Connor, Eileen, *see* O'Connor, Eily
  Rosaline
O'Connor, Eily Rosaline, 11.54
O'Connor, Feargus, 2.296
O'Connor, Francis, 2.296
O'Connor, Joseph Graham, 5.351
O'Connor, Kathleen Laetitia, 11.55
O'Connor, Michael, 5.352
O'Connor, Richard, 5.353
O'Connor, Richard Edward, 5.353, **11.56**
O'Connor, Roderic, 2.296
O'Connor, Roger, 2.296
O'Conor, Broughton Barnabas, 11.59
Oddie, James, 5.354
O'Doherty, Kevin Izod, 5.355
O'Doherty, Mary Eva, 5.355
O'Donnell, David George, 11.60
O'Donnell, Nicholas Michael, 11.60
O'Donnell, Thomas Joseph, 11.61
O'Donovan, Denis, 5.355
O'Donovan, John, 5.356
O'Dowd, Bernard Patrick, 11.62
O'Driscoll, Charles Xavier, 11.63
O'Driscoll, Terence, 1.323
O'Farrell, Henry James, 5.356
O'Farrell, Peter, 5.357
O'Farrell, William, 5.356
O'Ferrall, Ernest Francis, 11.64
Officer, Charles Myles, 5.357

Officer, Edward Cairns, 11.65
Officer, Mary Lillias, 5.358
Officer, Sir Robert, 2.297
Officer, Suetonius Henry, 5.357
O'Flaherty, Eliza, 2.298
O'Flaherty, Henry Charles, 2.298
O'Flynn, Jeremiah Francis, 2.299
Ogden, Anthony, 11.66
Ogden, James Ernest, 11.66
Ogg, Margaret Ann, 11.67
Ogilby, James Douglas, 11.68
Ogilvie, Albert George, 11.68
Ogilvie, Edward David Stewart, 5.358
Ogilvie, George, 11.70
Ogilvie, James, 2.300
Ogilvie, William Henry, 11.70
Ogilvy, Arthur James, 5.359
O'Grady, Sir James, 11.71
O'Grady, Louisa, 11.71
O'Grady, Michael, 5.360
O'Grady, Thomas, 5.361
O'Halloran, Thomas Shuldham, 2.300
O'Halloran, William Littlejohn, 2.301
O'Hara, Henry, 11.72
O'Hara, Henry Michael, 11.72
O'Hara, John Bernard, 11.72
O'Hara Wood, Arthur, 11.74
O'Hara Wood, Hector, 11.74
O'Hara Wood, Meryl Aitken, 11.75
O'Hara Wood, Pat, *see* O'Hara Wood,
  Hector
O'Haran, Denis Francis, 11.73
O'Hea, Timothy, 5.361
O'Kane, Thadeus, 5.362
O'Keefe, David John, 11.75
O'Keeffe (O'Keefe), David Augustus, 11.76
Old, Francis Edward, 11.76
Olden, Arthur Charles Niquet, 11.77
Oldfield, William Albert Stanley, 11.78
Oldham, James, 2.388
Oliphant, Ernest Henry Clark, 11.79
Oliver, Alexander, 5.362
Oliver, Charles Nicholson Jewel, 11.79
Oliver, Donald Percy, 11.80
Oliver, Maggie, 5.363
Olney, Sir Herbert Horace, 11.81
O'Loghlen, Sir Bryan, 5.364
O'Loghlen, Michael, 5.364
O'Loghlin, James, 11.82
O'Loghlin, James Vincent, 11.82
O'Loughlin, Laurence Theodore, 11.83
O'Mahony, Timothy, 5.366
O'Malley, King, 11.84
O'Meara, Martin, 11.86
O'Neil, Peter, 2.302
O'Neill, Charles Gordon, 5.367
O'Neill, George, 11.86
O'Neill, John Henry, 11.87
Onians, Edith Charlotte, 11.88
Onslow, Sir Alexander Campbell, 5.367
Onslow, Arthur Alexander Walton, 5.369
Onslow, Madeline Emma, Lady, 5.369
O'Quinn, James, *see* Quinn
Orchard, Richard Beaumont, 11.89

Orchard, William Arundel, 11.89
Ord, Harrison, 11.90
Ord, Sir Harry St George, 5.370
Ordell, Talone, 11.91
O'Reilly, Alfonso Bernard, 11.92
O'Reilly, Christopher, 5.370
O'Reilly, Dowell Philip, 5.372, **11.93**
O'Reilly, John Boyle, 5.371
O'Reilly, Maurice Joseph, 11.94
O'Reilly, Olive Kelynack, 11.95
O'Reilly, Rosa, 11.93
O'Reilly, Susannah Hennessy, 11.95
O'Reilly, Thomas, 5.372
O'Reilly, Walter Cresswell, 11.96
O'Reily, John, 11.96
Ormond, Francis (1829-1889), 5.372
Ormond, Francis (d.1875), 5.373
Orr, Alexander, 2.303
Orr, William (1843-1929), 11.97
Orr, William (1900-1954), 11.98
Orr, William Morgan, 2.302
Orsmond, John Muggridge, 2.599
Orton, Arthur, 5.374
Orton, Joseph Rennard, 2.303
Osborn, Theodore George Bentley, 11.99
Osborne, Ethel Elizabeth, 11.100
Osborne, George Davenport, 11.101
Osborne, George Samuel, 11.368
Osborne, Henry, 2.303
Osborne, Henry William (1865-1936), 11.102
Osborne, Henry William (book-keeper), 11.102
Osborne, James Bunbury Nott, 9.476
Osborne, John, 5.374
Osborne, John Percy, 11.103
Osborne, John Walter, 5.375
Osborne, Pat Hill, 2.304, **5.376**
Osborne, William Alexander, 11.103
Osburn, Lucy, 5.377
Osburne, Richard, 5.378
Oseland, Jane, *see* Barlee, Jane
O'Shanassy, Sir John, 4.110, **5.378**
O'Shaughnessy, Edward, 2.304
O'Shea, Dan, 9.188
O'Shea, Patrick Joseph Francis, 11.105
Oster, Philipp Jacob, **5.382**, 6.205
Oster, Philippe Jacques, 5.382
O'Sullivan, Edward William, 11.106
O'Sullivan, Patrick, 5.383
O'Sullivan, Richard, 5.384
O'Sullivan, Thomas, 11.109
Outhwaite, Ida Sherbourne, 11.109
Outtrim, Alfred Richard, 11.110
Outtrim, Elizabeth Rosa, 11.110
Outtrim, Frank Leon, 11.111
Ovens, John, 2.305
Owen, Albert John, 11.111
Owen, Gladys Mary, **10.566**, 11.114
Owen, Harrison, *see* Owen, Albert John
Owen, Sir Langer Meade Loftus, 11.113
Owen, Mary Louisa Dames, 11.114
Owen, Percy Thomas, 11.112
Owen, Richard, 1.85

Owen, Robert, 5.384
Owen, Robert Haylock, 11.112
Owen, Sir William, 11.113
Owen, Sir William Francis Langer, 11.115
Owens, John Downes, 5.385
Oxenham, Humphrey, 11.115
Oxenham, Justinian, 11.115
Oxley, John Joseph William Molesworth, 2.305
Packer, Charles (Stuart Shipley) Sandys, 5.387
Packer, Frederick Augustus Gow, 5.387
Packer, Robert Clyde, 11.117
Padbury, Walter, **5.388**, 8.34
Page, Alfred, 2.308
Page, Charles Service, 2.308
Page, Sir Earle Christmas Grafton, 11.118
Page, George, 2.308
Page, Harold Hillis, 11.122
Page, Robert, 11.123
Page, Rodger Clarence George, 11.124
Page, Samuel, 2.308
Paget, Arthur, 11.124
Paget, Walter Trueman, 11.124
Palfreyman, Achalen Woolliscroft, 11.125
Paling, Richard John, 5.390
Paling, William Henry, 5.389
Palmer, Sir Arthur Hunter, 5.390
Palmer, Charles Reginald, 11.128
Palmer, Edward Vivian, 11.126
Palmer, Frederick, 5.394
Palmer, George Eugene, 5.392
Palmer, George Thomas, 2.308
Palmer, Henry Wilfred, 11.128
Palmer, Sir James Frederick, 5.392
Palmer, Janet Gertrude, 11.127, **11.129**
Palmer, John, 2.309
Palmer, Joseph, 11.131
Palmer, Nettie, *see* Palmer, Janet Gertrude
Palmer, Philip, 2.311
Palmer, Rosina Martha Hosanah, 5.393
Palmer, Thomas (arr.1853), 11.131
Palmer, Thomas (1858-1927), 11.132
Palmer, Thomas Fyshe, 2.312
Palmer, Thomas McLeod, 5.394
Palmer, Vance, *see* Palmer, Edward Vivian
Palmerston, Christie, 5.395
Pamphlett, Thomas, 2.313
Pankhurst, Adela Constantia Mary, 12.372
Pankhurst, Christabel, 12.373
Pankhurst, Richard Marsden, 12.373
Pankhurst, Sylvia, 12.373
Pannett, Eva, 11.42
Panton, Ann Alison, 4.264
Panton, Joseph Anderson, 5.396
Pantoney, William, 2.101
Parer, Raymond John Paul, 11.133
Parker, Charles Avison, 11.134
Parker, Critchley, 11.137
Parker, Edward Stone, 5.396
Parker, Florence Mary, 11.135
Parker, Frank Critchley, 11.136
Parker, Harold, 11.137
Parker, Henry Thomas, 11.138

Parker, Sir Henry Watson, 5.397
Parker, Hubert Stanley Wyborn, 11.140
Parker, John, 11.138
Parker, K. Langloh, see Stow, Catherine
  Eliza Somerville
Parker, Langloh, 12.113
Parker, Sir Stephen Henry, **11.138**, 12.98
Parker, Stephen Stanley, 11.138
Parkes, Edmund Samuel, 5.398
Parkes, Sir Henry, 5.399
Parkes, Hilma Olivia Edla Johanna, 11.140
Parkes, Varney, 11.141
Parkhill, Sir Robert Archdale, 11.142
Parkin, William, 5.406
Parkinson, Charles Tasman, 11.143
Parkinson, Sydney, 2.314
Parks, Harold, see Edwards, George
Parnell, Edwin, 11.144
Parnell, John William, 11.144
Parramore, George, 2.314
Parramore, William Thomas, 2.314
Parrott, A. K., 11.146
Parrott, Amy, 11.146
Parrott, H. F., 11.146
Parrott, J. H., 11.146
Parrott, Thomas Samuel, 11.145
Parry, Annie Bertha, 11.146
Parry, Henry Hutton, 5.407
Parry, Sir William Edward, 2.315
Parry-Okeden, David, 11.147
Parry-Okeden, Herbert David, 11.148
Parry-Okeden, Rosalie Caroline, 11.147
Parry-Okeden, Uvedale Edward, 11.148
Parry-Okeden, William Edward, 11.147
Parsons, Charles Octavius, 2.316
Parsons, Sir Herbert Angas, 11.148
Parsons, John Langdon, 11.148
Parsons, Joseph, 11.150
Partridge, Bridget, 11.151
Partridge, Eric Honeywood, 11.152
Pasco, Crawford Atchison Denman, 5.409
Pasco, John, 5.409
Pasley, Charles, 5.409
Paten, Eunice Muriel Harriett Hunt,
  11.153
Paterson, Alexander Thomas, 11.153
Paterson, Andrew Barton, 11.154
Paterson, Andrew Bogle, 11.154
Paterson, Charles Stewart, 5.412
Paterson, Elizabeth, 2.319
Paterson, James, 5.411
Paterson, John Ford, 5.411
Paterson, John Waugh, 11.156
Paterson, Thomas, 11.157
Paterson, William (1755-1810), 2.317
Paterson, William (1847-1920), 11.158
Paton, Francis Hume Lyall, 11.159
Paton, Hugh, 11.160
Paton, John (1834-1914), 5.412
Paton, John (1867-1943), 11.161
Paton, John Gibson, 5.413
Paton, Robert Thomson, 11.162
Patrick, Mother, see Potter, Norah Mary
Patten, John Thomas, 11.162

Patterson, Ambrose McCarthy, 11.163
Patterson, Daniel Whittle Harvey, 11.165
Patterson, Gerald Leighton, 11.164
Patterson, Sir James Brown, 5.415
Patterson, John Hunter (1841-1930),
  11.165
Patterson, John Hunter (1882-1963),
  11.165
Patterson, Robert Charles, 11.166
Patteson, John Coleridge, 5.416
Pattison, James Grant, 11.167
Pattison, William, 5.417
Paul, Sir Charles Norman, 11.167
Paul, Mother (1865-1948), see Barron,
  Johanna
Paul, Mother Mary (1842?-1930), see
  Mulquin, Katherine
Pavy, Emily Dorothea, 11.168
Payne, Charles Alexander, 11.169
Payne, Ellen Nora, 11.169
Payne, Henry, 11.169
Payne, Herbert James Mockford, 11.170
Payne, Leslie Herbert, 11.171
Payne, Sir William Labatte Ryall, 11.171
Payten, Bayly William Renwick, 11.172
Payten, Thomas, 11.172
Peach, Henry, 11.172
Peacock, Sir Alexander James, 11.173
Peacock, George, 5.418
Peacock, Lucy Judge, 8.660
Peake, Archibald Henry, 11.175
Pearce, Alice, 5.419
Pearce, Sir George Foster, 11.177
Pearce, Harry, 5.419
Pearce, Henry John, 5.418
Pearce, Henry Robert, 11.182
Pearce, James, 11.183
Pearce, John, 11.183
Pearce, Lily, 5.419
Pearce, Samuel William, 11.183
Pearce, Sandy, see Pearce, Sidney Charles
Pearce, Sidney Charles, 11.184
Pearce, Simeon Henry, 5.419
Pearse, Albert William, 11.185
Pearse, Catherine, 11.186
Pearse, George Stapleton, 11.185
Pearse, Samuel George, 11.185
Pearse, William Silas, 5.420
Pearson, Alfred Naylor, 11.186
Pearson, Charles Henry, 5.421
Pearson, Edward John, 11.187
Pearson, Joseph, 11.187
Pearson, Josiah Brown, 5.426
Pearson, Thomas Edwin, 11.187
Pearson, William (1818-1893), 5.427
Pearson, William (1864-1919), 5.427
Pearson, William James, 11.188
Pease, Percy, 11.188
Peck, Harry Huntington, 5.428, **11.189**
Peck, John Henry, 11.189
Peck, John Murray, 5.427
Pedder, Sir John Lewes, 2.319
Peden, Barbara, 11.192
Peden, Sir John Beverley, 11.190

Peden, Margaret Elizabeth Maynard, 11.192
Pedley, Ethel Charlotte, 11.193
Peel, Thomas, 2.110, **2.320**
Peeler, Donald, 11.194
Peeler, Walter, 11.194
Pell, Gilbert Titus, 5.428
Pell, Morris Birkbeck, 5.428
Pelloe, Emily Harriet, 11.194
Pelsaert, Francisco, 2.322
Penfold, Arthur de Ramon, 11.195
Penfold, Christopher Rawson, 5.429
Penfold, Edwin Thomas, 11.196
Penfold, William Clark, 11.196
Penfold, William James, 11.197
Pennington, John Warburton, 11.198
Peppin, George, 5.430
Peppin, George Hall, 5.430
Percival, Arthur, 11.198
Percival, Edgar Wikner, 11.199
Perdriau, Edgar Martin, 11.200
Perdriau, Ernest Charles, 11.201
Perdriau, George Alexander, 11.201
Perdriau, Harold, 11.201
Perdriau, Henry, 11.200
Perdriau, Henry Carter, 11.200
Perdriau, Ralph Joseph, 11.201
Perdriau, Raymond, 11.201
Perdriau, Stephen Edward, 11.200
Perdriau, Walter Simpson, 11.201
Perkins, Alfred George, 11.203
Perkins, Arthur James, 11.201
Perkins, Frederick Thomas, 11.202
Perkins, John Arthur, 11.203
Perkins, Patrick, 5.431
Perkins, Thomas, 5.431
Permewan, John, 5.432
Péron, François, 2.323
Pérouse, see La Pérouse
Perry, Charles, 5.432
Perry, John, 11.204
Perry, Joseph Henry, 11.204
Perry, Orizaba George, 11.205
Perry, Reginald Harry, 11.205
Perry, Samuel Augustus, 2.324
Perry, Stanley Llewellyn, 11.206
Perry, Stanley Wesley, 11.205
Persse, De Burgh Fitzpatrick, 5.436
Pescott, Edward Edgar, 11.206
Pescott, Richard Thomas Martin, 11.207
Petchy, John, 2.325
Peter, John, 5.437
Peters, Frederick Augustus Bolles, 11.208
Peterson, Franklin George Reginald Sievright, 11.209
Peterson, Franklin Sievright, 11.208
Peterson, Georgette Augusta Christina, 11.208
Peterson, Isabel Varney Desmond, 10.555
Pethebridge, Sir Samuel Augustus, 11.209
Petherick, Edward Augustus, 5.438
Petre, Henry Aloysius, 11.210
Petrie, Andrew, 2.325
Petrie, Andrew Lang, 5.440

Petrie, John, 5.439
Petrie, Thomas, 2.326, **5.440**
Petterd, William Frederick, 5.441
Pflaum, Conrad Christian Theodor, 11.212
Pflaum, Friedrich Jacob Theodor, 11.211
Pflaum, Heinrich Adam Theodor, 11.211
Phelan, Patrick, 11.212
Phillip, Arthur, 2.326
Phillipps, Sir (William) Herbert, 11.213
Phillips, Sir Frederick Beaumont, 11.214
Phillips, Herbert Peter, 11.215
Phillips, John Hugh, 5.442
Phillips, Marion, 11.216
Phillips, Morris Mondle, 11.217
Phillips, Orwell, 11.218
Phillips, Owen Forbes, 11.219
Phillips, Ray, see Phillips, Rebecca
Phillips, Rebecca, 11.217, **11.218**
Phillips, Samuel James, 5.442
Phillips, Samuel Pole, 5.442
Philp, Sir Robert, 11.220
Phocas, Seraphim, 11.222
Phyllis, Sister, see Stevens, Jemima Elizabeth Mary
Pickering, Charles, 1.279
Picton, Edward Benjamin, 11.223
Piddington, Albert Bathurst, 11.224
Piddington, Marion Louisa, 11.226
Piddington, William Henry Burgess, 11.226
Piddington, William Jones Killick, 11.224
Piddington, William Richman, 5.443
Pidgeon, Elsie Clare, 11.227
Pidgeon, Nathaniel, 2.333
Pieman, The Flying, see King, William Francis
Piesse, Edmund Leolin, 11.227
Piesse, Frederick Henry, 11.229
Piesse, Frederick William, 11.227
Piesse, William Roper, 11.229
Pigdon, John, 5.444
Piggott, Sir Arthur Leary, 1.168
Piggott, M. D., 7.249
Pigot, Edward Francis, 11.230
Piguenit, Frederick Le Geyt, 5.444
Piguenit, Mary Ann, 5.444
Piguenit, William Charles, 5.444
Pike, George Herbert, 11.231
Pike, James Edward, 11.232
Pilcher, Charles Edward, 11.233
Pillars, Annie, 3.232
Pillinger, Alfred Thomas, 5.445
Pillinger, James, 5.445
Pinnock, James Denham (1810?-1875), 2.333
Pinnock, James Denham (jnr), 2.334
Pinnock, Robert Denham, 2.334
Pinschof, Carl Ludwig, 11.233
Piper, Arthur William, 11.235
Piper, Ernest John, 11.235
Piper, Hugh, 2.335
Piper, John, 2.334
Piper, Thomas, 11.235
Piquet, Jean Pierre, 11.236
Pitcairn, Robert, 2.336

Pitman, Alexander, 12.372
Pitman, Jacob, 5.446
Pitt Cobbett, William, see Cobbett
Pitt, Ernest Roland, 11.236
Pitt, George Matcham, 5.446
Pitt, Henry Arthur, 11.237
Pitt, Marie Elizabeth Josephine, 11.238
Pitt, Richard, 2.336
Pitt, William (1855-1918), 11.239
Pitt, William (d.1879), 11.239
Pittard, Alfred James, 11.241
Pittard, Alice Mary, 11.241
Pittman, Edward Fisher, 11.241
Plain, William, 11.242
Plant, Edmund Harris Thornburgh, 5.447
Plante, Ada Mary, 11.243
Platt, George, 2.599
Platt, John Laurio, 2.337
Playfair, Edmund John Bailey, 11.244
Playfair, John Thomas, 5.448
Playfair, Thomas Alfred (Creer) John,
   11.244
Playford, Thomas (1837-1915), 11.245
Playford, Thomas (d.1873), 11.245
Plume, Henry, 11.247
Plummer, Andrew, 5.448
Plummer, John, 11.248
Plunkett, John Hubert, 2.337
Pluto, Joe, 9.119
Poate, Frederick, 11.249
Poate, Sir Hugh Raymond Guy, 11.250
Pocock, George, 11.251
Pocock, Mary Anne, 11.251
Pohlman, Frederick Roper, 5.450
Pohlman, Robert Williams, 5.449
Poidevin, Leslie Oswald Sheridan, 11.252
Polding, John Bede, 2.340
Polini, Emelie Adeline, 11.252
Pollock, James Arthur, 11.253
Pomeroy, John, 11.254
Poole, Daniel, 11.255
Poole, Dora Francis, 11.257
Poole, Frederic Slaney, 11.255
Poole, George Thomas Temple, 11.257
Poole, Thomas Slaney, 11.255
Poore, John Legg, 5.450
Pope, Charles, 11.258
Pope, Cuthbert John, 11.258
Pope, Harold, 11.260
Porcelli, Pietro Giacomo, 11.261
Porter, Una Beatrice, 7.591
Porteus, Stanley David, 11.261
Portus, Garnet Vere, 11.262
Postle, Arthur Benjamin, 11.264
Potter, Charles Vincent, 11.264
Potter, Norah Mary, 11.265
Pottie, John, 5.451
Pottinger, Sir Frederick William, 5.451
Potts, George, 11.266
Potts, Henry William, 11.266
Poupinel, François Victor, 5.452
Powell, Edward, 2.347
Powell, James Alexander, 11.267
Powell, Lange Leopold, 11.268

Powell, Philippa Bull, see Bowden, Philippa
   Bull
Powell, Walter, 5.453
Power, Harold Septimus, 11.268
Power, Henry, 5.454
Power, John Joseph Wardell, 11.269
Power, Marguerite Helen, 11.270
Power, Robert, 2.348
Powers, Sir Charles, 11.271
Powlett, Frederick Armand, 2.349
Pownall, William Henry, 5.454
Poynton, Alexander, 11.272
Praed, Annie, 11.273
Praed, Rosa Caroline, 5.323, **11.273**
Pratt, Ambrose Goddard Hesketh, 11.274
Pratt, Frederick Vicary, 11.275
Pratt, John Jeffreys, see Camden, Earl
Pratt, Joseph Major, 11.276
Pratt, Rachel, 11.276
Pratt, Sir Thomas Simson, 5.455
Pratten, Herbert Edward, 11.277
Preece, Frederick William, 11.278
Preece, John Lloyd, 11.278
Preiss, Johann August Ludwig, 2.349
Prell, Charles Ernest, 11.279
Prendergast, George Michael, 11.280
Prendergast, Luke Thomas, 11.280
Prendiville, Redmond, 8.33
Prenzel, Robert Wilhelm, 11.282
Prescott, Charles John, 11.282
Preston, Jenico William Joseph, see
   Gormanston
Preston, Margaret Rose, 11.283
Preston Stanley, Millicent Fanny, 11.285
Price, Anne Elizabeth, 11.287-8
Price, Charles, 2.350
Price, Elizabeth, 2.227
Price, George Richard, 11.286
Price, James Franklin, 2.352
Price, John, 2.610
Price, John Frederick, 2.352
Price, John Giles, 2.351
Price, John Lloyd, 11.288
Price, Thomas, 11.287
Price, Thomas Caradoc Rose, 2.352,
   11.289
Prichard, Frederick John, 11.290
Prichard, Katharine Susannah, 11.291
Pridham, John Theodore, 11.293
Priestley, Henry, 11.294
Priestley, Henry James, 11.295
Priestley, Sir Raymond Edward, 11.295
Prieur, François Xavier, 2.352
Primrose, Archibald Philip, 5.456
Primrose, Hubert Leslie, 11.296
Pring, Ratcliffe, 5.457
Pring, Robert Darlow, 11.297
Prinsep, Charles Robert, 11.298
Prinsep, Henry Charles, 11.298
Prior, Samuel Henry, 11.299
Pritchard, George Baxter, 11.300
Proctor, Alethea Mary, 11.301
Propsting, William Bispham, 11.302
Proud, Cornelius, 11.168

Proud, Dorothea, *see* Pavy, Emily Dorothea
Proud, William James, 11.302
Prout, Alfred, 3.357
Prout, John Skinner, 2.353
Prout, Maria, 2.354
Prout, Sydney, 3.357
Prout, Victor Albert, 2.354
Prowse, John Henry, 11.303
Pryke, Dan, 11.304
Pryke, Frank, 11.304
Pryor, Oswald, 11.305
Puck, *see* Marlowe, Margaret Mary
Puckey, James, 1.252
Puckey, William, 1.252
Puddy, Albert, 11.305
Puddy, Maude Mary, 11.305
Pugh, Theophilus Parsons, 5.458
Pugh, William Russ, 2.355
Pulleine, Robert Henry, 11.306
Pulsford, Edward, 11.307
Pumpkin, 5.459
Purcell, James, 11.308
Purdy, John Smith, 11.308
Purser, Cecil, 11.309
Purton, David Gabriel, 11.310
Purves, James, 5.459
Purves, James Liddell, 5.459
Purves, John Mitchell, 5.461
Purves, William, 5.461
Purves Smith, Charles Roderick, 11.311
Purves Smith, Peter, *see* Purves Smith,
  Charles Roderick
Pury, Frédéric Guillaume de, *see* De Pury
Püttmann, Hermann, 5.461
Püttmann, Hermann Wilhelm, 5.462
Pye, Cecil Robert Arthur, 11.312
Pye, Emmeline, 11.312
Pye, Hugh, 11.313
Pye, James, 5.462
Pye, John, 5.463
Pyke, Vincent, 5.463
Quaife, Barzillai, 2.356
Quaife, Frederick Harrison, 2.357
Quaife, William Francis, 2.357
Queiros, Pedro Fernandez de, *see* Quiros
Quick, Balcombe, 11.315
Quick, Sir John, 11.316
Quick, William Abraham, 5.465
Quinlan, Timothy Francis, 8.91
Quinlivan, Thomas, 11.317
Quinn, Hugh, 11.318
Quinn, James, 5.366, **5.465**
Quinn, James Peter, 11.319
Quinn, John, 11.320
Quinn, Matthew, 5.466
Quinn, Patrick Edward, 11.321
Quinn, Roderic Joseph, 11.320
Quiros, Pedro Fernandez de, 2.357
Quong Tart, *see* Mei Quong Tart
Radcliffe-Brown, Alfred Reginald, **11.322**,
  12.397
Radford, Lewis Bostock, 11.322
Rae, Arthur Edward George, 11.323
Rae, John, 6.1

Raff, George, 6.2
Raine, John, 2.359
Raine, Thomas, 2.359
Ralston, Walter Vardon, 11.325
Ramaciotti, Gustave Mario, 11.325
Ramsay, Andrew Mitchell, 6.3
Ramsay, David, 2.361
Ramsay, Edward Pierson, 2.361, **6.3**
Ramsay, Hugh, 11.326
Ramsay, John (1841-1924), 11.328
Ramsay, Sir John (1872-1944), 11.327
Ramsay, Robert (1818-1910), 6.4
Ramsay, Robert (1842-1882), 6.5
Ramsay, William, 11.328
Ramsbotham, Joshua Fielden, 11.329
Ranclaud, Charles Mark, 11.329
Randell, George, 6.6
Randell, William Beavis, 6.6
Randell, William Richard, 6.6
Ranken, Arthur, 2.362
Ranken, George (1793-1860), 2.361
Ranken, George (1827-1895), 6.7
Ranken, Janet Ranken, 2.361-2
Rankin, Annabelle, 11.331
Rankin, Colin Dunlop Wilson, 11.330
Rankin, John, 11.331
Ranking, Robert Archibald, 11.332
Ransford, Vernon Seymour, 11.332
Ransom, Henry Alfred David, 7.646
Ransom, Thomas, 2.362
Raper, George, 2.363
Raphael, Joseph George, 6.8
Rason, Sir Cornthwaite Hector William
  James, 11.333
Rasp, Charles, **6.9**, 9.463
Rathie, Isabella, 3.516
Ratten, John Richard, 11.335
Ratten, Victor Richard, 11.334
Raven, William, 2.364
Rawlings, William, 11.335
Rawlings, William Reginald, **11.335**,
  12.219
Raws, Sir William Lennon, 11.336
Rawson, Sir Harry Holdsworth, 11.337
Rawson, Wilhelmina Frances, 11.338
Rayment, Percy Tarlton, 11.338
Raymond, James, 2.365
Rays, Marquis de, 6.9
Read, Charles Rudston, 6.10
Read, George, 1.429
Read, George Frederick, 2.365
Read, Henry, 6.10
Read, Irene Victoria, 11.339
Read, Richard (b.1765?), 2.366
Read, Richard (b.1796?), 2.367
Reade, Charles Compton, 11.340
Reading, Sir Claude Hill, 11.342
Reading, Fanny, 11.343
Real, Patrick, 11.344
Reay, William Thomas, 11.344
Rebell, Fred, 11.345
Rechner, Gustav Julius, 6.11
Redbeard, Ragnar, *see* Desmond, Arthur
Reddall, Thomas, 2.368

Rede, Robert William, 6.12
Redfern, William, 2.368
Redmond, Edward, 2.371
Redmond, John Edward, 6.12
Redmond, William Hoey Kearney, 6.12
Redmond, Winifred, 2.371
Reed, Hannah Elliot, see Boase, Hannah
 Elliot
Reed, Henry, 2.371
Reed, Joseph, 6.13
Reeks, Walter, 11.346
Rees, John, 6.14
Rees, Rowland, 6.15
Reeve, Edward, 6.16
Reibey, James Haydock, 2.374
Reibey, Mary, 2.373
Reibey, Thomas (1769-1811), 2.373
Reibey, Thomas (b.1796), 2.374
Reibey, Thomas (1821-1912), 6.17
Reid, Alexander, 2.375
Reid, Curtis Alexander, 6.18
Reid, David (1777-1840), 2.375
Reid, David (1820-1906), 6.17
Reid, Sir George Houstoun, 7.197, **11.347**
Reid, Jane Sinclair, 11.354
Reid, John (1825-1882), 6.18
Reid, John (1858-1919), 11.354
Reid, Mary, 2.375
Reid, Matthew, 11.355
Reid, Nellie Isobel, 11.357
Reid, Richard, see Read, Richard (b.1796?)
Reid, Robert, 11.356
Reid, Robert Dyce, 6.17
Reid, Roberta, see Reid, Jane Sinclair
Reid, Thomas, 2.376
Reid, Walter Ballantyne, 6.19
Reid, William, 1.127
Reilly, Joseph Thomas, 11.357
Reimann, Immanuel Gotthold, 11.358
Renard, Clement William, 6.20
Renard, Jules, 6.19
Rendall, Charles Henry, 11.359
Rene, Roy, 11.360
Rennie, Edward Henry, 11.361
Rennie, George Edward, 11.362
Rentoul, Annie Rattray, 11.109
Rentoul, Ida, see Outhwaite, Ida
 Sherbourne
Rentoul, John Laurence, 11.363
Rentoul, Thomas Craike, 11.365
Renwick, Sir Arthur, 6.20
Renwick, Elizabeth, Lady, 6.21
Resch, Edmund, 11.365
Resch, Emil Karl, 11.365
Reveley, Henry Willey, 2.376
Reymond, Joseph Bernard, 6.21
Reymond, Ralph Etienne Bernard, 6.22
Reynell, Carew, 11.366
Reynell, Gladys, 11.367
Reynell, John, 6.22
Reynell, Rupert, 11.367
Reynell, Walter, 6.23
Reynolds, Christopher Augustine, 6.23
Reynolds, Thomas, 6.23

Rhodes, Fred, 11.368
Rhodius, Charles, see Rodius
Ribush, Dolia, 11.369
Ricardo, Percy Ralph, 11.370
Rich, Sir George Edward, 11.371
Richard, George Anderson, 11.372
Richards, Henry Caselli, 11.373
Richards, Herbert Clarence, 11.375
Richards, Ranold, 11.374
Richards, Robert Stanley, 11.374
Richards, Thomas (1800-1877), 6.24
Richards, Thomas (1831-1898), 6.25
Richards, Tobias John Martin, 11.375
Richardson, Alexander Robert, 11.377
Richardson, Arnold Edwin Victor, 11.377
Richardson, Arthur Charles Jeston, 11.379
Richardson, Bill, 12.237
Richardson, Charles, 11.379
Richardson, Charles Douglas, 11.380
Richardson, Ethel Florence Lindesay,
 11.381
Richardson, Ethel Tracy, 11.384
Richardson, Henry Handel, see Richardson,
 Ethel Florence Lindesay
Richardson, Horace Frank, 11.384
Richardson, John, 6.26
Richardson, John Matthew, 2.377
Richardson, John Soame, 6.26
Richardson, Thomas Elliott, 11.380
Richardson, Victor York, 11.385
Richardson, Walter Lindesay, 11.381
Richmond, James, 6.27
Rickard, A. L., 11.387
Rickard, Sir Arthur, 11.386
Rickard, Douglas, 11.387
Rickards, Harry, 11.387
Riddell, Campbell Drummond, 2.377
Riddell, John Carre, 4.332, **6.28**
Riddell, Rodney Stuart, 2.378
Riddell, Thomas Milles Stratford, 2.378
Riddell, Thomas William Carre, 11.389
Riddell, Walter John Carre, 11.388
Riddle, Sir Ernest Cooper, 11.389
Riddoch, George, 11.390
Riddoch, John, 11.390
Ridgway, Charles Joseph, see Vaude,
 Charlie
Ridley, John, 2.379
Ridley, William, 6.29
Rigby, Edward Charles, 11.391
Rigg, Mary Lillias, 5.358
Rigg, William, 11.392
Rignall, George Richard, 6.30
Rignold, George, see Rignall, George
Riley, Alban Joseph, 6.30
Riley, Alexander, 2.379
Riley, Charles Owen Leaver, 11.393
Riley, Edward (1784-1825), 2.381
Riley, Edward (b.1806), 2.382
Riley, Eleanor Harriet, 6.31
Rintel, Moses, 6.31
Rintoul, Thomas, see Rentoul, Thomas
 Craike
Ripon, Earl of, see Goderich, Viscount

Rischbieth, Bessie Mabel, 11.394
Rischbieth, Henry Wills, 11.394
Risdale, Thomas, see Crowder, Thomas Ristol
Ritchie, Edgar Gowar, 11.396
Ritchie, Frederick Henry, 11.396
Ritchie, Sir George, 11.396
Ritchie, John (d.c1820), 2.382
Ritchie, John (d.1861), 6.32
Ritchie, Robert Adam, 6.32
Ritchie, Samuel Sextus, 6.32
Ritchie, Thomas, 2.382
Ritchie, William, 6.33
Rivers, Richard Godfrey, 11.397
Rivett, Albert, 11.398
Rivett, Sir Albert Cherbury David, 11.398
Rivett, Amy Christine, 11.401
Rivett, Doris Mary, 11.401
Rivett, Edward William, 11.401
Rivett, Eleanor Harriett, 11.401
Rivett, Elsie Grace, 11.401
Rivett, Olive Murray, 11.402
Rix, Henry Finch, 11.403
Rix, Hilda, see Nicholas, Emily Hilda
Rix Nicholas, Emily Hilda, see Nicholas, Emily Hilda
Roach, Bertie Smith, 11.403
Robb, John, 6.33
Robe, Frederick Holt, 2.383
Roberts, Abraham, 11.404
Roberts, Sir Alfred, 6.34
Roberts, Charles Fyshe, 6.35
Roberts, Charles James, 6.35
Roberts, Ernest Alfred, 11.405
Roberts, Gerald Alleyne, 11.408
Roberts, James Henry Cecil, 11.406
Roberts, Jane, 1.575
Roberts, John Garibaldi, 11.406
Roberts, John Levey, 2.322
Roberts, Mary Ellen, 11.407
Roberts, Mary Grant, 11.408
Roberts, Thomas Hope, 11.412
Roberts, Thomas William, 11.409
Roberts, William, 2.55
Roberts, William Joshua, 11.412
Robertson, Agnes Kelly, 3.200
Robertson, Alexander William, 6.36
Robertson, Constance, 11.413
Robertson, Edward, 11.413
Robertson, George (1825-1898), 5.309, **6.37**
Robertson, George (1860-1933), 11.414
Robertson, George Pringle, 6.46
Robertson, Gilbert, 2.384
Robertson, James (1781-1868), 6.38
Robertson, James (1848-1890), 6.46
Robertson, James (fl.1851-1861), 5.136
Robertson, James Campbell, 11.415
Robertson, James Robert Millar, 11.416
Robertson, Sir John (1816-1891), 6.38
Robertson, John (1837-1875), 6.46
Robertson, John (1856-1922), 11.417
Robertson, Lady, 6.46
Robertson, Sir Macpherson, 11.418

Robertson, Margery Fraser, 11.419
Robertson, Thorburn Brailsford, 11.420
Robertson, William (1798-1874), 6.46
Robertson, William (1839-1892), 6.46
Robertson, William Apperley Norton, 11.421
Robey, Ralph Mayer, 6.47
Robinson, Anthony Bennet, 11.428
Robinson, Sir Arthur, 11.422
Robinson, Edward Oswin, 11.423
Robinson, Frederick John, see Goderich, Viscount
Robinson, Frederick Walter, 11.424
Robinson, George Augustus, 2.385
Robinson, Gerald Henry, 11.429
Robinson, Harriet, 11.428
Robinson, Herbert Edward Cooper, 11.425
Robinson, Sir Hercules George Robert, **6.48**, 6.50
Robinson, Isabel, see Gray, Isabel
Robinson, Joseph Phelps, 2.387
Robinson of Kielder Forest and of Adelaide, Baron, see Robinson, Sir Roy Lister
Robinson, Lionel George, 11.429
Robinson, Michael Massey, 2.387
Robinson, Robert Thomson, 11.426
Robinson, Sir Roy Lister, 11.427
Robinson, Sir Thomas Bilbe, 11.427
Robinson, Sir William Cleaver Francis, 4.386, **6.50**
Robinson, William Sydney, 10.653, **11.428**
Robson, Edgar Iliff, 11.434
Robson, Ernest Iliff, 11.433
Robson, Gertrude, 11.433-4
Robson, William, 11.434
Robson, William Elliot Veitch, 11.434
Rocher, Jean-Louis, 6.51
Rodd, Brent Clements, 6.52
Rodd, John Tremayne, 6.52
Rodd, Nelle Marion, 7.283
Rodé, Franz Joseph August, 2.423
Rodgers, Arthur Stanislaus, 11.435
Rodius, Charles, 2.389
Rodway, Florence Aline, 11.436
Rodway, Leonard, 11.436
Roe, John Septimus, 2.390
Roe, Reginald Heber, 11.437
Roemer, Charles William, 2.392
Rofe, Thomas Ernest, 11.439
Rogers, Charles, 6.53
Rogers, Francis Edward, 11.440
Rogers, George Edgar, 11.440
Rogers, James, 11.441
Rogers, John Warrington, 6.53
Rogers, John William Foster, 2.393, **6.54**
Rogers, Sir Percival Halse, 11.442
Rogers, Richard Sanders, 11.443
Rogers, Thomas George, 2.392
Rogers, William Richard, 11.443
Rolando, Charles, 6.54
Rolland, Sir Francis William, 11.444
Rolland, Henry Maitland, 11.445
Rolleston, Christopher, 6.55

Rolph, Sir Gordon Burns, 11.446
Rolph, William Robert, 11.446
Romano, Azzalin Orlando, 11.447
Romilly, Hugh Hastings, 6.56
Roncoroni, Olga, 11.383
Roper, John, 6.57
Rosa, Samuel Albert, 11.447
Rose, Augustus Frederick, 11.449
Rose, David, 2.393
Rose, Edwin, 11.448
Rose, George Canler, 11.448
Rose, Herbert John, 11.449
Rose, John Charles, 11.449
Rose, Percival, 11.449
Rose, Robert Henry, **6.57**, 11.448
Rose, Thomas (1749?-1833), 2.394
Rose, Thomas (d.1837), 2.394
Rosebery, Earl of, *see* Primrose, Archibald
  Philip
Roseby, Ann, 6.59
Roseby, Gertrude Amy, 6.59
Roseby, John, 6.59
Roseby, Thomas (1844-1918), 6.58
Roseby, Thomas (d.1867), 6.58
Roseby, Thomas J., 6.59
Rosenhain, Walter, 11.450
Rosenthal, Sir Charles, 11.451
Rosman, Alice (Grant) Trevenen, 11.453
Rosman, Alice Mary Bowyer, 11.454
Rosmead, Baron, *see* Robinson, Sir
  Hercules George Robert
Ross, Alexander, 6.61
Ross, Alexander David, 11.454
Ross, Andrew Hendry, 6.59
Ross, Chisholm, 11.455
Ross, Edgar, 11.458
Ross, Emily, 6.62
Ross, Euphemia Welch, 11.455
Ross, Hugh Cokely, 2.395
Ross, Isabella Henrietta Younger, 11.456
Ross, James, 2.396
Ross, James Clark, 2.34
Ross, John (c1779-1800), 2.398
Ross, John (1817-1903), 6.60
Ross, John (1833-1920), 6.61
Ross, John Howlett, 11.457
Ross, Joseph Grafton, 6.62
Ross, Lloyd, 11.458
Ross, Robert (b.1740?), **2.397**, 2.328
Ross, Robert (1792-1862), 2.398, **6.62**
Ross, Sir Robert Dalrymple, 6.62
Ross, Robert Samuel, 11.457
Rossi, Francis Nicholas, 2.399
Rossi, Francis Robert Louis (Lewis), 6.63
Rossi, Maffio, 11.459
Rossiter, Thomas, 3.221
Ross-King, Alice, 11.459
Roth, Adam, 11.461
Roth, Alan, 11.461
Roth, Henry Ling, 11.461
Roth, Reuter Emerich, 11.462
Roth, Walter Edmund, 11.463
Roth, William, 11.461
Rothery, Frederick, 2.2

Rothery, William Montagu, 2.2
Rotton, Henry, 6.64
Rounsevell, John, 11.464
Rounsevell, William, 11.464
Rounsevell, William Benjamin, 11.464
Rous, Henry John, 2.400
Rouse, Leslie, 6.65
Rouse, Richard (1774-1852), 2.401
Rouse, Richard (1842-1903), 6.65
Rouse, Richard (1843-1906), 6.65
Rowan, Andrew, 6.65
Rowan, Ellis, *see* Rowan, Marian Ellis
Rowan, Frederic Charles, 11.465
Rowan, Marian Ellis, 11.465
Rowcroft, Charles, 2.402
Rowcroft, Thomas, 2.402
Rowe, George, 6.66
Rowe, George Curtis, 6.67
Rowe, Richard, 6.67
Rowe, Sarah Selina, 6.68
Rowe, Thomas, 6.68
Rowell, James, 11.466
Rowell, John, 11.466
Rowell, John Thomas Nightingale, 11.467
Rowell, William Nicholas, 11.467
Rowland, Caroline Ann, 11.468
Rowland, Percy Fritz, 11.469
Rowlandson, Alfred Cecil, 11.470
Rowley, Stanley Rupert, 11.470
Rowley, Thomas, 2.403
Rowntree, Amy, 11.471
Rowntree, Cameron Sutcliffe, 6.69
Rowntree, Frances (Fearn), 11.471
Rowntree, Thomas Stephenson, 6.69
Royston, John Robinson, 11.472
Ruatoka, 6.69
Rubbo, Antonio Salvatore Dattilo, **11.473**,
  11.644
Rubbo, Sydney, 11.474
Rubin, Bernard, 11.474
Rubin, Harold de Vahl, 11.474
Rubin, Mark, 11.474
Rubinstein, Helena, 11.475
Rudall, James Ferdinand, 6.70
Rudall, James Thomas, 6.70
Rudd, Steele, *see* Davis, Arthur Hoey
Rudd, William Henry, 11.477
Rudduck, Harold Sugden, 11.478
Rule, James, 6.71
Rumker, Christian Carl Ludwig, 2.403
Rumpf, Ann, 11.478
Rumpf, Johannes, 11.478
Rumpf, Maude, 11.479
Rumsby, Ann, 1.314
Rumsey, Herbert John, 11.479
Rundle, Jeremiah Brice, 6.71
Rupertswood, Baronet, *see* Clarke, Sir
  Rupert Turner Havelock
Rupp, Herman Montague Rucker, 11.480
Rusconi, Francis Philip, 11.481
Rusden, George Keylock, 6.72
Rusden, George William, 6.72
Rusden, Henry Keylock, 6.73
Ruse, James, 2.404

Russell, Alexander, 6.76
Russell, Barbara, *see* Brown, Janet le Brun
Russell, Bourn, 6.74
Russell, Delia Constance, 11.484
Russell, Edward John, 11.481
Russell, Francis Thomas Cusack, 2.405
Russell, George (1812-1888), 2.408
Russell, George (d.1914), 6.77
Russell, Henry Chamberlain, 6.74
Russell, Henry Stuart, **2.406**, 3.304
Russell, James, 6.75
Russell, James George, 11.482
Russell, Lord John, 2.407
Russell, John Peter, 11.483
Russell, Percy Joseph, 11.484
Russell, Sir Peter Nicol, 6.76
Russell, Philip (1796-1844), 2.408
Russell, Philip (1822?-1892), **6.77**, 6.127
Russell, Robert (1808-1900), 2.409
Russell, Robert (d.1840), 6.76
Russell, Robert Hamilton, 11.484
Russell, Stanley, 12.573
Russell, Thomas, 6.77
Russell, W. G. Stuart, 2.407
Ruth, Thomas Elias, 11.485
Rutherford, James, 6.78
Ruthven, William, 11.486
Rutledge, Sir Arthur, 11.487
Rutledge, Jane Ruth, 11.488
Rutledge, Thomas Lloyd Forster, 11.488
Rutledge, William, 2.411
Rutledge, William Woolls, 11.489
Ruwolt, Charles Ernest, 11.490
Ryan, Cecil Godfrey, 11.490
Ryan, Sir Charles Snodgrass, 11.491
Ryan, Edward John Francis, 11.492
Ryan, James, 11.493
Ryan, James Tobias, 6.78
Ryan, John, 11.493
Ryan, John Michael Tobin, 6.78
Ryan, John Tighe, 11.494
Ryan, Mary, 6.78
Ryan, Rupert Sumner, 11.492
Ryan, Thomas (1790-1846), 2.412
Ryan, Thomas (1870-1943), 11.495
Ryan, Thomas Joseph, 11.496
Ryder, John, 11.500
Rymill, John Riddoch, 11.501
Ryrie, Sir Granville de Laune, 11.502
Sachse, Arthur Otto, 11.505
Sadleir, Richard, 2.414
Sadler, Arthur Lindsay, 11.505
Sadler, James, 11.506
Sadler, Robert James, 11.506
Sadlier, Clifford William King, 11.507
St Clair, William Howard, 11.508
St Julian, Charles James Herbert de Courcy, 6.80
St Ledger, Anthony James Joseph, 11.508
Salier, George, 6.81
Salier, James Ebenezer, 6.81
Salier, John Jabez, 6.81
Salier, William George, 6.81

Salisbury, Alfred George, 11.509
Salisbury, Ishmael Ernest Eldon, 11.510
Salisbury, Marquis of, *see* Cecil, Robert Arthur Talbot Gascoyne
Salisbury, William Robert Peel, 11.510
Salmon, Charles Carty, 11.511
Salmon, Charles Frederick, 2.415
Salmon, Joseph, 2.415
Salmon, Thomas (1780?-1847), 2.414
Salmon, Thomas (1807-1868), 2.415
Salmond, Sir John William, 11.512
Salomons, Sir Julian Emanuel, 6.81
Salote, Queen of Tonga, 11.124
Saltau, Marcus, 11.513
Salter, Edward, 6.83
Salter, William, 6.83
Salting, George, 2.415
Salting, Severin Kanute, 2.415
Salting, William, 2.415
Salvado, Rosendo, 2.416
Sampson, Burford, 11.514
Sampson, George, 11.514
Samson, Lionel, 2.417
Samuel, Sir Saul, 6.84
Sanderson, Archibald, 11.515
Sanderson, Sir John, 11.516
Sanderson, Robert Fitzroy, 11.517
Sandes, Clare Louise, 11.519
Sandes, Francis Percival, 11.518
Sandes, John, 11.518
Sandford, Arthur Bruce, 11.520
Sandford, Augustus Henry, 11.519
Sandford, Daniel Fox, 6.85
Sandford, Horace Charles Augustus, 11.520
Sandford, Sir James Wallace, 11.520
Sandford, William, 11.521
Sandow, Eugene, 12.430
Sands, Herbert Guy, 6.86
Sands, John, 6.85
Sands, Robert, 6.86
Sandwich, Earl, *see* Montagu, John
Sani, Tomaso, 6.86
Sargent, Charlotte, 11.522
Sargent, Foster Henry Hartley, 11.522
Sargent, George, 11.522
Sargent, Oswald Hewlett, 11.523
Sargood, Sir Frederick Thomas, 6.87
Satō, Torajirō, 11.523
Saunders, Ambrose George Thomas, 11.524
Saunders, Edward, 4.272
Saunders, John, 2.418
Saunders, John Victor, 11.525
Saunders, Reg, 11.335
Savage, Arthur, 2.418
Savage, John, 2.419
Savage, Michael Joseph, 11.525
Savage, Robert, 6.88
Savery, Eliza Elliott, 2.420
Savery, Henry, 1.459, **2.419**
Sawers, John, 11.526
Saywell, Eliza Ann, 6.89
Saywell, George, 6.89

Saywell, Thomas, 6.89
Scaddan, John, 11.526
Scanlan, John Joseph, 11.529
Scanlan, Mary, 3.467
Scanlon, Michael, 5.7
Scantlebury Brown, Vera, 11.530
Scarlett, Robert, see Dalley-Scarlett
Sceusa, Francesco, 11.531
Schaeffer, Philip, see Schaffer
Schaffer, Philip, 2.420
Schardt, Susan Katherina, 11.532
Schauer, Amy, 11.532
Schauer, Minnie, 11.533
Schaw, Charles, 2.421
Schenk, Rodolphe Samuel, 11.533
Scherk, Theodor Johannes, 11.534
Schey, William Francis, 11.535
Schiassi, Omero, 11.536
Schirmeister, Carl Friedrich Alexander
  Franz, 6.90
Schlapp, Herman Henry, 11.537
Schleinitz, Georg Gustav, Freiherr von,
  6.90
Schlink, Sir Herbert Henry, 11.538
Schmidt, Karl Wilhelm Edward, 2.421
Schofield, Ellen, 2.424
Schofield, William, 2.423
Schomburgk, Alfred Otto, 6.91
Schomburgk, Moritz Richard, 6.91
Schuler, Gottlieb Frederich Henry, 11.539
Schulz, Adolf John, 11.540
Schurr, Felix, 6.92
Schutt, William John, 11.540
Schwarz, Walter Leslie, 11.541
Scobie, Grace Locke, 11.542
Scobie, James, 11.543
Scobie, Robert, 11.542
Sconce, Robert Clement, 2.424
Sconce, Robert Knox, 2.198, 2.424
Scotchman, Wild, see McPherson, James
  Alpin
Scott, Alexander Walker, 6.93
Scott, Allan Humphrey, 11.543
Scott, Andrew George, 6.94
Scott, Arthur, 6.97
Scott, Augusta Maria, 2.429
Scott, Daniel, 2.426
Scott, David Charles Frederick, 2.428
Scott, Ellis Martin, 2.426
Scott, Sir Ernest, 11.544
Scott, Eugene Montague, 6.95
Scott, Harriet, 6.93
Scott, Helena, 6.93
Scott, Helenus (1802-1879), 2.428
Scott, Helenus (d.1821), 2.428
Scott, Henry, 9.46
Scott, Henry James Herbert, 6.95
Scott, Herbert Hedley, 11.546
Scott, James (1790-1837), 2.427
Scott, James (d.1796), 2.427
Scott, James (1810-1884), 2.429
Scott, James Reid, 6.96
Scott, John McNaught, 12.102
Scott, Mary, 5.196

Scott, Robert, 2.428
Scott, Sir Robert Townley, 11.546
Scott, Rose, 11.547
Scott, Thomas, 2.429
Scott, Thomas Alison, 2.430
Scott, Thomas Hobbes, 2.431
Scott, Walter, 11.549
Scott, Walter Jervoise, 6.97
Scott, William, 6.97
Scott, William Henry, 11.549
Scott, William John Rendell, 11.550
Scratchley, Sir Peter Henry, 6.98
Scrivener, Charles Robert, 11.552
Scullin, James Henry, 8.483, **11.553**
Scurry, William Charles, 11.557
Scutt, Cecil Allison, 11.558
Seager, Alexandrine, 11.559
Seal, Charles, 2.433
Searcy, Alfred, 11.559
Searle, Henry Ernest, 6.99
Seccombe, William, 2.434
See, Sir John, 11.560
See Poy, Tom, 11.562
Seitz, Eleanor Ida Agnes, 11.564
Seitz, John Arnold, 11.563
Selfe, Norman, 6.100
Sellar, James Zimri, 11.564
Selle, Walter Albert, 11.564
Sellers, Maud, 8.490
Sellheim, Philip Frederic, 6.101
Sellheim, Victor Conradsdorf Morisset,
  11.565
Selwyn, Alfred Richard Cecil, 6.102
Selwyn, Arthur Edward, 6.103
Semmens, J. M., 12.361
Seppelt, Joseph Ernest, 6.104
Seppelt, Oscar Benno Pedro, 6.104
Sergeyev, Fedor Andreyevich, 11.567
Serisier, Jean Emile, 6.104
Serle, Dora Beatrice, 11.568
Serle, Edwin Hamilton, 11.569
Serle, Percival, 11.567
Serle, Walter Henry, 11.569
Serra, Joseph Benedict, 6.105
Service, James, 6.106
Service, Robert, 6.106
Sewell, Alice Maud, Lady, 11.569
Sewell, Sir Sidney Valentine, 11.569
Sexton, Gerald, see Buckley, Maurice
  Vincent
Sexton, Hannah Mary Helen, 11.570
Sexton, John Henry, 11.571
Seymour, Charles, 11.572
Seymour, David Thompson, 6.112
Seymour, John Alfred, 11.572
Seymour-Symers, Thomas Lyell,
  2.435
Shackell, James, 6.112
Shackleton, Ernest, 8.238
Shadforth, Henry, 2.435
Shadforth, Thomas (1771?-1862), 2.435
Shadforth, Thomas (d.c1855), 2.435
Shakespeare, Arthur Thomas, 11.573
Shakespeare, Thomas Mitchell, 11.573

Shanahan, Margaret, *see* Marlowe, Margaret Mary
Shang, Caleb James, 11.574
Shann, Edward Owen Giblin, 11.574
Shann, Frank, 11.576
Shapcott, Louis Edward, 11.577
Sharland, Anne Jane, 1.59
Sharland, John Frederic, 2.436
Sharland, William Stanley, 2.436
Sharman, James, 11.578
Sharman, Matthew Stanton, 11.579
Sharp, Cecil James, 11.579
Sharp, Gerald, 11.580
Sharp, Granville Gilbert, 11.582
Sharp, Lewis Hey, 11.582
Sharp, Percival John, 11.582
Sharp, William Hey, 11.581
Sharwood, William Henry, 11.582
Shaw, Archibald John, 11.583
Shaw, Ebenezer, 11.584
Shaw, Edna Mary Anna Jane, 11.584
Shaw, Edward Carr, 4.162
Shaw, Eleanor, 7.156
Shaw, George, 2.437
Shaw, Jonathon, 6.114
Shaw, Mabel Ann, 8.81
Shaw, Thomas (1800?-1865?), 2.437
Shaw, Thomas (1827-1907), 6.113
Shaw, Thomas (d.1860s), 2.438
Shaw, William Henry, 6.114
Shea, Ernest Herbert, 11.585
Shearer, David (1832-1891), 6.114
Shearer, David (1850-1936), 11.586
Shearer, John, 11.586
Shearston, John Samuel, 11.587
Shedden, Frederick, 12.504
Sheehan, Sir Henry John, 11.588
Sheehan, Michael, 9.558
Sheehy, Samuel John Austin, 6.115
Sheil, Laurence Bonaventure, 6.116
Sheldon, Sir Mark, 11.589
Sheldon, Mary, 11.590
Shelley, Elizabeth, 2.439
Shell(e)y, William, 2.438
Shellshear, Walter, 6.116
Shenton, Arthur, 6.117
Shenton, George (1811-1867), 2.439
Shenton, Sir George (1842-1909), 6.118
Shepherd, Arthur Edmund, 11.590
Shepherd, Malcolm Lindsay, 11.592
Shepherdson, John Banks, 2.440
Sheppard, Benjamin, 11.592
Sherbrooke, Viscount, *see* Lowe, Robert (1811-1892)
Sheridan, John Felix, 6.119
Sheridan, Richard Bingham, 6.119
Sherman, Louis, 10.493
Sherritt, Aaron, 5.7
Sherwin, Frances Amy Lillian, 2.442, **6.120**
Sherwin, Isaac, 2.441
Shields, Clive, 11.593
Shields, Sir Douglas Andrew, 11.594
Shields, Tasman, 11.595
Shiels, William, 11.595

Shiers, Walter Henry, 11.598
Shillinglaw, John Joseph, 6.121
Shirley, John, 11.598
Shirlow, John Alexander Thomas, 11.599
Shirlow, Robert, 11.599
Sholl, Horatio William, 11.600
Sholl, Richard Adolphus, 11.601
Sholl, Robert Frederick, 11.600
Sholl, Robert John, 6.121
Sholl, Trevarton Charles, 11.601
Shoobridge, Ebenezer, 11.601
Shoobridge, Louis Manton, 11.601
Shoobridge, Robert Wilkins Giblin, 11.601
Shoobridge, William, 2.442
Shoobridge, William Ebenezer, 11.601
Shore, Arnold Joseph Victor, 11.603
Short, Augustus, 6.122
Short, Benjamin, 6.123
Shortland, John (1739-1803), 2.442
Shortland, John (1769-1810), 2.443
Shout, Alfred John, 11.604
Sidaway, Robert, 2.444
Siddins, Richard, 2.444
Sidney, Samuel, 2.444
Siede, Julius, 6.124
Sievier, Robert Standish, 11.604
Silas, Ellis Luciano, 11.605
Silcock, Emma Caroline, 11.606
Sills, Robert, 2.597
Silverleaf, *see* Lloyd, Jessie Georgina
Simmons, Joseph, 2.445
Simoi, 11.607
Simonetti, Achille, 6.125
Simonov Peter, 11.607
Simons, John Joseph, 11.608
Simpkinson de Wesselow, Francis Guillemard, 2.446
Simpson, Alfred, 6.126
Simpson, Alfred Muller, 6.126
Simpson, Edward Percy, 11.609
Simpson, Edward Sydney, 11.610
Simpson, Sir George Bowen, 6.127
Simpson, Helen de Guerry, 11.611
Simpson, James, 2.447
Simpson, John, *see* Kirkpatrick, John Simpson
Simpson, Martha Margaret Mildred, 11.612
Simpson, Norah, 11.644
Simpson, Pierce (Percy), 1.111, 6.127
Simpson, Stephen, 2.448
Simson, Colin William, 6.128
Simson, John, 6.128
Simson, Robert, 6.127
Sinclair, Sir Colin Archibald, 11.613
Sinclair, Eric, 11.614
Sinclair, James, 6.128
Sinclair, William, 11.615
Sinclaire, Frederick, 11.615
Sinclair-Maclagan, Ewen George, 11.616
Singer, Violet, 7.398
Single, Clive Vallack, 10.361
Single, Verania, *see* McPhillamy

Singleton, Benjamin, 2.448
Singleton, John, 6.129
Singleton, William (arr.1792), 2.448
Singleton, William (arr.1851), 6.129
Sinnett, Frederick, 6.130
Sixsmith, William, 6.131
Sizer, Hubert Ebenezer, 11.618
Skeats, Ernest Willington, 11.619
Skene, Alexander John, 6.131
Skene, Thomas, 11.620
Skene, William, 11.620
Skerst, Arnold Oscar Hermann Gregory
  von, 11.621
Skertchly, Sydney Barber Josiah, 11.621
Skeyhill, Thomas John, 11.622
Skillen, Elizabeth, 11.623
Skinner, Henry Hawkins, 11.624
Skinner, Mary Louisa, 11.625
Skinner, Mollie, see Skinner, Mary Louisa
Skipper, John Michael, 6.132
Skipper, Spencer John, 6.133
Skirving, Robert Scot, 11.626
Skirving, William, 2.449
Skurrie, Joseph, 11.627
Skuthorp, Lance, 11.628
Skuthorp(e), Lancelot Albert, 11.627
Slade, Ernest Augustus, 2.450
Slade, Sir John, 2.450
Slade, William Ball, 11.628
Sladen, Sir Charles, 6.133
Sladen, Douglas Brooke Wheelton, 6.134
Slapoffski, Joseph Gustave, 11.629
Slattery, Joseph Patrick, 11.630
Slattery, Patrick Joseph, 6.135
Slattery, Thomas Michael, 11.631
Sleath, Richard, 11.632
Sleeman, John Harvey Crothers, 11.633
Sleigh, Sir Hamilton Morton Howard,
  11.634
Sleigh, Harold Crofton, 11.633
Sleigh, William Campbell, 6.135
Sligo, Archibald Douglas, 11.634
Sloane, Alexander, 11.635
Sloane, Thomas Gibson, 11.635
Sloman, Thomas Martin, 2.450
Sluice, Henry Vande, see Rene, Roy
Sly, Constance, 11.636
Sly, George James, 6.136, 11.636
Sly, Joseph, 6.136, 11.636
Sly, Joseph David, 6.136
Sly, Richard Meares, 11.636
Smalley, George Robarts, 6.136
Smart, Thomas Christie, 6.137
Smart, Thomas Ware, 6.138
Smeaton, Thomas Hyland, 11.636
Smith, Alexander John, 6.140
Smith, Alexander Kennedy, 6.139
Smith, Alfred Mica (Micaiah), 6.139
Smith, Andrew Bell, 11.654
Smith, Arthur Bruce, 11.637
Smith, Arthur Edward, 11.639
Smith, Bernhard, 6.140
Smith, Catherine Drummond, see Cotton,
  Catherine Drummond

Smith, Charles, 6.141
Smith, Charles Patrick, 11.640
Smith, Christian Brynhild Ochiltree Jollie,
  11.641
Smith, Edmund Edmonds, 11.637
Smith, Sir Edwin Thomas, 6.142
Smith, Fanny Cochrane, 11.642
Smith, Fergus Jago, 6.148
Smith, Francis Grey, 6.143
Smith, Sir Francis Villeneuve (1819-1909),
  6.144
Smith, Francis Villeneuve (1883-1956),
  11.642
Smith, Sir Gerard, 11.643
Smith, Grace Cossington, 11.644
Smith, Sir Grafton Elliot, 11.645
Smith, Henry George, 11.646
Smith, Henry Gilbert, 2.451
Smith, Henry Teesdale, 11.647
Smith, Issy, 11.649
Smith, Ivy Blanche Irene, 11.649
Smith, James (arr.1788), 1.312
Smith, James (1820-1910), 6.145
Smith, James (1827-1897), 5.3, **6.146**
Smith, Sir James John Joynton, 11.650
Smith, James MacCallum, 11.651
Smith, James William Norton, 6.147
Smith, John (1811-1895), 2.532, **6.148**
Smith, John (1821-1885), 6.148
Smith, John (arr.1832), 6.141
Smith, John Jennings, 6.143
Smith, John Lloyd, 6.154
Smith, John McGarvie, 11.652
Smith, John Thomas, 6.150
Smith, John Ure, 11.662
Smith, John William, 1.253
Smith, Julian Augustus Romaine, 11.653
Smith, Sir Keith Macpherson, 11.654
Smith, Louis Lawrence, 6.151
Smith, Louis Laybourne, 11.656
Smith, Louise, 6.152
Smith, Miles Staniforth Cater, 11.657
Smith, Molly Barr, 11.664
Smith, Norman Leslie, 11.658
Smith, Percival, 6.157
Smith, Philip Thomas, 2.452
Smith, Philosopher, see Smith, James
  (1827-1897)
Smith, Pierce, 6.153
Smith, Pierce Galliard, 6.152
Smith, Richard, 6.153
Smith, Robert, 11.658
Smith, Robert Barr, 6.153
Smith, Robert Burdett, 6.154
Smith, Robert Murray, 6.155
Smith, Robert Neil, 11.664
Smith, Sir Ross Macpherson, 11.654
Smith, Samuel, 6.157
Smith, Sappho, see Wildman, Alexina
  Maude
Smith, Shepherd, 6.157
Smith, Sidney (1837-1908), 6.157
Smith, Stephen Henry, 11.659
Smith, Sydney (1856-1934), 11.660

Smith, Sydney (1880-1972), 11.660
Smith, Sydney George Ure, 11.662
Smith, Thomas (1795-1842), 2.451
Smith, Thomas (1823-1900), 6.158
Smith, Thomas (1829-1882), 6.159
Smith, Thomas Jollie, 11.663
Smith, Thomas Whistler, 2.453
Smith, Tom Elder Barr, 11.664
Smith, Walter, 6.157
Smith, William, 1.252
Smith, William Beattie, 11.664
Smith, William Charles, 9.599
Smith, William Collard, 6.159
Smith, William Forgan, 11.665
Smith, William Henry Laird, 11.670
Smith, William Howard, 6.161
Smith, William Isaac Carr, 11.671
Smith, William John, 11.672
Smith, William Ramsay, 11.674
Smith, William Saumarez, 11.675
Smithies, Frederick, 11.677
Smyth, Arthur Bowes, 2.453
Smyth, Bridgetena (Brettena), 12.1
Smyth, Charles Edward Owen, 12.1
Smyth, John, 12.2
Smyth, Sir Nevill Maskelyn, 12.3
Smyth, Robert Brough, 6.161
Smythe, Carlyle Greenwood, 12.5
Smythe, Robert Sparrow, 12.4
Snodgrass, Kenneth, 2.454
Snodgrass, Peter, 2.455
Snook, Charles William, 12.5
Snow, Sir Gordon, 12.6
Snow, Sir Sydney, 12.6
Snowball, Oswald Robinson, 12.7
Snowball, William, 12.8
Snowden, Sir Arthur, 9.13, **12.8**
Soanes, John Thomas, *see* Wilson, John
   Thomas
Soares, Alberto Dias, 6.163
Sodeman, Arnold Karl, 12.9
Solander, Daniel, 2.456
Solly, Robert Henry, 12.10
Solomon, Albert Edgar, 12.11
Solomon, Ann, 2.457-8
Solomon, Emanuel, 6.163
Solomon, Esther, 12.12
Solomon, Ikey, *see* Solomon, Isaac
Solomon, Isaac, 2.457
Solomon, Joseph, 2.458
Solomon, Judah Moss, 6.164
Solomon, Samuel, *see* Sidney, Samuel
Solomon, Vaiben, 6.163
Solomon, Vaiben Louis, 6.164, **12.11**
Somers, Arthur Herbert Tennyson
   Somers-Cocks, 12.12
Somerset, Sir Henry Beaufort, 12.13
Somerset, Henry St John, 12.13
Somerville, Dorothy, 12.193
Somerville, George Cattell, 12.14
Somerville, John Blakely, 12.14
Somerville, William, 12.14
Sommerlad, Ernest Christian, 12.16
Soo Hoo Ten, *see* Ten, George Soo Hoo

Sorell, Julia, 1.30
Sorell, William (1775-1848), 2.459
Sorell, William (1800-1860), 2.462
Sorensen, Christense, 12.16
Sorenson, Edward Sylvester, 12.17
Sorlie, George Brown, 12.18
Soubeiran, Augustine, 12.19
Soul, Caleb, 6.164
Soul, Washington Handley, 6.165
Soundy, Sir John, 12.20
Souter, Charles Henry, 12.20
Souter, David Henry, 12.21
Southern, Clara, 12.22
Southwell, Daniel, 2.462
Soutter, Richard Ernest, 12.22
Soward, George Klewitz, 12.23
Sowden, Sir William John, 12.24
Sowerby, William, 6.165
Spain, Alfred, 12.25
Spain, David, 2.463
Spain, Staunton William, 12.25
Spain, William, 2.463
Spark, Alexander Brodie, 2.463
Sparks, Nicholas George, 12.26
Spaull, George Thomas, 12.26
Spears, Robert Adam, 12.27
Spedding, Quentin Shaddock, 12.28
Speight, Richard, **6.166**, 6.234
Spence, Catherine Helen, 6.167
Spence, David, 6.167
Spence, Francis, 12.30
Spence, George Heynes, 12.28
Spence, John, 12.29
Spence, Percy Frederick Seaton, 12.29
Spence, Robert William, 12.30
Spence, William Guthrie, 6.168
Spencer, Albert Henry, 12.31
Spencer, Cosens, 12.32
Spencer, Reuben, 12.33
Spencer, Sir Richard, 2.465
Spencer, Thomas Edward, 12.32
Spencer, Sir Walter Baldwin, 12.33
Spielvogel, Nathan Frederick, 12.36
Spieseke, F. W., 4.314
Spode, Josiah, 2.466
Spofforth, Frederick Robert, 6.170
Spooner, Eric Sydney, **12.37**, 12.76
Spragg, Alonzo Stephen, 12.38
Sprent, Charles Percy, 2.467
Sprent, James, 2.466
Spring, David Hugh, 6.171
Spring, Gerald, 6.171
Springthorpe, John William, 12.38
Spruson, Joseph John, 12.39
Spruson, Wilfred Joseph, 12.39
Spyer, Haden Daniel, 12.40
Squire, James, 2.467
Squires, Ernest Ker, 12.41
Stable, Jeremiah Joseph, 12.42
Stace, Arthur Malcolm, 12.42
Stackhouse, Alfred, 2.468
Stacy, Bertie Vandeleur, 12.43
Stacy, John Edward, 6.171
Stacy, Valentine Osborne, 12.43

Stainforth, Martin Frank, 12.44
Stanbury, James, 12.45
Standish, Frederick Charles, 6.172
Standley, Ida, 12.46
Stanfield, Daniel (c1790-1856), 2.469
Stanfield, Daniel (d.1826), 2.469
Stanford, Thomas Welton, 12.46
Stanford, William Walter Tyrell, 6.173
Stang, Eleanor Margrethe, 12.47
Stang, Rita, see Stang, Eleanor Margrethe
Stanley of Alderley, see Stanley, Arthur Lyulph
Stanley, Arthur Lyulph, 12.48
Stanley, Charles Roy, 12.48
Stanley, Edward George Geoffrey Smith, 2.470
Stanley, George Arthur Vickers, 12.49
Stanley, Owen, 2.470
Stansfield, William, 12.50
Stanton, George Henry, 6.174
Stanton, Richard Patrick Joseph, 12.51
Stapleton, Claude Augustine, 12.51
Stapley, Frank, 12.52
Stapylton, Granville William Chetwynd, 2.471
Starke, Elizabeth Jemima, 12.53
Starke, Sir Hayden Erskine, 12.53
Starling, John Henry, 12.54
Starr, James, 5.169
Statton, Percy Clyde, 12.54
Stawell, Florence Melian, 6.177, **12.55**
Stawell, Mary, Lady, 6.177
Stawell, Sir Richard Rawdon, 6.177, **12.56**
Stawell, William 6.l77
Stawell, Sir William Foster, 6.174
Stead, Christina, 12.58
Stead, David George, 12.57
Stedman, James, 12.58
Steel, John James, 6.178
Steel, Robert, 6.177
Steel, Thomas, 12.59
Steele, Alexander, 12.59
Steele, Bertram Dillon, 12.60
Steere, Sir James George Lee, 12.61
Steere, Lee, 12.61
Steinfeld, Emanuel, 6.178
Stenhouse, Nicol Drysdale, 6.179
Stephen, Sir Alfred, 2.478, 5.290, **6.180**
Stephen, Alfred Hamilton Hewlett, 6.187
Stephen, Caroline Sibella, Lady, 6.190
Stephen, Sir Colin Campbell, 6.192, **12.63**
Stephen, Edward Milner, 12.63
Stephen, Eleanor Martha, Lady, 6.181
Stephen, Francis, 2.478
Stephen, Sir George, 6.188
Stephen, George Milner, 2.472
Stephen, Harold, 4.228
Stephen, Sir James, 2.474
Stephen, James Wilberforce, 6.188
Stephen, John, 2.476
Stephen, Sir Matthew Henry, 6.190
Stephen, Montagu Consett, 6.191
Stephen, Patrick John, 12.64
Stephen, Reginald, 12.65

Stephen, Septimus Alfred, 6.191
Stephen, William Wilberforce, 6.192
Stephens, Alfred George, 12.66
Stephens, Alfred Ward, 2.479
Stephens, Arthur Augustus, 12.68
Stephens, Edward, 2.480
Stephens, Edward James, 6.193
Stephens, Henry Douglas, 12.69
Stephens, James, 6.194
Stephens, James Brunton, 6.195
Stephens, John, 2.480
Stephens, John Gower, 12.68
Stephens, John Raynor, 2.480
Stephens, Samuel, 2.481
Stephens, Samuel George, 12.66
Stephens, Thomas, 6.196
Stephens, Thomas Blacket, 6.196
Stephens, William John, 6.197
Stephensen, Percy Reginald, 12.70
Stephenson, Sir Arthur George, 12.71
Sternberg, Alexander, 12.72
Sternberg, Joseph, 12.72
Sterne, Elizabeth Anne Valentine, 12.73
Stevens, Arthur Borlase, 12.73
Stevens, Sir Bertram Sydney Barnsdale, 12.74
Stevens, Bertram William Mathyson Francis, 12.77
Stevens, Edward, 12.78
Stevens, Horace Ernest, 12.78
Stevens, Jemima Elizabeth Mary, 12.79
Stevenson, George, 2.481
Stevenson, George Ingram, 12.80
Stevenson, George John William, 2.482
Stevenson, James, 12.81
Stevenson, Jean, 9.304
Stevenson, John, 12.81
Stevenson, John Bryan, 12.81
Stevenson, Noel, 12.81
Steward, Sir George Charles Thomas, 12.81
Stewart, Alexander, 12.82
Stewart, Sir Alexander Anderson, 12.83
Stewart, Archibald, 12.84
Stewart, David, 7.329, **12.84**
Stewart, Eleanor Charlotte, 12.85
Stewart, Eleanor Towzey, 12.86
Stewart, Francis, 8.171
Stewart, Sir Frederick Harold, 12.87
Stewart, James, 12.92
Stewart, James Campbell, 12.89
Stewart, James Douglas, 6.199, **12.90**
Stewart, Jane, 12.84
Stewart, John (1810-1896), 6.198
Stewart, John (1832-1904), 6.199
Stewart, John McKellar, 12.91
Stewart, John Mitchell Young, 12.91
Stewart, Nellie, see Stewart, Eleanor Towzey
Stewart, Nora, see Stewart, Eleanor Charlotte
Stewart, Percy Gerald, 12.92
Stewart, William, 2.482
Sticht, Robert Carl, 12.93

Stieglitz, *see* Von Stieglitz
Stiles, Henry Tarlton, 2.483
Stillwell, Frank Leslie, 12.94
Stillwell, John, 12.95
Stirling, Edmund, 6.200
Stirling, Edward, 6.200
Stirling, Sir Edward Charles, 6.200
Stirling, Sir James, 2.484
Stirling, Sir John Lancelot, 6.200
Stirling, Nell, 8.416
Stodart, James, 12.95
Stodart, Robert Mackay, 12.96
Stoddard, Mary, 12.96
Stokes, Edward Sutherland, 12.97
Stokes, John Lort, 2.488
Stone, Sir Edward Albert, 12.98
Stone, Emily Mary Page, 12.99
Stone, Emma Constance, 12.98
Stone, George Frederick, 2.489
Stone, Grace Clara, 12.98
Stone, Louis, 12.100
Stone, William, 12.101
Stonehaven, John Lawrence Baird, 12.101
Stonehouse, Ethel Nhill Victoria, 12.102
Stoneman, Ethel Turner, 12.103
Stone-Wigg, Montagu John, 12.103
Stonor, Alban Charles, 2.489
Stopford, James, 12.104
Stopford, Robert, 12.105
Stopps, Arthur James, 4.178
Storey, Sir David, 12.105
Storey, John, 12.106
Storey, Sydney Albert Dawson, 12.108
Storey, Thomas, 12.108
Storkey, Percy Valentine, 12.108
Story, Ann Fawcett, 12.109
Story, George Fordyce, 2.490
Story, John Douglas, 12.110
Stott, Robert, 12.112
Stow, Augustine, 6.201
Stow, Catherine Eliza Somerville, 12.113
Stow, Jefferson Pickman, 6.201
Stow, Randolph Isham, 6.201
Stow, Thomas Quinton, 2.491
Strachan, Hugh Murray, 12.114
Strachan, James Ford, 2.492
Strachan, John, 6.202
Strachan, Lilias, 2.492
Stradbroke, George Edward John Mowbray
    Rous, 12.114
Stradbroke, Helena Violet Alice Keith,
    Lady, 12.115
Strahan, Sir George Cumine, 6.203
Stralia, Elsa, 12.115
Strange, Benjamin Edward, 12.116
Strange, Frederick, 2.493
Strangways, Henry Bull Templar, 6.204
Street, Geoffrey Austin, 12.117
Street, John Rendell, 12.118
Street, Sir Kenneth, 12.119
Street, Sir Laurence, 12.119
Street, Laurence Whistler, 12.119
Street, Sir Philip Whistler, 12.118
Streeton, Sir Arthur Ernest, 12.119

Strehlow, Carl Friedrich Theodor, 12.121
Strele, Anton, 6.205
Strempel, Carl Friedrich Adolph, 6.205
Stretch, John Francis, 12.122
Stretch, Theodore Carlos Benoni, 6.206
Strickland, Sir Edward, 6.207
Strickland, Sir Gerald, 12.123
Strickland, Henry Robert, 6.207
Strickland of Sizergh Castle, *see* Strickland,
    Sir Gerald
Strickland, William Henry John, 6.207
Strode, Thomas, 2.26
Strong, Sir Archibald Thomas, 6.210,
    12.124
Strong, Charles, 6.208
Strong, Herbert Augustus, **6.209**, 12.124
Strong, Walter Mersh, 12.125
Struth, John, 2.493
Strutt, William, 6.210
Strzelecki, Sir Paul Edmund de, 2.494
Stuart, Sir Alexander, 6.211
Stuart, Athol Hugh, 12.126
Stuart, Francis, 12.127
Stuart, Herbert Akroyd, 12.128
Stuart, John Alexander Salmon, 12.129
Stuart, John McDouall, 6.214
Stuart, Julian, *see* Stuart, John Alexander
    Salmon
Stuart, Sir Thomas Peter Anderson,
    12.130
Stuart, William, 12.132
Stukeley, Simon, *see* Savery, Henry
Sturgess, Reginald Ward, 12.132
Sturt, Charles, 2.495
Sturt, Evelyn Pitfield Shirley, 6.215
Sturt, Thomas Lenox Napier, 2.495
Stutchbury, Samuel, 6.216
Styles, James, 12.133
Sudds, Joseph, 1.285, 2.235
Suffolk, Owen Hargraves, 6.217
Sugden, Edward Holdsworth, 12.133
Sullivan, Arthur Percy, 12.135
Sullivan, James Forester, 6.218
Sullivan, Margaret Virginia, *see* Moore,
    Maggie
Sullivan, Thomas Barry, 6.219
Sulman, Florence, 12.136
Sulman, Sir John, 12.137
Summers, Charles, 6.219
Summers, Charles Francis, 6.220
Summers, Joseph, 6.220
Summons, Walter Ernest Isaac, 12.138
Sumsuma, 12.139
Supple, Gerald Henry, 6.221
Süssmilch, Adolph Carl von de Heyde,
    12.139
Sutherland, Alexander, 6.222
Sutherland, George (1855-1905), 6.223
Sutherland, George (arr.1864), 6.222,
    12.141
Sutherland, Jane, 6.223, **12.140**
Sutherland, John, 6.223
Sutherland, Sulina Murray MacDonald,
    6.225

Sutherland, William, 12.141
Sutton, Alfred, 6.227
Sutton, George Lowe, 12.142
Sutton, Harvey, 12.143
Sutton, Henry, 6.226
Sutton, Richard Henry, 6.226
Sutton, Robert, see Sievier, Robert
  Standish
Suttor, Sir Francis Bathurst, 6.227
Suttor, George, 2.498
Suttor, John Bligh (1809-1886), 6.229
Suttor, John Bligh (1859-1925), 6.229
Suttor, William Henry (1805-1877), 6.228
Suttor, William Henry (1834-1905), 6.229
Swadling, William Thomas, 12.145
Swain, Edward Harold Fulcher, 12.145
Swain, Herbert John, 12.146
Swallow, Thomas, 4.57, **6.230**
Swan, James, 6.230
Swanson, Donald Alexander, 12.147
Swanson, Sir John Warren, 12.147
Swanson, William, 12.147
Swanston, Charles, 2.500
Swanston, Charles Lambert, 2.501
Swanton, Mamie, see Swanton, Mary Hynes
Swanton, Mary Hynes, 12.148
Swayne, Edward Bowdich, 12.148
Sweet, George, 12.149
Sweet, Georgina, 12.149
Sweet, Samuel White, 6.231
Swinburne, George, 12.150
Sydenham of Combe, Baron, see Clarke, Sir
  George Sydenham
Sykes, Alfred Depledge, 12.152
Sylke, Ann, 2.174
Syme, David, 6.232
Syme, David York, 12.153
Syme, Ebenezer, 6.236
Syme, Sir Geoffrey, 12.154
Syme, Sir George Adlington, 12.155
Syme, George Alexander (1791-1845),
  6.232
Syme, George Alexander (1822-1894),
  6.235
Syme, Jane, 6.233
Syme, Joseph Cowen, 6.234
Syme, Oswald Julian, 12.155
Symers, Thomas, see Seymour-Symers,
  Thomas Lyell
Symes, Joseph, 6.237
Symon, Sir Josiah Henry, 12.156
Symonds, Saul, 12.158
Symons, John Christian, 6.237
Symons, William, 3.34
Symons, William John, 12.158
Synan, Mary, 12.159
Synnot, Monckton, 6.238
Taam Sze-Pui, see See Poy, Tom
Taber, Thomas, 2.502
Tait, Charles, 12.160
Tait, Edward Joseph, 12.160
Tait, Sir Frank Samuel, 12.160
Tait, George, 12.162
Tait, James McAlpine, 6.240

Tait, James Nevin, 12.160
Tait, John, 6.240
Tait, John Henry, 12.160
Tait, John Turnbull, 12.160
Tait, Sir Thomas James, 12.162
Takasuka, Jō, 12.163
Takasuka, Mario, 12.164
Takasuka, Sho, 12.164
Talbot, Albert Edward, 12.164
Talbot, John Richard, 6.241
Talbot, Margaret Jane, Lady, 12.165
Talbot, Sir Reginald Arthur James, 12.165
Talbot, Richard Gilbert, 2.503
Talbot, Samuel Robdard John Neil, 2.502
Talbot, Tom, 7.220
Talbot, William, 2.502
Tallis, Sir George, 12.165
Tanck, Johan Christian, 12.400
Tanner, Alfred John, 12.166
Tanner, William, 2.122
Taplin, George, 6.242
Tarczynski, Stanislaw Victor de, 12.167
Tardent, Henry Alexis, 12.167
Tarrant, Harley, 12.168
Tart, Quong, see Mei Quong Tart
Tasma, see Couvreur, Jessie Catherine
Tasman, Abel Janszoon, 2.503
Tate, Frank, 6.396, **12.169**
Tate, Henry, 12.172
Tate, Ralph, 6.243
Taubman, Claude Percival, 12.173
Taubman, George Henry, 12.173
Taubman, Henry George, 12.173
Taubman, Nathaniel James, 12.173
Tauchert, Arthur Michael, 12.173
Taverner, Sir John William, 12.174
Tayler, Lloyd, 6.244
Taylor, Adolphus George, 6.245
Taylor, Alfred Joseph, 6.246
Taylor, Sir Allen Arthur, 12.175
Taylor, David, 2.504
Taylor, Deighton, 4.378
Taylor, Florence Mary, **12.176**, 12.178
Taylor, George (1758-1828), 2.504
Taylor, George (d.1826), 2.504
Taylor, George (1861-1935), 12.177
Taylor, George Augustine, 12.176, **12.178**
Taylor, Harry Samuel, 12.179
Taylor, Headlie Shipard, 12.180
Taylor, Henry d'Esterre, 12.181
Taylor, Henry Joseph Stirling, 12.181
Taylor, Hugh (arr.1815), 6.247
Taylor, Hugh (1823-1897), 6.247
Taylor, Irene Frances, 12.182
Taylor, James (1820-1895), 6.248
Taylor, James (arr.1893), 12.185
Taylor, John, 2.504
Taylor, Joseph Leslie Theodore, 12.183
Taylor, Sir Patrick Gordon, 12.184
Taylor, Patrick Thomson, 12.185
Taylor, Rachel, see Henning, Rachel
  Biddulph
Taylor, Robert (1791-1861), 2.504
Taylor, Robert (1834-1907), 6.248

Taylor, Squizzy, *see* Taylor, Joseph Leslie Theodore
Taylor, Thomas Griffith, 12.185
Taylor, Thomas Johnstone, 9.140
Taylor, Thomas Joseph, 6.246
Taylor, William (1818-1903), 6.249
Taylor, William (1821-1902), 6.250
Taylor, William George, 12.188
Tazewell, Evelyn Ruth, 12.189
Teague, Violet Helen Evangeline, 12.189
Tebbutt, John, 6.251
Teddy the Jewboy, *see* Davis, Edward (1816-1841)
Teece, Richard, 12.190
Teece, Richard Clive, 12.190
Tegg, James, 2.504
Tegg, Samuel Augustus, 2.504
Tegg, Thomas, 2.504
Temple, David, 12.191
Temple-Poole, George Thomas, *see* Poole
Templeton, Andrew, 1.400
Templeton, Henry Barkley, 12.192
Templeton, Janet, 1.400-1
Templeton, John Montgomery, 6.252
Templeton, William, 6.253
Ten, George Soo Hoo, 6.253
Tench, Fisher, 2.506
Tench, Watkin, 2.506
Tenison-Woods, Julian Edmund, 6.254
Tenison Woods, Mary Cecil, 12.192
Tennant, Andrew, 6.255
Tennant, John, 6.255
Tennyson, Hallam, 12.194
Terry, Frederick Casemero (Charles), 6.256
Terry, John, 2.507
Terry, Leonard, 6.257
Terry, Rosetta, 2.508
Terry, Samuel, 2.508
Terry, Samuel Henry, 6.258
Terry, Thomas Charles, 6.259
Terry, William Henry, 6.259
Tewksbury, William Pearson, 12.195
Tewskbury, Alphonso Reed, 12.195
Thatcher, Charles Robert, 6.259
Thatcher, Griffithes Wheeler, 12.196
Thatcher, Richmond, 6.259
Theodore, Basil, 12.197
Theodore, Edward Granville, 12.197
Therry, John Joseph, 2.509
Therry, Sir Roger, 2.512
Thesiger, Frederick John Napier, *see* Chelmsford, Baron
Thickthorn, *see* De Vis, Charles Walter
Thirkell, Angela Margaret, 12.202
Thirkell, George Lancelot Allnutt, 12.202
Thomas, Arthur Nutter, 12.203
Thomas, Bartholomew Boyle, 2.516
Thomas, David John, 2.514
Thomas, Evan Henry, 2.515
Thomas, Jocelyn Henry Connor, 2.516
Thomas, Josiah, 12.203
Thomas, Julian, *see* James, John Stanley
Thomas, Lewis, 6.260

Thomas, Margaret, 6.261
Thomas, Mary, 6.263
Thomas, Mesac, 6.262
Thomas, Morgan, 6.263
Thomas, Richard, 12.204
Thomas, Robert, 6.263
Thomas, Sir Robert Kyffin, 6.264
Thomas, William, 2.518
Thomas, William Charles, 12.205
Thomas, William Kyffin, 6.264
Thompson, Andrew, 2.519
Thompson, Charles Victor, 12.206
Thompson, Clive Wentworth, 12.206
Thompson, David (1828-1889), 12.207
Thompson, David (1865-1916), 12.207
Thompson, Duncan Fulton, 12.208
Thompson, Edward Henry, 12.209
Thompson, Eliza, 1.68, 1.70
Thompson, Gerald Marr, 12.209
Thompson, James, 12.210
Thompson, John Ashburton, 12.211
Thompson, John Low, 6.265
Thompson, John Malbon, 6.265
Thompson, John Willis, 12.212
Thompson, Joseph, 6.266
Thompson, Matilda Louise, 12.212
Thompson, Patrick, 1.285
Thompson, R. W., 7.5
Thompson, Richard, 2.521
Thompson, William Bethel, 12.213
Thompson, William George, 12.213
Thomson, Adam (1813-1874), 6.267
Thomson, Adam (snr), 6.267
Thomson, Adam Compton, 2.521
Thomson, Alexander, 2.522
Thomson, Alexander Morrison, 6.268
Thomson, Annie Elizabeth, 6.267
Thomson, Dugald, 12.214
Thomson, Sir Edward Deas, 2.523
Thomson, George Edward, 6.268
Thomson, Herbert, 12.215
Thomson, James, 12.215
Thomson, James Alexander, 2.300, **2.527**
Thomson, James Park, 12.216
Thomson, Jane Elizabeth, *see* Young, Eliza
Thomson, Matthew Barclay, 6.272
Thomson, Robert, 6.269
Thomson, William, 6.270
Thorby, Harold Victor Campbell, 12.216
Thorn, George, 6.272
Thorn, George Henry, 6.272
Thorn, Sarah, *see* Thornton, Sarah
Thornber, Catherine Maria (1812?-1894), 12.217
Thornber, Catherine Maria (1837-1924), 12.217
Thornber, Ellen, 12.217
Thornber, Rachel Ann, 12.217
Thornber, Robert, 12.217
Thornton, George, 6.273
Thornton, Samuel, 6.274
Thornton, Sarah, 6.273
Thorpe, Harry, 12.218
Thow, William, 12.219

Thralrum, *see* Wilson, Mark
Threlfall, Sir Richard, 12.220
Threlkeld, Lancelot Edward, 2.528
Thring, Francis William, 12.221
Thring, Walter Hugh Charles Samuel, 12.222
Throsby, Charles, 2.530
Throssell, Frank Erick Cottrell, 12.223
Throssell, George, 12.223
Throssell, Hugo Vivian Hope, 12.223
Throssell, Michael, 12.223
Thrower, Thomas Henry, 12.225
Thunderbolt, Captain, *see* Ward, Frederick
Thurgood, Albert John, 12.225
Thurston, Frederick Arthur, 12.226
Thwaites, Frederick Joseph, 12.226
Thwaites, William, 12.227
Thynne, Andrew Joseph, 12.228
Tickell, Frederick, 12.229
Tietkens, William Harry, 6.275
Tighe, Atkinson Alfred Patrick, 6.276
Tighe, Robert, 6.276
Tildesley, Beatrice Maude, 12.230
Tildesley, Evelyn Mary, 12.230
Tilly, William Henry, 8.34, **12.231**
Tillyard, Pattie, 12.232
Tillyard, Robin John, 12.232
Timms, Edward Vivian, 12.233
Timperley, William Henry, 6.276
Tims, Martin, 2.531
Tindal, Charles Grant, 6.277
Tindal, Frederick Colquhoun, 6.277
Tinline, George, 6.278
Tisdall, Alice Constance, 12.234
Tisdall, Henry Thomas, 12.234
Tisdall, Lucy, 12.234
Tishler, Joseph, 12.235
Titheradge, George Sutton, 6.279
Tivey, Edwin, 12.236
Tjangamarra, 12.237
Todd, Sir Charles, 6.280
Todd, Ellen Joy, 12.238
Todd, Frederick Augustus, 12.237
Todd, Robert Henry, 12.238
Toft, John Percy Gilbert, 12.239
Toll, Frederick William, 12.240
Tolmer, Alexander, 6.282
Tolmie, James, 12.241
Tolmie, Roderick, 12.241
Tom, William, 2.532
Tomholt, Sydney John, 12.242
Tomkinson, Samuel, 6.283
Tompson, Charles (1784?-1871), 2.533
Tompson, Charles (1807-1883), 2.533
Toohey, James Matthew, 6.284
Toohey, John Thomas, 6.284
Toohey, Matthew, 6.284
Toomey, James Morton, 12.243
Toosey, James Denton, 2.533
Tooth, Atticus, 6.287
Tooth, Edwin, 6.285
Tooth, Frederick, 6.285
Tooth, John, 6.285
Tooth, Robert, 6.285

Tooth, Sir Robert Lucas Lucas-, 6.286
Tooth, William Butler, 6.287
Topp, Arthur Maning, 6.288
Topp, Charles Alfred, 6.289
Topp, Samuel St John, 6.288
Torode, Henry Kaines, 12.244
Torode, Walter Charles, 12.244
Torpy, James, 6.290
Torr, William George, 12.244
Torrance, George William, 6.290
Torreggiani, Elzear (Aloysius), 6.291
Torrens, Robert, 2.534
Torrens, Sir Robert Richard, 2.536, 4.436, **6.292**
Torres, Luiz Vaez de, 2.536
Touchstone, Tom, *see* Bury, Thomas
Tout, Sir Frederick Henry, 12.245
Toutcher, Charles, 12.246
Toutcher, Richard Frederick, 12.246
Town, Andrew, 6.294
Towner, Edgar Thomas, 12.247
Towns, Robert, 6.294
Townsend, Alfred Richard, 12.248
Townsend, George Wilfred Lambert, 12.249
Townsend, William, 6.296
Townson, John, **2.536**, 2.537
Townson, Robert, 2.537
Toynbee, Arnold, 12.547
Tozer, Sir Horace, 12.250
Tracey, Eliza, 12.250
Tracy, Richard Thomas, 6.297
Traeger, Alfred Hermann, 12.251
Traill, Jessie Constance Alicia, 12.252
Traill, John Charles Merriman, 12.252
Traill, William Henry, 6.298
Train, George Francis, 6.299
Tranter, Charles Herbert, 12.253
Treacy, Patrick Ambrose, 6.300
Treasure, Emmanuel, 12.254
Treasure, Harry Louis, 12.254
Treffene, Phillip, 12.372
Treflé, John Louis, 12.254
Tregurtha, Edward Primrose, 2.538
Treloar, George Devine, 12.255
Treloar, John Linton, 12.256
Trenerry, Horace Hurtle, 12.257
Trenwith, William Arthur, 12.258
Trethowan, Sir Arthur King, 12.260
Trethowan, Hubert Charles, 12.261
Trevascus, William Charles, 12.261
Treweek, Elsy, *see* Collier, Elsie Louise
Triaca, Camillo, 12.262
Trickett, Edward, 6.301
Trickett, Joseph, 6.302
Trickett, Oliver, 12.262
Trickett, William Joseph, 6.302
Trigg, Henry, 2.539
Triggs, Arthur Bryant, 12.263
Tritton, Duke, *see* Tritton, Harold Percy Croydon
Tritton, Harold Percy Croydon, 12.264
Troedel, Charles, *see* Troedel, Johannes Theodor Charles

Troedel, Johannes Theodor Charles, 6.302
Trollope, Anthony, 6.303
Trompf, Percival Albert, 12.264
Trooper Bluegum, see Hogue, Oliver
Trott, Albert Edwin, 12.265
Trott, George Henry Stevens, 12.265
Trouton, Frederick Henry, 6.304
Trower, Gerard, 12.266
Truganini, see Trugernanner
Trugernanner, 6.305
Truman, Ernest Edwin Philip, 12.266
Truman, John, 12.267
Trumble, Hugh, 12.268
Trumble, Thomas, 12.269
Trumper, Charles Thomas, 12.270
Trumper, Victor Thomas, 12.269
Truscott, William John, 12.272
Tryon, Sir George, 6.305
Tryon, George Clement, 6.306
Tryon, Henry, 12.272
Tubb, Frederick Harold, 12.273
Tubb, Harry, 12.273
Tuck, Marie Anne, 12.274
Tucker, Albert Edwin Elworthy Lee, 6.306
Tucker, Charles, 12.274
Tucker, Gerard Kennedy, 12.275
Tucker, Horace Finn, 12.275
Tucker, James, 2.539
Tucker, Thomas George, 12.277
Tucker, Thomas William, 2.26
Tucker, Tudor St George, 12.278
Tuckett, Francis Curtis, 12.279
Tuckett, Francis John, 12.279
Tuckett, Frederick William, 12.280
Tuckett, Joseph Helton, 12.280
Tuckett, Lewis, 12.279
Tuckett, Philip Samuel, 12.280
Tuckett, Richard Joseph, 12.280
Tuckfield, Francis, **2.540**, 12.280
Tuckfield, William John, 12.280
Tudor, Francis Gwynne, 12.281
Tufnell, Edward Wyndham, 6.307
Tulk, Augustus Henry, 6.308
Tulk, Charles Augustus, 6.308
Tulloch, Eric William, 12.282
Tully, William Alcock, 6.309
Tunbridge, Walter Howard, 12.283
Tunn, John Patrick, 12.284
Tunnecliffe, Thomas, 12.284
Turley, Joseph Henry Lewis, 9.656, **12.285**
Turnbull, Adam (1803-1891), 2.541
Turnbull, Adam (d.pre-1819), 2.541
Turnbull, Archibald, 12.286
Turnbull, Ernest, 12.287
Turnbull, Gilbert Munro, 12.287
Turner, Alfred Allatson, 6.310
Turner, Alfred Jefferis, 12.288
Turner, Charles Thomas Biass, 6.310
Turner, Dora Jeannette, 12.289
Turner, Ethel Mary, 12.290
Turner, Fred, 12.292
Turner, Sir George, 12.293
Turner, Henry Gyles, 6.311
Turner, James Alfred, 12.296

Turner, James Francis, 6.313
Turner, John William, 12.296
Turner, Lilian Wattnall, 12.290
Turner, Martha, 6.314
Turner, Walter James, 12.297
Turner, Walter James Redfern, 12.297
Turner, William, 6.315
Turriff, Haldane Colquhoun, 6.315
Tweddle, Isabel May, 12.298
Tweddle, Joseph Thornton, 12.298
Twopeny, Richard Ernest Nowell, 6.316
Twopeny, Thomas Nowell, 6.316
Tyas, John Walter, 6.317
Tye, Cyrus Willmot Oberon, 12.299
Tyers, Charles James, 2.542
Tyrrell, George, 12.300
Tyrrell, James Robert, 12.300
Tyrrell, Thomas James, 12.301
Tyrrell, William, 6.318
Tyson, Isabella, 6.319
Tyson, James, 6.319
Tyson, John, 6.319
Tyson, William, 6.319
Uhr, Wentworth D'Arcy, 6.321
Ullathorne, William Bernard, 2.544
Ulm, Charles Thomas Philippe, 9.599, **12.302**
Ulrich, Georg Heinrich Friedrich, 6.321
Ulrich, Theodore Friederick, 12.303
Unaipon, David, 12.303
Underwood, James, 2.546
Underwood, Joseph, 2.547
Unwin, Ernest Ewart, 12.305
Upfield, Arthur William, 12.305
Urquhart, Frederic Charles, 12.306
Using Daeng Rangka, 6.322
Uther, Reuben, 2.548
Vaccari, Gualtiero, 12.308
Vagabond, see James, John Stanley
Vale, Benjamin, 2.550
Vale, Grace, 6.324
Vale, May, 12.308
Vale, Richard Tayler, 6.324
Vale, William Mountford Kinsey, 6.324
Van Raalte, Henri Benedictus Salaman, 12.309
Vance, George Oakley, 6.325
Vancouver, George, 2.550
Vanzetti, Eugenio, 12.310
Vardon, Edward Charles, 12.311
Vardon, Joseph, 12.311
Varley, George Henry Gisborne, 12.311
Vaude, Charlie, 12.312
Vaughan, Crawford, 12.313
Vaughan, Dorothy, 12.315
Vaughan, Edmund, 6.326
Vaughan, John Howard, 12.313
Vaughan, Roger William Bede, 6.327
Vaughn, Robert Matterson, 6.329
Vaux, Hardy, 2.552
Vaux, James Hardy, 2.552
Vékey, Zsigmond, see Wekey, Sigismund
Venables, Henry Pares, 6.329
Venn, Henry Whittall, 12.316

Vennard, Alexander Vindex, 12.316
Venus, Winifred Sarah, 12.70
Verbrugghen, Henri Adrien Marie, 12.317
Verco, Sir Joseph Cooke, 12.318
Verdon, Sir George Frederic, 6.330
Verge, John, 2.553
Verjus, Henri Stanislas, 6.332
Verney, Kathleen, 11.15
Vernon, Geoffrey Hampden, 12.322
Vernon, Howard, 12.319
Vernon, Hugh Venables, 12.322
Vernon, Walter Liberty, 12.320
Verran, John, 12.322
Verran, John Stanley, 12.323
Vesta, see Allan, Stella May
Vezin, Eliza, see Young, Eliza
Vicars, John (1821-1894), 6.332
Vicars, Sir John (1857-1936), 12.324
Vicars, Sir William, 12.324
Vickers, Allan Robert Stanley, 12.324
Vickers, William, 12.325
Vickery, Ebenezer, 6.333
Victor, James Conway, 2.555
Vidal, Francis, 2.555
Vidal, Mary Theresa, 2.555
Vidler, Edward Alexander, 12.326
Vigano, Maria Teresa, 12.326
Vigano, Mario Antonio Francesco Battista
   Virginio, 12.326
Vincent, Alfred James, 12.327
Vincent, Edward, 12.328
Vincent, James, 12.328
Vincent, Mother, see Whitty, Ellen
Vincent, Roy Stanley, 12.328
Vincent, William, see Wallace, William
   Vincent
Viner, William Samuel, 12.329
Viney, Horace George, 12.330
Virgo, Emmeline Dorothy, 12.331
Virgo, John James, 12.330
Vlamingh, Willem de, 2.556
Vogel, Sir Julius, 6.334
Vogt, George Leonard, 12.331
Vogt, Johann Hermann, 12.331
Vogt, John, 12.331
Voigt, Emil Robert, 12.332
Von Doussa, Charles Louis, 12.332
Von Doussa, Emil Louis Alfred, 12.332
Von Doussa, Heinrich Albert Alfred,
   12.332
Von Schleinitz, Georg Gustav, see Schleinitz
Von Stieglitz, Charles Augustus, 2.557
Von Stieglitz, Emma, 2.557
Von Stieglitz, Francis Walter, 2.557
Von Stieglitz, Frederick Lewis, 2.556
Von Stieglitz, Henry Lewis, 2.557
Von Stieglitz, John Lewis, 2.557
Vonwiller, Oscar Ulrich, 12.333
Vosper, Frederick Charles Burleigh,
   12.334
Voss, Francis Henry Vivian, 12.335
Vosz, Heinrich Ludwig, 6.335
Waddell, Thomas, 12.337
Waddy, Percival Stacy, 12.338

Wade, Arthur, 12.338
Wade, Benjamin Martin, 12.339
Wade, Sir Charles Gregory, 12.340
Wade, John, 12.342
Wade, Leslie Augustus Burton, 12.342
Wade, Margaret, 12.342
Wade, Mary, 12.344
Wade, Sir Robert Blakeway, 12.343
Wade, Robert Thompson, 12.344
Wadsworth, Arthur, 12.345
Wager, Rhoda, 12.345
Wagner, Johann Gottfried, 2.422
Wainewright, Thomas Griffiths, 2.558
Wainwright, John William, 12.346
Wainwright, William Edward, 12.348
Waite, Edgar Ravenswood, 12.348
Waite, James Clarke, 6.336
Waite, Peter, 6.336
Waite, William Charles Nightingale, 12.349
Wakefield, Edward Gibbon, 2.559
Wakelin, Roland Shakespeare, 12.350
Walbey, John, see Warby, John
Walch, Charles Edward, 6.337
Walch, Garnet, 6.338
Walch, James William Henry, 6.338
Walder, Sir Samuel Robert, 12.351
Waldock, Arthur John, 12.352
Wales, Sir Alexander George, 12.353
Waley, Sir Frederick George, 12.354
Walker, Alan Cameron, 12.355
Walker, Allan Seymour, 12.355
Walker, Dame Eadith Campbell, 12.356
Walker, Fred (1884-1935), 12.357
Walker, Frederick (1820?-1866), 6.338
Walker, George, 6.344
Walker, George Washington, 2.562
Walker, Sir Harold Bridgwood, 12.358
Walker, Henry, 6.339
Walker, Hurtle Frank, 12.359
Walker, James (1795-1854), 6.341
Walker, James (arr.1823), 2.566
Walker, James (1863-1942), 12.360
Walker, James Backhouse, 6.340
Walker, James Thomas, 12.361
Walker, Jean Nellie Miles, 12.362
Walker, John (1799-1874), 2.563
Walker, John (1855-1941), 12.362
Walker, John William, 12.361
Walker, Lucy Arabella Stocks Wheatley, see
   Garvin
Walker, Philip Billingsley, 6.341
Walker, Richard Cornelius Critchett, 6.341
Walker, Robert Cooper, 6.341
Walker, Thomas (1791-1861), 2.564
Walker, Thomas (1804-1886), 2.565
Walker, Thomas (1858-1932), 6.342
Walker, W. H., see Ranken, George
   (1827-1895)
Walker, William (1787-1854), 2.566
Walker, William (1800-1855), 2.566
Walker, William (1828-1908), 6.344
Wall, Dorothy, 12.363
Wallace, Arthur Cooper, 12.364
Wallace, Arthur Knight, 7.18

Wallace, Donald Smith, 6.344
Wallace, Elisabeth (1814-1878), 2.568
Wallace, Elizabeth (1877-1969), see Ahern, Elizabeth
Wallace, George Stevenson, 12.365
Wallace, John Alston, 6.345
Wallace, Johnny, see Wallace, Arthur Cooper
Wallace, Sir Robert Strachan, 12.366
Wallace, William Vincent, 2.567
Wallen, Frank, 6.347
Wallen, Robert Elias, 6.346
Waller, Mervyn Napier, 12.367
Wallis, Alfred Russell, 12.367
Wallis, Frederick Samuel, 12.368
Wallis, James, 2.568
Wallis, William Dane, 12.369
Walpole, Herbert Reginald Robert Seymour, 12.370
Walsh, Henry Deane, 12.370
Walsh, James Morgan, 12.371
Walsh, John Joseph (1819-1895), 6.347
Walsh, John Joseph (1862-1926), 12.372
Walsh, Thomas, 12.372
Walsh, William Henry, 6.348
Walsh, William Horatio, 2.569
Walstab, George Arthur, 6.349
Walstab, John George, 6.349
Walter, William Ardagh Gardner, 12.374
Walters, George Thomas, 12.375
Walters, Henry Latimer, 12.376
Walton, Thomas Utrick, 12.376
Wand, John William Charles, 12.377
Wanliss, Cecil, 12.378
Wanliss, David Sydney, 12.378
Wanliss, Ewen, 12.378
Wanliss, Harold Boyd, 12.379
Wanliss, John Newton Wellesley, 12.379
Wanliss, Marion Boyd, 12.379
Wanliss, Neville, 12.378
Want, John Henry, 6.350, **12.380**
Want, Randolph John, 6.349
Warburton, Peter Egerton, 6.350
Warby, John, 2.570
Ward, Ebenezer, 6.351
Ward, Edward John, 9.664
Ward, Sir Edward Wolstenholme, 6.352
Ward, Elizabeth Jane, 12.381
Ward, Frederick, 6.353
Ward, Frederick Furner, 12.381
Ward, Frederick William, 12.382
Ward, Hugh Joseph, 12.383
Ward, Janet Penrose, 1.31
Ward, John Frederick, 12.383
Ward, Susanna M., 4.182
Wardell, Robert, **2.570**, 2.585
Wardell, William Wilkinson, 6.354
Wardill, Benjamin Johnston, 6.356
Wardill, Richard Wilson, 6.355
Wardlaw, Alan Lindsay, 12.385
Wark, Blair Anderson, 12.385
Warner, William Lloyd, 12.386
Warnes, Mary Jane, 12.387
Warren, Hubert Ernest de Mey, 12.387

Warren, William Henry, 6.356
Warung, Price, see Astley, William
Waterfield, William, 2.572
Waterhouse, Bertrand James, 12.388
Waterhouse, Eben Gowrie, 12.389
Waterhouse, Frederick George, 6.357
Waterhouse, George Marsden, 6.358
Waterhouse, Gustavus Athol, 12.390
Waterhouse, Henry, 2.573
Waterhouse, Jabez Bunting, 6.359
Waterhouse, John, 6.359
Waterhouse, Joseph, 6.359
Waterhouse, Samuel, 6.359
Waterhouse, Walter Lawry, 12.391
Waters, Edward Ernest, 6.360
Waterworth, Edith Alice, 12.392
Waterworth, John Newham, 12.392
Watkins, David, 12.393
Watkins, H. Gino, 11.501
Watkins, Jemima Gourlay, 12.566
Watling, Thomas, 2.574
Watriama, William Jacob, 12.394
Watsford, James, 6.361
Watsford, John, 6.361
Watson, Archibald, 12.394
Watson, Charles Henry, 12.396
Watson, Charles Vincent, 12.396
Watson, Elizabeth, see Brentnall, Elizabeth
Watson, Elliot Lovegood Grant, 12.397
Watson, George John, 6.361
Watson, Henry Greaves, 12.396
Watson, James, 4.145, **6.362**
Watson, James Frederick William, 12.398
Watson, James Henry, 12.399
Watson, John Boyd, 6.363
Watson, John Christian, 12.400
Watson, Mary Beatrice Phillips, 6.364
Watson, Phebe Naomi, 12.405
Watson, Robert, 2.575
Watson, Stanley Holm, 12.406
Watson, William, 12.407
Watson, William Thornton, 12.408
Watson, William Walker Russell, 12.409
Watt, Ernest Alexander Stuart, 12.410
Watt, Hugh, 12.410
Watt, James Michie, 12.412
Watt, John Brown, 6.365
Watt, Michael H., 12.416
Watt, Sir Robert Dickie, 12.410
Watt, Walter Oswald, 6.366, **12.411**
Watt, William Alexander, 12.412
Watt, William Shand, 12.416
Watterston, David, 12.417
Waugh, James Swanton, 6.366
Wawn, William Twizell, 6.366
Way, Arthur Sanders, 6.367
Way, James, 12.417
Way Lee, Yet Soo War, 12.420
Way, Sir Samuel James, 12.417
Waylen, Alfred Robert, 6.368
Wayn, Amelia Lucy, 12.420
Wayn, Arthur, 12.420
Wearing, William Alfred, 6.368
Wearne, James Teare, 12.421

Wearne, Joseph (1832-1884), 6.369
Wearne, Joseph (d.1856), 6.369
Wearne, Reginald, 12.421
Wearne, Thomas, 6.370
Wearne, Walter Ernest, 12.421
Wears, W. E. L., 12.574
Weatherburn, Charles Ernest, 12.422
Weatherly, Lionel James, 12.422
Weatherly, May Isabella, 12.423
Weatherly, William, 12.422
Weathers, Lawrence Carthage, 12.424
Weaver, Reginald Walter Darcy, 12.425
Webb, Ann, 6.372
Webb, Charles, 6.370
Webb, Chris, 12.426
Webb, Edmund, 6.371
Webb, Frederick William, 12.427
Webb, George Henry Frederick, 6.372
Webb, James, 6.370
Webb, Jessie Stobo Watson, 12.427
Webb, Thomas Prout, 6.372
Webb, William Alfred, 12.428
Webb, William Telford, 6.373
Webber, William Thomas Thornhill, 12.429
Weber, Clarence Alfred, **12.430**, 12.431
Weber, Horace George Martin, 12.430
Weber, Ivy Lavinia, 12.431
Webster, Alexander George, 6.374
Webster, Charles Ernest, 12.432
Webster, Edwin Herbert, 12.432
Webster, Ellen, 12.432
Webster, George Alexander, 12.432
Webster, Martha, *see* Turner, Martha
Webster, William, 12.433
Webster, William Maule (McDowell), 12.433
Wedge, John Helder, 2.575
Weedon, Sir Henry, 12.434
Weekes, Elias Carpenter, 6.375
Weigall, Albert Bythesea, 6.375
Weigall, Cecil Edward, 12.434
Weigall, Theyre à Beckett, 12.435
Weigall, Sir William Ernest George Archibald, 12.436
Weikert, Franz, 5.41
Weindorfer, Gustav, 12.436
Weingarth, John Leopold, 12.437
Weir, Stanley Price, 12.438
Wekey, Sigismund, 6.376
Welch, Eric Wilfred, 12.439
Weld, Filumena Mary, 6.379
Weld, Sir Frederick Aloysius, 6.377
Wellish, Edward Montague, 12.439
Wells, Lawrence Allen, 7.250, **12.440**
Wells, Samuel Pullen, 2.576
Wells, Thomas, 2.576
Welsby, Thomas, 12.441
Welsh, David Arthur, 12.441
Welsh, John, 2.577
Wemyss, William, 2.577
Wendt, Joachim Matthias, 12.442
Wenlock, Baron, *see* Lawley, Sir Arthur
Wentworth, D'Arcy, **2.579**, 2.582
Wentworth, William Charles, 2.582

Wentworth-Shields, Wentworth Francis, 12.443
Wenz, Emil, 12.444
Wenz, Paul, 12.444
Were, Jonathan Binns, 2.589
Werth, Elisabeth, 7.398
Wesché, Awdry Gordon, 12.445
Wesché, Phoebe Ellen, 12.445
Wesselow, *see* Simpkinson De Wesselow
West, John (1809-1873), 2.590
West, John (1856-1926), 12.445
West, John Edward, 12.446
West, Winifred Mary, 12.447
Westall, Richard, 2.592
Westall, William, 2.592
Westgarth, William, 6.379
Westmacott, Charles Babington, 12.448
Weston, Thomas Charles George, 12.449
Weston, William Pritchard, 2.593
Wetherspoon, John, 12.450
Wettenhall, Holford Highlord, 6.383
Wettenhall, Marcus Edwy, 12.450
Wettenhall, Mary Burgess, 6.383
Wettenhall, Roland Ravenscroft, 12.451
Whannell, Margaret, 5.161
Whatmore, Hugh Edward, 12.452
Wheatley, Frederick William, 12.452
Wheatley-Walker, Lucy, *see* Garvin, Lucy Arabella Stocks
Wheeler, Annie Margaret, 12.453
Wheeler, Charles Arthur, 12.454
Wheeler, John, 12.455
Wheeler, Victoria Julia, 12.454
Wheelwright, Horace (Horatio) William, 6.383
Wheen, Arthur Wesley, 12.455
Wheen, Harold, 12.457
Wheen, John Gladwell, 12.456
Whelan, James Paul, 12.457
Whiddon, Frank, 12.458
Whiddon, Horace William, 12.458
Whiddon, Samuel Thomas, 12.458
Whiddon, William Henry, 12.459
Whinham, John, 6.384
Whinham, Robert, 6.384
Whish, Claudius Buchanan, 6.385
White, Albert William, 6.391
White, Alexander Henry, 12.459
White, Alexander John Middleton, 12.460
White, Andrew Douglas(s), 2.595
White, Charles, 6.385
White, Cornelius, 12.472
White, Sir Cyril Brudenell Bingham, 12.460
White, Cyril Tenison, 3.74, **12.463**
White, Daniel, 12.464
White, Dinah Ann, 12.472
White, Dudley Persse, 12.462
White, Ellen Gould, 12.465
White, Emily Elizabeth, 6.388
White, Francis, 6.389
White, Francis Maloney, 6.386
White, George Boyle, 6.387
White, Gilbert, 12.466
White, Harold Fletcher, 12.466

White, Henry Eli, 12.467
White, Henry Luke, 12.468
White, James (1828-1890), 6.387
White, James (d.1842), 6.387
White, James (1861-1918), 12.470
White, James Charles, 6.389
White, James Cobb, 12.468
White, Jessie McHardy, 12.470
White, John (1756?-1832), 2.594
White, John (arr.1836), 6.390
White, John (1853-1922), 12.471
White, John Charles, 6.385
White, John Warren, 12.460
White, Myrtle Rose, 12.472
White, Robert Hoddle Driberg, 6.389
White, Samuel, 6.390
White, Samuel Albert, 12.472
White, William Clarence, 12.465
White, William Duckett, 6.391
Whitefoord, John, 2.595
Whitehead, Charles, 6.391
Whitehouse, Joseph Howell, 12.473
Whitelegge, Thomas, 12.474
Whitfeld, Hubert Edwin, 12.475
Whitfield, George, 6.392
Whitford, Stanley R., 12.475
Whitham, John Lawrence, 12.476
Whitington, Frederick Taylor, 12.477
Whittell, Hubert Massey, 12.478
Whittingham, Arthur Herbert, 12.478
Whittingham, George, 12.478
Whittle, Ivan Ernest, 12.479
Whittle, John Woods, 12.479
Whitton, Ivo Harrington, 12.480
Whitton, John, 6.393
Whitty, Ellen, 6.394
Whitworth, Robert Percy, 6.395
Whyte, James, 6.395
Whyte, Patrick, 6.396
Whyte, Thomas, 2.596
Whyte, William Farmer, 12.480
Wickens, Charles Henry, 12.481
Wickham, John Clements, 2.597
Wieck, George Frederick Gardells, 12.482
Wiedermann, Elise, 11.233
Wienholt, Arnold (1826-1895), 6.397
Wienholt, Arnold (1897-1940), 12.483
Wienholt, Edward, 6.397
Wight, George, 6.398
Wilcox, Dora, see Wilcox, Mary Theodora Joyce
Wilcox, Mary Theodora Joyce, 10.573
Wild(e), Joseph, 2.597
Wilder, Maurice, see Wilder-Neligan
Wilder-Neligan, Maurice, 12.484
Wildman, Alexina Maude, 12.485
Wilkes, William Charles, 6.398
Wilkie, Allan, 12.486
Wilkie, David Elliot, 6.399
Wilkie, Leslie Andrew Alexander, 12.487
Wilkin, Frederick John, 12.488
Wilkins, Ann, 6.400
Wilkins, Sir George Hubert, 12.488
Wilkins, William, 6.400

Wilkinson, Arthur George, 12.490
Wilkinson, Audrey Harold, 12.490
Wilkinson, Charles Smith, 6.402
Wilkinson, Christopher George, 12.491
Wilkinson, Dorothy Irene, 12.491
Wilkinson, Frederick Albert, 12.490
Wilkinson, George, see Davis, Edward (1816-1841)
Wilkinson, John Francis, 12.492
Wilkinson, Leslie, 12.492
Wilkinson, Robert Bliss, 6.402
Wilks, William Henry, 12.494
Willcock, John Collings, 12.494
Williams, Alfred, 12.495
Williams, Edward David, **12.496**, 12.506
Williams, Sir Edward Eyre, 6.403
Williams, Francis, 2.598
Williams, Francis Edgar, 12.497
Williams, George, 2.232
Williams, George Davies, 12.498
Williams, Harold John, 12.499
Williams, Harold Parkyn, 12.500
Williams, Harry Llewellyn Carlington, 12.501
Williams, Sir Hartley, 6.403
Williams, Henry Roberts, 12.501
Williams, James Hartwell, 6.404
Williams, John (1796-1839), 2.599
Williams, John (1797?-1872), 2.600
Williams, John (d.1832), see Welsh, John
Williams, John Chauner, 2.600
Williams, Louis Reginald, 11.38
Williams, Mary Boyd Burfitt, 12.502
Williams, Reuel, 6.405
Williams, Sir Richard, 12.502
Williams, Robert Ernest, 12.505
Williams, Susannah Jane, 12.506
Williams, Thomas, 6.405
Williams, Sir William Daniel Campbell, 12.506
Williams, William Henry, 12.508
Williams, William Lanyon, 12.501
Williams, Zephaniah, 1.419, **2.601**
Williamson, Francis Samuel, 12.509
Williamson, James, 2.602
Williamson, James Cassius, 5.279, **6.406**, 7.395
Willis, Albert Charles, 12.509
Willis, Edward, 6.407
Willis, Ernest Horatio, 12.511
Willis, Henry, 12.511
Willis, John Walpole, 2.602
Willis, Joseph Scaife, 6.408
Willis, Richard, 2.604
Willis, Robert, 6.409
Willis, William Nicholas, 12.512
Willmore, Henrietta, 9.473, **12.513**
Willmoth, Florence Adelaide, 12.586
Willmott, Francis Edward Sykes, 12.514
Willoughby, Howard, 6.409
Wills, Cedric, 2.606
Wills, Edward Spencer, 2.605
Wills, Elizabeth, 2.606
Wills, Horatio Spencer Howe, 2.605

Wills, Thomas Wentworth Spencer, 2.606, **6.409**
Wills, William, 6.410
Wills, William John, 6.410
Willshire, William Henry, 12.515
Willson, Robert William, 2.607
Wilmot, Frank Leslie Thompson, 12.515
Wilmot, Henry William, 12.515
Wilmot, Sir John Eardley, see Eardley-Wilmot
Wilmot, Robert, see Horton, Sir Robert Wilmot
Wilshire, Austin Forrest, 6.411
Wilshire, Esther, 2.609
Wilshire, James, 2.608
Wilshire, James Robert, 2.609, **6.411**
Wilshire, James Thompson, 6.412
Wilshire, William Pitt, 2.609
Wilsmore, Norman Thomas Mortimer, 12.517
Wilson, Alexander William, 12.518
Wilson, Arthur Mitchell, 12.518
Wilson, Charles Algernon, 2.612
Wilson, David, 12.519
Wilson, Dora Lynnell, 12.520
Wilson, Edward, 6.412
Wilson, Frank, 12.520
Wilson, Gordon Campbell, 12.521
Wilson, Grace Margaret, 12.522
Wilson, Henry Croasdaile, 2.609
Wilson, Herbert Ward, 12.523
Wilson, James Alexander Campbell, 12.524
Wilson, James Lockie, 12.525
Wilson, Sir James Milne, 6.415
Wilson, James Thomas, 12.525
Wilson, John (d.1800), 2.610
Wilson, John (d.c1834), 6.412
Wilson, John Bowie, 3.50, **6.416**
Wilson, John Bracebridge, 6.417
Wilson, John Purves, 12.527
Wilson, John Thomas, 2.610
Wilson, Lachlan Chisholm, 12.528
Wilson, Sir Leslie Orme, 12.528
Wilson, Margaret, 10.162
Wilson, Mark, 12.529
Wilson, Sir Reginald Victor, 12.530
Wilson, Sir Samuel, 6.418
Wilson, Theodore Percival, 2.612, 4.155
Wilson, Thomas, 2.611
Wilson, Thomas Braidwood, 2.612
Wilson, Walter Horatio, 12.531
Wilson, William Hardy, 12.531
Wilson, William Parkinson, 6.419
Wilton, Charles Pleydell Neale, 2.613
Wilton, Charles Richard, 12.533
Wilton, John Raymond, 12.533
Wilton, Olive Dorothea Graeme, 12.534
Wiltshire, Aubrey Roy Liddon, 12.535
Winchcombe, Frederick Earle, 12.536
Winder, Thomas White Melville, 2.613
Windeyer, Archibald, 2.614
Windeyer, Charles, 2.614
Windeyer, Henry, 12.540
Windeyer, John (1714-1794), 2.615

Windeyer, John (d.c1835), 2.614
Windeyer, John Cadell, 2.614, **12.537**
Windeyer, Mabel Fuller, 12.540
Windeyer, Margaret, 12.537
Windeyer, Maria, 2.617, 6.420
Windeyer, Mary Elizabeth, 6.422, **12.537**
Windeyer, Richard (1806-1847), 2.615
Windeyer, Richard (1868-1959), 12.539
Windeyer, Thomas Mark, 2.614
Windeyer, William Archibald, 12.539
Windeyer, Sir William Charles, 6.420
Windich, Tommy, 6.422
Windiitj, see Windich, Tommy
Windsor, Arthur Lloyd, 6.423
Winkfield, Mary, see Clark, Mary, Lady
Winn, Roy Coupland, 12.540
Winneke, Henry Christian, 12.541
Winspear, William Robert, 12.542
Winstanley, Eliza, see O'Flaherty, Eliza
Winter, Anthony William, 12.542
Winter, George, 12.543
Winter, James, 6.423
Winter, John, 6.423
Winter, Joseph (1844-1915), 6.425
Winter, Joseph (1853-1896), 12.543
Winter, Nick, see Winter, Anthony William
Winter, Samuel Pratt, 6.424
Winter, Samuel Vincent, 6.425
Winter-Irving, William Irving, 6.423
Wirth, George, 12.544
Wirth, John, 12.545
Wirth, Marizles, see Wirth, Mary Elizabeth Victoria
Wirth, Mary Elizabeth Victoria, 12.544
Wirth, May Emmeline, 12.544
Wirth, Philip Peter Jacob, 12.544
Wisdom, Evan Alexander, 12.546
Wisdom, Sir Robert, 3.282, **6.427**
Wise, Bernhard Ringrose, 12.546
Wise, Edward, 6.427
Wise, Frances Lucy Ann, 6.429
Wise, George Foster, 6.429
Wise, George Henry, 12.549
Wise, Percy William Charlton, 12.550
Wiseman, Jesse, 12.551
Wiseman, Solomon, 2.617
Wiseman, Thomas (1847-1941), 12.551
Wiseman, Thomas (snr), 12.551
Wishart, James, 2.231
Withers, Walter Herbert, 12.551
Withers, William Bramwell, 6.429
Withnell, Emma Mary, 6.430
Withnell, John, 6.430
Wittenoom, Sir Edward Charles (Horne), 12.553
Wittenoom, Frederick Dirck, 2.619
Wittenoom, Frederick Francis Burdett, 12.553
Wittenoom, John Burdett, 2.618
Wolfe, Herbert Austin, 12.554
Wolfskehl, William Ernest, 2.237
Wollaston, Sir Harry Newton Phillips, 12.555
Wollaston, John Ramsden, 2.619

Wollaston, Tullie Cornthwaite, 12.556
Wollstonecraft, Edward, 1.92, **2.620**
Wolseley, Frederick York, 6.431
Wolstenholme, Edmund Kay, 7.59
Wolstenholme, Maybanke, see Anderson,
    Maybanke Susannah
Wood, Essie, see Jennings, Elizabeth Esther
    Ellen
Wood, George Arnold, 12.556
Wood, Harrie, 6.432
Wood, John Dennistoun, 6.433
Wood, John Robert, 4.477
Wood, Leon, 12.306
Wood, Patrick, 6.433
Wood, Thomas, 12.558
Woodcock, Lucy Godiva, 12.559
Woodd, Henry Alexander, 12.560
Woodfull, Howard Thomas Colin, 12.561
Woodfull, Thomas Staines Brittingham,
    12.560
Woodfull, William Maldon, 12.560
Woodhouse, William John, 12.561
Woodriff, Daniel, 2.621
Woodriff, Daniel James, 2.622
Woodruff, Harold Addison, 12.562
Woods, Gordon, 12.564
Woods, James, 12.563
Woods, James Park, 12.564
Woods, John, 6.434
Woods, Julian Edmund Tenison-, see
    Tenison-Woods, Julian Edmund
Woods, Norman, 12.564
Woods, Percy William, 12.564
Woods, Roger Henry, 2.622
Woods, Walter Alan, 12.565
Woods, William Maitland, 12.566
Woodward, Bernard Henry, 12.567
Woodward, Frank Lee, 12.568
Woodward, Henry Page, 12.568
Woodward, Oliver Holmes, 12.569
Woodward, Samuel Pickworth, 12.567
Woolcock, John Laskey, 12.570
Woollard, Herbert Henry, 12.571
Woolley, Emmeline Mary Dogherty,
    11.193, **12.572**
Woolley, John, **6.435**, 12.572
Woolley, Thomas, 2.623
Woolls, William, 6.437
Woolner, Thomas, 6.438
Woolnough, Walter George, 12.572
Woore, Thomas, 6.439
Woorraddy, 6.305
Worgan, George Bouchier, 2.623
Wormald, Henry Percy, 12.573
Wormald, Joseph Dawson, 12.573
Worrall, Henry, 12.574
Worrall, John, 12.575
Worsnop, Thomas, 6.440
Wortman(n), Adolphus, 2.623
Wortman(n), Ignatz, 2.623
Wragge, Clement Lindley, 12.576
Wray, Frederick William, 12.577
Wray, Leonora, 12.578
Wreford, Sir Ernest Henry, 12.578

Wren, Arthur, 12.582
Wren, Charles William, 12.579
Wren, Ellen, 12.583
Wren, John, 9.527, **12.580**
Wren, Joseph, 12.582
Wrenfordsley, Sir Henry Thomas, 6.440
Wright, Colin William, 12.583
Wright, David McKee, 8.158, **12.584**
Wright, Edward, 2.624
Wright, Emily Hilda Rix, see Nicholas,
    Emily Hilda
Wright, Francis Augustus, 6.441
Wright, Horatio George Anthony, 6.442
Wright, John Arthur, 12.585
Wright, John Charles, 12.585
Wright, John James, 6.443
Wright, William, 3.302
Wright, William Henry, 6.444
Wrigley, Leslie James, 12.586
Wrixon, Sir Henry John, 6.445
Wroe, John, 2.625
Wunderlich, Alfred, 12.587
Wunderlich, Ernest (Henry Charles) Julius,
    12.587
Wunderlich, Frederick Otto, 12.587
Wyatt, Joseph, 2.625
Wyatt, William, 2.626
Wylde, Sir John, 2.627
Wylie, 2.629
Wylly, Guy George Egerton, 12.589
Wymark, Frederick Victor Grey, 12.590
Wyndham, George, 2.630
Wyndham, Margaret, 2.631
Wynn, David, 12.591
Wynn, Samuel, 12.590
Wynne, Agar, 12.591
Wynne, Watkin, 12.592
Wynyard, Edward Buckley, 2.631
Wyselaskie, John Dickson, 6.446
Ximenes, Ann, 2.298
Yabba, see Gascoigne, Stephen Harold
Yabsley, William, 6.448
Yagan, 2.632
Yelverton, Henry, 6.448
Yelverton, Henry John, 6.449
Yencken, Arthur Ferdinand, 12.594
Yencken, Edward Lowenstein, 12.594
Yewen, Alfred Gregory, 12.594
Yorick, see Reeve, Edward
Youl, Alfred, 12.595
Youl, Annette Frances, 12.595
Youl, Francis Victor Mansell, 12.595
Youl, Geoffrey Arthur Douglas, 12.595
Youl, Sir James Arndell, 6.449
Youl, John, 2.632
Youl, John Beresford Osmond, 12.595
Youl, Richard, 6.450
Young, Adolphus William, 2.633
Young, Charles, 12.600
Young, Charles Frederick Horace Frisby,
    6.450
Young, Charles Le Fanu, 4.372
Young, Edmund (Edmond) Mackenzie,
    6.451

Young, Eliza, 6.451
Young, Florence Maude, 12.596
Young, Florence Selina Harriet, 12.596
Young, Fox, 1.183
Young, Sir Frederick William, 12.597
Young, Sir Henry Edward Fox, 6.452
Young, James, 12.600
Young, James Henry, 6.453
Young, Jeanne Forster, *see* Young, Sarah
  Jane
Young, Sir John (1807-1876), 6.455
Young, John (1827-1907), 6.454
Young, John Lorenzo, 6.457
Young, Robert, 6.458
Young, Sarah Jane, 12.597
Young, Sir Walter James, 12.598
Young, William Blamire, 12.599
Young, William John (1850-1931), 12.600
Young, William John (1878-1942), 12.601
Young, William Ramsay, 12.601
Younger, Charles, 6.458
Younger, Montague Thomas Robson, 6.458
Younghusband, William, 3.324
Young Wai, John, 12.602

Yuill, William John, 12.603
Yuille, William Cross, 6.459
Yuranigh, 2.634
Zadow, Christiane Susanne Augustine,
  12.604
Zadow, Heinrich Christian Wilhelm,
  12.604
Zahel, Ethel May Eliza, 12.604
Zeal, Sir William Austin, 12.605
Zelman, Alberto, 6.461
Zelman, Samuel Victor Albert, 12.606
Zercho, Charles Henry, 12.607
Zercho, Frederick William, 12.607
Ziesemer, Friedrich Wilhelm Ernst, 12.608
Ziesemer, Theodor Martin Peter, 12.608
Zillman, Johann Leopold, 2.423
Zillman, Leopold, 2.423
Zimpel, Cecil Edward William, 12.609
Zimpel, William James, 12.608
Zouch, Henry, 6.461
Zox, Ephraim Laman (Lamen), 6.462
Zwar, Albert Michael, 12.609
Zwar, Henry Peter, 12.609
Zwar, Traugott Bernhard, 12.610

Places of Birth

ARGENTINA
Day, Robert Alexander, 8
Farrell, John, 4
AUSTRALIA
Rosa, Samuel Albert, 11
Wylie, 2
Yagan, 2
Yuranigh, 2
New South Wales
Batman, John, 1
Bettington, James Brindley, 3
Governor, Jimmy, 9
Grayndler, Edward, 9
Nanya, 10
Osburne, Richard, 5
ABERDEEN
Wallace, George Stevenson, 12
ADELONG
Prowse, John Henry, 11
Shaw, Archibald John, 11
ALBURY
Bunton, Haydn William, 7
Cass, Walter Edmund Hutchinson, 7
Dean, George, 8
Dwyer, Patrick Vincent, 8
Ferry, Michael Augustus, 8
Flannery, George Ernest, 8
Kirkpatrick, John, 9
Kraegen, Edward Charles, 9
McEachern, Walter Malcolm Neil, 10
Percival, Edgar Wikner, 11
Selle, Walter Albert, 11
ALEXANDRIA
Beeby, Sir George Stephenson, 7
Oldfield, William Albert Stanley, 11
Todd, Frederick Augustus, 12
ANNANDALE
Maxwell, Joseph, 10
Thorby, Harold Victor Campbell, 12
APPIN
Browne, Reginald Spencer, 7
ARALUEN
Connell, Cornelius Myles, 8
Lesina, Vincent Bernard, 10
ARMIDALE
Duncan, Walter Leslie, 8
Johnstone, John Lorimer Gibson, 9
Martyn, Athelstan Markham, 10
Proctor, Alethea Mary, 11
Sheldon, Sir Mark, 11
ASHFIELD
Akhurst, Daphne Jessie, 7
Auld, James Muir, 7
Corlette, James Montague Christian, 8
Litchfield, Jessie Sinclair, 10
Miles, Beatrice, 10
Ramsay, Edward Pierson, 6
ATTUNGA
Drummond, Stanley Gillick, 8

AUBURN
Blackburn, Doris, 7
BALGONIE
Taylor, George, 12
BALMAIN
Andrews, Ernest Clayton, 7
Boake, Barcroft Henry Thomas, 3
Bracegirdle, Sir Leighton Seymour, 7
Collins, Cuthbert Quinlan Dale, 8
Dryer, Albert Thomas, 8
Elliott, James Frederick, 8
Johnston, Thomas Harvey, 9
Loitte, Lavinia Florence de, 12
Lording, Rowland Edward, 10
Lyell, Lottie Edith, 10
McClintock, Albert Scott, 10
Manning, Charles James, 5
Messenger, Herbert Henry, 10
Molesworth, Voltaire, 10
Parker, Henry Thomas, 11
Perdriau, Henry, 11
Perdriau, Stephen Edward, 11
Reay, William Thomas, 11
Rennie, Edward Henry, 11
Rennie, George Edward, 11
Riley, Alban Joseph, 6
Sellheim, Victor Conradsdorf Morisset,
  11
Spedding, Quentin Shaddock, 12
Spence, Percy Frederick Seaton, 12
Spencer, Albert Henry, 12
Spofforth, Frederick Robert, 6
Thwaites, Frederick Joseph, 12
Watson, William Walker Russell, 12
BALRANALD
Cramsie, John Boyd, 8
BATHURST
Barton, Alan Sinclair Darvall, 7
Bean, Charles Edwin Woodrow, 7
Bonnor, George John, 3
Coates, Joseph Farrar, 8
Davis, William Walter, 8
Dettmann, Herbert Stanley, 8
Foley, Laurence, 4
Jones, Leslie John Roberts, 9
Livingston, Thomas, 10
McIntosh, Harold, 10
Meagher, Richard Denis, 10
Piddington, Albert Bathurst, 11
Suttor, Sir Francis Bathurst, 6
Thompson, Clive Wentworth, 12
Turner, Charles Thomas Biass, 6
Wade, Sir Robert Blakeway, 12
Wark, Blair Anderson, 12
White, Charles, 6
BAULKHAM HILLS
Suttor, William Henry (1805-1877), 6
BAW BAW
Fizelle, Reginald Cecil Grahame, 8

BEECROFT
  Catts, Dorothy Marguerite, 7
BELLEVUE HILL
  Fairfax, John Hubert Fraser, 8
BEN BULLEN
  Blackman, Meredith George, 7
BERRIMA
  Rosenthal, Sir Charles, 11
BINGARA
  Scott, William John Rendell, 11
BLUES POINT
  Mackaness, George, 10
  Webb, Chris, 12
BOMBALA
  Kerry, Charles Henry, 9
  Whyte, William Farmer, 12
BONDI
  Curlewis, Herbert Raine, 12
BONG BONG
  Chapman, Sir Austin, 7
BOOROWA
  Ashton, Frederick, 7
  Quinn, John, 11
BORO
  Gardiner, Francis, 4
BOTANY
  Corbett, Claude Gordon, 8
  Dixson, Emma Elizabeth, 8
  McHale, James Francis, 10
  Nelson, Harold George, 10
BOTOBOLAR
  Hickey, Simon, 9
BOURKE
  Foott, Cecil Henry, 8
  Saunders, Ambrose George Thomas, 11
BOWNING
  March, Frederick Hamilton, 10
BOWRAL
  De Maistre, LeRoy Leveson Laurent
    Joseph, 8
BRAIDWOOD
  Clarke, John, 3
  Clarke, Thomas, 3
  McGuigan, Brigid, 10
  Rich, Sir George Edward, 11
  Rusconi, Francis Philip, 11
BREEZA
  Hall, Benjamin, 4
BRICKFIELD HILL
  Fisher, Thomas, 4
BROCKLESBY
  Winter, Anthony William, 12
BROKEN BAY
  Stanbury, James, 12
BROKEN HILL
  Coates, James, 8
  Holman, Mary Alice, 9
  White, Myrtle Rose, 12
BROUGHTONS CREEK
  Lamond, Hector, 9
BRUSHGROVE
  Woolnough, Walter George, 12
BULLI
  Crawford, Thomas Simpson, 8

BUNDANOON
  Milne, Edmund Osborn, 10
BUNDARRA
  Leehy, Mary Agnes, 10
BUNGONIA
  Mitchell, James, 5
  Reid, Curtis Alexander, 6
  Reid, John, 6
  Reid, Robert Dyce, 6
BUNGOWANNAH
  Taylor, Headlie Shipard, 12
BURRAWANG
  McKivat, Christopher Hobart, 10
BURWOOD
  Booth, Mary, 7
  Jones, Sir Charles Lloyd, 9
  Kaleski, Robert Lucian Stanislaus, 9
  McKeown, Keith Collingwood, 10
  Nowland, Horace Henry, 11
  Palmer, Charles Reginald, 11
  Palmer, Henry Wilfred, 11
BYRON
  Ross, Chisholm, 11
  Sinclair, Sir Colin Archibald, 11
CABRAMATTA
  Driver, Richard, 4
CALABASH
  Tout, Sir Frederick Henry, 12
CAMBEWARRA
  Shepherd, Malcolm Lindsay, 11
CAMDEN PARK
  Dwyer, James Francis, 8
  Macarthur-Onslow, Francis Arthur, 10
  Macarthur-Onslow, George Macleay, 10
  Macarthur-Onslow, James William, 10
  Macarthur Onslow, Rosa Sibella, 10
CAMPBELLTOWN
  Leary, Joseph, 5
  Macdonald, Alexander Cameron, 5
  Payten, Thomas, 11
  Wilson, William Hardy, 12
CAMPERDOWN
  Bedford, George Randolph, 7
  Cotton, Frank Stanley, 8
  Lucas, John, 5
  Paul, Sir Charles Norman, 11
CANOWINDRA
  Field, Ernest, 8
CAPTAINS FLAT
  Weber, Ivy Lavinia, 12
CARCOAR
  Brady, Edwin James, 7
  Waddy, Percival Stacy, 12
CASINO
  Lumsdaine, John Sinclair, 10
CASTLE HILL
  Purser, Cecil, 11
CASTLEREAGH
  Shakespeare, Thomas Mitchell, 11
CHATSWOOD
  Peden, Margaret Elizabeth Maynard, 11
CHIPPENDALE
  Manning, Sir William Patrick, 10
  Naylor, Rupert Theodore, 10

Weatherburn, Charles Ernest, 12
CHURCH HILL
Spruson, Wilfred Joseph, 12
CLARENCE TOWN
Hogue, James Alexander, 9
COLYTON
Smith, Sydney (1856-1934), 11
CONCORD
McCulloch, Allan Riverstone, 10
CONDOBOLIN
Shakespeare, Arthur Thomas, 11
COOGEE
Stanley, George Arthur Vickers, 12
COOLAMATONG
Lynch, Thomas, 10
COOMA
Corey, Ernest Albert, 8
Fowler, Elizabeth Lilian Maud, 8
COONAMBLE
Tyrrell, Thomas James, 12
COOTAMUNDRA
Primrose, Hubert Leslie, 11
COPELAND
Muscio, Florence Mildred, 10
CORAKI
Flynn, Theodore Thomson, 8
CROOKWELL
Howard, Arthur Clifford, 9
Oakes, George Spencer, 11
CROYDON
Carne, Walter Mervyn, 7
Du Faur, Emmeline Freda, 8
Imlay, Norman George, 9
King, Olive May, 9
McPhillamy, Verania, 10
CURRAMBENE CREEK
Storey, John, 12
CURRAWANG
Jones, John Alexander Stammers, 9
Rickard, Sir Arthur, 11
DARLING POINT
Hordern, Anthony, 9
Hordern, Sir Samuel, 9
Hughes, Geoffrey Forrest, 9
DARLINGHURST
Ardill, George Edward, 7
Cohen, Sir Samuel Sydney, 8
Dalley-Scarlett, Robert, 8
De Lissa, Lillian Daphne, 8
Healy, Cecil Patrick, 9
Manning, Sir Henry Edward, 10
Neville, Dalton Thomas Walker, 11
Phillips, Orwell, 11
Quinn, Patrick Edward, 11
Russell, John Peter, 11
Simpson, Edward Percy, 11
Wellish, Edward Montague, 12
Windeyer, Richard, 12
Windeyer, William Archibald, 12
DARLINGTON
Challinor, Richard Westman, 7
Hawken, Roger William Hercules, 9
Moran, Herbert Michael, 10
Tyrrell, James Robert, 12

DARLINGTON POINT
Ferguson, William, 8
DEEPWATER
Mathews, Hamilton Bartlett, 10
DENHAM COURT
Woodd, Henry Alexander, 12
DENILIQUIN
Osborne, John Percy, 11
Tweddle, Isabel May, 12
DENMAN
Kibble, Nita Bernice, 9
DOUBLE BAY
Innes, Reginald Heath Long, 9
Jackson, Clements Frederick Vivian, 9
Littlejohn, Emma Linda Palmer, 10
Pearce, Henry Robert, 11
Pearce, Sidney Charles, 11
DUBBO
Bamford, Frederick William, 7
Burfitt, Walter Charles Fitzmaurice, 7
Leigh, Kathleen Mary Josephine, 10
Lihou, James Victor, 10
Lower, Leonard Waldemere, 10
Spears, Robert Adam, 12
DULWICH HILL
McKellar, John Alexander Ross, 10
DUNGOG
Burnage, Granville John, 7
Kenniff, Patrick, 9
Minns, Benjamin Edwin, 10
DURAL
Hunt, Alfred Edgar, 9
Hunt, John Charles, 9
DYRAABA
Sorenson, Edward Sylvester, 12
EAGLETON
Stuart, John Alexander Salmon, 12
ECCLESTON
Gillies, William Neil, 9
EDGECLIFF
Lassetter, Henry Beauchamp, 5
ELLALONG
Holden, Frances Gillam, 9
ENFIELD
Howell, George Julian, 9
Smith, Norman Leslie, 11
ENMORE
Bancks, James Charles, 7
Bryant, Charles David Jones, 7
ERSKINEVILLE
Stevens, Arthur Borlase, 12
FAIRY MEADOW
Lysaght, Andrew Augustus, 10
Miller, Sir Denison Samuel King, 10
FIVE DOCK
Howell-Price, John, 9
Tritton, Harold Percy Croydon, 12
Wilkinson, Audrey Harold, 12
FORBES
Aspinall, Jessie Strahorn, 7
Denison, Sir Hugh Robert, 8
Pratt, Ambrose Goddard Hesketh, 11
Webster, William Maule (McDowell), 12

FOUR-MILE CREEK
 Brown, John, 7
FROGMORE
 Willcock, John Collings, 12
GINNINDERRA
 Holland, Henry Edmund, 9
GLADESVILLE
 Herring, Sydney Charles Edgar, 9
GLEBE
 Barton, Sir Edmund, 7
 Breillat, Robert Graham, 3
 Halligan, Gerald Harnett, 9
 Halloran, Henry Ferdinand, 9
 Hurley, James Francis, 9
 Knox, Sir Errol Galbraith, 9
 Miller, David, 10
 Mills, Arthur James, 10
 O'Connor, Richard Edward, 11
 Swain, Edward Harold Fulcher, 12
 Taubman, Henry George, 12
 Want, John Henry, 12
GLEBE POINT
 Denham, Howard Kynaston, 8
GLEN INNES
 Kay, William Elphinstone, 9
 Matthews, Susan May, 10
GLENDONBROOK
 Scott, Rose, 11
GOCUP
 Perkins, John Arthur, 11
GOODOOGA
 Eather, Richmond Cornwallis, 8
GORDON
 Fitzsimons, Herbert Paton, 8
GOSFORD
 Ranclaud, Charles Mark, 11
GOULBURN
 Betts, Selwyn Frederic, 7
 Chisholm, Dame Alice Isabel, 7
 Collins, Charles, 3
 Emanuel, Isadore Samuel, 8
 Hoad, Sir John Charles, 9
 Long, Sydney, 10
 Rutledge, Thomas Lloyd Forster, 11
 Somerville, George Cattell, 12
 Wesché, Phoebe Ellen, 12
GRABBEN GULLEN
 Durack, Michael Patrick, 8
GRAFTON
 Cohen, Fanny, 8
 Cohen, John Jacob, 8
 Henry, Henry Goya, 9
 Page, Sir Earle Christmas Grafton, 11
 Page, Harold Hillis, 11
 Page, Rodger Clarence George, 11
 Searle, Henry Ernest, 6
 Smith, Sir Grafton Elliot, 11
GRANVILLE
 Hall, Arthur Charles, 9
 Woodcock, Lucy Godiva, 12
GREENWICH
 Trickett, Edward, 6
GRENFELL
 Lawson, Henry, 10

McCabe, Stanley Joseph, 10
GULGONG
 Spaull, George Thomas, 12
GUNBAR
 Jackson, John William Alexander, 9
GUNDAGAI
 MacPherson, Margaret, 10
GUNDAROO
 Dunn, William Fraser, 8
GUNNEDAH
 Rogers, Sir Percival Halse, 11
GUNNING
 Board, Ruby Willmet, 7
GUNTAWANG
 Rouse, Richard (1842-1903), 6
HARGRAVES
 Alanson, Alfred Godwin, 7
HARTLEY
 O'Reilly, Alfonso Bernard, 11
 Reid, Jane Sinclair, 11
HAWKESBURY RIVER
 Day, George, 4
 Hall, Thomas Simpson, 4
HAYDONTON
 Abbott, John Henry (Macartney), 7
HILL END
 Bath, Thomas Henry, 7
 Garvan, Sir John Joseph, 8
 Parry, Annie Bertha, 11
HOMEBUSH
 Kirkcaldie, Rosa Angela, 9
HUNTERS HILL
 Edgell, Robert Gordon, 8
INVERELL
 Duncan, Walter John Clare, 8
 Stevens, Bertram William Mathyson
  Francis, 12
JAMBEROO
 Cullen, Sir William Portus, 8
 Hyam, Solomon Herbert, 4
 Marks, Theodore John, 10
 Marks, Walter Moffitt, 10
 Morris, Robert Newton, 5
JUNEE
 Marks, Douglas Gray, 10
KELSO
 Lee, Ida Louisa, 10
KEMPS CREEK
 Bayly, Nicholas Paget, 3
KEMPSEY
 Gabriel, Charles Louis, 8
 Lovell, Henry Tasman, 10
KIAMA
 Carruthers, Sir Joseph Hector McNeil, 7
 Christmas, Harold Percival, 7
 Fuller, Colin Dunmore, 8
 Fuller, Sir George Warburton, 8
 Howell-Price, Frederick Phillimore, 9
 Howell-Price, Owen Glendower, 9
 Meares, Charles Edward Devenish, 10
KOGARAH
 Brown, David Michael, 7
KURRAJONG
 Skuthorp(e), Lancelot Albert, 11

LAMBTON
  Ainsworth, George Frederick, 7
  Larkin, Edward Rennix, 9
LEICHHARDT
  Benstead, Thomas Arthur, 7
  Bowles, William Leslie, 7
  Doyle, Stuart Frank, 8
  Leeson, Ida Emily, 10
LEWISHAM
  Drummond, David Henry, 8
LIMESTONE PLAINS
  MacPherson, John Alexander, 5
LINDFIELD
  Bryce, Lucy Meredith, 7
LIONSVILLE
  Bertie, Charles Henry, 7
LISMORE
  Carlton, James Andrew, 7
LITHGOW
  Donald, William Henry, 8
  Truscott, William John, 12
LIVERPOOL
  Coles, Sir Jenkin, 8
  Colls, Thomas, 3
  Cooper, Walter Hampson, 3
  Forbes, Frederick Augustus, 4
  Kennedy, Thomas, 9
LOCHINVAR
  Madsen, Sir John Percival Vaissing, 10
LUE
  Fairfax, Ruth Beatrice, 8
MACDONALDTOWN
  Tye, Cyrus Willmot Oberon, 12
MACKSVILLE
  Wallace, Arthur Cooper, 12
MAITLAND
  Bartlett, Charles Henry Falkner Hope,
    7
  Brown, Alexander, 7
  Campbell, Walter Scott, 7
  Colquhoun, Percy Brereton, 8
  Darcy, James Leslie, 8
  Dwyer, Joseph Wilfrid, 8
  Easterbrook, Claude Cadman, 8
  Edmunds, Walter, 8
  Enright, Walter John, 8
  Ewing, Robert, 8
  Fletcher, Lionel Bale, 8
  Grahame, William Calman, 9
  Hinder, Eleanor Mary, 9
  Lee, George Leonard, 10
  Macartney, Charles George, 10
  Marks, Ernest Samuel, 10
  Marks, Percy Joseph, 10
  Mein, Charles Stuart, 5
  Pilcher, Charles Edward, 11
  Russell, Henry Chamberlain, 6
  Viner, William Samuel, 12
  Waterhouse, Walter Lawry, 12
  White, Henry Luke, 12
  Wolfe, Herbert Austin, 12
  Wray, Leonora, 12
MANGOPLAH
  Pring, Robert Darlow, 11

MANLY
  Bardolph, Douglas Henry, 7
  Bardolph, Kenneth Edward Joseph, 7
  Lister, William Lister, 10
MANUS CREEK
  Bailey, John, 7
MARENGO
  Buttenshaw, Ernest Albert, 7
MARRICKVILLE
  Beardsmore, Robert Henry, 7
  Follett, Frank William, 8
  Kellermann, Annette Marie Sarah, 9
  Osborne, George Davenport, 11
MARSHALLMOUNT
  Osborne, Pat Hill, 5
MENAROO
  Horn, William Austin, 9
MEREWETHER
  Somerville, William, 12
MERRILLA
  Poidevin, Leslie Oswald Sheridan, 11
MERRIWA
  O'Brien, Catherine Cecily, 11
MERRYGOEN
  Mathews, Gregory Macalister, 10
MICHELAGO
  Ryrie, Sir Granville De Laune, 11
MILLERS FOREST
  Gillies, James Hynds, 9
MILLERS POINT
  Lamb, John de Villiers, 5
  Playfair, Thomas Alfred (Creer) John,
    11
MILLTHORPE
  Wilkinson, Arthur George, 12
MILTON
  Cambage, Richard Hind, 7
MINCHINBURY
  Gilbert, David John, 9
MINMI
  Estell, John, 8
  Wilson, Gordon Campbell, 12
MITTAGONG
  Armfield, Lillian May, 7
  Kaeppel, Carl Henry, 9
MOAMA
  Bruton, Dorothy Josephine, 7
  Fitzpatrick, John Charles Lucas, 8
  Patten, John Thomas, 11
  Rogers, James, 11
MOLONGLO PLAINS
  Wills, Thomas Wentworth Spencer, 6
MONGARLOWE
  Loughlin, Peter Ffrench, 10
MORPETH
  Kelly, John Edward, 5
  Portus, Garnet Vere, 11
MORUYA
  Brennan, Sarah Octavia, 7
MOSMAN
  Curlewis, Ethel Jean Sophia, 12
  Taylor, Sir Patrick Gordon, 12
MOSSMANS BAY
  Mosman, Hugh, 5

MOUNT WILSON
Howell-Price, Philip Llewellyn, 9
MUDGEE
Boswell, William Walter, 7
Bourne, Una Mabel, 7
Davidson, Sir Colin George Watt, 8
Mills, Arthur Edward, 10
Stacy, Bertie Vandeleur, 12
Stacy, Valentine Osborne, 12
Taylor, Adolphus George, 6
Willis, William Nicholas, 12
MULGOA
Callaghan, James Joseph, 7
Cox, Edward King, 3
Cox, George Henry, 3
Cox, James Charles, 3
MULGRAVE
Cunneen, James Augustine, 3
MULWALA
Palmer, George Eugene, 5
MURRUMBURRAH
Campbell, Alfred Walter, 7
Shaw, Edna Mary Anna Jane, 11
MUSWELLBROOK
Abbott, Sir Joseph Palmer, 3
Abbott, William Edward, 7
Cole, Percival Richard, 8
Ferguson, Sir David Gilbert, 8
MUTTONS FALLS
Durack, Ernest, 8
NARELLAN
Mathews, Robert Hamilton, 5
Sharman, James, 11
Tyson, James, 6
NARRABRI
Picton, Edward Benjamin, 11
Riddle, Sir Ernest Cooper, 11
NARRAMBLA
Paterson, Andrew Barton, 11
NARRANDERA
Beatty, Raymond Wesley, 7
NEUTRAL BAY
Bennett, Agnes Elizabeth Lloyd, 7
Smith, Grace Cossington, 11
Spain, Alfred, 12
Spain, Staunton William, 12
NEWCASTLE
Bingle, Walter David, 7
Brunker, James Nixon, 3
Goddard, Ernest James, 9
Gow, Robert Milne, 9
Henderson, George Cockburn, 9
Hickson, Robert Newburgh, 9
Ireland, Horace, 9
Longworth, Thomas, 10
Maxted, Edward, 10
Paton, John, 11
Pike, James Edward, 11
Robson, William, 11
Stewart, Sir Frederick Harold, 12
Stokes, Edward Sutherland, 12
Walters, Henry Latimer, 12
Winn, Roy Coupland, 12

NEWTOWN
Clark, Sir Reginald Marcus, 8
Dalyell, Elsie Jean, 8
Nangle, James, 10
Nock, Thomas, 11
NORTH SYDNEY
Charlton, Andrew Murray, 7
Childe, Vere Gordon, 7
Gregory, Jack Morrison, 9
NUMBA
O'Conor, Broughton Barnabas, 11
NUNDLE
Bourke, John Philip, 7
NYMAGEE
Cotton, Leo Arthur, 8
O'CONNELL PLAINS
Marsden, Samuel Edward, 5
OLDBURY
Atkinson, Caroline Louisa Waring, 3
Humphery, Frederick Thomas, 4
ORANGE
Edye, Sir Benjamin Thomas, 8
Gardiner, Albert, 8
Hamilton, John, 9
Jardine, Francis Lascelles, 4
PADDINGTON
Bannerman, Alexander Chalmers, 3
Campbell, Gerald Ross, 7
Gale, Walter Frederick, 8
Kenny, Thomas James Bede, 9
Kippax, Alan Falconer, 9
Lovely, Louise Nellie, 10
McCarthy, Dame Emma Maud, 10
Maughan, Sir David, 10
Parkhill, Sir Robert Archdale, 11
Penfold, William Clark, 11
Vonwiller, Oscar Ulrich, 12
Wildman, Alexina Maude, 12
PARKES
McGirr, John Joseph Gregory, 10
PARRAMATTA
Abbott, Joseph, 3
Ardill, George Edward, 7
Bowden, Eric Kendall, 7
Byrnes, William, 3
Cawood, Dorothy Gwendolen, 7
Clarke, George, 3
Fitzpatrick, Michael, 4
Hamilton, Hugh Montgomerie, 9
Hannell, James, 4
Hart, William Ewart, 9
Hill, George, 4
Hobson, Edmund Charles, 1
Hobson, Edward William, 1
Hume, Hamilton, 1
Kelly, James, 2
King, Arthur Septimus, 5
King, Copland, 9
King, John (1820-1895), 5
King, Philip Gidley, 5
King, William Essington, 5
Lee, Charles Alfred, 10
Macarthur, George Fairfowl, 5
Macarthur, James, 2

Macarthur, Sir William, 5
McCann, Peter, 10
McLaren, Sir John Gilbert, 10
Merriman, James, 5
Moore, William, 5
Oakes, George, 5
Rutledge, William Woolls, 11
Simpson, Sir George Bowen, 6
Stedman, James, 12
Tait, George, 12
Taylor, Hugh, 6
Turner, John William, 12
Watsford, John, 6
Youl, Sir James Arndell, 6
PASTORAL STATIONS
Carne, Joseph Edmund, 7
Cooper, Sir Pope Alexander, 8
Crommelin, Minard Fannie, 8
Dangar, Albert Augustus, 4
Dangar, Francis Richard, 4
De Beuzeville, Wilfred Alexander Watt, 8
Donnelly, John Francis, 8
Harrison, Henry Colden Antill, 4
Knight, Albert, 9
Lawson, Louisa, 10
Lee, George, 5
Mathias, Louis John, 10
Munro, Hugh Robert, 10
Newland, Victor Marra, 11
Officer, Edward Cairns, 11
Parry-Okeden, William Edward, 11
Weatherly, Lionel James, 12
Weaver, Reginald Walter Darcy, 12
Webb, Jessie Stobo Watson, 12
White, James Cobb, 12
PATERSON RIVER
Arnold, Richard Aldous, 7
PATRICKS PLAINS
Dutton, Charles Boydell, 4
PEEL
Handcock, Peter Joseph, 9
Suttor, William Henry (1834-1905), 6
PENNANT HILLS
Cox, Charles Frederick, 8
PENRITH
Bent, Sir Thomas, 3
Kater, Henry Edward, 5
Rutledge, Sir Arthur, 11
Ryan, James Tobias, 6
Stuart, Francis, 12
PETERSHAM
Anderson, Phyllis Margery, 7
Anthon, Daniel Herbert, 7
Chambers, Charles Haddon Spurgeon, 7
Duesbury, Frank Wentworth, 8
Hoskins, Sir Cecil Harold, 9
Kay, Alick Dudley, 9
Lenehan, Robert William, 10
Marr, Sir Charles William Clanan, 10
Morrison, Sibyl Enid Vera Munro, 10
Pratt, Frederick Vicary, 11
Tilly, William Henry, 12
Wise, Bernhard Ringrose, 12

PICTON
Antill, John Macquarie, 7
Cottrell, Ida Dorothy Ottley, 8
Haynes, Richard Septimus, 9
PITT TOWN
Ewing, Sir Thomas Thomson, 8
Terry, Samuel Henry, 6
POINT PIPER
Mackellar, Isobel Marion Dorothea, 10
PORT MACQUARIE
Becke, George Lewis, 7
Cohen, Henry Emanuel, 3
Tozer, Sir Horace, 12
PORT STEPHENS
Dangar, Frederick Holkham, 4
Dangar, Henry Cary, 4
POTTS POINT
Martin, Florence, 10
PROSPECT
Miller, Gustave Thomas Carlisle, 10
PURFLEET
Muscio, Bernard, 10
PYRMONT
Lawson, James Robert, 10
Murphy, George Francis, 10
Newling, Cecil Bede, 11
QUEANBEYAN
Schardt, Susan Katherina, 11
RAGLAN
Godfrey, Sidney George, 9
Kellett, Adelaide Maud, 9
RANDWICK
Peden, Sir John Beverley, 11
RAVENSWORTH
White, Francis, 6
RAYMOND TERRACE
Windeyer, John Cadell, 12
REDFERN
Cleary, William James, 8
Climpson, Joseph, 8
Crampton, Walter Russell, 8
Frost, Frederick Charlesworth, 8
Gascoigne, Stephen Harold, 8
Herrod, Ernest Edward, 9
Knibbs, Sir George Handley, 9
Lamaro, Joseph, 9
Law, Sydney James, 10
Owen, Sir Langer Meade Loftus, 11
Spragg, Alonzo Stephen, 12
Stace, Arthur Malcolm, 12
Stevens, Sir Bertram Sydney Barnsdale, 12
Williams, Mary Boyd Burfitt, 12
REEDY CREEK
Webster, Ellen, 12
RICHMOND
Bell, James Thomas Marsh, 7
Bowman, Alexander, 3
Bowman, George Pearce, 3
Bowman, Robert, 3
Faithfull, William Pitt, 4
Griffiths, John, 1
Howell-Price, Richmond Gordon, 9
Pitt, George Matcham, 5

Town, Andrew, 6
Walker, Allan Seymour, 12
RIVERINA
Huie, Alexander Gordon, 9
ROCK VIEW
Chaffey, Frank Augustus, 7
ROCKLEY
Boyce, Francis Stewart, 7
ROSE BAY
Dalley, John Bede, 8
Dumaresq, John Saumarez, 8
ROUCHEL BROOK
Cameron, Donald, 7
RUSHCUTTERS BAY
Burrell, Henry James, 7
RYDE
Farnell, Frank, 8
Gye, Harold Frederick Neville, 9
Kater, Sir Norman William, 9
Parkes, Varney, 11
RYLSTONE
D'Arcy, Dame Constance Elizabeth, 8
Moulds, Constance, 10
ST LEONARDS
Carter, Herbert Gordon, 7
Farnell, James Squire, 4
Massie, Robert John Allwright, 10
Matthews, Harley, 10
Pidgeon, Elsie Clare, 11
Stead, David George, 12
Wilson, James Lockie, 12
SAUMAREZ
White, Harold Fletcher, 12
SCONE
Baynton, Barbara Jane, 7
Munro, Edward Joy, 10
SHELLHARBOUR
Fitzgerald, John Daniel, 8
SINGLETON
Haynes, John, 4
Levien, Robert Henry, 10
Longworth, William (1892-1969), 10
Moore, Donald Ticehurst, 10
Wade, Sir Charles Gregory, 12
Wade, Leslie Augustus Burton, 12
SODWALLS
McLaughlin, Clara Jane, 10
SOFALA
Cummins, John, 8
Pryke, Frank, 11
SOUTH GUNDURIMBA
Bugden, Patrick Joseph, 7
SOUTH KINGSTON
Stephen, Sir Colin Campbell, 12
SOUTH KURRAJONG
Love, Nigel Borland, 10
SPIT ISLAND
Clark, James, 8
STANMORE
Beeby, Doris Isabel, 7
Harrison, Eric Fairweather, 9
Pridham, John Theodore, 11
STOCKTON
Lynn, Robert John, 10

STROUD
Dun, Percy Muir, 8
McRae, Christopher John, 10
White, James, 6
White, Robert Hoddle Driberg, 6
SUMMER HILL
Poate, Sir Hugh Raymond Guy, 11
Thompson, William Bethel, 12
Thurston, Frederick Arthur, 12
SUNNY CORNER
Wheen, Arthur Wesley, 12
SURRY HILLS
Allen, Sir George Wigram, 3
Baker, Reginald Leslie, 7
Ball, Richard Thomas, 7
Coleman, Percy Edmund Creed, 8
Donohoe, William Patrick, 8
Fallon, Cyril Joseph, 8
Green, Daniel Cooper, 9
Horder, Harold Norman, 9
Iredale, Francis Adams, 9
Lea, Arthur Mills, 10
Leist, Frederick William, 10
McMaster, Sir Frederick Duncan, 10
Maitland, Sir Herbert Lethington, 10
Monk, Cyril Farnsworth, 10
Nobbs, John, 11
Proud, William James, 11
Quinn, Roderic Joseph, 11
Robson, William Elliot Veitch, 11
Smith, Sydney (1880-1972), 11
Thrower, Thomas Henry, 12
SUTTON FOREST
Badgery, Henry Septimus, 3
SWALLOW CREEK
Lambert, William Henry, 9
Sydney
Aarons, Joseph, 3
Abbott, Gertrude, 7
Abigail, Ernest Robert, 7
Agnew, Roy (Robert) Ewing, 7
Alexander, Samuel, 7
Allan, Percy, 7
Anderson, Sir Robert Murray McCheyne, 7
Aronson, Zara, 7
Baker, William Harold, 7
Barbour, Eric Pitty, 7
Barraclough, Sir Samuel Henry Egerton, 7
Barton, George Burnett, 3
Benjamin, Arthur Leslie, 7
Black, Reginald James, 7
Blacket, Wilfred, 7
Boyle, Henry Frederick, 3
Brazier, John William, 3
Brennan, Christopher John, 7
Brereton, Ernest Le Gay, 7
Brereton, John Le Gay, 7
Brice, Katie Louisa, 7
Brown, Stephen Campbell, 3
Brownlow, Richard, 3
Bruton, Mary Catherine, 7
Buchanan, Gwynneth Vaughan, 7
Burdekin, Marshall, 3

Burdekin, Sydney, 3
Campbell, John, 1
Campbell, Robert (1804-1859), 1
Cavill, Richmond Theophilus, 7
Chandler, Thomas Charles, 7
Chapman, Edward Shirley, 7
Christian, Sydney Ernest, 7
Clamp, John Burcham, 8
Coghlan, Sir Timothy Augustine, 8
Cohen, George Judah, 8
Collins, Herbert Leslie, 8
Collins, Robert Martin, 3
Coppleson, Sir Victor Marcus, 8
Cotter, Albert, 8
Cowan, Theodora Esther, 8
Coward, Harry Keith, 8
Cowlishaw, James, 3
Cowlishaw, Leslie, 8
Cowper, Charles, 3
Cowper, William Macquarie, 3
Cropper, Charles William, 8
Dalley, William Bede, 4
Dangar, Thomas Gordon Gibbons, 4
Davidson, (Charles) Mark Anthony, 8
Davies, John, 4
De Mestre, Etienne Livingstone, 4
Deniehy, Daniel Henry, 4
Dibbs, Sir George Richard, 4
Dibbs, Sir Thomas Allwright, 4
Dixson, Sir Hugh, 8
Dixson, Thomas Storie, 8
Dixson, Sir William, 8
Donovan, Thomas Joseph, 8
Dove, Frederick Allan, 8
Dowling, Edward, 8
Dowling, Vincent James, 4
Dunningham, Sir John Montgomery, 8
Durack, Sarah, 8
Dutton, William, 1
Eagar, Geoffrey, 4
Fairfax, Sir James Oswald, 8
Fanning, Edward, 4
Fidler, Isabel Margaret, 8
Fletcher, John William, 8
Flood, Edward, 4
Fowler, Robert, 4
Fraser, John Edward, 8
Freehill, Francis Bede, 4
Freeman, Ambrose William, 8
Freeman, William Addison, 8
Garran, Sir Robert Randolph, 8
Garrick, Sir James Francis, 4
Gaunson, David, 4
Glencross, Eleanor, 9
Gordon, Sir Alexander, 9
Gore, St George Ralph, 4
Gould, Sir Albert John, 9
Gray, George Wilkie, 9
Greenway, Charles Capel, 4
Gregory, Edward James, 4
Gregory, Sydney Edward, 4
Gurner, Henry Field, 4
Hammond, Mark John, 4
Harris, Samuel Henry, 9

Heane, James, 9
Heney, Thomas William, 9
Hennessy, Arthur Stephen, 9
Heydon, Charles Gilbert, 9
Heydon, Louis Francis, 9
Hill, James Richard, 4
Hill, Richard, 4
Hogue, Oliver, 9
Holdsworth, Philip Joseph, 4
Holmes, William, 9
Hordern, Samuel, 4
Horniman, Vicary, 9
Houston, William, 4
Howe, George Terry, 1
Hughes, John Francis, 9
Hughes, Sir Thomas, 9
Hurley, John, 4
Innes, Sir Joseph George Long, 4
Ironside, Adelaide Eliza, 4
Jacobs, Jacob, 9
Jeanneret, Charles Edward, 4
Jones, Nina Eva Vida, 9
Jones, Sir Philip Sydney, 4
Jones, Rees Rutland, 9
Kavanagh, Edward John, 9
Kelly, Frederick Septimus, 9
Kelly, Thomas Herbert, 9
Kelly, William Henry, 9
Kenneally, James Joseph, 9
Kieran, Bernard Bede, 9
King, Sir George Eccles Kelso, 9
Knox, Sir Adrian, 9
Knox, Edward William, 9
Lackey, Sir John, 5
Lane, Frederick Claude Vivian, 9
Lang, John, 5
Lang, John Thomas, 9
Lees, Samuel Edward, 10
Lenehan, Henry Alfred, 10
Lewis, George, 10
Long, William Alexander, 5
Lord, George William, 5
McCoy, William Taylor, 10
McDonagh, Isabella Mercia, 10
McDonagh, Paulette de Vere, 10
McDonagh, Phyllis Glory, 10
McDonald, George Roy William, 10
McElhone, John, 5
McGlinn, John Patrick, 10
McIntosh, Hugh Donald, 10
Mackellar, Sir Charles Kinnaird, 10
Mackenzie, William Kenneth Seaforth, 10
McMahon, Gregan, 10
Mann, Gother Victor Fyers, 10
Manning, Emily Matilda, 5
Manning, Frederic, 10
Matthias, Elizabeth, 10
Maxted, Sydney, 10
Melville, Ninian, 5
Mills, Stephen, 10
Milson, James (1814-1903), 2
Mitchell, David Scott, 5
Mitchell, Ernest Meyer, 10
Moore, David, 5

Morehead, Boyd Dunlop, 5
Morgan, Frederick Augustus, 5
Mullins, John Lane, 10
Murray, George Gilbert Aimé, 10
Murray, Sir John Hubert Plunkett, 10
Nichols, George Robert, 5
Nicoll, Bruce Baird, 5
Noble, Montague Alfred, 11
Norton, Albert, 5
Norton, James, 5
O'Connell, Sir Maurice Charles, 5
Oliver, Alexander, 5
Oliver, Maggie, 5
O'Reilly, Dowell Philip, 11
O'Reilly, Susannah Hennessy, 11
O'Reilly, Walter Cresswell, 11
Payten, Bayly William Renwick, 11
Pearson, Joseph, 11
Peck, John Henry, 11
Penfold, Arthur de Ramon, 11
Perry, John, 11
Perry, Stanley Llewellyn, 11
Piddington, Marion Louisa, 11
Playfair, Edmund John Bailey, 11
Power, John Joseph Wardell, 11
Preston Stanley, Millicent Fanny, 11
Rawson, Wilhelmina Frances, 11
Read, Irene Victoria, 11
Reading, Sir Claude Hill, 11
Richards, Thomas, 6
Roberts, Charles James, 6
Robertson, Constance, 11
Robinson, Frederick Walter, 11
Rofe, Thomas Ernest, 11
Rogers, Francis Edward, 11
Roseby, Thomas, 6
Ross, Robert Samuel, 11
Sargent, Charlotte, 11
Schauer, Amy, 11
Scott, Harriet, 6
Scott, Helena, 6
Shearston, John Samuel, 11
Simpson, Helen de Guerry, 11
Sly, Joseph David, 6
Sly, Richard Meares, 11
Smart, Thomas Ware, 6
Smith, John McGarvie, 11
Smith, John Thomas, 6
Smith, Robert Burdett, 6
Stephen, Edward Milner, 12
Street, Sir Philip Whistler, 12
Süssmilch, Adolph Carl von de Heyde, 12
Swadling, William Thomas, 12
Symonds, Saul, 12
Taubman, George Henry, 12
Taubman, Nathaniel James, 12
Taylor, George Augustine, 12
Thompson, Charles Victor, 12
Thompson, John Malbon, 6
Thornton, George, 6
Tompson, Charles (1807-1883), 2
Tooth, Sir Robert Lucas Lucas-, 6
Trumper, Victor Thomas, 12
Turnbull, Archibald, 12

Walder, Sir Samuel Robert, 12
Walker, Dame Eadith Campbell, 12
Ward, Elizabeth Jane, 12
Watson, James Frederick William, 12
Watt, Ernest Alexander Stuart, 12
Wearne, Walter Ernest, 12
Webb, Frederick William, 12
Weigall, Cecil Edward, 12
Weingarth, John Leopold, 12
Wheeler, John, 12
Whiddon, Frank, 12
Whiddon, Horace William, 12
Whitfeld, Hubert Edwin, 12
Wilks, William Henry, 12
Williams, Sir William Daniel Campbell, 12
Wills, Horatio Spencer Howe, 2
Wilshire, James Robert, 6
Windeyer, Margaret, 12
Wirth, George, 12
Woods, Percy William, 12
Younger, Montague Thomas Robson, 6
TABULAM
Bruxner, Sir Michael Frederick, 7
Chauvel, Sir Henry George, 7
TALBINGO
Franklin, Stella Maria(n) Sarah Miles, 8
TAMBAROORA
Dwyer, Catherine Winifred, 8
Golding, Annie Mackenzie, 9
Golding, Isabella Theresa, 9
TAMWORTH
Curtis, George Silas, 8
Hyman, Arthur Wellesley, 9
TANGORIN
Skillen, Elizabeth, 11
TARCUTTA
Watson, Archibald, 12
TAREE
Boyce, Sir Harold Leslie, 7
TENT HILL
May, Sydney Lionel, 10
TENTERDEN
Wade, Benjamin Martin, 12
TENTERFIELD
MacKinnon, Eleanor Vokes Irby, 10
Sommerlad, Ernest Christian, 12
Woodward, Oliver Holmes, 12
THORNTHWAITE
Docker, Ernest Brougham, 8
TOONGABBIE
Pye, James, 5
TUENA
Mackness, Constance, 10
TUMBARUMBA
Dooley, John Braidwood, 8
TUMUT
Ryan, Edward John Francis, 11
Scott, Allan Humphrey, 11
ULLADULLA
Kendall, Thomas Henry, 5
ULTIMO
O'Shea, Patrick Joseph Francis, 11
URALLA
Vincent, Roy Stanley, 12

URANA
  Bishop, Charles George, 7
WAGGA WAGGA
  Bennett, Alfred Joshua, 7
  Catts, James Howard, 7
  Graham, Arthur Ernest James Charles King, 9
  Hardy, Charles Downey, 9
  Oakes, Charles William, 11
  Shaw, Ebenezer, 11
  Taylor, Sir Allen Arthur, 12
  Toomey, James Morton, 12
WALLA WALLA
  Brown, Thomas, 7
WALLENDBEEN
  Mackay, James Alexander Kenneth, 10
WALLSEND
  Currey, William Matthew, 8
  Jeffries, Clarence Smith, 9
  Watkins, David, 12
WARIALDA
  Kenny, Elizabeth, 9
  Munro, Grace Emily, 10
WARREN
  Bardsley, Warren, 7
  Body, Eliel Edmund Irving, 7
  Buckley, Alexander Henry, 7
  King, James Harold, 9
WATERLOO
  Spooner, Eric Sydney, 12
  Tauchert, Arthur Michael, 12
WATSONS BAY
  Creer, Herbert Victor, 8
  Creer, Reginald Charles, 8
WATTLE FLAT
  Oxenham, Humphrey, 11
  Suttor, John Bligh (1859-1925), 6
WAVERLEY
  Cobb, Chester Francis, 8
  Graves, James Joseph, 9
  Idriess, Ion Llewellyn, 9
  Leverrier, Francis Hewitt, 10
  Moore, John Drummond Macpherson, 10
  Waterhouse, Eben Gowrie, 12
  Waterhouse, Gustavus Athol, 12
WELLINGTON
  Davies, Charles Ellis, 8
  Gunther, William James, 4
  Harrison, Launcelot, 9
WENTWORTH
  Thring, Francis William, 12
WICKHAM
  Cheeseman, William Joseph Robert, 7
  Clark, James William, 8
WILBERFORCE
  Baldwin, Charles, 3
WILLOUGHBY
  Mashman, Ernest James Theodore, 10
  Vincent, James, 12
WINDSOR
  Bourne, Joseph Orton, 3
  Bradley, William, 3
  Bridges, Frederick, 3
  Broughton, Thomas Stafford, 3

  Butler, Thomas John, 7
  Cope, William, 8
  Dick, James Adam, 8
  Egan, Daniel, 4
  Fiaschi, Piero Francis Bruno, 8
  Fitzgerald, Robert, 4
  Fleming, Joseph, 4
  Garnsey, Arthur Henry, 8
  Harpur, Charles, 1
  McPhillamy, John Smith, 5
  O'Callaghan, Thomas, 11
  Pye, Cecil Robert Arthur, 11
  Rouse, Richard (1843-1906), 6
  Scrivener, Charles Robert, 11
  Stewart, James Douglas, 12
  Tebbutt, John, 6
  Templeton, Henry Barkley, 12
  Ward, Frederick, 6
WINGHAM
  Board, Peter, 7
  Higgs, William Guy, 9
WOLLOMBI
  Smith, Stephen Henry, 11
WOLLONGONG
  Ewing, John, 8
  Ewing, Norman Kirkwood, 8
  Fidler, Mabel Maude, 8
  Garrett, Thomas William, 8
  Gregory, David William, 4
  Osborne, John, 5
  Owen, Percy Thomas, 11
  Owen, Robert Haylock, 11
WOLUMLA
  Maddock, Sarah, 10
WOMBAT
  Lazzarini, Carlo Camillo, 10
WOODHOUSELEE
  Gilmore, Dame Mary Jean, 9
WOODLANDS
  Nichols, Reginald Gordon Clement, 11
WOOLLAHRA
  Connell, Hugh John, 8
  Latimer, Hugh, 10
  Mort, Eirene, 10
  Simpson, Edward Sydney, 11
  Street, Geoffrey Austin, 12
  Williams, Harold John, 12
WOOLLOOMOOLOO
  Corbett, William Francis, 8
  Lockyer, Sir Nicholas Colston, 10
  Miles, William John, 10
  Sargent, Foster Henry Hartley, 11
  Stewart, Eleanor Towzey, 12
  Teece, Richard Clive, 12
  Whiddon, William Henry, 12
YAMBA
  Cayley, Neville William, 7
YASS
  Costello, John, 3
  Cusack, John Joseph, 8
  Hartigan, Patrick Joseph, 9
  Mackay, Donald George, 10
  Merriman, Sir Walter Thomas, 10

YASS PLAINS
  McKinnon, Thomas Firmin, 10
YOUNG
  Campbell, Eric, 7
  Creal, Rose Ann, 8
  Hickson, Ella Violet, 9
  Ness, John Thomas, 11
  Rowley, Stanley Rupert, 11
ZETLAND
  Mailey, Alfred Arthur, 10
Northern Territory
WIGHU
  Mondalmi, 10
Queensland
  Grant, Douglas, 9
ALBERT RIVER
  Cran, James, 8
ALLORA
  Connolly, Sir James Daniel, 8
AYR
  Benjamin, Louis Reginald Samuel, 7
BLACKALL
  Dash, John, 8
BOULIA
  Noble, James, 11
BOWEN
  Salisbury, Alfred George, 11
  Toll, Frederick William, 12
Brisbane
  Allan, Robert Marshall, 7
  Appel, John George, 7
  Bailey, John Frederick, 7
  Balsillie, John Graeme, 7
  Baylebridge, William, 7
  Baynes, Ernest, 7
  Baynes, George, 7
  Beal, George Lansley, 7
  Benjamin, David Samuel, 7
  Birkbeck, Gilbert Samuel Colin Latona, 7
  Booth, Doris Regina, 7
  Bourne, Eleanor Elizabeth, 7
  Bourne, George Herbert, 7
  Boyd, Edith Susan, 7
  Burke, John Edward, 7
  Byrnes, Thomas Joseph, 7
  Cameron, Sir Donald Charles, 7
  Campbell, Charles William, 7
  Campbell, John Dunmore, 7
  Carroll, John, 7
  Carter, Hubert Reginald, 7
  Chisholm, Alexander, 7
  Cocks, Nicholas John, 8
  Collins, John William Fitzclarence, 8
  Cullen, Edward Alexander Ernest, 8
  Davidson, Sir Alfred Charles, 8
  Dixon, Graham Patrick, 8
  Duhig, James Vincent, 8
  East, Hubert Fraser, 8
  Feez, Adolph Frederick Milford, 8
  Forbes, Arthur Edward, 8
  Forsyth, John Keatly, 8
  Green, William Herbert, 9
  Hall, Francis Richard, 9
  Hall, Thomas Ramsay, 9

  Heagney, Muriel Agnes, 9
  Holmes à Court, Alan Worsley, 9
  Hughes, Francis Augustus, 9
  Hughes, Fred William, 9
  Jackson, Sidney William, 9
  Jennings, Elizabeth Esther Ellen, 4
  Keatinge, Maurice Barber Bevan, 9
  King, Reginald Macdonnell, 9
  Kingsford Smith, Sir Charles Edward, 9
  Larkin, Herbert Joseph, 9
  Love, Sir Joseph Clifton, 10
  Macandie, George Lionel, 10
  Macgroarty, Neil Francis, 10
  Macleod, Thomas, 10
  Marks, Alexander Hammett, 10
  Marks, Gladys Hope, 10
  Marshall, William Henry George, 5
  Mayne, James O'Neil, 10
  Mayne, Mary Emelia, 10
  Ogg, Margaret Ann, 11
  Phillips, Herbert Peter, 11
  Piddington, William Henry Burgess, 11
  Powers, Sir Charles, 11
  Stodart, Robert Mackay, 12
  White, Cyril Tenison, 12
  Wieck, George Frederick Gardells, 12
  Wilson, Grace Margaret, 12
BROMELTON
  Praed, Rosa Caroline, 11
BUNDABERG
  Hinkler, Herbert John Louis, 9
  Moncrieff, Gladys Lillian, 10
  Palmer, Edward Vivian, 11
  Toft, John Percy Gilbert, 12
  Wirth, May Emmeline, 12
CABOOLTURE
  Case, James Thomas, 7
  Currie, Patrick, 8
  Payne, Sir William Labatte Ryall, 11
CHARTERS TOWERS
  Douglas, Roger, 8
  Heron, Alexander Robert, 9
  Mills, Charles, 10
  Quinn, Hugh, 11
  Stapleton, Claude Augustine, 12
  Timms, Edward Vivian, 12
COALFALLS
  Blair, Sir James William, 7
CONDAMINE
  Lukin, Lionel Oscar, 10
COOKTOWN
  Musgrave, Anthony, 10
COPPERFIELD
  Mackay, George Hugh Alexander, 10
CUNGUMBOGAN
  Lawton, Thomas, 10
DALBY
  Pocock, Mary Anne, 11
  Wirth, Mary Elizabeth Victoria, 12
DEEBING CREEK
  Richards, Ranold, 11
DRAYTON
  Davis, Arthur Hoey, 8
  Purcell, James, 11

EAGLE FARM
Cross, Zora Bernice May, 8
EMERALD
Sterne, Elizabeth Anne Valentine, 12
ENOGGERA
Paten, Eunice Muriel Harriett Hunt, 11
FORTITUDE VALLEY
Shang, Caleb James, 11
Somerset, Henry St John, 12
GATTON
Carroll, Edward John, 7
Huntingfield, William Charles Arcedeckne, 9
GAYNDAH
Jones, Alfred James, 9
HERBERTON
Blakey, Othman Frank, 7
IPSWICH
Archibald, Robert John, 7
Ashton, James, 7
Bell, Joshua Thomas, 7
Brand, Charles Henry, 7
Burdett, Basil, 7
Cribb, Henry Smart, 8
Cribb, James Clarke, 8
Edwards, Lewis David, 8
Gall, William, 8
Gibson, Elizabeth Dickson, 8
Gibson, John Lockhart, 8
Gill, James Howard, 4
Hancock, Josias Henry, 9
Hargreaves, William Arthur, 9
McGill, Alec Douglas, 10
McVicars, John, 10
O'Sullivan, Thomas, 11
Sandes, Francis Percival, 11
Thorn, George Henry, 6
Welsby, Thomas, 12
Williams, Harold Parkyn, 12
IRVINEBANK
Dalziel, Henry, 8
KELVIN GROVE
Broadbent, Joseph Edward, 7
Lilley, Charles Mitford, 10
Lilley, Kathleen Mitford, 10
KILCOY
Butler, Arthur Graham, 7
KILLARNEY
Howe, John Robert, 9
LAIDLEY
Cahill, Patrick, 7
LOGAN RIVER
Wilson, Lachlan Chisholm, 12
LUTWYCHE
Macrossan, Hugh Denis, 10
MACKAY
Coyne, David Emmet, 8
Gorman, John Thomas, 9
Hynes, Maurice Patrick, 9
Zahel, Ethel May Eliza, 12
MARY RIVER
Kirwan, Michael Joseph, 9
MARYBOROUGH
Brennan, Frank Tennison, 7

Christie, Robert, 7
Edkins, Edward Rowland Huey, 8
Harricks, Dudley Francis John, 9
Heath, Albert Edward, 9
McDowall, Valentine, 10
Stephensen, Percy Reginald, 12
MILTON
Moore, William, 10
MORINISH
McMaster, Sir Fergus, 10
MOUNT PERRY
Keys, Constance Mabel, 9
NUNDAH
Moroney, Timothy, 10
OXLEY
Wright, Colin William, 12
OXLEY CREEK
Fowles, Edwin Wesley Howard, 8
PASTORAL STATIONS
Bell, Bertram Charles, 7
Bell, Ernest Thomas, 7
Blacklock, Walter, 7
Collins, William, 3
Cran, Robert (1856–1940), 8
Cunningham, Arthur Henry Wickham, 8
Dallas, Roderic Stanley, 8
Edkins, Boyd Robertson Huey, 8
Farber, Henry Christian, 8
Hobler, George Alexander, 9
Hunt, Atlee Arthur, 9
Imlay, Alexander Peter, 9
Macartney, Henry Dundas Keith, 10
Morgan, Sir Arthur, 10
Towner, Edgar Thomas, 12
Uhr, Wentworth D'Arcy, 6
Vennard, Alexander Vindex, 12
Wheeler, Annie Margaret, 12
Wienholt, Arnold, 12
PETRIE
Brier, Percy, 7
PIMPAMA
Lahey, Frances Vida, 9
Lahey, Romeo Watkins, 9
PITTSWORTH
Ziesemer, Friedrich Wilhelm Ernst, 12
Ziesemer, Theodor Martin Peter, 12
RAVENSWOOD
McKelvey, Sir John Lawrance, 10
REDBANK PLAINS
Carroll, Daniel Joseph, 7
REDLAND BAY
Newton, Frank Graham, 11
ROCKHAMPTON
Dawson, Andrew, 8
Dibdin, Edward John, 8
Feez, Arthur Herman Henry Milford, 8
Fisher, Mary Lucy, 8
Larcombe, James, 9
Powell, Lange Leopold, 11
Stopford, James, 12
ROCKLEA
McDonald, Sydney Fancourt, 10
ST GEORGE
Ferry, Thomas Arthur, 8

ST LAWRENCE
McCormack, William, 10
SANDGATE
Bradfield, John Job Crew, 7
Locke, Helena Sumner, 10
Sorensen, Christense, 12
Townsend, George Wilfred Lambert, 12
SPRING HILL
Jolly, William Alfred, 9
Pethebridge, Sir Samuel Augustus, 11
SPRINGSIDE
Postle, Arthur Benjamin, 11
TEXAS
McDougall, Charles Edward, 10
TIARO
Glasgow, Sir Thomas William, 9
TINANA
Bulcock, Emily Hemans, 7
TOOWONG
Knowles, Sir George Shaw, 9
TOOWOOMBA
Annand, Frederick William Gadsby, 7
Annand, James Douglas, 7
Bailey, Margaret Ann Montgomery, 7
Dunn, Andrew (1880-1956), 8
Dunn, William Herbert Alan, 8
Griffiths, Alfred Atherton, 9
Griffiths, George Herbert, 9
Groom, Henry Littleton, 9
Groom, Sir Littleton Ernest, 9
Hall, Elsie Maude Stanley, 9
Hilder, Jesse Jewhurst, 9
Imlay, Ellen Jeanie, 9
Leahy, Michael James, 10
McCawley, Thomas William, 10
Moran, Charles John, 10
Robertson, James Campbell, 11
Sachse, Arthur Otto, 11
Schwarz, Walter Leslie, 11
Stephens, Alfred George, 12
TOWNSVILLE
McSharry, Terence Patrick, 10
WARWICK
Chauvel, Charles Edward, 7
Fletcher, James Lionel, 8
Foster, William James, 8
Oxenham, Justinian, 11
Phillips, Owen Forbes, 11
Thompson, Duncan Fulton, 12
WINTON
Noble, Angelina, 11
WOODFORD
Gilbert, Edward, 9
South Australia
Cunningham, James, 8
Hamilton, Frank, 9
Keynes, Richard Robinson, 9
ABERDEEN
Gerard, Alfred Edward, 8
Adelaide
Bagot, Walter Hervey, 7
Baker, Sir Richard Chaffey, 7
Barwell, Sir Henry Newman, 7
Batchelor, Egerton Lee, 7

Belt, Francis Walter, 7
Benjamin, Sophia, 7
Benny, Susan Grace, 7
Birrell, Frederick William, 7
Boas, Isaac Herbert, 7
Bonython, Sir John Lavington, 7
Bottrill, David Hughes, 7
Bowen, Esther Gwendolyn, 7
Bragg, Sir William Lawrence, 7
Bray, Sir John Cox, 3
Butler, Charles Philip, 7
Cawthorne, Charles Witto-Witto, 7
Chanter, John Moore, 7
Chapple, Phoebe, 7
Claxton, Norman, 8
Cobbett, William Pitt, 8
Cooke, William Ernest, 8
Cotton, Francis, 8
Crowder, Frederick Thomas, 8
Darling, Harold Gordon, 8
Davidson, Ethel Sarah, 8
Dawson, Peter Smith, 8
De Mole, Lancelot Eldin, 8
Dean, Edwin Theyer, 8
Denny, William Joseph, 8
Denton, James Samuel, 8
Doolette, Dorham Longford, 8
Downer, Sir John William, 8
Edwards, Albert Augustine, 8
Fiveash, Rosa Catherine, 8
Gepp, Sir Herbert William, 8
Giffen, George, 4
Giles, Clement, 9
Gooch, Walter, 9
Gramp, Gustav, 4
Hawker, James Clarence, 9
Hay, Clifford Henderson, 9
Hill, Clement, 9
Hill, Lionel Laughton, 9
Holden, Leslie Hubert, 9
Holmes, Marion Phoebe, 9
Howell, Cedric Ernest, 9
Hudd, Sir Herbert Sydney, 9
Inwood, Reginald Roy, 9
Jacobs, Samuel Joshua, 9
Johnson, Joseph Colin Francis, 9
Kingston, Charles Cameron, 9
McCallum, Alexander, 10
Macgeorge, Norman, 10
Mayo, George Elton, 10
Mayo, Helen Mary, 10
Mead, Gertrude Ella, 10
Moriarty, Daniel, 10
Morice, Louise, 10
Nicholls, Elizabeth Webb, 11
Northmore, Sir John Alfred, 11
Parsons, Sir Herbert Angas, 11
Pavy, Emily Dorothea, 11
Phillipps, Sir (William) Herbert, 11
Prendergast, George Michael, 11
Rene, Roy, 11
Richardson, Arnold Edwin Victor, 11
Rischbieth, Bessie Mabel, 11
Rogers, Richard Sanders, 11

Rounsevell, William Benjamin, 11
Sharp, Granville Gilbert, 11
Smith, Francis Villeneuve, 11
Smith, Sir Keith Macpherson, 11
Smith, Sir Ross Macpherson, 11
Solomon, Vaiben Louis, 12
Standley, Ida, 12
Stralia, Elsa, 12
Taylor, Harry Samuel, 12
Tenison Woods, Mary Cecil, 12
Torode, Walter Charles, 12
Trenerry, Horace Hurtle, 12
Vaughan, Crawford, 12
Venn, Henry Whittall, 12
Von Doussa, Heinrich Albert Alfred, 12
Waite, William Charles Nightingale, 12
Watson, Phebe Naomi, 12
Whitington, Frederick Taylor, 12
Willshire, William Henry, 12
Wilson, Sir Reginald Victor, 12
Wreford, Sir Ernest Henry, 12
Wren, Charles William, 12
ALBERTON
Buck, Robert Henry, 7
ANGASTON
Hague, William, 9
Johnson, Edward Angas, 9
Nesbit, (Edward) Paris(s), 11
ARDROSSAN
Gordon, Sir Thomas Stewart, 9
ATHELSTONE
Kidman, Sir Sidney, 9
AUBURN
Dennis, Clarence Michael James, 8
Jones, Ernest, 9
BALHANNAH
Grasby, William Catton, 9
BEAUMONT
Cleland, Edward Erskine, 8
BLACK ROCK
Jones, Hooper Josse Brewster, 9
BLYTH
Young, Sir Frederick William, 12
BOWDEN
Matters, Muriel Lilah, 10
Ward, Frederick Furner, 12
BRIDGEWATER
Morris, Albert, 10
BRIGHTON
Lewis, John, 10
Prior, Samuel Henry, 11
BROMPTON
Puddy, Maude Mary, 11
BURNSIDE
Black, Dorothea Foster, 7
Melrose, Charles James, 10
BURRA
Lewis, Essington, 10
CALLINGTON
Sexton, John Henry, 11
CAMPBELLTOWN
Dean, George Henry, 8
CARRIETON
Hillary, Michael Thomas, 9

CLARE
Adey, William James, 7
Bell, Peter Albany, 7
Hawker, Charles Allan Seymour, 9
Hawker, Edward William, 9
Simons, John Joseph, 11
COLLEGE PARK
Holden, Sir Edward Wheewall, 9
COROMANDEL VALLEY
Laffer, George Richards, 9
CUDLEE CREEK
Kelly, Robert, 9
EASTWOOD
Irwin, Leighton Major Francis, 9
ECHUNGA
Hack, Wilton, 4
ENCOUNTER BAY
Stow, Catherine Eliza Somerville, 12
FORRESTON
Day, Theodore Ernest, 8
FULLARTON
Verco, Sir Joseph Cooke, 12
Warnes, Mary Jane, 12
GAWLER
Butler, Sir Richard Layton, 7
Coombe, Ephraim Henry, 8
Duffield, Walter Geoffrey, 8
Ifould, William Herbert, 9
Richards, Herbert Clarence, 11
Stable, Jeremiah Joseph, 12
GILBERTON
Blakeley, Arthur, 7
Blakeley, Frederick, 7
GLANVILLE
McCann, William Francis James, 10
GLEN OSMOND
Boothby, Guy Newell, 7
Darling, Joseph, 8
Gill, Thomas, 9
GLENELG
Kingsmill, Sir Walter, 9
Niall, James Mansfield, 11
Niall, Kenneth Mansfield, 11
Nicholson, Reginald Chapman, 11
Preece, John Lloyd, 11
Reynell, Gladys, 11
Virgo, John James, 12
GOLDEN GROVE
Gillen, Peter Paul, 9
GOODWOOD
Leahy, Thomas Joseph, 10
GOOLWA
Lindsay, David, 10
Ritchie, Sir George, 11
GUMERACHA
O'Loghlin, James Vincent, 11
HACKNEY
Melbourne, Alexander Clifford Vernon, 10
HAHNDORF
Reimann, Immanuel Gotthold, 11
Von Doussa, Charles Louis, 12
HAMILTON
Barnes, John, 7

HAPPY VALLEY
  Holder, Sir Frederick William, 9
HARTLEY VALE
  Hannaford, George, 9
HEMINGTON
  Daly, John Joseph, 8
HENLEY BEACH
  Bagot, Edward Daniel Alexander, 7
HINDMARSH
  McCloughry, Edgar James, 10
  Vardon, Edward Charles, 12
  Vardon, Joseph, 12
JAMESTOWN
  McCann, Sir Charles Francis Gerald, 10
JUNGGURUMBAR
  Milerum, 10
KANGARILLA
  Dashwood, Charles James, 8
KAPUNDA
  Benham, Ellen Ida, 7
  Bruce, Sir Wallace, 7
  Rosman, Alice (Grant) Trevenen, 11
  Wheatley, Frederick William, 12
  Zwar, Traugott Bernhard, 12
KENSINGTON
  Fox, Sir Frank Ignatius, 8
  Holden, Henry James, 9
  Newland, Sir Henry Simpson, 11
KENT TOWN
  Basedow, Herbert, 7
  Blacket, John, 7
  Edwards, George, 8
  Hales, Alfred Arthur Greenwood, 9
KNIGHTSBRIDGE
  McCloughry, Wilfred Ashton, 10
KOOLUNGA
  Moyes, Morton Henry, 10
KOORINGA
  Holmes, Marion Louisa, 9
LINDEN PARK
  Hay, William Goss, 9
LITTLE PARA
  Gillen, Francis James, 9
MACCLESFIELD
  Robinson, Sir Roy Lister, 11
  Wallis, Frederick Samuel, 12
MAGILL
  Murray, Sir George John Robert, 10
  Reynell, Carew, 11
  Walker, Hurtle Frank, 12
MALVERN
  Williams, Francis Edgar, 12
MANNAHILL
  Hannaford, Ernest Hayler, 9
MANOORA
  Miethke, Adelaide Laetitia, 10
MARDON
  James, Frederick Alexander, 9
MEADOWS
  Brooks, George Vickery, 7
MERRINDIE
  Kelly, William Stanley, 9
MINTARO
  Brown, William Jethro, 7

  Jolly, Norman William, 9
MITCHAM
  Ambrose, Theodore, 7
  Downes, Rupert Major, 8
  Finlayson, John Harvey, 4
  Jones, Doris Egerton, 9
  Thornber, Ellen, 12
MODBURY
  Cudmore, Daniel Henry, 8
MONTACUTE
  Richards, Tobias John Martin, 11
MOONTA
  Cocks, Fanny Kate Boadicea, 8
  Craigie, Edward John, 8
  Marquet, Claude Arthur, 10
  Pryor, Oswald, 11
  Richards, Robert Stanley, 11
  Scaddan, John, 11
  Verran, John Stanley, 12
  Whitford, Stanley R., 12
  Williams, Sir Richard, 12
  Young, Sir Walter James, 12
MOUNT BARKER
  May, William Lewis, 10
  Mitchell, Samuel James, 10
  Pearce, Sir George Foster, 11
  Searcy, Alfred, 11
MOUNT BRYAN
  Wilkins, Sir George Hubert, 12
MOUNT GAMBIER
  Daley, Jane, 8
  Hone, Frank Sandland, 9
  Jarvis, Eric Roy, 9
  Leane, Allan William, 10
  Livingston, John, 10
  Mann, Edward Alexander, 10
  Mann, Sir Frederick Wollaston, 10
  Steele, Alexander, 12
MOUNT TORRENS
  Tuck, Marie Anne, 12
MURRAY BRIDGE
  Wilson, Mark, 12
NAILSWORTH
  Thomas, Robert Kyffin, 6
NAIRNE
  Hocking, Sidney Edwin, 9
NARACOORTE
  McLachlan, Alexander John, 10
  Wainwright, John William, 12
NATIVE VALLEY
  Mills, William George James, 10
NORWOOD
  à Beckett, Ada Mary, 7
  Blundell, Reginald Pole, 7
  Cleland, Sir John Burton, 8
  Homburg, Hermann Robert, 9
  Howie, Laurence Hotham, 9
  Jauncey, Leslie Cyril, 9
  Moulden, Sir Frank Beaumont, 10
  Shepherd, Arthur Edmund, 11
  Shiers, Walter Henry, 11
  Soward, George Klewitz, 12
  Vaughan, Dorothy, 12
  Vaughan, John Howard, 12

Weir, Stanley Price, 12
NURIOOTPA
  Davey, Constance Muriel, 8
PARKSIDE
  Richardson, Victor York, 11
  Viney, Horace George, 12
  Watson, Stanley Holm, 12
  Weber, Horace George Martin, 12
PASTORAL STATIONS
  Chewings, Charles, 7
PENOLA
  Neilson, John Shaw, 10
  Rymill, John Riddoch, 11
PENWORTHAM
  Roach, Bertie Smith, 11
PINE HUT
  Davey, Arnold Edwin, 8
POINT MCLEAY
  Unaipon, David, 12
PORT ADELAIDE
  Duncan, Annie Jane, 8
  Lundie, Francis Walter, 10
  Mack, Amy Eleanor, 10
  Matson, Phillip Henry, 10
  Preston, Margaret Rose, 11
  Theodore, Edward Granville, 12
  Willis, Henry, 12
PORT ELLIOT
  Anstey, Edward Alfred, 7
  Boxall, Arthur d'Auvergne, 7
PORT GAWLER
  Cowan, Sir John, 8
PORT LINCOLN
  Wollaston, Tullie Cornthwaite, 12
PORT PIRIE
  Cairns, Sir Hugh William Bell, 7
  Stewart, Eleanor Charlotte, 12
PROSPECT
  Brookman, William Gordon, 7
  Leane, Edwin Thomas, 10
  Leane, Sir Raymond Lionel, 10
  Sullivan, Arthur Percy, 12
REEDBEDS
  White, Samuel Albert, 12
RENMARK
  Madigan, Cecil Thomas, 10
REYNELLA
  Reynell, Walter, 6
RIVERTON
  Cooper, Robert Joel, 8
  Gordon, Sir David John, 9
ROBE
  Campbell, Donald, 7
ROSEBANK
  Melrose, Sir John, 10
ST IVES
  Williams, Alfred, 12
SALISBURY
  Davy, Ruby Claudia Emily, 8
  Nock, Horace Keyworth, 11
SEVENHILL
  Jacob, Caroline, 9
SMITHFIELD
  Baker, Thomas Charles Richmond, 7

Cheney, Sydney Albert, 7
STEPNEY
  Schulz, Adolf John, 11
STRATHALBYN
  Goode, Agnes Knight, 9
  Herbert, Charles Edward, 9
  Poole, Thomas Slaney, 11
  Stirling, Sir Edward Charles, 6
  Stirling, Sir John Lancelot, 6
STURT
  Bottrill, Frank, 7
TANTANOOLA
  McNeill, John James, 10
TEROWIE
  Jenkins, Sir George Frederick, 9
  Lacey, Andrew William, 9
TRURO
  Crick, William Patrick, 8
  Kauffmann, John, 9
TWO WELLS
  Woods, James Park, 12
UNLEY
  Davey, Phillip, 8
  Smith, Louis Laybourne, 11
  Young, Sarah Jane, 12
VIRGINIA
  O'Loughlin, Laurence Theodore, 11
WALKERVILLE
  Hill, Henry John, 4
  Tucker, Charles, 12
WALLAROO
  Kneebone, Henry, 9
WATRABA
  Arnold, Thomas Francis, 7
WILD HORSE PLAINS
  Lyons, Herbert William, 10
WOODVILLE
  Blackburn, Arthur Seaforth, 7
  Creswell, John, 8
  Smith, Tom Elder Barr, 11
YALLUM PARK
  Wells, Lawrence Allen, 12
YANKALILLA
  Clayton, Arthur Ross, 8
YORKETOWN
  Butler, Henry John, 7
YUNTA
  Gerard, Edwin Field, 8
Tasmania
  Casey, Richard Gardiner, 3
  Clark, Charles George Henry Carr, 3
  Clark, George John Edwin, 3
  Hassell, John Frederick Tasman, 4
  Jones, Auber George, 4
  McWilliams, William James, 10
  Morris, Augustus, 5
  Thomson, Jane Elizabeth, 6
  Trugernanner, 6
ANTILL PONDS
  Pillinger, Alfred Thomas, 5
AVOCA
  Wardlaw, Alan Lindsay, 12
BAGDAD
  Armytage, Charles Henry, 3

Armytage, Frederick William, 3
Blacklow, Archibald Clifford, 7
Butler, William Frederick Dennis, 7
BATTERY POINT
Cunningham, Sir Edward Sheldon, 8
BEACONSFIELD
Statton, Percy Clyde, 12
BELLERIVE
McAulay, Alexander Leicester, 10
BLESSINGTON
Morrison, Edward Charles, 10
BOTHWELL
Lascelles, Edward Harewood, 5
Wood, John Dennistoun, 6
BREAM CREEK
Dunbabin, Thomas Charles, 8
BRIDGEWATER
Earle, John, 8
Hayes, John Blyth, 9
BRIGHTON
Chalmers, Frederick Royden, 7
Desailly, George Peter, 4
Devine, Edward, 4
Lord, John Ernest Cecil, 10
BROADMARSH
Culley, Charles Ernest, 8
Walch, Garnet, 6
CAMBRIDGE
Dunbabin, Robert Leslie, 8
CAMPANIA
Brock, Harold James, 7
Brock, Henry Eric, 7
CAMPBELL TOWN
Gatty, Harold Charles, 8
McGee, Lewis, 10
Power, Marguerite Helen, 11
CARRICK
Rolph, William Robert, 11
CLARENDON
Miller, Montague David, 10
CONSTITUTION HILL
Carter, Samuel, 3
CULLENSWOOD
Legge, William Vincent, 5
DELORAINE
Loftus-Hills, Clive, 10
DEVONPORT
McCall, Sir John, 10
EVANDALE
Murray, Henry William, 10
FLINDERS ISLAND
Smith, Fanny Cochrane, 11
FRANKLIN
Longman, Irene Maud, 10
GEORGE TOWN
Smith, James, 6
Youl, Richard, 6
GLENORCHY
Barclay, Charles James, 3
GORDON
Atkinson, Henry Brune, 7
GREAT SWANPORT
Lyne, Sir William John, 10

HADSPEN
Reibey, Thomas, 6
HAMILTON
Bethune, Frank Pogson, 7
Bethune, John Walter, 7
HAREFIELD
Groom, Arthur Champion, 9
Hobart
Abbott, Percy Phipps, 7
Alderman, Walter William, 7
Barclay, David, 7
Benson, Lucy Charlotte, 7
Best, Amy Jane, 3
Bridges, Hilda Maggie, 7
Bridges, Royal Tasman (Roy), 7
Brient, Lachlan John, 7
Brown, Nicholas John, 3
Buckland, John Vansittart, 3
Buckland, William Harvey, 3
Burgess, William Henry, 3
Burn, Alan, 7
Carmichael, Ambrose Campbell, 7
Clark, Andrew Inglis, 3
Clark, James Purcell, 8
Clarke, Joseph, 3
Crisp, Sir Harold, 8
Crowther, Edward Lodewyk, 3
Curr, Edward Micklethwaite, 3
Daly, Clarence Wells, 8
Davies, Joseph, 4
Dobson, Alfred, 4
Dobson, Frank Stanley, 4
Dobson, Henry, 8
Eady, Charles John, 8
Elliott, Charles Hazell, 8
Fitzgerald, George Parker, 4
Flynn, Errol Leslie, 8
Giblin, Lyndhurst Falkiner, 8
Giblin, Ronald Worthy, 8
Giblin, William Robert, 4
Grant, Charles William, 9
Hamilton, John, 4
Hawthorn, Arthur George Clarence, 9
Henderson, Jessie Isabel, 9
Higgins, Arthur Embery, 9
Higgins, Ernest Henry, 9
Higgins, Tasman George, 9
Hogan, Percival James Nelson, 9
Hopkins, John Rout, 4
Hull, Arthur Francis Basset, 9
James, Tristram Bernard Wordsworth, 9
John, Cecilia Annie, 9
Jones, Sir Henry, 9
Jones, John Percy, 9
Keating, John Henry, 9
Lewis, Sir Neil Elliott, 10
Lord, Clive Errol, 10
Lovett, Mildred Esther, 10
Lyons, Thomas, 10
McCann, Edward John, 10
McGregor, Martin Robert, 10
Mack, Marie Louise Hamilton, 10
McVilly, Cecil Leventhorpe, 10
Mather, Joseph Francis, 10

Miles, Edward Thomas, 10
Murdoch, Thomas (1868-1946), 10
Nicholas, Harold Sprent, 11
Ogilvie, Albert George, 11
Oliver, Charles Nicholson Jewel, 11
Packer, Robert Clyde, 11
Palmer, Rosina Martha Hosanah, 5
Pattison, William, 5
Payne, Herbert James Mockford, 11
Petterd, William Frederick, 5
Piguenit, William Charles, 5
Pike, George Herbert, 11
Price, Thomas Caradoc Rose, 11
Propsting, William Bispham, 11
Roberts, Gerald Alleyne, 11
Roberts, Mary Grant, 11
Rodway, Florence Aline, 11
Rowntree, Amy, 11
Shann, Edward Owen Giblin, 11
Shann, Frank, 11
Smith, Ivy Blanche Irene, 11
Stephen, Alfred Hamilton Hewlett, 6
Stephen, Sir Matthew Henry, 6
Stephen, Montagu Consett, 6
Stephen, William Wilberforce, 6
Stone, Emma Constance, 12
Stone, Grace Clara, 12
Stone, William, 12
Taylor, Alfred Joseph, 6
Thompson, John Willis, 12
Walker, Alan Cameron, 12
Walker, James Backhouse, 6
Webster, Charles Ernest, 12
Webster, Edwin Herbert, 12
Wylly, Guy George Egerton, 12
HUON ISLAND
Whittle, John Woods, 12
HUONVILLE
Sherwin, Frances Amy Lillian, 6
KANGAROO POINT
Murray, Pembroke Lathrop, 10
LAUNCESTON
Archer, William, 3
Clarke, Charles James, 8
Collins, George Thomas, 8
Crick, Stanley Sadler, 8
Dry, Sir Richard, 1
Edwards, William Burton, 8
Emmett, Evelyn Temple, 8
Evans, Alexander Arthur, 8
Fysh, Sir Wilmot Hudson, 8
Gordon, Bernard Sidney, 9
Grubb, Frederick William, 4
Henty, Henry, 4
Henty, Thomas, 4
Israel, John William, 9
James, Sir Claude Ernest Weymouth, 9
Langham, Frederick, 5
Lilly, James, 5
Littler, Charles Augustus Murray, 10
Littler, Frank Mervyn, 10
Lloyd, Jessie Georgina, 5
Lukin, Gresley, 5
McDonald, Edgar Arthur, 10

Martin, Edward Fowell, 10
Meston, Archibald Lawrence, 10
Mills, Charles Frederick, 2
Mills, John Brabyn, 2
Monds, Albert William, 10
Monds, Thomas Wilkes, 2
Oakden, Percy, 5
O'Sullivan, Edward William, 11
Rolph, Sir Gordon Burns, 11
Sadler, Robert James, 11
Sampson, Burford, 11
Shields, Tasman, 11
Trenwith, William Arthur, 12
Vincent, Alfred James, 12
Wiseman, Thomas, 12
LILLICOS SIDING
Lillico, Sir Alexander, 10
LONGFORD
Lee, Sir Walter Henry, 10
O'Keefe, David John, 11
Solomon, Albert Edgar, 12
LOVELY BANKS
Clarke, Sir William John, 3
MACQUARIE PLAINS
Nichols, Hubert Allan, 11
MELTON MOWBRAY
Bisdee, John Hutton, 7
NEW NORFOLK
Brown, Walter Ernest, 7
Moore, Thomas Bather, 10
Officer, Charles Myles, 5
Officer, Suetonius Henry, 5
Shoobridge, Louis Manton, 11
NEW TOWN
Piesse, Edmund Leolin, 11
Stephens, Arthur Augustus, 12
Tazewell, Evelyn Ruth, 12
NILE
Cameron, Cyril St Clair, 7
Cameron, Donald Norman, 7
OUSE
Gellibrand, Sir John, 8
PERTH
Houghton, Sydney Robert, 9
Lewis, Arndell Neil, 10
Ritchie, William, 6
Youl, Alfred, 12
PIPERS RIVER
Counsel, Edward Albert, 8
Deacon, Clare, 8
PORT ARTHUR
Dobson, Emily, 8
Fraser, Simon Alexander, 8
PORT ESPERANCE
Rivett, Sir Albert Cherbury David, 11
Rivett, Eleanor Harriett, 11
PORT SORELL
Walker, Jean Nellie Miles, 12
PORTLAND
Turner, Dora Jeannette, 12
RECHERCHE
McDougall, Stanley Robert, 10
RICHMOND
Johnstone, Robert Arthur, 4

Shoobridge, Robert Wilkins Giblin, 11
Shoobridge, William Ebenezer, 11
RINGAROOMA
Conder, Walter Tasman, 8
Gaby, Alfred Edward, 8
RIVER DON
Heritage, Francis Bede, 9
ROSEVILLE
Parker, Florence Mary, 11
SANDY BAY
O'Neill, John Henry, 11
SIDMOUTH
Dadson, Leslie, 8
SORELL
Wettenhall, Holford Highlord, 6
STANLEY
Lyons, Joseph Aloysius, 10
TABLE CAPE
Alexander, Frederick Matthias, 7
TORQUAY
Holyman, James, 9
Holyman, Thomas Henry, 9
Holyman, William, 9
TUNNACK
Nettlefold, Isaac Robert, 11
Nettlefold, Sir Thomas Sydney Richard,
11
ULVERSTONE
Smithies, Frederick, 11
WESTBURY
Harrap, George Edward, 9
Payne, Ellen Nora, 11
Smith, William Henry Laird, 11
WYNYARD
Palfreyman, Achalen Woolliscroft, 11
Victoria
Chidley, William James, 7
Cooper, William, 8
Minchin, Alfred Corker, 10
ALBERTON
Blanc, Gustave, 7
ALEXANDRA
Leckie, John William, 10
ALPHINGTON
Minifie, Richard Pearman, 10
AMHERST
Salmon, Charles Carty, 11
ARARAT
Falkiner, Franc Brereton Sadleir, 8
Falkiner, Otway Rothwell, 8
Grano, Paul Langton, 9
Keegan, Thomas Michael, 9
Lyell, George, 10
Scobie, James, 11
Trumble, Thomas, 12
Ulrich, Theodore Friederick, 12
ARMADALE
Ham, Wilbur Lincoln, 9
ASCOT
Holdsworth, Albert Armytage, 9
McRae, James, 10
Pye, Hugh, 11
ASCOT VALE
Latham, Sir John Greig, 10

ASHBY
Clark, Donald, 8
AVOCA
Fenton, James Edward, 8
Green, Albert Ernest, 9
AVON PLAINS
Fleming, William Montgomerie, 8
BACCHUS MARSH
Cuthbertson, Margaret Gardiner, 8
Grant, Sir Kerr, 9
Heagney, Patrick Reginald, 9
BAGSHOT
Ingram, George Mawby, 9
BALD HILLS
Temple, David, 12
BALLAN
Lay, Percy, 10
BALLARAT
Ahern, Elizabeth, 7
Archer, Francis Henry Joseph, 7
Bailey, Arthur Rudolph, 7
Bailey, Henry Stephen, 7
Baird, Adam, 7
Brazenor, William, 7
Carmichael, Grace Elizabeth Jennings, 7
Corbould, William Henry, 8
Crouch, Richard Armstrong, 8
Daglish, Henry, 8
Davies, David, 8
Dunstan, William, 8
Dyson, Ambrose Arthur, 8
Dyson, William Henry, 8
Gaunt, Sir Guy Reginald Archer, 8
Gellatly, Francis Mephan, 8
Hagelthorn, Frederick William, 9
Halley, Ida Gertrude Margaret, 9
Hardie, John Leslie, 9
Henderson, Isabella Thomson, 9
Herbert, Harold Brocklebank, 9
Holman, Ada Augusta, 9
King, George Raymond, 9
Kirton, Joseph William, 9
Leach, John Albert, 10
Lemmone, John, 10
Longstaff, William Frederick, 10
McWhae, Sir John, 10
Meagher, Richard James, 10
Miller, Horatio Clive, 10
Moss, Alice Frances Mabel, 10
Nicholas, Emily Hilda, 11
Nicholls, Sir Herbert, 11
Nicholls, William Henry, 11
Olden, Arthur Charles Niquet, 11
Olney, Sir Herbert Horace, 11
Palmer, Thomas, 11
Perry, Reginald Harry, 11
Phillips, Sir Frederick Beaumont, 11
Pittard, Alfred James, 11
Robertson, Sir Macpherson, 11
Ross-King, Alice, 11
Seager, Alexandrine, 11
Sewell, Sir Sidney Valentine, 11
Sharwood, William Henry, 11
Snow, Sir Sydney, 12

Spielvogel, Nathan Frederick, 12
Summons, Walter Ernest Isaac, 12
Sutton, Henry, 6
Thompson, Matilda Louise, 12
Treloar, George Devine, 12
Tulloch, Eric William, 12
Vale, May, 12
Wanliss, Cecil, 12
Wanliss, Harold Boyd, 12
Weatherly, May Isabella, 12
White, Alexander Henry, 12
Williams, Robert Ernest, 12
BALWYN
Bennett, Alfred Edward, 7
Broinowski, Robert Arthur, 7
BAMGANIE
Lasseter, Lewis Herbert, 9
BARFOLD
Watt, William Alexander, 12
BARKERS CREEK
Peeler, Walter, 11
Zercho, Charles Henry, 12
Zercho, Frederick William, 12
BEAUFORT
Heathershaw, James Thomas, 9
Lapsley, James McFarlane, 9
O'Connell, Cecily Maude Mary, 11
O'Dowd, Bernard Patrick, 11
Trompf, Percival Albert, 12
Tuckett, Francis John, 12
BEECHWORTH
Clemens, Sir William James, 8
Foster, Alfred William, 8
Gaunt, Sir Ernest Frederick Augustus,
8
Macnamara, Dame Annie Jean, 10
Rivett, Doris Mary, 11
Wirth, Philip Peter Jacob, 12
BELFAST, see also Port Fairy
Stewart, James Campbell, 12
Tuckfield, William John, 12
Wilton, John Raymond, 12
BELLARINE
Levien, Cecil John, 10
BENALLA
Robertson, Edward, 11
BENDIGO, see also Sandhurst
Bowman, David, 7
Cockerill, George, 8
Cohn, Carola, 8
Dyett, Sir Gilbert Joseph Cullen, 8
Foy, Mark, 8
Hunter, John Irvine, 9
Salisbury, William Robert Peel, 11
BEREMBOKE
Black, Percy Charles Herbert, 7
BERWICK
Brisbane, William Peter, 7
Holt, Michael, 9
BEVERIDGE
Jones, Harold Edward, 9
Kelly, Edward, 5
BITTERN
Greaves, William Clement, 9

BOLWARRAH
Hyett, Francis William, 9
BOORCAN
Mackinnon, Donald, 10
BOORT
Morris, Myra Evelyn, 10
BOOSEY
McNamara, David John, 10
BORUNG
Borella, Albert Chalmers, 7
BOX HILL
Porteus, Stanley David, 11
Stephenson, Sir Arthur George, 12
BRIGHTON
Campbell, Archibald George, 7
Clark, Alister, 8
Crowther, George O'Dell, 8
Crowther, Henry Arnold, 8
Cumbrae Stewart, Janet Agnes, 8
Cumbrae-Stewart, Zina Beatrice Selwyn,
8
Grainger, George Percy, 9
Grieve, Robert Cuthbert, 9
Hammond, Robert Brodribb Stewart, 9
Harford, Lesbia Venner, 9
Hawker, Harry George, 9
Henderson, Kingsley Anketell, 9
Kelly, Sir George Dalziel, 9
Le Souef, William Henry Dudley, 10
Rogers, William Richard, 11
Ryan, Cecil Godfrey, 11
Taylor, Joseph Leslie Theodore, 12
Traill, Jessie Constance Alicia, 12
Weber, Clarence Alfred, 12
BROADFORD
Zwar, Albert Michael, 12
Zwar, Henry Peter, 12
BRUNSWICK
Barnett, Frederick Oswald, 7
Cleary, Patrick Scott, 8
Eggleston, Sir Frederick William, 8
Rivett, Elsie Grace, 11
Sweet, Georgina, 12
Winchcombe, Frederick Earle, 12
BULLDOG
Keegan, John Walter, 9
BULLENGAROOK
O'Donnell, David George, 11
O'Donnell, Nicholas Michael, 11
BULLOCK CREEK
Campbell, John Archibald, 7
BULUMWAAL
Pitt, Marie Elizabeth Josephine, 11
BUNGAREE
Avery, David, 7
BUNINYONG
McClelland, David John, 10
O'Donnell, Thomas Joseph, 11
Pye, Emmeline, 11
Reid, John, 11
BURWOOD
Hoadley, Charles Archibald Brookes, 9
CAMBERWELL
Sadlier, Clifford William King, 11

CAMPBELLFIELD
Canning, Alfred Wernam, 7
CANIAMBO
Vickers, Allan Robert Stanley, 12
CARISBROOK
Aston, Matilda Ann, 7
Long, George Merrick, 10
Russell, Percy Joseph, 11
CARLTON
Allen, Sir Carleton Kemp, 7
Baldwin, Joseph Mason, 7
Barrett, John George, 7
Brenan, Jennie Frances, 7
Broinowski, Leopold Thomas, 7
Brunton, Sir William, 7
Cole, Frank Hobill, 8
Denehy, Charles Aloysius, 8
Ellis, Constance, 8
Evergood, Miles, 8
Forbes, Catherine Ellen, 8
Gray, Ethel, 9
Greig, Stella Fida, 9
Gunn, Jeannie, 9
Lemmon, John, 10
MacDonald, James Stuart, 10
Mair, Alexander, 10
Morell, Sir Stephen Joseph, 10
Mummery, Joseph Browning, 10
Murdoch, Madoline, 10
Newman-Morris, Sir John, 11
Outhwaite, Ida Sherbourne, 11
Robinson, Sir Arthur, 11
Robinson, Gerald Henry, 11
Rowell, John Thomas Nightingale, 11
Rowell, William Nicholas, 11
Rubin, Bernard, 11
Scurry, William Charles, 11
Seitz, John Arnold, 11
Snowball, William, 12
Wallis, Alfred Russell, 12
Wilson, James Alexander Campbell, 12
CARRANBALLAC
Chirnside, John Percy, 7
CARRS PLAINS
Wettenhall, Marcus Edwy, 12
Wettenhall, Roland Ravenscroft, 12
CASTERTON
Beckett, Clarice Marjoribanks, 7
Hervey, Grant, 9
CASTLEMAINE
Arthur, John Andrew, 7
Barnes, George Powell, 7
Barnes, Walter Henry, 7
Card, Mary, 7
Elkington, John Simeon Colebrook, 8
Embley, Edward Henry, 8
Emery, George Edwin, 8
Harrison, Eric, 9
Higgins, Sir John Michael, 9
Laver, Alfred Edmund, 10
Laver, Frank Jonas, 10
Laver, William Adolphus, 10
McCay, Adam Cairns, 10
McCay, Delamore William, 10

Murphy, Edwin Greenslade, 10
Poynton, Alexander, 11
Sowden, Sir William John, 12
Sutton, Harvey, 12
Tait, Charles, 12
Tait, Edward Joseph, 12
Tait, James Nevin, 12
Tait, John Henry, 12
Tate, Frank, 12
Thompson, David (1865-1916), 12
Williams, Susannah Jane, 12
CAULFIELD
Duffy, Sir Charles Leonard Gavan, 8
Grimwade, Sir Wilfrid Russell, 9
Groom, Arthur, 9
Hart, John Stephen, 9
Hart, Thomas Stephen, 9
Jones, Allan Murray, 9
Munro, David Hugh, 10
Munro, James Leslie, 10
CERES
McCann, Wesley Burrett, 10
CHARLTON
De Garis, Mary Clementina, 8
Elliott, Harold Edward, 8
Lind, Sir Albert Eli, 10
Martyn, Nellie Constance, 10
CHILTERN
Cook, Robert, 8
Gaunt, Cecil Robert, 8
Harris, Sir John Richards, 9
CHILWELL
Bennett, Henry Gilbert, 7
CHINAMAN CREEK
Laver, Charles William, 10
CHINAMANS FLAT
Worrall, John, 12
CHINTIN
Allan, John, 7
CHUTE
Callister, Cyril Percy, 7
CLEAR LAKE
Bussau, Sir Albert Louis, 7
CLIFTON HILL
Welch, Eric Wilfred, 12
CLUNES
Beadle, Jane, 7
Jobson, Alexander, 9
Jobson, Nancy, 9
Lewis, Robert, 10
Longstaff, Sir John Campbell, 10
Tarrant, Harley, 12
COBRAM
Hughes, Ernest Selwyn, 9
COCKATOO
Gilbert, Charles Marsh (Nash) Web, 9
Orchard, Richard Beaumont, 11
COGHILLS CREEK
Tunnecliffe, Thomas, 12
COLAC
Pitt, Henry Arthur, 11
COLLINGWOOD
Alcock, Randal James, 7
Andrade, David Alfred, 7

Andrade, William Charles, 7
Best, Sir Robert Wallace, 7
Boyd, Emma Minnie, 7
Chinn, Henry, 7
Cohen, Montague, 8
Collier, Frederick Redmond, 8
Crawford, Thomas William, 8
Dartnell, William Thomas, 8
Deakin, Alfred, 8
Edwards, Percy Malcolm, 8
Gabriel, Charles John, 8
Lee, Walter Henry (1889-1968), 10
McComas, Robert Bond Wesley, 10
Patterson, John Hunter (1841-1930), 11
Ross, John Howlett, 11
Ruthven, William, 11
Ryder, John, 11
Thatcher, Griffithes Wheeler, 12
Trott, Albert Edwin, 12
Trott, George Henry Stevens, 12
Trumble, Hugh, 12
Wilkinson, John Francis, 12
Wilmot, Frank Leslie Thompson, 12
Wren, John, 12
CORINDHAP
Laidler, Thomas Percival, 9
CRESWICK
Laby, Thomas Howell, 9
Lindsay, Sir Ernest Daryl, 10
Lindsay, Sir Lionel Arthur, 10
Lindsay, Norman Alfred Williams, 10
Lindsay, Percival Charles, 10
Peacock, Sir Alexander James, 11
Richard, George Anderson, 11
Robertson, John, 11
Starke, Sir Hayden Erskine, 12
CROSBIE
Hansen, Martin Peter, 9
CROWLANDS
Blackwood, Robert Officer, 7
CROYDON
Goble, Stanley James, 9
DANDENONG
Henley, Frank Le Leu, 9
DAYLESFORD
Patterson, Ambrose McCarthy, 11
Rowlandson, Alfred Cecil, 11
DEANS MARSH
Lawrence, Marjorie Florence, 10
DENISON
McWilliam, John James, 10
DIGBY
Lawton, John Thomas, 10
DIMBOOLA
Traeger, Alfred Hermann, 12
DINGEE
Old, Francis Edward, 11
DONALD
Dunstan, Sir Albert Arthur, 8
Guthrie, James Francis, 9
DRYSDALE
Cherry, Percy Herbert, 7
DUNACH
Fenner, Charles Albert Edward, 8

DUNEED
Streeton, Sir Arthur Ernest, 12
DUNOLLY
Boan, Henry, 7
Hill, William Caldwell, 9
Lawson, Sir Harry Sutherland Wightman, 10
McBride, Sir Peter, 10
DURDIDWARRAH
Ogden, James Ernest, 11
DURHAM LEAD
Baragwanath, William, 7
Lamble, George Edwin, 9
EAGLEHAWK
Hall, John Joseph, 9
Leggo, Arthur Victor, 10
Leggo, Henry Madren, 10
Symons, William John, 12
EDENHOPE
Hankinson, Robert Henry, 9
ELDORADO
Dunstan, William John, 8
ELLERSLIE
Barber, John Andrew, 7
ELLIMINYT
Murray, Russell Mervyn, 10
ELSTERNWICK
Serle, Percival, 11
Weigall, Theyre à Beckett, 12
Williams, Harry Llewellyn Carlington, 12
ELWOOD
Le Souef, Ernest Albert, 10
EMERALD HILL
Albiston, Arthur Edward, 7
Barrett, Edith Helen, 7
Barrett, Sir James William, 7
Clendinnen, Frederick John, 8
Coates, George James, 8
Coningham, Arthur, 8
Cox, Erle, 8
McNicoll, Sir Walter Ramsay, 10
Robertson, Margery Fraser, 11
EMU CREEK
Brennan, Anna Teresa, 7
Brennan, Francis, 7
ERCILDOUNE
Livingstone-Learmonth, Frederick Valiant Cotton, 10
EVERTON
Mackay, John Hilton, 10
FITZROY
Balfour, James Lawson, 7
Birtles, Francis Edwin, 7
Blackett, William Arthur Mordey, 7
Blackham, John McCarthy, 3
Campbell, Archibald James, 7
Conrick, Horatio Victor Patrick, 8
Fox, Emanuel Phillips, 8
Harker, Constance Elizabeth, 9
Hewlett, Herbert Maunsell, 9
Horsfall, Alfred Herbert, 9
Hume, Walter Reginald, 9
Kershaw, James Andrew, 9
Kiernan, Esmond Laurence, 9

Lewis, Fred, 10
McBeath, Sir William George, 10
Macdonald, Donald Alaster, 10
Mackennal, Sir Edgar Bertram, 10
McKillop, Mary Helen, 5
Muskett, Alice Jane, 10
Richardson, Ethel Florence Lindesay, 11
Sanderson, Robert Fitzroy, 11
Shea, Ernest Herbert, 11
Tomholt, Sydney John, 12
Tucker, Albert Edwin Elworthy Lee, 6
Webb, Thomas Prout, 6
Williams, Sir Hartley, 6
Williamson, Francis Samuel, 12
FLEMINGTON
Mathews, Robert Henry, 10
FOOTSCRAY
Behan, Sir John Clifford Valentine, 7
Campbell, Edward, 7
Cobb, Victor Ernest, 8
Holme, Ernest Rudolph, 9
Holme, John Barton, 9
Paterson, Alexander Thomas, 11
Sandford, Sir James Wallace, 11
Stewart, Percy Gerald, 12
FRANKLINFORD
Judkins, William Henry, 9
GAFFNEYS CREEK
Cohen, Laurence, 8
GARDINER
Chandler, Alfred Elliott, 7
GEELONG
Allen, George Thomas, 7
Allen, Sir Harry Brookes, 7
Asche, Thomas Stange(r) Heiss Oscar, 7
Ashton, James, 7
Battye, James Sykes, 7
Beggs, Theodore, 7
Broadbent, George Robert, 7
Bromilow, William Edward, 7
Brownlee, John Donald Mackenzie, 7
Currie, Sir (Henry) Alan, 8
Currie, John Lang, 8
Davies, Sir Matthew Henry, 4
Evans, Daniel Edward, 8
Hall, Thomas Sergeant, 9
Hancock, William, 9
Hitchcock, Howard, 9
Hodge, Charles Reynolds, 9
Holden, Albert Thomas, 9
Holden, George Frederick, 9
Kernot, Maurice Edwin, 9
Leckie, Alexander Joseph, 10
Mauger, Samuel, 10
Moore, Caroline Ellen, 10
Owen, Albert John, 11
Pescott, Edward Edgar, 11
Richardson, Horace Frank, 11
Rodgers, Arthur Stanislaus, 11
Rolland, Sir Francis William, 11
Stephen, Reginald, 12
Strachan, Hugh Murray, 12
Stretch, John Francis, 12
Turner, Walter James, 12

Walsh, James Morgan, 12
GISBORNE
Cherry, Thomas, 7
Gibson, William Gerrand, 8
Peck, Harry Huntington, 11
GLENDARUEL
Judkins, George Alfred, 9
GLENLYON
Macfarlan, Sir James Ross, 10
GLENMAGGIE
Fullerton, Mary Eliza, 8
GOBUR
Bromham, Ada, 7
GOLDSBOROUGH
Sleeman, John Harvey Crothers, 11
GOULBURN VALLEY
Winter, Joseph, 6
Winter, Samuel Vincent, 6
GRASSDALE
Coldham, Walter Timon, 8
GREENSBOROUGH
Starling, John Henry, 12
GROVEDALE
Heyer, Johannes, 9
HAMILTON
Boxer, Walter Henry, 7
Layh, Herbert Thomas Christoph, 10
Mott, Hamilton Charnock, 10
Shields, Clive, 11
HAPPY VALLEY
Annear, Harold Desbrowe, 7
HARCOURT
James, William Edward, 9
HARRIETVILLE
Hall, David Robert, 9
HARROW
Davidson, James Edward, 8
HAWTHORN
Alcock, Alfred Upton, 7
Ampt, Gustav Adolph, 7
Barrett, Charles Leslie, 7
Baynes, Harry, 7
Buckley, Maurice Vincent, 7
Creswick, Alexander Thomson, 8
Derham, Enid, 8
Gullett, Lucy Edith, 9
Kauper, Henry Alexis, 9
Little, Robert Alexander, 10
Longford, Raymond John Walter Hollis, 10
McCrae, Hugh Raymond, 10
McCubbin, Louis Frederick, 10
McDougall, Dugald Gordon, 10
Meeson, Dora, 8
Minogue, Henry, 10
Pattison, James Grant, 11
Sodeman, Arnold Karl, 12
Stillwell, Frank Leslie, 12
Walker, Fred, 12
HEALESVILLE
Lalor, Vivian William, 9
White, Jessie McHardy, 12
HEATHCOTE
Cocks, Sir Arthur Alfred Clement, 8

McCormack, William Thomas
   Bartholomew, 10
HEIDELBERG
   Lewis, Edward Powell, 10
HERNE HILL
   Armstrong, Edmund La Touche, 7
HIGHTON
   Newland, James Ernest, 11
HOMEBUSH
   Goudie, Sir George Louis, 9
   Kenyon, Alfred Stephen, 9
HORSHAM
   Watson, Charles Vincent, 12
   Woollard, Herbert Henry, 12
HOTHAM
   Anderson, Valentine George, 7
   Cattanach, William, 7
   Lawrence, Charles Edward, 10
HUNTLY
   Davidson, William St John Stevens,
   8
INDIGO
   Gaunt, Mary Eliza Bakewell, 8
INGLEWOOD
   Blackburn, Maurice McCrae, 7
   Tivey, Edwin, 12
ITALIAN GULLY
   Roberts, John Garibaldi, 11
   Roberts, William Joshua, 11
KANGAROO FLAT
   Luxton, Sir Harold Daniel, 10
   Wickens, Charles Henry, 12
KANGAROO GROUND
   Furphy, John, 4
KANIVA
   Leason, Percy Alexander, 10
KENSINGTON
   Hardwick, Arthur Ernest, 9
KEW
   Alsop, Rodney Howard, 7
   Bell, George Frederick Henry, 7
   Brodzky, Horace Ascher, 7
   Carson, Duncan, 7
   Carter, Norman St Clair, 7
   Dodd, Arthur William, 8
   Langley, Hudson John Watson, 9
   Miller, Everard Studley, 10
   Moore, James Lorenzo, 10
   Murphy, Arthur William, 10
   Ratten, Victor Richard, 11
   Ritchie, Edgar Gowar, 11
   St Clair, William Howard, 11
   Stawell, Florence Melian, 12
   Stawell, Sir Richard Rawdon, 12
   Waldock, Arthur John, 12
KILDARE
   Archibald, Jules François, 3
KILMORE
   Burston, James, 7
   Davis, Charles Herbert, 8
   Finlay, Mary McKenzie, 8
   Kerr, William Warren, 9
   Lade, Frank, 9
   MacKenzie, Sir William Colin, 10

KINGSTON
   Hodgson, William Roy, 9
   Shapcott, Louis Edward, 11
   Smith, Miles Staniforth Cater, 11
KOROIT
   Crowe, Robert, 8
   Murray, John, 10
KYNETON
   Argyle, Sir Stanley Seymour, 7
   Armstrong, Warwick Windridge, 7
   Burton, Alexander Stewart, 7
   Elliott, Robert Charles Dunlop, 8
   Gregory, Henry, 9
   Le Couteur, Philip Ridgeway, 10
   Minogue, Michael Andrew, 10
   Southern, Clara, 12
LAKE TYERS
   Thorpe, Harry, 12
LAL LAL
   Hall, Robert, 9
LANCEFIELD
   Lockwood, Alfred Wright, 10
   Moore, Eleanor May, 10
   Onians, Edith Charlotte, 11
   Wilson, Alexander William, 12
LANDSBOROUGH
   Morgan, Godfrey, 10
LEARMONTH
   McDougall, John Keith, 10
LETHBRIDGE
   Elmslie, George Alexander, 8
LINTON
   Charlton, Matthew, 7
   Scantlebury Brown, Vera, 11
LITTLE RIVER
   Devine, Sir Hugh Berchmans, 8
   Tranter, Charles Herbert, 12
LONGWOOD
   Tubb, Frederick Harold, 12
   Wiltshire, Aubrey Roy Liddon, 12
LOWER JORDAN
   Martin, Lewis Ormsby, 10
MACORNA
   Schenk, Rodolphe Samuel, 11
MAGPIE
   Hill, William Duguid, 9
MAJORCA
   Nicholas, Alfred Michael, 11
   Nicholas, George Richard Rich, 11
MALDON
   Brigden, James Bristock, 7
   Daley, Charles Studdy, 8
   Hain, Gladys Adeline, 9
   Michell, John Henry, 10
   Woodfull, William Maldon, 12
MALVERN
   Newton, Sir Hibbert Alan Stephen, 11
MANSFIELD
   McMillan, Samuel, 10
MARRAWEENEY
   Tuckett, Lewis, 12
MARYBOROUGH
   Allen, Horace William, 7
   Allen, Leslie Holdsworth, 7

Healy, George Daniel, 9
Osborne, Henry William, 11
Toutcher, Richard Frederick, 12
Melbourne
Allen, Mary Cecil, 7
Baskerville, Margaret Francis Ellen, 7
Bear, Annette Ellen, 7
Beaurepaire, Sir Francis Joseph Edmund, 7
Brahe, Mary Hannah, 7
Bruche, Sir Julius Henry, 7
Cameron, Donald James, 7
Campbell, Elizabeth, 7
Carson, David, 3
Carter, Bryce Morrow, 7
Carter, Francis Mowat, 7
Castles, Amy Eliza, 7
Cazaly, Roy, 7
Clarke, William, 3
Clarke, William Lionel Russell, 8
Cockram, Thomas (1860-1920), 8
Code, Edward Percival, 8
Cohen, Isaac Henry, 8
Coyne, John Harry, 8
Cumming, Thomas Forrest, 3
Davies, Sir John George, 8
De Garis, Clement John, 8
Duggan, William Joseph, 8
Dyer, Louise Berta Mosson Hanson, 8
Dymock, William, 8
Fetherston, Richard Herbert Joseph, 8
Flynn, Julia Teresa, 8
Foxton, Justin Fox Greenlaw, 8
French, Charles Hamilton, 8
Frewin, Kenneth Moreton, 8
Froggatt, Walter Wilson, 8
Geach, Portia Swanston, 8
Gibson, Robert, 8
Grice, Sir John, 9
Grover, Montague MacGregor, 9
Hall, Eliza Rowdon, 9
Hamilton, John, 4
Hamilton, William, 9
Harper, Margaret Hilda, 9
Harris, Alfred, 9
Haynes, Thomas Watson, 9
Hennessy, Sir David Valentine, 9
Hentze, Margaret Edith, 9
Hodgson, Richard, 4
Hood, Sir Joseph Henry, 9
Hordern, Anthony (1842-1886), 4
Howard, Henry, 9
Irvine, Hans William Henry, 9
Irving, Godfrey George Howy, 9
Isaacs, Sir Isaac Alfred, 9
Johnston, Charles Melbourne, 9
Johnston, George Jameson, 9
Kellaway, Charles Halliley, 9
Kennedy, Colin, 9
Kennedy, John, 9
Knox, William, 9
Kruse, Johann Secundus, 5
Labilliere, Francis Peter, 5
Le Souef, Albert Sherbourne, 10

Lindrum, Frederick William, 10
Lonergan, John Joseph, 10
McCracken, Alexander, 10
McCubbin, Frederick, 10
McDonald, Charles, 10
Macintyre, Ronald George, 10
McPherson, Sir William Murray, 10
Mahony, Daniel James, 10
Mahony, Francis, 10
Maloney, William Robert, 10
Mattingley, Arthur Herbert Evelyn, 10
Meyer, Felix Henry, 10
Mitchell, Isabel Mary, 10
Mitchell, Janet Charlotte, 10
Monash, Sir John, 10
Murdoch, Sir Keith Arthur, 10
Nathan, Sir Charles Samuel, 10
Norriss, Elizabeth May, 12
O'Ferrall, Ernest Francis, 11
Oliphant, Ernest Henry Clark, 11
Oliver, Donald Percy, 11
Parer, Raymond John Paul, 11
Parnell, John William, 11
Patterson, John Hunter (1882-1963), 11
Patterson, Robert Charles, 11
Pitt, William, 11
Pittman, Edward Fisher, 11
Purves, James Liddell, 5
Purves Smith, Charles Roderick, 11
Quinn, James Peter, 11
Ralston, Walter Vardon, 11
Richardson, Ethel Tracy, 11
Riddell, Walter John Carre, 11
Rigby, Edward Charles, 11
Robinson, William Sydney, 11
Rowan, Marian Ellis, 11
Russell, Delia Constance Law, 11
Saunders, John Victor, 11
Scanlan, John Joseph, 11
Serle, Dora Beatrice, 11
Sexton, Hannah Mary Helen, 11
Shields, Sir Douglas Andrew, 11
Smyth, Bridgetena (Brettena), 12
Swanton, Mary Hynes, 12
Syme, Sir Geoffrey, 12
Taverner, Sir John William, 12
Taylor, Henry Joseph Stirling, 12
Teague, Violet Helen Evangeline, 12
Thurgood, Albert John, 12
Thwaites, William, 12
Toohey, James Matthew, 6
Turner, Sir George, 12
Turner, Walter James Redfern, 12
Vernon, Howard, 12
Weedon, Sir Henry, 12
Wilkie, Leslie Andrew Alexander, 12
Wilson, Arthur Mitchell, 12
Wise, George Henry, 12
Young, Florence Maude, 12
Zelman, Samuel Victor Albert, 12
MELTON
Richards, Henry Caselli, 11
MERINO
Smith, Henry Teesdale, 11

METCALFE
  Rentoul, Thomas Craike, 11
MICKLEHAM
  Cole, George Henry, 8
MIDDLE PARK
  Ulm, Charles Thomas Philippe, 12
MILAWA
  Murdoch, Thomas (1876-1961), 10
MOLIAGUL
  Flynn, John, 8
  Lane, Zebina Bartholomew, 9
MOONEE PONDS
  Albiston, Walter, 7
  Edgerton, Eric Henry Drummond, 8
  Hailes, William Allan, 9
  Kennedy, Thomas James, 9
  Kinnear, Edward Hore, 9
  Kinnear, Henry Humphrey, 9
  McDowall, Archibald, 10
  Whitton, Ivo Harrington, 12
MOOROOPNA
  Mills, Richard Charles, 10
MORNINGTON
  Stone, Emily Mary Page, 12
MORRISON
  Dyson, Edward George, 8
MOUNT ARARAT
  West, John, 12
MULGRAVE
  Woods, Walter Alan, 12
MUMBANNAR
  Pratt, Rachel, 11
MYRTLEFORD
  Lowerson, Albert David, 10
NAVARRE
  Pennington, John Warburton, 11
NEW CHUM
  Lazarus, Daniel Barnet, 10
NEWBRIDGE
  Bayley, Arthur Wellesley, 7
NEWPORT
  Sturgess, Reginald Ward, 12
NEWTOWN
  Fairbairn, Sir George, 8
  Kernot, Wilfred Noyce, 9
  Morrison, Charles Norman, 10
  Morrison, George Ernest, 10
NHILL
  Stonehouse, Ethel Nhill Victoria, 12
NORTHCOTE
  Latham, Richard Thomas Edwin, 10
NORVAL
  Burke, Thomas Michael, 7
OAKLEIGH
  Mustar, Ernest Andrew, 10
OSBORNS FLAT
  Bosch, George Henry, 7
PARKVILLE
  Smith, Christian Brynhild Ochiltree Jollie,
    11
PASTORAL STATIONS
  Austin, Edward Arthur, 7
  Beggs, Hugh Norman, 7
  Beggs, Robert Gottlieb, 7

  Brennan, Thomas Cornelius, 7
  Brennan, William Adrian, 7
  Cameron, Alexander, 7
  Clarke, Janet Marion, 3
  Connolly, Eric Alfred, 8
  Davidson, James, 8
  Dunhill, Sir Thomas Peel, 8
  Hood, Robert Alexander David, 9
  McArthur, Sir William Gilbert Stewart,
    10
  McLeod, Donald Norman, 10
  Manifold, Edward, 10
  Manifold, James Chester, 10
  Manifold, William Thomson, 10
  Maygar, Leslie Cecil, 10
  Mullagh, Johnny, 5
  Patterson, Daniel Whittle Harvey, 11
  Rankin, John, 11
  Ryan, Sir Charles Snodgrass, 11
  Sanderson, Archibald, 11
  Sanderson, Sir John, 11
  Skene, Thomas, 11
  Wallace, Donald Smith, 6
  White, Dudley Persse, 12
PEG LEG
  Watson, William, 12
PENSHURST
  Treflé, John Louis, 12
  Waller, Mervyn Napier, 12
PLEASANT CREEK, *see also* Stawell
  Grant, William, 9
POMBORNEIT
  McNamara, Daniel Laurence, 10
POOTILLA
  Bourchier, Sir Murray William James,
    7
PORT FAIRY, *see also* Belfast
  Moloney, Parker John, 10
  Rupp, Herman Montague Rucker, 11
  Ryan, Thomas Joseph, 11
PORT MELBOURNE
  Deane, Percival Edgar, 8
  Johnson, Florence Ethel, 9
  Langley, George Furner, 9
  Treloar, John Linton, 12
  Turnbull, Ernest, 12
PORTLAND
  Cussen, Sir Leo Finn Bernard, 8
  Goldstein, Vida Jane Mary, 9
  Hales, Thomas, 4
  McKillop, Donald, 5
PRAHRAN
  Bayles, Norman, 7
  Beckett, William James, 7
  Cobby, Arthur Henry, 8
  Cook, Bertie Stuart Baxter, 8
  James, Winifred Llewellyn, 9
  Knox, Sir George Hodges, 9
  Marden, John, 10
  Murphy, George Read, 10
  Rentoul, Annie Rattray, 11
  Stevens, Horace Ernest, 12
  Tate, Henry, 12
  Thomson, Herbert, 12

Warren, Hubert Ernest de Mey, 12
Winter, Joseph, 12
PRESTON
Patterson, Gerald Leighton, 11
PURDEET
Donaldson, John, 4
PURNIM
Rawlings, William Reginald, 11
QUEENSCLIFF
Baillieu, William Lawrence, 7
Champion de Crespigny, Sir Constantine
  Trent, 7
RAYWOOD
Donaldson, John, 8
McKay, Hugh Victor, 10
RHEOLA
Gunn, John, 9
RICHMOND
Ashworth, Thomas Ramsden, 7
Austral, Florence Mary, 7
Bale, Alice Marian Ellen, 7
Campbell, Thomas Irving, 7
Dodd, Josiah Eustace, 8
Dunkley, Louisa Margaret, 8
Fairbairn, Frederick William, 8
Forster, Thomas Richmond, 8
Fuhrman, Osmond Charles William, 8
Gratton, Norman Murray Gladstone, 9
Henry, Alice, 9
Hill, Alfred Francis, 9
Melba, Dame Nellie, 10
Miles, John Campbell, 10
Miller, Sir Edward, 10
Mullaly, John Charles, 10
O'Connor, Eily Rosaline, 11
Parker, Frank Critchley, 11
Perry, Stanley Wesley, 11
Schutt, William John, 11
Smith, Robert, 11
Tait, Sir Frank Samuel, 12
Taylor, Henry D'Esterre, 12
Wales, Sir Alexander George, 12
Wrigley, Leslie James, 12
ROSEBROOK
Goble, Joseph Hunter, 9
ROSEDALE
Buntine, Walter Murray, 7
RUSHWORTH
McNamara, Frank Hubert, 10
ST ARNAUD
McPherson, Sir Clive, 10
White, Sir Cyril Brudenell Bingham,
  12
ST KILDA
Bage, Anna Frederika, 7
Barnett, Henry Walter, 7
Bennett, James Mallett, 7
Boyd, William Merric, 7
Brookes, Sir Norman Everard, 7
Bruce, Stanley Melbourne, 7
Bunny, Rupert Charles Wulsten, 7
Clapp, Sir Harold Winthrop, 8
Cohen, Harold Edward, 8
Connibere, Sir Charles Wellington, 8

Connibere, Frederick George, 8
Gillespie, Sir Robert Winton, 9
Grimwade, Edward Norton, 9
Grimwade, Harold William, 9
Lavater, Louis Isidore, 10
McInnes, William Beckwith, 10
Marlowe, Margaret Mary, 10
Mulvany, Edward Joseph, 10
O'Hara Wood, Hector, 11
O'Keeffe, David Augustus, 11
Pelloe, Emily Harriet, 11
Phillips, Marion, 11
Phillips, Morris Mondle, 11
Prell, Charles Ernest, 11
Robertson, William Apperley Norton,
  11
Sheehan, Sir Henry John, 11
Sloane, Thomas Gibson, 11
Taylor, Irene Frances, 12
SALE
Bell, Sir George John, 7
Bruce, Minnie (Mary) Grant, 7
Chomley, Charles Henry, 7
Leslie, William Durham, 10
SANDFORD
Jackson, Ernest Sandford, 9
SANDHURST, see also Bendigo
Anderson, William, 7
Andrews, John Arthur, 7
Atkinson, Evelyn John Rupert, 7
Boyland, John, 7
Brookes, Herbert Robinson, 7
Dethridge, George James, 8
Duffy, Maurice Boyce, 8
Dyason, Edward Clarence Evelyn, 8
Findley, Edward, 8
Herman, Hyman, 9
Jess, Sir Carl Herman, 9
Kirkby, Sydney James, 9
Mackey, Sir John Emanuel, 10
MacMahon, Charles, 10
MacMahon, James, 10
Meudell, George Dick, 10
Moffitt, Ernest Edward, 10
Mollison, Crawford Henry, 10
Moore, William George, 10
Morres, Elsie Frances, 10
Murdoch, William David, 10
Murdoch, William Lloyd, 5
O'Hara, John Bernard, 11
Palmer, Janet Gertrude, 11
Perry, Orizaba George, 11
Swanson, Donald Alexander, 12
Swanson, Sir John Warren, 12
SANDRIDGE
Newman, Leslie John William, 11
SANDRINGHAM
MacNeil, Neil Harcourt, 10
SCARSDALE
McGrath, David Charles, 10
SEBASTIAN
Yuill, William John, 12
SEBASTOPOL
Collins, James Richard, 8

Jensen, Jens August, 9
Stewart, Archibald, 12
Thomas, William Charles, 12
SEVEN CREEKS
Gilpin, Oliver, 9
SEYMOUR
Buggy, Edward Hugh, 7
SHEPPARTON
Trevascus, William Charles, 12
SKIPTON
Aitken, George Lewis, 7
SMEATON
McClelland, Hugh, 10
SMYTHESDALE
Lynch, Arthur Alfred, 10
SOUTH YARRA
Brodzky, Leon Herbert Spencer, 7
Brookes, Ivy, 7
Clendinnen, Leslie John, 8
Cumpston, John Howard Lidgett, 8
Dethridge, John Stewart, 8
Hughes, Agnes Eva, 9
Knox, Sir Robert Wilson, 9
Lind, Edmund Frank, 10
Merrett, Sir Charles Edward, 10
Murphy, Herbert Dyce, 10
Ransford, Vernon Seymour, 11
Stang, Eleanor Margrethe, 12
Strong, Sir Archibald Thomas, 12
Tucker, Gerard Kennedy, 12
Tuckett, Joseph Helton, 12
Willis, Ernest Horatio, 12
SPRING HILL
Sewell, Alice Maud, 11
Trethowan, Sir Arthur King, 12
STAWELL, *see also* Pleasant Creek
Brennan, Edward Thomas, 7
Cato, Frederick John, 7
Cooch, Alexander, 8
Croll, Robert Henderson, 8
Hutchinson, William, 9
Whelan, James Paul, 12
Wymark, Frederick Victor Grey, 12
STRATHBOGIE
Mackrell, Edwin Joseph, 10
STRATHLODDON
Pitt, Ernest Roland, 11
STUART MILL
Macdonell, Donald, 10
SUNBURY
Clarke, Sir Francis Grenville, 8
Clarke, Sir Rupert Turner Havelock, 8
Shirlow, John Alexander Thomas, 11
SUTHERLAND PLAINS
Duggan, Bernard Oscar Charles, 8
SUTTON GRANGE
Kellow, Henry Brown, 9
SWAN HILL
McDonald, Arthur Stephen, 10
TAGGERTY
Bowen, Rowland Griffiths, 7
TALBOT
Griffiths, Philip Lewis, 9
Winneke, Henry Christian, 12

TARADALE
McNamara, William Henry Thomas, 10
Wray, Frederick William, 12
TARRAVILLE
Crossley, Ada Jemima, 8
TATONG
Savage, Michael Joseph, 11
TATURA
Mactier, Robert, 10
TERANG
Conacher, Charles William Davy, 8
Duigan, John Robertson, 8
Edwards, John Harold McKenzie, 8
Skeyhill, Thomas John, 11
TOOLAMBA
Gullett, Sir Henry Somer, 9
TOOLLEEN
Downey, Michael Henry, 8
TOORAK
Fairbairn, Stephen, 8
Harper, Robert Rainy, 9
Scott, Henry James Herbert, 6
TRAWALLA
Scullin, James Henry, 11
UPPER MURRAY
Jephcott, Sydney Wheeler, 9
VAUGHAN
Dunstan, Benjamin, 8
VIOLET TOWN
Tuckett, Philip Samuel, 12
WALHALLA
Tisdall, Alice Constance, 12
WALLACE
Hogan, Edmond John, 9
WALLAN WALLAN
Long, Charles Richard, 10
WANDILIGONG
Roberts, Mary Ellen, 11
Treasure, Harry Louis, 12
WANGARATTA
Ah Ket, William, 7
WARRAGUL
Greeves, Edward Goderich, 9
WARRNAMBOOL
Dickson, James, 8
Forth, Nowell Barnard de Lancey, 8
Manifold, Sir Walter Synnot, 10
Oakley, Robert McKeeman, 11
Ross, Isabella Henrietta Younger, 11
Russell, Edward John, 11
Saltau, Marcus, 11
Stewart, John McKellar, 12
WATERLOO
Chinnery, Ernest William Pearson, 7
Moore, John Charles, 10
WHITTLESEA
Lockwood, Joseph, 10
WILLIAMSTOWN
Barbour, George Pitty, 7
Draper, Alexander Frederick, 8
Guerin, Julia Margaret, 9
Levien, Jonas Felix Australia, 5
Mullen, Leslie Miltiades, 10
Stephens, Henry Douglas, 12

Syme, David York, 12
Tudor, Francis Gwynne, 12
Wilsmore, Norman Thomas Mortimer, 12
WINCHELSEA
Austin, Austin Albert, 7
Austin, Edwin Henry, 7
Jacka, Albert, 9
WINDSOR
Hughes, Frederic Godfrey, 9
O'Driscoll, Charles Xavier, 11
Shore, Arnold Joseph Victor, 11
Wadsworth, Arthur, 12
WODONGA
Schlink, Sir Herbert Henry, 11
WOODS POINT
Knowles, Marion, 9
WOODSTOCK
Collier, Phillip, 8
WOORAGEE
Billson, Alfred Arthur, 7
YACKANDANDAH
Tewksbury, William Pearson, 12
Tewskbury, Alphonso Reed, 12
YAMBUK
Watson, Charles Henry, 12
YAN YEAN
McPhee, Sir John Cameron, 10
YARRA GLEN
Furphy, Joseph, 8
YARRAWONGA
Frazer, Charles Edward, 8
Rivett, Amy Christine, 11
Rivett, Edward William, 11
Rivett, Olive Murray, 11
YEA
McLeish, Duncan, 10
Western Australia
Bussell, William John, 7
Harris, William, 9
Monger, John Henry, 5
Tjangamarra, 12
ALBANY
Fowles, Herbert James, 8
Hassell, Albert Young, 4
Maley, John Stephen, 5
AUSTRALIND
Rose, Edwin, 11
Rose, George Canler, 11
BEVERLEY
Lee Steere, Sir Ernest Augustus, 10
BUNBURY
Forrest, Sir John (1847-1918), 8
Johnston, Harry Frederick, 9
Sholl, Richard Adolphus, 11
Sholl, Robert Frederick, 11
BUSSELTON
Drake-Brockman, Edmund Alfred, 8
COLD HARBOUR
Parker, Sir Stephen Henry, 11
COOLGARDIE
Tuckett, Francis Curtis, 12
DARDANUP
Mitchell, Sir James, 10

FREMANTLE
Boyle, Ignatius George, 7
Dempster, Charles Edward, 4
Marmion, William Edward, 10
Moore, Sir Newton James, 10
Paterson, William, 11
Pearse, William Silas, 5
Snook, Charles William, 12
Wittenoom, Sir Edward Charles (Horne), 12
Yelverton, Henry John, 6
GERALDTON
Chase, Muriel Jean Eliot, 7
Cowan, Edith Dircksey, 8
Gale, Charles Frederick, 8
Gale, Walter Augustus, 8
Johnston, Edward Bertram, 9
Lawrence, Gordon Ord, 10
Murphy, Bennett Francis, 10
GREENOUGH
Farrelly, Mary Martha, 8
GUILDFORD
Hackett, Deborah Vernon, 9
Harper, Charles Walter, 9
Withnell, Emma Mary, 6
GWAMBYGINE
Wittenoom, Frederick Francis Burdett, 12
JARRAHDALE
Martin, William Clarence, 10
KALGOORLIE
Lindrum, Walter Albert, 10
KELLERBERRIN
Windich, Tommy, 6
MOKINE
Wollaston, Sir Harry Newton Phillips, 12
NORTHAM
Drake-Brockman, Frederick Slade, 8
Piesse, Frederick Henry, 11
Throssell, Hugo Vivian Hope, 12
NORTHAMPTON
Drew, John Michael, 8
OAKOVER
Moore, William Dalgety, 5
Perth
Bell, Frederick William, 7
Chipper, Donald John, 7
Ferguson, Charles William, 4
James, Sir Walter Hartwell, 9
Leake, George, 10
Lefroy, Sir Henry Bruce, 10
Linton, James Alexander Barrow, 10
North, Charles Frederic, 11
Parker, Hubert Stanley Wyborn, 11
Shenton, Sir George, 6
Sholl, Horatio William, 11
Skinner, Mary Louisa, 11
Stone, Sir Edward Albert, 12
Stoneman, Ethel Turner, 12
Strickland, William Henry John, 6
Wallis, William Dane, 12
PICTON
Forrest, Alexander, 8
POINT WALTER
Waylen, Alfred Robert, 6

TOODYAY
  Harper, Charles, 4
UPPER SWAN
  Carson, Alfred, 7
YORK
  Brown, Maitland, 3
  McCarthy, Lawrence Dominic, 10
  Monger, Alexander Joseph, 10
  Monger, Frederick Charles, 10
AUSTRIA, *see also* Austro-Hungarian
  Empire
  Guerard, Johann Joseph Eugen von, 4
AUSTRO-HUNGARIAN EMPIRE
  Breinl, Anton, 7
  Brunnich, Johannes Christian, 7
  Daneš, Jirí Václav, 8
  Degotardi, John, 4
  D'Hage, Ludwig, 8
  Freedman, David Isaac, 8
  Goll, Edward, 9
  Kranewitter, Aloysius, 5
  Makutz, Bela, 5
  Peterson, Georgette Augusta Christina,
    11
  Pinschof, Carl Ludwig, 11
  Rubinstein, Helena, 11
  Strele, Anton, 6
  Weindorfer, Gustav, 12
  Wiedermann, Elise, 11
  Wortman, Adolphus, 2
  Zelman, Alberto, 6
  Zimpel, William James, 12
AZORES
  Gordon, Adam Lindsay, 4
BELGIUM
  Armit, William Edington, 3
  Bernacchi, Louis Charles, 7
  De Bavay, Auguste Joseph François, 8
  Dechaineux, Florent Vincent Emile
    Lucien, 8
  Drury, Albert Victor, 4
  Drury, Edward Robert, 4
  Lodewyckx, Augustin, 10
  Mouton, Jean Baptiste Octave, 10
  Renard, Jules, 6
  Verbrugghen, Henri Adrien Marie, 12
BRAZIL
  Richardson, Arthur Charles Jeston, 11
  Sharman, Matthew Stanton, 11
CANADA
  Abbott, Edward, 1
  Broome, Sir Frederick Napier, 3
  Brown, Henry Yorke Lyell, 7
  Burrowes, Robert, 3
  Chaffey, George, 7
  Chaffey, William Benjamin, 7
  Crews, John Branscombe, 3
  Dalgety, Frederick Gonnerman, 4
  Darling, Sir Charles Henry, 4
  De Chair, Sir Dudley Rawson Stratford,
    8
  Fraser, Sir Simon, 4
  Gilbert, John, 4
  Harris, Richard Deodatus Poulett, 4

  Hunt, John Horbury, 4
  Kelly, Ethel Knight, 9
  Lane, Zebina, 9
  Lawson, Abercrombie Anstruther, 10
  Molloy, Thomas George Anstruther, 10
  Prieur, François Xavier, 2
  Redfern, William, 2
  Seymour, John Alfred, 11
  Smith, Charles Patrick, 11
  Tait, Sir Thomas James, 12
  Zouch, Henry, 6
CAPE COLONY, *see also* South Africa
  Blyth, John, 3
  Donnithorne, Eliza Emily, 4
  Ebden, Charles Hotson, 1
  Gunn, Ronald Campbell, 1
  Halloran, Henry, 4
  Miller, Edmund Morris, 10
  White, Gilbert, 12
CASTELORIZO
  Michelides, Peter Spero, 10
CEYLON
  Christie, William Harvie, 3
  Goodwin, Sir Thomas Herbert John
    Chapman, 9
  Ligar, Charles Whybrow, 5
  Robinson, Lionel George, 11
  White, James Charles, 6
CHANNEL ISLES
  Armstrong, Richard Ramsay, 3
  Bidmead, Martha Sarah, 7
  Broun, Peter Nicholas, 1
  Caire, Nicholas John, 3
  Campbell, Oswald Rose, 3
  Carey, George Jackson, 3
  Collett, Herbert Brayley, 8
  Cotton, Alfred John, 8
  De Garis, Elisha Clement, 8
  De La Condamine, Thomas, 1
  Douglas, Alexander Douglas, 4
  Fink, Benjamin Josman, 4
  Fink, Theodore, 8
  Harry, Gilbert, 9
  Hodel, Joseph, 9
  Kennedy, Edmund Besley Court, 2
  Laurens, John, 5
  Smith, William Saumarez, 11
CHILE
  Watson, John Christian, 12
CHINA
  Ah Mouy, Louis, 3
  Cheong Cheok Hong, 3
  Chin Kaw, 7
  Kwok Bew, 9
  Leon, Andrew, 5
  Mei Quong Tart, 5
  See Poy, Tom, 11
  Ten, George Soo Hoo, 6
  Tickell, Frederick, 12
  Turner, Alfred Jefferis, 12
  Way Lee, Yet Soo War, 12
  Young Wai, John, 12
COOK ISLANDS
  Ruatoka, 6

DALMATIA
Jasprizza, Nicholas, 4
DENMARK
Bjelke-Petersen, Hans Christian, 7
Bjelke-Petersen, Marie Caroline, 7
Jensen, Harald Ingemann, 9
Jensen, Joergen Christian, 9
Jorgenson, Jorgen, 2
Knox, Sir Edward, 5
Koerstz, Christian Christiansen, 9
Nielsen, Niels Rasmus Wilson, 11
Salting, Severin Kanute, 2
DUTCH EAST INDIES
Using, Daeng Rangka, 6
EGYPT
Perkins, Arthur James, 11
Smith, Issy, 11
ENGLAND
Allen, William, 1
Allison, William Race, 1
Barrow, John Henry, 3
Bayley, Sir Lyttleton Holyoake, 3
Bedford, Sir Frederick George Denham, 7
Belstead, Charles Torrens, 3
Best, Charles, 1
Best, Henry, 1
Boothby, Benjamin (1831-1883), 3
Boothby, Josiah, 3
Boothby, Thomas Wilde, 3
Boothby, William Robinson, 3
Boyd, Edward, 1
Brockman, Edmund Ralph, 3
Brown, James, 3
Burbury, Thomas, 1
Burnett, James Charles, 3
Busby, William, 3
Cadman, John, 1
Cathcart, James Faucitt, 3
Cathcart, Mary Fanny, 3
Challinor, Henry, 3
Challis, John Henry, 3
Cross, John, 1
Crouch, James Joseph, 3
Dana, Henry Edward Pulteney, 1
Darrell, George Frederick Price, 4
De Little, Robert, 1
De Satgé, Oscar John, 4
Degraves, William, 4
Dennys, Charles John, 4
Desailly, Francis William Wisdom, 4
Dowling, Robert Hawker, 4
Driscoll, Cornelius, 1
Eddy, Edward Miller Gard, 8
Edwards, Sir James Bevan, 4
Farmer, Sir William, 4
Fulton, Henry, 1
Garvin, Lucy Arabella Stocks, 8
Gellibrand, Joseph Tice, 1
Gilbert, John, 1
Gould, Charles, 4
Griffiths, Jonathan, 1
Grose, Francis, 1
Hallen, Ambrose, 1
Hallen, Edward, 1

Harrap, Alfred, 4
Hart, John, 4
Hawkins, Thomas Fitzherbert, 1
Hume, Fergusson Wright, 4
Hunt, Charles Cooke, 4
James, Henry Kerrison, 4
Kay, William Porden, 2
Kempt, John Francis, 5
Knowles, Conrad Theodore, 2
Landor, Edward Willson, 2
Leake, George, 2
McCrone, Francis Nesbitt, 2
Merewether, Francis Lewis Shaw, 5
Montefiore, Dorothy Frances, 10
Moore, Thomas, 2
Nairn, William, 2
Nettleton, Charles, 5
O'Flaherty, Eliza, 2
Palmer, John, 2
Perdriau, Henry Carter, 11
Praed, Annie, 11
Reveley, Henry Willey, 2
Reynolds, Thomas, 6
Robey, Ralph Mayer, 6
Robinson, Michael Massey, 2
Shadforth, Thomas, 2
Singleton, Benjamin, 2
Stephens, Samuel, 2
Sweet, George, 12
Thompson, Richard, 2
Tolmer, Alexander, 6
Uther, Reuben, 2
Wardell, Robert, 2
West, John, 2
Williams, Sir Edward Eyre, 6
Windeyer, Archibald, 2
Woolley, Emmeline Mary Dogherty, 12
Woolley, Thomas, 2
London
à Beckett, Sir Thomas, 3
à Beckett, Thomas Turner, 3
à Beckett, Sir William, 3
Abel, Charles William, 7
Abigail, Francis, 3
Abrahams, Joseph, 7
Adcock, William Eddrup, 7
Alexander, Maurice, 8
Allan, George Leavis, 3
Alt, Augustus Theodore Henry, 1
Andrews, Cecil Rollo Payton, 7
Anstey, Francis George, 7
Archer, William Henry, 3
Atkins, Thomas, 1
Babbage, Benjamin Herschel, 3
Baker, Shirley Waldemar, 3
Barnett, Neville George, 3
Bassett, William Frederick, 3
Bateman, John, 1
Batty, Francis de Witt, 7
Beamont, John, 1
Beauchamp, Earl, 7
Beazley, William David, 7
Bedford, Edward Samuel Pickard, 3
Belbin, James, 1

London

Belmore, Earl of, 3
Benjamin, Sir Benjamin, 3
Bent, Andrew, 1
Bernays, Lewis Adolphus, 3
Berry, Sir Graham, 3
Beuzeville, James, 3
Bevan, Theodore Francis, 3
Birnie, Richard, 3
Black, Maurice Hume, 3
Bland, William, 1
Bonython, Sir John Langdon, 7
Boyce, Charles, 3
Boyce, Thomas Burnham, 3
Boyd, Benjamin, 1
Bracewell, David, 1
Bradley, Henry Burton, 3
Brodribb, William Adams, 3
Brown, Gilbert Wilson, 3
Browne, Thomas Alexander, 3
Butler, Henry, 3
Byatt, John, 7
Campion, Sir William Robert, 7
Cannan, Kearsey, 3
Canterbury, Viscount, 3
Carlile, Sir Edward, 7
Carnegie, David Wynford, 7
Carrington, Francis Thomas Dean, 3
Cassell, James Horatio Nelson, 3
Chalmers, William, 3
Chelmsford, Baron, 7
Chester, Henry Marjoribanks, 3
Child, Coles, 3
Childers, Hugh Culling Eardley, 3
Chubb, Charles Edward, 3
Clark, Alfred Thomas, 3
Clark, Charles, 3
Clark, Thomas, 3
Clunies Ross, William John, 8
Cohen, Edward, 3
Collins, David, 1
Colvin, Sir Ragnar Musgrave, 8
Conder, Charles Edward, 3
Cooke, Ebenezer, 3
Cooper, Robert, 1
Coote, William, 3
Cope, Thomas Spencer, 3
Cotton, Francis, 1
Cox, Francis William, 3
Cribb, Thomas Bridson, 8
Crommelin, George Whiting, 3
Crossley, George, 1
Crouch, Thomas James, 3
Curtis, Anthony, 1
Dacre, Ranulph, 1
Daplyn, Alfred James, 4
Dashwood, George Frederick, 1
Davidson, John Ewen, 8
Davies, John, 4
Davies, Maurice Coleman, 4
Davis, Alexander Barnard, 4
Davis, Charles, 8
De Bernales, Claude Albo, 8
De Boos, Charles Edward Augustus, 4
De Lissa, Alfred, 4

Deane, John Philip, 1
Deffell, George Hibbert, 4
Denison, Sir William Thomas, 4
Denman, Thomas, Baron, 8
Dilke, Sir Charles Wentworth, 4
Docker, Joseph, 4
Donaldson, St Clair George Alfred, 8
Douglas, John, 4
Dowling, Sir James, 1
Dowling, James Sheen, 4
Drake, James George, 8
Du Croz, Frederick Augustus, 4
Du Faur, Frederick Eccleston, 4
Dudley, William Humble Ward, Earl, 8
Dugdale, Henrietta Augusta, 4
Duterrau, Benjamin, 1
Dwight, Henry Tolman, 4
Eardley-Wilmot, Sir John Eardley, 1
Earle, Augustus, 1
Ebsworth, Frederick Louis, 4
Ebsworth, Octavius Bayliffe, 4
Elphinstone, Augustus Cecil, 8
Elsey, Joseph Ravenscroft, 4
Evans, George Essex, 8
Eyre, John (1768-1854), 1
Fawkner, John Pascoe, 1
Feakes, Henry James, 8
Fehon, William Meeke, 8
Fisher, Charles Brown, 4
Fitch, Algernon Sydney, 8
Fitzhardinge, William George Augustus,
    4
Flower, Horace, 4
Forwood, Walter Weech, 4
Fowler, Francis Edmund Town, 4
Francis, James Goodall, 4
Freeling, Sir Arthur Henry, 4
Fuller, Sir Benjamin John, 8
Fuller, John, 8
Garran, Andrew, 4
Gibbes, John George Nathaniel, 1
Gibson, Alexander James, 8
Gibson, William Alfred, 8
Gilles, Osmond, 1
Gladman, Frederick John, 4
Goderich, Viscount, 1
Goldsmith, Frederick William, 9
Gordon, Alexander, 4
Gosling, John William, 1
Goulburn, Henry, 1
Goyder, George Woodroffe, 4
Griffiths, George Richard, 1
Grubb, William Dawson, 4
Gurney, Theodore Thomas, 4
Haddon, Robert Joseph, 9
Hall, Edward Smith, 1
Hall, William, 1
Hall, William Shakespeare, 4
Halley, Jacob John, 4
Hanson, Sir Richard Davies, 4
Hare, Charles Simeon, 4
Harper, Herbert Reah, 9
Harris, Alexander, 1
Harris, George, 4

Harris, John, 4
Hart, William, 4
Hawker, George Charles, 4
Head, Frederick Waldegrave, 9
Heales, Richard, 4
Henderson, John Baillie, 4
Hill, Richard, 1
Hobbs, Sir Joseph John Talbot, 9
Hobbs, William, 4
Hodgson, William, 4
Holroyd, Arthur Todd, 4
Hordern, Anthony (1819-1876), 4
Horsley, Charles Edward, 4
Hose, Henry Judge, 4
Hosking, John, 1
Hoskins, Charles Henry, 9
Hoskins, James, 4
Hudson, Henry, 4
Hull, Hugh Munro, 4
Hunt, Henry Ambrose, 9
Hutt, John, 1
Jackson, Samuel, 2
Jersey, Sir Victor Albert George
    Child-Villiers, 9
Johnson, Robert Ebenezer, 4
Jordan, Sir Frederick Richard, 9
Joseph, Samuel Aaron, 4
Kay, Joseph Henry, 2
Kemp, Charles, 2
Kiek, Edward Sidney, 9
King, William Francis, 5
Kirk, Maria Elizabeth, 9
Kirkpatrick, Andrew Alexander, 9
Knight, John George, 5
Knipe, John Hanlon, 5
Korff, John, 5
Lake, George Hingston, 9
Lamb, Edward William, 5
Lamb, Walter, 5
Lambe, David, 2
Lamington, Baron, 9
Landseer, Albert Henry, 9
Langlands, Henry, 2
Lansell, Sir George Victor, 9
Laporte, François Louis Nompar de
    Caumont, 5
Lascelles, Thomas Allen, 2
La Trobe, Charles Joseph, 2
Lawley, Sir Arthur, 10
Lawlor, Adrian, 10
Ledger, Charles, 5
Levey, Barnett, 2
Levey, George Collins, 5
Levy, Sir Daniel, 10
Levy, Lewis Wolfe, 5
Lewis, Mortimer William, 2
Linton, James Walter Robert, 10
Loader, Thomas, 5
Lochée, Francis, 2
Loyau, George Ettienne, 5
Lutwyche, Alfred James Peter, 5
Lyne, Charles Emanuel, 10
McCrae, Georgiana Huntly, 2
McDonnell, Percy Stanislaus, 5

McEacharn, Sir Malcolm Donald, 10
McKinley, Alexander, 5
Macleay, Sir George, 2
Macleay, William Sharp, 2
Macleod, William, 10
Marconi, Joseph Cornelius, 10
Marryat, Charles, 10
Marshall-Hall, George William Louis, 10
Martens, Conrad, 2
Martindale, Ben Hay, 5
Matheson, Sir Alexander Perceval, 10
Mathews, Julia, 5
Merewether, Edward Christopher, 5
Michael, James Lionel, 5
Michie, Sir Archibald, 5
Middleton, George Augustus, 2
Miller, Granville George, 5
Miller, Maxwell, 5
Miller, Robert Byron, 5
Mocatta, George Gershon, 5
Mollison, Alexander Fullerton, 2
Molloy, John, 2
Montefiore, Joseph Barrow, 2
Moore, Sir William Harrison, 10
Morphett, Sir John, 2
Nathan, Charles, 5
Neale, William Lewis, 10
Neighbour, George Henry, 10
Newcastle-under-Lyme, Henry Pelham
    Fiennes Pelham Clinton, 5
Newcomb, Caroline Elizabeth, 1
Nicholls, Charles Frederick, 5
Nicholls, Henry Richard, 5
Norman, Sir Henry Wylie, 11
Normanby, George Augustus Constantine
    Phipps, 5
Orchard, William Arundel, 11
Outtrim, Alfred Richard, 11
Outtrim, Frank Leon, 11
Page, Samuel, 2
Palmer, Joseph, 11
Palmer, Thomas McLeod, 5
Parker, Edward Stone, 5
Patteson, John Coleridge, 5
Pedder, Sir John Lewes, 2
Perry, Charles, 5
Piddington, William Richman, 5
Plummer, John, 11
Pohlman, Robert Williams, 5
Powell, James Alexander, 11
Pratt, Joseph Major, 11
Price, Charles, 5
Primrose, Archibald Philip, 5
Ramsay, Robert, 6
Raphael, Joseph George, 6
Read, George Frederick, 2
Read, Richard (b.1765?), 2
Riley, Alexander, 2
Riley, Edward, 2
Roberts, Ernest Alfred, 11
Roberts, James Henry Cecil, 11
Robinson, George Augustus, 2
Rogers, Charles, 6
Rogers, George Edgar, 11

Romilly, Hugh Hastings, 6
Roth, Henry Ling, 11
Roth, Walter Edmund, 11
Rowcroft, Charles, 2
Samuel, Sir Saul, 6
Saunders, John, 2
Scott, Eugene Montague, 6
Scott, Herbert Hedley, 11
Shellshear, Walter, 6
Sheppard, Benjamin, 11
Shillinglaw, John Joseph, 6
Short, Benjamin, 6
Sievier, Robert Standish, 11
Silas, Ellis Luciano, 11
Simpkinson de Wesselow, Francis
  Guillemard, 2
Simpson, Alfred, 6
Simpson, Alfred Muller, 6
Skinner, Henry Hawkins, 11
Sladen, Douglas Brooke Wheelton, 6
Slapoffski, Joseph Gustave, 11
Smith, Sir James John Joynton, 11
Smith, Louis Lawrence, 6
Smyth, Sir Nevill Maskelyn, 12
Smythe, Robert Sparrow, 12
Solomon, Emanuel, 6
Solomon, Isaac, 2
Solomon, Judah Moss, 6
Soul, Caleb, 6
Soul, Washington Handley, 6
Stanford, William Walter Tyrell, 6
Stanley, Arthur Lyulph, 12
Stephen, James Wilberforce, 6
Stephens, Edward, 2
Stephens, Edward James, 6
Stevens, Edward, 12
Story, George Fordyce, 2
Stradbroke, George Edward John
  Mowbray Rous, 12
Stutchbury, Samuel, 6
Taber, Thomas, 2
Talbot, Sir Reginald Arthur James, 12
Tayler, Lloyd, 6
Taylor, James, 6
Tegg, James, 2
Tegg, Samuel Augustus, 2
Tenison-Woods, Julian Edmund, 6
Thomas, William Kyffin, 6
Thompson, Joseph, 6
Thomson, Alexander Morrison, 6
Thornton, Samuel, 6
Todd, Robert Henry, 12
Traill, William Henry, 6
Trollope, Anthony, 6
Turner, Martha, 6
Tyers, Charles James, 2
Tyrrell, William, 6
Vale, Benjamin, 2
Vale, Richard Tayler, 6
Vale, William Mountford Kinsey, 6
Vance, George Oakley, 6
Varley, George Henry Gisborne, 12
Vaude, Charlie, 12
Venables, Henry Pares, 6

Vickery, Ebenezer, 6
Victor, James Conway, 2
Vidler, Edward Alexander, 12
Vogel, Sir Julius, 6
Wakefield, Edward Gibbon, 2
Waley, Sir Frederick George, 12
Walker, George Washington, 2
Walsh, William Horatio, 2
Want, Randolph John, 6
Waterhouse, Frederick George, 6
Waterhouse, Jabez Bunting, 6
Wearing, William Alfred, 6
Webber, William Thomas Thornhill, 12
Webster, Alexander George, 6
Weeks, Elias Carpenter, 6
Weigall, Sir William Ernest George
  Archibald, 12
Westmacott, Charles Babington, 12
Whatmore, Hugh Edward, 12
Whish, Claudius Buchanan, 6
White, Francis Maloney, 6
Whitehead, Charles, 6
Willmore, Henrietta, 12
Wilson, Sir Leslie Orme, 12
Winder, Thomas White Melville, 2
Windeyer, Richard, 2
Wollaston, John Ramsden, 2
Woods, William Maitland, 12
Wright, Francis Augustus, 6
Wylde, Sir John, 2
Wynne, Agar, 12
Yelverton, Henry, 6
Youl, John, 2
Young, John Lorenzo, 6
Bedfordshire
Macqueen, Thomas Potter, 2
AMPTHILL
Lee, Benjamin, 5
BEDFORD
Chapman, Thomas Daniel, 3
Luffman, Lauretta Caroline Maria, 10
Parrott, Thomas Samuel, 11
BIGGLESWADE
Foster, Hubert John, 8
Manton, John Allen, 2
Sandford, Augustus Henry, 11
ICKWELL
Palmer, Thomas Fyshe, 2
Roberts, Charles Fyshe, 6
LUTON
McAulay, Alexander, 10
WHIPSNADE
Eyre, Edward John, 1
WILSHAMSTEAD
Morgan, Sir William, 5
Berkshire
ABINGDON
Barron, Ellen, 7
ALDERMASTON
Lawes, William George, 5
EARLY
Geake, William Henry Gregory, 8
HARE HATCH
Young, Adolphus William, 2

MILTON
  Walsh, William Henry, 6
NEWBURY
  Bicheno, James Ebenezer, 1
  Dalrymple, David Hay, 8
  Roe, John Septimus, 2
READING
  Packer, Charles (Stuart Shipley) Sandys, 5
  Packer, Frederick Augustus Gow, 5
  Rayment, Percy Tarlton, 11
  Swallow, Thomas, 6
SANDHURST
  Matthews, Charles Henry Selfe, 10
  Sands, John, 6
  Wright, William Henry, 6
WALTHAM ST LAWRENCE
  Micklem, Philip Arthur, 10
WANTAGE
  Harvey, Lewis Jarvis, 9
WINDSOR
  Edinburgh, Alfred Ernest Albert, Duke of, 4
  Gowrie, Sir Alexander Gore Arkwright Hore-Ruthven, 9
Buckinghamshire
  Kirby, Joseph Coles, 5
AYLESBURY
  Barker, Edward, 3
  Barker, William, 3
  Browne, Sir Thomas Gore, 3
  Grimes, Charles, 1
  Parker, Harold, 11
BIERTON
  Shaw, George, 2
BURNHAM
  Tucker, Thomas George, 12
DORNEY
  Scott, Sir Robert Townley, 11
GREAT MARLOW
  Calder, James Erskine, 1
  Grant, Charles Henry, 9
  Terry, Frederick Casemero, 6
HIGH WYCOMBE
  Vernon, Walter Liberty, 12
HUGHENDON
  Clubbe, Sir Charles Percy Barlee, 8
IBSTONE
  Brewis, Charles Richard Wynn, 7
LITTLE MISSENDEN
  Austin, Baron Herbert, 3
SHABBINGTON
  Goddard, Benjamin, 9
SLOUGH
  Lovekin, Arthur, 10
STRATFORD STONY
  Chapman, Sir Robert William, 7
TYLERS HILL
  Hoare, Benjamin, 9
WINGRAVE
  Pearce, Samuel William, 11
WINSLOW
  Grace, Joseph Neal, 9
Cambridgeshire
  Carter, Charles, 3

CAMBRIDGE
  Dixon, Horace Henry, 8
  Montagu, Algernon Sidney, 2
  Sizer, Hubert Ebenezer, 11
  Smith, Francis Grey, 6
  Tucker, Horace Finn, 12
  Wilkin, Frederick John, 12
COTTENHAM
  Rowell, James, 11
ELY
  Peach, Henry, 11
HORNINGSEA
  Moore, Joshua John, 2
LITTLINGTON
  Kimpton, William Stephen, 5
MELBOURNE
  Mortlock, William Ranson, 5
STAPLEFORD
  Balls-Headley, Walter, 3
WHITTLESEY
  Hemmant, William, 4
Cheshire
  Barnes, William, 1
  Clay, Henry Ebenezer, 3
  Mitchell, Joseph Earl Cherry, 5
BIRKENHEAD
  Connah, Thomas William, 8
  Dexter, Walter Ernest, 8
  Keane, Edward Vivien Harvey, 5
  Poole, Daniel, 11
BOLLINGTON
  Smith, William Collard, 6
BRIMSTAGE
  Davidson, James, 8
CHESTER
  Brierly, Sir Oswald Walters, 3
  Lloyd, Henry Grant, 5
  Tench, Watkin, 2
  Trouton, Frederick Henry, 6
CHILDER THORNTON
  Sharp, Gerald, 11
HYDE
  Bradley, Joseph, 7
  Ives, Joshua, 9
KINGSLEY
  Burrows, John, 3
LISCARD
  Miller, William, 5
LOSTOCK GRALAM
  Bolton, William Kinsey, 7
MARTON
  Buckley, William, 1
NEWTON-BY-CHESTER
  Anderson, Sir David Murray, 7
NORTHWICH
  Warburton, Peter Egerton, 6
OXTON
  Walker, John, 12
SALE MOOR
  Frodsham, George Horsfall, 8
SANDBACH
  Burgess, Henry Thomas, 7
STOCKPORT
  Brooks, Joseph, 7

Lamb, Sir Horace, 5
Leadbeater, Charles Webster, 10
Whitelegge, Thomas, 12
WALLASEY
Spence, George Heynes, 12
Cornwall
Cornish, William Crocker, 3
Roberts, Abraham, 11
Rundle, Jeremiah Brice, 6
Symons, John Christian, 6
BLISLAND
Tom, William, 2
BODMIN
Coode, Sir John, 3
Gale, John, 4
Lawry, Walter, 2
BREAGE
Eade, Joel, 4
CALLINGTON
Bice, Sir John George, 7
CAMBORNE
Bennett, Samuel, 3
Thomas, Josiah, 12
FIDDLERS GREEN
Watson, Mary Beatrice Phillips, 6
FOUNDRY
Martin, James, 5
GERMOE
Tuckfield, Francis, 2
GLUVIAN
Carvosso, Benjamin, 1
GWENNAP
Verran, John, 12
HELSTON
Fitzsimmons, Robert, 8
KILKHAMPTON
Dunstan, Edward Tremayne, 8
LANDRAKE
Palmer, Philip, 2
LAUNCESTON
King, Philip Gidley, 2
Parsons, John Langdon, 11
Ruse, James, 2
LISKEARD
Clemes, Samuel, 8
Webb, Edmund, 6
LUDGVAN
Curnow, James Henry, 8
MADRON
Jenkin, John Grenfell, 9
MT PERRANZABULOE
Allen, Joseph Francis, 7
MYLOR
Boucaut, Sir James Penn, 3
NEWLYN
Kelynack, William, 5
Tregurtha, Edward Primrose, 2
PENZANCE
Booth, Herbert Henry, 7
Dennis, Alexander, 4
Permewan, John, 5
Rowe, Thomas, 6
Waterhouse, George Marsden, 6

PERRAN-ZABULOE
May, Frederick, 5
PONSANOOTH
Wearne, Joseph, 6
REDRUTH
Gribble, John Brown, 4
ST CLEMENT
Woolcock, John Laskey, 12
ST DOMINICK
Vosper, Frederick Charles Burleigh, 12
ST ENODER
Bassett, Samuel Symons, 7
Bassett, William Augustus, 7
ST ERTH
Charleston, David Morley, 7
ST IVES
Curnow, William, 8
Quick, Sir John, 11
ST JUST
Williams, Henry Roberts, 12
ST JUST IN PENRITH
Angwin, William Charles, 7
ST KEVERNE
Smith, John, 6
ST KEW
Braddon, Sir Edward Nicholas Coventry, 7
ST NEOT
Dangar, Henry, 1
Dangar, William John, 4
TRANNACK
Davey, Edwin, 8
TREGONY
Rounsevell, John, 11
TRURO
Bath, Henry, 3
Matthews, Daniel, 5
WHEAL HOPE
Hooper, Richard, 9
Cumberland
Grainger, Henry William Allerdale, 9
Harrison, John, 4
AIKTON
Nicholson, John Barnes, 11
BOOTLE
Grice, Richard, 4
BRAITHWAITE
Barnes, Henry, 3
BRAMPTON
Penfold, William James, 11
BROMFIELD
Irving, Clark, 4
CARLISLE
Graham, Margaret, 9
Molloy, Georgiana, 2
Nanson, John Leighton, 10
CASTLE SOWERBY
Sowerby, William, 6
COCKERMOUTH
Nicholson, Sir Charles, 2
GARRIGILL
Hutchinson, William Alston, 4
GLASSONBY
Beatham, Robert Matthew, 7

HAILE
  Cameron, Samuel Sherwen, 7
HARRINGTON
  Henry, Ernest, 4
HORNSBY
  Willis, Edward, 6
IREBY
  Cape, William, 1
LAMPLUGH
  Nicholson, Germain, 5
PENRITH
  Lamb, John, 2
  Nanson, Edward John, 10
STAINBURN
  Iredale, Tom, 9
WESTWARD
  Bragg, Sir William Henry, 7
WHITEHAVEN
  Huddart, James, 4
  McBryde, Duncan Elphinstone, 10
  Magrath, Edward Crawford, 10
  Nesbitt, Thomas Huggins, 11
  Nicholson, William, 5
  Waite, James Clarke, 6
WIGTON
  Graves, John Woodcock, 4
WORKINGTON
  Gainford, Thomas, 4
Derbyshire
  Bateman, Edward La Trobe, 3
BASLOW
  Barker, Frederic, 3
BELPER
  Hollis, Robert, 9
CHESTERFIELD
  Cutts, William Henry, 3
  Miller, Emma, 10
DERBY
  Fleming, John William, 8
  Jeffries, Lewis Wibmer, 9
  Waterfield, William, 2
HEANOR
  Howitt, Godfrey, 4
  Howitt, Richard, 4
  Howitt, William, 4
MATLOCK
  Gell, John Philip, 1
MATLOCK BATH
  Flower, Willoughby, 8
RIDDINGS
  Brentnall, Frederick Thomas, 3
TICKNALL
  Armytage, George, 1
Devon
  Bowden, Thomas, 1
  Cory, Edward Gostwyck, 1
  Dawbin, Annie Maria, 1
  Ewing, Thomas James, 1
  Helpman, Benjamin Franklin, 1
  Macarthur, Elizabeth, 2
  Matthews, William, 5
  Parkes, Edmund Samuel, 5
ABBOTSHAM
  Piper, Thomas, 11

ALPHINGTON
  Manning, Sir William Montagu, 5
ASHBURTON
  Eales, John, 1
  Facy, Peter, 4
AVETON GIFFORD
  Ruth, Thomas Elias, 11
BARNSTAPLE
  Hitchcock, George Michelmore, 4
  Jewell, Richard Roach, 4
  Rodd, Brent Clements, 6
BIDEFORD
  Braund, George Frederick, 7
  Haverfield, Robert Ross, 4
BONDLEIGH
  Dunn, John (1802-1894), 4
BRIDGERULE
  Luxton, Thomas, 5
BUCKFASTLEIGH
  Tryon, Henry, 12
CLYST ST MARY
  Strong, Herbert Augustus, 6
COCKINGTON
  Luffman, Charles, 10
CREDITON
  Pring, Ratcliffe, 5
  Rudall, James Thomas, 6
DARTINGTON
  Froude, James Anthony, 4
DARTMOUTH
  Crook, William Pascoe, 1
DAWLISH
  Walker, Frederick, 6
DEVONPORT
  Crawford, Andrew, 3
  Hampden, Sir Henry Robert Brand, 9
  Jones, Charles Edwin, 4
EAST STONEHOUSE
  Elliott, Gilbert Charles Edward, 8
  Watson, James Henry, 12
EXBOURNE
  Cawker, Thomas, 3
EXETER
  Bidwill, John Carne, 1
  Cockburn-Campbell, Sir Thomas, 3
  Cole, Joseph Stear Carlyon, 8
  Francis, Leonard, 8
  Glyde, Lavington, 4
  Leakey, Caroline Woolmer, 5
  Manning, Edye, 2
  Manning, James Alexander Louis, 5
  Milford, Samuel Frederick, 5
  Quick, William Abraham, 5
  Rowe, George Curtis, 6
  Salter, Edward, 6
  Salter, William, 6
  Short, Augustus, 6
  Sloman, Thomas Martin, 2
GITTISHAM
  Hardy, Thomas, 4
GREAT TORRINGTON
  Palmer, Sir James Frederick, 5
HARBERTONFORD
  Colton, Sir John, 3

HARTLAND
  Scott, William, 6
HATHERLEIGH
  King, Anna Josepha, 2
HEAVITREE
  Haydon, George Henry, 4
HELE BROADCLIST
  Connibere, Ernest William Richards, 8
HONITON
  Tindal, Charles Grant, 6
HORRABRIDGE
  Hancock, Henry Richard, 4
ILFRACOMBE
  Reynell, John, 6
IPPLEPEN
  Langler, Sir Alfred, 9
IVYBRIDGE
  Huxham, John Saunders, 9
MILTON DAMEREL
  Anderson, Ernest Augustus, 7
MODBURY
  Bickford, James, 3
NEWTON ABBOT
  D'Arcy, William Knox, 8
NEWTON TRACEY
  Scott, Walter, 11
NEWTON-BUSHELL
  Gullett, Henry, 9
OTTERY ST MARY
  Davy, Edward, 1
PAIGNTON
  Dulhunty, Robert Venour, 1
PLYMOUTH
  Arthur, Sir George, 1
  Arthur, Henry, 1
  Bennett, George, 1
  Bligh, William, 1
  Derry, John Dickson, 4
  Dickson, Sir James Robert, 8
  Heydon, Jabez King, 1
  Hobbs, James, 1
  Lockyer, Edmund, 2
  Macarthur, Hannibal Hawkins, 2
  Neales, John Bentham, 2
  Pasco, Crawford Atchison Denman,
    5
  Prout, John Skinner, 2
  Reid, David, 6
  Rivers, Richard Godfrey, 11
  Seccombe, William, 2
  Shortland, John, 2
  Steele, Bertram Dillon, 12
  Wyatt, William, 2
PLYMPTON
  Icely, Thomas, 2
PLYMPTON ST MAURICE
  Yabsley, William, 6
PLYMSTOCK
  Trethowan, Hubert Charles, 12
POUGHILL
  Rumpf, Ann, 11
SAMPFORD SPINEY
  Cann, John Henry, 7
  Cann, William Henry, 7

SHALDON
  Fox, Henry Thomas, 4
SIDBURY
  Randell, William Richard, 6
SOUTH MOLTON
  Pearce, John, 11
STOKE DAMEREL
  Wise, Percy William Charlton, 12
TAVISTOCK
  Torr, William George, 12
  Wilder-Neligan, Maurice, 12
TEIGNMOUTH
  Ham, Thomas, 4
  Strutt, William, 6
TIVERTON
  Boyce, Francis Bertie, 7
  Brooks, William, 7
  Govett, William Romaine, 1
  Harriman, Benjamin Cosway, 4
  Pitt, Richard, 2
TOPSHAM
  Brooks, Richard, 1
TORQUAY
  Barry, John Arthur, 7
  Hutton, Sir Edward Thomas Henry, 9
  Rodway, Leonard, 11
  Whitworth, Robert Percy, 6
TORRINGTON
  Buzacott, Charles Hardie, 3
  Sandford, William, 11
  Vidal, Mary Theresa, 2
TOTNES
  Wills, William John, 6
Dorset
  Parry-Okeden, David, 11
  Sturt, Evelyn Pitfield Shirley, 6
BEAMINSTER
  Holden, John Rose, 1
BLANDFORD
  Keynes, Joseph, 9
  Roe, Reginald Heber, 11
  Rose, Thomas, 2
BRIDPORT
  Male, Arthur, 10
  Prescott, Charles John, 11
BROADWAY
  Holman, Richard Charles Frederick, 9
CHIDEOCK
  Weld, Sir Frederick Aloysius, 6
DORCHESTER
  Roberts, Thomas William, 11
  Shirley, John, 11
  Soundy, Sir John, 12
IWERNE
  Hull, George, 1
JORDAN HILL
  Sandford, Daniel Fox, 6
LYME REGIS
  Gould, John, 1
  Nicholson, John Henry, 5
MORDEN
  Smith, Sidney, 6
POOLE
  Barling, Joseph, 3

Cribb, Benjamin, 3
Cribb, Robert, 3
PORTLAND
Symes, Joseph, 6
SHERBORNE
Day, Ernest Charles, 8
SWANAGE
Hixson, Francis, 4
King, Henry, 9
TOLPUDDLE
Loveless, George, 2
WAREHAM
Smith, Samuel, 6
WEYMOUTH
Highett, John, 4
Highett, William, 4
WIMBORNE
Cox, William, 1
WIMBORNE MINSTER
Druitt, Thomas, 4
Durham
Curley, James, 3
Smith, Shepherd, 6
Turner, William, 6
BARNARD CASTLE
Brown, George, 3
BISHOP AUCKLAND
Hay, Robert Snowdon, 9
BOLDON
Wawn, William Twizell, 6
CARR HILL
Dobson, Sir William Lambert, 4
DARLINGTON
Dixon, Robert, 1
DURHAM
Dodds, Sir John Stokell, 4
EGGLESTONE
Headlam, Charles, 4
ESCOMB
Brentnall, Thomas, 7
FERRY HILL
Winspear, William Robert, 12
GATESHEAD
Dodds, Thomas Henry, 8
HARTLEPOOL
Atkinson, Meredith, 7
HEBBURN
Maughan, James, 5
HEDLEYHOPE
Lee, John Robert, 10
HYLTON
Brown, Sir Harry Percy, 7
LITTLE CHILTON
Longmore, Lydia, 10
LOW FELL
Lawson, William, 10
LUMLEY
Cole, George Ward, 1
MONKWEARMOUTH
Forster, Anthony, 4
Wilson, Frank, 12
RYHOPE
Crosby, William, 3

RYTON
Young, Robert, 6
SEDGEFIELD
Maxwell, Walter, 10
SHIELDS
Kirkpatrick, John Simpson, 9
SHILDON
Harrison, Sir John, 9
SOUTH SHIELDS
Forsyth, George, 4
McColl, James Hiers, 10
STILLINGTON
Johnson, George, 9
SUNDERLAND
Ashcroft, Edgar Arthur, 7
Robson, Ernest Iliff, 11
Rowntree, Thomas Stephenson, 6
TUDHOE
Adamson, John, 7
WALKERFELD
Hawdon, Joseph, 1
WEST BOLDON
Ridley, John, 2
WINLATON
Tweddle, Joseph Thornton, 12
WOLSINGHAM
Snowball, Oswald Robinson, 12
Essex
Houlding, John Richard, 4
Wiseman, Solomon, 2
BLACK NOTLEY
Wynne, Watkin, 12
BOCKING
Hopkins, Felicia, 9
BURNHAM
Elliott, Sizar, 4
CHELMSFORD
Fegan, John Lionel, 8
COLCHESTER
Ashton, James Henry, 7
Clark, George Daniel, 8
Dowling, Thomas, 4
DEDHAM
Downes, Major Francis, 4
ELMDON
Litchfield, James, 5
EPPING
Andrews, Richard Bullock, 3
GOSFIELD
Robertson, George, 11
GREAT BADDOW
Duffield, Walter, 4
GREAT BENTLEY
Dawson, Robert, 1
Dawson, Robert Barrington, 4
GREAT CLACTON
Osborn, Theodore George Bentley, 11
GREAT TEY
Hills, John Francis, 9
GREAT WAKERING
Collin, William, 3
HALSTEAD
Davies, George Schoen, 4
Davies, Sir John Mark, 4

Davies, Joseph Bartlett, 4
HARTFORD END
Ridley, William, 6
HARWICH
Garrard, Jacob, 4
INGATESTONE
Petre, Henry Aloysius, 11
LEIGH
Armstrong, William George, 7
LOUGHTON
Hamilton, Edward William Terrick, 4
MALDON
Champ, William Thomas Napier, 3
Cottee, William Alfred, 3
Felton, Alfred, 4
ROCHFORD
Kernot, Charles, 5
Kernot, William Charles, 5
ROMFORD
Andrews, Edward William, 3
Petchy, John, 2
ROXWELL
Bramston, Sir John, 3
SOUTHMINSTER
Blackett, Cuthbert Robert, 3
STRATFORD
Stanton, George Henry, 6
Whittell, Hubert Massey, 12
TOLLESHUNT D'ARCY
Smyth, Arthur Bowes, 2
UPTON
Blackburn, James, 1
WALTHAMSTOW
Taylor, Thomas Griffith, 12
WANSTEAD
Barlow, Andrew Henry, 7
Evans, Ada Emily, 8
Lucas, Walter Henry, 10
WEST HAM
Buxton, Sir Thomas Fowell, 7
WITHAM
Coote, Audley, 3
Gloucestershire
Fraser, Sir Malcolm, 4
McArthur, David Charteris, 5
Salmon, Thomas, 2
Trigg, Henry, 2
ALDERLY
Hale, Mathew Blagden, 4
ASHBROOK
Creed, John Mildred, 3
BERRY HILL
Garnsey, Charles Frederick, 4
BRISTOL
Benham, Frederic Charles Courtenay, 7
Brodribb, Thomas, 3
Brown, Francis Ernest, 7
Cayley, Henry Priaulx, 7
Derham, Frederick Thomas, 4
Fewings, Eliza Ann, 8
Fisher, James Cowley Morgan, 4
Freeman, William Glover Webb, 4
Giles, Ernest, 4
Gill, William Wyatt, 4

Greville, Edward, 4
Griffiths, George Washington, 9
Henning, Rachel Biddulph, 4
Jefferis, James, 4
Lane, Ernest Henry, 9
Lane, William, 9
Loftus, Lord Augustus William Frederick
  Spencer, 5
Neild, John Cash, 10
O'Grady, Sir James, 11
Rees, John, 6
Sampson, George, 11
Stiles, Henry Tarlton, 2
Thatcher, Charles Robert, 6
Tucker, James, 2
Warren, William Henry, 6
BURTON ST MICHAEL
Turley, Joseph Henry Lewis, 12
CHELTENHAM
Belisario, John, 3
Dun, William Sutherland, 8
Etheridge, Robert, 8
Gregory, Henry Gregory, 1
Meeks, Sir Alfred William, 10
CLIFTON
Coneybeer, Frederick William, 8
Jose, Arthur Wilberforce, 9
Lysaght, Herbert Royse, 10
Nicholson, Mark, 5
DOWN END
King, Joseph, 9
FAIRFORD
Cowley, Sir Alfred Sandlings, 3, 8
GLOUCESTER
Dowling, Henry (1810-1885), 1
Parker, Charles Avison, 11
LECKHAMPTON
Townsend, Alfred Richard, 12
LYDNEY
Thomas, Richard, 12
MAISEMORE
Harmer, John Reginald, 9
MANGOTSFIELD
Greenway, Francis, 1
Pratten, Herbert Edward, 11
NAILSWORTH
Smith, James William Norton, 6
OLDLAND
Wheen, Harold, 12
RANDWICK
Pearce, Simeon Henry, 5
STOWE
Wilton, Charles Pleydell Neale, 2
STROUD
Browne, Eyles Irwin Caulfield, 3
TEWKESBURY
Preece, Frederick William, 11
Priestley, Sir Raymond Edward, 11
ULEY
Garlick, Daniel, 4
WESTBURY
Sleigh, Harold Crofton, 11
WESTBURY-UPON-TRYM
Mais, Henry Coathupe, 5

WOODCHESTER
Moreton, Berkeley Basil, 5
WOTTON
Fosbery, Edmund Walcott, 4
Hampshire
Verge, John, 2
ALDERSHOTT
Arthur, Richard, 7
Cohen, Francis Lyon, 8
ALVERSTOKE
Butters, Sir John Henry, 7
Clifton, Marshall Waller, 3
Galway, Sir Henry Lionel, 8
Gibbs, Herbert William, 8
ASHE
Lefroy, Sir John Henry, 5
BASINGSTOKE
Booth, Charles O'Hara, 1
BERAIS TOWN
Skeats, Ernest Willington, 11
BOURNEMOUTH
Watt, Walter Oswald, 12
CARISBROOKE
Poore, John Legg, 5
Wise, Edward, 6
CHRISTCHURCH
Reeks, Walter, 11
CLANFIELD
Poate, Frederick, 11
COWES
Jeffreys, Charles, 2
Jervois, Sir William Francis Drummond, 4
Spain, William, 2
EXBURY
Bundey, Sir William Henry, 3
FRESHWATER
Somers, Arthur Herbert Tennyson
Somers-Cocks, 12
GOSPORT
Goldfinch, Sir Philip Henry Macarthur, 9
Hargraves, Edward Hammond, 4
Upfield, Arthur William, 12
HARDWAY
Macgregor, Lewis Richard, 10
HIGHCLERE CASTLE
Carnarvon, Earl of, 3
ISLE OF WIGHT
Elyard, Samuel, 4
MILTON
Randell, George, 6
MINSTEAD IN THE NEW FOREST
Broomfield, Frederick John, 7
MOORCOURT
Young, James Henry, 6
MUDDIFORD
Henderson, Sir Edmund Yeamans Walcott, 4
NEWPORT
Babbidge, Benjamin Harris, 3
ODIHAM
Newland, Ridgway William, 2
PETERSFIELD
Morgan, John, 2

Woolley, John, 6
PORTSEA
Ayers, Sir Henry, 3
Boyd, James Arthur, 7
Bussell, Alfred Pickmore, 3
Bussell, John Garrett, 1
Dowse, Richard, 8
Sparks, Nicholas George, 12
Sweet, Samuel White, 6
Titheradge, George Sutton, 6
PORTSMOUTH
Dickens, Charles, 4
Illingworth, Nelson William, 9
Jeffery, Walter James, 9
Leak, John, 10
Stephens, Alfred Ward, 2
Way, Sir Samuel James, 12
RYDE
Du Cane, Sir Charles, 4
SOUTHAMPTON
Hodgkinson, Clement, 4
SOUTHSEA
Clarke, Sir Andrew, 3
Hyde, Sir George Francis, 9
STOCKBRIDGE
Thorn, George, 6
STOKE
Bentham, George, 3
STONEHAM
Aslatt, Harold Francis, 7
STUBBINGTON
Boyes, George Thomas William Blamey, 1
WHITCHURCH
Withers, William Bramwell, 6
WICKHAM
Draper, Daniel James, 1
WINCHESTER
Kentish, Nathaniel Lipscomb, 2
Pinnock, James Denham, 2
Robinson, Herbert Edward Cooper, 11
Shenton, Arthur, 6
Shenton, George, 2
Woolls, William, 6
Herefordshire
Clint, Raphael, 1
Hayward, Charles Wiltens Andrée, 9
COURTFIELD
Vaughan, Edmund, 6
Vaughan, Roger William Bede, 6
HINTON
Goode, Sir Charles Henry, 4
KINGTON
Hall, Walter Russell, 9
LEDBURY
Ballard, Robert, 3
LEOMINSTER
Smith, Thomas (1823-1900), 6
Smith, Thomas (1829-1882), 6
RODD
Thornber, Catherine Maria (1812?-1894), 12
WOLFERFLOW
Colebatch, Sir Harry Pateshall, 8

Hertfordshire
BALDOCK
  Fossey, Joseph, 1
BRICKENDON
  Andrews, Arthur, 7
BUNTINGFORD
  Stow, Jefferson Pickman Augustine, 6
ESSENDON
  Green, Richard, 4
HATFIELD
  Cecil, Robert Arthur Talbot Gascoyne, 3
HEMEL HEMPSTEAD
  Fowler, Hugh Lionel, 8
HERTFORD
  Archer, Joseph, 1
  Rose, Herbert John, 11
  Westall, William, 2
HODDESDON
  Gosse, William Christie, 4
REDHILL
  Adams, George, 3
RICKMANSWORTH
  Bunce, Daniel, 1
  Fellows, Thomas Howard, 4
  Hodgson, Sir Arthur, 4
TRING
  Pope, Cuthbert John, 11
WATFORD
  Howard, Amos William, 9
Huntingdonshire
DIDDINGTON
  Linton, Sydney, 5
GREAT STAUGHTON
  Giles, William, 1
HEMINGFORD ABBOTS
  Daintree, Richard, 4
KIMBOLTON
  Raws, Sir William Lennon, 11
SAINT BENEDICT
  McNess, Sir Charles, 10
ST IVES
  Carter, Arthur John, 7
YELLING
  See, Sir John, 11
Kent
  Atkinson, James, 1
  Blackman, James, 1
  Buckland, Thomas, 3
  Forster, Sir Henry William, 8
  Goodchap, Charles Augustus, 4
  Gregson, Jesse, 4
  Kane, Benjamin Francis, 5
ALLHALLOWS
  Phillip, Arthur, 2
BORSTAL
  Tillyard, Pattie, 12
BOUGHTON-UNDER-BLEAN
  Berry, Henry, 3
BRADBOURNE
  Young, Sir Henry Edward Fox, 6
BRASTED
  Marchant, George, 10
  Smith, Richard, 6

BROMLEY
  Morton, Frank, 10
  Sulman, Florence, 12
BROMPTON
  Palmer, George Thomas, 2
CANTERBURY
  Beaney, James George, 3
  Buchanan, Florence Griffiths, 7
  Davies, Robert Rowland, 1
  Kingsford, Richard Ash, 5
  Mate, Thomas Hodges, 5
  Nathan, Isaac, 2
CHARTHAM HATCH
  Cheel, Edwin, 7
CHATHAM
  Pasley, Charles, 5
CLAPHAM
  Cooper, Lilian Violet, 8
CRANBROOK
  Tooth, Atticus, 6
  Tooth, John, 6
  Tooth, William Butler, 6
DARTFORD
  Snowden, Sir Arthur, 12
DEAL
  Millen, Edward Davis, 10
DEPTFORD
  Hopkins, Henry, 1
DOVER
  Finnis, John, 1
  Hamilton, Henry, 9
  Tunbridge, Walter Howard, 12
  Wright, John Arthur, 12
EASTWELL
  Finch-Hatton, Harold Heneage, 4
EDENBRIDGE
  Nash, Robert, 2
ELLINGTON
  Leake, John, 2
  Solly, Robert Henry, 12
ELTHAM
  Bridges, Sir Tom Molesworth, 7
  Latham, John, 2
ERITH
  Swayne, Edward Bowdich, 12
FARNINGHAM
  Russell, Robert Hamilton, 11
FAVERSHAM
  Buss, Frederic William, 7
  Piper, Arthur William, 11
  Smith, Philip Thomas, 2
FOLKESTONE
  Blackall, William Edward, 7
  Unwin, Ernest Ewart, 12
FOOTS CRAY
  Young, John, 6
FORDWICH
  Blaxland, Gregory, 1
FOREST HILL
  Corin, William, 8
FRINDSBURY
  Morey, Edward, 5
GILLINGHAM
  Bingle, John, 1

GRAVESEND
 Davis, Edward, 1
 Langton, Edward, 5
 Nicholson, Edmund James Houghton, 11
 Pritchard, George Baxter, 11
GREENHITHE
 Blackburn, Sir Charles Bickerton, 7
GREENWICH
 Douglass, Benjamin, 4
 Hargrave, John Fletcher, 4
 Hargrave, Lawrence, 9
 Hart, Fritz Bennicke, 9
 McDougall, Frank Lidgett, 10
 Moor, Henry, 2
 Ritchie, Samuel Sextus, 6
 Smith, Bernhard, 6
 Sulman, Sir John, 12
 Todd, Ellen Joy, 12
HYTHE
 Latham, Sir Charles George, 10
LENHAM
 Quaife, Barzillai, 2
LEWISHAM
 French, Charles, 8
 George, Madeline Rees, 8
 Mann, John Frederick, 5
 Parker, Sir Henry Watson, 5
 Wentworth-Shields, Wentworth Francis,
 12
LEYSDOWN
 Gowlland, John Thomas Ewing, 4
LITTLEBOURNE
 Smith, Henry George, 11
LOOSE
 Smith, James, 6
MAIDSTONE
 Buckland, Sir Thomas, 7
 Masters, George, 5
 Poole, Frederic Slaney, 11
 Wright, Horatio George Anthony, 6
MARGATE
 Lansell, George, 5
NEWINGTON
 Catt, Alfred, 3
NORTH CRAY
 Ord, Sir Harry St George, 5
PEMBURY
 Butler, Robert John Cuthbert, 7
PENGE
 Barton, Russell, 3
PLUMSTEAD
 Clark, Sir Ernest, 8
RAMSGATE
 Coxen, Charles, 3
 Goodman, Sir William George Toop, 9
 Gould, Elizabeth, 1
RINGWOULD
 Gipps, Sir George, 1
RIPPLE
 Sladen, Sir Charles, 6
ROCHESTER
 Cracknell, Edward Charles, 3
 Elyard, William, 4
 Heaton, Sir John Henniker, 4

 Jaques, Theodore James, 4
 Sconce, Robert Knox, 2
ST PAULS CRAY
 Bull, John Wrathall, 1
SANDGATE
 Le Souef, Albert Alexander Cochrane, 5
SEVENOAKS
 Chapman, Edgar, 3
STAPLEHURST
 Cotton, George Witherage, 3
SYDENHAM
 Gibbs, Cecilia May, 8
 Potter, Charles Vincent, 11
TENTERDEN
 Cole, Edward William, 3
 Finn, Henry, 8
TUNBRIDGE WELLS
 Boreham, Frank William, 7
 Langridge, George David, 5
 Stone-Wigg, Montagu John, 12
WOOLWICH
 Baker, Richard Thomas, 7
 Bannerman, Charles, 3
 Crawford, Emma, 8
 Martin, Arthur Patchett, 5
 Rix, Henry Finch, 11
Lancashire
 Atherton, John, 3
 Bleasdale, John Ignatius, 3
 Cowper, Sir Charles, 3
ARDWICK
 McConnel, David Cannon, 5
 Voigt, Emil Robert, 12
ASHTON-UNDER-LYNE
 Hinchcliffe, Albert, 9
 Lees, Harrington Clare, 10
BIRKDALE
 Bold, William Ernest, 7
BLACKBURN
 Anderson, William Acland Douglas, 3
 Wisdom, Sir Robert, 6
BOLTON
 Claxton, Marshall, 3
 Cooper, Daniel, 1
 Hopwood, Henry, 4
 Mort, Thomas Sutcliffe, 5
 Wright, John Charles, 12
BOLTON-LE-MOORS
 Cooper, Sir Daniel, 3
BROUGHTON
 Kemp, Henry Hardie, 9
BURY
 Reibey, Mary, 2
 Verdon, Sir George Frederic, 6
CASTLETON
 Waterworth, Edith Alice, 12
CHEETHAM
 Gould, Nathaniel, 9
CHORLEY
 Wood, Thomas, 12
CHORLTON-CUM-HARDY
 Nicholson, George Gibb, 11
CHORLTON-ON-MEDLOCK
 Neil, Edwin Lee, 10

Pankhurst, Adela Constantia Mary, 12
CLITHEROE
Bulcock, Robert, 3
Oddie, James, 5
DALTON
O'Connell, Michael William, 11
DALTON-IN-FURNESS
Airey, Peter, 7
DIDSBURY
Ewen, John Carr, 8
EVERTON
Price, John Lloyd, 11
Sutton, George Lowe, 12
Wardill, Benjamin Johnston, 6
Webster, William, 12
GARSTON
Hall, Lindsay Bernard, 9
HARPURHAY
Thornber, Catherine Maria (1837-1924), 12
Thornber, Rachel Ann, 12
HARTSHEAD
Worrall, Henry, 12
HOLLOWFORTH
Threlfall, Sir Richard, 12
KIRKDALE
Dunn, James Patrick Digger, 8
KNOWSLEY
Stanley, Edward George Geoffrey Smith, 2
LANCASTER
Carruthers, George Simpson, 7
Mansergh, James, 5
LIVERPOOL
Aspinall, Butler Cole, 3
Astley, William, 3
Bibb, John, 1
Boote, Henry Ernest, 7
Brennan, Peter Joseph, 3
Bushell, Philip Howard, 7
Casey, Cornelius Gavin, 1
Clark, John James, 3
Cohen, Sir Lewis, 8
Crompton, Joseph, 3
Crooke, Edward, 3
Donaghy, John, 4
Evans, Sir John William, 8
Ford, Richard, 4
Garrett, Thomas, 4
Gould, William Buelow, 1
Hodges, Sir Henry Edward Agincourt, 9
Johnson, Edwin, 4
Jones, Richard (1816-1892), 2
Kerferd, George Briscoe, 5
Kirwan, Sir John Waters, 9
Latham, Edward, 5
Levi, Nathaniel, 5
Moffitt, William, 2
Polding, John Bede, 2
Rawson, Sir Harry Holdsworth, 11
Rigg, William, 11
Scott, Daniel, 2
Smith, Robert Murray, 6
Sorlie, George Brown, 12

Walters, George Thomas, 12
Wardill, Richard Wilson, 6
White, James, 12
Woods, John, 6
Zox, Ephraim Laman, 6
MANCHESTER
Bleakley, John William, 7
Brady, Alfred Barton, 7
Broadhurst, Charles Edward, 3
Brookes, William, 3
Calvert, John Jackson, 3
Davies, William, 4
Henn, Percy Umfreville, 9
Houghton, Thomas John, 9
Howitt, William, 9
Kiek, Winifred, 9
Kitson, Sir Albert Ernest, 9
Laing, Charles, 2
Makinson, Thomas Cooper, 2
Nolan, Sara Susan, 11
Pownall, William Henry, 5
Read, Henry, 6
Sprent, James, 2
NEWTON
Ward, John Frederick, 12
OLDHAM
Irving, James Washington, 9
PATRICROFT
Dendy, Arthur, 8
PEELFOLD
Peel, Thomas, 2
PRESCOT
Bellew, Harold Kyrle Money, 7
PRESTON
Craven, Richard, 8
Hebblethwaite, James, 9
Walker, Thomas, 6
PRESTWICH-CUM-OLDHAM
Barber, George Walter, 7
ROCHDALE
Irving, James, 9
Stephens, Thomas Blacket, 6
SALFORD
Kenny, Augustus Leo, 9
Talbot, Albert Edward, 12
Wood, George Arnold, 12
SOUTHPORT
Halfey, John, 4
STRETFORD
Spencer, Sir Walter Baldwin, 12
Waters, Edward Ernest, 6
TODMORDEN
Greenwood, James, 4
TOTTINGTON
Duckworth, Arthur, 8
TOXTETH PARK
Banfield, Edmund James, 7
Dakin, William John, 8
Ewart, Alfred James, 8
Mansfield, Ralph, 2
Stevenson, John Bryan, 12
Wilkie, Allan, 12
TUE BROOK
Long, Richard Hooppell, 10

UPHOLLAND
Berry, Richard James Arthur, 7
Stopford, Robert, 12
Wilkinson, Dorothy Irene, 12
WALTON-ON-THE-HILL
Smith, William John, 11
WARRINGTON
Draper, Thomas Percy, 8
Morris, George Francis, 5
WAVERTREE
Brookfield, Percival Stanley, 7
Sixsmith, William, 6
WEST DERBY
Thow, William, 12
Whitehouse, Joseph Howell, 12
WHITTINGTON
Cowper, William, 1
WIGAN
Standish, Frederick Charles, 6
WITHINGTON
Young, William John (1878-1942), 12
WORSLEY
Longworth, William (1846-1928), 10
Leicestershire
ANSTY
Skertchly, Sydney Barber Josiah, 11
ASHBY-DE-LA-ZOUCH
Deeming, Frederick, 8
Fleming, Sir Valentine, 4
BURBAGE
Hurst, George, 4
GLENFIELD
Throsby, Charles, 2
GROBY
Everard, John, 4
HOUGHTON-ON-THE-HILL
Glover, John, 1
LEICESTER
Billson, John William, 7
Hassell, George Frederick, 9
Mitchell, Sir William Henry Fancourt, 5
Stone, Louis, 12
LOUGHBOROUGH
Barrett, Walter Franklyn, 7
Lincolnshire
Billson, George, 7
Burton, Henry, 3
Willson, Robert William, 2
ASWARBY
Bass, George, 1
BARROW-ON-HUMBER
Hardey, Joseph, 1
BARTON-ON-HUMBER
Holyman, William, 4
DONINGTON
Flinders, Matthew, 1
GRANTHAM
Fitchett, William Henry, 8
Milson, James (1783-1872), 2
Wand, John William Charles, 12
GRIMSBY
Dickinson, Edward Alexander, 8
HORNCASTLE
Williams, Thomas, 6

LINCOLN
Jordan, Henry, 4
Turner, Lilian Wattnall, 12
LOUTH
Badham, Edith Annesley, 7
Goe, Field Flowers, 9
Gresswell, Dan Astley, 9
Stuart, Athol Hugh, 12
MARKET DEEPING
Hardwicke, Charles Browne, 1
NORTH THORESBY
Kendall, Thomas, 2
REDBOURNE
Howe, John, 1
SCOTTON
Brumby, James, 1
SPILSBY
Bayldon, Francis Joseph, 7
Franklin, Sir John, 1
STAMFORD
Johnston, Joseph, 4
SUTTON
Gore, John, 4
SWINDERBY
Clarke, Sir George Sydenham, 8
Middlesex
Baker, Ezekiel Alexander, 3
Wrenfordsley, Sir Henry Thomas, 6
ACTON
Pedley, Ethel Charlotte, 11
Spyer, Haden Daniel, 12
ALDGATE
Kemp, Anthony Fenn, 2
BETHNAL GREEN
Crofts, Charles Alfred, 8
Griffiths, John Alfred, 9
Playford, Thomas, 11
BOW
Gregory, John Walter, 9
Robertson, Sir John, 6
CAMDEN TOWN
Chapman, Frederick, 7
McMillan, Sir Robert Furse, 10
Richardson, Charles, 11
CHELSEA
Chapman, Israel, 1
Guilfoyle, William Robert, 4
Liardet, Wilbraham Frederick Evelyn,
2
Newdegate, Sir Francis Alexander
Newdigate, 11
Nicolay, Charles Grenfell, 5
Peake, Archibald Henry, 11
Stonehaven, John Lawrence Baird, 12
Suttor, George, 2
Triggs, Arthur Bryant, 12
CHISWICK
Horne, Thomas, 4
CLERKENWELL
Hancock, John, 9
Innes-Noad, Sidney Reginald, 9
Lowe, Robert (1783-1832), 2
COVENT GARDEN
Wilson, Edward, 6

CROUCH END
  Pearse, Albert William, 11
CROUCH HILL
  Priestley, Henry James, 11
EALING
  Chapman, Henry George, 7
  Cronin, Bernard Charles, 8
  Huxley, Thomas Henry, 1
  Pope, Harold, 11
EDMONTON
  Horne, Richard Henry, 4
ENFIELD
  Biscoe, John, 1
  Mendes da Costa, Benjamin, 5
FINCHLEY
  Lawson, William, 2
  Medland, Lilian Marguerite, 9
  Suffolk, Owen Hargraves, 6
  Tucker, Tudor St George, 12
FINSBURY
  Roberts, Sir Alfred, 6
FULHAM
  Dorrington, Albert, 8
  Gunter, Howel, 9
  Henslowe, Francis Hartwell, 1
HACKNEY
  Asher, Morris, 3
  Bailey, Frederick Manson, 3
  Bainton, Edgar Leslie, 7
  Barnard, James, 1
  Biggs, Leonard Vivian, 7
  Bunning, Robert, 7
  Dowse, Thomas, 4
  Gillbee, William, 4
  Goddard, Henry Arthur, 9
  Jones, Frederic Wood, 9
  Legge, James Gordon, 10
  Martin, Sir Charles James, 10
  Miller, Frederick, 2
  Sadler, Arthur Lindsay, 11
  Thomas, Arthur Nutter, 12
  Voss, Francis Henry Vivian, 12
HALLIFORD
  Russell, Henry Stuart, 2
HAMMERSMITH
  McKenzie, Alexander Kenneth, 2
  Stacy, John Edward, 6
HAMPSTEAD
  Brinsmead, Horace Clowes, 7
  Haines, William Clark, 4
  Harvey, Sir John Musgrave, 9
  Masson, Sir David Orme, 10
HAMPTON WICK
  Coombes, Richard, 8
HIGHBURY
  Fysh, Sir Philip Oakley, 8
  Soares, Alberto Dias, 6
HIGHGATE
  Couvreur, Jessie Catherine, 3
HOLBORN
  Barry, Alfred, 3
  Garling, Frederick, 1
HORNSEY
  Smith, Thomas Whistler, 2

HOUNSLOW
  Butler, Gamaliel, 1
  Pearce, Henry John, 5
HOXTON
  Bedggood, John Charles, 3
  Collick, Edward Mallan, 8
  Jefferies, Richard Thomas, 9
HOXTON NEW TOWN
  Schey, William Francis, 11
  Whiddon, Samuel Thomas, 12
HOXTON OLD TOWN
  Spencer, Thomas Edward, 12
ISLINGTON
  Armit, Henry William, 7
  Ashton, Julian Howard, 7
  Barnes, Gustave Adrian, 7
  Bowser, Sir John, 7
  Camfield, Julius Henry, 7
  Crisp, Christopher, 3
  Flack, Edwin Harold, 8
  Garratt, Charles Clement, 8
  Hobler, George, 1
  Kennerley, Alfred, 5
  Michell, Anthony George Maldon, 10
  Pearson, Charles Henry, 5
  Richardson, Alexander Robert, 11
  Richardson, Charles Douglas, 11
  Rowland, Percy Fritz, 11
  Smith, Arthur Edward, 11
  Terry, William Henry, 6
  Tietkens, William Harry, 6
  Todd, Sir Charles, 6
  Woodward, Bernard Henry, 12
  Wunderlich, Alfred, 12
  Wunderlich, Ernest (Henry Charles)
    Julius, 12
  Wunderlich, Frederick Otto, 12
KENSINGTON
  à Beckett, William Arthur Callander,
    3
  Brooker, Thomas Henry, 7
  Budd, Richard Hale, 3
  Cavill, Frederick, 7
  Clarke, Marcus Andrew Hislop, 3
  Harris, Lawrence Herschel Levi, 9
  Marsh, Stephen Hale Alonzo, 5
  North, Frederic Dudley, 11
  Thirkell, Angela Margaret, 12
  Thompson, John Ashburton, 12
  Turner, Henry Gyles, 6
  Wood, Harrie, 6
  Wynyard, Edward Buckley, 2
KENTISH TOWN
  Calvert, Albert Frederick, 7
  Ewart, Florence Maud, 8
  Jackson, Sir Cyril, 9
  Montford, Paul Raphael, 10
  Rowland, Caroline Ann, 11
LALEHAM
  Arnold, Thomas, 1
LINCOLNS INN FIELDS
  Marriott, Fitzherbert Adams, 2
MAIDA VALE
  Keysor, Leonard Maurice, 9

MARYLEBONE
  Cumberlege, Claude Lionel, 8
  Northcote, Sir Henry Stafford, 11
MAYFAIR
  Russell, Lord John, 2
MILE END
  Green, Solomon, 9
  Pope, Charles, 11
MILE END OLD TOWN
  Wager, Rhoda, 12
NEW SOUTHGATE
  Wilkinson, Leslie, 12
OLD BRENTFORD
  Hartley, John Anderson, 4
PADDINGTON
  Nathan, Sir Matthew, 10
  Thompson, Gerald Marr, 12
PIMLICO
  Bennett, Mary Montgomerie, 7
  Browne, William Henry, 7
  Hughes, William Morris, 9
  Smith, Sir Gerard, 11
PONDERS END
  Chambers, James, 3
  Chambers, John, 3
POPLAR
  Wardell, William Wilkinson, 6
POYLE
  Weston, Thomas Charles George, 12
RATCLIFF
  Delany, John Albert, 4
ST CATHERINES
  Burford, William Henville, 1
ST GEORGE IN THE EAST
  Steward, Sir George Charles Thomas,
    12
ST JAMES
  Clisby, Harriet Jemima Winifred, 3
ST JOHNS WOOD
  Maiden, Joseph Henry, 10
  White, Samuel, 6
ST PANCRAS
  Archibald, William Oliver, 7
  Chapple, Frederic, 7
  Fincham, George, 4
  Furber, Thomas Frederick, 8
  Holman, William Arthur, 9
  Irving, Martin Howy, 4
SHADWELL
  Bruce, George, 1
SHOREDITCH
  Neitenstein, Frederick William, 10
  Weston, William Pritchard, 2
SOHO
  Barker, Thomas, 1
STAINES
  Watson, Elliot Lovegood Grant, 12
STEPNEY
  Massina, Alfred Henry, 5
STOKE NEWINGTON
  De Hamel, Lancel Victor, 8
  Leake, George Walpole, 5
  Leake, Sir Luke Samuel, 5
  Smith, Sydney George Ure, 11

SUNBURY
  Fisher, Sir James Hurtle, 1
  Fisk, Sir Ernest Thomas, 8
TEDDINGTON
  Hurst, John Herbert, 9
  Selfe, Norman, 6
TOTTENHAM
  Farr, George Henry, 4
  Ogilvie, Edward David Stewart, 5
  Powell, Walter, 5
  Walstab, George Arthur, 6
  Williams, John (1796-1839), 2
TURNHAM GREEN
  Liversidge, Archibald, 5
TWICKENHAM
  Glossop, John Collings Taswell, 9
  Tennyson, Hallam, 12
UPPER HOLLOWAY
  Wainwright, William Edward, 12
UXBRIDGE
  Fox, Ethel Carrick, 8
WAPPING
  Orton, Arthur, 5
WESTMINSTER
  Ball, Percival, 7
  Banks, Sir Joseph, 1
  Broughton, William Grant, 1
  Brownlow, Frederick Hugh Cust, 7
  Hay, Robert William, 1
  Hoddle, Robert, 1
  Thomas, William, 2
  Ward, Ebenezer, 6
  Windeyer, Sir William Charles, 6
WHITECHAPEL
  Edments, Alfred, 8
  Joyce, Alfred, 2
  Paget, Walter Trueman, 11
  Sternberg, Joseph, 12
WHITEHALL
  Carington, Rupert Clement George, 7
  Carrington, Charles Robert, 3
Monmouthshire
  Parsons, Charles Octavius, 2
ABERTILLERY
  Davies, William, 8
ABERYSTRUTH
  Gould, Ellen Julia, 9
BLAINA
  Davies, David Mortimer, 4
CHEPSTOW
  David, Charles St John, 8
  Stephens, James, 6
MACHEN LOWER
  Morgans, Alfred Edward, 10
NANTYGLO
  James, David, 9
NEWPORT
  Frost, John, 1
PENROSE
  Feetham, John Oliver, 8
PONTYPOOL
  Steel, Robert, 6
USK
  Davis, Charles Henry, 1

WHITCHURCH
  Prichard, Frederick John, 11
Norfolk
  Custance, John Daniel, 3
FOULSHAM
  Middleton, John, 5
FRAMINGHAM-PIGOT
  Plume, Henry, 11
GOODERSTONE
  Jessep, Thomas, 9
HANWORTH
  Heath, George Poynter, 4
HARLESTON
  Grimwade, Frederick Sheppard,
  4
HEYDON
  Richardson, John Soame, 6
KINGS LYNN
  Toosey, James Denton, 2
  Vancouver, George, 2
NORWICH
  Bevan, Louisa Jane, 7
  Holt, Joseph Thomas, 4
  Howchin, Walter, 9
  Julius, Sir George Alfred, 9
  Rivett, Albert, 11
  Skipper, John Michael, 6
  Tillyard, Robin John, 12
  Woodward, Henry Page, 12
PULHAM
  Carron, William, 3
SAHAM TONEY
  Woodward, Frank Lee, 12
ST FAITH
  Beaumont, Edward Armes, 3
ST GERMANS
  Cambridge, Ada, 3
STALHAM
  Silcock, Emma Caroline, 11
THORPE-NEXT-NORWICH
  Douglas, Sir Adye, 4
TOPCROFT
  Cowles, Charles, 3
WHISSONSETT
  Seal, Charles, 2
WORSTEAD
  Stirling, Edmund, 6
YARMOUTH
  Hovell, William Hilton, 1
  Smith, William Howard, 6
  Smith, William Isaac Carr, 11
  Turner, James Francis, 6
Northamptonshire
BARNACK
  Kingsley, Henry, 5
BLISWORTH
  Gadsden, Jabez, 8
BULWICK
  Tryon, Sir George, 6
CRANSLEY
  Morley, William, 10
KETTERING
  Briggs, Sir Henry, 7
  Gotch, John Speechly, 4

NORTHAMPTON
  Chisholm, Caroline, 1
  Scott, Sir Ernest, 11
PETERBOROUGH
  Goodman, George, 4
  Wilson, William Parkinson, 6
POTTERSPURY
  Wilkinson, Charles Smith, 6
ROTHERSTHORPE
  Manning, Frederic Norton, 5
TANSOR
  Wheelwright, Horace William, 6
WELLINGBOROUGH
  Keartland, George Arthur, 9
Northumberland
  Clark, Robert, 3
  Pigdon, John, 5
  Stewart, John (1810-1896), 6
ALNWICK
  Bosanquet, Sir Day Hort, 7
  Busby, John, 1
  Newbigin, William Johnstone, 11
  Patterson, Sir James Brown, 5
  Tate, Ralph, 6
BEADNELL
  Kerr, George, 9
BERWICK-UPON-TWEED
  Mather, Robert, 2
  Stevenson, George, 2
  Swanston, Charles, 2
BROOMHAUGH
  Potts, Henry William, 11
CRAMLINGTON
  Cann, George, 7
FORD
  Neville, Auber Octavius, 11
HAZLERIGG
  Bird, Bolton Stafford, 3
HOWICK
  Grey, Henry George, 1
LONG BENTON
  Bigge, John Thomas, 1
LONG HORSLEY
  Towns, Robert, 6
MORPETH
  Purdy, John Smith, 11
NEWCASTLE-UPON-TYNE
  Alderson, William Maddison, 3
  Angas, George Fife, 1
  Angas, George French, 1
  Angas, John Howard, 3
  Binney, Thomas, 3
  Green, James, 9
  Harcus, William, 4
  Johnson, Sir William Elliot, 9
  Kent, William, 2
  Lilley, Sir Charles, 5
  Lothian, Thomas Carlyle, 10
  Mennell, Philip Dearman, 10
  Swinburne, George, 12
  Thompson, Edward Henry, 12
  Wilson, Dora Lynnell, 12
NORHAM
  Rule, James, 6

NORTH SHIELDS
  Moulton, James Egan, 5
  Salmond, Sir John William, 11
  Stephens, John, 2
ROTHBURY
  Forster, William Mark, 4
SHARPERTON
  Whinham, John, 6
TYNEMOUTH
  Owen, Robert, 5
WALKER
  Lightfoot, Gerald, 10
  Smith, William Beattie, 11
WALLSEND
  Smyth, Robert Brough, 6
WILLINGTON
  Fryar, William, 4
Nottinghamshire
  Dexter, Caroline, 4
BALDERTON
  Walpole, Herbert Reginald Robert
  Seymour, 12
BASFORD
  Platt, John Laurio, 2
BEESTON
  Brooks, Samuel Wood, 3
BINGHAM
  Lowe, Robert (1811-1892),
  2
BURTON-JOYCE
  Rolleston, Christopher, 6
COTGRAVE
  Mordaunt, Evelyn May, 10
EAST RETFORD
  Hindley, William George, 9
FARNSFIELD
  Gregory, Sir Augustus Charles, 4
LENTON
  Bancroft, Thomas Lane, 7
MANSFIELD
  Radford, Lewis Bostock, 11
NEWARK
  Bland, Revett Henry, 3
  Eggleston, John, 4
  Wittenoom, John Burdett, 2
NOTTINGHAM
  Earp, George Frederick, 8
  Hatfield, William, 9
  Howitt, Alfred William, 4
  Hunter, Henry, 4
  Plant, Edmund Harris Thornburgh,
  5
  Strange, Frederick, 2
RADFORD
  Saywell, Thomas, 6
SHERWOOD
  Syme, Sir George Adlington, 12
Oxfordshire
  Rouse, Richard, 2
  Stonor, Alban Charles, 2
ARNCOTT
  Greaves, Edwin, 9
BANBURY
  Smalley, George Roberts, 6

BICESTER
  Collingridge de Tourcey, George
  Alphonse, 8
BURDROP
  Manning, James, 5
CASSINGTON
  Fry, James, 4
CHIPPING NORTON
  Darnell-Smith, George Percy, 8
CULHAM
  Phillips, Samuel Pole, 5
GREAT ROLLRIGHT
  Rendall, Charles Henry, 11
HENLEY-UPON-THAMES
  Cooper, Sir Charles, 1
KELMSCOTT
  Scott, Thomas Hobbes, 2
NEITHROP
  Clarke, Marian, 8
OXFORD
  Embling, Thomas, 4
  Robinson, Edward Oswin, 11
SHIRBURN
  Davenport, Sir Samuel, 4
STADHAMPTON
  Butler, Sir Richard, 7
STONESFIELD
  Padbury, Walter, 5
Rutland
LITTLE CASTERTON
  Twopeny, Richard Ernest Nowell, 6
UPPINGHAM
  Green, Samuel, 4
Shropshire
  Owens, John Downes, 5
  Powlett, Frederick Armand, 2
ACTON ROUND
  Lloyd, Charles William, 5
BRIDGNORTH
  Andrew, Henry Martyn, 3
  Edkins, Edward Rowland, 4
CHETWYND
  Bagshaw, John Stokes, 3
CHIRBURY
  Jones, Richard (1786-1852), 2
CONDOVER
  Huffer, John, 4
LLANYMYNECH
  Thomas, Robert, 6
LUDLOW
  Badham, Charles, 3
OSWESTRY
  Davies, Edward Harold, 8
  Lewis, Richard, 2
SHRAWARDINE
  Tanner, Alfred John, 12
TICKLETON
  Buddicom, Robert Arthur, 7
WELLINGTON
  Vickers, William, 12
Somerset
  Anstey, Thomas, 1
  Clarke, William John Turner, 1
  Corfield, William Henry, 3

ABBOTS LEIGH
  Bright, Charles Edward, 3
ALLERFORD
  Moresby, John, 5
BALTONSBOROUGH
  Austin, Albert, 3
  Austin, James, 1
  Austin, Sidney, 7
  Austin, Thomas, 1
BATH
  Blackmore, Edwin Gordon, 3
  Broadhurst, Edward, 3
  Elliston, William Gore, 1
  Ferres, John, 4
  Havelock, Sir Arthur Elibank, 9
  Keene, William, 5
  Ley, Thomas John, 10
  Macarthur, Sir Edward, 5
  Parry, Sir William Edward, 2
  Peacock, George, 5
  Ricardo, Percy Ralph, 11
  Tufnell, Edward Wyndham, 6
  Wilton, Olive Dorothea Graeme, 12
BEDMINSTER
  Dunn, Edward John, 8
  Taylor, Florence Mary, 12
BRIDGWATER
  Morant, Harry Harbord, 10
BURNHAM
  Petherick, Edward Augustus, 5
BUTCOMBE
  Savery, Henry, 2
CHARLTON MACKRELL
  Summers, Charles, 6
  Summers, Joseph, 6
CHEW MAGNA
  Collins, Sir Robert Henry Muirhead, 8
CHILCOTE
  Robinson, Anthony Bennet, 11
CLEVE YATTON
  Rason, Sir Cornthwaite Hector William James, 11
COMBE ST NICHOLAS
  Aplin, William, 3
CURRY-MALLET
  Mead, Silas, 5
DULVERTON
  Peppin, George Hall, 5
EXETER
  Kyngdon, Leslie Herbert, 9
FROME-SELWOOD
  Rotton, Henry, 6
GLASTONBURY
  Parkin, William, 5
ILMINSTER
  Baker, John, 3
KILMINGTON
  Selwyn, Alfred Richard Cecil, 6
  Selwyn, Arthur Edward, 6
LANGPORT
  Denham, Digby Frank, 8
LOCKING
  Reeve, Edward, 6

MARTOCK
  Adams, Robert Patten, 3
MONTACUTE
  Baker, Thomas, 7
  Langdon, William, 2
NAILSEA
  Newton, Frederick Robert, 5
OLDMIXON
  Bisdee, Edward, 1
  Bisdee, John, 1
PENSFORD ST THOMAS
  Butler, Walter Richmond, 7
PERRITON
  Gill, Samuel Thomas, 1
ROADWATER
  Langdon, Thomas, 9
SHAPWICK
  Strangways, Henry Bull Templar, 6
SHEPTON-MALLET
  Pyke, Vincent, 5
STOGURSEY
  Howse, Sir Neville Reginald, 9
STON EASTON
  Dowling, Henry (1780-1869), 1
TAUNTON
  Clarke, Jacob Richard, 3
  Cleland, George Fullerton, 3
  Fletcher, Charles Brunsden, 8
  Harding, George Rogers, 4
  Lassetter, Frederic, 5
  North, John Britty, 5
TWERTON
  Shackell, James, 6
WELLINGTON
  Were, Jonathan Binns, 2
WELLS
  Bowen, George Meares Countess, 1
  Murray-Prior, Thomas Lodge, 5
  Stephen, George Milner, 2
  Williams, John (1797?-1872), 2
WESTON-SUPER-MARE
  Love, Ernest Frederick John, 10
  Truman, Ernest Edwin Philip, 12
WIDCOMBE
  Nairn, William Edward, 5
WILTON
  Walter, William Ardagh Gardner, 12
YEOVIL
  Adams, Walter, 3
  Baker, Henry Herbert, 7
  Slade, William Ball, 11
Staffordshire
  Bromley, Frederick Hadkinson, 7
  Lycett, Joseph, 2
  Windeyer, Charles, 2
BIDDULPH
  Cockram, Thomas (1831-1912), 8
BILSTON
  Ham, Theophilus Job, 4
BURSLEM
  Baddeley, John Marcus, 7
  Pulsford, Edward, 11
  Sherwin, Isaac, 2

DILHORNE
  Flowers, Fred, 8
  Loton, Sir William Thorley, 10
  Walker, Sir Harold Bridgwood, 12
DUDLEY
  Rhodes, Fred, 11
FAZELEY
  Jones, Kathleen Annie Gilman, 9
HANDSWORTH
  Hammond, George Meysey, 9
HANLEY
  Newland, Simpson, 11
  Shelley, William, 2
LEEK
  Gaunt, William Henry, 4
LICHFIELD
  Bird, Samuel Dougan, 3
  Simpson, Stephen, 2
MILTON
  Leigh, Samuel, 2
PENKRIDGE
  Girdlestone, Henry, 9
SANDON
  Bonney, Charles, 3
SHELTON
  Knight, John James, 9
SILVERDALE
  Cook, Sir Joseph, 8
STAFFORD
  Brassey, Thomas, 7
STONE
  Cooper, Thomas, 3
TAMWORTH
  Edden, Alfred, 8
UPPER GORNALL
  Jones, William Ernest, 9
WALSALL
  Gray, John Edward, 1
  Hill, Kate, 9
  James, John Stanley, 4
  Smith, Sir Edwin Thomas, 6
WEDNESBURY
  Danks, John, 4
  Hill, Thomas, 9
WEST BROMWICH
  George, William James, 8
WILLENHALL
  Lewis, William Howard Horatio, 10
  Tildesley, Beatrice Maude, 12
  Tildesley, Evelyn Mary, 12
WOLVERHAMPTON
  Barney, George, 1
  Springthorpe, John William, 12
Suffolk
ALDEBURGH
  Stevens, Jemima Elizabeth Mary,
    12
ALPHETON
  Gardener, Alfred Henry, 4
BARNINGHAM
  Fison, Lorimer, 4
BECCLES
  Arnold, Joseph, 1
  Rede, Robert William, 6

DENNINGTON
  Hotham, Sir Charles, 4
EAST BERGHOLT
  Clarke, William Branwhite, 3
ELLOUGH
  Arnold, William Munnings, 3
FRAMLINGHAM
  Stow, Randolph Isham, 6
HADLEIGH
  Stow, Thomas Quinton, 2
  Woolner, Thomas, 6
HALESWORTH
  Hooker, Sir Joseph Dalton, 4
HONINGTON
  Hayward, Thomas, 4
IPSWICH
  Backhouse, Alfred Paxton, 7
  Backhouse, Benjamin, 7
  Gocher, William Henry, 9
  Maitland, Edward, 5
KIRKLEY
  Castleton, Claud Charles, 7
  Willmott, Francis Edward Sykes, 12
LOWESTOFT
  Brunning, George, 3
MILDENHALL
  Adams, Philip Francis, 3
NACTON
  Catchpole, Margaret, 1
NEEDHAM MARKET
  Best, Dudley Robert William, 7
STANTON
  Rose, Robert Henry, 6
SUDBURY
  Breillat, Thomas Chaplin, 3
  Button, Henry, 3
  Webb, Charles, 6
SYLEHAM
  Mann, Charles, 2
WORLINGWORTH
  Barlee, Sir Frederick Palgrave, 3
Surrey
  Holroyd, Sir Edward Dundas, 4
  Moore, Henry Byron, 5
  Wilkes, William Charles, 6
ADDLESTONE
  Ashton, Julian Rossi, 7
ALBURY
  Green, Arthur Vincent, 9
BALHAM HILL
  Cotton, John, 1
BANSTEAD
  Brown, Herbert Basil, 7
BERMONDSEY
  Booth, John, 3
  Broome, George Herbert, 7
  Underwood, James, 2
BRIXTON
  Allard, Sir George Mason, 7
  Hawkins, Herbert Middleton, 9
  Nash, Clifford Harris, 10
  Tyas, John Walter, 6
  Yencken, Edward Lowenstein,
    12

CAMBERWELL
Devine, Matilda, 8
Levey, James Alfred, 10
Massy-Greene, Sir Walter, 10
Sharp, Cecil James, 11
Smith, Julian Augustus Romaine, 11
Stackhouse, Alfred, 2
Strong, Walter Mersh, 12
Thomson, Dugald, 12
CHERTSEY
Beach, William, 3
CHRISTCHURCH
Leighton, Arthur Edgar, 10
CLAPHAM COMMON
Deane, Henry, 8
CRANLEIGH
Ellery, Robert Lewis John, 4
CROYDON
Archer, Edward Walker, 7
Archer, Robert Stubbs, 7
Biddell, Walter (Vivian Harcourt), 7
Coxen, Henry William, 3
Ellis, Henry Havelock, 4
Haddon, Frederick William, 4
Hinton, Howard, 9
Jones, Inigo Owen, 9
Styles, James, 12
Thomas, Margaret, 6
Yewen, Alfred Gregory, 12
DENMARK HILL
Barron, Sir Harry, 7
DORKING
Way, Arthur Sanders, 6
DULWICH
Glennie, Benjamin, 4
EGHAM
Coxen, Walter Adams, 8
Lindeman, Henry John, 5
FARNHAM
Moss, William, 5
Onslow, Sir Alexander Campbell, 5
FRENSHAM
West, Winifred Mary, 12
GUILDFORD
Goodenough, James Graham, 4
KENNINGTON
Chapman, Henry Samuel, 3
Hussey, Henry, 4
Ord, Harrison, 11
Russell, Robert, 2
KEW
Davis, John King, 8
KINGSTON-UPON-THAMES
Anderson, Maybanke Susannah, 7
Maxwell-Mahon, William Ion, 10
Taplin, George, 6
LAMBETH
Jenks, Edward, 9
Mirams, James, 5
Mutch, Thomas Davies, 10
Stephen, Sir James, 2
Swain, Herbert John, 12
Van Raalte, Henri Benedictus Salaman, 12
Webb, George Henry Frederick, 6

West, John Edward, 12
Wilkins, William, 6
LEITH HILL
Rusden, George William, 6
Rusden, Henry Keylock, 6
LINGFIELD
Bonwick, James, 3
MITCHAM
Keats, Horace Stanley, 9
NEW-CROSS
Bartley, Nehemiah, 3
NEWINGTON BUTTS
Dale, Robert William, 4
NORWOOD
Lloyd, George Alfred, 5
OCKLEY
Steere, Sir James George Lee, 12
PECKHAM
Evans, Matilda Jane, 4
PLAISTOW
Ashby, Edwin, 7
REIGATE
Cramp, Karl Reginald, 8
RICHMOND
Best, Henry, 3
Best, Joseph, 3
Bird, Frederic Dougan, 7
Glover, Charles Richmond John, 9
Hawes, John Cyril, 9
Mitchell, Sir Edward Fancourt, 10
Russell, James George, 11
Tulk, Augustus Henry, 6
Wainewright, Thomas Griffiths, 2
ROTHERHITHE
Robinson, Sir Thomas Bilbe, 11
Smith, Arthur Bruce, 11
Smith, Edmund Edmonds, 11
SAINT JOHNS
Brown, Joseph Tilley, 7
SOUTHWARK
Alston, James, 7
Ash, George, 7
Blacket, Edmund Thomas, 3
Moulden, Beaumont Arnold, 10
Sholl, Robert John, 6
Threlkeld, Lancelot Edward, 2
Townsend, William, 6
STREATHAM
Game, Sir Philip Woolcott, 8
SURBITON
Franklin, Richard Penrose, 8
Musgrove, George, 5
VAUXHALL
Sellar, James Zimri, 11
WALWORTH
Cape, William Timothy, 1
Favenc, Ernest, 4
Michel, Louis John, 5
Sargood, Sir Frederick Thomas, 6
WANDSWORTH
Danglow, Jacob, 8
D'Arcy-Irvine, Gerard Addington, 8
WIMBLEDON
Agar, Wilfred Eade, 7

Cunningham, Allan, 1
Cunningham, Richard, 1
WONERSH
Arundale, George Sydney, 7
Sussex
Barker, Stephen, 7
Mollison, William Thomas, 2
ALFRISTON
Jenner, Caleb Joshua, 4
BRIGHTON
Collings, Joseph Silver, 8
Gill, Harry Pelling, 9
Hall, George Wilson, 4
Herbert, Sir Robert George Wyndham, 4
Jenner, Isaac Walter, 9
Molineux, Albert, 5
Norton, John, 11
Roth, Reuter Emerich, 11
Taylor, Robert, 6
Thatcher, Richmond, 6
BUXTED
Windeyer, Mary Elizabeth, 12
CHICHESTER
Florance, Thomas, 1
Hack, John Barton, 1
EASTBOURNE
Hamlyn-Harris, Ronald, 9
Lane-Poole, Charles Edward, 9
HASTINGS
Ranking, Robert Archibald, 11
Vernon, Geoffrey Hampden, 12
HORSHAM
Dampier, Alfred, 4
Jull, Martin Edward, 9
HOVE
Stapley, Frank, 12
HUNSTON
Spencer, Cosens, 12
HURSTPIERPOINT
Campion, Frederick Henry, 7
LEWES
Gwynne, Edward Castres, 4
LINDFIELD
Smith, Sir Francis Villeneuve, 6
PETWORTH
Halford, George Britton, 4
RYE
Dawes, Nathaniel, 8
Elkington, John Simeon, 8
ST LEONARDS-ON-SEA
Marks, Charles Ferdinand, 10
Urquhart, Frederic Charles, 12
ST MARY-IN-THE-CASTLE
Story, Ann Fawcett, 12
Vernon, Hugh Venables, 12
SALEHURST
Caffyn, Stephen Mannington, 3
STEYNING
Bannister, Saxe, 1
Coppin, George Selth, 3
Polini, Emelie Adeline, 11
UPPER LANCING
Cutlack, Frederic Morley, 8

WADHURST
Fairbairn, James Valentine, 8
WARTLING
Chataway, Thomas Drinkwater, 7
WILLINGDON
Hoadley, Abel, 9
WORTHING
Chatfield, Florence, 7
Henty, Herbert James, 4
Warwick
Fairfax, John, 4
Parkes, Sir Henry, 5
ANSLEY
Hutchins, William, 1
ASTON
Arnold, Ellen, 7
Chataway, James Vincent, 7
Floyd, Alfred Ernest, 8
Hunt, Philip Charles Holmes, 9
Paterson, Thomas, 11
Radcliffe-Brown, Alfred Reginald, 11
BIRMINGHAM
Aaron, Isaac, 1
Abbott, Joseph Henry, 3
Baines, Sarah Jane, 7
Blyth, Sir Arthur, 3
Blyth, Neville, 3
Clark, Caroline Emily, 3
Clark, John Howard, 3
Derrington, Edwin Henry, 4
De Vis, Charles Walter, 4
Grimley, Frank, 9
Ham, Cornelius Job, 4
Jukes, Joseph Beete, 2
Loynes, James, 10
Meredith, George, 2
Meredith, Louisa Ann, 5
Perry, Joseph Henry, 11
Rignall, George Richard, 6
Riley, Charles Owen Leaver, 11
Salomons, Sir Julian Emanuel, 6
Sullivan, Thomas Barry, 6
Willoughby, Howard, 6
Wilson, John Thomas, 2
COLESHILL
Dale, John, 8
COMBE FIELDS
Truman, John, 12
COVENTRY
Eyre, John (b.1771), 1
Hassall, Rowland, 1
Hassall, Thomas, 1
Iliffe, John, 9
ERDINGTON
Fullwood, Albert Henry, 8
Kelly, Robert Hume Vandeleur, 9
FOLESHILL
Mann, Thomas, 10
Oakes, Francis, 2
Sargent, George, 11
GLASCOTE
Dumolo, Elsie, 8
Dumolo, Nona, 8

HANDSWORTH
  Hodgkinson, William Oswald, 4
KINGSBURY
  Cary, Henry, 3
LEAMINGTON
  Rumsey, Herbert John, 11
LEAMINGTON SPA
  Fairfax, Sir James Reading, 8
LEAMINGTON-HASTINGS
  Cain, Sir Jonathon Robert, 7
NUNEATON
  Dorsey, William McTaggart, 4
SOLIHULL
  Timperley, William Henry, 6
STRATFORD
  Rickards, Harry, 11
STRATFORD-ON-AVON
  Lucas, Arthur Henry Shakespeare, 10
SUTTON COLDFIELD
  Bock, Thomas, 1
TAMWORTH
  Dumolo, Harriet Alice, 8
  Withers, Walter Herbert, 12
WITTON
  Clements, Frederick Moore, 8

Westmorland
AMBLESIDE
  Kendall, Ernest Arthur, 9
CLIFTON
  Woodhouse, William John, 12
CROSSTHWAITE
  Barker, Tom, 7
DOCKER
  Farrer, William James, 8
FIRBANK
  Clarke, Henry Lowther, 8
KENDAL
  Forrest, Robert, 1
KIRKBY LONSDALE
  Pease, Percy, 11
LEVENS
  Stephens, Thomas, 6
  Stephens, William John, 6
MAULDS MEABURN
  Brunskill, Anthony, 7
NEWBY
  Docker, Joseph, 1
WINDERMERE
  Forrest, Edward Barrow, 8

Wiltshire
  Boyd, Theodore Penleigh, 7
  Browne, John Harris, 3
  Browne, William James, 3
  Clutterbuck, Katherine Mary, 8
  Goold, Stephen Styles, 4
  Henley, Sir Thomas, 9
  Marsh, Matthew Henry, 5
BEANACRE
  Nash, James, 5
BRADFORD
  Thring, Walter Hugh Charles Samuel, 12
CALNE
  Nichols, Isaac, 2

CORSHAM
  Fuller, Sir John Michael Fleetwood, 8
DEVIZES
  Cox, James, 1
  Lewis, Charles Ferris, 5
DINTON
  Wyndham, George, 2
EDEN VALE
  Hayter, Henry Heylyn, 4
FONTHILL-GIFFORD
  Combes, Edward, 3
HEYTESBURY
  Longman, Albert Heber, 10
LUDGERSHALL
  Everett, Edwin, 4
  Everett, George, 4
  Everett, John, 4
MARLBOROUGH
  Carter, Herbert James, 7
  Halcomb, Frederick, 9
NORTH SAVERNAKE
  Collins, Henry Michael, 8
PUCKSHIPTON
  Gilbert, Joseph, 4
SALISBURY
  Angel, Henry, 3
  Bean, Isabelle, 7
TROWBRIDGE
  Pitman, Jacob, 5
WESTBURY
  Perkins, Frederick Thomas, 11
  Rudduck, Harold Sugden, 11
  Zeal, Sir William Austin, 12
WILTON
  Chermside, Sir Herbert Charles, 7

Worcestershire
  Holden, George Kenyon, 4
BROMSGROVE
  Maund, John, 5
CLAINES
  Joseland, Richard George Howard, 9
DUDLEY
  Angliss, Sir William Charles, 7
EVESHAM
  Cheeke, Alfred, 3
GREAT MALVERN
  Blanch, George Ernest, 7
KIDDERMINSTER
  Ross, Joseph Grafton, 6
KINGS NORTON
  Williams, William Henry, 12
MARTLEY
  Stainforth, Martin Frank, 12
OLDBURY
  Davis, Joseph, 8
REDDITCH
  Davis, Thomas Martin, 8
SELLY OAK
  Sargent, Oswald Hewlett, 11
STOURBRIDGE
  Wragge, Clement Lindley, 12
WORCESTER
  Stretch, Theodore Carlos Benoni, 6

Yorkshire
Buckley, Henry, 3
Chambers, Thomas, 3
Hannan, Joseph Francis, 9
Shaw, Thomas, 2
Wade, John, 12
Walker, Thomas, 2
BALBY
Turner, Ethel Mary, 12
BARNSLEY
Farrar, Ernest Henry, 8
St Ledger, Anthony James Joseph, 11
BAWTRY
Brereton, John Le Gay, 3
BEVERLEY
Boyce, William Binnington, 3
BIRKBY
Maitland, Andrew Gibb, 10
BIRSTALL
Shaw, Thomas, 6
BOLTON
Flegg, Henry, 8
BOWLING
Wroe, John, 2
BRADFORD
Demaine, William Halliwell, 8
Jowett, Edmund, 9
Priestley, Henry, 11
Turner, James Alfred, 12
Wilson, Herbert Ward, 12
BRIDLINGTON
Trickett, Oliver, 12
BRIGHOUSE
Fisher, Joseph, 4
BURTON-SALMON
Turner, Fred, 12
CAMPSALL
Bowker, Richard Ryther Steer, 3
CLIFTON
Ashton, Sir John William, 7
CRAVEN
Caley, George, 1
DONCASTER
Boothby, Benjamin (1803-1868), 3
Braim, Thomas Henry, 3
Neild, James Edward, 5
Reed, Henry, 2
Rowe, Richard, 6
Young, Charles Frederick Horace Frisby,
  6
DUDLEY HILL
Schofield, William, 2
EAST HESLERTON
Shepherdson, John Banks, 2
ECCLESALL BIERLOW
Glauert, Ludwig, 9
Wheen, John Gladwell, 12
ECCLESFIELD
Ogden, Anthony, 11
Sugden, Edward Holdsworth, 12
ECCLESHILL
Mercer, John Edward, 10
FARSLEY
Marsden, Samuel, 2

FELIX-KIRK
Darvall, Sir John Bayley, 4
FILEY
Farthing, William Armstrong, 4
FORCETT
Gordon, James, 1
GOODMANHAM
Foster, Richard Witty, 8
HALIFAX
Greenup, Richard, 4
Lawson, James, 10
Lord, David, 2
Stuart, Herbert Akroyd, 12
Wade, Arthur, 12
Waterhouse, Joseph, 6
HALTON
Pearson, Alfred Naylor, 11
HARDEN
Laycock, Frederick, 10
HARROGATE
Kennion, George Wyndham, 5
HAWORTH
Horsfall, John Sutcliffe, 4
HAYTON
Read, Charles Rudston, 6
HEATON
Laycock, Burdett, 10
HIGH GREEN
Copley, William, 8
HONLEY
Booth, Norman Parr, 7
HOOK
Trower, Gerard, 12
HORBURY
Holt, Thomas, 4
HORTON
Illingworth, Frederick, 9
HUDDERSFIELD
Coates, Joseph, 3
North, Alexander, 11
Topp, Arthur Maning, 6
Topp, Charles Alfred, 6
Topp, Samuel St John, 6
HULL
Bromby, Charles Henry, 3
Bromby, John Edward, 3
Copeland, Henry, 3
Gleadow, John Ward, 1
Gresham, William Hutchison, 4
Orton, Joseph Rennard, 2
Soutter, Richard Ernest, 12
HUNDERTHWAITE
Bayles, William, 3
KINGSTON-UPON-HULL
Sharp, William Hey, 11
KINGTHORPE
Airey, Henry Parke, 7
KIRBY WISKE
Armitage, Frederick, 3
KIRKHAM ABBEY
Oxley, John Joseph William Molesworth,
  2
KNARESBOROUGH
Greeves, Augustus Frederick Adolphus, 4

KNAYTON
  Taylor, William George, 12
LAZENBY
  Burton, John Wear, 7
LEEDS
  Adam, George Rothwell Wilson, 7
  Appleton, William Thomas, 7
  Bayldon, Arthur Albert Dawson, 7
  Bosisto, Joseph, 3
  Bruce, Theodore, 7
  Dixon, Francis Burdett, 4
  Gatliff, John Henry, 8
  Osborne, Ethel Elizabeth, 11
  Osburn, Lucy, 5
  Rogers, John William Foster, 6
  Waite, Edgar Ravenswood, 12
  Waterhouse, Bertrand James, 12
LEPTON
  Sykes, Alfred Depledge, 12
LONDESBOROUGH
  Young, William Blamire, 12
MANNINGHAM
  Gant, Tetley, 8
MARTON
  Cook, James, 1
MASHAM
  Carter, Thomas, 7
  Hedley, Charles, 9
MELTHAM
  Hirst, Godfrey, 9
MIDDLESBOROUGH
  Hornung, Ernest William, 9
  Kilburn, John George, 9
MIRFIELD
  Ingham, William Bairstow, 4
NEW WORTLEY
  May, Philip William, 5
OTLEY
  Calvert, James Snowden, 3
PATELEY-BRIDGE
  Harker, George, 4
PICKERING
  Calvert, James, 3
POCKLINGTON
  Ullathorne, William Bernard, 2
PONTEFRACT
  Howe, Michael, 1
POPPLETON NETHER
  Camidge, Charles Edward, 7
RICHMOND
  Humble, George Bland, 4
RIPON
  Bickersteth, Kenneth Julian Faithfull, 7
SCARBOROUGH
  Gatenby, Andrew, 1
  Naylor, Henry Darnley, 10
  Terry, Leonard, 6
  Waterworth, John Newham, 12
SELBY
  Speight, Richard, 6
SHEFFIELD
  Bavister, Thomas, 7
  Chapman, Samuel, 3
  Curr, Edward, 1

  Gillott, Sir Samuel, 9
  Hutton, George Samuel, 9
  Moorhouse, James, 5
  Rudd, William Henry, 11
  Woodruff, Harold Addison, 12
SHIPLEY
  Goldsbrough, Richard, 4
  Mawson, Sir Douglas, 10
SILSDEN
  Heaton, Herbert, 9
SOUTHOWRAM
  Aspinall, Arthur Ashworth, 7
STAINFORTH
  Maudsley, Sir Henry Carr, 10
SUNNY BANK
  Kendall, William Tyson, 9
SWINEFLEET
  Faulding, Francis Hardey, 4
TERRINGTON
  Bustard, William, 7
THORNTON-IN-CRAVEN
  Carr, William James, 7
THORNTON-STEWARD
  Humble, William, 4
TICKHILL
  Hill, Charles Lumley, 4
TODMORDEN
  Ramsbotham, Joshua Fielden, 11
TRANBY
  Metcalfe, Michael, 5
WADSLEY
  Howard, Stanley, 4
WADSWORTH
  Stansfield, William, 12
WAKEFIELD
  Scutt, Cecil Allison, 11
  Walker, Henry, 6
  Whitton, John, 6
WHITBY
  Clarkson, Sir William, 8
WIGGLESWORTH
  Lancaster, Samuel, 9
WORRALL
  Grayson, Henry Joseph, 9
WORTLEY
  Worsnop, Thomas, 6
YORK
  Benson, Louisa, 7
  Berry, William, 7
  Brown, James Drysdale, 7
FIJI
  Kesteven, Hereward Leighton, 9
  Moore, Samuel Wilkinson, 10
  Prichard, Katharine Susannah, 11
FINLAND
  Nobelius, Carl Axel, 5
FRANCE
  Baudin, Nicolas Thomas, 1
  Blosseville, Jules Poret de, 1
  Bochsa, Robert Nicholas Charles, 3
  Boismenu, Alain Marie Guynot de, 7
  Boyd, William Alexander Jenyns, 7
  Bruny D'Entrecasteaux, Joseph-Antoine
    Raymond, 1

Cameron, Ewen Wallace, 3
Caron, Leon Francis Victor, 3
Chabrillan, Céleste de, 3
Champion de Crespigny, Philip, 7
Clarke, George O'Malley, 3
Couppé, Louis, 8
Fauchery, Antoine Julien, 4
Forrest, Haughton, 8
Freycinet, Louis-Claude Desaulses de, 1
Gibson, William Ralph Boyce, 8
Gsell, Francis Xavier, 9
Haly, Charles Robert, 4
Henry, Lucien Felix, 4
Huon de Kerrilleau, Gabriel Louis Marie, 1
Joubert, Jules François de Sales, 4
Krause, Ferdinand Moritz, 5
La Billardière, Jacques-Julien Houtou de, 2
La Pérouse, Jean-François de Galaup, 2
Laboureyas, Pierre, 5
Le Rennetel, Pierre François, 10
Marin la Meslée, Edmond Marie, 5
Monnier, Joseph, 5
Nicolle, Eugène Dominique, 5
Noblet, Marie Thérèse Augustine, 11
Oster, Philipp Jacob, 5
Péron, François, 2
Piquet, Jean Pierre, 11
Poupinel, François Victor, 5
Rays, Marquis de, 6
Reymond, Joseph Bernard, 6
Rocher, Jean-Louis, 6
Rossi, Francis Nicholas, 2
St Julian, Charles James Herbert de Courcy, 6
Schurr, Felix, 6
Scratchley, Sir Peter Henry, 6
Serisier, Jean Emile, 6
Soubeiran, Augustine, 12
Turner, Alfred Allatson, 6
Weigall, Albert Bythesea, 6
Wenz, Paul, 12

GERMANY/GERMAN STATES
Freeman, Paul, 8
Menge, Johann, 2
Sellheim, Philip Frederic, 6
Wayn, Amelia Lucy, 12
Baden
Jerger, Charles Adolph, 9
Müller, Frederick, 10
Roth, Adam, 11
Bavaria
Flierl, Johann, 8
Gramp, Johann, 4
Leidig, Georg Friedrich, 10
Neumayer, Georg Balthasar von, 5
Brunswick
Homburg, Robert, 9
Krefft, Johann Ludwig Gerard, 5
Hamburg
Heysen, Sir Wilhelm Ernst Hans Franz, 9
Holtermann, Bernhardt Otto, 4
Josephson, Joshua Frey, 4
Koch, John Augustus Bernard, 9

Lempriere, Thomas James, 2
Sinnett, Frederick, 6
Troedel, Johannes Theodor Charles, 6
Hanover
Eggers, Karl Friedrich Wilhelm, 4
Foelsche, Paul Heinrich Matthias, 4
Gerstaecker, Friedrich, 4
Holtze, Maurice William, 9
Kayser, Heinrich Wilhelm Ferdinand, 5
Michaelis, Moritz, 5
Preiss, Johann August Ludwig, 2
Vosz, Heinrich Ludwig, 6
Hesse-Darmstadt
Becker, Ludwig, 3
Hernsheim, Eduard, 4
Holstein
Pflaum, Friedrich Jacob Theodor, 11
Scherk, Theodor Johannes, 11
Magdeburg
Handt, Johann Christian Simon, 1
Mecklenburg
Bauer, Ferdinand Lukas, 1
Bracker, Frederick John Henry, 3
Mecklenburg-Schwerin
Herz, Julius, 4
Mueller, Baron Sir Ferdinand Jakob Heinrich von, 5
Nickel, Theodor August Friedrich Wilhelm, 11
Ruwolt, Charles Ernest, 11
Nassau
Zadow, Christiane Susanne Augustine, 12
Oldenburg
Menkens, Frederick Burnhardt, 5
Prussia
Appel, George, 3
Auricht, Johann Christian, 3
Basedow, Martin Peter Friedrich, 7
Blandowski, William, 3
Boehm, Traugott Wilhelm, 7
Brache, Jacob, 3
Brodzky, Maurice, 7
Buring, Adolph Wilhelm Rudolph, 3
Buring, Hermann Paul Leopold, 3
Buring, Theodor Gustav Hermann, 3
Castella, Charles Hubert de, 3
Castella, Paul Frédéric de, 3
De Pury, Frédéric Guillaume, 4
Finsch, Otto, 4
Forster, Johann Georg(e) Adam, 1
Forster, Johann Reinhold, 1
Goethe, Matthias, 4
Haller, John Friederick, 1
Helms, Richard, 4
Herlitz, Hermann, 4
Herz, Max Markus, 9
Hirsch, Maximilian, 9
Hirschfeld, Eugen, 9
Hoffnung, Sigmond, 4
Hübbe, Ulrich, 4
Kates, Francis Benjamin, 5
Kavel, August Ludwig Christian, 2
Krome, Otto Georg Hermann Dittmar, 9
Leichhardt, Friedrich Wilhelm Ludwig, 2

Liebe, Friederich Wilhelm Gustav, 10
Lindt, John William, 5
Linger, Carl Ferdinand August, 5
McNamara, Matilda Emilie Bertha, 10
Muecke, Carl Wilhelm Ludwig, 5
Muecke, Hugo Carl Emil, 10
Prenzel, Robert Wilhelm, 11
Puttmann, Hermann, 5
Rechner, Gustav Julius, 6
Resch, Edmund, 11
Rodius, Charles, 2
Rosenhain, Walter, 11
Rumker, Christian Carl Ludwig, 2
Schaffer, Philip, 2
Schirmeister, Carl Friedrich Alexander
    Franz, 6
Schleinitz, Georg Gustav Freiherr von, 6
Schmidt, Karl Wilhelm Edward, 2
Seppelt, Joseph Ernest, 6
Seppelt, Oscar Benno Pedro, 6
Steinfeld, Emanuel, 6
Strehlow, Carl Friedrich Theodor, 12
Strempel, Carl Friedrich, 6
Ulrich, Georg Heinrich Friedrich, 6
Vogt, George Leonard, 12
Wendt, Joachim Matthias, 12
Saxony
Dietrich, Amalie, 4
Hagenauer, Friedrich August, 4
Heinicke, August Moritz Hermann, 9
Heyne, Ernst Bernhard, 4
Schomburgk, Moritz Richard, 6
Siede, Julius, 6
Schleswig
Krichauff, Friedrich Eduard Heinrich
    Wulf, 5
Silesia
Strzelecki, Sir Paul Edmund de, 2
Thuringian States
Heidenreich, Georg Adam, 4
Westphalia
Backhaus, George Henry, 3
Württemberg
Eipper, Christopher, 1
Elsasser, Carl Gottlieb, 4
Leibius, Charles Adolph, 5
Rasp, Charles, 6
Resch, Emil Karl, 11
Schuler, Gottlieb Frederich Henry, 11
GREECE
Comino, Athanassio, 8
Comino, John, 8
Freeleagus, Christy Kosmas, 8
Knetes, Christophoros, 9
Lucas, Antony John Jereos, 10
GUIANA
Cameron, John, 7
HOLLAND/NETHERLANDS
Ainsworth, Alfred Bower, 7
Boas, Abraham Tobias, 7
Crowther, William Lodewyk, 3
Delprat, Guillaume Daniel, 8
Houtman, Frederik de, 1
Paling, William Henry, 5

Pelsaert, Francisco, 2
Tasman, Abel Janszoon, 2
HUNGARY, *see also* Austro-Hungarian
Empire
Wekey, Sigismund, 6
INDIA
Allan, James Thomas, 3
Allardyce, Sir William Lamond, 7
Angelo, Edward Houghton, 7
Bean, Edwin, 4
Beg, Wazir, 3
Bejah, Dervish, 7
Bignold, Hugh Baron, 7
Birdwood, William Riddell, 7
Braddon, Sir Henry Yule, 7
Cavenagh, George, 1
Champion, Henry Hyde, 7
Clogstoun, Henry Oliver, 8
Close, Edward Charles, 1
Cooke, Cecil Pybus, 3
Coverdale, John, 1
Cunningham, Hastings, 3
Eames, William L'Estrange, 8
Field, Edward Percy, 8
Forster, William, 4
French, Sir John Russell, 8
Geils, Andrew, 1
Glasfurd, Duncan John, 9
Glenelg, Baron, 1
Godfrey, Frederick Race, 4
Gordon, Grosvenor George Stuart,
    9
Griffen Foley, James Joseph, 9
Hopkins, Francis Rawdon Chesney,
    4
Jacob, Archibald Hamilton, 4
Lee, John Henry Alexander, 10
Lorimer, Philip Durham, 5
Mackie, William Henry, 2
Macnaghten, Charles Melville, 10
Mault, Alfred, 5
Montagu, John, 2
Montgomery, Henry Hutchinson, 10
Morris, Edward Ellis, 5
Ogilvy, Arthur James, 5
O'Halloran, Thomas Shuldham, 2
Onslow, Arthur Alexander Walton, 5
Ordell, Talone, 11
Payne, Henry, 11
Pottinger, Sir Frederick William, 5
Prinsep, Henry Charles, 11
Scobie, Grace Locke, 11
Scott, Alexander Walker, 6
Scott, Helenus, 2
Scott, Robert, 2
Smythe, Carlyle Greenwood, 12
Squires, Ernest Ker, 12
Sturt, Charles, 2
Tracey, Eliza, 12
Walch, Charles Edward, 6
Ward, Sir Edward Wolstenholme, 6
Wesché, Awdry Gordon, 12
Whitham, John Lawrence, 12
Young, Sir John, 6

IRELAND

Allen, William Bell, 3
Bowen, Sir George Ferguson, 3
Brenan, John Ryan, 1
Burns, John Fitzgerald, 3
Cairns, Sir William Wellington, 3
Cleburne, Richard, 1
Considen, Dennis, 1
Cudmore, Daniel Michael Paul, 8
Cussen, Patrick Edward, 1
Darley, Sir Frederick Matthew, 4
Doyne, William Thomas, 4
Druitt, George, 1
Hennessy, John Francis, 9
Hogan, Patrick Gould, 1
Kelly, David Frederick, 5
Kelly, William, 5
Meehan, James, 2
Moloney, Patrick, 5
Murnin, Michael Egan, 5
Nobbs, George Hunn, 2
O'Halloran, William Littlejohn, 2
Osborne, John Walter, 5
O'Shaughnessy, Edward, 2
Power, Robert, 2
Reid, Thomas, 2
Ryan, Thomas, 11
Thompson, David (1828-1889), 12
Torrens, Robert, 2
Von Stieglitz, Frederick Lewis, 2

Dublin

Adamson, Travers, 3
Armstrong, Thomas Henry, 7
Atkins, John Ringrose, 3
Barlow, Christopher George, 7
Barlow, William, 7
Barrett, John Joseph, 3
Barrington, George, 1
Belcher, George Frederick, 3
Bell, Barbara, 7
Blackall, Samuel Wensley, 3
Boulger, Edward Vaughan, 3
Bourke, Sir Richard, 1
Brooke, Gustavus Vaughan, 3
Browne, Fielding, 1
Bryan, William, 1
Buchanan, Nathaniel, 3
Buchanan, William Frederick, 3
Burrowes, John, 3
Bury, Thomas, 3
Byrne, Frederick, 7
Byrne, Joseph Patrick, 3
Carroll, Robert Joseph, 7
Chomley, Hussey Malone, 3
Costello, James Jasper, 8
Darley, Benjamin, 4
De Burgh, Ernest Macartney, 8
Dobbie, Edward David, 8
Donohoe, John, 1
Douglass, Henry Grattan, 1
Dowling, Christopher Vincent, 4
Duffy, Charles Gavan, 8
Duffy, Sir Frank Gavan, 8
Duffy, John Gavan, 4

Dwyer-Gray, Edmund John Chisholm, 8
Eades, Richard, 4
Faucett, Peter, 4
Fitzpatrick, Columbus, 4
Fitzpatrick, John, 4
Foster, John Leslie Fitzgerald Vesey, 4
Foy, Francis, 8
Frayne, Ursula, 4
Gardiner, John, 1
Garland, David John, 8
Geoghegan, Patrick Bonaventure, 4
Gore, St George Richard, 4
Greene, Molesworth Richard, 4
Hancock, William John, 9
Higinbotham, George, 4
Higinbotham, Thomas, 4
Howard, Charles Beaumont, 1
Ievers, Robert Lancelot, 4
Keenan, Sir Norbert Michael, 9
Kelly, Nicholas William, 9
Kelly, William, 5
Lee, Alfred, 10
Leeper, Alexander, 10
Le Fanu, Henry Frewen, 10
Lennon, William, 10
Lyster, William Saurin, 5
Macartney, Hussey Burgh, 5
Macartney, Sir William Grey Ellison, 10
McCathie, Harriette Adelaide, 10
McCoy, Sir Frederick, 5
MacDonnell, Randal, 5
MacDonnell, Sir Richard Graves, 5
Mayne, William Colburn, 5
Mills, Peter, 2
Molesworth, Hickman, 10
Molesworth, Sir Robert, 5
Monahan, Thomas, 5
Moncrieff, Alexander Bain, 10
Moore, James (1807-1895), 5
Moore, Joseph Sheridan, 5
Mullan, John, 10
Mullen, Samuel, 5
Murphy, William Emmett, 5
Nash, Richard West, 2
O'Connor, Michael, 5
O'Doherty, Kevin Izod, 5
O'Farrell, Henry James, 5
O'Loghlen, Sir Bryan, 5
Reilly, Joseph Thomas, 11
Reynolds, Christopher Augustine, 6
Richardson, Walter Lindesay, 11
Rogers, Thomas George, 2
Seymour, Charles, 11
Singleton, John, 6
Sleigh, William Campbell, 6
Tully, William Alcock, 6
Wade, Robert Thompson, 12
Walsh, Henry Deane, 12
Wrixon, Sir Henry John, 6

Antrim

Griffin, Thomas John Augustus, 4
McIntyre, William, 5
Thomas, Evan Henry, 2

BALLYCLARE
Agnew, Sir James Willson, 3
BALLYCLOGHAN
Wilson, Sir Samuel, 6
BALLYMENA
Angus, Samuel, 7
BALLYNURE
McCay, Sir James Whiteside, 10
BELFAST
Allen, Alfred, 3
Allen, William Johnston, 3
Bailey, William, 1
Cairnduff, Alexander, 1
Campbell, Francis Rawdon Hastings, 3
Cooke, John, 8
Crawford, Alexander, 8
Kirkpatrick, Mary, 9
Langwell, Hugh, 9
Montgomery, Sydney Hamilton Rowan, 10
Newell, Hugh Hamilton, 11
Ogilby, James Douglas, 11
Shaw, William Henry, 6
Thomson, Robert, 6
Whitfield, George, 6
Young, William John (1850-1931), 12
CARRICKFERGUS
Jamison, Sir John, 2
CLOONA
Grimshaw, Beatrice Ethel, 9
TULLYNEWY
Harper, Nathaniel White, 9
McCaughey, Sir Samuel, 5
Armagh
Dunlop, Eliza Hamilton, 1
Lennon, Hugh, 5
Palmer, Sir Arthur Hunter, 5
Synnot, Monckton, 6
ARMAGH
Benson, John Robinson, 3
Lee, David, 5
LURGAN
Thompson, William George, 12
MARKETHILL
Glassey, Thomas, 9
NEWRY
Gunn, William, 1
PORTADOWN
Watson, James, 6
Wentworth, D'Arcy, 2
Carlow
BALLYDARTON
Watson, George John, 6
LEIGHLINBRIDGE
Moran, Patrick Francis, 10
Cavan
Brady, John, 1
Divine, Nicholas, 1
Donohoe, James Joseph, 8
BAILIEBOROUGH
Hamilton, Alexander Greenlaw, 9
BELTURBET
Hearn, William Edward, 4

COOTEHILL
Deane, John Horace, 8
GALLON ETRA
Lucas, Sir Edward, 10
KILLESHANDRA
Gibney, Matthew, 8
VIRGINIA
Lynch, Annie, 10
Clare
Allman, Francis, 1
Casey, Gilbert Stephen, 7
Crotty, James, 8
Crowe, William, 8
Haugh, Denis Robert, 9
Quinlivan, Thomas, 11
BROADFORD
Abbott, Robert Palmer, 3
DROMOLAND
O'Brien, William Smith, 2
ENNIS
Baker, Thomas, 7
Graham, James, 4
McDonnell, Francis, 10
ENNISTYMON
Thynne, Andrew Joseph, 12
KILKEE
Foran, Martin Henry, 8
KILLALOE
Minahan, Patrick Joseph, 10
KILRUSH
Meagher, John, 10
QUIN
Hannan, Patrick, 9
ROCKFOREST
Bagot, Edward Meade, 3
RUAN
Clune, Patrick Joseph, 8
SCARRIFF
Durack, Patrick, 4
TROMRA
Casey, James Joseph, 3
Cork
Atkin, Robert Travers, 3
Cuthbert, John, 3
Fitzgibbon, Edmund Gerald, 4
Goold, James Alipius, 4
Moriarty, Abram Orpen, 5
Moriarty, Merion Marshall, 5
Murphy, Sir Francis, 5
O'Connor, Richard, 5
O'Neil, Peter, 2
Supple, Gerald Henry, 6
Torrens, Sir Robert Richard, 6
BALLYCLOUGH
Barry, Sir Redmond, 3
BALLYMACODA
Ahern, Thomas, 7
BANDON
Kingston, Sir George Strickland, 2
BANTRY
Cotter, Thomas Young, 1
Desmond, Anna Maria, 8
O'Hea, Timothy, 5
O'Sullivan, Richard, 5

White, George Boyle, 6
BELLMOUNT
  Murphy, Daniel, 5
BLARNEY
  McCarthy, Charles, 5
BUTTEVANT
  Forrest, John, 4
CHARLEVILLE
  Mannix, Daniel, 10
CLONMEL
  Curran, John (Michael) Milne, 3
CLOYNE
  Lawless, Clement Francis, 2
  Lawless, Paul, 2
  Madden, Sir John, 10
CORK
  Barry, Zachary, 3
  Bride, Thomas Francis, 3
  Carew-Smyth, Ponsonby May, 7
  Carey, John Randal, 7
  Dacey, John Rowland, 8
  Goldstein, Jacob Robert Yannasch, 9
  Henderson, Anketell Matthew, 9
  Hungerford, Thomas, 4
  Madden, Sir Frank, 10
  Madden, Walter, 10
  O'Hara, Henry Michael, 11
  Sadleir, Richard, 2
  Sandes, John, 11
  Savage, Robert, 6
  Sheehy, Samuel John Austin, 6
  Spence, Robert William, 12
  Talbot, John Richard, 6
  Therry, Sir Roger, 2
CREAGH
  Macartney, John Arthur, 5
DOUGLAS
  Pollock, James Arthur, 11
FERMOY
  Throssell, George, 12
  Torpy, James, 6
FREEMOUNT
  Barry, John, 7
JAMESBROOK
  Goold-Adams, Sir Hamilton John,
  9
KILMURRY
  Doyle, Jeremiah Joseph, 8
KINSALE
  Burke, John, 7
  Gibbons, Geraldine Scholastica, 4
  O'Donovan, Denis, 5
MACROOM
  Horgan, John, 9
MALLOW
  Browne, William Henry, 1
  Buckley, Mars, 3
  Whyte, Patrick, 6
MIDLETON
  Martin, Sir James, 5
MITCHELSTOWN
  Dunne, John, 8
OLDCOURT
  Stawell, Sir William Foster, 6

QUEENSTOWN
  O'Reilly, Maurice Joseph, 11
RATHARD
  O'Mahony, Timothy, 5
SCHULL
  Leahy, John, 10
SPRINGFIELD
  Coveny, Robert, 3
TIMOLEAGUE
  Fihelly, John Arthur, 8
YOUGHAL
  Walsh, Thomas, 12
Donegal
BALLINTRA
  Moubray, Thomas, 5
BALLYSHANNON
  Coane, John Montgomery, 8
CREESLOUGH
  Macrossan, John Murtagh, 5
GLENTIES
  MacDevitt, Edward O'Donnell, 5
GREENCASTLE
  Fitzsimons, William Robert, 8
LISFANNON
  Dill Macky, William Marcus, 8
PETTIGOE
  Corrigan, James, 3
RAMELTON
  Gwynn, Sir Charles William, 9
Down
  Magarey, Thomas, 2
BALLYMACARNE
  Moore, Charles, 5
BALLYNAHINCH
  Gordon, Samuel Deane, 4
BALLYNASKEAGH
  Wright, David McKee, 12
BANBRIDGE
  McIlrath, Sir Martin, 10
  McIlrath, William, 10
  Walker, James, 12
CULTRA
  Kennedy, Sir Arthur Edward, 5
  Kennedy, Hugh, 5
DROMARA
  King, John Charles, 2
DROMORE
  Frazer, John, 4
DRUMGOOLAND
  Mulligan, James Venture, 5
DUNDRUM
  Pigot, Edward Francis, 11
HILLSBOROUGH
  Fowler, Thomas Walker, 8
  Hume, Andrew Hamilton, 1
HOLYWOOD
  Macartney, Sir Edward Henry, 10
  Osborne, William Alexander, 11
LISTOODER
  Newell, John, 5
NEWRY
  Glenny, Henry, 4
  Irvine, Sir William Hill, 9
  Jennings, Sir Patrick Alfred, 4

McMinn, Gilbert Rotherdale, 5
McMinn, William, 5
NEWTOWNARDS
Higgins, Henry Bournes, 9
PORTAFERRY
Glass, Hugh, 4
RATHFRYLAND
Scott, Andrew George, 6
SAINTFIELD
Gledson, David Alexander, 9
Dublin
KINGSTOWN
Wolseley, Frederick York, 6
PALMERSTON
Doyle, Cyrus Matthew, 1
RATHMINES
Bennett, William Christopher, 3
Torrance, George William, 6
SANDFORD
Doolette, Sir George Philip, 8
Fermanagh
Mason, Francis Conway, 5
Ryan, Thomas, 2
AGHAVEA
Burley, Johnston, 7
ENNISKILLEN
Brady, Joseph, 3
Latimer, William Fleming, 10
McArthur, Alexander, 5
McCarron, John Francis, 5
O'Haran, Denis Francis, 11
HILLGROVE
Allingham, Christopher, 3
KILLESHER
Maguire, James Bernard, 10
ST CATHERINES
Ovens, John, 2
Galway
Fitzgerald, Nicholas, 4
Ireland, Richard Davies, 4
Lardner, John, 5
Walsh, John Joseph, 6
ARDFRY
Daly, Sir Dominick, 4
BALLINASLOE
Kelly, Anthony Edwin Bowes, 9
BALLYMORE
Seymour, David Thompson, 6
GORT
Glynn, Patrick McMahon, 9
LISMANNY
Gowrie, Zara Eileen, Lady, 9
MOYLOUGH
Carr, Thomas Joseph, 7
MOYODE CASTLE
Persse, De Burgh Fitzpatrick, 5
SAINTCLERANS
Burke, Robert O'Hara, 3
TONACURRA
Delany, Patrick, 8
TUAM
Finney, Thomas, 4
Kerry
Hickson, Robert Rowan Purdon, 4

Moriarty, Edward Orpen, 5
O'Connell, Sir Maurice Charles Philip, 2
O'Flynn, Jeremiah Francis, 2
CAHERSIVEEN
Connor, Daniel, 8
CASTLEMAINE
O'Sullivan, Patrick, 5
Spring, Gerald, 6
DINGLE
Kennedy, John Joseph, 9
Moriarty, William, 2
O'Kane, Thadeus, 5
KILLARNEY
Eagar, Edward, 1
LISTOWEL
Moore, James (1834-1904), 5
TRALEE
Chute, Sir Trevor, 3
Fitzgerald, Robert David, 4
Kildare
Bell, Sir Joshua Peter, 3
BALLITORE
Cullen, Paul, 3
EADESTOWN
Quinn, Matthew, 5
FONTSTOWN
Bagot, Robert Cooper, 3
HARRISTOWN
Byron, John Joseph, 7
JOHNSTOWN
MacCullagh, John Christian, 5
KILDARE
Griffith, Charles James, 4
NEWBRIDGE
Partridge, Bridget, 11
Strange, Benjamin Edward, 12
NURNEY
Bagot, Charles Harvey, 1
RATHBANE
Quinn, James, 5
Kilkenny
Butler, Edward, 3
McKenna, Martin, 5
BALLYCALLAN
Dunne, William John, 4
CALLAN
Tallis, Sir George, 12
CASTLECOMER
Brophy, Daniel, 3
CASTLEWARREN
Loughlin, Martin, 5
FERRYBANK
Smyth, Charles Edward Owen, 12
JOHNSTOWN
Phelan, Patrick, 11
KILKENNY
Brennan, Martin, 7
Hackett, William Philip, 9
Kinchela, John, 2
Morison, Alexander, 5
Murphy, Jeremiah Matthias, 10
O'Reily, John, 11
Kings County
Bermingham, Patrick, 3

O'Connor, Joseph Graham, 5
EDENDERRY
  Killian, Andrew, 9
FANCROFT
  Bergin, Michael, 7
KILLURIN
  Mahon, Hugh, 10
LUSMAGH
  O'Grady, Thomas, 5
MOYSTOWN DEMESNE
  Foy, Mark, 4
PHILIPSTOWN
  Dunne, Patrick, 4
TULLAMORE
  Fitzgerald, Sir Thomas Naghten, 4
  Hely, Hovenden, 4
  Jageurs, Morgan Peter, 9
  Webb, William Telford, 6
Leitrim
BROOKLAWN
  Bruce, John Munro, 3
KILTYCLOGHER
  Keaney, Paul Francis, 9
MOHILL
  Murphy, Peter, 10
Limerick
  Barlow, Mary Kate, 7
  Bindon, Samuel Henry, 3
  Gunson, John Michael, 4
  Hales, Francis, 4
  Hayes, Catherine, 4
  Hurley, John, 4
  Montez, Lola, 5
  Synan, Mary, 12
ADARE
  Mulquin, Katherine, 10
BALLYSTEEN
  Murray, Sir Terence Aubrey, 2
CAPPAGH
  Garvan, James Patrick, 4
DUNTRYLEAGUE
  Dalton, James, 4
KILFINNANE
  Walsh, John Joseph, 12
KILLILA
  Duhig, Sir James, 8
LIMERICK
  Baylee, Pery, 1
  Corbett, James Francis, 8
  Finnerty, John Michael, 8
  Hanran, Patrick Francis, 9
  Ievers, William, 4
  Lefroy, Anthony O'Grady, 5
  Ryan, John, 11
  Toohey, John Thomas, 6
  Tracy, Richard Thomas, 6
MOUNT COOTE
  King, Henry Edward, 5
PALLAS GREAN
  Real, Patrick, 11
SUMMERVILLE
  Harvey, William Henry, 4
Londonderry
  McGowan, Samuel Walker, 5

Millen, John Dunlop, 10
  Robb, John, 6
AGHADOWEY
  Fullerton, James, 4
ARTICLAVE
  Anderson, Robert Stirling Hore, 3
BALLYKELLY
  Forrest, John, 8
  Forrest, William, 8
BALLYRONAN
  Charles, Samuel, 3
CAMNISH
  Mitchel, John, 2
COLERAINE
  Lyle, Sir Thomas Ranken, 10
  McFarland, Alfred, 5
  McKenny, John, 2
  Young, Edmund Mackenzie, 6
CULLYCAPPLE
  Thomson, James, 12
DUNGIVEN
  Little, Robert, 5
GARVAGH
  Rentoul, John Laurence, 11
LONDONDERRY
  Cabena, William Whyte, 7
  McMillan, Sir William, 10
  Miller, Henry, 5
  Woore, Thomas, 6
MAGHERA
  Clarke, Henry, 3
  Harris, John, 4
  Shiels, William, 11
MAGHERAFELT
  Harris, Sir Matthew, 9
MONEYMORE
  Harris, John, 1
Longford
  Crawford, George John, 3
CLOONTAMORE
  Potter, Norah Mary, 11
EDGEWORTHSTOWN
  Byrnes, James, 3
LONGFORD
  Dooley, James Thomas, 8
  Morgan, James, 5
Louth
COLLON
  Greene, George Henry, 9
DROGHEDA
  Davitt, Arthur, 4
  Hardman, Edward Townley, 4
  O'Reilly, John Boyle, 5
  Thompson, James, 12
DUNDALK
  Foster, Roland, 8
RATHESCAR
  Foster, William John, 4
Mayo
  Considine, Michael Patrick, 8
  Kelly, Alicia Mary, 9
  McEvilly, Walter O'Malley, 5
BALLINA
  Wright, John James, 6

CASTLEBAR
  Brennan, Louis, 3
  Sheridan, Richard Bingham, 6
CLAREMORRIS
  Gray, Moses Wilson, 4
HOLLYMOUNT
  Love, Wilton Wood Russell, 10
  O'Brien, Cornelius, 2
  O'Brien, Henry, 2
Meath
  Balfe, John Donnellan, 3
  Corrigan, Tom, 3
  Halloran, Laurence Hynes, 1
AGHER
  Winter, Samuel Pratt, 6
BALLYBEG
  O'Reilly, Christopher, 5
CASTLETOWN
  O'Connor, Charles Yelverton, 11
GORMANSTON
  Gormanston, Jenico William Joseph
    Preston, 9
MARTINSTOWN
  Sheridan, John Felix, 6
NAVAN
  Daley, Victor James William Patrick, 8
  Murphy, Francis, 2
Monaghan
  Blair, David, 3
  Conolly, Philip, 1
  Duffy, Sir Charles Gavan, 4
  Lee, Mary, 10
  Longmore, Francis, 5
  Waddell, Thomas, 12
BALLYBAY
  Gray, James, 4
  Robinson, Robert Thomson, 11
CARRICKMACROSS
  Fitzgerald, Thomas Henry, 4
MONAGHAN
  McCourt, William Joseph, 10
TYDAVNET
  Storey, Sir David, 12
Queens County
MARYBOROUGH
  Erskine, James, 1
  Graves, James Abraham Howlin, 4
MOUNTMELLICK
  Beale, Octavius Charles, 7
RAHEEN
  Lalor, Peter, 5
ROSENALLIS
  Meredith, John Baldwin Hoystead,
    10
Roscommon
  Strickland, Sir Edward, 6
ATHLONE
  Beattie, Joseph Aloysius, 7
  Bruce, John, 3
  Bull, John Edward Newell, 3
  Crummer, James Henry, 1
  Fallon, James Thomas, 4
BALLYFARNAN
  East, Hubert, 8

BALLYMACURLY
  Beirne, Thomas Charles, 7
BOYLE
  Cuthbert, Sir Henry, 3
COOLTEIGE
  Blakeney, Charles William, 3
ELPHIN
  Flanagan, Roderick, 4
  Gormly, James, 4
FRENCHPARK
  O'Grady, Michael, 5
GRANNY
  Liston, John James, 10
KINGSLAND
  Harrington, William Frederick, 9
MOUNTPLUNKETT
  Plunkett, John Hubert, 2
ROSCOMMON
  French, Sir George Arthur, 8
STROKESTOWN
  Cahill, William Geoffrey, 7
  Stanton, Richard Patrick Joseph,
    12
Sligo
  Farleigh, John Gibson, 8
  Kemble, Myra, 5
CASTLETOWN
  Fenton, Michael, 1
SLIGO
  Henry, William, 1
  Higgins, Patrick, 4
Tipperary
  Bates, Daisy May, 7
  Edgar, Alexander Robert, 8
  Falkiner, Franc Sadlier, 4
  Hoolan, John, 9
  Minchin, William, 2
ARDSALLAGH
  McEncroe, John, 2
BALLYNAHOW
  O'Shanassy, Sir John, 5
CAPPAGH-WHITE
  Givens, Thomas, 9
  Hunt, Thomas, 4
CARRICK-ON-SUIR
  Dwyer, Sir Walter, 8
CASHEL
  Perkins, Patrick, 5
CLONMEL
  Dodery, William, 4
  Martin, David, 10
CLONOULTY
  Ryan, John Tighe, 11
DOON
  Ryan, James, 11
FETHARD
  Burges, William, 1
  MacCarthy, Charles William, 10
GLENOUGH
  Fahey, John, 8
GREENANE
  Slattery, Thomas Michael, 11
GREENHILLS
  Minchin, Richard Ernest, 5

LISDALEEN
Lanigan, William, 5
LORRHA
O'Meara, Martin, 11
NENAGH
Hogan, James Francis, 4
Slattery, Patrick Joseph, 6
ROSCREA
White, Daniel, 12
THURLES
Treacy, Patrick Ambrose, 6
TIPPERARY
Daly, Anne, 8
Finn, Edmund, 1
Knaggs, Samuel Thomas, 5
O'Connor, Daniel, 5
Tyrone
Hely, Frederick Augustus, 1
King, John (1841-1872), 5
McCrea, William, 5
Morrow, James, 5
AGHYARAN
Forsyth, Samuel, 8
BALLYGAWLEY
Crookes, John, 1
MacRory, Margaret, 10
CASTLEDERG
Devine, William, 8
CLOGHLIN
Montague, Alexander, 5
COAGH
Marks, John, 5
DONEMANA
Moore, George Fletcher, 2
DUNGANNON
Clement, Dixie Paumier, 8
Cordner, William John, 3
O'Neill, George, 11
FINTONA
King, George (1813-1899), 5
Love, James Robinson, 5
GORTMORE
Morrison, Askin, 5
KILDRESS
Black, William Robert, 7
KILLETTER
Love, James Robert Beattie, 10
MOY
Davidson, William, 8
OMAGH
Ellis, Henry Augustus, 8
McCutcheon, Robert George, 10
MacFarland, Sir John Henry, 10
MacMahon, Sir Charles, 5
Rowan, Frederic Charles, 11
Simpson, Martha Margaret Mildred,
11
Waterford
Kean, Charles John, 5
Wallace, William Vincent, 2
BALLYVADDEN
O'Donovan, John, 5
CAPPOQUIN
Baker, Catherine, 7

CLONMEL
Archdall, Mervyn, 7
KNOCKALISHEEN
Barron, Johanna, 7
LISMORE
Duggan, Edmund, 8
WATERFORD
Dalton, Joseph, 4
Hobson, William, 1
Kelly, Michael, 9
Meagher, Thomas Francis, 2
Moore, Nicholas, 10
Power, Henry, 5
Slattery, Joseph Patrick, 11
Sullivan, James Forester, 6
Tisdall, Henry Thomas, 12
Westmeath
Donaldson, Robert Thomas, 8
Griffith, Arthur Hill, 9
McAlroy, Michael, 5
ATHLONE
Kelly, Thomas Hussey, 5
Moffatt, Thomas de Lacy, 5
DARDISTOWN
Fetherstonhaugh, Cuthbert, 4
GLENCARA
Kelly, Robert Vandeleur, 9
MOATE
Clibborn, Thomas Strettel, 3
White, William Duckett, 6
MOYVORE
Higgins, Joseph, 9
MULLINGAR
Gannon, Michael, 4
ROSMEAD
Robinson, Sir Hercules George Robert,
6
Robinson, Sir William Cleaver Francis, 6
SKEARK
Lynch, Patrick Joseph, 10
Wexford
Barry, Mary Gonzaga, 3
Frencham, Henry, 4
Hayes, Michael, 1
Pidgeon, Nathaniel, 2
ARTRAMONT
Le Hunte, Sir George Ruthven, 10
BALLYTRENT
Redmond, John Edward, 6
Redmond, William Hoey Kearney, 6
BARRYSTOWN
Crane, Martin, 3
CASTLEBRIDGE
Dixon, James, 1
ENNISCORTHY
Cash, Martin, 1
Esmond, James William, 4
James, Charles Henry, 4
GOREY
Owen, Sir William, 11
NEWTOWNBARRY
Waugh, James Swanton, 6
OILGATE
Whitty, Ellen, 6

WEXFORD
  Dry, Richard, 1
  Sheil, Laurence Bonaventure, 6
Wicklow
  Fishbourne, John William Yorke, 8
  Folingsby, George Frederick, 4
  Murray, James, 5
BRAY
  Hackett, Sir John Winthrop, 9
DUNLAVIN
  Fenton, James, 4
KILQUADE
  Cullen, John Hugh, 8
WICKLOW
  Chomley, Arthur Wolfe, 3
ISLE OF MAN
  Adamson, Lawrence Arthur, 7
  Ashton, James, 7
  Cain, William, 3
  Clucas, Robert John Miller, 8
  Hoff, George Rayner, 9
  Kermode, Robert Quale, 2
  Kermode, William, 2
  McBurney, Mona Margaret, 10
  O'Reilly, Thomas, 5
ITALY, *see also* Austro-Hungarian Empire
  Bernacchi, Angelo Giulio Diego, 7
  Porcelli, Pietro Giacomo, 11
  Ramaciotti, Gustave Mario, 11
  Romano, Azzalin Orlando, 11
  Schiassi, Omero, 11
  Triaca, Camillo, 12
  Vaccari, Gualtiero, 12
  Vigano, Mario Antonio Francesco Battista
    Virginio, 12
Lombardy
  Rossi, Maffio, 11
  Vanzetti, Eugenio, 12
Papal States
  Anivitti, Giulio, 3
  Cani, John, 3
  Carboni, Raffaello, 3
  Torreggiani, Elzear, 6
Parma
  Hazon, Roberto, 9
  Marina, Carlo, 5
Rome
  James, John Charles Horsey, 4
  Poole, George Thomas Temple, 11
  Simonetti, Achille, 6
Sardinia
  D'Albertis, Luigi Maria, 4
  Verjus, Henri Stanislas, 6
Sicily
  Sceusa, Francesco, 11
Tuscany
  Baracchi, Pietro Paolo Giovanni Ernesto,
    7
  Catani, Carlo Giorgio Domenico Enrico, 7
  Checchi, Ettore, 7
  De Salis, Leopold Fabius Dietegan Fane, 4
  Fiaschi, Thomas Henry, 8
  Nerli, Girolamo Pieri Ballati, 10
  Newbery, James Cosmo, 5

  Rolando, Charles, 6
  Sani, Tomaso, 6
Two Sicilies
  Baccarini, Antonio, 7
  Rubbo, Antonio Salvatore Dattilo, 11
JAPAN
  Freame, Wykeham Henry Koba, 8
  Kashiwagi, Taira, 9
  Kitamura, Toranosuke, 9
  Komine, Isokichi, 9
  McLaren, Charles Inglis, 10
  McLaren, Samuel Bruce, 10
  Muramats, Jirō, 10
  Satō, Torajirō, 11
  Takasuka, Jō, 12
LEBANON
  Mansour, Sylwanos, 10
MALAY PENINSULA
  Eredia, Manuel Godinho de, 1
  Light, William, 2
  Lowe Kong Meng, 5
MALTA
  Adams, Francis William Lauderdale,
    3
  Davidson, Sir Walter Edward, 8
  Strickland, Sir Gerald, 12
MAURITIUS
  Brownrigg, Marcus Blake, 3
  Corby, John McKenzie, 8
  Despeissis, Jean Marie Adrian, 8
  Guthrie, Frederick Bickell, 9
  Rossi, Francis Robert Louis, 6
NATAL, *see also* South Africa
  Royston, John Robinson, 11
NEW CALEDONIA
  Watriama, William Jacob, 12
NEW GUINEA
  Ahuia Ova, 7
  Hides, Jack Gordon, 9
  Simoi, 11
NEW HEBRIDES
  Paton, Francis Hume Lyall, 11
NEW IRELAND
  Sumsuma, 12
NEW ZEALAND
  Desmond, Arthur, 8
AKAROA
  Green, Percy Gordon, 9
AUCKLAND
  Bailey, Albert Edward, 7
  Bessell-Browne, Alfred Joseph, 7
  Davy, Thomas Arthur Lewis, 8
  Fletcher, Joseph James, 8
  Lynas, William James Dalton, 10
  McGuinness, Arthur, 10
CANTERBURY
  Cumbrae-Stewart, Francis William Sutton,
    8
CAVERSHAM
  Grimmett, Clarence Victor, 9
CHRISTCHURCH
  Amadio, John (Bell), 7
  Ashbolt, Sir Alfred Henry, 7
  Barnett, Percy Neville, 7

Deamer, Mary Elizabeth Kathleen Dulcie, 8
Garsia, Rupert Clare, 8
Price, George Richard, 11
Rae, Arthur Edward George, 11
COLLINGWOOD
Devanny, Jane, 8
COROMANDEL
Fraser, Sir Colin, 8
DUNEDIN
Dods, Robert Smith, 8
Duncan, George Smith, 4
Greville, Henrietta, 9
Hungerford, Richard Colin Campbell, 9
Low, Sir David Alexander Cecil, 10
Mussen, Sir Gerald, 10
Percival, Arthur, 11
Power, Harold Septimus, 11
Quick, Balcombe, 11
Sligo, Archibald Douglas, 11
Tishler, Joseph, 12
Wheeler, Charles Arthur, 12
White, Henry Eli, 12
Whittingham, Arthur Herbert, 12
GISBORNE
Gruner, Elioth Lauritz Leganyer, 9
Partridge, Eric Honeywood, 11
GREEN ISLAND
Watt, William Shand, 12
GREYTOWN
Wakelin, Roland Shakespeare, 12
HAMILTON
Pearson, Thomas Edwin, 11
HAMPDEN
Joyce, Edmund Michael, 9
HAWERA
Parkinson, Charles Tasman, 11
HOKITIKA
O'Connor, Kathleen Laetitia, 11
INVERCARGILL
Angus, John Henry Smith, 7
Conyers, Evelyn Augusta, 8
Ferguson, Eustace William, 8
Mehaffey, Maurice William, 10
Monckton, Charles Arthur Whitmore, 10
Pomeroy, John, 11
Reade, Charles Compton, 11
KAIAPOI
Allan, Stella May, 7
Bavin, Sir Thomas Rainsford, 7
Champion, Herbert William, 7
KAIKOURA
Cooke, Thomas, 8
KARANGAHAKE
Stanley, Charles Roy, 12
KIHIKIHI
Cook, James Newton Haxton Hume, 8
KILBIRNIE
Wall, Dorothy, 12
LAWRENCE
Adams, Arthur Henry, 7
LEESTON
Hutchens, Francis, 9
Kneeshaw, Frederick Percival, 9

MILTON
Calder, William, 7
MOTUEKA
Young, Florence Selina Harriet, 12
NAPIER
Moore, Arthur Edward, 10
Storkey, Percy Valentine, 12
NELSON
Watson, William Thornton, 12
OAMARU
Bee, James, 7
Green, Florence Emily, 9
Scott, William Henry, 11
OPOHO
Boyd, Arthur Merric, 7
OTAHUHU
Hayes-Williams, William Gordon, 9
PAIHIA
Teece, Richard, 12
PALMERSTON NORTH
Linton, Sir Richard, 10
PAPAKURA VALLEY
Gardiner, James, 8
Sinclaire, Frederick, 11
PICTON
Pulleine, Robert Henry, 11
ROSS
Lockington, William Joseph, 10
ST BATHANS
Purton, David Gabriel, 11
TARANAKI
Ward, Frederick William, 12
TE KOPURU
Weathers, Lawrence Carthage, 12
TEMUKA
Plante, Ada May, 11
THAMES
Dunstan, Thomas, 8
TIMARU
MacKenzie, Seaforth Simpson, 10
WAIMATAITAI
Gibb, William, 8
WAINUI
Moore, Annie May, 10
Moore, Minnie Louise, 10
WANGANUI
Johnson, William Dartnell, 9
WELLINGTON
Cazneaux, Harold Pierce, 7
Marks, Percy, 10
Shout, Alfred John, 11
WESTPORT
Hallahan, Walter Rewi, 9
WHITIANGA
Hanna, George Patrick, 9
WOODVILLE
O'Brien, John Patrick, 11
NORFOLK ISLAND
Kearney, William, 2
King, Phillip Parker, 2
Lee, William, 2
Lucas, James, 2
Nobbs, Charles Chase Ray, 11

NORWAY
Asche, Thomas, 7
Borchgrevink, Carsten Egeberg, 7
Dannevig, Harald Kristian, 8
Lumholtz, Carl Sophus, 5
OTTOMAN EMPIRE
Phocas, Seraphim, 11
POLAND, *see also* Austro-Hungarian
Empire; Prussia; Russia
Broinowski, Gracius Joseph, 3
Goldhar, Pinchas, 9
Kossak, Ladislaus Sylvester, 5
Kubary, John Stanislaw, 5
Rubin, Mark, 11
Tarczynski, Stanislaw Victor de, 12
Wynn, Samuel, 12
Galicia and Lodomeria
Lhotsky, John, 2
PORTUGAL
Grey, Sir George, 1
Loureiro, Artur Jose, 5
Quiros, Pedro Fernandez de, 1
Snodgrass, Peter, 2
RUSSIA
Albert, Michel François, 7
Antonieff, Valentin Andreevich, 7
Ball, George, 7
Bellingshausen, Faddei Faddeevich, 1
Chevalier, Nicholas, 3
Coppleson, Albert Abraham, 8
Falk, Leib Aisack, 8
Glass, Barnet, 9
King, George (1814-1894), 5
Lambert, George Washington Thomas, 9
Margolin, Eliezer, 10
Mikluho-Maklai, Nicholai Nicholaievich, 5
Myer, Simcha Baevski, 10
Noskowski, Ladislas Adam de, 11
Parsons, Joseph, 11
Reading, Fanny, 11
Rebell, Fred, 11
Ribush, Dolia, 11
Sergeyev, Fedor Andreyevich, 11
Simonov, Peter, 11
Skerst, Arnold Oscar Hermann Gregory
von, 11
SCOTLAND
Bell, William Montgomerie, 1
Bethune, Walter Angus, 1
Brown, John Ednie, 3
Burn, David, 1
Dalrymple, George Augustus Frederick
Elphin, 4
Dempster, James McLean, 4
Drysdale, George Russell, 4
Drysdale, John, 4
Drysdale, William, 4
Dunn, John, 1
Falconer, William Rose, 4
Forlonge, William, 1
Fraser, Peter Gordon, 1
Grant, Kenneth McDonald, 9
Howe, William, 1
Imlay, Alexander, 2

Imlay, George, 2
Imlay, Peter, 2
Landale, Thomas, 2
Learmonth, Peter, 5
Learmonth, William, 5
Lithgow, William, 2
McLachlan, Charles, 2
McLean, Alexander Grant, 5
Muir, Thomas, 2
Murray, Reginald Augustus Frederick,
5
Paterson, William, 2
Ross, Robert (b.1740?), 2
Smart, Thomas Christie, 6
Thomson, James Park, 12
Weatherly, William, 12
Aberdeenshire
Black, Morrice Alexander, 3
Cumming, John, 3
Dalgarno, Isabella, 4
Kerr, Peter, 5
Mackay, Angus, 5
Ormond, Francis, 5
Panton, Joseph Anderson, 5
ABERDEEN
Beattie, John Watt, 7
Cran, John, 8
Deuchar, John, 4
Gordon, Patrick Robertson, 4
Hutchison, James, 9
Jamieson, William, 9
MacGillivray, John, 2
McPherson, John Abel, 10
Mathew, John, 10
Miller, Alexander, 10
Milligan, Stanley Lyndall, 10
Mitchell, William, 5
Nelson, Wallace Alexander, 10
Rae, John, 6
Reid, David, 2
Skene, Alexander John, 6
Souter, Charles Henry, 12
Souter, David Henry, 12
Stewart, Sir Alexander Anderson,
12
Thomson, Alexander, 2
BALLATER
Cameron, James, 3
CRATHIE
Michie, John Lundie, 10
DONSIDE
Meston, Archibald, 5
DRUMBLADE
Forbes, Henry Ogg, 4
ELLON
Garland, James, 4
FOVERAN
Lyall, William, 5
McGaw, Andrew Kidd, 10
FRASERBURGH
Strahan, Sir George Cumine, 6
INSCH
Collie, Alexander, 1
Thompson, John Low, 6

KEIG
  Bruce, Alexander, 3
KEITHHALL
  Angus, William, 7
KING EDWARD
  Smith, William Ramsay, 11
LUMSDEN
  Stuart, William, 12
OLD DEER
  Wallace, Sir Robert Strachan, 12
PETERCULTER
  Smith, John, 6
PETERHEAD
  Stephen, Patrick John, 12
PITSLIGO
  Murdoch, Patrick John, 10
ROSEHEARTY
  Murdoch, Sir Walter Logie Forbes, 10
SHIELS
  Ferguson, John, 8
TARLAND
  Stewart, John Mitchell Young, 12
TILLYFOURIE
  McCombie, Thomas, 5
TOWIE
  Cran, Robert (1821-1894), 8
  Duncan, William Augustine, 1
  MacGregor, Sir William, 5
TURRIFF
  Littlejohn, William Still, 10
  Riddoch, George, 11
  Riddoch, John, 11
UDNY
  Woods, James, 12
WARTHILL
  Leslie, Patrick, 2
WOODSIDE
  Milne, John Alexander, 10
YTHSIE
  Hay, Sir John, 4
Argyll
  Hook, Charles, 1
  McIntyre, Duncan, 5
  McLachlan, Lachlan, 5
  McNab, Duncan, 5
APPIN
  McDonald, Hugh, 2
ARDRISHAIG
  Chalmers, James, 3
DUNOON
  McLaurin, James, 5
INNELLAN
  Smith, Thomas Jollie, 11
INVERARY
  Campbell, Envidale Savage Norman,
    3
ISLE OF ISLAY
  McDougall, Archibald Campbell, 5
KILBRIDEMORE
  Black, Niel, 3
KILMUN
  McGregor, Gregor, 10
LOCHGILPHEAD
  Campbell, James Lang, 7

MULL
  Campbell, Alexander, 1
NORTH KNAPDALE
  MacCormick, Sir Alexander, 10
OBAN
  McLean, Allan, 10
SANDBANK
  McKinlay, John, 5
ULVA
  Macquarie, Lachlan, 2
Ayrshire
  McCracken, Robert, 5
  McLerie, John, 5
  Ranken, George, 2
  Ranken, George, 6
  Whitefoord, John, 2
ARDROSSAN
  Craig, Robert Gordon, 8
AYR
  Blair, John, 7
  Lennox, David, 2
  McIlwraith, Andrew, 10
  McIlwraith, John, 5
  McIlwraith, Sir Thomas, 5
BEITH
  Barbour, Robert, 3
BOURTREE HILL
  Orr, William (1843-1929), 11
CATRINE
  Nimmo, John, 5
CROSSHOUSE
  Fisher, Andrew, 8
DAILLY
  Strong, Charles, 6
DALMELLINGTON
  Reid, Matthew, 11
DALRY
  Dunlop, James, 1
GALSTON
  Paterson, James, 5
  Rankin, Colin Dunlop Wilson, 11
GIRVAN
  Anderson, John Wilson, 3
IRVINE
  Fullarton, Robert Russell, 4
  Jack, Robert Logan, 4
  McGavin, Matthew, 5
  McLean, Margaret, 10
  Wilson, John Bowie, 6
KELBURNE
  Goldie, Andrew, 4
KILMARNOCK
  Dow, John Lamont, 4
  Nelson, Sir Hugh Muir, 10
KILMAURS
  Gibson, Angus, 4
  Templeton, John Montgomery, 6
  Watt, Sir Robert Dickie, 12
KILWINNING
  Service, James, 6
KIRKOSWALD
  Blackwood, James, 3
  Blackwood, John Hutchison, 3
  Willis, Joseph Scaife, 6

LARGS
  Brisbane, Sir Thomas Makdougall, 1
MAUCHLINE
  Murray, John, 10
MAYBOLE
  Piper, John, 2
MUIRKIRK
  Maclanachan, James, 5
  Ross, Andrew Hendry, 6
NEWMILNS
  Moffat, John, 10
RICCARTON
  Spence, John, 12
SALTCOATS
  Currie, Archibald, 3
  McAlpine, Daniel, 10
  Main, Hugh, 10
STEVENSTON
  Landsborough, William, 5
STEWARTON
  Brown, David Laughland, 3
  Kerr, James Semple, 9
TARBOLTON
  Hood, Sir Alexander Jarvie, 9
TROON
  Hardie, John Jackson, 9

Banffshire
  Cuming, James, 8
ARNDILLY
  Black, Alexander, 3
BANFF
  Melvin, Joseph Dalgarno, 10
  Wilson, Sir James Milne, 6
BOHARM
  Forbes, William Anderson, 4
BUCKIE
  Bennett, George Henry, 7
FORDYCE
  Garland, John, 8
FORGIE
  Gregor, John, 1
INCHDREWER CASTLE
  Scott, James, 2
INVERAVON
  Mitchell, Sir William, 10

Berwick
  Fairbairn, George, 4
  Struth, John, 2
AUCHINCRAW
  Greenfield, Alexander Mackay, 9
COLDSTREAM
  Stenhouse, Nicol Drysdale, 6
  Thomson, Adam, 6
CORSBIE
  Cockburn, Sir John Alexander, 8
DUNSE
  Bell, Thomas, 1
  Guthrie, Thomas, 4
EARLSTON
  Scott, James Reid, 6
FOULDEN
  Christison, Robert, 3
LONGFORMACUS
  Hood, Robert, 9

Bute
ISLE OF ARRAN
  Macredie, William, 5
LAG
  Mackinnon, Daniel, 5
Caithness
  Larnach, Donald, 5
  McLeod, Donald, 10
AUCHINGILL
  Larnach, John, 2
CANISBAY
  Shearer, David, 6
THRUMSTER
  Innes, Archibald Clunes, 2
THURSO
  Angus, David Mackenzie, 7
WICK
  Macleay, Sir William John, 5
  Sutherland, John, 6
  Symon, Sir Josiah Henry, 12

Clackmannanshire
ALLOA
  Dalgleish, Daniel Cameron, 4
CLACKMANNAN
  Christie, John Mitchell, 7
TILLICOULTRY
  Vicars, Sir John, 12
  Vicars, Sir William, 12

Dumbartonshire
BONHILL
  Harrison, James, 1
CARDROSS
  Erskine, John Elphinstone, 4
  Yuille, William Cross, 6
DUMBARTON
  Sutherland, George, 6
  White, John, 12
HELENSBURGH
  Carslaw, Horatio Scott, 7
KIRKINTILLOCH
  Munro, David, 5
MILNGAVIE
  McNaughtan, Alexander, 5
OLD KILPATRICK
  Pottie, John, 5
ROSNEATH
  Fell, William Scott, 8

Dumfriesshire
  Hetherington, Irving, 4
  Lorimer, Sir James, 5
  McLean, William, 5
  Milligan, Joseph, 2
  Watling, Thomas, 2
ANNANDALE
  Johnston, George, 2
DALSWINTON
  Cunningham, Peter Miller, 1
DUMFRIES
  Halliday, William, 4
  Macvitie, Thomas, 2
  Stuart, Sir Thomas Peter Anderson,
    12
KIRKMAHOE
  Paton, John Gibson, 5

LANGHOLM
  Smith, Pierce Galliard, 6
LOCHMABEN
  Johnstone, Thomas, 4
MIDDLEBIE
  Bell, Jane, 7
  Bell, John, 1
MOFFAT
  Armstrong, Robert Grieve, 3
  Armstrong, William, 3
MONIAIVE
  Wilson, James Thomas, 12
SANQUHAR
  Bell, James, 3
  Wyselaskie, John Dickson, 6
SPEDLINS TOWER
  Jardine, John, 4
Elginshire
  Dallachy, John, 4
  Morrison, George, 5
  Murdoch, John Smith, 10
ALTYRE
  Sinclair, James, 6
EDINKILLIE
  Morrison, Alexander, 5
ELGIN
  Elder, Sir James Alexander Mackenzie, 8
  Hardie, Sir David, 9
  Macdonald, Benjamin Wickham, 10
  Spark, Alexander Brodie, 2
FORRES
  Campbell, William Douglas, 1
  Raff, George, 6
GARMOUTH
  Forsyth, Archibald, 4
RELUGAS
  Campbell, Alexander, 3
Fife
  Berry, Alexander, 1
  Kenny, John, 2
  Mitchell, James, 2
  Petrie, Andrew, 2
  Simson, Robert, 6
ANSTRUTHER
  Duncan, Sir John James, 4
  Murray, David, 5
CERES
  Sleath, Richard, 11
CRAIL
  Crombie, James, 8
  Gosman, Alexander, 4
CUPAR
  Barclay, Andrew, 1
  Greig, Jane Stocks, 9
DUNFERMLINE
  Beveridge, Peter, 3
  Binns, Kenneth, 7
  Bowling, Peter, 7
  Collier, James, 8
  Hay, Alexander, 1
DYSART
  Stuart, John McDouall, 6
FREUCHIE
  Richardson, John, 6

GUARDBRIDGE
  Kellow, Henry Arthur, 9
HILTON
  Pearson, William, 5
KENNOWAY
  Hill, James Peter, 9
KILCONQUHAR
  MacLaurin, Sir Henry Normand, 10
KILRENNY
  Fowler, David, 4
  Fowler, George Swan, 4
KINGHORN
  Clark, Alexander Russell, 1
  Davidson, John, 4
KIRKCALDY
  Elder, Alexander Lang, 4
  Elder, George, 4
  Elder, Sir Thomas, 4
  Elder, William, 4
  Kirkcaldie, David, 9
  Russell, Sir Peter Nicol, 6
  Waite, Peter, 6
LEVEN
  Reid, Robert, 11
NEWBURGH
  Amess, Samuel, 3
  Lyell, Andrew, 5
  Wetherspoon, John, 12
PATHHEAD
  Arnott, William, 3
PITTENWEEM
  Hughes, Sir Walter Watson, 4
RAITH
  Munro Ferguson, Sir Ronald Craufurd, 10
ST ANDREWS
  Black, John, 3
Forfarshire
  Mitchell, David, 5
  Mitchell, Thomas, 10
ARBROATH
  Barnet, James Johnstone, 3
  Gordon, George, 4
  Macdonald, Louisa, 10
AUCHMITHIE
  Gilruth, John Anderson, 9
BRECHIN
  Grimm, George, 4
  Kidd, John, 5
  Seymour-Symers, Thomas Lyell, 2
BROUGHTY FERRY
  Greig, Clara Puella, 9
  Greig, Grata Flos Matilda, 9
  Greig, Janet Lindsay, 9
CUPAR-ANGUS
  Don, Charles Jardine, 4
DUNDEE
  Banks, Elizabeth Lindsay, 3
  Bennet, David, 3
  Elder, David, 4
  Ferguson, John, 1
  Fulton, Thomas, 4
  Langlands, George, 5
  Mealmaker, George, 2
  Moore, Charles, 5

Murray, Stuart, 5
Officer, Sir Robert, 2
Paterson, John Ford, 5
EDZELL
  Inglis, James, 4
FORFAR
  Howe, James Henderson, 9
KIRRIEMUIR
  Smith, Charles, 6
MENMUIR
  Anderson, Peter Corsar, 7
MONTROSE
  Aikenhead, James, 1
  Anderson, William, 3
  Ballow, David Keith, 1
  Maxwell, George Arnot, 10
  Strachan, James Ford, 2
  Strachan, John, 6
  Syme, George Alexander, 6
  Welsh, David Arthur, 12
Haddingtonshire
BARNS
  Watterston, David, 12
COCKBURNSPATH
  Chirnside, Andrew Spencer, 3
  Chirnside, Thomas, 3
COCKENZIE
  Cadell, Francis, 3
HADDINGTON
  Purves, William, 5
  Skirving, Robert Scot, 11
  Wight, George, 6
  Wilkie, David Elliot, 6
HUMBIE
  Reid, Alexander, 2
NORTH BERWICK
  Syme, David, 6
  Syme, Ebenezer, 6
PENSTON
  Archibald, John, 7
Inverness-shire
  Macdonald, Alexander Rose, 5
  Mackay, John, 5
  McPherson, James Alpin, 5
  Melville, Francis, 5
ALDOURIE
  Fraser, Alexander, 4
ALVIE
  Grant, James Macpherson, 4
  Robertson, William, 6
BROADFORD
  Mackinnon, Sir Lauchlan Charles, 10
CONNAGE
  Johnston, Robert Mackenzie, 9
GLEN BRITTLE
  McMillan, Angus, 2
INVERNESS
  Fraser, Simon, 4
  Grant, Alexander Charles, 9
  Grant, Donald McLennan, 9
  Smith, James MacCallum, 11
  Wisdom, Evan Alexander, 12
ISLE OF SKYE
  Martin, Catherine Edith Macauley, 10

KILBRIDE
  Mackinnon, Lauchlan, 5
KILMALLIE
  Cameron, Charles, 1
KILMONIVAIG
  Cameron, Ewen Hugh, 3
  McIntyre, William, 5
KILMUIR
  McLean, John Donald, 5
KINGUSSIE
  Ross, John (1833-1920), 6
LAKEFIELD
  Maclean, Harold, 5
PORTREE
  Cameron, Donald (1838-1916), 3
Kincardine
FETTERCAIRN
  Mackie, George, 5
FETTERESSO
  Duff, Sir Robert William, 8
  Murdoch, James, 10
FORDOUN
  Cameron, Donald (1814-1890), 3
NIGG
  Garden, John Smith, 8
  Stott, Robert, 12
Kinross-shire
KINROSS
  Campbell, John Fauna, 7
Kirkcudbrightshire
KIRKBEAN
  Murray, Andrew, 5
KIRKCUDBRIGHT
  Anderson, Samuel, 1
Lanark
  Brown, Alexander, 3
  Brown, James, 3
  Kent, William George Carlile, 2
AIRDRIE
  De Largie, Hugh, 8
  Gillies, John, 9
  Lang, Matthew, 5
AUCHTERHEAD
  McDonald, Lewis, 10
BAILIESTON
  Mitchell, John, 10
BELLSHILL
  Orr, William (1900-1954), 11
BIGGAR
  McKenzie, William, 10
BOTHWELL
  Fisken, Archibald, 4
BROOMIELAW
  Davis, James, 1
CAMBUSNETHAN
  Morton, William Lockhart, 5
CARSTAIRS
  Chumleigh, Harold Vere, 7
CHRYSTON
  Buchanan, James, 3
COATBRIDGE
  Young, William Ramsay, 12
CRAIGEND
  Mitchell, Sir Thomas Livingstone, 2

DALSERF
  Henderson, William, 4
FORTH
  Ramsay, John, 11
GLASGOW
  Anderson, Sir Francis, 7
  Brookman, Sir George, 7
  Bruce, John Leck, 7
  Buchanan, Benjamin, 3
  Campbell, Allan, 7
  Campbell, Colin, 3
  Charteris, Archibald Hamilton, 7
  Colquhoun, Alexander, 8
  Cuthbertson, James Lister, 3
  Duncan, Handasyde, 1
  Edmond, James, 8
  Foott, Mary Hannay, 4
  Gardner, John, 4
  Gardner, William, 1
  Gibson, William, 8
  Gillies, Duncan, 4
  Gilmore, Hugh, 4
  Harper, Andrew, 9
  Harper, Robert, 9
  Howie, Sir Archibald, 9
  Jull, Roberta Henrietta Margaritta, 9
  Kennedy, Malcolm, 9
  Khull, Edward, 5
  Kirkland, Katherine, 2
  Lithgow, Alexander Frame, 10
  Lyon, John Lamb, 10
  Macadam, John, 5
  Macalister, Arthur, 5
  McBurney, Samuel, 5
  MacCallum, Sir Mungo William, 10
  McColl, Hugh, 5
  McCulloch, George, 5
  McCulloch, Sir James, 5
  MacDougall, James, 10
  McGarvie, John, 2
  McGarvie, William, 2
  McGibbon, John, 5
  McIntyre, Sir John, 5
  MacKay, William John, 10
  McLachlan, Duncan Clark, 10
  Mair, William, 5
  Milne, Sir William, 5
  O'Neill, Charles Gordon, 5
  Peter, John, 5
  Philp, Sir Robert, 11
  Ramsay, Hugh, 11
  Ramsay, Sir John, 11
  Ramsay, William, 11
  Renwick, Sir Arthur, 6
  Robertson, George, 6
  Ross, Alexander David, 11
  Scott, Thomas Alison, 2
  Skurrie, Joseph, 11
  Smeaton, Thomas Hyland, 11
  Steel, Thomas, 12
  Sutherland, Alexander, 6
  Sutherland, William, 12
  Swan, James, 6
  Tait, James McAlpine, 6

  Taylor, William, 6
  Templeton, William, 6
  Tunn, John Patrick, 12
  Walker, William, 6
  Wilson, David, 12
GOVAN
  Fawsitt, Charles Edward, 8
  Hay, James, 9
  Taylor, Patrick Thomson, 12
HAMILTON
  Arnot, Arthur James, 7
  Farrell, John, 8
  Mather, John, 10
KELVINSIDE
  Stevenson, George Ingram, 12
MILLHOLM
  Fowler, James Mackinnon, 8
PARTICK
  Guthrie, Robert Storrie, 9
RUTHERGLEN
  Jackson, Archibald, 9
  McCorkindale, Isabella, 10
  Wallace, John Alston, 6
SHETTLESTON
  Ramsay, Andrew Mitchell, 6
SPRINGBURN
  Hunter, James Aitchison Johnston, 9
STONEHOUSE
  Anderson, John, 7
TOLLCROSS
  Smyth, John, 12
Linlithgowshire
  Johnston, James Stewart, 4
BO'NESS
  Stephens, James Brunton, 6
BONNYTOUN
  Dawson, James, 4
BORROWSTOUNNESS
  Gilfillan, Robert, 4
BROXBURN
  Nelson, Charles, 10
CATHLAW
  Hamilton, Thomas Ferrier, 4
LINLITHGOW
  Frater, William, 8
  Graham, George, 9
QUEENSFERRY
  Miller, Robert William, 10
SOUTH QUEENSFERRY
  Hopetoun, John Adrian Louis Hope, 9
UPHALL
  Wilson, Thomas Braidwood, 2
Mid-Lothian
BORTHWICK
  Clunie, James Oliphant, 1
BUCCLEUCH
  Turnbull, Adam, 2
DALKEITH
  Fletcher, James, 4
  Plummer, Andrew, 5
  Wilson, John Purves, 12
Edinburgh
  Addis, William (Edward), 7

Allan, William, 3
Balfour, James, 3
Baylis, Henry, 3
Black, George Mure, 7
Bowes, Euphemia Bridges, 7
Brown, Margaret Hamilton, 7
Browne, Hugh Junor, 3
Bruce, John Vans Agnew, 3
Buchanan, David, 3
Buncle, John, 3
Busby, James, 1
Cameron, Angus, 3
Cameron, Donald (1780-1857), 3
Campbell, Alexander James, 3
Carmichael, Sir Thomas David Gibson, 7
Darling, John (1852-1914), 4
Darling, John (1831-1905), 4
Denovan, William Dixon Campbell, 4
Dixson, Hugh, 4
Dowie, John Alexander, 4
Dunlop, James Matthew, 8
Dunlop, William Philip, 8
Dymock, David Lindsay, 4
Earsman, William Paisley, 8
Edmondstone, George, 4
Elder, James, 1
Fergusson, Sir James, 4
Geikie, Archibald Constable, 4
Graham, Sir James, 4
Henry, Frederick Ormiston, 9
Innes, Frederick Maitland, 4
Ivory, Francis Jeffrey, 4
Ivory, James, 4
Kerr, David McFarlane McLachlan, 9
Kilgour, Alexander James, 9
Kintore, Algernon Hawkins Thomond
  Keith-Falconer, 5
Lazar, John, 2
Loch, Henry Brougham, 5
Lyall, James, 5
MacGillivray, Paul Howard, 5
Mackie, Alexander, 10
Macknight, Charles Hamilton, 5
McMillan, Robert, 10
Maconochie, Alexander, 2
Meldrum, Duncan Max, 10
Morehead, Robert Archibald Alison, 2
Murdoch, Sir James Anderson, 10
Murray, Hugh, 2
Murray, John, 2
Parkinson, Sydney, 2
Paton, Robert Thomson, 11
Peterson, Franklin Sievright, 11
Petrie, John, 5
Petrie, Thomas, 5
Pitcairn, Robert, 2
Rintel, Moses, 6
Robertson, Thorburn Brailsford, 11
Sinclair-Maclagan, Ewen George, 11
Stewart, John (1832-1904), 6
Stodart, James, 12
Stoddard, Mary, 12
Stuart, Sir Alexander, 6

Thomson, Sir Edward Deas, 2
Traill, John Charles Merriman, 12
Walker, James Thomas, 12
Watt, John Brown, 6
Westgarth, William, 6
Winter, James, 6
Winter-Irving, William Irving, 6
Wormald, Henry Percy, 12
Wormald, Joseph Dawson, 12
GREENLAW
Whyte, James, 6
Haswell, William Aitcheson, 9
HAWTHORNDEN
Drummond, James, 1
KINGS KNOWE
Miles, William, 5
LEITH
Boyd, Archibald, 1
Esson, Thomas Louis Buvelot, 8
Ewan, James, 4
Goodlet, John Hay, 4
Hunter, John, 1
Lowe, William, 2
McCrae, George Gordon, 5
Ross, Robert (1792-1862), 2
Stewart, David, 12
Walker, Thomas, 2
Wickham, John Clements, 2
MUSSELBURGH
Lindesay, Sir Patrick, 2
NEW HAILES
Dalrymple, Alexander, 1
PORTO-BELLO
Mackenzie, Sir Evan, 5
WEST CALDER
Mackersey, John, 2
Nairn
AULDEARN
Macintosh, John, 5
CAWDOR
Newland(s), Sir John, 11
Orkney
Shearer, David, 11
Shearer, John, 11
EDAY
Spence, William Guthrie, 6
ORPHIR
Anderson, John Gerard, 3
STENNESS
Anderson, Charles, 7
Peeblesshire
Plain, William, 11
HORSBURGH CASTLE
Mills, Charles, 5
PEEBLES
Borthwick, Thomas, 7
SKIRLING MAINS
Paterson, John Waugh, 11
Perthshire
Gibson, David, 1
Laidley, James, 2
McIntyre, Peter, 2
Menzies, Sir Charles, 2
Ramsay, David, 2

ABERFOYLE
  Campbell, William, 3
ALYTH
  Ewart, David, 4
ARDOCH
  Kinross, John, 5
AUCHTERARDER
  Angus, James, 7
  Campbell, James, 7
BALVAIRD
  Taylor, George, 2
BLAIR GOWRIE
  Butters, James Stewart, 3
BLAIR-ATHOLL
  Frazer, Charles, 1
BRIDGEND
  Ross, John (1817-1903), 6
CALLANDER
  Marshall, Norman, 10
CAPUTH
  Stewart, Alexander, 12
CRIEFF
  McLellan, William, 5
CUPAR ANGUS
  Clark, William Nairne, 1
  Thomson, George Edward, 6
DUNBLANE
  Vicars, John, 6
DUNKELD
  Kennedy, Alexander, 5
DUNNING
  Bon, Ann Fraser, 7
FORTINGAL
  McDougall, Robert, 5
GASK
  McLaren, Samuel Gilfillan, 10
INVERGOWRIE
  Smith, William Forgan, 11
KENMORE
  Ferguson, John, 8
LAWGROVE
  Black, George, 3
LEARAN
  MacGregor, Duncan, 5
LOGIE-ALMOND
  Cameron, James, 7
LONGFORGAN
  Cairns, Adam, 3
MEIGLE
  Mitchell, Robert, 10
MONZIEVAIRD
  Baxter, Alexander Macduff, 1
OCHTERTYRE
  Murray, Sir George, 2
PERTH
  Kethel, Alexander, 9
  McLaren, David, 2
  Smith, Alfred Mica, 6
  Wanliss, David Sydney, 12
PITLOCHRY
  McCash, John McDonald, 10
RHYND
  Balmain, William, 1
  Ritchie, Thomas, 2

Renfrewshire
BARRHEAD
  Henderson, John Brownlie, 9
BRIDGE OF WEIR
  Gay, William, 8
EASTWOOD
  Boyd, Adam Alexander, 7
GREENOCK
  Bridges, Sir William Throsby, 7
  Caird, George Sutherland, 3
  Campbell, Robert (1789-1851), 1
  Campbell, Robert (1769-1846), 1
  Dunn, Andrew (1854-1934), 8
  Lang, John Dunmore, 2
  Walton, Thomas Utrick, 12
JOHNSTONE
  Macfarlane, Samuel, 5
  Reid, Sir George Houstoun, 11
KILMALCOLM
  Gordon, Sir John Hannah, 9
LANGSIDE
  Adam, David Stow, 7
  Fell, David, 8
LOCHWINNOCH
  Smith, Robert Barr, 6
PAISLEY
  Barr, John Mitchell, 3
  Bell, Alexander Foulis, 7
  McGregor, Alexander, 5
  Paton, Hugh, 11
  Ritchie, Robert Adam, 6
  Snodgrass, Kenneth, 2
  Thomson, William, 6
  Turriff, Haldane Colquhoun, 6
  Watson, John Boyd, 6
PORT-GLASGOW
  McCormick, Peter Dodds, 10
RENFREW
  Robertson, James Robert Millar, 11
WEST GREENOCK
  Sinclair, Eric, 11
Ross
  McLeay, Alexander, 2
APPLECROSS
  Mackenzie, Roderick, 10
COUL
  Mackenzie, Sir Robert Ramsay, 5
DINGWALL
  McNeil, Neil, 5
KINRIVE
  MacBain, Sir James, 5
TAIN
  Munro, Andrew Watson, 10
Roxburghshire
ABBOTSFORD
  Harper, George, 1
CAULDMILL
  Smith, Alexander Kennedy, 6
CAVERS
  Armstrong, James, 3
COMELY BANK
  Laurie, Henry, 10
EDGERSTON
  Leitch, Sir Walter, 10

EDNAM
Walker, John, 2
HAWICK
Ramsay, Robert, 6
Tennant, Andrew, 6
JEDBURGH
Story, John Douglas, 12
Tinline, George, 6
KELSO
Fairbairn, Charles, 8
Ogilvie, William Henry, 11
LINTHILL
Riddell, John Carre, 6
MAXTON
Haining, Robert, 1
MELROSE
Amos, Adam, 1
Campbell, Frederick Alexander, 7
Laidlaw, Thomas, 5
Mein, James, 2
Spence, Catherine Helen, 6
Tait, John, 6
MOREBATTLE
Hope, Robert Culbertson, 4
ROXBURGH
Brunton, Thomas, 3
SOUTHDEAN
Richmond, James, 6
STOBS
Eliott, Gilbert, 4
WILTON
Reid, Walter Ballantyne, 6
Selkirkshire
Lowrie, William, 10
SELKIRK
Lang, Gideon Scott, 2
YARROW
Currie, John Lang, 3
Shetland Isles
BRESSAY
Hamilton, Sir Robert George Crookshank, 4
LERWICK
Henry, John, 9
SCATSTA
Irvine, Robert Francis, 9
UNST
Johnson, John Andrew, 9
Stirlingshire
Calder, George, 7
Paton, John, 5
BALDERNOCK
Gillison, Andrew, 9
BANNOCKBURN
Gardner, Robert, 8
McArthur, John, 10
CAMELON
Anderson, John, 1
CHARTERSHALL
Clow, James, 1
FALKIRK
Cowie, James, 3
Ferguson, Mephan, 4
Gibson, Sir Robert, 8

Gilchrist, John, 1
Kidston, William, 9
Marshall, James Waddell, 5
Russell, James, 6
GRANGEMOUTH
Fairley, Sir Andrew Walker, 8
NEWTOWN OF FINTRY
Love, James Simpson, 10
POLMONT
Burns, Sir James, 7
STIRLING
Drummond, Ralph, 1
Fraser, Archibald Colquhoun, 4
Macansh, John Donald, 5
Nisbet, James Hume, 11
Sawers, John, 11
WEST PLEAN
Forsyth, James, 8
Sutherland
Munro, James, 5
CULGOWER
Sutherland, Sulina Murray MacDonald, 6
DORNOCH
Sinclair, William, 11
GOLSPIE
Muirden, William, 10
KEOLDALE
Anderson, Joseph, 1
LAIRG
Matheson, John, 5
ROGART
McKenzie, Hugh, 10
Wigtonshire
Auld, Patrick, 3
Kerr, William, 2
McCulloch, William, 5
McMeckan, James, 5
STRANRAER
Cosh, James, 3
WIGTON
Black, John McConnell, 7
SOCIETY ISLANDS
Barff, Henry Ebenezer, 7
SOLOMON ISLANDS
Fatnowna, John Kwailiu Abelfai, 8
SOUTH AFRICA, *see also* Cape Colony; Natal
Fairbridge, Kingsley Ogilvie, 8
Kellaway, Cecil Lauriston, 9
SPAIN
Creswell, Sir William Rooke, 8
Frome, Edward Charles, 1
Gordon, Joseph Maria, 9
Griver, Martin, 4
Rees, Rowland, 6
Salvado, Rosendo, 2
Serra, Joseph Benedict, 6
Trickett, William Joseph, 6
ST HELENA
Balcombe, Alexander Beatson, 3
STRAITS SETTLEMENT
Carpenter, Sir Walter Randolph, 7
SWEDEN
Friström, Carl Magnus Oscar, 8

Jonsson, Nils Josef, 9
Kopsen, William, 9
Parkes, Hilma Olivia Edla Johanna, 11
Solander, Daniel, 2
SWITZERLAND
Albert, Jacques, 7
Bainton, John Richard, 7
Bugnion, François Louis, 3
Buvelot, Abram-Louis, 3
De Rougemont, Louis, 8
Franki, James Peter, 8
Tardent, Henry Alexis, 12
TURKEY, *see* Ottoman Empire
UNITED STATES OF AMERICA
Antill, Henry Colden, 1
Badger, Joseph Stillman, 7
Bond, George Alan, 7
Booth, Edwin Thomas, 3
Boucicault, Dionysius George, 3
Bouton, Wilbur Knibloe, 7
Bradley, Luther, 7
Bunker, Eber, 1
Clapp, Francis Boardman, 3
Clark, Hubert Lyman, 8
Cobb, Freeman, 3
Cobb, Nathan Augustus, 8
Cook, Solomon, 3
Cuming, James, 8
Dana, James Dwight, 1
Davidson, Daniel Sutherland, 8
Dean, Horace, 4
Dickinson, Sidney, 8
Duryea, Townsend, 4
Gairdner, Gordon, 1
George, Henry, 4
Gore, Thomas Jefferson, 4
Graebner, Carl Friedrich, 9
Griffin, Walter Burley, 9
Hall, Hayden Hezekiah, 4
Hardacre, Herbert Freemont, 9
Hart, Alfred, 9
Hayes, William Henry, 4
Hoover, Herbert Clark, 9
Hopkins, Livingston York, 4
Jefferson, Joseph, 4
Jeffries, Maud Evelyn Craven, 9
Jenkins, John Greeley, 9
Johns, Frederick, 9
Kruttschnitt, Julius, 9
Laseron, Charles Francis, 9
Mead, Elwood, 10
Montgomery, Walter, 5
Moore, Maggie, 5
Morton, Alexander, 10
O'Malley, King, 11
Peck, John Murray, 5
Pell, Morris Birkbeck, 5
Peters, Frederick Augustus Bolles, 11
Rutherford, James, 6
Schlapp, Herman Henry, 11
Stanford, Thomas Welton, 12
Sticht, Robert Carl, 12
Sutherland, Jane, 12
Taylor, William, 6

Train, George Francis, 6
Vaughn, Robert Matterson, 6
Ward, Hugh Joseph, 12
Warner, William Lloyd, 12
Webb, William Alfred, 12
White, Ellen Gould, 12
Williams, James Hartwell, 6
Williamson, James Cassius, 6
WALES
Johns, Joseph Bolitho, 4
Perry, Samuel Augustus, 2
Anglesey
BEAUMARIS
Lyster, John Sanderson, 10
HOLYHEAD
Goodisson, Lillie Elizabeth, 9
NEWBOROUGH
Jones, William, 9
Brecon
LLANIGON
Bruntnell, Albert, 7
Cardigan
ABERYSTWITH
Douglas, William Bloomfield, 4
Granville, Cecil Horace Plantagenet, 9
Thomas, Mesac, 6
LLANRHYSTYD
Lewis, David Edward, 10
NEW QUAY
Gordon, Margaret Jane, 9
TALYBONT
Thomas, Lewis, 6
Carmarthen
LAUGHARNE
Cox, Sir Edward John Owen, 8
Wienholt, Arnold, 6
Wienholt, Edward, 6
LLANELLY
Bevan, Llewelyn David, 7
LLANGADOCK
Thomas, David John, 2
Carnarvon
LLANDUDNO
Turnbull, Gilbert Munro, 12
Denbighz
HARWD BRYMBO
Price, Thomas, 11
RHOS-Y-MEDRE
Wilson, Walter Horatio, 12
RUTHIN
Jones, Joseph, 4
WREXHAM
Maurice, Price, 5
Tomkinson, Samuel, 6
Flint
BUCKLEY
Birks, Frederick, 7
Glamorgan
BRIDGEND
Collier, Jenkin, 3
GLYN NEATH
Thomas, Morgan, 6
HIRWAIN
John, Morgan Bevan, 9

MAESTEG
  Bracy, Henry, 7
MERTHYR-TYDFIL
  Griffith, Sir Samuel Walker, 9
  Williams, Zephaniah, 2
PENARTH
  Pearse, Samuel George, 11
ST FAGANS
  David, Sir Tannatt William Edgeworth, 8
SWANSEA
  Beor, Henry Rogers, 3
  Dumaresq, Edward, 1
TONYREFAIL
  Willis, Albert Charles, 12
Montgomery
NEWTOWN
  Humffray, John Basson, 4
TALERDDIG
  Williams, Edward David, 12
Pembrokeshire
  Meredith, Charles, 5
HAVERFORDWEST
  Baillieu, James George, 7
LLAWHADEN
  Brigstocke, Charles Ferdinand, 1
PEMBROKE
  Johns, Peter, 4
  Lord, Edward, 2
ST DOGMAELS
  Williams, George Davies, 12
Radnor
GLADESTRY
  Burgoyne, Thomas, 7
PRESTEIGN
  Griffiths, Thomas, 9
WEST INDIES
  Alleyne, Haynes Gibbes, 3
  Allwood, Robert, 1
  Broome, Mary Anne, 3
  Buhôt, John, 3
  Burnside, Robert Bruce, 7
  Burt, Octavius, 7
  Burt, Septimus, 7
  Carter, Godfrey Downes, 3

  Cowen, Sir Frederick Hymen, 3
  Crowther, George Henry, 8
  Dickinson, Sir John Nodes, 4
  Dillon, Peter, 1
  Doorly, James Gerald Stokely, 8
  Fletcher, Joseph Horner, 4
  Howe, George, 1
  Isaacs, Robert Macintosh, 4
  Jackson, Peter, 9
  Lambie, Charles George, 9
  Montefiore, Eliezer Levi, 5
  Montefiore, Jacob Levi, 5
  Musgrave, Sir Anthony, 5
  Parry, Henry Hutton, 5
  Pugh, Theophilus Parsons, 5
  Robertson, Gilbert, 2
  Ross, Sir Robert Dalrymple, 6
  Schaw, Charles, 2
  Sorell, William, 2
  Stephen, Sir Alfred, 6
  Stephen, Sir George, 6
  Wallen, Robert Elias, 6
AT SEA
  Anderson, Henry Charles Lennox, 7
  Campbell, Charles, 1
  Carr-Boyd, William Henry James, 3
  Clare, Chapman James, 8
  Cudmore, James Francis, 8
  De Mestre, Prosper, 1
  Finniss, Boyle Travers, 1
  Griffiths, Albert, 9
  Hooley, Edward Timothy, 4
  Hunter, John McEwan, 9
  King, Robert Lethbridge, 5
  McGowen, James Sinclair Taylor, 10
  McGregor, John Gibson, 5
  Nickle, Sir Robert, 5
  Robertson, Alexander William, 6
  Spruson, Joseph John, 12
  Tighe, Atkinson Alfred Patrick, 6
  Tolmie, James, 12
  Walker, Richard Cornelius Critchett, 6
  Windsor, Arthur Lloyd, 6

Occupations

CATEGORIES

Accountant
Actor
Actuary
Administrator
Advertising agent
Advocate-general
Air Force officer
Ambulance driver
Anarchist
Anatomist
Anthropologist
Apiarist
Aquaculturist
Arbitrator
Archaeologist
Archbishop
Architect
Art teacher
Artist
Astronomer
Asylum superintendent
Athlete
Auctioneer
Auditor
Aviator
Axeman
Bacteriologist
Baker
Bank clerk
Banker
Baseballer
Bibliographer
Billiards player
Biochemist
Biographer
Biologist
Bishop
Blacksmith
Boilermaker
Bookmaker
Bookseller
Bootmaker
Botanist
Boxer
Brewer
Builder
Bushranger
Businessman
Butcher
Camel driver
Canner
Canteen superintendent
Cardinal
Carpenter
Carrier
Cartoonist
Caterer
Chaplain
Charcoal burner

Charity worker
Chemist
Chess master
Circus proprietor
Civil official
Clergy
Clerk
Coach driver
Coach proprietor
Coachbuilder
Collector
Colonial secretary
Colonizer
Commercial traveller
Commissariat official
Community leader
Company chairman
Company director
Company manager
Company secretary
Company superintendent
Conservationist
Consul
Contractor
Convict administrator
Co-operative advocate
Cricketer
Criminal
Critic
Cryptographer
Cyclist
Dance teacher
Dancer
Decorator
Dentist
Designer
Diarist
Diplomat
Distiller
Dog-breeder
Dog racer
Domestic servant
Draper
Draughtsman
Drover
Eccentric
Economist
Editor
Educationist
Electoral reformer
Electrician
Employment agent
Engineer
Entertainer
Entertainment entrepreneur
Entomologist
Epidemiologist
Estate agent
Eugenicist

Explorer
Exporter
Factory inspector
Farmer
Ferry employee
Ferry master
Ferry proprietor
Film censor
Film-maker
Financier
Fire officer
Fitter
Folklorist
Football administrator
Footballer
Forester
Gallery curator
Gallery director
Gambler
Garage proprietor
Geographer
Geologist
Goldfields commissioner
Golfer
Government adviser
Governor
Governor-general
Governor's wife
Greengrocer
Grocer
Gunsmith
Hairdresser
Hansard reporter
Harbourmaster
Historian
Hockey player
Homoeopath
Horticulturist
Hospital administrator
Hospital founder
Hotelkeeper
House-painter
Hunter
Hydrographer
Illustrator
Immigration agent
Immigration promoter
Indexer
Industrialist
Insurance agent
Insurance manager
Intelligence agent
Inventor
Ironfounder
Ironmonger
Irrigationist
Ivory turner
Jeweller
Jockey

166

Journalist
Judge
Judge-advocate
Labourer
Land agent
Land developer
Landholder
Lawyer
Lexicographer
Librarian
Lieut-governor
Lifesaver
Lighthouse-keeper
Linguist
Lottery promoter
Magistrate
Maltster
Manufacturer
Marine
Mariner
Marksman
Mason
Masseur
Mathematician
Mayor
Mechanic
Medical practitioner
Merchant
Metallurgist
Meteorologist
Miller
Milliner
Mine director
Mine engineer
Mine manager
Mine proprietor
Miner
Mineralogist
Mining entrepreneur
Mining official
Missionary
Motor dealer
Motor racer
Mountaineer
Murderer
Museum curator
Museum director
Music publisher
Music seller
Music teacher
Musician
Musicologist
Naturalist
Naval officer
Navigator
News agent
Newsagent
Newspaper editor
Newspaper employee
Newspaper proprietor
Nurse
Omnibus proprietor
Ophthalmologist
Optician
Orchardist
Organbuilder
Ornithologist
Pacifist

Palaeontologist
Pastoralist
Patent attorney
Pathologist
Patron
Pearler
Penal reformer
Pharmacist
Philologist
Philosopher
Photographer
Physicist
Physiologist
Physiotherapist
Pioneer settler
Planter
Plasterer
Plumber
Police commissioner
Police officer
Political activist
Political party organizer
Politician
Potter
Preacher
Premier
Prime Minister
Printer
Prison administrator
Professor
Prospector
Prostitute
Protector of Aborigines
Psychiatrist
Psychical researcher
Psychologist
Public servant
Publisher
Rabbi
Rabbiter
Racehorse trainer
Radio broadcaster
Radiologist
Railway worker
Railways commissioner
Refiner
Religious brother
Religious sister
Restaurateur
Retailer
Rower
Rural worker
Saddler
Salvationist
Scholar
School principal
School proprietor
Scientist
Sculptor
Sealer
Secularist
Seismologist
Selector
Sericulturist
Shearer
Sheep-breeder
Ship chandler
Ship-owner

Shipbuilder
Shipping agent
Silversmith
Singer
Socialist
Sociologist
Soldier
Spelaeologist
Spiritualist
Sports administrator
Sports instructor
Statistician
Stenographer
Stock and station agent
Stock-breeder
Stockbroker
Storekeeper
Suffragist
Surfer
Surveyor
Swimmer
Tailor
Tanner
Taxi proprietor
Taxidermist
Teacher
Technical educator
Telegraphist
Temperance advocate
Tennis player
Theatre proprietor
Theatrical manager
Theatrical producer
Theologian
Theosophist
Tinsmith
Town clerk
Town planner
Trade unionist
Trader
Transportee
Trepanger
Trotting official
Trotting trainer
Undertaker
University administrator
University teacher
Veterinary inspector
Veterinary surgeon
Vigneron
Violin-maker
Visitor
Walker
Watchmaker
Weaver
Welfare worker
Whaler
Wheat-breeder
Wheelwright
Women's rights activist
Woodcarver
Woolbroker
Writer
Yachtsman
Zoo director
Zoologist

ACCOUNTANT

Allard, Sir George Mason, 7
Barnett, Frederick Oswald, 7
Braund, George Frederick*, 7
Brentnall, Thomas, 7
Carmichael, Ambrose Campbell*, 7
Clark, John Howard, 3
Cooke, Ebenezer*, 3
Crick, Stanley Sadler, 8
Davies, Joseph Bartlett, 4
Dibdin, Edward John, 8
Duesbury, Frank Wentworth, 8
Eagar, Geoffrey*, 4
Elder, David, 4
Evans, Alexander Arthur*, 8
Fell, David*, 8
Fisher, Joseph*, 4
Flack, Edwin Harold, 8
Ford, Richard, 4
Gilfillan, Robert, 4
Glyde, Lavington*, 4
Greenfield, Alexander Mackay, 9
Hack, John Barton, 1
Hare, Charles Simeon*, 4
Haynes, Thomas Watson, 9
Hunter, James Aitchison Johnston*, 9
Hutton, George Samuel, 9
Jobson, Alexander, 9
Jolly, William Alfred*, 9
Langton, Edward*, 5
Latimer, Hugh*, 10
Lording, Rowland Edward, 10
Macdonald, Alexander Cameron, 5
Martin, Edward Fowell, 10
Meudell, George Dick, 10
Miles, William John, 10
Moore, Donald Ticehurst, 10
Neil, Edwin Lee, 10
Roberts, John Garibaldi, 11
Robson, William*, 11
Serle, Percival, 11
Spooner, Eric Sydney*, 12
Stevenson, George Ingram, 12
Taylor, Patrick Thomson*, 12
Toll, Frederick William, 12
Trethowan, Hubert Charles, 12
Triggs, Arthur Bryant, 12
Tweddle, Joseph Thornton, 12
Wells, Thomas, 2
Welsby, Thomas*, 12
Wheeler, John*, 12
Wormald, Henry Percy, 12

ACTOR

Asche, Thomas Stange(r) Heiss Oscar, 7
Atkins, John Ringrose, 3
Bailey, Albert Edward, 7
Baker, Reginald Leslie, 7
Bellew, Harold Kyrle Money, 7
Booth, Edwin Thomas, 3
Boucicault, Dionysius George, 3
Brooke, Gustavus Vaughan, 3
Brough, Lionel Robert, 3
Cathcart, James Faucitt, 3
Cathcart, Mary Fanny, 3

Coppin, George Selth*, 3
Dampier, Alfred, 4
Duggan, Edmund, 8
Flynn, Errol Leslie, 8
Holt, Joseph Thomas, 4
Jefferson, Joseph, 4
Jeffries, Maud Evelyn Craven, 9
Jennings, Elizabeth Esther Ellen, 4
Kean, Charles John, 5
Kellaway, Cecil Lauriston, 9
Kellermann, Annette Marie Sarah, 9
Kelly, Ethel Knight, 9
Kemble, Myra, 5
Knowles, Conrad Theodore, 2
Lazar, John, 2
Longford, Raymond John Walter Hollis, 10
Lovely, Louise Nellie, 10
Lyell, Lottie Edith, 10
McCrone, Francis Nesbitt, 2
McDonagh, Isabella Mercia, 10
McMahon, Gregan, 10
Marlowe, Margaret Mary, 10
Mathews, Julia, 5
Maxwell-Mahon, William Ion, 10
Montgomery, Walter, 5
Moore, Caroline Ellen, 10
Moore, Maggie, 5
O'Flaherty, Eliza, 2
Oliver, Maggie, 5
Ordell, Talone, 11
Parkinson, Charles Tasman, 11
Polini, Emelie Adeline, 11
Rignall, George Richard, 6
Rowe, George Curtis, 6
Simmons, Joseph, 2
Stewart, Eleanor Towzey, 12
Sullivan, Thomas Barry, 6
Tauchert, Arthur Michael, 12
Titheradge, George Sutton, 6
Treloar, George Devine, 12
Ward, Hugh Joseph, 12
Westmacott, Charles Babington, 12
Wilkie, Allan, 12
Williamson, James Cassius, 6
Wilton, Olive Dorothea Graeme, 12
Young, Florence Maude, 12

ACTRESS, see Actor

ACTUARY

Black, Morrice Alexander, 3
Teece, Richard, 12
Templeton, John Montgomery, 6
Thomson, Robert, 6
Wickens, Charles Henry, 12

ADMINISTRATOR

Nauru

Chalmers, Frederick Royden, 7

Norfolk Island

Bennett, Alfred Joshua, 7
Herbert, Charles Edward*, 9
Parnell, John William, 11
Sellheim, Victor Conradsdorf Morisset, 11

Northern Territory

Gilruth, John Anderson, 9
Smith, Miles Staniforth Cater*, 11

Urquhart, Frederic Charles, 12
Papua and/or New Guinea
Douglas, John*, 4
Griffiths, Thomas, 9
Johnston, George Jameson, 9
Le Hunte, Sir George Ruthven, 10
Levien, Cecil John, 10
MacGregor, Sir William, 5
MacKenzie, Seaforth Simpson, 10
McNicoll, Sir Walter Ramsay*, 10
Murray, Sir John Hubert Plunkett, 10
Pethebridge, Sir Samuel Augustus, 11
Romilly, Hugh Hastings, 6
Scratchley, Sir Peter Henry, 6
Townsend, George Wilfred Lambert, 12
Wilder-Neligan, Maurice, 12
Wisdom, Evan Alexander*, 12
Tasmania
Lefroy, Sir John Henry, 5
ADVERTISING AGENT
Gotch, John Speechly, 4
Paton, Hugh, 11
Smith, Sydney George Ure, 11
Stanley, Charles Roy, 12
ADVOCATE-GENERAL, see also
Judge-advocate
Mackie, William Henry, 2
Mann, Charles (1799-1860), 2
Nash, Richard West, 2
AIR FORCE OFFICER
Baker, Thomas Charles Richmond, 7
Bell, Bertram Charles, 7
Bennett, James Mallett, 7
Butler, Henry John, 7
Chinnery, Ernest William Pearson, 7
Christie, Robert, 7
Cobby, Arthur Henry, 8
Collins, John William Fitzclarence, 8
Dallas, Roderic Stanley, 8
Duigan, John Robertson, 8
Fairbairn, James Valentine*, 8
Goble, Stanley James, 9
Harrison, Eric, 9
Hinkler, Herbert John Louis, 9
Holden, Leslie Hubert, 9
Howell, Cedric Ernest, 9
Hughes, Geoffrey Forrest, 9
Jones, Allan Murray, 9
Jones, Leslie John Roberts, 9
Kingsford Smith, Sir Charles Edward, 9
Knox, Sir Errol Galbraith, 9
Larkin, Herbert Joseph, 9
Little, Robert Alexander, 10
Love, Nigel Borland, 10
McCloughry, Edgar James, 10
McCloughry, Wilfred Ashton, 10
MacLeod, Thomas, 10
McNamara, Frank (Francis) Hubert, 10
Miller, Horatio Clive, 10
Minifie, Richard Pearman, 10
Murphy, Arthur William, 10
Mustar, Ernest Andrew, 10
O'Hara Wood, Hector, 11
Parer, Raymond John Paul, 11

Percival, Edgar Wikner, 11
Petre, Henry Aloysius, 11
Phillips, Sir Frederick Beaumont, 11
Shiers, Walter Henry, 11
Smith, Sir Keith Macpherson, 11
Smith, Sir Ross Macpherson, 11
Snook, Charles William, 12
Taylor, Sir Patrick Gordon, 12
Thompson, William Bethel, 12
Watt, Walter Oswald, 12
Williams, Sir Richard, 12
Wilson, Gordon Campbell, 12
AMBULANCE DRIVER
King, Olive May, 9
ANARCHIST
Andrade, David Alfred, 7
Andrews, John Arthur, 7
ANATOMIST
Berry, Richard James Arthur, 7
Kesteven, Hereward Leighton, 9
Wilson, James Thomas, 12
Woollard, Herbert Henry, 12
ANTHROPOLOGIST
Basedow, Herbert, 7
Bates, Daisy May, 7
Chewings, Charles, 7
Chinnery, Ernest William Pearson, 7
Davidson, Daniel Sutherland, 8
Dawson, James, 4
Finsch, Otto, 4
Fison, Lorimer, 4
Gillen, Francis James, 9
Howitt, Alfred William, 4
Jones, Frederic Wood, 9
Kubary, John Stanislaw, 5
Mathew, John, 10
Mathews, Robert Hamilton, 5
Mikluho-Maklai, Nicholai Nicholaievich,
   5
Milerum, 10
Radcliffe-Brown, Alfred Reginald, 11
Roth, Henry Ling, 11
Roth, Walter Edmund, 11
Smith, Sir Grafton Elliot, 11
Smith, William Ramsay, 11
Spencer, Sir Walter Baldwin, 12
Stow, Catherine Eliza Somerville, 12
Strehlow, Carl Friedrich Theodor, 12
Strong, Walter Mersh, 12
Warner, William Lloyd, 12
Williams, Francis Edgar, 12
APIARIST
Hannaford, Ernest Hayler*, 9
Rayment, Percy Tarlton, 11
AQUACULTURIST
Dannevig, Harald Kristian, 8
Youl, Sir James Arndell, 6
ARBITRATOR
Gillies, William Neil*, 9
Lyell, Andrew*, 5
Spencer, Thomas Edward, 12
Wallis, Alfred Russell, 12
ARCHAEOLOGIST
Childe, Vere Gordon, 7

ARCHBISHOP, *see also* Cardinal
Anglican
Clarke, Henry Lowther, 8
Donaldson, St Clair George Alfred, 8
Head, Frederick Waldegrave, 9
Le Fanu, Henry Frewen, 10
Lees, Harrington Clare, 10
Riley, Charles Owen Leaver, 11
Smith, William Saumarez, 11
Wand, John William Charles, 12
Wright, John Charles, 12
Catholic
Carr, Thomas Joseph, 7
Clune, Patrick Joseph, 8
Couppé, Louis, 8
Cullen, Paul, 3
Delany, Patrick, 8
Duhig, Sir James, 8
Goold, James Alipius, 4
Kelly, Michael, 9
Killian, Andrew, 9
Mannix, Daniel, 10
Murphy, Daniel, 5
O'Reily, John, 11
Polding, John Bede, 2
Reynolds, Christopher Augustine, 6
Spence, Robert William, 12
Vaughan, Roger Wiliam Bede, 6
ARCHITECT
Allen, Joseph Francis*, 7
Alsop, Rodney Howard, 7
Annear, Harold Desbrowe, 7
Archer, John Lee, 1
Archer, William*, 3
Ashworth, Thomas Ramsden*, 7
Atkinson, Charles, 1
Backhouse, Benjamin, 7
Bagot, Walter Hervey, 7
Bardolph, Kenneth Edward Joseph*, 7
Barnet, James Johnstone, 3
Bibb, John, 1
Blackburn, James, 1
Blacket, Edmund Thomas, 3
Blackett, William Arthur Mordey, 7
Brady, Alfred Barton, 7
Butler, Walter Richmond, 7
Clamp, John Burcham, 8
Clark, John James, 3
Cohen, John Jacob*, 8
Cowlishaw, James*, 3
De Little, Robert, 1
Dods, Robert Smith, 8
Eade, Joel, 4
Garlick, Daniel, 4
Greenway, Francis, 1
Griffin, Marion Lucy Mahony, 9
Griffin, Walter Burley, 9
Haddon, Robert Joseph, 9
Hall, Francis Richard, 9
Hall, Thomas Ramsay, 9
Hallen, Ambrose, 1
Hallen, Edward, 1
Hawes, John Cyril, 9
Henderson, Anketell Matthew, 9

Henderson, Kingsley Anketell, 9
Hennessy, John Francis, 9
Hickson, Robert Newburgh, 9
Hobbs, Sir Joseph John Talbot, 9
Hunt, John Horbury, 4
Hunter, Henry, 4
Hurst, John Herbert, 9
Irwin, Leighton Major Francis, 9
Jackson, Samuel, 2
Jewell, Richard Roach, 4
Joseland, Richard George Howard, 9
Kay, William Porden, 2
Kemp, Henry Hardie, 9
Kerr, Peter, 5
King, George Raymond, 9
Kirkpatrick, John, 9
Knight, John George, 5
Koch, John Augustus Bernard, 9
Laing, Charles, 2
Laing, Henry, 2
Lambe, David, 2
Lewis, Mortimer William, 2
Lord, Clive Errol, 10
McMinn, William, 5
Mann, Gother Victor Fyers, 10
Manning, James, 5
Marks, Theodore John, 10
Menkens, Frederick Burnhardt, 5
Moore, John Drummond Macpherson, 10
Murdoch, John Smith, 10
Nangle, James, 10
North, Alexander, 11
Oakden, Percy, 5
Parkes, Varney*, 11
Petrie, Andrew, 2
Pitman, Jacob, 5
Pitt, William (1855-1918), 11
Poole, George Thomas Temple, 11
Powell, Lange Leopold, 11
Reed, Joseph, 6
Rees, Rowland*, 6
Rosenthal, Sir Charles*, 11
Rowe, Thomas, 6
Russell, Robert, 2
Smeaton, Thomas Hyland*, 11
Smith, Louis Laybourne, 11
Soares, Alberto Dias, 6
Soward, George Klewitz, 12
Spain, Alfred, 12
Stapley, Frank, 12
Stephenson, Sir Arthur George, 12
Sulman, Sir John, 12
Tayler, Lloyd, 6
Taylor, Florence Mary, 12
Terry, Leonard, 6
Thomson, James Alexander, 2
Tucker, James, 2
Tunbridge, Walter Howard, 12
Turnbull, Gilbert Munro, 12
Verge, John, 2
Vernon, Hugh Venables, 12
Vernon, Walter Liberty, 12
Walker, Alan Cameron, 12
Wardell, William Wilkinson, 6

Waterhouse, Bertrand James, 12
Webb, Charles, 6
Webb, James, 6
White, Francis Maloney, 6
White, Henry Eli, 12
Wilkinson, Leslie, 12
Willis, Ernest Horatio, 12
Wilson, William Hardy, 12
ARMY OFFICER, see Soldier
ART TEACHER
Allen, Mary Cecil, 7
Anivitti, Giulio, 3
Ashton, Julian Rossi, 7
Balfour, James Lawson, 7
Bell, George Frederick Henry, 7
Boxall, Arthur d'Auvergne, 7
Clark, Thomas, 3
Dechaineux, Florent Vincent Emile
  Lucien, 8
Folingsby, George Frederick, 4
Fowles, Joseph, 1
Fox, Emanuel Phillips, 8
Gill, Harry Pelling, 9
Hack, Wilton, 4
Hall, Lindsay Bernard, 9
Harvey, Lewis Jarvis, 9
Haydon, George Henry, 4
Henry, Lucien Felix, 4
Hoff, George Rayner, 9
Howie, Laurence Hotham, 9
McCubbin, Frederick, 10
Macgeorge, Norman, 10
Mather, John, 10
Meldrum, Duncan Max, 10
Payne, Ellen Nora, 11
Rivers, Richard Godfrey, 11
Rodius, Charles, 2
Rowell, John Thomas Nightingale, 11
Rubbo, Antonio Salvatore Dattilo, 11
Serle, Dora Beatrice, 11
Shirlow, John Alexander Thomas, 11
Van Raalte, Henri Benedictus Salaman, 12
Waite, James Clarke, 6
Withers, Walter Herbert, 12
ARTIST, see also Cartoonist; Illustrator;
Potter; Sculptor; Silversmith; Wood-
carver
Allen, Mary Cecil, 7
Angas, George French, 1
Anivitti, Giulio, 3
Ashton, James, 7
Ashton, Sir John William, 7
Ashton, Julian Howard, 7
Ashton, Julian Rossi, 7
Auld, James Muir, 7
Bale, Alice Marian Ellen, 7
Balfour, James Lawson, 7
Barnes, Gustave Adrian, 7
Bateman, Edward La Trobe, 3
Bauer, Ferdinand Lukas, 1
Becker, Ludwig, 3
Beckett, Clarice Marjoribanks, 7
Bell, George Frederick Henry, 7
Black, Dorothea Foster, 7

Bock, Thomas, 1
Bowen, Esther Gwendolyn, 7
Boxall, Arthur d'Auvergne, 7
Boyd, Arthur Merric, 7
Boyd, Emma Minnie, 7
Boyd, Theodore Penleigh, 7
Brierly, Sir Oswald Walters, 3
Brodzky, Horace Ascher, 7
Broinowski, Gracius Joseph, 3
Bryant, Charles David Jones, 7
Bunny, Rupert Charles Wulsten, 7
Bustard, William, 7
Buvelot, Abram-Louis, 3
Campbell, Oswald Rose, 3
Carter, Norman St Clair, 7
Cayley, Neville William, 7
Chapman, Thomas Evans, 1
Chevalier, Nicholas, 3
Chidley, William James, 7
Clark, Thomas, 3
Claxton, Marshall, 3
Clint, Raphael, 1
Coates, George James, 8
Cobb, Victor Ernest, 8
Collingridge de Tourcey, George
  Alphonse, 8
Colquhoun, Alexander, 8
Combes, Edward*, 3
Conder, Charles Edward, 3
Cumbrae Stewart, Janet Agnes, 8
Daplyn, Alfred James, 4
Davies, David, 8
De Maistre, LeRoy Leveson Laurent
  Joseph, 8
Dowling, Robert Hawker, 4
Duterrau, Benjamin, 1
Earle, Augustus, 1
Elyard, Samuel, 4
Eyre, John (b.1771), 1
Fizelle, Reginald Cecil Grahame, 8
Folingsby, George Frederick, 4
Forrest, Haughton, 8
Fowles, Joseph, 1
Fox, Emanuel Phillips, 8
Fox, Ethel Carrick, 8
Frater, William, 8
Friström, Carl Magnus Oscar, 8
Fullwood, Albert Henry, 8
Garling, Frederick (1806–1873), 1
Geach, Portia Swanston, 8
Gibbs, Herbert William, 8
Gibson, Elizabeth Dickson, 8
Gill, Harry Pelling, 9
Gill, Samuel Thomas, 1
Glover, John, 1
Gocher, William Henry, 9
Gould, Elizabeth, 1
Gould, William Buelow, 1
Grove, James, 1
Gruner, Elioth Lauritz Leganyer, 9
Guerard, Johann Joseph Eugen von, 4
Gye, Harold Frederick Neville, 9
Hall, Lindsay Bernard, 9
Ham, Thomas, 4

Haydon, George Henry, 4
Henry, Lucien Felix, 4
Herbert, Harold Brocklebank, 9
Heysen, Sir Wilhelm Ernst Hans Franz, 9
Hilder, Jesse Jewhurst, 9
Hill, Samuel Prout, 1
Hipkiss, Richard, 1
Howie, Laurence Hotham, 9
Ironside, Adelaide Eliza, 4
Jenner, Isaac Walter, 9
Lahey, Frances Vida, 9
Lambert, George Washington Thomas, 9
Lawlor, Adrian, 10
Leason, Percy Alexander, 10
Leist, Frederick William, 10
Lewin, John William, 2
Liardet, Wilbraham Frederick Evelyn, 2
Lindsay, Sir Ernest Daryl, 10
Lindsay, Sir Lionel Arthur, 10
Lindsay, Norman Alfred Williams, 10
Lindsay, Percival Charles, 10
Lindsay, Raymond, 10
Lindsay, Ruby, 10
Linton, James Walter Robert, 10
Lister, William Lister, 10
Lloyd, Henry Grant, 5
Long, Sydney, 10
Longstaff, Sir John Campbell, 10
Longstaff, William Frederick, 10
Loureiro, Artur Jose, 5
Lovett, Mildred Esther, 10
Lycett, Joseph, 2
Lyon, John Lamb, 10
McCrae, Georgiana Huntly, 2
McCubbin, Frederick, 10
McCubbin, Louis Frederick, 10
Macgeorge, Norman, 10
McInnes, William Beckwith, 10
Macleod, William, 10
Mahony, Francis, 10
Martens, Conrad, 2
Mather, John, 10
May, Philip William, 5
Medland, Lilian Marguerite, 9
Meeson, Dora, 8
Meldrum, Duncan Max, 10
Minns, Benjamin Edwin, 10
Moffitt, Ernest Edward, 10
Moore, Gladys Mary, 10
Moore, John Drummond Macpherson, 10
Mort, Eirene, 10
Muskett, Alice Jane, 10
Nerli, Girolamo Pieri Ballati, 10
Nicholas, Emily Hilda, 11
Nisbet, James Hume, 11
Norriss, Elizabeth May, 12
O'Connell, Michael William, 11
O'Connor, Kathleen Laetitia, 11
Officer, Edward Cairns, 11
Owen, Gladys Mary, 10
Paterson, John Ford, 5
Patterson, Ambrose McCarthy, 11
Pelloe, Emily Harriet, 11
Piguenit, William Charles, 5

Plante, Ada May, 11
Power, Harold Septimus, 11
Power, John Joseph Wardell, 11
Preston, Margaret Rose, 11
Proctor, Alethea Mary, 11
Prout, John Skinner, 2
Purves Smith, Charles Roderick (Peter), 11
Quinn, James Peter, 11
Ramsay, Hugh, 11
Raper, George, 2
Read, Richard (b.1765?), 2
Read, Richard (b.1796?), 2
Richardson, Charles Douglas, 11
Rivers, Richard Godfrey, 11
Roberts, Thomas William, 11
Rodius, Charles, 2
Rodway, Florence Aline, 11
Rolando, Charles, 6
Rowan, Marian Ellis, 11
Rowe, George, 6
Rowell, John Thomas Nightingale, 11
Rowell, William Nicholas, 11
Rubbo, Antonio Salvatore Dattilo, 11
Russell, John Peter, 11
Russell, Robert, 2
Scott, Harriet, 6
Scott, Helena, 6
Serle, Dora Beatrice, 11
Shirlow, John Alexander Thomas, 11
Shore, Arnold Joseph Victor, 11
Silas, Ellis Luciano, 11
Simpkinson de Wesselow, Francis Guillemard, 2
Skipper, John Michael, 6
Smith, Bernhard, 6
Smith, Grace Cossington, 11
Smith, Sydney George Ure, 11
Souter, David Henry, 12
Southern, Clara, 12
Spence, Percy Frederick Seaton, 12
Stainforth, Martin Frank, 12
Stoddard, Mary, 12
Strange, Frederick, 2
Streeton, Sir Arthur Ernest, 12
Strutt, William, 6
Sturgess, Reginald Ward, 12
Sutherland, Jane, 12
Teague, Violet Helen Evangeline, 12
Terry, Frederick Casemero, 6
Thomas, Margaret, 6
Traill, Jessie Constance Alicia, 12
Trenerry, Horace Hurtle, 12
Trompf, Percival Albert, 12
Tuck, Marie Anne, 12
Tucker, Tudor St George, 12
Turner, James Alfred, 12
Tweddle, Isabel May, 12
Vale, May, 12
Van Raalte, Henri Benedictus Salaman, 12
Vigano, Maria Teresa, 12
Wainewright, Thomas Griffiths, 2
Waite, James Clarke, 6
Wakelin, Roland Shakespeare, 12

Waller, Mervyn Napier, 12
Watling, Thomas, 2
Westall, William, 2
Wheeler, Charles Arthur, 12
Wilkie, Leslie Andrew Alexander, 12
Wilson, Dora Lynnell, 12
Withers, Walter Herbert, 12
Young, William Blamire, 12

ASSAYER, *see* Metallurgist

ASTRONOMER
Abbott, Francis, 3
Adams, Philip Francis, 3
Baldwin, Joseph Mason, 7
Baracchi, Pietro Paolo Giovanni Ernesto, 7
Brooks, Joseph, 7
Cooke, William Ernest, 8
Duffield, Walter Geoffrey, 8
Dunlop, James, 1
Ellery, Robert Lewis John, 4
Gale, Walter Frederick, 8
Lenehan, Henry Alfred, 10
Rumker, Christian Carl Ludwig, 2
Russell, Henry Chamberlain, 6
Scott, William, 6
Smalley, George Robarts, 6
Tebbutt, John, 6
Todd, Sir Charles, 6

ASYLUM SUPERINTENDENT
Coverdale, John, 1
Laver, Alfred Edmund, 10
Suttor, George, 2

ATHLETE
Carlton, James Andrew, 7
Donaldson, John, 8
Flack, Edwin Harold, 8
Marks, Ernest Samuel*, 10
Miller, William, 5
Postle, Arthur Benjamin, 11
Rowley, Stanley Rupert, 11
Weber, Clarence Alfred, 12
Wettenhall, Marcus Edwy*, 12
Winter, Anthony William, 12

AUCTIONEER
Brown, Frederick*, 3
Bruce, Theodore*, 7
Chanter, John Moore*, 7
Chapman, Sir Austin*, 7
Cox, John Edward, 1
Crouch, George Stanton, 3
Curtis, George Silas*, 8
Donnelly, John Francis, 8
Dowse, Thomas, 4
Dymock, David Lindsay, 4
Fraser, Alexander*, 4
Fryett, Richard William, 1
Gardiner, James*, 8
Greenfield, Alexander Mackay, 9
Ham, Cornelius Job*, 4
Heydon, Jabez King, 1
Hipkiss, Richard, 1
Howe, John, 1
King, John Charles*, 2
Knipe, John Hanlon, 5

Lawson, James Robert, 10
Lewis, Richard, 2
Livingston, John*, 10
Lloyd, George Alfred*, 5
Lowes, Thomas Yardley, 2
Lyons, Samuel, 2
McComas, John Wesley, 10
McPherson, Sir Clive, 10
Mitchell, Samuel James*, 10
Moore, Charles (1820-1895)*, 5
Neales, John Bentham*, 2
North, John Britty, 5
O'Connor, Daniel*, 5
Outtrim, Alfred Richard*, 11
Shackell, James, 6
Simmons, Joseph, 2
Smith, Sydney (1856-1934)*, 11
Smith, William Collard*, 6
Solomon, Judah Moss*, 6
Solomon, Vaiben Louis*, 12
Stanton, Richard Patrick Joseph, 12
Stow, Jefferson Pickman, 6
Thomas, Evan Henry, 2
Townsend, William*, 6
Tuckett, Joseph Helton, 12
Waite, William Charles Nightingale, 12

AUDITOR
Carson, David, 3
Lithgow, William, 2

AVIATOR
Butler, Henry John, 7
Douglas, Roger, 8
Duigan, John Robertson, 8
Follett, Frank William, 8
Frewin, Kenneth Moreton, 8
Fysh, Sir Wilmot Hudson, 8
Gatty, Harold Charles, 8
Hargrave, Lawrence, 9
Hart, William Ewart, 9
Hawker, Harry George, 9
Henry, Henry Goya, 9
Hinkler, Herbert John Louis, 9
Holden, Leslie Hubert, 9
Kingsford Smith, Sir Charles Edward, 9
Larkin, Herbert Joseph, 9
Love, Nigel Borland, 10
MacLeod, Thomas, 10
Melrose, Charles James, 10
Miller, Horatio Clive, 10
Mustar, Ernest Andrew, 10
Parer, Raymond John Paul, 11
Percival, Edgar Wikner, 11
Smith, Sir Keith Macpherson, 11
Smith, Sir Ross Macpherson, 11
Snook, Charles William, 12
Taylor, Sir Patrick Gordon, 12
Ulm, Charles Thomas Philippe, 12
Wilson, Gordon Campbell, 12
Woods, James, 12

AXEMAN
Blanc, Gustave, 7

BACTERIOLOGIST
Borthwick, Thomas, 7
Cherry, Thomas, 7

De Bavay, Auguste Joseph François, 8
Penfold, William James, 11
Smith, John McGarvie, 11
BAKER
Arnott, William, 3
Brunton, Thomas*, 3
Crews, John Branscombe*, 3
Cribb, Robert*, 3
Fawkner, John Pascoe*, 1
Goddard, Benjamin, 9
Kimpton, William Stephen, 5
Mitchell, William, 5
Oliver, Donald Percy, 11
Rose, Thomas (d.1837), 2
Sargent, Charlotte, 11
Sargent, Foster Henry Hartley, 11
Sargent, George, 11
Sidaway, Robert, 2
BANK CLERK
Barnett, Percy Neville, 7
Bayly, Nicholas, 1
Brookes, William*, 3
Duncan, Walter John Clare, 8
Hilder, Jesse Jewhurst, 9
Layh, Herbert Thomas Christoph, 10
Neville, Dalton Thomas Walker, 11
Treloar, George Devine, 12
BANKER
Adey, Stephen, 1
Aikenhead, James*, 1
Angas, George Fife*, 1
Annand, Frederick William Gadsby, 7
Barclay, Charles James, 3
Barclay, David, 7
Barlow, Andrew Henry*, 7
Black, Reginald James*, 7
Blackwood, James, 3
Boucher, Charles, 1
Boucher, Frederick, 1
Bourne, George Herbert, 7
Breillat, Robert Graham, 3
Brown, James Drysdale*, 7
Brown, Joseph Tilley*, 7
Buckland, Thomas, 3
Champion de Crespigny, Philip, 7
Clarke, William*, 3
Cohen, George Judah, 8
Cooch, Alexander, 8
Cottee, William Alfred, 3
Cribb, Henry Smart, 8
Cribb, Thomas Bridson*, 8
Davidson, Sir Alfred Charles, 8
Davies, George Schoen, 4
Dibbs, Sir Thomas Allwright, 4
Dowling, Henry (1810-1885)*, 1
Driscoll, Cornelius, 1
Drury, Edward Robert, 4
Dunn, John, 1
Emery, George Edwin, 8
French, Sir John Russell, 8
Gale, Walter Frederick, 8
Gatliff, John Henry, 8
Gibson, Sir Robert, 8
Griffiths, George Richard, 1

Hall, Edward Smith, 1
Hamilton, William Henry, 1
Healy, George Daniel, 9
Henty, Charles Shum*, 1
Highett, William*, 4
Hill, James Richard, 4
Knox, Sir Edward*, 5
Larnach, Donald, 5
Leake, John, 2
Lennon, William*, 10
Lochée, Francis, 2
Lyons, Thomas, 10
McArthur, David Charteris, 5
McKellar, John Alexander Ross, 10
McKenzie, Alexander Kenneth, 2
Macvitie, Thomas, 2
Massy-Greene, Sir Walter*, 10
Matheson, John, 5
Mercer, George Duncan, 2
Miller, Sir Denison Samuel King, 10
Miller, Sir Edward*, 10
Miller, Everard Studley, 10
Moore, James (1807-1895), 5
Oakden, Philip, 2
Parkes, Edmund Samuel, 5
Paterson, William*, 11
Piddington, William Henry Burgess*, 11
Ralston, Walter Vardon, 11
Read, George Frederick, 2
Reading, Sir Claude Hill, 11
Riddle, Sir Ernest Cooper, 11
Robinson, Joseph Phelps, 2
Rutledge, William*, 2
Sawers, John, 11
Sheehan, Sir Henry John, 11
Sherwin, Isaac, 2
Sloman, Thomas Martin, 2
Smith, Francis Grey, 6
Smith, Henry Gilbert*, 2
Smith, Shepherd, 6
Smith, Thomas Whistler*, 2
Stephens, Edward, 2
Stuart, Sir Alexander*, 6
Sullivan, Arthur Percy, 12
Swanston, Charles, 2
Taylor, Henry D'Esterre, 12
Tinline, George, 6
Tomkinson, Samuel*, 6
Tranter, Charles Herbert, 12
Turner, Charles Thomas Biass, 6
Turner, Henry Gyles, 6
Verdon, Sir George Frederic*, 6
Walker, James Thomas*, 12
Walker, John*, 2
Walker, Thomas (1804-1886), 2
White, Robert Hoddle Driberg*, 6
Williams, Francis, 2
Wiltshire, Aubrey Roy Liddon, 12
Wreford, Sir Ernest Henry, 12
Wren, Charles William, 12
BARRISTER, *see* Lawyer
BASEBALLER
Claxton, Norman, 8

BIBLIOGRAPHER
Miller, Edmund Morris, 10
Petherick, Edward Augustus, 5
BILLIARDS PLAYER
Lindrum, Frederick William (1888-1958), 10
Lindrum, Walter Albert, 10
BIOCHEMIST
Priestley, Henry, 11
Robertson, Thorburn Brailsford, 11
Young, William John, 12
BIOGRAPHER
Johns, Frederick, 9
Mennell, Philip Dearman, 10
Serle, Percival, 11
BIOLOGIST, *see also* Botanist; Zoologist
Darnell-Smith, George Percy, 8
Fletcher, Joseph James, 8
Goddard, Ernest James, 9
Johnston, Thomas Harvey, 9
Lucas, Arthur Henry Shakespeare, 10
Stutchbury, Samuel, 6
BISHOP, *see also* Archbishop; Cardinal
Anglican
Anderson, Ernest Augustus, 7
Armstrong, Thomas Henry, 7
Barker, Frederic, 3
Barlow, Christopher George, 7
Barry, Alfred, 3
Batty, Francis de Witt, 7
Bromby, Charles Henry, 3
Broughton, William Grant, 1
Camidge, Charles Edward, 7
Chalmers, William, 3
D'Arcy-Irvine, Gerard Addington, 8
Dawes, Nathaniel, 8
Dixon, Horace Henry, 8
Feetham, John Oliver, 8
Frodsham, George Horsfall, 8
Goe, Field Flowers, 9
Goldsmith, Frederick William, 9
Green, Arthur Vincent, 9
Hale, Mathew Blagden, 4
Harmer, John Reginald, 9
Hart, John Stephen, 9
Hay, Robert Snowdon, 9
Kennion, George Wyndham, 5
Kirkby, Sydney James, 9
Linton, Sydney, 5
Long, George Merrick, 10
Marsden, Samuel Edward, 5
Mercer, John Edward, 10
Montgomery, Henry Hutchinson, 10
Moorhouse, James, 5
Nixon, Francis Russell, 2
Parry, Henry Hutton, 5
Patteson, John Coleridge, 5
Pearson, Josiah Brown, 5
Perry, Charles, 5
Radford, Lewis Bostock, 11
Sandford, Daniel Fox, 6
Sharp, Gerald, 11
Short, Augustus, 6
Stanton, George Henry, 6

Stephen, Reginald, 12
Stone-Wigg, Montagu John, 12
Stretch, John Francis, 12
Thomas, Arthur Nutter, 12
Thomas, Mesac, 6
Thomas, Richard, 12
Thornton, Samuel, 6
Trower, Gerard, 12
Tufnell, Edward Wyndham, 6
Turner, James Francis, 6
Tyrrell, William, 6
Webber, William Thomas Thornhill, 12
Wentworth-Shields, Wentworth Francis, 12
White, Gilbert, 12
Catholic
Barry, John, 7
Boismenu, Alain Marie Guynot de, 7
Brady, John, 1
Byrne, Joseph Patrick, 3
Cani, John, 3
Corbett, James Francis, 8
Crane, Martin, 3
Davis, Charles Henry, 1
Doyle, Jeremiah Joseph, 8
Dunne, John, 8
Dwyer, Joseph Wilfrid, 8
Dwyer, Patrick Vincent, 8
Geoghegan, Patrick Bonaventure, 4
Gibney, Matthew, 8
Griver, Martin, 4
Gsell, Francis Xavier, 9
Higgins, Joseph, 9
Lanigan, William, 5
Moore, James (1834-1904), 5
Murphy, Francis, 2
Murray, James, 5
O'Connor, Michael, 5
O'Mahony, Timothy, 5
Phelan, Patrick, 11
Quinn, James, 5
Quinn, Matthew, 5
Serra, Joseph Benedict, 6
Sheil, Laurence Bonaventure, 6
Torreggiani, Elzear, 6
Willson, Robert William, 2
Greek Orthodox
Knetes, Christophoros, 9
BLACKSMITH
Adams, Walter*, 3
Babbidge, Benjamin Harris, 3
Beach, William, 3
Bice, Sir John George*, 7
Bottrill, Frank, 7
Cook, Solomon, 3
Davis, James, 1
Furphy, John, 4
Handcock, Peter Joseph, 9
Hervey, Grant (Madison), 9
Kerr, George*, 9
Munro, David, 5
BOILERMAKER
Storey, John*, 12

BOOKMAKER
Dunningham, Sir John Montgomery*, 8
Green, Solomon, 1
Kerr, David McFarlane McLachlan, 9
Naylor, Rupert Theodore, 10
Oxenham, Humphrey, 11
Shang, Caleb James, 11
Sievier, Robert Standish, 11
Thompson, Joseph, 6
Thurgood, Albert John, 12
Wren, John, 12
BOOKSELLER
Andrade, David Alfred, 7
Andrade, William Charles, 7
Angus, David Mackenzie, 7
Clarke, Jacob Richard, 3
Cole, Edward William, 3
Dwight, Henry Tolman, 4
Dymock, William, 8
Humffray, John Basson*, 4
Kidston, William*, 9
Laidler, Thomas Percival, 9
McGarvie, William, 2
McNamara, Matilda Emilie Bertha, 10
McNamara, William Henry Thomas, 10
Moffitt, William, 2
Mullen, Samuel, 5
Perkins, John Arthur*, 11
Petherick, Edward Augustus, 5
Piddington, William Richman*, 5
Preece, Frederick William, 11
Preece, John Lloyd, 11
Robertson, George, 6
Robertson, George, 11
Rowlandson, Alfred Cecil, 11
Serle, Percival, 11
Spencer, Albert Henry, 12
Tegg, James, 2
Tegg, Samuel Augustus, 2
Tyrrell, James Robert, 12
Vale, Richard Tayler*, 6
Vale, William Mountford Kinsey*, 6
Walch, Charles Edward, 6
Wilmot, Frank Leslie Thompson, 12
Wymark, Frederick Victor Grey, 12
BOOTMAKER
Fisher, Thomas, 4
Fleming, John William, 8
Picton, Edward Benjamin, 11
Townsend, William*, 6
Trenwith, William Arthur*, 12
Tunnecliffe, Thomas*, 12
BOTANIST
Atkinson, Henry Brune, 7
Bailey, Frederick Manson, 3
Bailey, John Frederick, 7
Baker, Richard Thomas, 7
Banks, Sir Joseph, 1
Bentham, George, 3
Betche, Ernst, 3
Bidwill, John Carne, 1
Black, John McConnell, 7
Blackall, William Edward, 7
Brown, Robert, 1

Bunce, Daniel, 1
Burton, David, 1
Caley, George, 1
Calvert, James Snowden, 3
Cambage, Richard Hind, 7
Carne, Walter Mervyn, 7
Carron, William, 3
Cheel, Edwin, 7
Cunningham, Allan, 1
Cunningham, Richard, 1
Dallachy, John, 4
Deane, Henry, 8
Drummond, James (1784-1863), 1
Ewart, Alfred James, 8
Frazer, Charles, 1
Guilfoyle, William Robert, 4
Gunn, Ronald Campbell*, 1
Harvey, William Henry, 4
Heyne, Ernst Bernhard, 4
Hirschfeld, Eugen, 9
Holtze, Maurice William, 9
Hooker, Sir Joseph Dalton, 4
Lawson, Abercrombie Anstruther, 10
Maiden, Joseph Henry, 10
Molloy, Georgiana, 2
Moore, Charles (1820-1905), 5
Morris, Albert, 10
Mueller, Baron Sir Ferdinand Jakob
  Heinrich von, 5
Nicholls, William Henry, 11
Osborn, Theodore George Bentley, 11
Pelloe, Emily Harriet, 11
Rodway, Leonard, 11
Rogers, Richard Sanders, 11
Rupp, Herman Montague Rucker, 11
Sargent, Oswald Hewlett, 11
Schomburgk, Moritz Richard, 6
Tate, Ralph, 6
Tisdall, Henry Thomas, 12
Turner, Fred, 12
White, Cyril Tenison, 12
Woolls, William, 6
BOXER
Baker, Reginald Leslie, 7
Baker, William Harold, 7
Christie, John Mitchell, 7
Darcy, James Leslie, 8
Fitzsimmons, Robert, 8
Foley, Laurence, 4
Godfrey, Sidney George, 9
Griffiths, Albert, 9
Hardwick, Arthur Ernest, 9
Jackson, Peter, 9
Miller, William, 5
Richards, Ranold, 11
Sharman, James, 11
BREWER
Barnes, William (1791?-1848), 1
Billson, Alfred Arthur*, 7
Billson, George*, 7
Boston, John, 1
Chapman, Edgar, 3
De Bavay, Auguste Joseph François, 8
Farrell, John, 4

Fitzgerald, Nicholas*, 4
Gatehouse, George, 1
Graham, Charles James*, 4
Gray, George Wilkie*, 9
Jacobs, Samuel Joshua, 9
Jones, John Alexander Stammers, 9
Kerferd, George Briscoe*, 5
Latham, Edward, 5
McCracken, Alexander, 10
McCracken, Robert, 5
McHale, James Francis, 10
Mackay, Martin, 5
Perkins, Patrick*, 5
Phillips, Orwell, 11
Pinschof, Carl Ludwig, 11
Resch, Edmund, 11
Resch, Emil, 11
Smith, Sir Edwin Thomas*, 6
Squire, James, 2
Tewksbury, Alphonso Reed, 12
Toohey, James Matthew*, 6
Toohey, John Thomas*, 6
Tooth, Edwin, 6
Tooth, Frederick, 6
Tooth, John, 6
Tooth, Robert*, 6
Tooth, Sir Robert Lucas Lucas-*, 6
Tulloch, Eric William, 12
Walker, John*, 2
Wilson, Sir James Milne*, 6
BUCKJUMPER, *see* Entertainer
BUILDER
Amess, Samuel, 3
Anderson, William*, 3
Angwin, William Charles*, 7
Anstey, Edward Alfred*, 7
Bloodsworth, James, 1
Burgoyne, Thomas*, 7
Byrnes, James (1806-1886)*, 3
Cain, William*, 3
Cockram, Thomas (1831-1912), 8
Cockram, Thomas (1860-1920), 8
Cornish, William Crocker, 3
Cox, William, 1
De Little, Robert, 1
Ewen, John Carr, 8
Fitzpatrick, Columbus, 4
Flood, Edward*, 4
Foley, Laurence, 4
Gannon, Michael, 4
Garlick, Daniel, 4
Harrison, Sir John, 9
Henley, Sir Thomas*, 9
Howie, Sir Archibald*, 9
Hudson, Henry, 4
Johnson, William Dartnell*, 9
Joubert, Jules François de Sales, 4
Keane, Edward Vivien Harvey*, 5
Lennox, David, 2
Liebe, Friederich Wilhelm Gustav, 10
Loynes, James, 10
Lucas, John*, 5
Lucas, Nathaniel, 2

McCann, Peter, 10
Mitchell, David, 5
O'Grady, Thomas, 5
Petrie, Andrew, 2
Petrie, John, 5
Pigdon, John, 5
Pitman, Jacob, 5
Robinson, George Augustus, 2
Spencer, Thomas Edward, 12
Stuart, William, 12
Sutherland, John*, 6
Swanson, Donald Alexander, 12
Swanson, Sir John Warren, 12
Thompson, David (1828-1889), 12
Thomson, James Alexander, 2
Torode, Walter Charles, 12
Trigg, Henry, 2
Vaughn, Robert Matterson*, 6
Verge, John, 2
Wade, Benjamin Martin*, 12
Walker, James, 12
White, Henry Eli, 12
Young, John, 6
BUSHRANGER
Brady, Matthew, 1
Cash, Martin, 1
Clarke, John (1846?-1867), 3
Clarke, Thomas, 3
Davis, Edward, 1
Donohoe, John, 1
Gardiner, Francis, 4
Gilbert, John, 4
Governor, Jimmy, 9
Hall, Benjamin, 4
Howe, Michael, 1
Johns, Joseph Bolitho, 4
Kelly, Edward, 5
McPherson, (James) Alpin, 5
Melville, Francis, 5
Power, Henry, 5
Scott, Andrew George, 6
Ward, Frederick, 6
BUSINESSMAN, *see also* Company—
chairman, director, manager; Financier;
Industrialist; Manufacturer; Merchant;
Retailer
Anderson, Sir Robert Murray McCheyne,
7
Ashbolt, Sir Alfred Henry, 7
Bagot, Edward Daniel Alexander*, 7
Beaurepaire, Sir Francis Joseph Edmund*,
7
Boyd, James Arthur*, 7
Connibere, Sir Charles Wellington, 8
Curnow, James Henry, 8
Gardner, Robert, 8
Grant, Kenneth McDonald*, 9
Hodel, Joseph*, 9
Jones, William, 9
Levi, Nathaniel*, 5
Moore, Henry Byron, 5
Nobbs, Charles Chase Ray, 11
Rounsevell, John*, 11
Smith, Robert Barr, 6

BUTCHER
Angliss, Sir William Charles, 7
Austin, James (1810-1896), 1
Baynes, Ernest, 7
Baynes, George, 7
Baynes, Harry, 7
Clarke, William John Turner, 1
Edmondstone, George*, 4
Hardacre, Herbert Freemont*, 9
Hill, George*, 4
Hill, Richard*, 4
Langton, Edward*, 5
O'Connor, Daniel*, 5
Orton, Arthur, 5
Patterson, Sir James Brown*, 5
Pattison, William*, 5
Playfair, (John) Thomas*, 5
Ryan, James Tobias*, 6
Taylor, Hugh*, 6
Tighe, Atkinson Alfred Patrick*, 6
Ulrich, Theodore Friederick, 12
Young, William Ramsay, 12
CAMEL DRIVER
Allum, Mahomet, 7
Bejah, Dervish, 7
Mahomet, Faiz, 10
CANNER
Broadhurst, Charles Edward, 3
Walker, Fred, 12
fruit
Fairley, Sir Andrew Walker, 8
Lamb, Walter, 5
Laver, Ralph Herbert, 10
meat
Elliott, Sizar, 4
Ritchie, Samuel Sextus, 6
Tindal, Charles Grant, 6
CANTEEN SUPERINTENDENT
Chisholm, Dame Alice Isabel, 7
McPhillamy, Verania, 10
CARDINAL
Moran, Patrick Francis, 10
CARPENTER
Ah Mouy, Louis, 3
Arscott, John, 1
Bamford, Frederick William*, 7
Baughan, John, 1
Cooke, Thomas, 8
Cotton, George Witherage*, 3
Ferguson, John (1830-1906)*, 8
Gardiner, Albert*, 8
Huie, Alexander Gordon, 9
Ingram, George Mawby, 9
Lalor, Vivian William, 9
Long, Richard Hooppell, 10
Lucas, Nathaniel, 2
Pearce, Sir George Foster*, 11
Reid, Matthew*, 11
Rogers, George Edgar, 11
Shout, Alfred John, 11
Stewart, David, 12
CARRIER
Barton, Russell*, 3
Hall, Walter Russell, 9

Ingham, William Bairstow, 4
McCulloch, James, 5
McCulloch, William*, 5
Mahomet, Faiz, 10
Permewan, John, 5
Tewksbury, William Pearson, 12
Wiseman, Thomas, 12
Wright, Francis Augustus*, 6
CARTOONIST
Bancks, James Charles, 7
Bradley, Luther, 7
Carrington, Francis Thomas Dean, 3
Case, James Thomas, 7
Dyson, Ambrose Arthur, 8
Dyson, William Henry, 8
Hopkins, Livingston York, 4
Jonsson, Nils Josef, 9
Low, Sir David Alexander Cecil, 10
Mailey, Alfred Arthur, 10
Marquet, Claude Arthur, 10
Pryor, Oswald, 11
Scott, Eugene Montague, 6
Strange, Benjamin Edward, 12
Taylor, George Augustine, 12
Vincent, Alfred James, 12
CATERER, *see also* Restaurateur
Aronson, Zara, 7
Bell, Peter Albany, 7
Pomeroy, John, 11
Sargent, Charlotte, 11
Sargent, George, 11
Skinner, Henry Hawkins*, 11
Sterne, Elizabeth Anne Valentine, 12
CHAPLAIN
Bain, James, 1
South African War
Collick, Edward Mallan, 8
Frodsham, George Horsfall, 8
Holden, Albert Thomas, 9
Rose, Herbert John, 11
Wray, Frederick William, 12
World War I
Bergin, Michael, 7
Bethune, John Walter, 7
Collick, Edward Mallan, 8
Danglow, Jacob, 8
Devine, William, 8
Dexter, Walter Ernest, 8
Fahey, John, 8
Forbes, Arthur Edward, 8
Gillison, Andrew, 9
Green, James, 9
Holden, Albert Thomas, 9
Kennedy, John Joseph, 9
Long, George Merrick, 10
McKenzie, William, 10
O'Donnell, Thomas Joseph, 11
Paton, Francis Hume Lyall, 11
Rentoul, Thomas Craike, 11
Rolland, Sir Francis William, 11
Talbot, Albert Edward, 12
Woods, William Maitland, 12
Wray, Frederick William, 12

CHARCOAL BURNER
Fisher, James Cowley Morgan, 4
CHARITY WORKER
Alston, Mary, 7
Aronson, Zara, 7
Barlow, Mary Kate, 7
Benjamin, David Samuel, 7
Bevan, Louisa Jane, 7
Chisholm, Dame Alice Isabel, 7
Cumbrae-Stewart, Zina Beatrice Selwyn, 8
Denman, Gertrude Mary, Lady, 8
Dudley, Rachel, Lady, 8
Fairfax, Ruth Beatrice, 8
Goode, Sir Charles Henry*, 4
Gordon, Margaret Jane, 9
Gowrie, Zara Eileen, Lady, 9
Hackett, Deborah Vernon, 9
Holmes, Marion Louisa, 9
Holmes, Marion Phoebe, 9
Hughes, Agnes Eva, 9
King, Anna Josepha, 2
Lee, Minnie, 10
Levey, James Alfred, 10
Macarthur Onslow, Rosa Sibella, 10
MacKinnon, Eleanor Vokes Irby, 10
Masson, Mary, Lady, 10
Mitchell, Eliza Fraser, Lady, 10
Moore, Gladys Mary, 10
Moss, Alice Frances Mabel, 10
Munro, Grace Emily, 10
Munro Ferguson, Helen Hermione, Lady, 10
Newman-Morris, Sir John, 11
Oakden, Philip, 2
O'Neil, Charles Gordon, 5
Owen, Gladys Mary, 10
Parker, Florence Mary, 11
Phillips, Rebecca, 11
Read, Irene Victoria, 11
Ross, Euphemia Welch, 11
Russell, Delia Constance, 11
Sewell, Alice Maud, Lady, 11
Smith, Ivy Blanche Irene, 11
Sterne, Elizabeth Anne Valentine, 12
Tillyard, Pattie, 12
Vaughan, Dorothy, 12
Virgo, John James, 12
Ward, Elizabeth Jane, 12
Weber, Ivy Lavinia*, 12
Wesché, Phoebe Ellen, 12
Windeyer, Mary Elizabeth, 12
Young, Sarah Jane, 12
CHEMIST, see also Pharmacist
Ampt, Gustav Adolph, 7
Anderson, Valentine George, 7
Avery, David, 7
Benjamin, Louis Reginald Samuel, 7
Boas, Isaac Herbert, 7
Booth, Norman Parr, 7
Brünnich, Johannes Christian, 7
Callister, Cyril Percy, 7
Challinor, Richard Westman, 7
Elliott, James Frederick, 8
Faulding, Francis Hardey, 4

Grimwade, Sir Wilfrid Russell, 9
Guthrie, Frederick Bickell, 9
Hargreaves, William Arthur, 9
Hart, Alfred, 9
Henderson, John Brownlie, 9
Leibius, Charles Adolph, 5
Macadam, John*, 5
Mann, Edward Alexander*, 10
Masson, Sir David Orme, 10
Masson, Sir James Irvine Orme, 10
Maund, John, 5
Maxwell, Walter, 10
Newbery, James Cosmo, 5
Pearson, Alfred Naylor, 11
Penfold, Arthur de Ramon, 11
Potter, Charles Vincent, 11
Rennie, Edward Henry, 11
Rivett, Sir Albert Cherbury David, 11
Simpson, Edward Sydney, 11
Smith, Alfred Mica, 6
Smith, Henry George, 11
Steel, Thomas, 12
Sutherland, William, 12
Thomson, Alexander Morrison, 6
Walton, Thomas Utrick, 12
Wilsmore, Norman Thomas Mortimer, 12
CHESS MASTER
Viner, William Samuel, 12
CIRCUS PROPRIETOR
Ashton, Frederick, 7
Ashton, James, 7
Ashton, James Henry, 7
Burton, Henry, 3
Wirth, George, 12
Wirth, Mary Elizabeth Victoria, 12
Wirth, Philip Peter Jacob, 12
CIVIL OFFICIAL
Angus, William*, 7
Armstrong, William George, 7
Bannister, Saxe, 1
Barber, George Walter, 7
Baxter, Alexander Macduff, 1
Beamont, John, 1
Bell, Alexander Foulis, 7
Bell, Frederick William, 7
Bigge, John Thomas, 1
Boyes, George Thomas William Blamey, 1
Brennan, Edward Thomas*, 7
Brinsmead, Horace Clowes, 7
Bromley, Edward Foord, 1
Brookes, Herbert Robinson, 7
Busby, James, 1
Butters, Sir John Henry, 7
Cameron, Alexander, 7
Campbell, John Thomas, 1
Carey, George Jackson, 3
Cattanach, William, 7
Cherry, Thomas, 7
Cheyne, Alexander, 1
Cleary, William James, 8
Cobby, Arthur Henry, 8
Collicott, John Thomas, 1
Cordeaux, William, 1
Crawford, Alexander, 8

Cumpston, John Howard Lidgett, 8
Dannevig, Harald Kristian, 8
Davis, John King, 8
Despeissis, Jean Marie Adrian, 8
Downes, Major Francis, 4
Drummond, John, 1
Dulhunty, Robert Venour, 1
Elkington, John Simeon Colebrook, 8
Emmett, Evelyn Temple, 8
Fairley, Sir Andrew Walker, 8
Farnell, Frank*, 8
Fereday, Dudley, 1
Fisher, Sir James Hurtle*, 1
Fraser, Peter Gordon, 1
Garrick, Sir James Francis*, 4
Gibson, Sir Robert, 8
Gilbert, David John, 9
Gilles, Osmond, 1
Gordon, Sir Thomas Stewart*, 9
Gore, William, 1
Gregory, John, 1
Gresswell, Dan Astley, 9
Griffith, Arthur Hill*, 9
Hargreaves, William Arthur, 9
Holden, George Frederick*, 9
James, Sir Claude Ernest Weymouth*, 9
Kay, Alick Dudley*, 9
Kerr, William Warren, 9
Kinchela, John, 2
Langwell, Hugh*, 9
Leighton, Arthur Edgar, 10
Lewis, Essington, 10
Lowrie, William, 10
McCrea, William, 5
McGowan, Samuel Walker, 5
Meagher, Richard James, 10
Molineux, Albert, 5
Moloney, Parker John, 10
Monash, Sir John, 10
Murray, Stuart, 5
Nepean, Evan, 2
Pearson, Alfred Naylor, 11
Perkins, Arthur James, 11
Piesse, Edmund Leolin, 11
Piper, John, 2
Pittman, Edward Fisher, 11
Purcell, James, 11
Purdy, John Smith, 11
Raymond, James, 2
Richardson, Arnold Edwin Victor, 11
Riddell, Campbell Drummond*, 2
Riddell, Walter John Carre, 11
Rigby, Edward Charles, 11
Rivett, Sir Albert Cherbury David, 11
Robertson, Edward, 11
Robinson, Edward Oswin, 11
Robinson, Sir Thomas Bilbe, 11
Rouse, Richard, 2
Shepherdson, John Banks, 2
Simpson, James, 2
Simpson, Stephen, 2
Spencer, Sir Richard, 2
Stable, Jeremiah Joseph, 12
Stephen, Sir James, 2

Stone, George Frederick, 2
Sturt, Charles, 2
Taylor, Henry Joseph Stirling, 12
Thomas, Jocelyn Henry Connor, 2
Tims, Martin, 2
Tyers, Charles James, 2
Walker, James, 12
Ward, Sir Edward Wolstenholme*, 6
Whiddon, William Henry, 12
Williams, Sir Richard, 12
Young, Adolphus William, 2
CLERGY, *see also* Archbishop; Bishop;
Cardinal; Chaplain; Missionary; Preacher;
Rabbi; Religious brother; Religious sister;
Salvationist
Anglican
Allwood, Robert, 1
Archdall, Mervyn, 7
Armitage, Frederick, 3
Atkins, Thomas, 1
Atkinson, Henry Brune, 7
Bailey, William, 1
Barry, Zachary, 3
Bedford, William, 1
Bethune, Frank Pogson, 7
Bethune, John Walter, 7
Bolden, John Satterthwaite, 1
Boyce, Francis Bertie, 7
Braim, Thomas Henry, 3
Brigstocke, Charles Ferdinand, 1
Bromby, John Edward, 3
Brown, Francis Ernest, 7
Brown, James (1820-1895), 3
Browne, William Henry, 1
Brownrigg, Marcus Blake, 3
Burrowes, John, 3
Bussell, William John, 7
Campbell, Colin*, 3
Campion, Frederick Henry, 7
Cartwright, Robert, 1
Cary, Henry, 3
Child, Coles, 3
Clarke, William Branwhite, 3
Collick, Edward Mallan, 8
Cowper, William, 1
Cowper, William Macquarie, 3
Cox, Frederick Holdslip, 1
Cross, John, 1
Davies, Robert Rowland, 1
Dexter, Walter Ernest, 8
Docker, Joseph, 1
Druitt, Thomas, 4
Ewing, Thomas James, 1
Farr, George Henry, 4
Flower, Willoughby, 8
Forrest, Robert, 1
Fry, Henry Phibbs, 1
Fulton, Henry, 1
Garland, David John, 8
Garnsey, Arthur Henry, 8
Garnsey, Charles Frederick, 4
Gell, John Philip, 1
Girdlestone, Henry, 9
Glennie, Benjamin, 4

Goodman, George, 4
Green, Samuel, 4
Greenway, Charles Capel, 4
Gregor, John, 1
Gunther, William James, 4
Hales, Francis, 4
Hammond, Robert Brodribb Stewart, 9
Hancock, William, 9
Handfield, Henry Hewett Paulet, 4
Harris, Richard Deodatus Poulett, 4
Hassall, Thomas, 1
Hebblethwaite, James, 9
Henn, Percy Umfreville, 9
Hill, Richard, 1
Hindley, William George, 9
Hodgson, William, 4
Hose, Henry Judge, 4
Howard, Charles Beaumont, 1
Howard, Stanley, 4
Hughes, Ernest Selwyn, 9
Hutchins, William, 1
Johnson, Richard, 2
Jose, George Herbert, 9
Kane, Henry Plow, 2
King, George (1813-1899), 5
King, Robert Lethbridge, 5
Knopwood, Robert, 2
Lamble, George Edwin, 9
Macarthur, George Fairfowl, 5
Macartney, Hussey Burgh, 5
MacCullagh, John Christian, 5
Makinson, Thomas Cooper, 2
Marriott, Fitzherbert Adams, 2
Marryat, Charles, 10
Marsden, Samuel, 2
Matthews, Charles Henry Selfe, 10
Micklem, Philip Arthur, 10
Middleton, George Augustus, 2
Nash, Clifford Harris, 10
Newton, Frederick Robert, 5
Nichols, Reginald Gordon Clement, 11
Nicolay, Charles Grenfell, 5
Noble, James, 11
Oakes, George Spencer, 11
O'Reilly, Thomas, 5
Palmer, Philip, 2
Parkinson, Charles Tasman, 11
Perkins, Frederick Thomas, 11
Plume, Henry, 11
Poole, Frederic Slaney, 11
Portus, Garnet Vere, 11
Pownall, William Henry, 5
Read, Henry, 6
Reddall, Thomas, 2
Reibey, Thomas*, 6
Rogers, Thomas George, 2
Rose, Herbert John, 11
Rupp, Herman Montague Rucker, 11
Russell, Francis Thomas Cusack, 2
Sconce, Robert Knox, 2
Scott, Thomas Hobbes, 2
Scott, William, 6
Selwyn, Arthur Edward, 6

Sharp, William Hey, 11
Smith, Pierce Galliard, 6
Smith, Thomas (1829-1882), 6
Smith, William Isaac Carr, 11
Soares, Alberto Dias, 6
Sowerby, William, 6
Stackhouse, Alfred, 2
Stephen, Alfred Hamilton Hewlett, 6
Stiles, Henry Tarlton, 2
Stretch, Theodore Carlos Benoni, 6
Sykes, Alfred Depledge, 12
Talbot, Albert Edward, 12
Taylor, Robert, 6
Thompson, Edward Henry, 12
Thomson, Adam Compton, 2
Torrance, George William, 6
Tucker, Gerard Kennedy, 12
Tucker, Horace Finn, 12
Vale, Benjamin, 2
Vance, George Oakley, 6
Waddy, Percival Stacy, 12
Wade, Robert Thompson, 12
Walsh, William Horatio, 2
Warren, Hubert Ernest de Mey, 12
Whitington, Frederick Taylor, 12
Wilton, Charles Pleydell Neale, 2
Wise, Percy William Charlton, 12
Wittenoom, John Burdett, 2
Wollaston, John Ramsden, 2
Woodd, Henry Alexander, 12
Woods, William Maitland, 12
Woolley, John, 6
Woolls, William, 6
Wray, Frederick William, 12
Youl, John, 2
Zercho, Charles Henry, 12

Australian Church
Addis, William (Edward), 7
Strong, Charles, 6

Baptist
Boreham, Frank William, 7
Chapman, Samuel, 3
Clark, Charles, 3
Dowling, Henry (1780-1869), 1
Goble, Joseph Hunter, 9
Greenwood, James*, 4
Mead, Silas, 5
Parsons, John Langdon*, 11
Ruth, Thomas Elias, 11
Saunders, John, 2
Sexton, John Henry, 11
Syme, George Alexander, 6
Waldock, Arthur John, 12
Wilkin, Frederick John, 12

Catholic
Backhaus, George Henry, 3
Bergin, Michael, 7
Bermingham, Patrick, 3
Bleasdale, John Ignatius, 3
Byrne, Frederick, 7
Carlton, James Andrew, 7
Conolly, Philip, 1
Cullen, John Hugh, 8
Curran, John (Michael) Milne, 3

Dalton, Joseph, 4
Devine, William, 8
Dixon, James, 1
Dowling, Christopher Vincent, 4
Dunne, Patrick, 4
Dunne, William John, 4
Fahey, John, 8
Fitzpatrick, John, 4
Forrest, John, 4
Gregory, Henry Gregory, 1
Hackett, William Philip, 9
Hall, William, 1
Harold, James, 1
Hartigan, Patrick Joseph, 9
Hawes, John Cyril, 9
Jerger, Charles Adolph, 9
Kelly, William (1823-1909), 5
Kennedy, John Joseph, 9
Kenny, John, 2
Kranewitter, Aloysius, 5
Le Rennetel, Pierre François, 10
Lockington, William Joseph, 10
Lonergan, John Joseph, 10
McAlroy, Michael, 5
McEncroe, John, 2
McKillop, Donald, 5
Monnier, Joseph, 5
Murphy, Jeremiah Matthias, 10
O'Donnell, Thomas Joseph, 11
O'Donovan, John, 5
O'Flynn, Jeremiah Francis, 2
O'Haran, Denis Francis, 11
O'Neil, Peter, 2
O'Neill, George, 11
O'Reilly, Maurice Joseph, 11
Pigot, Edward Francis, 11
Piquet, Jean Pierre, 11
Poupinel, François Victor, 5
Rocher, Jean-Louis, 6
Ryan, James, 11
Salvado, Rosendo, 2
Schurr, Felix, 6
Shaw, Archibald John, 11
Sheehy, Samuel John Austin, 6
Sheridan, John Felix, 6
Slattery, Joseph Patrick, 11
Slattery, Patrick Joseph, 6
Strele, Anton, 6
Tenison-Woods, Julian Edmund, 6
Therry, John Joseph, 2
Ullathorne, William Bernard, 2
Vaughan, Edmund, 6
Christian Socialist
Turnbull, Archibald, 12
Churches of Christ
Forbes, Arthur Edward, 8
Garden, John Smith*, 8
Gore, Thomas Jefferson, 4
Congregational
Albiston, Walter, 7
Barrow, John Henry*, 3
Bevan, Llewellyn David, 7
Binney, Thomas, 3
Bird, Bolton Stafford*, 3

Clarke, George (1823-1913), 3
Cocks, Nicholas John, 8
Cover, James Fleet, 1
Cox, Francis William, 3
Dale, Robert William, 4
Davies, David Mortimer*, 4
Dowie, John Alexander, 4
Dunstan, Edward Tremayne, 8
Fletcher, Lionel Bale, 8
Fletcher, William Roby, 4
Gainford, Thomas, 4
Gosman, Alexander, 4
Halley, Jacob John, 4
Harcus, William, 4
Hebblethwaite, James, 9
Jefferis, James, 4
Johnston, Joseph, 4
Kiek, Edward Sidney, 9
Kiek, Winifred, 9
King, James Harold, 9
King, Joseph, 9
Kirby, Joseph Coles, 5
Miller, Frederick, 2
Morison, Alexander, 5
Morley, William, 10
Morris, Robert Newton, 5
Moss, William, 5
Newland, Ridgway William, 2
Poore, John Legg, 5
Pratt, Frederick Vicary, 11
Price, Charles, 2
Quaife, Barzillai, 2
Rivett, Albert, 11
Roseby, Thomas, 6
Ross, Robert (1792-1862), 2
Ruth, Thomas Elias, 11
Stow, Thomas Quinton, 2
Sykes, Alfred Depledge, 12
Thatcher, Griffithes Wheeler, 12
Threlkeld, Lancelot Edward, 2
Waterfield, William, 2
West, John, 2
Wight, George, 6
Wright, David McKee, 12
Greek Orthodox
Phocas, Seraphim, 11
Lutheran
Auricht, Johann Christian, 3
Fritzsche, Gotthard Daniel, 2
Goethe, Matthias, 4
Graebner, Carl Friedrich, 9
Heidenreich, Georg Adam, 4
Heidenreich, Johannes Heinrich Siegfried, 4
Herlitz, Hermann, 4
Kavel, August Ludwig Christian, 2
Leidig, Georg Friedrich, 10
Nickel, Theodor August Friedrich Wilhelm, 11
Oster, Philipp Jacob, 5
Rechner, Gustav Julius, 6
Schirmeister, Carl Friedrich Alexander Franz, 6
Strempel, Carl Friedrich Adolph, 6

Melkite
Mansour, Sylwanos, 10
Methodist
Adamson, John*, 7
Albiston, Arthur Edward, 7
Bath, Henry, 3
Bickford, James, 3
Blacket, John, 7
Boyce, William Binnington, 3
Brentnall, Frederick Thomas*, 3
Burgess, Henry Thomas, 7
Burton, John Wear, 7
Butters, William, 3
Cann, William Henry, 7
Carvosso, Benjamin, 1
Cole, George Henry, 8
Curnow, William, 8
Draper, Daniel James, 1
Drummond, Stanley Gillick, 8
Edgar, Alexander Robert, 8
Eggleston, John, 4
Fitchett, William Henry, 8
Fletcher, Joseph Horner, 4
Forsyth, Samuel, 8
Gilmore, Hugh, 4
Green, James, 9
Holden, Albert Thomas, 9
Howard, Henry, 9
Howchin, Walter, 9
Hurst, George, 4
Jenkin, John Grenfell, 9
Judkins, George Alfred, 9
Kelynack, William, 5
Lade, Frank, 9
McKenny, John, 2
Manton, John Allen, 2
Maughan, James, 5
Osborne, John, 5
Piper, Thomas, 11
Prescott, Charles John, 11
Quick, William Abraham, 5
Rentoul, Thomas Craike, 11
Robson, William*, 11
Rutledge, Sir Arthur*, 11
Rutledge, William Woolls, 11
Stephen, Patrick John, 12
Sugden, Edward Holdsworth, 12
Symons, John Christian, 6
Taylor, William George, 12
Walker, William (1800-1855), 2
Ward, Frederick William, 12
Waterhouse, Jabez Bunting, 6
Waterhouse, Joseph, 6
Waterhouse, Samuel, 6
Watsford, John, 6
Waugh, James Swanton, 6
Wheen, Harold, 12
Wheen, John Gladwell, 12
Worrall, Henry, 12
Young, Robert, 6
Presbyterian
Aspinall, Arthur Ashworth, 7
Barber, John Andrew, 7
Beg, Wazir, 3

Blair, David*, 3
Cairns, Adam, 3
Cameron, James, 3
Campbell, Alexander James, 3
Clow, James, 1
Cosh, James, 3
Crawford, Thomas Simpson*, 8
Davidson, John, 4
Dill Macky, William Marcus, 8
Drummond, Ralph, 1
Eipper, Christopher, 1
Ferguson, John (1852-1925), 8
Flynn, John, 8
Forbes, James, 1
Fullerton, James, 4
Gardner, John, 4
Garrett, James, 1
Geikie, Archibald Constable, 4
Gillison, Andrew, 9
Grimm, George, 4
Haining, Robert, 1
Henderson, William, 4
Hetherington, Irving, 4
Heyer, Johannes, 9
Howard, Henry, 9
Johnstone, Thomas, 4
Kinross, John, 5
Lang, John Dunmore*, 2
Lawton, John Thomas, 10
Lillie, John, 2
Lyall, James, 5
Macarthur, Archibald, 2
McGarvie, John, 2
McGavin, Matthew, 5
McGibbon, John, 5
Macintyre, Ronald George, 10
McIntyre, William (1805-1870), 5
Mackersey, John, 2
Mackie, George, 5
McLaren, Samuel Gilfillan, 10
Mathew, John, 10
Mitchell, Robert, 10
Murdoch, Patrick John, 10
Paton, Francis Hume Lyall, 11
Purves, William, 5
Ramsay, Andrew Mitchell, 6
Rentoul, John Laurence, 11
Ridley, William, 6
Rolland, Sir Francis William, 11
Seymour, John Alfred, 11
Shearer, David, 6
Smith, Thomas Jollie, 11
Steel, Robert, 6
Tait, George, 12
Thomson, Adam, 6
Turnbull, Adam (1803-1891), 2
Walker, John, 12
Young Wai, John, 12
Russian Orthodox
Antonieff, Valentin Andreevich, 7
Seventh Day Adventist
Watson, Charles Henry, 12
Tabor
Muecke, Carl Wilhelm Ludwig, 5

Unitarian
Palmer, Thomas Fyshe, 2
Sinclaire, Frederick, 11
Walters, George Thomas, 12
CLERK
Anthon, Daniel Herbert, 7
Boxer, Walter Henry, 7
James, Henry Kerrison, 4
Kay, Alick Dudley*, 9
Lawson, William, 10
Murray, Robert William Felton Lathrop, 2
Suffolk, Owen Hargraves, 6
Taber, Thomas, 2
Tait, John Henry, 12
Ulrich, Theodore Friederick, 12
Vaux, James Hardy, 2
Verran, John Stanley*, 12
Wallis, William Dane, 12
Walsh, John Joseph, 6
COACH DRIVER
Devine, Edward, 4
COACH PROPRIETOR
Cawker, Thomas, 3
Chambers, James, 3
Clapp, Francis Boardman, 3
Cobb, Freeman, 3
Cox, John Edward, 1
Gormly, James*, 4
Hill, Henry John, 4
Hurley, John (1796-1882)*, 4
Liardet, Wilbraham Frederick Evelyn, 2
Page, Samuel, 2
Peck, John Murray, 5
Raine, John, 2
Robertson, Alexander William, 6
Rogers, Charles, 6
Rotton, Henry*, 6
Rutherford, James, 6
Thompson, John Willis, 12
Watson, George John, 6
Wiseman, Thomas, 12
COACHBUILDER
Cusack, John Joseph*, 8
Heales, Richard*, 4
McMillan, Samuel, 10
White, Daniel, 12
COLLECTOR
Andrews, Arthur, 7
Dixson, Sir William, 8
Glover, Charles Richmond John, 9
Lee, Alfred, 10
Mackaness, George, 10
Mitchell, David Scott, 5
Petherick, Edward Augustus, 5
Roberts, John Garibaldi, 11
COLONIAL SECRETARY
New South Wales
Goulburn, Frederick, 1
McLeay, Alexander, 2
Thomson, Sir Edward Deas, 2
Port Phillip
Lonsdale, William, 2
South Australia
Gouger, Robert, 1

Van Diemen's Land
Bicheno, James Ebenezer, 1
Burnett, John, 1
Chapman, Henry Samuel*, 3
Montagu, John, 2
Western Australia
Barlee, Sir Frederick Palgrave, 3
Broun, Peter Nicholas, 1
COLONIZER
Angas, George Fife*, 1
Bacon, Anthony, 1
Clifton, Marshall Waller, 3
Gouger, Robert, 1
Macqueen, Thomas Potter, 2
Peel, Thomas, 2
Rays, Marquis de, 6
Torrens, Robert, 2
Wakefield, Edward Gibbon, 2
COMMERCIAL TRAVELLER
Kenny, Thomas James Bede, 9
McCarthy, Lawrence Dominic, 10
COMMISSARIAT OFFICIAL
Allan, David, 1
Archer, Thomas (1790-1850), 1
Broughton, William, 1
Drennan, Frederick, 1
Fosbrook, Leonard, 1
Hull, George, 1
Laidley, James, 2
Lempriere, Thomas James, 2
Miller, Andrew, 2
Miller, George, 2
Palmer, John, 2
Parsons, Charles Octavius, 2
Walker, Thomas (1791-1861), 2
Wemyss, William, 2
Williamson, James, 2
Wilshire, James, 2
COMMUNITY LEADER
Benny, Susan Grace, 7
Dyett, Sir Gilbert Joseph Cullen, 8
Fairfax, Ruth Beatrice, 8
Fatnowna, John Kwailiu Abelfai, 8
Hoadley, Charles Archibald Brookes, 9
Sumsuma, 12
Warnes, Mary Jane, 12
Aboriginal
Arabanoo, 1
Barak, William, 3
Bennelong, 1
Biraban, 1
Bungaree, 1
Colebe, 1
Cooper, William, 8
Mondalmi, 10
Nanya, 10
Smith, Fanny Cochrane, 11
Tjangamarra, 12
Trugernanner, 6
Unaipon, David, 12
Wilson, Mark, 12
Yagan, 2
Chinese
Ah Mouy, Louis, 3

Cheong Cheok Hong, 3
Chin Kaw, 7
Lowe Kong Meng, 5
Way Lee, Yet Soo War, 12
Greek
Comino, John, 8
Freeleagus, Christy Kosmas, 8
Lucas, Antony John Jereos, 10
Irish
Dryer, Albert Thomas, 8
Jageurs, Morgan Peter, 9
O'Donnell, Nicholas Michael, 11
Italian
Baccarini, Antonio, 7
Vaccari, Gualtiero, 12
Japanese
Kashiwagi, Taira, 9
Jewish
Benjamin, Sir Benjamin*, 3
Cohen, Edward*, 3
Reading, Fanny, 11
Symonds, Saul, 12
Wynn, Samuel, 12
COMPANY CHAIRMAN
Angus, John Henry Smith, 7
Ayers, Sir Henry*, 3
Baillieu, Clive Latham, 7
Brown, Sir Harry Percy, 7
Bruce, Stanley Melbourne*, 7
Currie, Archibald, 3
Darling, Harold Gordon, 8
Ewan, James, 4
Fraser, Sir Colin, 8
Freeman, William Addison, 8
Fysh, Sir Wilmot Hudson, 8
Gordon, Sir Thomas Stewart*, 9
Gotch, John Speechly, 4
Grant, Charles William*, 9
Gray, George Wilkie*, 9
Grice, Sir John, 9
Grimwade, Edward Norton, 9
Grimwade, Harold William, 9
Grimwade, Sir Wilfrid Russell, 9
Harper, Charles Walter, 9
Haynes, Thomas Watson, 9
Higgins, Sir John Michael, 9
Holdsworth, Albert Armytage, 9
Hughes, Sir Thomas*, 9
Jones, Allan Murray, 9
Knox, Edward William, 9
Lee Steere, Sir Ernest Augustus, 10
McMaster, Sir Fergus, 10
Manifold, James Chester*, 10
Massie, Robert John Allwright, 10
Niall, James Mansfield, 11
Palfreyman, Achalen Woolliscroft, 11
Patterson, Gerald Leighton, 11
Pigdon, John, 5
Purcell, James, 11
Rankin, John, 11
Sanderson, Robert Fitzroy, 11
Sheldon, Sir Mark, 11
Stewart, Sir Alexander Anderson, 12
Swinburne, George*, 12

Taubman, Henry George, 12
Taylor, Patrick Thomson*, 12
Tewksbury, Alphonso Reed, 12
Theodore, Edward Granville*, 12
Vardon, Edward Charles*, 12
Wales, Sir Alexander George*, 12
Waley, Sir Frederick George, 12
Webster, Charles Ernest, 12
Weedon, Sir Henry*, 12
Welsby, Thomas*, 12
White, John*, 12
Winchcombe, Frederick Earle*, 12
Wormald, Joseph Dawson, 12
Young, Sir Walter James, 12
COMPANY DIRECTOR
Allen, Sir George Wigram*, 3
Archer, Robert Stubbs, 7
Baker, John*, 3
Balfour, James*, 3
Benn, John, 3
Bernacchi, Angelo Giulio Diego, 7
Blackwood, Arthur Ranken, 7
Blackwood, Robert Officer, 7
Blair, James, 1
Bonython, Sir John Lavington, 7
Brentnall, Frederick Thomas*, 3
Brewster, John Gray, 3
Brophy, Daniel*, 3
Bruce, Sir Wallace, 7
Buchanan, Benjamin, 3
Buckland, Sir Thomas, 7
Cain, William*, 3
Caird, George Sutherland, 3
Campbell, Alexander*, 3
Casey, Richard Gardiner*, 3
Clark, James William, 8
Clarke, Sir Francis Grenville*, 8
Cohen, Montague, 8
Cowlishaw, James*, 3
Cran, John, 8
Dixson, Sir William, 8
Drysdale, William, 4
Elliott, Robert Charles Dunlop*, 8
Farnell, James Squire*, 4
Forrest, Edward Barrow*, 8
Francis, James Goodall*, 4
Fraser, John Edward, 8
Frazer, John*, 4
Godfrey, Frederick Race*, 4
Grant, Alexander Charles, 9
Grant, Charles Henry*, 9
Green, William Herbert*, 9
Halfey, John*, 4
Hallen, Ambrose, 1
Hamilton, Edward William Terrick, 4
Hamilton, John (1834-1924)*, 4
Hinton, Howard, 9
Holden, John Rose, 1
Hughes, Frederic Godfrey, 9
Hutchinson, William, 1
Irving, Clark*, 4
Jamieson, William, 9
Jenner, Caleb Joshua*, 4
Kelly, Anthony Edwin Bowes, 9

Kelly, Sir George Dalziel, 9
Kelly, Thomas Herbert, 9
Kelly, Thomas Hussey, 5
Kemp, Charles, 2
King, Sir George Eccles Kelso, 9
Knox, Sir Robert Wilson, 9
Lamb, John de Villiers, 5
Lasseter, Henry Beauchamp, 5
Levien, Jonas Felix Australia*, 5
Longworth, William (1892-1969), 10
Luxton, Sir Harold Daniel*, 10
Lyons, Herbert William*, 10
Lyons, Thomas, 10
McBryde, Duncan Elphinstone*, 10
McDonald, George Roy William*, 10
Mackellar, Sir Charles Kinnaird*, 10
McLachlan, Charles, 2
McPhee, Sir John Cameron*, 10
Macqueen, Thomas Potter, 2
Marks, Theodore John, 10
Massy-Greene, Sir Walter*, 10
Metcalfe, Michael, 5
Milson, James (1814-1903), 2
Mitchell, William, 5
Morell, Sir Stephen Joseph, 10
Muecke, Hugo Carl Emil*, 10
Murphy, Peter*, 10
Neil, Edwin Lee, 10
Niall, Kenneth Mansfield, 11
Nimmo, John*, 5
Persse, De Burgh Fitzpatrick*, 5
Pinnock, James Denham*, 2
Raws, Sir William Lennon, 11
Reading, Sir Claude Hill, 11
Reid, John, 11
Robinson, Gerald Henry, 11
Robinson, Sir Thomas Bilbe, 11
Rounsevell, William Benjamin*, 11
Rowan, Andrew, 6
Salting, Severin Kanute, 2
Sandford, Sir James Wallace*, 11
Shadforth, Thomas, 2
Simpson, Edward Percy, 11
Smith, James MacCallum*, 11
Smith, Thomas Whistler*, 2
Smith, Tom Elder Barr, 11
Spence, John, 11
Strachan, Hugh Murray, 12
Strickland, William Henry John, 6
Syme, David York, 12
Symons, William John, 12
Templeton, William, 6
Tooth, Frederick, 6
Tweddle, Joseph Thornton, 12
Vicars, Sir William, 12
Walder, Sir Samuel Robert*, 12
Waterhouse, Gustavus Athol, 12
Watson, John Boyd, 6
Watson, John Christian*, 12
Watt, John Brown*, 6
Watt, Walter Oswald, 12
Webster, Edwin Herbert, 12
Willis, Joseph Scaife, 6
Wilson, John Thomas, 2

Wilson, Lachlan Chisholm, 12
Wilson, Sir Reginald Victor*, 12
Wittenoom, Sir Edward Charles*, 12
Wormald, Henry Percy, 12
Zeal, Sir William Austin*, 12
COMPANY MANAGER
Adey, Stephen, 1
Ainsworth, George Frederick, 7
Badger, Joseph Stillman, 7
Bell, Alexander Foulis, 7
Blackwood, James, 3
Braddon, Sir Henry Yule*, 7
Brown, John, 1
Carter, Arthur John, 7
Chapman, Edward Shirley, 7
Cleary, William James, 8
Clibborn, Thomas Strettel, 3
Conacher, Charles William, 8
Cottee, William Alfred, 3
Cowper, Sir Charles*, 3
Creswell, John, 8
Crick, Stanley Sadler, 8
Curr, Edward, 1
Davies, George Schoen, 4
Dawson, Robert, 1
Dunstan, William, 8
Elphinstone, Augustus Cecil*, 8
Fisk, Sir Ernest Thomas, 8
Fletcher, John William*, 8
Forsyth, James*, 8
Gepp, Sir Herbert William, 8
Gibson, James Alexander (1814-1860), 1
Giles, William, 1
Goldfinch, Sir Philip Henry Macarthur*, 9
Goldie, Alexander, 1
Grieve, Robert Cuthbert, 9
Harper, Robert Rainy, 9
Kemble, Francis, 2
King, Phillip Parker, 2
McColl, James Hiers*, 10
Macdonald, Benjamin Wickham, 10
McGaw, Andrew Kidd, 10
McLachlan, Charles, 2
McLaren, David, 2
Marks, Douglas Gray, 10
Morehead, Robert Archibald Alison, 2
Osborne, Henry William, 11
Perry, Stanley Wesley, 11
Ranclaud, Charles Mark, 11
Ross, Joseph Grafton, 6
Rowan, Frederic Charles, 11
Schwarz, Walter Leslie, 11
Smith, James William Norton*, 6
Stephens, Samuel, 2
Stuart, Athol Hugh, 12
Trouton, Frederick Henry, 6
Ward, Frederick Furner, 12
Watson, Charles Henry, 12
Wesché, Awdry Gordon, 12
Wheeler, John*, 12
Whitton, Ivo Harrington, 12
Wilson, Alexander William, 12
Wittenoom, Frederick Francis Burdett, 12

COMPANY SECRETARY
Aikenhead, James*, 1
Austin, Edward Arthur*, 7
Brazenor, William, 7
Breillat, Robert Graham, 3
Bright, Charles, 3
Henley, Frank Le Leu, 9
Hughes, Francis Augustus, 9
King, Sir George Eccles Kelso, 9
Knox, William*, 9
Meagher, Richard James, 10
Somerville, George Cattell, 12
Walpole, Herbert Reginald Robert
Seymour, 12
COMPANY SUPERINTENDENT
Gregson, Jesse, 4
Hodgson, Sir Arthur*, 4
Livingstone-Learmonth, Frederick Valiant
Cotton, 10
Merewether, Edward Christopher,
5
Parry, Sir William Edward, 2
COMPOSER, *see* Musician
CONCHOLOGIST, *see* Zoologist
CONDUCTOR, *see* Musician
CONSERVATIONIST
Crommelin, Minard Fannie, 8
Gooch, Walter, 9
Groom, Arthur, 9
Lewis, Fred, 10
CONSUL
Appel, George, 3
Williams, James Hartwell, 6
CONTRACTOR
Buckley, Maurice Vincent, 7
Governor, Jimmy, 9
Hall, Hayden Hezekiah, 4
James, David*, 9
Pearce, John, 11
Whelan, James Paul, 12
railway
Angus, James, 7
Bruce, John Vans Agnew, 3
Cain, William*, 3
Collier, Jenkin, 3
Fraser, Sir Simon*, 4
Higgins, Patrick*, 4
McNeil, Neil, 5
Munro, David, 5
O'Grady, Thomas, 5
Robb, John, 6
Smith, Henry Teesdale*, 11
Styles, James*, 12
CONVICT, *see* Transportee
CONVICT ADMINISTRATOR
Baylee, Pery, 1
Blackman, James (1792?-1868), 1
Booth, Charles O'Hara, 1
Clunie, James Oliphant, 1
Crowder, Thomas Ristol, 1
Divine, Nicholas, 1
Gunn, William, 1
Hampton, John Stephen, 1
Hely, Frederick Augustus, 1

Henderson, Sir Edmund Yeamans Walcott,
4
Hume, Andrew Hamilton, 1
Hutchinson, William, 1
Lord, Thomas Daunt, 2
Mason, Martin, 2
Menzies, Sir Charles, 2
Price, John Giles, 2
Slade, Ernest Augustus, 2
Spode, Josiah, 2
Woods, Roger Henry, 2
CO-OPERATIVE ADVOCATE
Dymock, David Lindsay, 4
Meares, Charles Edward Devenish, 10
Ross, John (1833-1920), 6
Wilson, Alexander William, 12
Wilson, David, 12
CRICKETER
Armstrong, Warwick Windridge, 7
Bannerman, Alexander, 3
Bannerman, Charles, 3
Barbour, Eric Pitty, 7
Bardsley, Warren, 7
Blackham, John McCarthy, 3
Bonnor, George, 3
Boyle, Henry Frederick, 3
Claxton, Norman, 8
Coates, Joseph, 3
Collins, Herbert Leslie, 8
Coningham, Arthur, 8
Cotter, Albert, 8
Darling, Joseph*, 8
Eady, Charles John*, 8
Garrett, Thomas William, 8
Giffen, George, 4
Gilbert, Edward, 9
Gregory, David William, 4
Gregory, Edward James, 4
Gregory, Jack Morrison, 9
Gregory, Sydney Edward, 4
Grimmett, Clarence, 9
Hill, Clement, 9
Iredale, Francis Adams, 9
Jackson, Archibald, 9
Jones, Ernest, 9
Kippax, Alan Falconer, 9
Laver, Frank Jonas, 10
Macartney, Charles George, 10
McCabe, Stanley Joseph, 10
McDonald, Edgar Arthur, 10
McDonnell, Percy Stanislaus, 5
Mailey, Alfred Arthur, 10
Mullagh, Johnny, 5
Murdoch, William Lloyd, 5
Noble, Montague Alfred, 11
Oldfield, William Albert Stanley, 11
Palmer, George Eugene, 5
Peden, Margaret Elizabeth Maynard, 11
Poidevin, Leslie Oswald Sheridan, 11
Ransford, Vernon Seymour, 11
Richardson, Victor York, 11
Ryder, John, 11
Saunders, John Victor, 11
Scott, Henry James Herbert, 6

Spofforth, Frederick Robert, 6
Trott, Albert Edwin, 12
Trott, George Henry Stevens, 12
Trumble, Hugh, 12
Trumper, Victor Thomas, 12
Turner, Charles Thomas Biass, 6
Wardill, Richard Wilson, 6
Wills, Thomas Wentworth Spencer, 6
Woodfull, William Maldon, 12
Worrall, John, 12
CRIMINAL, *see also* Bushranger;
Murderer; Prostitute; Transportee
Coates, James, 8
Crouch, James Joseph, 3
Dean, George, 8
Devine, Matilda, 8
Leigh, Kathleeen Mary Josephine, 10
Miles, Beatrice, 10
O'Farrell, Henry James, 5
Orton, Arthur, 5
Taylor, Joseph Leslie Theodore, 12
Williams, Francis, 2
CRITIC
Buchanan, David*, 3
Burdett, Basil, 7
Carrington, Francis Thomas Dean, 3
Colquhoun, Alexander, 8
Dickinson, Sidney, 8
Griffen Foley, James Joseph, 9
Kellow, Henry Arthur, 9
Lawlor, Adrian, 10
Lindsay, Sir Lionel Arthur, 10
MacDonald, James Stuart, 10
Moore, William George, 10
Neild, James Edward, 5
Palmer, Janet Gertrude, 11
Shore, Arnold Joseph Victor, 11
Sinnett, Frederick, 6
Smythe, Carlyle Greenwood, 12
Stephens, Alfred George, 12
Stevens, Bertram William Mathyson
  Francis, 12
Tate, Henry, 12
Thompson, Gerald Marr, 12
Tomholt, Sydney John, 12
Turner, Walter James Redfern, 12
Williams, William Henry, 12
CRYPTOGRAPHER
Wheatley, Frederick William, 12
CYCLIST
Birtles, Francis Edwin, 7
Broadbent, George Robert, 7
Maddock, Sarah, 10
Pearson, Joseph, 11
Richardson, Arthur Charles Jeston, 11
Spears, Robert Adam, 12
DANCE TEACHER
Brenan, Jennie Frances, 7
Stewart, Eleanor Charlotte, 12
DANCER
Montez, Lola, 5
Young, Eliza, 6
DECORATOR
Smith, William Forgan*, 11

DENTIST
Belisario, John, 3
Davidson, William St John Stevens, 8
Fitzsimons, William Robert*, 8
Hart, William Ewart, 9
Iliffe, John, 9
Jordan, Henry*, 4
Lawrence, Gordon Ord, 10
Mills, Arthur James, 10
Noble, Montague Alfred, 11
Olden, Arthur Charles Niquet, 11
Peach, Henry, 11
Potts, Henry William, 11
Praed, Annie, 11
Rodway, Leonard, 11
Stevens, Horace Ernest, 12
Tuckfield, William John, 12
Watson, William Walker Russell, 12
Wilson, James Alexander Campbell, 12
DESIGNER
Buring, Adolph Wilhelm Rudolph, 3
Card, Mary, 7
Frater, William, 8
Gibson, Sir Robert, 8
Wager, Rhoda, 12
DIARIST
Boyes, George Thomas William Blamey, 1
Clark, Ralph, 1
Dawbin, Annie Maria, 1
Knopwood, Robert, 2
Lempriere, Thomas James, 2
McCrae, Georgiana Huntly, 2
Moore, George Fletcher, 2
Southwell, Daniel, 2
DIPLOMAT, *see also* Consul
Brigden, James Bristock, 7
Bruce, Stanley Melbourne*, 7
Eggleston, Sir Frederic William, 8
Fuhrman, Osmond Charles William, 8
Glasgow, Sir Thomas William*, 9
Hodgson, William Roy, 9
Laporte, François Louis Nompar de
  Caumont, 5
Latham, Sir John Greig*, 10
Leeper, Alexander Wigram Allen, 10
Reid, Sir George Houstoun*, 11
Robinson, William Sydney, 11
Simonov, Peter, 11
DISTILLER
Browne, Hugh Junor, 3
Cooper, Robert, 1
De Gillern, William, 1
Lowes, Thomas Yardley, 2
Underwood, James, 2
DOG-BREEDER
Hall, Thomas Simpson, 4
Kaleski, Robert Lucian Stanislaus, 9
Moore, James Lorenzo, 10
Quinn, John, 11
DOG RACER
Gardener, Alfred Henry, 4
DOMESTIC SERVANT
Catchpole, Margaret, 1
Smith, Fanny Cochrane, 11

White, Myrtle Rose, 12
DRAPER
Buckley, Mars, 3
Cain, Sir Jonathon Robert, 7
Chisholm, Alexander, 7
Cooper, Thomas*, 3
Dickson, James, 8
East, Hubert, 8
East, Hubert Fraser, 8
Foy, Mark, 4
Hemmant, William*, 4
Hitchcock, Walter Michelmore, 4
Hordern, Anthony (1819-1876), 4
Kingsford, Richard Ash*, 5
Latimer, William Fleming*, 10
Law, Sydney James, 10
Lewis, David Edward, 10
Lucas, Sir Edward*, 10
Lyell, Andrew*, 5
McDonnell, Francis*, 10
Marshall, James Waddell, 5
Moore, Charles (1820-1895)*, 5
Moubray, Thomas, 5
Murray, David*, 5
O'Shanassy, Sir John*, 5
Parkin, William*, 5
Payne, Herbert James Mockford*, 11
Pearson, Joseph, 11
Riley, Alban Joseph*, 6
Smyth, Bridgetena, 12
Soundy, Sir John*, 12
Stewart, Alexander, 12
Terry, William Henry, 6
Walker, George Washington, 2
Webb, Edmund*, 6
DRAUGHTSMAN
Goldstein, Jacob Robert Yannasch, 9
Grant, Douglas, 9
DROVER
Bonney, Charles*, 3
Hawdon, Joseph, 1
Laver, Charles William, 10
Ross, John (1817-1903), 6
Uhr, Wentworth D'Arcy, 6
Ward, Frederick, 6
ECCENTRIC
Chidley, William James, 7
Donnithorne, Eliza Emily, 4
Miles, Beatrice, 10
Stace, Arthur Malcolm, 12
ECONOMIST
Benham, Frederic Charles Courtenay, 7
Brigden, James Bristock, 7
Duckworth, Arthur, 8
Dyason, Edward Clarence Evelyn, 8
Giblin, Lyndhurst Falkiner*, 8
Hearn, William Edward*, 4
Heaton, Herbert, 9
Hirsch, Maximilian*, 9
Irvine, Robert Francis, 9
Jauncey, Leslie Cyril, 9
Jevons, William Stanley, 4
McDougall, Frank Lidgett, 10
Mills, Richard Charles, 10

Pinschof, Carl Ludwig, 11
Shann, Edward Owen Giblin, 11
Torrens, Robert, 2
Wainwright, John William, 12
EDITOR, *see also* Newspaper editor
Auricht, Johann Christian, 3
Fletcher, Joseph James, 8
Kentish, Nathaniel Lipscomb, 2
Pearse, Albert William, 11
EDUCATIONIST, *see also* School
principal; Teacher; Technical educator
Behan, Sir John Clifford Valentine, 7
Mills, Richard Charles, 10
New South Wales
Atkinson, Meredith, 7
Benjamin, Sophia, 7
Board, Peter, 7
Bridges, Frederick, 3
Carmichael, Henry, 1
Coburn, Isaac, 3
Cole, Percival Richard, 8
Cramp, Karl Reginald, 8
Huffer, John, 4
Johnson, Edwin, 4
Macdonald, Louisa, 10
McIntyre, William (1830-1911), 5
Mackaness, George, 10
Mackie, Alexander, 10
Morris, Robert Newton, 5
Newling, Cecil Bede, 11
Potts, Henry William, 11
Reddall, Thomas, 2
Rogers, John William Foster*, 6
Sharp, William Hey, 11
Simpson, Martha Margaret Mildred, 11
Smith, Stephen Henry, 11
Spaull, George Thomas, 12
Stewart, David, 12
Turner, John William, 12
West, Winifred Mary, 12
Wilkins, William, 6
Queensland
Anderson, John Gerard, 3
Barrett, John Joseph, 3
Crawford, Emma, 8
Edwards, Lewis David, 8
Ewart, David, 4
MacDonnell, Randal, 5
McKenna, Bernard (Joseph), 10
Roe, Reginald Heber, 11
Shirley, John, 11
South Australia
Adey, William James, 7
Grasby, William Catton, 9
Hartley, John Anderson, 4
Longmore, Lydia, 10
McCoy, William Taylor, 10
Miethke, Adelaide Laetitia, 10
Muecke, Carl Wilhelm Ludwig, 5
Neale, William Lewis, 10
Schulz, Adolf John, 11
Tenison-Woods, Julian Edmund, 6
Watson, Phebe Naomi, 12
Williams, Alfred, 12

Wyatt, William, 2
Tasmania
Arnold, Thomas, 1
Brooks, George Vickery, 7
Johnson, John Andrew, 9
Kane, Benjamin Francis, 5
McCoy, William Taylor, 10
Meston, Archibald Lawrence, 10
Parker, Henry Thomas, 11
Rowntree, Amy, 11
Rule, James, 6
Stephens, Thomas, 6
Turner, Dora Jeannette, 12
Victoria
Bell, Barbara, 7
Benson, Louisa, 7
Brodribb, Thomas, 3
Brown, Gilbert Wilson, 3
Budd, Richard Hale, 3
Byatt, John, 7
Campbell, Colin*, 3
Carew-Smyth, Ponsonby May, 7
Corrigan, James, 3
Davitt, Arthur, 4
Flynn, Julia Theresa, 8
Forbes, Catherine Ellen, 8
Gladman, Frederick John, 4
Hansen, Martin Peter, 9
Leeper, Alexander, 10
Long, Charles Richard, 10
MacFarland, Sir John Henry, 10
McLaren, Samuel Gilfillan, 10
McRae, James, 10
Mulquin, Katherine, 10
O'Driscoll, Charles Xavier, 11
Pearson, Charles Henry*, 5
Pye, Emmeline, 11
Rix, Henry Finch, 11
Robertson, John, 11
Robertson, Margery Fraser, 11
Rusden, George William, 6
Seitz, John Arnold, 11
Smyth, John, 12
Sugden, Edward Holdsworth, 12
Tate, Frank, 12
Thompson, John Low, 6
Topp, Charles Alfred, 6
Treacy, Patrick Ambrose, 6
Venables, Henry Pares, 6
Wrigley, Leslie James, 12
Western Australia
Andrews, Cecil Rollo Paton, 7
Jackson, Sir Cyril, 9
Shearer, David, 6
ELECTORAL REFORMER
Nanson, Edward John, 10
Young, Sarah Jane, 12
ELECTRICIAN
Smith, William Henry Laird*, 11
EMBRYOLOGIST, *see* Zoologist
EMPLOYMENT AGENT
Benny, Susan Grace, 7
Seager, Alexandrine, 11
Tracey, Eliza, 12

ENGINEER, *see also* Mine engineer
Ainsworth, Alfred Bower, 7
Alcock, Alfred Upton, 7
Allan, Percy, 7
Allen, Alfred*, 3
Allen, Joseph Francis*, 7
Archer, John Lee, 1
Arnot, Arthur James, 7
Ashcroft, Edgar Arthur, 7
Austin, Baron Herbert, 3
Babbage, Benjamin Herschel*, 3
Badger, Joseph Stillman, 7
Bagot, Robert Cooper, 3
Bainton, John Richard, 7
Baird, Adam, 7
Ball, Richard Thomas*, 7
Ballard, Robert, 3
Balsillie, John Graeme, 7
Barker, Thomas*, 1
Barney, George, 1
Barraclough, Sir Samuel Henry Egerton, 7
Barrallier, Francis Luis, 1
Bell, Thomas, 1
Bennet, David, 3
Bennett, William Christopher, 3
Berry, William, 7
Blackburn, James, 1
Blakey, Othman Frank, 7
Boothby, Benjamin, 3
Braché, Jacob, 3
Bradfield, John Job Crew, 7
Brady, Alfred Barton, 7
Brady, Joseph, 3
Brennan, Louis, 3
Brown, Sir Harry Percy, 7
Bruce, John Leck, 7
Burn, Alan, 7
Busby, John, 1
Butters, Sir John Henry, 7
Calder, William, 7
Campbell, Edward (1883-1944), 7
Campbell, Frederick Alexander, 7
Carter, Herbert Gordon, 7
Catani, Carlo Giorgio Domenico Enrico, 7
Chaffey, George, 7
Chapman, Sir Robert William, 7
Charleston, David Morley*, 7
Checchi, Ettore, 7
Cheyne, Alexander, 1
Chinn, Henry, 7
Clark, Alexander Russell, 1
Clogstoun, Henry Oliver, 8
Close, Edward Charles, 1
Coane, John Montgomery, 8
Combes, Edward*, 3
Coode, Sir John, 3
Cook, Solomon, 3
Coote, William, 3
Corbould, William Henry, 8
Corby, John McKenzie, 8
Corin, William, 8
Corlette, James Montagu Christian, 8
Cotton, Hugh Calveley, 1
Cracknell, Edward Charles, 3

Cullen, Edward Alexander Ernest, 8
Currie, Sir (Henry) Alan, 8
Dalgleish, Daniel Cameron*, 4
David, Charles St John, 8
Davidson, William, 8
Davis, Joseph, 8
Dawes, William, 1
Deane, Henry, 8
De Burgh, Ernest Macartney, 8
Degraves, Peter, 1
De Mole, Lancelot Eldin, 8
Derry, John Dickson, 4
Dethridge, John Stewart, 8
Dickson, John, 1
Doyne, William Thomas, 4
Druitt, George, 1
Duigan, John Robertson, 8
Dumaresq, William John*, 1
Duncan, George Smith, 4
Edgell, Robert Gordon, 8
Evans, Daniel Edward, 8
Falconer, William Rose, 4
Fisk, Sir Ernest Thomas, 8
Flegg, Henry, 8
Forwood, Walter Weech, 4
Fowler, Thomas Walker, 8
Franki, James Peter, 8
Fraser, Sir Malcolm*, 4
Freeling, Sir Arthur Henry, 4
Garrard, Jacob*, 4
Geake, William Henry Gregory, 8
George, William James*, 8
Gibson, Alexander James, 8
Goodman, Sir William George Toop, 9
Gordon, George, 4
Grant, Charles Henry*, 9
Griffiths, John Alfred, 9
Halligan, Gerald Harnett, 9
Hancock, William John, 9
Harper, Herbert Reah, 9
Harricks, Dudley Francis John, 9
Hawken, Roger William Hercules, 9
Henderson, John Baillie, 4
Herman, Hyman, 9
Hickson, Robert Rowan Purdon, 4
Higinbotham, Thomas, 4
Hill, Thomas, 9
Hobler, George Alexander, 9
Hudson, Henry, 4
Hunt, Philip Charles Holmes, 9
Jackson, Clements Frederick Vivian, 9
Johns, Peter, 4
Jones, Leslie John Roberts, 9
Julius, Sir George Alfred, 9
Kauper, Henry Alexis, 9
Kay, William Porden, 2
Kayser, Heinrich Wilhelm Ferdinand, 5
Keane, Edward Vivien Harvey*, 5
Kelsall, Roger, 2
Kennedy, Colin, 9
Kenyon, Alfred Stephen, 9
Kernot, Maurice Edwin, 9
Kernot, Wilfred Noyce, 9
Kernot, William Charles, 5

Kingston, Sir George Strickland*, 2
Kneeshaw, Frederick Percival*, 9
Krausé, Ferdinand Moritz, 5
Lahey, Romeo Watkins, 9
Lee, John Robert*, 10
Leighton, Arthur Edgar, 10
Lennox, David, 2
Lewis, Edward Powell, 10
Lynch, Arthur Alfred, 10
Lynch, Patrick Joseph*, 10
McClelland, David John, 10
McCormack, William Thomas
  Bartholomew, 10
McDonald, Arthur Stephen, 10
McGowan, Samuel Walker, 5
Mackay, John Hilton, 10
Mais, Henry Coathupe, 5
Maley, John Stephen, 5
Mansergh, James, 5
Martindale, Ben Hay, 5
Massie, Robert John Allwright, 10
Mault, Alfred, 5
May, Frederick, 5
Mead, Elwood, 10
Mehaffey, Maurice William, 10
Michell, Anthony George Maldon, 10
Millen, John Dunlop, 10
Monash, Sir John, 10
Moncrieff, Alexander Bain, 10
Moriarty, Edward Orpen, 5
Munro, David, 5
Murdoch, Thomas (1876-1961), 10
Murphy, Arthur William, 10
Murray, Stuart, 5
Newbigin, William Johnstone, 11
Newell, Hugh Hamilton, 11
Nicolle, Eugène Dominique, 5
O'Connor, Charles Yelverton, 11
O'Neil, Charles Gordon, 5
Ovens, John, 2
Owen, Percy Thomas, 11
Parrott, Thomas Samuel, 11
Pasley, Charles, 5
Patterson, Robert Charles, 11
Payne, Henry, 11
Percival, Edgar Wikner, 11
Perry, Stanley Llewellyn, 11
Phillips, Herbert Peter, 11
Ramsbotham, Joshua Fielden, 11
Reveley, Henry Willey, 2
Ritchie, Edgar Gowar, 11
Russell, John Peter, 11
Ruwolt, Charles Ernest, 11
Sachse, Arthur Otto*, 11
Scott, William Henry, 11
Scratchley, Sir Peter Henry, 6
Selfe, Norman, 6
Shaw, Ebenezer, 11
Shaw, William Henry, 6
Shellshear, Walter, 6
Shiers, Walter Henry, 11
Shoobridge, William Ebenezer*, 11
Smith, Alexander Kennedy*, 6
Somerville, William, 12

Stewart, Sir Alexander Anderson, 12
Stone, William, 12
Struth, John, 2
Stuart, Herbert Akroyd, 12
Styles, James*, 12
Swain, Herbert John, 12
Swinburne, George*, 12
Thompson, David (1865-1916), 12
Thompson, James, 12
Thomson, Herbert, 12
Thomson, James Alexander, 2
Thow, William, 12
Threlfall, Sir Richard, 12
Thwaites, William, 12
Todd, Sir Charles, 6
Traeger, Alfred Hermann, 12
Victor, James Conway, 2
Voigt, Emil Robert, 12
Wade, Leslie Augustus Burton, 12
Wainwright, William Edward, 12
Walsh, Henry Deane, 12
Walton, Thomas Utrick, 12
Warren, William Henry, 6
Watson, Stanley Holm, 12
Whitton, John, 6
Woods, John*, 6
Wright, John Arthur*, 12
Zeal, Sir William Austin*, 12

ENTERTAINER, see also Actor; Singer
Edwards, George, 8
Farber, Henry Christian, 8
Hanna, George Patrick, 9
Latham, Sir Charles George*, 10
Lawrence, Charles Edward, 10
Lumsdaine, John Sinclair, 10
Rene, Roy, 11
Rickards, Harry, 11
Sharman, James, 11
Skuthorp(e), Lancelot Albert, 11
Sorlie, George Brown, 12
Tauchert, Arthur Michael, 12
Thatcher, Charles Robert, 6
Vaude, Charlie, 12
Wallace, George Stevenson, 12
Wirth, Mary Elizabeth Victoria, 12
Wirth, May Emmeline, 12
Young, Charles Frederick Horace Frisby, 6

ENTERTAINMENT ENTREPRENEUR
Anderson, William, 7
Bailey, Albert Edward, 7
Baker, Reginald Leslie, 7
Carroll, Daniel Joseph, 7
Carroll, Edward John, 7
Cawthorne, Charles Witto-Witto, 7
Coppin, George Selth*, 3
Doyle, Stuart Frank, 8
Fuller, Sir Benjamin John, 8
Fuller, John (1879-1959), 8
Green, Daniel Cooper, 9
Hill, William Duguid, 9
Lyster, William Saurin, 5
McCann, Bernard Aloysius, 10
McIntosh, Hugh Donald*, 10

MacMahon, Charles, 10
MacMahon, James, 10
Naylor, Rupert Theodore, 10
Perry, Orizaba George, 11
Perry, Reginald Harry, 11
Smythe, Robert Sparrow, 12
Sorlie, George Brown, 12
Spencer, Cosens, 12
Tait, Charles, 12
Tait, Edward Joseph, 12
Tait, Sir Frank Samuel, 12
Tait, James Nevin, 12
Tait, John Henry, 12
Tallis, Sir George, 12
Thring, Francis William, 12
Turnbull, Ernest, 12
Ward, Hugh Joseph, 12
Wren, John, 12

ENTOMOLOGIST
Carter, Herbert James, 7
Davidson, James, 8
Ferguson, Eustace William, 8
French, Charles, 8
French, Charles Hamilton, 8
Froggatt, Walter Wilson, 8
Hamlyn-Harris, Ronald, 9
Kershaw, James Andrew, 9
Lea, Arthur Mills, 10
Littler, Frank Mervyn, 10
McKeown, Keith Collingwood, 10
McLeay, Alexander, 2
Masters, George, 5
Musgrave, Anthony, 10
Newman, Leslie John William, 11
Rayment, Percy Tarlton, 11
Scott, Alexander Walker*, 6
Sloane, Thomas Gibson, 11
Thompson, Edward Henry, 12
Tillyard, Robin John, 12
Tryon, Henry, 12
Turner, Alfred Jefferis, 12
Waterhouse, Gustavus Athol, 12

EPIDEMIOLOGIST
Thompson, John Ashburton, 12
Thomson, William, 6

ESTATE AGENT
Anderson, John Wilson, 3
Ashby, Edwin, 7
Baillieu, William Lawrence*, 7
Beazley, William David*, 7
Bruntnell, Albert*, 7
Burke, Thomas Michael, 7
Collicott, John Thomas, 1
Crews, John Branscombe*, 3
Cribb, Robert*, 3
Dickson, Sir James Robert*, 8
Halloran, Henry Ferdinand, 9
Hawkins, Herbert Middleton*, 9
Herring, Sydney Charles Edgar, 9
Ievers, George Hawkins, 4
Ievers, William (1818-1901), 4
Ievers, William (1839-1895)*, 4
Illingworth, Frederick*, 9
Kirton, Joseph William*, 9

Knipe, John Hanlon, 5
Lang, John Thomas*, 9
Langridge, George David*, 5
Law, Sydney James, 10
Lewis, Charles Ferris, 5
Patterson, Sir James Brown*, 5
Pratt, Joseph Major*, 11
Ramsay, John, 11
Rickard, Sir Arthur, 11
Ryan, Thomas*, 11
St Clair, William Howard, 11
Scherk, Theodor Johannes*, 11
Smart, Thomas Ware*, 6
Stanton, Richard Patrick Joseph, 12
Weaver, Reginald Walter Darcy*, 12
ETHNOGRAPHER, *see* Anthropologist
ETHNOLOGIST, *see* Anthropologist
EUGENICIST
Goodisson, Lillie Elizabeth, 9
Piddington, Marion Louisa, 11
EVANGELIST, *see* Preacher
EXPLORER
Allan, James Thomas, 3
Allingham, Christopher, 3
Anderson, Samuel, 1
Babbage, Benjamin Herschel*, 3
Barker, Collet, 1
Barrallier, Francis Luis, 1
Bass, George, 1
Becker, Ludwig, 3
Bell, Archibald (1804–1883)*, 1
Bellingshausen, Faddei Faddeevich, 1
Bernacchi, Louis Charles, 7
Bevan, Theodore Francis, 3
Bishop, Peter, 1
Blackman, James (1792?–1868), 1
Blaxland, Gregory, 1
Blosseville, Jules Poret de, 1
Borchgrevink, Carsten Egeberg, 7
Brown, Maitland*, 3
Browne, John Harris, 3
Bruny D'Entrecasteaux, Joseph-Antoine
  Raymond, 1
Buchanan, Nathaniel, 3
Burke, Robert O'Hara, 3
Burnett, James Charles, 3
Calvert, Albert Frederick, 7
Calvert, James Snowden, 3
Carnegie, David Wynford, 7
Carr-Boyd, William Henry, 3
Carron, William, 3
Cook, James, 1
Cunningham, Allan, 1
D'Albertis, Luigi Maria, 4
Dalrymple, George Augustus Frederick
  Elphinstone*, 4
Dampier, William, 1
Darke, John Charles, 1
Davis, John King, 8
Dempster, Andrew*, 4
Dempster, Charles Edward*, 4
Douglas, Alexander Douglas, 4
Drake-Brockman, Frederick Slade, 8
Elsey, Joseph Ravenscroft, 4

Eyre, Edward John, 1
Favenc, Ernest, 4
Flinders, Matthew, 1
Forbes, Henry Ogg, 4
Forrest, Alexander*, 8
Forrest, Sir John*, 8
Gilbert, John, 1
Giles, Ernest, 4
Gosse, William Christie, 4
Gregory, Sir Augustus Charles, 4
Gregory, John Walter, 9
Grey, Sir George, 1
Hacking, Henry, 1
Hall, William Shakespeare, 4
Hann, Frank Hugh, 4
Hann, William, 4
Hayes, Sir John, 1
Hellyer, Henry, 1
Hely, Hovenden*, 4
Henry, Ernest, 4
Hides, Jack Gordon, 9
Hoadley, Charles Archibald Brookes, 9
Hobbs, James, 1
Hodgkinson, William Oswald*, 4
Hodgson, Christopher Pemberton, 4
Hooley, Edward Timothy*, 4
Houtman, Frederick de, 1
Hovell, William Hilton, 1
Howitt, Alfred William, 4
Hume, Hamilton, 1
Hunt, Charles Cooke, 4
Jack, Robert Logan, 4
Jackey Jackey, 2
Janssen, Willem, 2
Johnstone, Robert Arthur, 4
Jorgenson, Jorgen, 2
Kennedy, Edmund Besley Court, 2
King, John (1841–1872), 5
Landsborough, William, 5
La Pérouse, Jean-François de Galaup, 2
Lawson, William, 2
Laycock, Thomas (1786?–1823), 2
Lazarev, Mikhail Petrovich, 2
Leahy, Michael James, 10
Leichhardt, Friedrich Wilhelm Ludwig, 2
Lindsay, David, 10
Logan, Patrick, 2
McIntyre, Duncan, 5
McKay, Alexander, 2
Mackay, Donald George, 10
Mackay, John, 5
McKinlay, John, 5
Macleay, Sir George*, 2
McMillan, Angus*, 2
Madigan, Cecil Thomas, 10
Mann, John Frederick, 5
Mawson, Sir Douglas, 10
Meehan, James, 2
Meston, Archibald*, 5
Mikluho-Maklai, Nicholai Nicholaievich, 5
Mitchell, Sir Thomas Livingstone, 2
Moore, Thomas Bather, 10
Moresby, John, 5
Morton, William Lockhart, 5

Moyes, Morton Henry, 10
Murray, John, 2
O'Hea, Timothy, 5
Oxley, John Joseph William Molesworth, 2
Palmerston, Christie, 5
Péron, François, 2
Petrie, Thomas, 5
Quiros, Pedro Fernandez de, 2
Roe, John Septimus, 2
Roper, John, 6
Ross, John (1817-1903), 6
Russell, Henry Stuart, 2
Rymill, John Riddoch, 11
Scott, James (1810-1884), 2
Scott, James Reid*, 6
Smith, James (1827-1897)*, 6
Stapylton, Granville William Chetwynd, 2
Stokes, John Lort, 2
Strachan, John, 6
Strzelecki, Sir Paul Edmund de, 2
Stuart, John McDouall, 6
Sturt, Charles, 2
Tasman, Abel Janszoon, 2
Throsby, Charles, 2
Tietkens, William Harry, 6
Torres, Luis Vaez de, 2
Turner, Alfred Allatson, 6
Vlamingh, Willem de, 2
Warburton, Peter Egerton, 6
Warby, John, 2
Wedge, John Helder*, 2
Wells, Lawrence Allen, 12
Wentworth, William Charles*, 2
Wild(e), Joseph, 2
Wilkins, Sir George Hubert, 12
Wills, William John, 6
Wilson, John, 2
Windich, Tommy, 6
Wylie, 2
Yuranigh, 2

EXPORTER
Crompton, Joseph, 3
Darling, John (1831-1905)*, 4
Livingston, Thomas*, 10
Love, James Simpson, 10
Reilly, Joseph Thomas, 11

meat
Angliss, Sir William Charles, 7
Armytage, Frederick William, 3
Baynes, Harry, 7
Collins, Robert, 3
Collins, Robert Martin, 3
Cooke, John, 8
Cox, Sir Edward John Owen*, 8
Cramsie, John Boyd, 8
Deane, John Horace, 8
Elder, Sir James Alexander Mackenzie, 8
Forrest, William*, 8
McIlwraith, Andrew, 10
Playfair, Thomas Alfred (Creer) John*, 11

FACTORY INSPECTOR
Cuthbertson, Margaret Gardiner, 8
Duncan, Annie Jane, 8
Levey, James Alfred, 10

Ord, Harrison, 11
Scobie, Grace Locke, 11
Zadow, Christiane Susanne Augustine, 12

FARMER, *see also* Selector

King Island
Crowe, Robert, 8

New South Wales
Allman, Francis, 1
Anderson, Henry Charles Lennox, 7
Ardill, George Edward (1889-1964)*, 7
Arndell, Thomas, 1
Atkinson, James, 1
Bell, Archibald (1804-1883)*, 1
Berry, David, 3
Blackman, James (1792?-1868), 1
Bowen, George Meares Countess, 1
Bowman, John, 1
Brabyn, John, 1
Broinowski, Gracius Joseph, 3
Brunskill, Anthony, 7
Buckley, Alexander Henry, 7
Bunker, Eber, 1
Buttenshaw, Ernest Albert*, 7
Chaffey, Frank Augustus*, 7
Charles, Samuel*, 3
Clarke, Henry*, 3
Cowper, Sir Charles*, 3
Crossley, George, 1
Cunneen, James Augustine*, 3
Davies, Arthur, 1
Dodd, Henry Edward, 1
Drummond, David Henry*, 8
Dymock, David Lindsay, 4
Elliott, (William) Edward, 1
Evans, George William, 1
Everingham, Matthew James, 1
Faithful, William, 1
Field, Ernest, 8
Fuller, Colin Dunmore, 8
Gerard, Edwin Field, 8
Gibson, Robert, 8
Hardie, John Jackson, 9
Harris, John (1754-1838), 1
Hawkins, Thomas Fitzherbert, 1
Holt, Joseph, 1
Howe, William, 1
Jephcott, Sydney Wheeler, 9
Johnston, George (1764-1823), 2
Johnston, George (1790-1820), 2
Kennerley, Alfred*, 5
Kent, Thomas, 2
Kidd, John*, 5
Larra, James, 2
Ledger, Charles, 5
Lee, John Robert*, 10
Legge, James Gordon, 10
McIntyre, William (1830-1911), 5
Marks, John*, 5
Marsden, Samuel, 2
Mein, James, 2
Milson, James (1783-1872), 2
Moore, Thomas, 2
Morgan, Molly, 2

Nock, Horace Keyworth*, 11
Oakes, Francis, 2
Powell, Edward, 2
Ranken, George, 2
Rose, Thomas (1749?-1833), 2
Rouse, Richard, 2
Ruse, James, 2
Schaffer, Philip, 2
Scott, Alexander Walker*, 6
Skirving, William, 2
Squire, James, 2
Suttor, George, 2
Thompson, Andrew, 2
Thorby, Harold Victor Campbell*, 12
Tom, William, 2
Townsend, Alfred Richard, 12
Townson, Robert, 2
Verge, John, 2
Vincent, James, 12
Viner, William Samuel, 12
Wetherspoon, John*, 12
Williamson, James, 2
Wilson, Thomas Braidwood, 2
Winder, Thomas White Melville, 2
Wyndham, George, 2
Yabsley, William, 6

Norfolk Island
Stanfield, Daniel (d.1826), 2
Tims, Martin, 2

Queensland
Appel, John George*, 7
Arnold, Thomas Francis, 7
Bell, Bertram Charles, 7
Boyd, William Alexander Jenyns, 7
Dalziel, Henry, 8
Davis, Arthur Hoey, 8
Gordon, Bernard Sidney, 9
Harry, Gilbert, 9
Lawton, Thomas, 10
McConnel, David Cannon, 5
Milne, John Alexander, 10
Moore, Arthur Edward*, 10
O'Reilly, Alfonso Bernard, 11
Paget, Walter Trueman*, 11
Postle, Arthur Benjamin, 11
Purcell, James, 11
Roberts, James Henry Cecil*, 11
Soutter, Richard Ernest, 12
Stapleton, Claude Augustine, 12
Tardent, Henry Alexis, 12
Thomas, Lewis*, 6
Ziesemer, Friedrich Wilhelm Ernst, 12
Ziesemer, Theodor Martin Peter, 12

South Australia
Angus, William*, 7
Buddicom, Robert Arthur, 7
Bull, John Wrathall, 1
Copley, William*, 8
Hack, John Barton, 1
Hannaford, George, 9
Hardy, Arthur*, 4
Howe, James Henderson*, 9
Krichauf, Friedrich Eduard Heinrich
 Wulf*, 5

Livingston, John*, 10
Lyons, Herbert William*, 10
Mitchell, Thomas, 10
O'Loughlin, Laurence Theodore*,
 11
Pearce, John, 11
Rymill, John Riddoch, 11

Tasmania
Amos, Adam, 1
Archer, Joseph, 1
Archer, Thomas (1790-1850), 1
Armytage, George, 1
Bartley, Theodore Bryant, 1
Batman, John, 1
Belbin, James, 1
Bethune, Frank Pogson, 7
Bisdee, Edward*, 1
Bisdee, John, 1
Bisdee, John Hutton, 7
Bryan, William, 1
Cameron, Donald Norman*, 7
Cotton, Francis, 1
Cronin, Bernard Charles, 8
Crouch, George Stanton, 3
Dadson, Leslie, 8
De Gillern, William, 1
Dry, Sir Richard*, 1
Fenton, James, 4
Gatenby, Andrew, 1
Gill, Henry Horatio*, 4
Goldie, Alexander, 1
Gordon, James, 1
Guest, George, 1
Gunning, George Weston, 1
Harrap, Alfred, 4
Hayes, John Blyth*, 9
Kearney, William, 2
Lambe, David, 2
Lascelles, Thomas Allen, 2
Lee, Sir Walter Henry*, 10
Lillico, Sir Alexander*, 10
McCarty, Denis, 2
McKay, Alexander, 2
Maclanachan, James*, 5
Massey, Thomas, 2
Mather, Robert, 2
Maum, William James, 2
Meredith, George, 2
Murdoch, James, 2
O'Reilly, Christopher*, 5
Pitt, Richard, 2
Reibey, Thomas*, 6
Robertson, Gilbert, 2
Rose, David, 2
Shoobridge, William, 2
Smith, James (1827-1897)*, 6
Smith, William Henry Laird*, 11
Stanfield, Daniel (d.1856), 2
Statton, Percy Clyde, 12
Taylor, George, 2
Terry, John, 2
Wardlaw, Alan Lindsay*, 12
Weindorfer, Gustav, 12
Whyte, Thomas, 2

Victoria
Allan, John*, 7
Anderson, John Wilson, 3
Anderson, Samuel, 1
Anderson, William*, 3
Baker, Thomas (1840-1923)*, 7
Blanc, Gustave, 7
Borella, Albert Chalmers, 7
Bruce, Alexander, 3
Buchanan, James*, 3
Bussau, Sir Albert Louis, 7
Cameron, Ewen Hugh*, 3
Cameron, James*, 7
Chanter, John Moore*, 7
Chomley, Charles Henry, 7
Clarke, Charles James, 8
Cook, Robert*, 8
Crowe, William, 8
Duggan, Bernard Oscar Charles, 8
Dunstan, Sir Albert Arthur*, 8
Dutton, William, 1
Fry, James, 4
Gibson, William Gerrand*, 8
Goudie, Sir George Louis*, 9
Graham, George*, 9
Harker, George*, 4
Hill, William Caldwell*, 9
Howitt, Richard, 4
Joyce, Alfred, 2
Kennedy, Thomas James*, 9
Kirkland, Katherine, 2
Lay, Percy, 10
Lind, Sir Albert Eli*, 10
Longmore, Francis*, 5
Lowerson, Albert David, 10
Lyall, William*, 5
McClelland, Hugh*, 10
McCulloch, James, 5
McGregor, Martin Robert*, 10
Mackrell, Edwin Joseph*, 10
McLeod, Donald Norman*, 10
O'Farrell, Henry James, 5
Old, Francis Edward*, 11
Orr, William (1843-1929)*, 11
Palmer, Thomas McLeod, 5
Paterson, Thomas*, 11
Plain, William*, 11
Plummer, Andrew, 5
Quinlivan, Thomas, 11
Rankin, John, 11
Rees, John*, 6
Rodgers, Arthur Stanislaus*, 11
Rogers, James, 11
Sanderson, Robert Fitzroy, 11
Stewart, Percy Gerald*, 12
Takasuka, Jō, 12
Tubb, Frederick Harold, 12
Webb, William Telford*, 6
West, John, 12
Wettenhall, Marcus Edwy*, 12
Wilson, Alexander William, 12
Wilson, David, 12
Wilson, Edward, 6

Western Australia
Bath, Thomas Henry*, 7
Brockman, Edmund Ralph*, 3
Burley, Johnston, 7
Cockburn-Campbell, Sir Thomas*, 3
Denton, James Samuel*, 8
Hardey, Joseph, 1
Hayward, Thomas*, 4
Latham, Sir Charles George*, 10
Liebe, Friederich Wilhelm Gustav, 10
Macgregor, Lewis Richard, 10
Monger, John Henry*, 5
Moran, Charles John*, 10
Paterson, William*, 11
Prowse, John Henry*, 11
Rose, Robert Henry, 6
Snook, Charles William, 12
Taylor, Henry Joseph Stirling, 12
Throssell, Hugo Vivian Hope, 12
Truman, John, 12
FEMINIST, *see* Women's rights activist
FERRY EMPLOYEE
Webb, Chris, 12
FERRY MASTER
Dean, George, 8
Randell, George*, 6
FERRY PROPRIETOR
Austin, James (1776-1831), 1
Milson, James (1814-1903), 2
Thomson, Dugald*, 12
FILM CENSOR
O'Reilly, Walter Cresswell, 11
FILM-MAKER
Barrett, Walter Franklyn, 7
Chauvel, Charles Edward, 7
Crick, Stanley Sadler, 8
Doyle, Stuart Frank, 8
Gibson, William Alfred, 8
Higgins, Arthur Embery, 9
Higgins, Ernest Henry, 9
Higgins, Tasman George, 9
Hurley, James Francis, 9
Longford, Raymond John Walter Hollis, 10
Lyell, Lottie Edith, 10
McDonagh, Isabella Mercia, 10
McDonagh, Paulette de Vere, 10
McDonagh, Phyllis Glory, 10
MacMahon, Charles, 10
Ordell, Talone, 11
Perry, Joseph Henry, 11
Perry, Orizaba George, 11
Perry, Reginald Harry, 11
Tait, Charles, 12
Thring, Francis William, 12
FINANCIER
Baillieu, William Lawrence*, 7
Braddon, Sir Henry Yule*, 7
Bright, Charles Edward, 3
Campbell, Robert (1789-1851), 1
Campbell, William*, 3
Coates, James, 8
Connor, Daniel, 8
Coote, Audley*, 3
Dalgety, Frank Gonnerman, 4

De Garis, Clement John, 8
Fisher, Thomas, 4
Forrest, Alexander*, 8
Forster, Anthony*, 4
Garvan, Sir John Joseph, 8
Glass, Hugh, 4
Harper, Nathaniel White*, 9
Holt, Thomas*, 4
Humphery, Frederick Thomas*, 4
James, Charles Henry*, 4
Lyell, Andrew*, 5
McIlwraith, Sir Thomas*, 5
Manning, Sir William Patrick*, 10
Matheson, Sir Alexander Perceval*, 10
Miller, Henry*, 5
Mirams, James*, 5
Molloy, Thomas George Anstruther*, 10
Montefiore, Jacob Levi*, 5
Montefiore, Joseph Barrow, 2
Morehead, Robert Archibald Alison, 2
Mort, Thomas Sutcliffe, 5
Munro, James*, 5
Philp, Sir Robert*, 11
Roemer, Charles William, 2
Rofe, Thomas Ernest, 11
Rumpf, Ann, 11
Vanzetti, Eugenio, 12
Wren, John, 12
Young, Edmund Mackenzie, 6
Zox, Ephraim Laman*, 6
FIRE OFFICER
Lapsley, James McFarlane, 9
Sparks, Nicholas George, 12
Winter, Anthony William, 12
FITTER
Graves, James Joseph*, 9
FOLKLORIST
Sharp, Cecil James, 11
FOOTBALL ADMINISTRATOR
Flegg, Henry, 8
Larkin, Edward Rennix*, 9
FOOTBALLER
Australian Rules
Bunton, Haydn William, 7
Cazaly, Roy, 7
Greeves, Edward Goderich, 9
Harrison, Henry Colden Antill, 4
Leahy, Thomas Joseph, 10
Lee, Walter Henry (1889-1968), 10
McClelland, William Caldwell, 10
McHale, James Francis, 10
McNamara, David John, 10
Matson, Phillip Henry, 10
Moriarty, Daniel, 10
Richardson, Victor York, 11
Thurgood, Albert John, 12
Truscott, William John, 12
Worrall, John, 12
Rugby League
Brown, David Michael, 7
Fihelly, John Arthur*, 8
Gorman, John Thomas, 9
Hennessy, Arthur Stephen, 9
Horder, Harold Norman, 9

McKivat, Christopher Hobart, 10
Messenger, Herbert Henry, 10
Pearce, Sidney Charles, 11
Thompson, Duncan Fulton, 12
Rugby Union
Baker, Reginald Leslie, 7
Colquhoun, Percy Brereton*, 8
Lawton, Thomas, 10
McKivat, Christopher Hobart, 10
Spragg, Alonzo Stephen, 12
Wade, Leslie Augustus Burton, 12
Wallace, Arthur Cooper, 12
FORESTER
Brown, John Ednie, 3
De Beuzeville, Wilfred Alexander Watt, 8
Jolly, Norman William, 9
Lane-Poole, Charles Edward, 9
McDougall, Stanley Robert, 10
Robinson, Sir Roy Lister, 11
Swain, Edward Harold Fulcher, 12
GALLERY CURATOR
Gill, Harry Pelling, 9
Van Raalte, Henri Benedictus Salaman, 12
GALLERY DIRECTOR
Burdett, Basil, 7
Hall, Lindsay Bernard, 9
McCubbin, Louis Frederick*, 10
MacDonald, James Stuart, 10
Mann, Gother Victor Fyers, 10
Montefiore, Eliezer Levi, 5
GAMBLER
Connolly, Eric Alfred, 8
GARAGE PROPRIETOR
Leak, John, 10
Margolin, Eliezer, 10
GEOGRAPHER
Daneš, Jiří Václav, 8
Fenner, Charles Albert Edward, 8
Lee, Ida Louisa, 10
Macdonald, Alexander Cameron, 5
Maconochie, Alexander, 2
Marin la Meslée, Edmond Marie, 5
Taylor, Thomas Griffith, 12
Thomson, James Park, 12
Wilkins, Sir George Hubert, 12
GEOLOGIST, *see also* Mineralogist;
Palaeontologist; Seismologist
Andrews, Ernest Clayton, 7
Baragwanath, William, 7
Basedow, Herbert*, 7
Brown, Henry Yorke Lyell, 7
Carne, Joseph Edmund, 7
Chewings, Charles, 7
Clarke, William Branwhite, 3
Curran, John (Michael) Milne, 3
Daintree, Richard, 4
Dana, James Dwight, 1
David, Sir Tannatt William Edgeworth, 8
Dunn, Edward John, 8
Dunstan, Benjamin, 8
Fraser, Sir Colin, 8
Gould, Charles, 4
Gregory, John Walter, 9
Hardman, Edward Townley, 4

Herman, Hyman, 9
Howchin, Walter, 9
Jack, Robert Logan, 4
Jensen, Harald Ingemann, 9
Jukes, Joseph Beete, 2
Keene, William, 5
Kitson, Sir Albert Ernest, 9
Krausé, Ferdinand Moritz, 5
Laseron, Charles Francis, 9
Lewis, Arndell Neil*, 10
Loftus-Hills, Clive, 10
Madigan, Cecil Thomas, 10
Mahony, Daniel James, 10
Maitland, Andrew Gibb, 10
Mawson, Sir Douglas, 10
Menge, Johann, 2
Murray, Reginald Augustus Frederick, 5
Nicolay, Charles Grenfell, 5
Osborne, George Davenport, 11
Pittman, Edward Fisher, 11
Priestley, Sir Raymond Edward, 11
Pritchard, George Baxter, 11
Richards, Henry Caselli, 11
Selwyn, Alfred Richard Cecil, 6
Skeats, Ernest Willington, 11
Skertchly, Sydney Barber Josiah, 11
Stanley, George Arthur Vickers, 12
Stephen, George Milner*, 2
Stillwell, Frank Leslie, 12
Strzelecki, Sir Paul Edmund de, 2
Stutchbury, Samuel, 6
Süssmilch, Adolph Carl von de Heyde, 12
Sweet, George, 12
Tate, Ralph, 6
Tenison-Woods, Julian Edmund, 6
Thomson, Alexander Morrison, 6
Ulrich, Georg Heinrich Friedrich, 6
Wade, Arthur, 12
Wilkinson, Charles Smith, 6
Woodward, Henry Page, 12
Woolnough, Walter George, 12

GOLDFIELDS COMMISSIONER

Anderson, William Acland Douglas, 3
Browne, Thomas Alexander, 3
Bull, John Edward Newell, 3
Clarke, George O'Malley, 3
Douglas, John*, 4
Griffin, Thomas John Augustus, 4
Hardy, John Richard, 4
Horne, Richard Henry, 4
Jardine, John, 4
King, William Essington, 5
Maclean, Harold, 5
Panton, Joseph Anderson, 5
Powlett, Frederick Armand, 2
Pring, Ratcliffe*, 5
Rede, Robert William, 6
Smith, Bernhard, 6
Standish, Frederick Charles, 6
Templeton, William, 6
Wright, William Henry, 6
Zouch, Henry, 6

GOLFER

Whitton, Ivo Harrington, 12

Williams, Harry Llewellyn Carlington, 12
Wray, Leonora, 12

GOVERNMENT ADVISER

Anderson, Sir Robert Murray McCheyne, 7
Elder, Sir James Alexander Mackenzie, 8
Leitch, Sir Walter, 10
Maxwell, Walter, 10
Morrison, George Ernest, 10

GOVERNOR, see also Lieut-governor; Governor-General

New South Wales

Anderson, Sir David Murray, 7
Beauchamp, Earl, 7
Belmore, Earl of, 3
Bligh, William, 1
Bourke, Sir Richard, 1
Brisbane, Sir Thomas Makdougall, 1
Carrington, Charles Robert, 3
Chelmsford, Baron, 7
Darling, Sir Ralph, 1
Davidson, Sir Walter Edward, 8
De Chair, Sir Dudley Rawson Stratford, 8
Duff, Sir Robert William, 8
Game, Sir Philip Woolcott, 8
Gipps, Sir George, 1
Hampden, Sir Henry Robert Brand, Viscount, 9
Hunter, John (1737-1821), 1
Jersey, Sir Victor Albert George Child-Villiers, 9
King, Philip Gidley, 2
Loftus, Lord Augustus William Frederick Spencer, 5
Macquarie, Lachlan (1762-1824), 2
Phillip, Arthur, 2
Rawson, Sir Harry Holdsworth, 11
Robinson, Sir Hercules George Robert, 6
Strickland, Sir Gerald, 12
Young, Sir John, 6

New Zealand

Hobson, William, 1

Papua and/or New Guinea

Schleinitz, Georg Gustav Freiherr von, 6

Queensland

Blackall, Samuel Wensley, 3
Bowen, Sir George Ferguson, 3
Cairns, Sir William Wellington, 3
Chelmsford, Baron, 7
Chermside, Sir Herbert Charles, 7
Goodwin, Sir Thomas Herbert John Chapman, 9
Goold-Adams, Sir Hamilton, 9
Kennedy, Sir Arthur Edward, 5
Lamington, Baron, 9
MacGregor, Sir William, 5
Musgrave, Sir Anthony, 5
Nathan, Sir Matthew, 10
Norman, Sir Henry Wylie, 11
Normanby, George Augustine Constantine Phipps, 5
Wilson, Sir Leslie Orme, 12

South Australia

Bosanquet, Sir Day Hort, 7

Bridges, Sir (George) Tom Molesworth, 7
Buxton, Sir Thomas Fowell, 7
Daly, Sir Dominick, 4
Fergusson, Sir James, 4
Galway, Sir Henry Lionel, 8
Gawler, George, 1
Grey, Sir George, 1
Hindmarsh, Sir John, 1
Jervois, Sir William Francis Drummond, 4
Kintore, Algernon Hawkins Thomond
  Keith-Falconer, Earl, 5
Le Hunte, Sir George Ruthven, 10
MacDonnell, Sir Richard Graves, 5
Musgrave, Sir Anthony, 5
Robinson, Sir William Cleaver Francis, 6
Tennyson, Hallam, Baron, 12
Weigall, Sir William Ernest George
  Archibald, 12

Tasmania
Allardyce, Sir William Lamond, 7
Barron, Sir Harry, 7
Browne, Sir Thomas Gore, 3
Clark, Sir Ernest, 8
Du Cane, Sir Charles, 4
Gormanston, Jenico William Joseph
  Preston, Viscount, 9
Hamilton, Sir Robert George Crookshank,
  4
Havelock, Sir Arthur Elibank, 9
Macartney, Sir William Grey Ellison, 10
Newdegate, Sir Francis Alexander
  Newdigate, 11
O'Grady, Sir James, 11
Strahan, Sir George Cumine, 6
Strickland, Sir Gerald, 12
Weld, Sir Frederick Aloysius, 6
Young, Sir Henry Edward Fox, 6

Victoria
Barkly, Sir Henry, 3
Bowen, Sir George Ferguson, 3
Brassey, Thomas, Earl, 7
Canterbury, Viscount, 3
Carmichael, Sir Thomas David Gibson, 7
Clarke, Sir George Sydenham, 8
Darling, Sir Charles Henry, 4
Fuller, Sir John Michael Fleetwood, 8
Hotham, Sir Charles, 4
Huntingfield, William Charles Arcedeckne
  Vanneck, 9
Loch, Henry Brougham, 5
Normanby, George Augustine Constantine
  Phipps, 5
Somers, Arthur Herbert Tennyson
  Somers-Cocks, 12
Stanley, Arthur Lyulph, 12
Stradbroke, George Edward John
  Mowbray Rous, 12
Talbot, Sir Reginald Arthur James, 12

Western Australia
Barron, Sir Harry, 7
Bedford, Sir Frederick George Denham, 7
Broome, Sir Frederick Napier, 3
Campion, Sir William Robert, 7
Clarke, Andrew, 1

FitzGerald, Charles, 1
Hampton, John Stephen, 1
Hutt, John, 1
Kennedy, Sir Arthur Edward, 5
Lawley, Sir Arthur, 10
Macartney, Sir William Grey Ellison, 10
Mitchell, Sir James, 10
Newdegate, Sir Francis Alexander
  Newdigate, 11
Ord, Sir Harry St George, 5
Robinson, Sir William Cleaver Francis, 6
Smith, Sir Gerard, 11
Stirling, Sir James, 2
Strickland, Sir Gerald, 12
Weld, Sir Frederick Aloysius, 6

GOVERNOR-GENERAL
Denison, Sir William Thomas, 4
Denman, Thomas, Baron, 8
Dudley, William Humble Ward, Earl, 8
FitzRoy, Sir Charles Augustus, 1
Forster, Sir Henry William, Baron, 8
Gowrie, Sir Alexander Gore Arkwright
  Hore-Ruthven, Earl, 9
Hopetoun, John Adrian Louis, Earl, 9
Isaacs, Sir Isaac Alfred*, 9
Munro Ferguson, Sir Ronald Craufurd, 10
Northcote, Sir Henry Stafford, 11
Stonehaven, John Lawrence Baird, 12
Tennyson, Hallam, Baron, 12

GOVERNOR'S WIFE
Broome, Mary Anne, 3
Denman, Gertrude Mary, 8
Franklin, Lady Jane, 1
Gowrie, Zara Eileen, 9
Macquarie, Elizabeth Henrietta, 2
Munro Ferguson, Helen Hermione, 10

GRAZIER, *see* Pastoralist

GREENGROCER
Laver, Ralph Herbert, 10

GROCER
Brown, Walter Ernest, 7
Burgess, William Henry (1847-1917)*, 3
Cato, Frederick John, 7
Fowler, David, 4
Hay, Alexander*, 1
Laurens, John*, 5
Maguire, James Bernard, 10
Morgan, Sir William*, 5
Nicholas, Alfred Michael, 11
Nicholson, Germain, 5
Nicholson, William*, 5
Prieur, François Xavier, 2
Reynolds, Thomas*, 6
Scullin, James Henry*, 11
Temple, David, 12
Watson, William*, 12
Wilson, Sir Reginald Victor*, 12

GUNSMITH
Cowles, Charles, 3
Whitfield, George, 6

HAIRDRESSER
Liston, John James, 10

HANSARD REPORTER
Johns, Frederick, 9

HARBOURMASTER
Campbell, Alexander, 1
Collins, William, 1
Douglas, William Bloomfield, 4
Friend, Matthew Curling, 1
Helpman, Benjamin Franklin, 1
Kelly, James, 2
Lucas, James, 2
Mackay, John, 5
Mills, Peter, 2
Moriarty, Merion Marshall*, 5
Scott, Daniel, 2
Watson, Robert, 2

HEADMASTER, see School principal
HEADMISTRESS, see School principal

HISTORIAN
Andrews, Arthur, 7
Barton, George Burnett, 3
Bean, Charles Edwin Woodrow, 7
Beattie, John Watt, 7
Bennett, Samuel, 3
Bertie, Charles Henry, 7
Bonwick, James, 3
Butler, Arthur Graham, 7
Cameron, James, 3
Childe, Vere Gordon, 7
Collingridge de Tourcey, George
  Alphonse, 8
Cowlishaw, Leslie, 8
Cramp, Karl Reginald, 8
Cutlack, Frederic Morley, 8
Favenc, Ernest, 4
Flanagan, Roderick, 4
Froude, James Anthony, 4
Giblin, Ronald Worthy, 8
Gullett, Sir Henry Somer*, 9
Henderson, George Cockburn, 9
Hentze, Margaret Edith, 9
Hussey, Henry, 4
Jacobs, Joseph, 9
Jose, Arthur Wilberforce, 9
Kenny, John, 2
Kenyon, Alfred Stephen, 9
Lang, John Dunmore*, 2
Marks, Percy Joseph, 10
Melbourne, Alexander Clifford Vernon, 10
Meston, Archibald Lawrence, 10
Murdoch, James, 10
Mutch, Thomas Davies*, 10
Osburne, Richard, 5
Pearson, Charles Henry*, 5
Portus, Garnet Vere, 11
Rumsey, Herbert John, 11
Rusden, George William, 6
Russell, Henry Stuart, 2
Scott, Sir Ernest, 11
Shillinglaw, John Joseph, 6
Turner, Henry Gyles, 6
Walker, Allan Seymour, 12
Walker, James Backhouse, 6
Watson, James Frederick William, 12
Watson, James Henry, 12
Wayn, Amelia Lucy, 12
Webb, Jessie Stobo Watson, 12

West, John, 2
Westgarth, William*, 6
White, Charles, 6
Withers, William Bramwell, 6
Wood, George Arnold, 12

HOCKEY PLAYER
Tazewell, Evelyn Ruth, 12
West, Winifred Mary, 12

HOMOEOPATH
Bouton, Wilbur Knibloe, 7
Simpson, Stephen, 2

HORTICULTURIST
Bent, Sir Thomas*, 3
Brunning, George, 3
Camfield, Julius Henry, 7
Chandler, Alfred Elliott*, 7
Clark, Alister, 8
Cox, Samuel Emanuel, 1
Dallachy, John, 4
French, Charles, 8
Grayson, Henry Joseph, 9
Guilfoyle, William Robert, 4
Heyne, Ernst Bernhard, 4
Howard, Amos William, 9
Littlejohn, Robert, 2
Luffman(n), Charles (Bogue), 10
Maxwell, Joseph, 10
Moore, Charles (1820-1905), 5
Nobelius, Carl Axel, 5
Pescott, Edward Edgar, 11
Richardson, John Matthew, 2
Rumsey, Herbert John, 11
Sinclair, James, 6
Sturgess, Reginald Ward, 12
Thorpe, Harry, 12
Turner, Fred, 12
Turner, William*, 6
Waterhouse, Eben Gowrie, 12
West, John, 12
Weston, Thomas Charles George, 12

HOSPITAL ADMINISTRATOR
Ievers, Robert Lancelot, 4
Lynch, Annie, 10
Paul, Sir Charles Norman, 11
Schlink, Sir Herbert Henry, 11
Stuart, Sir Thomas Peter Anderson, 12

HOSPITAL FOUNDER
Abbott, Gertrude, 7
Daly, Anne, 8
Schardt, Susan Katherina, 11

HOTELKEEPER
Adams, George, 3
Asche, Thomas, 7
Asher, Morris*, 3
Austin, James (1776-1831), 1
Baillieu, James George, 7
Best, Henry, 1
Boyle, Ignatius George*, 7
Brennan, Peter Joseph, 3
Burrowes, Robert*, 3
Cadman, John, 1
Calder, George, 7
Cawker, Thomas, 3
Collits, Pierce, 1

Colls, Thomas*, 3
Connor, Daniel, 8
Cox, John Edward, 1
Curtis, Anthony, 1
Davies, John (1813-1872)*, 4
Deane, John Philip, 1
Dodery, William*, 4
Edwards, Albert Augustine*, 8
Fawkner, John Pascoe*, 1
Gannon, Michael, 4
Gorman, John Thomas, 9
Gray, Isabel, 9
Greeves, Augustus Frederick Adolphus*, 4
Groom, William Henry*, 4
Hannell, James*, 4
Harris, John (fl.1783-1803), 1
Hayes, Michael, 1
Heagney, Patrick Reginald, 9
Hill, George*, 4
Holtermann, Bernhardt Otto*, 4
Hopwood, Henry, 4
Howe, John Robert, 9
Humffray, John Basson*, 4
Hurley, John (1796-1882)*, 4
Jensen, Jens August*, 9
Johnston, James Stewart*, 4
Larra, James, 2
Lawson, James, 10
Leahy, John*, 10
Liardet, Wilbraham Frederick Evelyn, 2
Liston, John James, 10
Lucas, John*, 5
Lysaght, Andrew*, 10
McClintock, Albert Scott, 10
Merriman, James*, 5
Michel, Louis John, 5
Monahan, Thomas, 5
Morell, Sir Stephen Joseph, 10
Morgan, Frederick Augustus, 5
Morgan, Molly, 2
Murphy, Peter*, 10
Nichols, Isaac, 2
Page, Samuel, 2
Powell, Edward, 2
Ransom, Thomas, 2
Raphael, Joseph George*, 6
Redmond, Edward, 2
Reibey, Mary, 2
Resch, Edmund, 11
Roberts, Charles James*, 6
Rose, Thomas (d.1837), 2
Rotton, Henry*, 6
Ryan, James Tobias*, 6
Sidaway, Robert, 2
Smith, Sir James John Joynton*, 11
Smith, John Thomas*, 6
Sorenson, Edward Sylvester, 12
Strickland, William Henry John, 6
Tait, John, 6
Terry, Samuel, 2
Thompson, John Willis, 12
Thorn, George*, 6
Torpy, James*, 6

Tracey, Eliza, 12
Trickett, Edward, 6
Wallace, John Alston*, 6
Weekes, Elias Carpenter*, 6
Weindorfer, Gustav, 12
Welch, Eric Wilfred, 12
Wisdom, Evan Alexander*, 12
Wiseman, Thomas, 12
HOUSE-PAINTER
Goold, Stephen Styles*, 4
HUNTER
Cahill, Patrick, 7
Cooper, Robert Joel, 8
Robinson, Edward Oswin, 11
HYDROGRAPHER
Blackwood, Francis Price, 1
Dalrymple, Alexander, 1
Flinders, Matthew, 1
Halligan, Gerald Harnett, 9
King, Phillip Parker, 2
Moresby, John, 5
Schleinitz, Georg Gustav Freiherr von, 6
Stokes, John Lort, 2
Vancouver, George, 2
ILLUSTRATOR
Ashton, George Rossi, 7
Bustard, William, 7
Carrington, Francis Thomas Dean, 3
Fiveash, Rosa Catherine, 8
Gibbs, Cecilia May, 8
Outhwaite, Ida Sherbourne, 11
Parkinson, Sydney, 2
Scott, Eugene Montague, 6
Tillyard, Pattie, 12
Wall, Dorothy, 12
IMMIGRATION AGENT
Brown, John, 1
Dashwood, George Frederick, 1
Jordan, Henry*, 4
McLaren, David, 2
Pinnock, James Denham*, 2
Wise, George Foster, 6
IMMIGRATION PROMOTER
Crawford, Andrew*, 3
Lang, John Dunmore*, 2
INDEXER
James, Henry Kerrison, 4
James, John Charles Horsey, 4
INDUSTRIALIST
Brock, Harold James, 7
Delprat, Guillaume, 8
Gillies, James Hynds, 9
Hughes, Fred William, 9
Lewis, Essington, 10
Longworth, Thomas (1857-1927), 10
Longworth, William (1846-1928), 10
Mitchell, James*, 2
Mussen, Sir Gerald, 10
Robinson, William Sydney, 11
INSURANCE AGENT
Bright, Charles Edward, 3
Fox, Henry Thomas, 4
Garvan, James Patrick*, 4
Glenny, Henry, 4

Neild, John Cash*, 10
O'Malley, King*, 11
Prowse, John Henry*, 11
Scott, William John Rendell, 11
Short, Benjamin, 6
Whittle, John Woods, 12
INSURANCE MANAGER
Macredie, William, 5
O'Grady, Michael, 5
Smithies, Frederick, 11
Spence, George Heynes, 12
Tunn, John Patrick, 12
INTELLIGENCE AGENT
Murphy, Herbert Dyce, 10
INVENTOR
Alcock, Alfred Upton, 7
Balsillie, John Graeme, 7
Bottrill, Frank, 7
Brennan, Louis, 3
Bull, John Wrathall, 1
Buncle, John, 3
Davidson, James, 8
De Mole, Lancelot Eldin, 8
Frewin, Kenneth Moreton, 8
Geake, William Henry Gregory, 8
Grayson, Henry Joseph, 9
Harrison, James*, 1
Howard, Arthur Clifford, 9
Hume, Walter Reginald, 9
Julius, Sir George Alfred, 9
Kauper, Henry Alexis, 9
Koerstz, Christian Christiansen, 9
Lapsley, James McFarlane, 9
McComas, John Wesley, 10
McMillan, Samuel, 10
Michell, Anthony George Maldon, 10
Morrow, James, 5
Morton, William Lockhart, 5
Murphy, George Read, 10
Nicolle, Eugène Dominique, 5
Osborne, John Walter, 5
Pomeroy, John, 11
Quinlivan, Thomas, 11
Ridley, John, 2
Savage, Robert, 6
Shaw, Archibald John, 11
Shearer, David, 11
Shearer, John, 11
Sutton, Henry, 6
Taylor, Headlie Shipard, 12
Traeger, Alfred Hermann, 12
Unaipon, David, 12
Wolseley, Frederick York, 6
Woods, John*, 6
IRONFOUNDER
Babbidge, Benjamin Harris, 3
Ferguson, Mephan, 4
Fulton, Thomas, 4
Furphy, John, 4
Gibson, Sir Robert, 8
Griffiths, Alfred Atherton, 9
Griffiths, George Herbert, 9
Griffiths, George Washington, 9
Harrington, William Frederick, 9

Hoskins, Cecil Harold, 9
Hoskins, Charles Henry, 9
Humble, William, 4
John, Morgan Bevan, 9
Langlands, Henry*, 2
Oddie, James, 5
Russell, Sir Peter Nicol, 6
Shaw, William Henry, 6
Wearne, Thomas, 6
IRONMONGER
Blyth, Sir Arthur*, 3
Blyth, Neville*, 3
Brookes, William*, 3
Davies, John (1839-1896)*, 4
Grimley, Frank, 9
Hart, William*, 4
Hopkins, Henry, 1
Jenner, Caleb Joshua*, 4
Loader, Thomas*, 5
Macintosh, John*, 5
McLean, William, 5
McNess, Sir Charles, 10
Powell, Walter, 5
Weekes, Elias Carpenter*, 6
Wilson, John Thomas, 2
Woolley, Thomas, 2
Younger, Montague Thomas Robson, 6
IRRIGATIONIST
Carter, Samuel, 3
Chaffey, George, 7
Chaffey, William Benjamin, 7
De Garis, Elisha Clement, 8
McColl, Hugh*, 5
Mead, Elwood, 10
West, John, 12
IVORY TURNER
Parkes, Sir Henry*, 5
JEWELLER
Hutchinson, William, 9
Lazar, John, 2
McCann, Arthur Francis, 10
Marks, Percy, 10
Oakes, Charles William*, 11
Orchard, Richard Beaumont*, 11
Proud, William James, 11
Smith, John McGarvie, 11
Wager, Rhoda, 12
JOCKEY
Connell, Cornelius Myles, 8
Corrigan, Tom, 3
Hales, Thomas, 4
Lewis, Robert, 10
Munro, David Hugh, 10
Munro, James Leslie, 10
Pike, James Edward, 11
Rene, Roy, 11
Stephen, Sir Colin Campbell, 12
Taylor, Joseph Leslie Theodore, 12
JOURNALIST, *see also* Newspaper editor
Aaron, Isaac, 1
Adams, Arthur Henry, 7
Adcock, William Eddrup, 7
Allan, Stella May, 7
Andrews, John Arthur, 7

Archibald, Jules François, 3
Armit, Henry William, 7
Armit, William Edington, 3
Aronson, Zara, 7
Ashton, Julian Howard, 7
Aspinall, Butler Cole*, 3
Astley, William, 3
Balfe, John Donnellan*, 3
Barnett, Charles Leslie, 7
Barry, John Arthur, 7
Barton, George Burnett, 3
Bean, Charles Edwin Woodrow, 7
Bedford, George Randolph*, 7
Birnie, Richard, 3
Black, George Mure*, 7
Black, John McConnell, 7
Blair, David*, 3
Bottrill, David Hughes, 7
Boyd, William Alexander Jenyns, 7
Brady, Edwin James, 7
Brennan, William Adrian, 7
Brentnall, Frederick Thomas*, 3
Bridges, Royal Tasman, 7
Brient, Albert Lachlan, 7
Brient, Lachlan John, 7
Bright, Charles, 3
Brodzky, Leon Herbert Spencer, 7
Brodzky, Maurice, 7
Broinowski, Leopold Thomas, 7
Brooke, John Henry*, 3
Brooks, Samuel Wood*, 3
Broomfield, Frederick John, 7
Browne, Reginald Spencer, 7
Bruce, Minnie Grant, 7
Buggy, Edward Hugh, 7
Bulcock, Emily Hemans, 7
Burdett, Basil, 7
Bury, Thomas, 3
Butler, Charles Philip, 7
Champion, Henry Hyde, 7
Chase, Muriel Jean Eliot, 7
Clarke, Marcus Andrew Hislop, 3
Cleary, Patrick Scott, 8
Clisby, Harriet Jemima Winifred, 3
Cockerill, George, 8
Collins, Cuthbert Quinlan Dale, 8
Cook, Bertie Stuart Baxter, 8
Coombe, Ephraim Henry*, 8
Coombes, Richard, 8
Cooper, Walter Hampson*, 3
Coote, William, 3
Corbett, Claude Gordon, 8
Corbett, William Francis, 8
Cotton, Francis*, 8
Cox, Erle, 8
Crampton, Walter Russell, 8
Crouch, James Joseph, 3
Cutlack, Frederic Morley, 8
Daley, Victor James William Patrick, 8
Dalley, John Bede, 8
Dalley, William Bede*, 4
Deakin, Alfred*, 8
Dean, Horace, 4
De Boos, Charles Edward Augustus, 4

Denovan, William Dixon Campbell*, 4
Dickinson, Sidney, 8
Donald, William Henry, 8
Dorrington, Albert, 8
Dow, John Lamont*, 4
Drake, James George*, 8
Duffy, Sir Charles Gavan*, 4
Dunbabin, Thomas Charles, 8
Duncan, William Augustine, 1
Edmond, James, 8
Farrell, John, 4
Favenc, Ernest, 4
Ferry, Michael Augustus, 8
Finn, Edmund, 1
Fitzgerald, John Daniel*, 8
Flanagan, Roderick, 4
Foott, Mary Hannay, 4
Foran, Martin Henry, 8
Fowler, Francis Edmund Town, 4
Fox, Sir Frank Ignatius, 8
Gellatly, Francis Mephan, 8
Gilbert, David John, 9
Gordon, Sir David John*, 9
Gould, Nathaniel, 9
Grainger, Henry William Allerdale*, 9
Grasby, William Catton, 9
Gray, Moses Wilson*, 4
Gullett, Sir Henry Somer*, 9
Gunson, William Henry, 4
Hain, Gladys Adeline, 9
Hales, Alfred Arthur Greenwood, 9
Hall, George Wilson*, 4
Hall, John Joseph, 9
Halloran, Laurence Hynes, 1
Harpur, Joseph Jehoshaphat*, 1
Haynes, John*, 4
Heaton, Sir John Henniker, 4
Henry, Alice, 9
Hervey, Grant (Madison), 9
Higinbotham, George*, 4
Hoare, Benjamin, 9
Hodgkinson, William Oswald*, 4
Hogan, James Francis, 4
Hogue, Oliver, 9
Holdsworth, Philip Joseph, 4
Holman, Ada Augusta, 9
Hübbe, Ulrich, 4
Innes, Frederick Maitland*, 4
Jefferis, James, 4
Johnson, Joseph Colin Francis*, 9
Kemp, Charles, 2
Lane, Ernest Henry, 9
Leckie, Hattie Martha, 10
Lesina, Vincent Bernard, 10
Levey, George Collins*, 5
Loyau, George Ettienne, 5
Lyne, Charles Emanuel, 10
McCay, Adam Cairns, 10
McCay, Delamore William, 10
McCombie, Thomas*, 5
McDonagh, Phyllis Glory, 10
Macdonald, Donald Alaster, 10
Mack, Marie Louise Hamilton, 10
McKinnon, Thomas Firmin, 10

McMillan, Robert, 10
Mahon, Hugh*, 10
Mailey, Alfred Arthur, 10
Manning, Emily Matilda, 5
Marlowe, Margaret Mary, 10
Matthews, Harley, 10
Melvin, Joseph Dalgarno, 10
Miller, Maxwell*, 5
Mitchel, John, 2
Mitchell, Janet Charlotte, 10
Molesworth, Voltaire*, 10
Moore, William George, 10
Morgan, John, 2
Moriarty, Daniel, 10
Morrison, George Ernest, 10
Morton, Frank, 10
Murphy, Edwin Greenslade, 10
Murray, Pembroke Lathrop, 10
Murray, Robert William Felton Lathrop, 2
Mussen, Sir Gerald, 10
Mutch, Thomas Davies*, 10
Nanson, Janet, 10
Nanson, John Leighton*, 10
Nash, Richard West, 2
Nelson, Wallace Alexander*, 10
Nicholas, Harold Sprent*, 11
Nicholls, Charles Frederick, 5
Nichols, Hubert Allan*, 11
Noskowski, Ladislas Adam de, 11
O'Ferrall, Ernest Francis, 11
O'Keefe, David John, 11
O'Reilly, John Boyle, 5
Osborne, Henry William, 11
Osborne, John, 5
O'Sullivan, Edward William*, 11
Owen, Albert John (Harrison), 11
Parkes, Sir Henry*, 5
Paterson, Andrew Barton, 11
Pattison, James Grant, 11
Pearson, Charles Henry*, 5
Pelloe, Emily Harriet, 11
Pitt, Marie Elizabeth Josephine, 11
Plummer, John, 11
Pratt, Ambrose Goddard Hesketh, 11
Püttmann, Hermann, 5
Quaife, Barzillai, 2
Quinn, Patrick Edward*, 11
Reay, William Thomas*, 11
Reeve, Edward, 6
Rhodes, Fred, 11
Robertson, Constance, 11
Robinson, Anthony Bennet, 11
Robinson, William Sydney, 11
Rosa, Samuel Albert, 11
Rosman, Alice (Grant) Trevenen, 11
Ross, John Howlett, 11
Ross, Robert Samuel, 11
Rowe, Richard, 6
St Julian, Charles James Herbert de Courcy, 6
Sanderson, Archibald*, 11
Sandes, John, 11
Savage, Robert, 6

Scott, Sir Ernest, 11
Sergeyev, Fedor Andreyevich, 11
Sievier, Robert Standish, 11
Sinclaire, Frederick, 11
Sizer, Hubert Ebenezer*, 11
Skerst, Arnold Oscar Hermann Gregory von, 11
Sleeman, John Harvey Crothers, 11
Smith, Charles Patrick, 11
Smythe, Robert Sparrow, 12
Stephens, Alfred George, 12
Stow, Jefferson Pickman, 6
Stuart, Athol Hugh, 12
Stuart, John Alexander Salmon*, 12
Supple, Gerald Henry, 6
Sutherland, Alexander, 6
Sutherland, George, 6
Syme, Ebenezer*, 6
Taylor, Hugh*, 6
Taylor, Irene Frances, 12
Thatcher, Richmond, 6
Thompson, Gerald Marr, 12
Thompson, Richard, 2
Todd, Ellen Joy, 12
Topp, Arthur Maning, 6
Twopeny, Richard Ernest Nowell, 6
Vaughan, Crawford*, 12
Vennard, Alexander Vindex, 12
Vidler, Edward Alexander, 12
Viney, Horace George, 12
Vogel, Sir Julius*, 6
Walch, Garnet, 6
Walker, Thomas*, 6
Wallen, Robert Elias, 6
Walsh, John Joseph, 6
Walsh, Thomas, 12
Walstab, George Arthur, 6
Waters, Edward Ernest, 6
Welch, Eric Wilfred, 12
West, John, 12
Whitington, Frederick Taylor, 12
Whitworth, Robert Percy, 6
Whyte, William Farmer, 12
Wight, George, 6
Wildman, Alexina Maude, 12
Wilkins, Sir George Hubert, 12
Winspear, William Robert, 12
Winter, Joseph*, 12
Withers, William Bramwell, 6
Wolfe, Herbert Austin, 12
Worrall, John, 12
Wright, David McKee, 12
Wynne, Watkin, 12
Yewen, Alfred Gregory, 12

JUDGE

Commonwealth

Barton, Sir Edmund*, 7
Beeby, Sir George Stephenson*, 7
Dethridge, George James, 8
Drake-Brockman, Edmund Alfred*, 8
Duffy, Sir Frank Gavan, 8
Foster, Alfred William, 8
Griffith, Sir Samuel Walker*, 9
Higgins, Henry Bournes*, 9

Isaacs, Sir Isaac Alfred*, 9
Knox, Sir Adrian*, 9
Latham, Sir John Greig*, 10
O'Connor, Richard Edward*, 11
Powers, Sir Charles*, 11
Rich, Sir George Edward, 11
Starke, Sir Hayden Erskine, 12
Fiji
St Julian, Charles James Herbert de
  Courcy, 6
New South Wales
à Beckett, Sir Thomas, 3
Backhouse, Alfred Paxton, 7
Beeby, Sir George Stephenson*, 7
Bent, Jeffery Hart, 1
Betts, Selwyn Frederic, 7
Boyce, Francis Stewart*, 7
Burton, Sir William Westbrooke*, 1
Callaghan, Thomas, 1
Campbell, James Lang, 7
Cary, Henry, 3
Cheeke, Alfred, 3
Cohen, Henry Emanuel*, 3
Cohen, John Jacob*, 8
Cullen, Sir William Portus*, 8
Curlewis, Herbert Raine, 12
Darley, Sir Frederick Matthew*, 4
Davidson, Sir Colin George Watt, 8
Deffell, George Hibbert, 4
Dickinson, Sir John Nodes*, 4
Docker, Ernest Brougham, 8
Dowling, Sir James, 1
Dowling, James Sheen, 4
Edmunds, Walter, 8
Faucett, Peter, 4
Ferguson, Sir David Gilbert, 8
Field, Barron, 1
Forbes, Sir Francis, 1
Gordon, Sir Alexander, 9
Hamilton, Hugh Montgomerie, 9
Hargrave, John Fletcher*, 4
Harvey, Sir John Musgrave, 9
Heydon, Charles Gilbert*, 9
Innes, Sir Joseph George Long*, 4
Innes, Reginald Heath Long, 9
Jordan, Sir Frederick Richard, 9
Josephson, Joshua Frey*, 4
Lamaro, Joseph*, 9
McFarland, Alfred, 5
Manning, Charles James, 5
Manning, Sir William Montagu*, 5
Martin, Sir James*, 5
Milford, Samuel Frederick, 5
Nicholas, Harold Sprent*, 11
Owen, Sir Langer Meade Loftus, 11
Owen, Robert*, 5
Owen, Sir William, 11
Piddington, Albert Bathurst*, 11
Pike, George Herbert, 11
Pring, Robert Darlow, 11
Rogers, Francis Edward, 11
Rogers, Sir Percival Halse, 11
Simpson, Sir George Bowen*, 6
Sly, Richard Meares, 11

Stacy, Bertie Vandeleur, 12
Stephen, Sir Alfred*, 6
Stephen, Edward Milner, 12
Stephen, John, 2
Stephen, Sir Matthew Henry*, 6
Storkey, Percy Valentine, 12
Street, Sir Philip Whistler, 12
Therry, Sir Roger*, 2
Wade, Sir Charles Gregory*, 12
Willis, John Walpole, 2
Windeyer, Sir William Charles*, 6
Wise, Edward*, 6
Wylde, Sir John, 2
New Zealand
Salmond, Sir John William, 11
Norfolk Island
Browne, Fielding, 1
Northern Territory
Dashwood, Charles James*, 8
Mitchell, Samuel James*, 10
Papua and/or New Guinea
Griffiths, Philip Lewis, 9
Herbert, Charles Edward*, 9
Phillips, Sir Frederick Beaumont,
  11
Wanliss, David Sydney, 12
Queensland
Blair, Sir James William*, 7
Blakeney, Charles William*, 3
Chubb, Charles Edward*, 3
Cockle, Sir James, 3
Cooper, Sir Pope Alexander*, 8
Griffith, Sir Samuel Walker*, 9
Harding, George Rogers, 4
Innes, Sir Joseph George Long*, 4
Lilley, Sir Charles*, 5
Lukin, Lionel Oscar, 10
Lutwyche, Alfred James Peter, 5
McCawley, Thomas William, 10
Macrossan, Hugh Denis*, 10
Mein, Charles Stuart*, 5
Miller, Granville George, 5
O'Sullivan, Thomas*, 11
Real, Patrick, 11
Rutledge, Sir Arthur*, 11
South Australia
Boothby, Benjamin, 3
Boucaut, Sir James Penn*, 3
Bundey, Sir William Henry*, 3
Cleland, Edward Erskine, 8
Cooper, Sir Charles, 1
Crawford, George John, 3
Gordon, Sir John Hannah*, 9
Gwynne, Edward Castres*, 4
Hanson, Sir Richard Davies*, 4
Homburg, Robert*, 9
Jeffcott, Sir John William, 2
Murray, Sir George John Robert, 10
Parsons, Sir Herbert Angas*, 11
Piper, Arthur William, 11
Poole, Thomas Slaney, 11
Stow, Randolph Isham*, 6
Way, Sir Samuel James*, 12
Wearing, William Alfred, 6

Tasmania
Adams, Robert Patten*, 3
Clark, Andrew Inglis*, 3
Crisp, Sir Harold, 8
Dobbie, Edward David, 8
Dobson, Sir William Lambert*, 4
Dodds, Sir John Stokell*, 4
Fleming, Sir Valentine, 4
Giblin, William Robert*, 4
Horne, Thomas, 4
Montagu, Algernon Sidney, 2
Nicholls, Sir Herbert*, 11
Pedder, Sir John Lewes, 2
Rogers, John Warrington*, 6
Smith, Sir Francis Villeneuve*, 6
Stephen, Sir Alfred*, 6
Victoria
à Beckett, Sir William, 3
Barry, Sir Redmond, 3
Bindon, Samuel Henry*, 3
Casey, James Joseph*, 3
Chapman, Henry Samuel*, 3
Chomley, Arthur Wolfe, 3
Cope, Thomas Spencer, 3
Cussen, Sir Leo Finn Bernard, 8
Duffy, Sir Charles Leonard Gavan, 8
Fellows, Thomas Howard*, 4
Foster, Alfred William, 8
Gaunt, William Henry, 4
Higinbotham, George*, 4
Hodges, Sir Henry Edwin Agincourt, 9
Holroyd, Sir Edward Dundas, 4
Hood, Sir Joseph Henry, 9
Irvine, Sir William Hill, 9
Jeffcott, Sir William, 2
Kerferd, George Briscoe*, 5
McArthur, Sir William Gilbert Stewart, 10
Macfarlan, Sir James Ross, 10
Madden, Sir John (1844-1918)*, 10
Mann, Sir Frederick Wollaston, 10
Molesworth, Hickman, 10
Molesworth, Sir Robert, 5
Pohlman, Robert Williams*, 5
Schutt, William John, 11
Stawell, Sir William Foster*, 6
Stephen, James Wilberforce*, 6
Webb, George Henry Frederick, 6
Williams, Sir Edward Eyre, 6
Williams, Sir Hartley, 6
Winneke, Henry Christian, 12
Western Australia
Burnside, Robert Bruce, 7
Burt, Sir Archibald Paull, 3
Draper, Thomas Percy*, 8
Dwyer, Sir Walter*, 8
Hensman, Alfred Peach*, 4
McMillan, Sir Robert Furse, 10
Northmore, Sir John Alfred, 11
Onslow, Sir Alexander Campbell, 5
Parker, Sir Stephen Henry*, 11
Stone, Sir Edward Albert, 12
Wrenfordsley, Sir Henry Thomas, 6
JUDGE-ADVOCATE, *see also*
Advocate-general

Abbott, Edward, 1
Atkins, Richard, 1
Bate, Samuel, 1
Bent, Ellis, 1
Dore, Richard, 1
Hibbins, Thomas, 1
Wylde, Sir John, 2
LABOURER
Brown, Herbert Basil, 7
Hamilton, John, 9
Kennedy, Thomas, 9
McGregor, Gregor*, 10
Mathias, Louis John, 10
Richards, Ranold, 11
Ryan, Edward John Francis, 11
LAND AGENT
Cunneen, James Augustine*, 3
Fitzpatrick, Michael*, 4
Garrett, Thomas*, 4
Gibson, Robert, 8
Hübbe, Ulrich, 4
Willis, William Nicholas*, 12
LAND DEVELOPER
Bent, Sir Thomas*, 3
Fink, Benjamin Josman*, 4
James, Charles Henry*, 4
Joubert, Jules François de Sales, 4
Pearce, Simeon Henry, 5
Rickard, Sir Arthur, 11
Saywell, Thomas, 6
LANDHOLDER
Allison, William Race*, 1
Anderson, Joseph, 1
Anstey, Thomas, 1
Archer, William*, 3
Austin, James (1776-1831), 1
Balmain, William, 1
Barclay, Andrew, 1
Bartley, Nehemiah, 3
Bayly, Nicholas, 1
Berry, David, 3
Bingle, John, 1
Brooks, Richard, 1
Burbury, Thomas, 1
Bussell, John Garrett*, 1
Cameron, Donald (1780-1857), 3
Cameron, Donald (1814-1890)*, 3
Campbell, Envidale Savage Norman, 3
Clark, Alister, 8
Clarke, Joseph, 3
Clarke, Sir William John*, 3
Dangar, Francis Richard, 4
Davidson, Walter Stevenson, 1
Druitt, George, 1
Dumaresq, Edward, 1
Fenton, Michael*, 1
Fryett, Richard William, 1
Gilles, Osmond, 1
Gregson, Thomas George, 1
Hely, Hovenden*, 4
Icely, Thomas*, 2
Jamison, Sir John, 2
Johnston, Esther, 2
Kermode, Robert Quayle*, 2

Kermode, William, 2
King, Anna Josepha, 2
Langdon, William*, 2
Lawrence, William Effingham, 2
Laycock, Thomas (1756?-1809), 2
Learmonth, Andrew James, 2
Learmonth, John, 2
Lockyer, Edmund, 2
Lord, David, 2
Lord, Thomas Daunt, 2
Loton, William Thorley*, 10
Lyttleton, William Thomas, 2
McIntyre, Peter, 2
McKenzie, Alexander Kenneth, 2
Mackenzie, David, 2
Meares, Richard Goldsmith, 2
Meehan, James, 2
Mercer, George, 2
Mercer, William Drummond, 2
Molloy, John, 2
Monahan, Thomas, 5
Moriarty, William, 2
Morphett, Sir John*, 2
Morrison, Askin*, 5
Mudie, James, 2
Murdoch, Peter, 2
Murray, Robert William Felton Lathrop, 2
Nicholson, Sir Charles*, 2
O'Connor, Roderic, 2
Orr, William Morgan, 2
Owen, Robert*, 5
Palmer, George Thomas, 2
Palmer, John, 2
Peel, Thomas, 2
Petchy, John, 2
Piper, John, 2
Platt, John Laurio, 2
Redmond, Edward, 2
Ritchie, Thomas, 2
Robinson, Joseph Phelps, 2
Roemer, Charles William, 2
Rose, Thomas (d.1837), 2
Rossi, Francis Robert Louis, 6
Rowcroft, Charles, 2
Rowley, Thomas, 2
Rutledge, William*, 2
Salmon, Thomas, 2
Salting, Severin Kanute, 2
Scott, Helenus (1802-1879), 2
Scott, Robert, 2
Scott, Thomas, 2
Singleton, Benjamin, 2
Smith, John Thomas*, 6
Smith, Philip Thomas, 2
Spark, Alexander Brodie, 2
Spencer, Sir Richard, 2
Spode, Josiah, 2
Terry, Samuel, 2
Terry, Samuel Henry*, 6
Thomas, Bartholomew Boyle, 2
Thomas, Jocelyn Henry Connor, 2
Thorn, George*, 6
Throsby, Charles, 2
Toosey, James Denton, 2

Tooth, Sir Robert Lucas Lucas-*, 6
Townson, John, 2
Uther, Reuben, 2
Walker, Thomas (1791-1861), 2
Warby, John, 2
Wentworth, William Charles*, 2
Willis, Richard, 2
Windeyer, Archibald, 2
Windeyer, Richard, 2
Wollstonecraft, Edward, 2
Wyatt, William, 2
LAWYER, see also Judge; Magistrate
Abbott, Sir Joseph Palmer*, 3
Abbott, Percy Phipps*, 7
Abbott, Robert Palmer*, 3
à Beckett, Thomas Turner*, 3
à Beckett, William Arthur Callander*, 3
Abigail, Ernest Robert, 7
Adamson, Travers*, 3
Ah Ket, William, 7
Allen, George*, 1
Allen, Sir George Wigram*, 3
Allport, Joseph, 1
Allport, Morton, 3
Anderson, Robert Stirling Hore*, 3
Andrews, Richard Bullock*, 3
Appel, John George*, 7
Arthur, John Andrew*, 7
Ash, George*, 7
Aspinall, Butler Cole*, 3
Baker, Sir Richard Chaffey*, 7
Bannister, Saxe, 1
Barlow, William, 7
Barton, George Burnett, 3
Barwell, Sir Henry Newman*, 7
Bavin, Sir Thomas Rainsford*, 7
Baxter, Alexander Macduff, 1
Bayles, Norman*, 7
Bayley, Sir Lyttleton Holyoake*, 3
Belt, Francis Walter, 7
Beor, Henry Rogers*, 3
Best, Sir Robert Wallace*, 7
Bignold, Hugh Baron, 7
Birnie, Richard, 3
Blackburn, Arthur Seaforth, 7
Blackburn, Maurice McCrae*, 7
Blacket, Wilfred, 7
Bowden, Eric Kendall*, 7
Bradley, Henry Burton, 3
Bramston, Sir John*, 3
Bray, Sir John Cox*, 3
Brennan, Anna Teresa, 7
Brennan, Francis*, 7
Brennan, Frank Tennison*, 7
Brennan, Thomas Cornelius*, 7
Broadhurst, Edward*, 3
Brown, Frederick*, 3
Brown, James Drysdale*, 7
Brown, Stephen Campbell*, 3
Browne, Eyles Irwin Caulfield*, 3
Buchanan, David*, 3
Bunny, Brice Frederick*, 3
Burdekin, Marshall*, 3
Butler, Edward*, 3

Butler, Gamaliel, 1
Butler, William Frederick Dennis, 7
Byrnes, Thomas Joseph*, 7
Cameron, Alexander, 7
Campbell, Donald*, 7
Campbell, Gerald Ross, 7
Carlile, Sir Edward, 7
Carruthers, Sir Joseph Hector McNeil*, 7
Charteris, Archibald Hamilton, 7
Chartres, George, 1
Clark, James Purcell, 8
Clark, William Nairne, 1
Cohen, Harold Edward*, 8
Cohen, Isaac Henry*, 8
Cohen, Montague, 8
Coldham, Walter Timon, 8
Collins, George Thomas*, 8
Colquhoun, Percy Brereton*, 8
Cope, William, 8
Crawford, Thomas Simpson*, 8
Crick, William Patrick*, 8
Crossley, George, 1
Crouch, Richard Armstrong*, 8
Crowther, George O'Dell, 8
Cumbrae-Stewart, Francis William Sutton, 8
Cuthbert, Sir Henry*, 3
Dalley, William Bede*, 4
Daly, John Joseph*, 8
Dangar, Henry Cary*, 4
D'Arcy, William Knox, 8
Darvall, Sir John Bayley*, 4
Davies, Sir John Mark*, 4
Davies, Sir Matthew Henry*, 4
Davis, Charles Herbert, 8
Davy, Thomas Arthur Lewis*, 8
Deakin, Alfred*, 8
De Lissa, Alfred, 4
Deniehy, Daniel Henry*, 4
Denny, William Joseph*, 8
Dobson, Alfred*, 4
Dobson, Frank Stanley*, 4
Dobson, Henry*, 8
Douglas, Sir Adye*, 4
Downer, Sir John William*, 8
Drake, James George*, 8
Driver, Richard*, 4
Duffy, Sir Charles Gavan*, 4
Duffy, John Gavan, 4
Eady, Charles John*, 8
Eagar, Edward, 1
Eggleston, Sir Frederic William, 8
Elliott, Harold Edward*, 8
Enright, Walter John, 8
Evans, Ada Emily, 8
Evans, George Samuel*, 4
Feez, Adolph Frederick Milford, 8
Feez, Arthur Herman Henry Milford, 8
Field, Edward Percy, 8
Fink, Theodore*, 8
Fitzhardinge, William George Augustus, 4
Flannery, George Ernest, 8
Foster, William John*, 4
Fowles, Edwin Wesley Howard*, 8

Foxton, Justin Fox Greenlaw*, 8
Freehill, Francis Bede, 4
Freeman, William Addison, 8
Gant, Tetley*, 8
Garland, John*, 8
Garling, Frederick (1775-1848), 1
Garran, Sir Robert Randolph, 8
Garrett, Thomas William, 8
Garrick, Sir James Francis*, 4
Gaunson, David*, 4
Gellibrand, Joseph Tice, 1
Gill, James Howard, 4
Gillott, Sir Samuel*, 9
Gleadow, John Ward*, 1
Glynn, Patrick McMahon*, 9
Gordon, Alexander, 4
Gould, Sir Albert John*, 9
Grant, James Macpherson*, 4
Gray, Moses Wilson*, 4
Greig, Grata Flos Matilda, 9
Greig, Stella Fida, 9
Groom, Sir Littleton Ernest*, 9
Grubb, Frederick William*, 4
Grubb, William Dawson*, 4
Gurner, Henry Field, 4
Gurner, John, 1
Hain, Gladys Adeline, 9
Hall, David Robert*, 9
Ham, Wilbur Lincoln, 9
Hardy, Arthur*, 4
Hawker, Edward William*, 9
Hawthorn, Arthur George Clarence*, 9
Hayes-Williams, William Gordon, 9
Haynes, Richard Septimus*, 9
Hearn, William Edward*, 4
Henty, William, 1
Heydon, Louis Francis*, 9
Holden, George Kenyon*, 4
Holman, William Arthur*, 9
Holme, John Barton, 9
Holroyd, Arthur Todd*, 4
Homburg, Hermann Robert*, 9
Hone, Joseph, 1
Horgan, John, 9
Hübbe, Ulrich, 4
Hughes, Geoffrey Forrest, 9
Hughes, John Francis*, 9
Hughes, Sir Thomas*, 9
Hunt, Atlee Arthur, 9
Hyman, Arthur Wellesley, 9
Ireland, Horace, 9
Ireland, Richard Davies*, 4
Isaacs, Robert Macintosh*, 4
James, Sir Walter Hartwell*, 9
Jaques, Theodore James, 4
Johnson, Robert Ebenezer*, 4
Johnstone, John Lorimer Gibson, 9
Jones, Rees Rutland*, 9
Keating, John Henry, 9
Keenan, Sir Norbert Michael*, 9
King, Reginald Macdonnell*, 9
Kingston, Charles Cameron*, 9
Knowles, Sir George Shaw, 9
Labilliere, Francis Peter, 5

Landor, Edward Willson, 2
Lang, John, 5
Lawson, Sir Harry Sutherland Wightman*, 10
Leake, George*, 10
Leake, George Walpole*, 5
Leary, Joseph*, 5
Lenehan, Robert William, 10
Leverrier, Francis Hewitt, 10
Levien, Robert Henry*, 10
Levy, Sir Daniel*, 10
Lewis, Arndell Neil*, 10
Lewis, Sir Neil Elliott*, 10
Ley, Thomas John*, 10
Little, Robert, 5
Lochée, Francis, 2
Lowe, Robert (1811-1892)*, 2
Lysaght, Andrew Augustus*, 10
Macalister, Arthur*, 5
Macartney, Sir Edward Henry*, 10
McCann, William Francis James, 10
McCay, Sir James Whiteside*, 10
MacDevitt, Edward O'Donnell*, 5
Macdowell, Edward, 2
McGill, Alec Douglas, 10
Macgroarty, Neil Francis*, 10
Mackaness, John, 2
Mackenzie, William Kenneth Seaforth, 10
Mackinnon, Donald*, 10
Mackinnon, Lauchlan Kenneth Scobie, 10
McLachlan, Alexander John*, 10
MacLeod, Thomas, 10
Macnaghten, Charles Melville, 10
Madden, Sir Frank*, 10
Mann, Charles (1799-1860), 2
Manning, Sir Henry Edward*, 10
Marks, Percy Joseph, 10
Marks, Walter Moffitt*, 10
Martin, Lewis Ormsby*, 10
Maughan, Sir David, 10
Maxwell, George Arnot*, 10
Meagher, Richard Denis*, 10
Michael, James Lionel, 5
Michie, Sir Archibald*, 5
Miller, Robert Byron*, 5
Minogue, Henry, 10
Mitchell, Sir Edward Fancourt, 10
Mitchell, Ernest Meyer*, 10
Moor, Henry*, 2
Moore, George Fletcher, 2
Moore, Sir William Harrison, 10
Moore, William Henry, 2
Morrison, Sibyl Enid Vera Munro, 10
Moulden, Beaumont Arnold*, 10
Moulden, Sir Frank Beaumont, 10
Muir, Thomas, 2
Mullins, John Lane*, 10
Neighbour, George Henry, 10
Nesbit, (Edward) Paris(s), 11
Nichols, George Robert*, 5
Nobbs, John (1845-1921)*, 11
Norton, James*, 2
Norton, James, 5
O'Conor, Broughton Barnabas*, 11

Ogilvie, Albert George*, 11
O'Loghlen, Sir Bryan*, 5
Parker, Hubert Stanley Wyborn*, 11
Parramore, William Thomas, 2
Paterson, Andrew Barton, 11
Pavy, Emily Dorothea, 11
Peden, Sir John Beverley*, 11
Petre, Henry Aloysius, 11
Phillips, Morris Mondle, 11
Piesse, Edmund Leolin, 11
Pilcher, Charles Edward*, 11
Pitcairn, Robert, 2
Plunkett, John Hubert*, 2
Pratt, Ambrose Goddard Hesketh, 11
Primrose, Hubert Leslie*, 11
Pring, Ratcliffe*, 5
Propsting, William Bispham*, 11
Purves, James Liddell*, 5
Quick, Sir John*, 11
Ramaciotti, Gustave Mario, 11
Ramsay, Robert (1842-1882)*, 6
Riddell, Walter John Carre, 11
Rigby, Edward Charles, 11
Ritchie, William, 6
Robertson, William (1839-1892)*, 6
Robinson, Sir Arthur*, 11
Robinson, Robert Thomson*, 11
Robson, William Elliot Veitch*, 11
Rodd, Brent Clements, 6
Rofe, Thomas Ernest, 11
Ross, Hugh Cokeley, 2
Russell, James George, 11
Russell, Percy Joseph, 11
Ryan, Thomas Joseph*, 11
St Ledger, Anthony James*, 11
Salomons, Sir Julian Emanuel*, 6
Sanderson, Archibald*, 11
Sharwood, William Henry, 11
Shields, Tasman*, 11
Shiels, William*, 11
Simpson, Edward Percy, 11
Sinclair, Sir Colin Archibald*, 11
Skipper, John Michael, 6
Sladen, Sir Charles*, 6
Slattery, Thomas Michael*, 11
Sleigh, William Campbell*, 6
Sly, Joseph David, 6
Smith, Arthur Bruce*, 11
Smith, Christian Brynhild Ochiltree Jollie, 11
Smith, Francis Villeneuve, 11
Smith, Philip Thomas, 2
Smith, Robert Burdett*, 6
Snowball, Oswald Robinson*, 12
Snowden, Sir Arthur*, 12
Solomon, Albert Edgar*, 12
Stenhouse, Nicol Drysdale, 6
Stephen, Sir Colin Campbell, 12
Stephen, Sir George, 6
Stephen, George Milner*, 2
Stephen, Montagu Consett*, 6
Stephen, Septimus Alfred*, 6
Stonor, Alban Charles, 2
Strangways, Henry Bull Templar*, 6

Symon, Sir Josiah Henry*, 12
Symonds, Saul, 12
Teece, Richard Clive, 12
Tenison Woods, Mary Cecil, 12
Thomas, Evan Henry, 2
Thompson, John Malbon*, 6
Thynne, Andrew Joseph*, 12
Todd, Robert Henry, 12
Topp, Samuel St John, 6
Tout, Sir Frederick Henry*, 12
Tozer, Sir Horace*, 12
Trickett, William Joseph*, 6
Turner, Sir George*, 12
Vaughan, John Howard*, 12
Von Doussa, Charles Louis*, 12
Walker, James Backhouse, 6
Walker, William*, 6
Wallace, Arthur Cooper, 12
Wanliss, John Newton Wellesley, 12
Want, John Henry*, 12
Want, Randolph John*, 6
Wardell, Robert, 2
Webb, Thomas Prout, 6
Weigall, Cecil Edward, 12
Weigall, Theyre à Beckett, 12
Wentworth, William Charles*, 2
Wilson, Lachlan Chisholm, 12
Wilson, Thomas, 2
Wilson, Walter Horatio*, 12
Windeyer, Richard, 2
Windeyer, Richard, 12
Windeyer, William Archibald, 12
Wisdom, Sir Robert*, 6
Wise, Bernhard Ringrose*, 12
Wise, George Henry*, 12
Wollaston, Sir Harry Newton Phillips, 12
Wood, John Dennistoun*, 6
Woolcock, John Laskey, 12
Wrixon, Sir Henry John*, 6
Wynne, Agar*, 12
Young, Adolphus William, 2
Young, Sir Frederick William*, 12

LEXICOGRAPHER
Mathews, Robert Henry, 10
Partridge, Eric Honeywood, 11

LIBRARIAN
Anderson, Henry Charles Lennox, 7
Armstrong, Edmund la Touche, 7
Battye, James Sykes, 7
Bertie, Charles Henry, 7
Binns, Kenneth, 7
Brereton, John Le Gay, 7
Bride, Thomas Francis, 3
Clucas, Robert John Miller, 8
Ifould, William Herbert, 9
Kibble, Nita Bernice, 9
Leeson, Ida Emily, 10
McClintock, Albert Scott, 10
McEvilly, Walter O'Malley, 5
Martens, Conrad, 2
Miller, Edmund Morris, 10
Miller, Maxwell*, 5
Morice, James Percy, 10
O'Donovan, Denis, 5

Pitt, Ernest Roland, 11
Smith, James (1820-1910), 6
Taylor, Alfred Joseph, 6
Tulk, Augustus Henry, 6
Wadsworth, Arthur, 12
Walker, Robert Cooper, 6
Wheen, Arthur Wesley, 12
Windeyer, Margaret, 12

LIEUT-GOVERNOR
New South Wales
Erskine, James, 1
Grose, Francis, 1
Molle, George James, 2
Paterson, William, 2
Ross, Robert (b.1740?), 2
Stewart, William, 2
Street, Sir Philip Whistler, 12
South Australia
Robe, Frederick Holt, 2
Young, Sir Henry Edward Fox, 6
Van Diemen's Land
Arthur, Sir George, 1
Collins, David, 1
Davey, Thomas, 1
Denison, Sir William Thomas, 4
Eardley-Wilmot, Sir John Eardley, 1
Franklin, Sir John, 1
Snodgrass, Kenneth, 2
Sorell, William (1775-1848), 2
Victoria
La Trobe, Charles Joseph, 2

LIFESAVER
Biddell, Walter, 7

LIGHTHOUSE-KEEPER
Baillieu, James George, 7
Fowles, Herbert James, 8
Siddins, Richard, 2

LINGUIST
Ahuia Ova, 7
Menge, Johann, 2
Tilly, William Henry, 12
Way, Arthur Sanders, 6

LOTTERY PROMOTER
Adams, George, 3

MAGISTRATE
Allman, Francis, 1
Antill, Henry Colden, 1
Arndell, Thomas, 1
Arthur, Charles, 1
Barclay, Andrew, 1
Baylis, Henry, 3
Bell, Archibald (1773-1837), 1
Blair, James, 1
Brenan, John Ryan, 1
Brown, Maitland*, 3
Browne, Thomas Alexander, 3
Burges, William, 1
Campbell, Pieter Laurentz, 1
Clarke, George O'Malley, 3
Close, Edward Charles, 1
Cowper, Charles*, 3
Cox, William, 1
Crummer, James Henry, 1
Day, Edward Denny, 1

De Boos, Charles Edward Augustus, 4
Douglass, Henry Grattan*, 1
Dulhunty, Robert Venour, 1
Faunce, Alured Tasker, 1
Forster, Matthew, 1
Fyans, Foster, 1
Gordon, James, 1
Gunn, William, 1
Haly, Charles Robert*, 4
Hardy, John Richard, 4
Hume, Hamilton, 1
Humphrey, Adolarius William Henry, 1
Innes, Archibald Clunes, 2
James, John Charles Horsey, 4
Jardine, Francis Lascelles, 4
Jardine, John, 4
Landor, Edward Willson, 2
Langlands, George, 5
Leake, George Walpole*, 5
Lockyer, Edmund, 2
McLachlan, Lachlan, 5
Mason, Martin, 2
Mason, Thomas, 2
Miles, William Augustus, 2
Molloy, John, 2
Monckton, Charles Arthur Whitmore, 10
Moore, Thomas, 2
Mulgrave, Peter Archer, 2
Pasco, Crawford Atchison Denman, 5
Powlett, Frederick Armand, 2
Price, John Giles, 2
Pugh, Theophilus Parsons*, 5
Ranking, Robert Archibald, 11
Read, Charles Rudston, 6
Reeve, Edward, 6
Schaw, Charles, 2
Shepherdson, John Banks, 2
Simpson, James, 2
Slade, Ernest Augustus, 2
Stow, Jefferson Pickman, 6
Sturt, Evelyn Pitfield Shirley, 6
Tighe, Atkinson Alfred Patrick*, 6
Walter, William Ardagh Gardner, 12
White, James Charles, 6
Whitefoord, John, 2
Wickham, John Clements, 2
Wilson, Henry Croasdaile, 2
Windeyer, Charles, 2
MALTSTER
Burston, James, 7
White, Alexander Henry, 12
MANUFACTURER, *see also* Industrialist;
Ironfounder; Refiner
Alston, James, 7
Ashworth, Thomas Ramsden*, 7
Austin, Baron Herbert, 3
Baker, Thomas (1854-1928), 7
Beale, Octavius Charles, 7
Benjamin, Louis Reginald Samuel, 7
Bennett, George Henry*, 7
Berry, Henry, 3
Bond, George Alan, 7
Brunton, Sir William, 7
Crompton, Joseph, 3

Danks, John, 4
Degraves, Peter, 1
Derham, Frederick Thomas*, 4
Ebsworth, Frederick Louis, 4
Felton, Alfred, 4
Forwood, Walter Weech, 4
Gadsden, Jabez, 8
Gerard, Alfred Edward, 8
Gibson, William, 8
Goodlet, John Hay, 4
Grimwade, Frederick Sheppard*, 4
Grove, James, 1
Hudson, Henry, 4
Johns, Peter, 4
Johnston, Charles Melbourne, 9
Kent, Thomas, 2
Kopsen, William, 9
Leckie, John William*, 10
Lord, Simeon, 2
Lysaght, Herbert Royse, 10
MacDougall, James, 10
McIlwraith, John, 5
Makutz, Bela, 5
Marchant, George, 10
Marconi, Joseph Cornelius, 10
Martyn, Nellie Constance, 10
Mitchell, David, 5
Mitchell, Joseph Earl Cherry*, 5
Muller, Frederick, 10
Penfold, William Clark, 11
Phillips, Orwell, 11
Ramsay, William, 11
Ricardo, Percy Ralph, 11
Ritchie, Robert Adam*, 6
Rubinstein, Helena, 11
Rumpf, Ann, 11
Sandford, William, 11
Sands, John, 6
Shaw, Archibald John, 11
Simpson, Alfred Muller*, 6
Sinclair, William, 11
Smith, William John, 11
Struth, John, 2
Sweet, George, 12
Thompson, David (1865-1916), 12
Uther, Reuben, 2
Vickery, Ebenezer*, 6
Vogt, George Leonard, 12
Walder, Sir Samuel Robert*, 12
Wormald, Henry Percy, 12
Wormald, Joseph Dawson, 12
Wortman(n), Adolphus, 2
Wortman(n), Ignatz, 2
Wrigley, Leslie James, 12
Wunderlich, Alfred, 12
Wunderlich, Ernest (Henry Charles), 12
Wunderlich, Frederick Otto, 12
aircraft
Larkin, Herbert Joseph, 9
Percival, Edgar Wikner, 11
boots
Abbott, Joseph Henry*, 3
Abigail, Francis*, 3
Alderson, William Maddison*, 3

Bedggood, John Charles, 3
Cabena, William Whyte, 7
Hayes, Michael, 1
Minahan, Patrick Joseph*, 10
Ryder, John, 11
Whiddon, Samuel Thomas*, 12
candles
Burford, William Henville, 1
Loader, Thomas*, 5
cars
Lewis, William Howard Horatio, 10
Tarrant, Harley, 12
Thomson, Herbert, 12
cement
McCann, Peter, 10
McCann, Wesley Burrett, 10
Mills, Charles, 10
chemicals
Cuming, James (1835-1911), 8
Cuming, James (1861-1920), 8
Leggo, Arthur Victor, 10
cloth
Barker, Thomas*, 1
Byrnes, James (1806-1886)*, 3
Ebsworth, Octavius Bayliffe, 4
Hirst, Godfrey, 9
Hughes, Fred William, 9
Laycock, Burdett, 10
Laycock, Frederick, 10
Vicars, Sir John, 12
Vicars, John, 6
Vicars, Sir William, 12
Williams, Edward David*, 12
clothing
Edwards, Percy Malcolm, 8
Murray, David*, 5
Myer, Elcon Baevski, 10
Stewart, Alexander, 12
Stuart, Francis*, 12
Thompson, Matilda Louise, 12
Woods, Percy William, 12
dairy products
Crawford, Alexander, 8
Crowe, Robert, 8
Graham, Arthur Ernest James Charles
  King, 9
Livingston, Thomas*, 10
Mackrell, Edwin Joseph*, 10
Wilson, David, 12
foodstuffs
Arnott, William, 3
Bell, Peter Albany, 7
Biddell, Walter, 7
Edgell, Robert Gordon, 8
Hoadley, Abel, 9
Leggo, Henry Madren, 10
Love, Sir Joseph Clifton, 10
Peters, Frederick Augustus Bolles, 11
Pratten, Herbert Edward*, 11
Ribush, Dolia, 11
Robertson, Sir Macpherson, 11
Stedman, James, 12
Swallow, Thomas, 6
Wade, Benjamin Martin*, 12

Walker, Fred, 12
Watson, William*, 12
White, William Clarence, 12
furniture
Prenzel, Robert Wilhelm, 11
Rogers, Charles, 6
Steinfeld, Emanuel*, 6
Zimpel, William James, 12
hats
Mauger, Samuel*, 10
Sanderson, Robert Fitzroy, 11
Uther, Reuben, 2
jam
Jones, Sir Henry, 9
Palfreyman, Achalen Woolliscroft, 11
Peacock, George, 5
Reynolds, Thomas*, 6
leather goods
Hickey, Simon*, 9
Olney, Sir Herbert Horace*, 11
machinery
Bagshaw, John Stokes, 3
Buncle, John, 3
Koerstz, Christian Christiansen, 9
Leitch, Sir Walter, 10
Lennon, Hugh, 5
Lewis, Edward Powell, 10
Lyell, George, 10
McKay, Hugh Victor, 10
Martin, James*, 5
May, Frederick, 5
Morrow, James, 5
Ridley, John, 2
Rigg, William*, 11
Roberts, Abraham, 11
Ruwolt, Charles Ernest, 11
Salisbury, William Robert Peel, 11
Shearer, David, 11
Shearer, John, 11
Taylor, Headlie Shipard, 12
Thompson, David (1828-1889), 12
motor bodies
Holden, Sir Edward Wheewall*, 9
Holden, Henry James, 9
Richards, Herbert Clarence*, 11
Richards, Tobias John Martin, 11
paint
Taubman, George Henry, 12
Taubman, Nathaniel James, 12
Vosz, Heinrich Ludwig, 6
pharmaceuticals
Elliott, James Frederick, 8
Faulding, Francis Hardey, 4
Nicholas, Alfred Michael, 11
Nicholas, George Richard Rich, 11
Soul, Caleb, 6
Soul, Washington Handley, 6
pipes
Hume, Walter Reginald, 9
Nettlefold, Isaac Robert, 11
Nettlefold, Sir Thomas Sydney Richard,
  11
pottery
Fowler, Robert*, 4

King, James (1800-1857), 2
Mashman, Ernest James Theodore, 10
rope
Donaghy, John*, 4
Forsyth, Archibald*, 4
Kinnear, Edward Hore, 9
Kinnear, Henry Humphrey, 9
rubber
Glass, Barnet, 9
Perdriau, Henry, 11
soap
Allen, Alfred*, 3
Allen, William Bell*, 3
Allen, William Johnston*, 3
Hutchinson, William Alston*, 4
Lansell, George, 5
Pearson, Thomas Edwin, 11
Walker, Henry, 6
tobacco
Denison, Sir Hugh Robert, 8
Dixson, Sir Hugh, 8
Dixson, Hugh, 4
Michelides, Peter Spero, 10
MARINE
Childs, Joseph, 1
Clark, Ralph, 1
Davey, Thomas, 1
Dawes, William, 1
Easty, John, 1
Johnston, George (1764-1823), 2
Lord, Edward, 2
Menzies, Sir Charles, 2
Mudie, James, 2
Nepean, Nicholas, 2
Ross, Robert (b.1740?), 2
Scott, James (d.1796), 2
Stanfield, Daniel (d.1826), 2
Tench, Watkin, 2
MARINER
Allen, William, 1
Anstey, Francis George*, 7
Barclay, Andrew, 1
Bass, George, 1
Baudin, Nicolas Thomas, 1
Bayldon, Francis Joseph, 7
Biscoe, John, 1
Bruce, George, 1
Bruny D'Entrecasteaux, Joseph-Antoine
  Raymond, 1
Burke, John, 7
Cadell, Francis, 3
Calder, George, 7
Charles, Samuel*, 3
Clare, Chapman James, 8
Clark, Alfred Thomas*, 3
Collin, William, 3
Coote, Audley*, 3
Corby, John McKenzie, 8
Creer, Herbert Victor, 8
Creer, Reginald Charles, 8
Darley, Benjamin, 4
Davis, John King, 8
Dempster, James McLean, 4
Dexter, Walter Ernest, 8

Doorly, James Gerald Stokely, 8
Elder, William, 4
Evans, Sir John William*, 8
Fox, Henry Thomas, 4
Gatty, Harold Charles, 8
Hacking, Henry, 1
Hart, John*, 4
Hayes, William Henry, 4
Helpman, Benjamin Franklin, 1
Henry, Henry Goya, 9
Hernsheim, Eduard, 4
Holyman, Thomas Henry, 9
Holyman, William, 4
Hovell, William Hilton, 1
Janssen, Willem, 2
Jones, William, 9
Jorgenson, Jorgen, 2
Kelly, James, 2
La Pérouse, Jean-François de Galaup, 2
Lee, John Henry Alexander, 10
Mackay, John, 5
McMeckan, James, 5
Morrill, James, 2
Murray, John, 2
Pearse, Albert William, 11
Pelsaert, Francisco, 2
Poole, Daniel, 11
Raine, Thomas, 2
Raven, William, 2
Rebell, Fred, 11
Rhodes, Fred, 11
Rowntree, Thomas Stephenson, 6
Seymour-Symers, Thomas Lyell, 2
Siddins, Richard, 2
Smith, William Howard, 6
Strachan, John, 6
Sumsuma, 12
Sweet, Samuel White, 6
Tasman, Abel Janszoon, 2
Tregurtha, Edward Primrose, 2
Trouton, Frederick Henry, 6
Walsh, Thomas, 12
Wawn, William Twizell, 6
Welsh, John, 2
Whyte, Thomas, 2
MARKSMAN
Brownlow, Richard (1832-1873), 3
MASON
Dixon, Francis Burdett, 4
Don, Charles Jardine*, 4
Jageurs, Morgan Peter, 9
Lynch, John, 2
McGregor, Gregor*, 10
Price, Thomas*, 11
Roseby, John*, 6
Rusconi, Francis Philip, 11
Smith, Thomas (1823-1900), 6
Stanford, William Walter Tyrell, 6
MASSEUR
Cazaly, Roy, 7
MATHEMATICIAN
Carslaw, Horatio Scott, 7
Cockle, Sir James, 3
Gurney, Theodore Thomas, 4

Lamb, Sir Horace, 5
McLaren, Samuel Bruce, 10
Michell, John Henry, 10
Pell, Morris Birkbeck, 5
Weatherburn, Charles Ernest, 12
Wellish, Edward Montague, 12
Wilton, John Raymond, 12
MATRON, *see* Nurse
MAYOR
Adelaide
Bruce, Sir Wallace, 7
Cain, Sir Jonathon Robert, 7
Glover, Charles Richmond John, 9
Moulden, Sir Frank Beaumont, 10
Brisbane
Jolly, William Alfred*, 9
Jones, Alfred James*, 9
Petrie, John, 5
Cairns
Draper, Alexander Frederick John, 8
Geelong
Hitchcock, Howard, 9
Hawthorn
Rigby, Edward Charles, 11
Melbourne
Brunton, Sir William, 7
Cabena, William Whyte, 7
Hennessy, Sir David Valentine, 9
Moor, Henry*, 2
Morell, Sir Stephen Joseph, 10
Moubray, Thomas, 5
Sydney
Harris, John (1838-1911)*, 4
Harris, Sir Matthew*, 9
Macdermott, Henry, 2
Williamstown
Liston, John James, 10
MECHANIC
Bennett, James Mallett, 7
MEDICAL PRACTITIONER, *see also*
Homoeopath; Ophthalmologist;
Pathologist
Aaron, Isaac, 1
Adam, George Rothwell Wilson, 7
Agnew, Sir James Willson*, 3
Allan, Robert Marshall, 7
Alleyne, Haynes Gibbes, 3
Allum, Mahomet, 7
Ambrose, Theodore, 7
Andrews, Arthur, 7
Armit, Henry William, 7
Armstrong, William George, 7
Arndell, Thomas, 1
Arnold, Joseph, 1
Arthur, Richard*, 7
Aspinall, Jessie Strahorn, 7
Ballow, David Keith, 1
Balls-Headley, Walter, 3
Balmain, William, 1
Bancroft, Joseph, 3
Bancroft, Thomas Lane, 7
Barber, George Walter, 7
Barbour, Eric Pitty, 7
Barker, Edward, 3

Barker, William, 3
Barrett, Edith Helen, 7
Barton, Alan Sinclair Darvall, 7
Basedow, Herbert*, 7
Bass, George, 1
Bassett, William Frederick, 3
Beaney, James George*, 3
Beattie, Joseph Aloysius, 7
Bedford, Edward Samuel Pickard*, 3
Bennett, Agnes Elizabeth Lloyd, 7
Benson, John Robinson*, 3
Berry, Richard James Arthur, 7
Birch, Thomas William, 1
Bird, Frederic Dougan, 7
Bird, Samuel Dougan, 3
Blackall, William Edward, 7
Blackburn, Sir Charles Bickerton, 7
Bland, William*, 1
Booth, Mary, 7
Bourne, Eleanor Elizabeth, 7
Bowden, Edmund, 1
Bowden, Matthew, 1
Bowker, Richard Ryther Steer*, 3
Bowman, James, 1
Bowman, Robert, 3
Breinl, Anton, 7
Brennan, Edward Thomas*, 7
Brereton, John Le Gay, 3
Brice, Katie Louisa, 7
Bromley, Edward Foord, 1
Browne, John Harris, 3
Browne, William James*, 3
Browning, Colin Arrott, 1
Brownless, Sir Anthony Colling, 3
Burfitt, Walter Charles Fitzmaurice, 7
Butler, Arthur Graham, 7
Butler, Henry*, 3
Caffyn, Stephen Mannington, 3
Cairns, Sir Hugh William Bell, 7
Cameron, Donald (1780-1857), 3
Campbell, Alfred Walter, 7
Campbell, Allan, 7
Campbell, Francis Rawdon Hastings, 3
Cannan, Kearsey, 3
Casey, Cornelius Gavin, 1
Challinor, Henry*, 3
Chambers, Thomas, 3
Champion de Crespigny, Sir Constantine
   Trent, 7
Chapple, Phoebe, 7
Clayton, Arthur Ross, 8
Clement, Dixie Paumier, 8
Clisby, Harriet Jemima Winifred, 3
Clubbe, Sir Charles Percy Barlee, 8
Cockburn, Sir John Alexander*, 8
Cole, Frank Hobill, 8
Collie, Alexander, 1
Conrick, Horatio Victor Patrick, 8
Considen, Dennis, 1
Cooper, Lilian Violet, 8
Coppleson, Sir Victor Marcus, 8
Cotter, Thomas Young, 1
Coverdale, John, 1
Cowlishaw, Leslie, 8

Cox, James Charles, 3
Craig, Robert Gordon, 8
Creed, John Mildred*, 3
Crowther, Edward Lodewyk*, 3
Crowther, William Lodewyk*, 3
Cunningham, Peter Miller, 1
Cussen, Patrick Edward, 1
Cuts, William Henry, 3
Dale, John, 8
D'Arcy, Dame Constance Elizabeth, 8
Davy, Edward, 1
Dean, Horace, 4
De Garis, Mary Clementina, 8
Denham, Howard Kynaston, 8
Devine, Sir Hugh Berchmans, 8
Dick, James Adam, 8
Dixon, Graham Patrick, 8
Dixson, Thomas Storie, 8
Dobie, John, 1
Docker, Joseph*, 4
Dorsey, William McTaggart, 4
Douglass, Henry Grattan*, 1
Dowie, John Alexander, 4
Downes, Rupert Major, 8
Dryer, Albert Thomas, 8
Duncan, Handasyde, 1
Dunhill, Sir Thomas Peel, 8
Eades, Richard, 4
Eames, William L'Estrange, 8
Edye, Sir Benjamin Thomas, 8
Ellis, Constance, 8
Ellis, Henry Augustus*, 8
Elsey, Joseph Ravenscroft, 4
Embley, Edward Henry, 8
Embling, Thomas, 4
Fallon, Cyril Joseph*, 8
Ferguson, John, 1
Fetherston, Richard Herbert Joseph*, 8
Fiaschi, Piero Francis Bruno, 8
Fiaschi, Thomas Henry, 8
Fishbourne, John William Yorke, 8
FitzGerald, Sir Thomas Naghten, 4
Gabriel, Charles Louis, 8
Gillbee, William, 4
Graham, Sir James*, 4
Greenup, Richard, 4
Greeves, Augustus Frederick Adolphus*, 4
Greig, Jane Stocks, 9
Greig, Janet Lindsay, 9
Gresswell, Dan Astley, 9
Gullett, Lucy Edith, 9
Gunson, John Michael, 4
Hailes, William Allan, 9
Hall, Edward Swarbreck, 1
Hall, James, 1
Halley, Ida Gertrude Margaret, 9
Hamilton, John (1841-1916)*, 4
Hampton, John Stephen, 1
Hardie, Sir David, 9
Harper, Margaret Hilda, 9
Harris, John (1754-1838), 1
Harris, Sir John Richards*, 9
Harris, Samuel Henry, 9

Herz, Max Markus, 9
Hirschfeld, Eugen, 9
Hobbs, William, 4
Hobson, Edmund Charles, 1
Holmes à Court, Alan Worsley, 9
Hone, Frank Sandland, 9
Hood, Sir Alexander Harvie, 9
Hope, Robert Culbertson*, 4
Hopley, William, 1
Horrocks, Joseph Lucas, 4
Howitt, Godfrey, 4
Howse, Sir Neville Reginald*, 9
Imlay, Alexander, 2
Imlay, George, 2
Irving, John, 2
Jackson, Ernest Sandford, 9
Jamison, Sir John, 2
Jamison, Thomas, 2
Jeffries, Lewis Wibmer, 9
Johnson, Edward Angas, 9
Jones, Sir Philip Sydney, 4
Jull, Roberta Henrietta Margaritta, 9
Kay, William Elphinstone, 9
Kelly, Robert Vandeleur, 9
Kenny, Augustus Leo, 9
Kesteven, Hereward Leighton, 9
Knaggs, Samuel Thomas, 5
Lambie, Charles George, 9
Landale, Thomas, 2
Laver, Charles William, 10
Leitch, Emily Bertha, Lady, 10
Lilley, Charles Mitford, 10
Lind, Edmund Frank, 10
Lindeman, Henry John, 5
Love, Wilton Wood Russell, 10
Luttrell, Edward, 2
McCall, Sir John*, 10
McCarthy, Charles, 5
MacCarthy, Charles William, 10
McClelland, William Caldwell, 10
MacCormick, Sir Alexander, 10
McCrea, William, 5
McDonald, Sydney Fancourt, 10
MacGillivray, Paul Howard, 5
Mackellar, Sir Charles Kinnaird*, 10
McKelvey, Sir John Lawrance, 10
MacKenzie, Sir William Colin, 10
McLaren, Charles Inglis, 10
MacLaurin, Sir Henry Normand*, 10
Macnamara, Dame Annie Jean, 10
Maitland, Sir Herbert Lethington, 10
Maloney, William Robert (Nuttall)*, 10
Manning, Frederic Norton, 5
Marks, Alexander Hammett, 10
Marks, Charles Ferdinand*, 10
Mason, Martin, 2
Maudsley, Sir Henry Carr, 10
Maund, John, 5
Mayne, James O'Neil, 10
Mayo, Helen Mary, 10
Mead, Gertrude Ella, 10
Meredith, John Baldwin Hoystead, 10
Meyer, Felix Henry, 10
Mileham, James, 2

Milligan, Joseph, 2
Mills, Arthur Edward, 10
Mitchell, James*, 2
Moloney, Patrick, 5
Moore, William, 10
Moran, Herbert Michael, 10
Mountgarrett, Jacob, 2
Munro, Andrew Watson, 10
Murdoch, James, 2
Murphy, Sir Francis*, 5
Nathan, Charles, 5
Newland, Sir Henry Simpson, 11
Newman-Morris, Sir John, 11
Newton, Sir Hibbert Alan Stephen, 11
Nicholson, Sir Charles*, 2
O'Doherty, Kevin Izod*, 5
O'Donnell, Nicholas Michael, 11
Officer, Sir Robert*, 2
O'Hara, Henry Michael, 11
O'Reilly, Susannah Hennessy, 11
Osborne, Ethel Elizabeth, 11
O'Shea, Patrick Joseph Francis, 11
Owens, John Downes*, 5
Page, Sir Earle Christmas Grafton*, 11
Palmer, Charles Reginald, 11
Palmer, Henry Wilfred, 11
Palmer, Sir James Frederick*, 5
Paton, Robert Thomson, 11
Paul, Sir Charles Norman, 11
Penfold, Christopher Rawson, 5
Plummer, Andrew, 5
Poate, Sir Hugh Raymond Guy, 11
Poidevin, Leslie Oswald Sheridan, 11
Power, John Joseph Wardell, 11
Pugh, William Russ, 2
Pulleine, Robert Henry, 11
Purser, Cecil, 11
Pye, Cecil Robert Arthur, 11
Quick, Balcombe, 11
Ramsay, David, 2
Ramsay, Sir John, 11
Ratten, Victor Richard, 11
Read, Henry, 6
Reading, Fanny, 11
Redfern, William, 2
Reid, David, 2
Reid, Thomas, 2
Rennie, George Edward, 11
Renwick, Sir Arthur*, 6
Richardson, Walter Lindesay, 11
Rivett, Amy Christine, 11
Rivett, Edward William, 11
Roberts, Sir Alfred, 6
Robertson, Edward, 11
Rogers, Richard Sanders, 11
Ross, Andrew Hendry*, 6
Ross, Isabella Henrietta Younger, 11
Roth, Reuter Emerich, 11
Roth, Walter Edmund, 11
Russell, Robert Hamilton, 11
Ryan, Sir Charles Snodgrass, 11
Salmon, Charles Carty*, 11
Sandes, Francis Percival, 11
Savage, Arthur, 2

Savage, John, 2
Scantlebury Brown, Vera, 11
Schlink, Sir Herbert Henry, 11
Scott, Henry James Herbert, 6
Scott, James (1790-1837), 2
Seccombe, William, 2
Sewell, Sir Sidney Valentine, 11
Sexton, Hannah Mary Helen, 11
Sharp, Granville Gilbert, 11
Shepherd, Arthur Edmund, 11
Shields, Clive*, 11
Shields, Sir Douglas Andrew, 11
Singleton, John, 6
Skirving, Robert Scot, 11
Smart, Thomas Christie, 6
Smith, Julian Augustus Romaine, 11
Smith, Louis Lawrence*, 6
Smith, William Ramsay, 11
Smyth, Arthur Bowes, 2
Snowball, William, 12
Souter, Charles Henry, 12
Springthorpe, John William, 12
Stacy, John Edward, 6
Stacy, Valentine Osborne, 12
Stang, Eleanor Margrethe, 12
Stawell, Sir Richard Rawdon, 12
Stephens, Henry Douglas, 12
Stewart, John Mitchell Young, 12
Stirling, Sir Edward Charles*, 6
Stokes, Edward Sutherland, 12
Stone, Emily Mary Page, 12
Stone, Emma Constance, 12
Stone, Grace Clara, 12
Stopford, Robert*, 12
Story, George Fordyce, 2
Strong, Walter Mersh, 12
Summons, Walter Ernest Isaac, 12
Sutton, Harvey, 12
Syme, Sir George Adlington, 12
Thomas, David John, 2
Thomas, Morgan, 6
Thompson, Clive Wentworth, 12
Thompson, John Ashburton, 12
Thomson, Alexander*, 2
Thomson, William, 6
Throsby, Charles, 2
Todd, Robert Henry, 12
Tracy, Richard Thomas, 6
Turnbull, Adam (1803-1891), 2
Turner, Alfred Jefferis, 12
Verco, Sir Joseph Cooke, 12
Vickers, Allan Robert Stanley, 12
Voss, Francis Henry Vivian, 12
Wade, Sir Robert Blakeway, 12
Walker, Allan Seymour, 12
Wanliss, Marion Boyd, 12
Watson, James Frederick William, 12
Waylen, Alfred Robert, 6
Welsh, David Arthur, 12
Wentworth, D'Arcy, 2
Wettenhall, Roland Ravenscroft, 12
White, John, 2
Wilkie, David Elliot*, 6
Wilkinson, John Francis, 12

Williams, Mary Boyd Burfitt, 12
Williams, Sir William Daniel Campbell, 12
Wilson, Arthur Mitchell, 12
Wilson, Thomas Braidwood, 2
Windeyer, John Cadell, 12
Worgan, George Bouchier, 2
Wright, Edward, 2
Wright, Horatio George Anthony, 6
Wunderlich, Frederick Otto, 12
Wyatt, William, 2
Youl, Richard, 6
Zwar, Traugott Bernhard, 12
military
Barber, George Walter, 7
Barrett, Sir James William, 7
Barton, Alan Sinclair Darvall, 7
Bennett, Agnes Elizabeth Lloyd, 7
Bird, Frederic Dougan, 7
Blackall, William Edward, 7
Blackburn, Sir Charles Bickerton, 7
Butler, Arthur Graham, 7
Cairns, Sir Hugh William Bell, 7
Campbell, Alfred Walter, 7
Champion de Crespigny, Sir Constantine
   Trent, 7
Cherry, Thomas, 7
Clayton, Arthur Ross, 8
Conrick, Horatio Victor Patrick, 8
Coppleson, Sir Victor Marcus, 8
Cowlishaw, Leslie, 8
Dick, James Adam, 8
Dixon, Graham Patrick, 8
Downes, Rupert Major, 8
Downey, Michael Henry, 8
Duhig, James Vincent, 8
Eames, William L'Estrange, 8
Ferguson, Eustace William, 8
Fetherston, Richard Herbert Joseph*, 8
Fiaschi, Piero Francis Bruno, 8
Fiaschi, Thomas Henry, 8
Gibson, John Lockhart, 8
Hailes, William Allan, 9
Holmes à Court, Alan Worsley, 9
Horsfall, Alfred Herbert, 9
Howse, Sir Neville Reginald*, 9
Jackson, Ernest Sandford, 9
Jeffries, Lewis Wibmer, 9
Kater, Sir Norman William*, 9
Kay, William Elphinstone, 9
Kellaway, Charles Halliley, 9
Kelly, Robert Vandeleur, 9
Lilley, Charles Mitford, 10
McDonald, Sydney Fancourt, 10
Marks, Alexander Hammett, 10
Martin, Sir Charles James, 10
Newland, Sir Henry Simpson, 11
Newton, Sir Hibbert Alan Stephen, 11
O'Shea, Patrick Joseph Francis, 11
Poate, Sir Hugh Raymond Guy, 11
Purdy, John Smith, 11
Quick, Balcombe, 11
Roth, Reuter Emerich, 11
Shepherd, Arthur Edmund, 11
Sinclair, Eric, 11

Smith, William Ramsay, 11
Springthorpe, John William, 12
Stacy, Valentine Osborne, 12
Stawell, Sir Richard Rawdon, 12
Stewart, John Mitchell Young, 12
Summons, Walter Ernest Isaac, 12
Sutton, Harvey, 12
Syme, Sir George Adlington, 12
Thompson, Clive Wentworth, 12
Wade, Sir Robert Blakeway, 12
Wettenhall, Roland Ravenscroft, 12
Williams, Sir William Daniel Campbell, 12
Wilson, Arthur Mitchell, 12
Winn, Roy Coupland, 12
Woollard, Herbert Henry, 12
Zwar, Traugott Bernhard, 12
MERCHANT, *see also* Exporter
Andrews, Edward William, 3
Angas, George Fife*, 1
Appel, George, 3
Baccarini, Antonio, 7
Baker, Alice, 7
Baker, Thomas (1854-1928), 7
Balfour, James*, 3
Bartley, Nehemiah, 3
Bateman, John, 1
Bateman, John Wesley, 1
Bayles, William*, 3
Bell, John, 1
Bell, William Montgomerie*, 1
Benjamin, Samuel, 1
Berry, Alexander*, 1
Bessell-Browne, Alfred Joseph, 7
Bethune, Walter Angus, 1
Bettington, James Brindley (1796-1857), 3
Bingle, John, 1
Birch, Thomas William, 1
Birnie, James, 1
Blaxcell, Garnham, 1
Blaxland, John, 1
Blyth, John, 3
Bosch, George Henry, 7
Boston, John, 1
Boyd, Benjamin, 1
Boyle, Henry Frederick, 3
Breillat, Thomas Chaplin, 3
Bright, Charles Edward, 3
Broadhurst, Charles Edward, 3
Broadhurst, Florance Constantine, 3
Brooker, Thomas Henry*, 7
Brooks, Richard, 1
Brooks, Samuel Wood*, 3
Brown, Alexander, 3
Brown, David Laughland, 3
Brown, James (1816-1894)*, 3
Buchanan, Benjamin, 3
Buckland, Thomas, 3
Buckley, Henry*, 3
Cabena, William Whyte, 7
Caird, George Sutherland, 3
Cameron, Ewen Wallace, 3
Campbell, Alexander*, 3
Campbell, James, 7
Campbell, John (1802-1886)*, 1

Campbell, Robert (1769-1846), 1
Campbell, Robert (1789-1851), 1
Campbell, Robert (1804-1859), 1
Carpenter, Sir Walter Randolph, 7
Challis, John Henry, 3
Chapman, Thomas Daniel*, 3
Cleburne, Richard*, 1
Cocks, Sir Arthur Alfred Clement*, 8
Cohen, Edward*, 3
Cohen, George Judah, 8
Cohen, Sir Lewis*, 8
Cohen, Sir Samuel Sydney, 8
Cole, George Ward*, 1
Cooper, Daniel, 1
Cooper, Sir Daniel*, 3
Cooper, Robert, 1
Cox, James, 1
Cribb, Benjamin*, 3
Crookes, John*, 1
Crosby, William (1832-1910)*, 3
Cummins, John, 8
Dacre, Ranulph, 1
Dalgety, Frank Gonnerman, 4
Dalton, James, 4
Dangar, Frederick Holkham, 4
Davidson, Walter Stevenson, 1
Degraves, William*, 4
De Mestre, Prosper, 1
Dibbs, Sir George Richard*, 4
Dickson, James*, 4
Donaldson, Sir Stuart Alexander
  (1812-1867)*, 4
Dowse, Thomas, 4
Du Croz, Frederick Augustus, 4
Egan, Daniel*, 4
Elder, Alexander Lang, 4
Elder, David, 4
Elder, George, 4
Elder, William, 4
Elliott, Sizar, 4
Fanning, Edward, 4
Fanning, William, 4
Fell, William Scott*, 8
Felton, Alfred, 4
Forster, William Mark, 4
Frazer, John*, 4
Fysh, Sir Philip Oakley*, 8
Gilchrist, John, 1
Giles, Clement*, 9
Gilfillan, Robert, 4
Glass, Hugh, 4
Glyde, Lavington*, 4
Goddard, Henry Arthur, 9
Goode, Sir Charles Henry*, 4
Gordon, Samuel Deane*, 4
Gosling, John William, 1
Graham, James*, 4
Green, Richard, 4
Greenfield, Alexander Mackay, 9
Grice, Richard, 4
Griffiths, George Richard, 1
Grimwade, Frederick Sheppard*, 4
Hack, John Barton, 1
Hagen, Jacob, 1

Hall, Hayden Hezekiah, 4
Haller, John Friederick, 1
Hamilton, John (1834-1924)*, 4
Harrap, Alfred, 4
Harris, George*, 4
Harris, John (1819-1895), 4
Hart, John*, 4
Hayward, Thomas*, 4
Henry, John*, 9
Henty, Henry*, 4
Henty, Herbert James, 4
Henty, James*, 1
Henty, Stephen George*, 1
Hoffnung, Sigmond, 4
Hogan, Michael, 1
Holtermann, Bernhardt Otto*, 4
Hook, Charles, 1
Hosking, John (1806-1882), 1
Hunter, John McEwan*, 9
Ingle, John, 2
Jacka, Albert, 9
Jenkins, John Greeley*, 9
Jenkins, Robert, 2
Jones, David, 2
Jones, Joseph*, 4
Jones, Richard (1786-1852), 2
Joseph, Samuel Aaron*, 4
Kable, Henry, 2
Kemp, Anthony Fenn, 2
Kent, Thomas, 2
Kermode, William, 2
Keysor, Leonard Maurice, 9
King, George (1814-1894)*, 5
King, James (1800-1857), 2
Lamb, John, 2
Lamb, Walter, 5
Landseer, Albert Henry*, 9
Larra, James, 2
Lawrence, William Effingham, 2
Leake, George, 2
Leake, Sir Luke Samuel*, 5
Lee, Alfred, 10
Lempriere, Thomas James, 2
Lennon, William*, 10
Levey, Barnett, 2
Levey, Solomon, 2
Lewis, Richard, 2
Lloyd, George Alfred*, 5
Loane, Ro(w)land Walpole, 2
Lord, Edward, 2
Lord, Simeon, 2
Lorimer, Sir James*, 5
Loton, Sir William Thorley*, 10
Lovell, Esh, 2
Lowe Kong Meng, 5
Lowes, Thomas Yardley, 2
McArthur, Alexander*, 5
Macarthur, Hannibal Hawkins, 2
MacBain, Sir James, 5
McBeath, Sir William George, 10
McCulloch, Sir James*, 5
McElhone, John*, 5
McGregor, Alexander*, 5
McIntyre, Sir John*, 5

McLachlan, Charles, 2
McMillan, Sir William, 10
McNaughtan, Alexander, 5
McPherson, Sir William Murray, 10
Macvitie, Thomas, 2
Mair, Alexander*, 10
Manning, Edye, 2
Meeks, Sir Alfred William*, 10
Mendes da Costa, Benjamin, 5
Merrett, Sir Charles Edward, 10
Metcalfe, Michael, 5
Michaelis, Moritz, 5
Milson, James (1814-1903), 2
Monger, John Henry*, 5
Montefiore, Eliezer Levi, 5
Montefiore, Jacob Levi*, 5
Montefiore, Joseph Barrow, 2
Moore, David*, 5
Moore, William Dalgety*, 5
Morris, George Francis, 5
Morrison, Askin*, 5
Mosman, Archibald, 2
Muecke, Hugo Carl Emil*, 10
Murdoch, Thomas (1868-1946)*, 10
Murnin, Michael Egan, 5
Murray, David*, 5
Nathan, Sir Charles Samuel*, 10
Nettlefold, Isaac Robert, 11
Nettlefold, Sir Thomas Sydney Richard, 11
Nicholson, Edmund James Houghton, 11
Oakden, Philip, 2
Orr, William Morgan, 2
Paling, William Henry, 5
Paterson, James, 5
Paton, John, 11
Pearse, William Silas*, 5
Pease, Percy*, 11
Perdriau, Henry, 11
Petchy, John, 2
Petterd, William Frederick, 5
Phillipps, Sir (William) Herbert, 11
Philp, Sir Robert*, 11
Pinschof, Carl Ludwig, 11
Pittard, Alfred James*, 11
Raff, George*, 6
Raine, John, 2
Raine, Thomas, 2
Ramsay, David, 2
Raven, William, 2
Read, George Frederick, 2
Reed, Henry, 2
Reibey, Mary, 2
Reid, John, 11
Reid, Robert*, 11
Reid, Walter Ballantyne, 6
Riley, Alexander, 2
Riley, Edward, 2
Robey, Ralph Mayer*, 6
Robinson, Anthony Bennet, 11
Roemer, Charles William, 2
Rossi, Maffio, 11
Rowan, Andrew, 6
Rudd, William Henry, 11

Rundle, Jeremiah Brice*, 6
Rutledge, William*, 2
Salier, George*, 6
Salier, James Ebenezer, 6
Salmon, Thomas, 2
Samson, Lionel, 2
Samuel, Sir Saul*, 6
Sandford, Sir James Wallace*, 11
Saywell, Thomas, 6
Scott, Ellis Martin, 2
Seal, Charles, 2
Shenton, George, 2
Shenton, Sir George*, 6
Sherwin, Isaac, 2
Sleigh, Harold Crofton, 11
Smith, Charles, 6
Smith, Henry Gilbert*, 2
Smith, Richard, 6
Smith, Robert Murray*, 6
Smith, Thomas Whistler*, 2
Solomon, Emanuel*, 6
Spark, Alexander Brodie, 2
Spragg, Alonzo Stephen, 12
Stevens, Edward, 12
Stodart, James*, 12
Storey, Sir David*, 12
Stuart, Sir Alexander*, 6
Swanston, Charles, 2
Terry, Samuel, 2
Thompson, William George*, 12
Thomson, Dugald*, 12
Thornton, George*, 6
Throssell, George*, 12
Tooth, John, 6
Towns, Robert*, 6
Train, George Francis, 6
Underwood, James, 2
Underwood, Joseph, 2
Vaccari, Gualtiero, 12
Vickery, Ebenezer*, 6
Walker, Fred, 12
Walker, Thomas (1804-1886), 2
Walker, William (1787-1854), 2
Waterhouse, George Marsden*, 6
Watson, James*, 6
Watt, John Brown*, 6
Way Lee, Yet Soo War, 12
Westgarth, William*, 6
Wilks, William Henry*, 12
Williams, Francis, 2
Williams, James Hartwell, 6
Willis, Joseph Scaife, 6
Winder, Thomas White Melville, 2
Wiseman, Solomon, 2
Wollaston, Tullie Cornthwaite, 12
Wollstonecraft, Edward, 2
Woolley, Thomas, 2
Yencken, Edward Lowenstein, 12
Young, Adolphus William, 2
coffee
Leggo, Henry Madren, 10
Nimmo, John*, 5
fruit
De Garis, Elisha Clement, 8

James, Frederick Alexander, 9
Jessep, Thomas*, 9
Kwok Bew, 9
furniture
Beckett, William James*, 7
Steinfeld, Emanuel*, 6
grain
Bell, James*, 3
Darling, John (1831-1905)*, 4
Darling, John (1852-1914)*, 4
Harker, George*, 4
Langdon, Thomas*, 9
O'Farrell, Henry James, 5
grocery
Alcock, Randal James, 7
Coveny, Robert, 3
Fowler, David, 4
Fowler, George Swan*, 4
Freeleagus, Christy Kosmas, 8
Gow, Robert Milne, 9
Ireland, Horace, 9
Love, James Robinson, 5
McIlrath, Sir Martin, 10
McIlrath, William, 10
Rickard, Sir Arthur, 11
hardware
Colton, Sir John*, 3
Davis, Charles, 8
Earp, George Frederick, 8
Lasseter, Frederic, 5
Luxton, Sir Harold Daniel*, 10
oyster
Comino, Athanassio, 8
Comino, John, 8
paper
Dunlop, James Matthew, 8
Dunlop, William Philip (1877-1954), 8
Linton, Sir Richard*, 10
Paterson, Alexander Thomas, 11
produce
Barnes, George Powell*, 7
Bulcock, Robert*, 3
Clarke, Henry*, 3
Denham, Digby Frank*, 8
Harrap, George Edward, 9
Hyam, Solomon Herbert*, 4
Littler, Robert Alexander, 10
Mocatta, George Gershon, 5
Ness, John Thomas*, 11
Richardson, Horace Frank*, 11
Russell, James*, 6
Saltau, Marcus*, 11
See, Sir John*, 11
Watt, William Alexander*, 12
softgoods
Barbour, Robert*, 3
Bruce, John Munro, 3
Connibere, Ernest William Richards, 8
Connibere, Frederick George, 8
Doolette, Sir George Philip, 8
Sargood, Sir Frederick Thomas*, 6
tea
Ah Mouy, Louis, 3
Benjamin, Sir Benjamin*, 3

Benn, John, 3
Bushell, Philip Howard, 7
Harper, Robert*, 9
Haugh, Denis Robert, 9
Inglis, James*, 4
Innes-Noad, Sidney Reginald*, 9
Love, Sir Joseph Clifton, 10
Mei Quong Tart, 5
Sellar, James Zimri*, 11
Service, James*, 6
Tait, Sir Frank Samuel, 12
Ten, George Soo Hoo, 6
timber
Booth, John*, 3
Bunning, Robert, 7
Davies, Maurice Coleman, 4
Facy, Peter (1822-1890), 4
Goodlet, John Hay, 4
Ham, Theophilus Job, 4
Hancock, Josias Henry, 9
Hardy, Charles Downey*, 9
Heath, Albert Edward, 9
Kethel, Alexander*, 9
Lahey, Romeo Watkins, 9
McNeil, Neil, 5
Marshall, James Waddell, 5
Taylor, Sir Allen Arthur*, 12
Whelan, James Paul, 12
Yelverton, Henry, 6
wine
Auld, Patrick, 3
Best, Dudley Robert William, 7
Buring, Adolph Wilhelm Rudolph, 3
Buring, Hermann Paul Leopold, 3
Buring, Theodor Gustav Hermann, 3
Burnage, Granville John, 7
Carter, Godfrey Downes*, 3
Cleland, George Fullerton, 3
Fallon, James Thomas*, 4
Kerferd, George Briscoe*, 5
Lalor, Peter*, 5
Lang, Matthew*, 5
Macdermott, Henry, 2
MacDougall, James, 10
McWilliam, John James, 10
Milne, Sir William*, 5
Murray, Hugh, 2
North, John Britty, 5
Ogilvie, James, 2
Palmer, Sir James Frederick*, 5
Wunderlich, Ernest (Henry Charles)
   Julius, 12
Wynn, Samuel, 12
wool
Elder, Sir Thomas*, 4
Flower, Horace, 4
Gooch, Walter, 9
Holt, Thomas*, 4
Hopkins, Henry, 1
Kitamura, Toranosuke, 9
Laycock, Frederick, 10
Marks, Ernest Samuel*, 10
Sanderson, Sir John, 11
Shaw, Thomas (1800?-1865?), 2

Smith, Robert, 11
Watson, Charles Henry, 12
Webster, Alexander George, 6
Whiddon, Frank, 12
Whiddon, Horace William, 12
METALLURGIST
Ashcroft, Edgar Arthur, 7
Delprat, Guillaume, 8
Gepp, Sir Herbert William, 8
Gillies, James Hynds, 9
Hallahan, Walter Rewi, 9
Hawker, Edward William*, 9
Higgins, Sir John Michael, 9
Leggo, Arthur Victor, 10
Morris, Albert, 10
Richard, George Anderson, 11
Rosenhain, Walter, 11
Schlapp, Herman Henry, 11
Smith, John McGarvie, 11
Somerset, Henry St John, 12
Sticht, Robert Carl, 12
Woodward, Bernard Henry, 12
Woodward, Oliver Holmes, 12
METEOROLOGIST
Abbott, Francis, 3
Hunt, Henry Ambrose, 9
Jevons, William Stanley, 4
Jones, Inigo Owen, 9
Russell, Henry Chamberlain, 6
Smyth, Robert Brough, 6
Todd, Sir Charles, 6
Watt, William Shand, 12
Wragge, Clement Lindley, 12
MILLER
Pflaum, Friedrich Jacob Theodor*, 11
Wade, John, 12
flour
Amos, Adam, 1
Archibald, John*, 7
Archibald, Robert John, 7
Barker, Thomas*, 1
Breillat, Thomas Chaplin, 3
Brunton, Thomas*, 3
Burns, John Fitzgerald, 3
Burrows, John, 3
Clark, Charles George Henry Carr*, 3
Davey, Arnold Edwin, 8
Davey, Edwin, 8
Day, George*, 4
Degraves, William*, 4
Dickson, John, 1
Duffield, Walter*, 4
Dunn, John (1802-1894)*, 4
Dunn, John (1830-1902)*, 4
Fry, James, 4
Gatenby, Andrew, 1
Gillespie, Sir Robert Winton, 9
Heidenreich, Franz Theodor Paul, 4
Highett, John, 4
Kater, Henry Edward, 5
Kates, Francis Benjamin*, 5
Kimpton, William Stephen, 5
Larnach, Donald, 5
Learmonth, Peter, 5

Love, Nigel Borland, 10
McLaurin, James, 5
Magarey, Thomas*, 2
Minifie, Richard Pearman, 10
Monds, Albert William, 10
Monds, Thomas Wilkes, 2
Nash, Robert, 2
O'Loghlin, James Vincent*, 11
Padbury, Walter*, 5
Raine, John, 2
Reid, John, 6
Ridley, John, 2
Shenton, George, 2
Singleton, Benjamin, 2
Struth, John, 2
Terry, John, 2
Thompson, David (1828-1889), 12
Walker, John*, 2
Wearne, Joseph (1832-1884)*, 6
Winder, Thomas White Melville, 2
sugar
Brünnich, Johannes Christian, 7
Buss, Frederic William, 7
Cowley, Sir Alfred Sandlings*, 3
Cran, Robert (1821-1894), 8
Davidson, John Ewen, 8
Draper, Alexander Frederick John, 8
Drysdale, George Russell, 4
Drysdale, John, 4
Hope, Louis*, 4
Ross, Joseph Grafton, 6
timber
Barbour, Robert*, 3
Bunning, Robert, 7
Campbell, Charles William, 7
Campbell, James, 7
Campbell, John Dunmore*, 7
Davies, Maurice Coleman, 4
Dun, Percy Muir, 8
Gainford, Thomas, 4
Goodlet, John Hay, 4
Grubb, William Dawson*, 4
Prieur, François Xavier, 2
Reymond, Joseph Bernard*, 6
Sampson, Burford*, 11
Smith, Henry Teesdale*, 11
Swayne, Edward Bowdich*, 12
Wade, Benjamin Martin*, 12
Wilson, Frank*, 12
Yelverton, Henry John*, 6
MILLINER, *see also* Manufacturer, hats
Johnston, Esther, 2
Ward, Elizabeth Jane, 12
MINE DIRECTOR
Allen, William, 1
Bedford, George Randolph*, 7
Bland, Revett Henry, 3
Brophy, Daniel*, 3
D'Arcy, William Knox, 8
Garrett, Thomas*, 4
Hackett, Deborah Vernon, 9
Hart, William*, 4
Horn, William Austin*, 9
Kelly, Anthony Edwin Bowes, 9

Kruttschnitt, Julius, 9
Lazarus, Daniel Barnet*, 10
McCulloch, George, 5
McLellan, William*, 5
Moore, Sir Newton James*, 10
Morgans, Alfred Edward*, 10
Patterson, Daniel Whittle Harvey, 11
Pattison, William*, 5
Pratt, Ambrose Goddard Hesketh, 11
Tucker, Charles*, 12
Von Doussa, Heinrich Albert Alfred*, 12
Wilson, Frank*, 12

MINE ENGINEER
Boyd, Adam Alexander, 7
Braché, Jacob, 3
Brereton, Ernest Le Gay, 7
Calvert, Albert Frederick, 7
Freeman, Ambrose William, 8
Hoover, Herbert Clark, 9
Lane, Zebina, 9
Murray, Russell Mervyn, 10
O'Reilly, Christopher*, 5
Plant, Edmund Harris Thornburgh*, 5
Richardson, Arthur Charles Jeston, 11
Robertson, James Robert Millar, 11
Ryan, Cecil Godfrey, 11
Smyth, Robert Brough, 6
Watt, William Shand, 12
Woodward, Henry Page, 12

MINE MANAGER
Brookes, Herbert Robinson, 7
Broome, George Herbert, 7
Buckland, Sir Thomas, 7
Corbould, William Henry, 8
Davies, Joseph, 4
Doolette, Dorham Longford, 8
Freeman, Ambrose William, 8
Hancock, Henry Richard, 4
Hare, Charles Simeon*, 4
Harper, Nathaniel White*, 9
Jamieson, William, 9
Kayser, Heinrich Wilhelm Ferdinand, 5
Kruttschnitt, Julius, 9
Lane, Zebina Bartholomew*, 9
Miles, Edward Thomas*, 10
Moore, Samuel Wilkinson*, 10
Rankin, Colin Dunlop Wilson*, 11
Richard, George Anderson, 11
Ryan, Cecil Godfrey, 11
Stephen, George Milner*, 2
Sticht, Robert Carl, 12
Thomson, James, 12
Treloar, George Devine, 12
Wainwright, William Edward, 12
Waley, Sir Frederick George, 12
Wekey, Sigismund, 6
Whitfeld, Hubert Edwin, 12
Williams, Henry Roberts*, 12
Wittenoom, Frederick Francis Burdett, 12
Woodward, Oliver Holmes, 12

MINE PROPRIETOR
Bagot, Charles Hervey*, 1
Barton, Russell*, 3
Black, William Robert, 7

Brown, Alexander, 3
Brown, Alexander*, 7
Brown, James (1816-1894), 3
Brown, John, 7
Craven, Richard, 8
Farthing, William Armstrong, 4
Fletcher, James*, 4
Hall, Walter Russell, 9
Horrocks, Joseph Lucas, 4
Hughes, Sir Walter Watson, 4
Hurley, John (1844-1911)*, 4
James, David*, 9
Lewis, Charles Ferris, 5
Longworth, Thomas (1857-1927), 10
Longworth, William (1846-1928), 10
Lynn, Robert John*, 10
Miller, Robert William, 10
Moffat, John, 10
Morgan, Frederick Augustus, 5
Mosman, Hugh*, 5
Neales, John Bentham*, 2
North, John Britty, 5
Philp, Sir Robert*, 11
Plant, Edmund Harris Thornburgh*, 5
Robertson, James Robert Millar, 11
Tewksbury, William Pearson, 12
Thomas, Lewis*, 6
Vickery, Ebenezer*, 6
Weatherly, William, 12
Webster, William*, 12
Williams, Zephaniah, 2
Wren, John, 12

MINER
coal
Bowling, Peter, 7
Cann, John Henry*, 7
Curley, James*, 3
Edden, Alfred*, 8
Estell, John*, 8
Fegan, John Lionel*, 8
Fisher, Andrew*, 8
Fletcher, James*, 4
McVicars, John, 10
Nelson, Charles, 10
Orr, William (1900-1954), 11
Turner, William*, 6
Williams, John (1797?-1872), 2
Willis, Albert Charles*, 12
Winspear, William Robert, 12
copper
Henry, Ernest, 4
Verran, John*, 12
gold
Abbott, Joseph Henry*, 3
Ah Mouy, Louis, 3
Barr, John Mitchell*, 3
Bath, Thomas Henry*, 7
Black, Percy Charles Herbert, 7
Booth, Doris Regina, 7
Bourke, John Philip, 7
Browne, William Henry*, 7
Carboni, Raffaello, 3
Carnegie, David Wynford, 7
Deane, John Horace, 8

Denovan, William Dixon Campbell*, 4
Esmond, James William, 4
Finch-Hatton, Harold Heneage, 4
Frencham, Henry, 4
Gillies, Duncan*, 4
Givens, Thomas*, 9
Hammond, Mark John*, 4
Haverfield, Robert Ross, 4
Holtermann, Bernhardt Otto*, 4
Hoskins, James*, 4
Howitt, William, 4
Lalor, Peter*, 5
McIntyre, Sir John*, 5
Pryke, Frank, 11
Scaddan, John*, 11
Sellar, James Zimri*, 11
Skurrie, Joseph, 11
Taylor, George*, 12
Thomson, George Edward, 6
Torpy, James*, 6
Vaughn, Robert Matterson*, 6
Watson, William Thornton, 12
Wood, Harrie, 6
opal
Blakeley, Frederick, 7
tin
Carson, David, 3
Lynas, William James Dalton, 10
MINERALOGIST
Anderson, Charles, 7
Baker, Ezekiel Alexander*, 3
Humphrey, Adolarius William Henry, 1
Liversidge, Archibald, 5
Ulrich, Georg Heinrich Friedrich, 6
MINING ENTREPRENEUR
Brookman, Sir George*, 7
Brookman, William Gordon, 7
Carson, David, 3
Copeland, Henry*, 3
De Bernales, Claude Albo, 8
Doolette, Sir George Philip, 8
Hack, Wilton, 4
Lansell, George, 5
Levien, Cecil John, 10
Loughlin, Martin, 5
Monger, Frederick Charles*, 10
Morey, Edward*, 5
Nicholls, Charles Frederick, 5
Orr, William (1843-1929)*, 11
Sligo, Archibald Douglas, 11
Vanzetti, Eugenio, 12
Wallace, John Alston*, 6
Watson, John Boyd, 6
MINING OFFICIAL, see also Goldfields
  commissioner
Finnerty, John Michael, 8
Fryar, William*, 4
Hodgkinson, William Oswald*, 4
Jackson, Clements Frederick Vivian, 9
Sellheim, Philip Frederic, 6
MISSIONARY, see also Preacher
Abel, Charles William, 7
Arnold, Ellen, 7
Backhouse, James, 1

Baker, Shirley Waldemar, 3
Bromilow, William Edward, 7
Brooks, Samuel Wood*, 3
Brown, George, 3
Buchanan, Florence Griffiths, 7
Bugnion, François Louis, 3
Cairnduff, Alexander, 1
Calvert, James, 3
Chalmers, James, 3
Cheong Cheok Hong, 3
Clemes, Samuel, 8
Crook, William Pascoe, 1
Elder, James, 1
Eyre, John (1768-1854), 1
Fison, Lorimer, 4
Flierl, Johann, 8
Flynn, John, 8
Gill, William Wyatt, 4
Gribble, John Brown, 4
Gsell, Francis Xavier, 9
Gyles, John, 1
Hack, Wilton, 4
Hagenauer, Friedrich August, 4
Handt, Johann Christian Simon, 1
Harris, John (1754-1819), 1
Henry, William, 1
Kendall, Thomas, 2
King, Copland, 9
Langham, Frederick, 5
Lawes, William George, 5
Lawry, Walter, 2
Leigh, Samuel, 2
Long, Olive Murray, 11
Love, James Robert Beattie, 10
Lovell, Esh, 2
Macfarlane, Samuel, 5
McLaren, Charles Inglis, 10
McNab, Duncan, 5
Mansfield, Ralph, 2
Mathews, Robert Henry, 10
Matthews, Daniel, 5
Moore, William, 5
Moulton, James Egan, 5
Nicholson, Reginald Chapman, 11
Nobbs, George Hunn, 2
Noble, Angelina, 11
Oakes, Francis, 2
Orton, Joseph Rennard, 2
Page, Rodger Clarence George, 11
Paton, Francis Hume Lyall, 11
Paton, John Gibson, 5
Rivett, Eleanor Harriett, 11
Ruatoka, 6
Schenk, Rodolphe, 11
Schmidt, Karl Wilhelm Edward, 2
Schofield, William, 2
Shearston, John Samuel, 11
Shelley, William, 2
Strehlow, Carl Friedrich Theodor, 12
Taplin, George, 6
Ten, George Soo Hoo, 6
Tuckfield, Francis, 2
Verjus, Henri Stanislas, 6
Warren, Hubert Ernest de Mey, 12

Williams, John (1796-1839), 2
Williams, Thomas, 6
Youl, John, 2
Young, Florence Selina Harriet, 12
MOTOR DEALER, see also Garage proprietor
Cheney, Sydney Albert, 7
Kellow, Henry Brown, 9
Lewis, William Howard Horatio, 10
Smith, Norman Leslie, 11
MOTOR RACER
Benstead, Thomas Arthur, 7
Edkins, Boyd Robertson Huey, 8
Jones, Nina Eva Vida, 9
Rubin, Bernard, 11
Smith, Norman Leslie, 11
Thompson, William Bethel, 12
Wilkinson, Arthur George, 12
MOUNTAINEER
Du Faur, Emmeline Freda, 8
MURDERER
Deeming, Frederick, 8
Griffin, Thomas John Augustus, 4
Kenniff, James, 9
Kenniff, Patrick, 9
Ley, Thomas John*, 10
Sodeman, Arnold Karl, 12
MUSEUM CURATOR
Baker, Richard Thomas, 7
Carne, Joseph Edmund, 7
De Vis, Charles Walter, 4
Etheridge, Robert, 8
Glauert, Ludwig, 9
Krefft, Johann Ludwig Gerard, 5
Masters, George, 5
Reeve, Edward, 6
Roth, Henry Ling, 11
Scott, Herbert Hedley, 11
Waterhouse, Frederick George, 6
MUSEUM DIRECTOR
Anderson, Charles, 7
Forbes, Henry Ogg, 4
Longman, Albert Heber, 10
Lord, Clive Errol, 10
McCoy, Sir Frederick, 5
Morton, Alexander, 10
Penfold, Arthur de Ramon, 11
Stirling, Sir Edward Charles*, 6
Waite, Edgar Ravenswood, 12
Woodward, Bernard Henry, 12
MUSIC PUBLISHER
Albert, Michel François, 7
Clarke, Jacob Richard, 3
Dyer, Louise Berta Mosson Hanson, 8
MUSIC SELLER
Allan, George Leavis, 3
Cawthorne, Charles Witto-Witto, 7
MUSIC TEACHER
Albert, Michel François, 7
Allan, George Leavis, 3
Bainton, Edgar Leslie, 7
Beatty, Raymond Wesley, 7
Carter, Bryce Morrow, 7

Carter, Francis Mowat, 7
Code, Edward Percival, 8
Dalley-Scarlett, Robert, 8
Davy, Ruby Claudia Emily, 8
D'Hage, Ludwig, 8
Elsasser, Carl Gottlieb, 4
Foster, Roland, 8
Francis, Leonard, 8
Goll, Edward, 9
Hazon, Roberto, 9
Heinicke, August Moritz Hermann, 9
Leckie, Alexander Joseph, 10
McBurney, Samuel, 5
May, Sydney Lionel, 10
Orchard, William Arundel, 11
Puddy, Maude Mary, 11
Reimann, Immanuel Gotthold, 11
Sampson, George, 11
Verbrugghen, Henri Adrien Marie, 12
Wallace, William Vincent, 2
Wiedermann, Elise, 11
Willmore, Henrietta, 12
Woolley, Emmeline Mary Dogherty, 12
MUSICIAN, see also Singer
Agnew, Roy Ewing, 7
Amadio, John (Bell), 7
Bainton, Edgar Leslie, 7
Barnes, Gustave Adrian, 7
Barnett, Neville George, 3
Benjamin, Arthur Leslie, 7
Benson, Lucy Charlotte, 7
Bochsa, Robert Nicholas Charles, 3
Bourne, Una Mabel, 7
Bradley, Joseph, 7
Brahe, Mary Hannah, 7
Brier, Percy, 7
Brookes, Ivy, 7
Campbell, Elizabeth, 7
Caron, Leon Francis Victor, 3
Carter, Bryce Morrow, 7
Carter, Francis Mowat, 7
Cawthorne, Charles Witto-Witto, 7
Code, Edward Percival, 8
Cordner, William John, 3
Cowen, Sir Frederick Hymen, 3
Dalley-Scarlett, Robert, 8
Davies, Edward Harold, 8
Davy, Ruby Claudia Emily, 8
Dawson, Peter Smith, 8
Deane, John Philip, 1
Delany, John Albert, 4
D'Hage, Ludwig, 8
Diggles, Silvester, 4
Elsasser, Carl Gottlieb, 4
Ewart, Florence Maud, 8
Floyd, Alfred Ernest, 8
Francis, Leonard, 8
Fraser, Simon Alexander, 8
Goll, Edward, 9
Grainger, George Percy, 9
Graves, John Woodcock, 4
Hall, Elsie Maude Stanley, 9
Hart, Fritz Bennicke, 9
Hazon, Roberto, 9

Heinicke, August Moritz Hermann, 9
Henslowe, Francis Hartwell, 1
Herz, Julius, 4
Hill, Alfred Francis, 9
Horsley, Charles Edward, 4
Hutchens, Francis, 9
Ives, Joshua, 9
Jefferies, Richard Thomas, 9
Jones, Hooper Josse Brewster, 9
Keats, Horace Stanley, 9
Kelly, Frederick Septimus, 9
Kurse, Johann Secundus, 5
Lavater, Louis Isidore, 10
Laver, William Adolphus, 10
Leckie, Alexander Joseph, 10
Lee, David, 5
Lemmone, John, 10
Linger, Carl Ferdinand August, 5
Lithgow, Alexander Frame, 10
Lumsdaine, John Sinclair, 10
McBurney, Mona Margaret, 10
McCann, Arthur Francis, 10
McCann, Edward John, 10
McCormick, Peter Dodds, 10
Marsh, Stephen Hale Alonzo, 5
Marshall-Hall, George William Louis, 10
May, Sydney Lionel, 10
Monk, Cyril Farnsworth, 10
Murdoch, William David, 10
Nathan, Isaac, 2
Orchard, William Arundel, 11
Packer, Charles (Stuart Shipley) Sandys, 5
Packer, Frederick Augustus Gow, 5
Paling, William Henry, 5
Pedley, Ethel Charlotte, 11
Peterson, Franklin Sievright, 11
Peterson, Georgette Augusta Christina, 11
Peterson, Isabel Varney Desmond, 10
Puddy, Maude Mary, 11
Reimann, Immanuel Gotthold, 11
Sampson, George, 11
Sharp, Cecil James, 11
Siede, Julius, 6
Slapoffski, Joseph Gustave, 11
Summers, Joseph, 6
Tarczynski, Stanislaw Victor de, 12
Tate, Henry, 12
Torrance, George William, 6
Truman, Ernest Edwin Philip, 12
Turner, Walter James, 12
Verbrugghen, Henri Adrien Marie, 12
Wallace, William Vincent, 2
Weber, Horace George Martin, 12
Willmore, Henrietta, 12
Wirth, George, 12
Wirth, Philip Peter Jacob, 12
Wood, Thomas, 12
Woolley, Emmeline Mary Dogherty, 12
Younger, Montague Thomas Robson, 6
Zelman, Alberto, 6
Zelman, Samuel Victor Albert, 12

MUSICOLOGIST
Tate, Henry, 12

NATURALIST
Allport, Morton, 3
Angas, George French, 1
Archer, William*, 3
Arnold, Joseph, 1
Ashby, Edwin, 7
Atkinson, Caroline Louisa Waring, 3
Backhouse, James, 1
Barnett, Charles Leslie, 7
Baudin, Nicolas Thomas, 1
Becker, Ludwig, 3
Bennett, George, 1
Best, Dudley Robert William, 7
Bicheno, James Ebenezer, 1
Blandowski, William, 3
Buddicom, Robert Arthur, 7
Burrell, Henry James, 7
Coxen, Charles*, 3
Crowther, William Lodewyk*, 3
Darwin, Charles Robert, 1
Dietrich, Amalie, 4
Diggles, Silvester, 4
Elsey, Joseph Ravenscroft, 4
Enright, Walter John, 8
Fitzgerald, Robert David, 4
Forster, Johann Reinhold, 1
French, Charles Hamilton, 8
Freycinet, Louis-Claude Desaulses de, 1
Gilbert, John, 1
Goldie, Andrew, 4
Hamilton, Alexander Greenlaw, 9
Harper, George, 1
Hart, Thomas Stephen, 9
Hedley, Charles, 9
Helms, Richard, 4
Hobson, Edmund Charles, 1
Howitt, Alfred William, 4
Howitt, Godfrey, 4
Hull, Arthur Francis Basset, 9
Huxley, Thomas Henry, 1
Johnston(e), Robert Mackenzie, 9
Kubary, John Stanislaw, 5
La Billardière, Jacques-Julien Houtou de, 2
Laporte, François Louis Nompar de Caumont, 5
Leach, John Albert, 10
Legge, William Vincent, 5
Leichhardt, Friedrich Wilhelm Ludwig, 2
Lewin, John William, 2
Lhotsky, John, 2
Lord, Clive Errol, 10
Lumholtz, Carl Sophus, 5
Lyell, George, 10
MacGillivray, John, 2
MacGillivray, Paul Howard, 5
Macleay, Sir William John*, 5
Macleay, William Sharp, 2
Morton, Alexander, 10
Parkinson, Sydney, 2
Péron, François, 2
Pescott, Edward Edgar, 11
Petterd, William Frederick, 5
Preiss, Johann August Ludwig, 2
Pulleine, Robert Henry, 11

Rowan, Marian Ellis, 11
Scott, Harriet, 6
Shaw, George, 2
Solander, Daniel, 2
Stead, David George, 12
Steel, Thomas, 12
Story, George Fordyce, 2
Waterhouse, Frederick George, 6
Weindorfer, Gustav, 12
Wheelwright, Horace William, 6
White, John, 2
Whitelegge, Thomas, 12
Wilson, Herbert Ward, 12
Wilson, John Bracebridge, 6

NAVAL OFFICER
Anderson, Sir David Murray, 7
Armstrong, Richard Ramsay, 3
Ball, Henry Lidgbird, 1
Belt, Francis Walter, 7
Blackwood, Francis Price, 1
Bligh, William, 1
Bowen, John, 1
Bowen, Rowland Griffiths, 7
Bracegirdle, Sir Leighton Seymour, 7
Bradley, William, 1
Bremer, Sir James John Gordon, 1
Brewer, Henry, 1
Brewis, Charles Richard Wynn, 7
Brownlow, Frederick Hugh Cust, 7
Carr, William James, 7
Cayley, Henry Priaulx, 7
Clare, Chapman James, 8
Clarkson, Sir William, 8
Collins, Sir Robert Henry Muirhead, 8
Colvin, Sir Ragnar Musgrave, 8
Creer, Herbert Victor, 8
Creer, Reginald Charles, 8
Creswell, Sir William Rooke, 8
Cumberlege, Claude Lionel, 8
Davies, Arthur, 1
Dobie, John, 1
Douglas, William Bloomfield, 4
Dumaresq, John Saumarez, 8
Erskine, James Elphinstone, 4
Erskine, John Elphinstone, 4
Feakes, Henry James, 8
Flinders, Matthew, 1
Fullarton, Robert Russell, 4
Garsia, Rupert Clarke, 8
Gaunt, Sir Ernest Frederick, 8
Gaunt, Sir Guy Reginald Archer, 8
Glossop, John Collings Taswell, 9
Goodenough, James Graham, 4
Gowlland, John Thomas Ewing, 4
Grant, James, 1
Hardwicke, Charles Browne, 1
Heath, George Poynter, 4
Hixson, Francis, 4
Hobson, William, 1
Hogan, Percival James Nelson, 9
Howell-Price, John, 9
Hunter, John (1737-1821), 1
Hyde, Sir George Francis, 9
Jeffreys, Charles, 2

Kay, Joseph Henry, 2
Kelly, Frederick Septimus, 9
Kent, William (1751-1812), 2
Kent, William George Carlile, 2
King, Phillip Parker, 2
Knatchbull, John, 2
Lamb, John, 2
Lazarev, Mikhail Petrovich, 2
McCrea, William, 5
Maconochie, Alexander, 2
Moresby, John, 5
Moriarty, William, 2
Moyes, Morton Henry, 10
Onslow, Arthur Alexander Walton*, 5
Oxley, John Joseph William Molesworth, 2
Parker, Charles Avison, 11
Parry, Sir William Edward, 2
Pasco, Crawford Atchison Denman, 5
Phillip, Arthur, 2
Pope, Cuthbert John, 11
Raper, George, 2
Rawson, Sir Harry Holdsworth, 11
Read, Charles Rudston, 6
Ritchie, Thomas, 2
Roe, John Septimus, 2
Rous, Henry John, 2
Sadleir, Richard*, 2
Shortland, John (1739-1803), 2
Shortland, John (1769-1810), 2
Simpkinson de Wesselow, Francis
    Guillemard, 2
Southwell, Daniel, 2
Spain, Staunton William, 12
Stanley, Owen, 2
Stevenson, John Bryan, 12
Thring, Walter Hugh Charles Samuel, 12
Tickell, Frederick, 12
Tryon, Sir George, 6
Vancouver, George, 2
Waterhouse, Henry, 2
Wickham, John Clements, 2
Williams, George Davies, 12
Woodriff, Daniel, 2
Woore, Thomas, 6

NAVIGATOR
Gatty, Harold Charles, 8

NEWS AGENT
Collins, Henry Michael, 8
Gotch, John Speechly, 4
Greville, Edward*, 4

NEWSAGENT
Mackay, George Hugh Alexander*, 10
Vickers, William, 12

NEWSPAPER EDITOR
Aikenhead, James*, 1
Andrews, Edward William, 3
Arden, George, 1
Bardolph, Douglas Henry*, 7
Barr, John Mitchell*, 3
Biggs, Leonard Vivian, 7
Bonython, Sir John Langdon*, 7
Bonython, Sir John Lavington, 7
Boote, Henry Ernest, 7
Bowser, Sir John*, 7

Newspaper proprietor

Campbell, Donald*, 7
Carson, Alfred, 7
Cavenagh, George, 1
Chomley, Charles Henry, 7
Cockburn-Campbell, Sir Thomas*, 3
Crisp, Christopher, 3
Cunningham, Sir Edward Sheldon, 8
Curnow, William, 8
Davidson, James Edward, 8
Drew, John Michael*, 8
Dwyer-Gray, Edmund John Chisholm*, 8
Elliston, William Gore*, 1
Evans, George Samuel*, 4
Finlayson, John Harvey, 4
Fletcher, Charles Brunsdon, 8
Forster, Anthony*, 4
Gale, John*, 4
Garran, Andrew*, 4
Goldhar, Pinchas, 9
Goodwin, William Lushington*, 1
Grover, Montague MacGregor, 9
Gullett, Henry*, 9
Hackett, Sir John Winthrop*, 9
Haddon, Frederick William, 4
Hall, Edward Smith, 1
Harcus, William, 4
Harris, Alfred, 9
Haverfield, Robert Ross, 4
Hayward, Charles Wiltens Andrée, 9
Heney, Thomas William, 9
Hogue, James Alexander*, 9
Holland, Henry Edmund*, 9
Howe, George, 1
Howe, Robert, 1
Jackson, John Alexander, 2
Jeffery, Walter James, 9
Kerr, William, 2
Kirwan, Sir John Waters*, 9
Kneebone, Henry*, 9
Knight, John James, 9
Knox, Sir Errol Galbraith, 9
Lamond, Hector*, 9
Lane, William, 9
Langler, Sir Alfred, 9
Lochée, Francis, 2
Lovekin, Arthur, 10
Lukin, Gresley, 5
Macdougall, John Campbell, 2
Macdowell, Thomas, 2
McWilliams, John James*, 10
Mansfield, Ralph, 2
Martin, Sir James*, 5
Meston, Archibald*, 5
Millen, Edward Davis*, 10
Muecke, Carl Wilhelm Ludwig, 5
Murray, Andrew, 5
Nicholls, Henry Richard, 5
Norton, John*, 11
O'Kane, Thadeus, 5
Oliphant, Ernest Henry Clark, 11
O'Shaughnessy, Edward, 2
Prichard, Frederick John, 11
Prior, Samuel Henry, 11
Pugh, Theophilus Parsons*, 5

Robertson, Gilbert, 2
Ross, James, 2
Ryan, James*, 11
Ryan, John Tighe, 11
Schuler, Gottlieb Frederick Henry, 11
Scullin, James Henry*, 11
Simonov, Peter, 11
Sinnett, Frederick, 6
Smith, James (1820-1910), 6
Sowden, Sir William John, 12
Spedding, Quentin Shaddock, 12
Stephens, John, 2
Stevenson, George, 2
Syme, George Alexander, 6
Tardent, Henry Alexis, 12
Taylor, Adolphus George*, 6
Thomas, Evan Henry, 2
Thompson, Charles Victor*, 12
Thomson, James, 12
Tolmie, James*, 12
Traill, William Henry*, 6
Vosper, Frederick Charles Burleigh*, 12
Ward, Frederick William, 12
Wardell, Robert, 2
Watterston, David, 12
West, John, 2
White, Charles, 6
Wilkes, William Charles, 6
Williams, Harold Parkyn, 12
Williams, Robert Ernest, 12
Willoughby, Howard, 6
Windsor, Arthur Lloyd, 6
Woods, Walter Alan*, 12

NEWSPAPER EMPLOYEE
Howell, George Julian, 9
McArthur, John (1875-1947), 10

NEWSPAPER PROPRIETOR
Andrews, Edward William, 3
Ash, George*, 7
Ashton, James*, 7
Atkin, Robert Travers*, 3
Barrow, John Henry*, 3
Basedow, Martin Peter Friedrich*, 7
Bennett, Samuel, 3
Bent, Andrew, 1
Berry, Sir Graham*, 3
Blair, John, 7
Boyce, Charles, 3
Boyce, Thomas Burnham, 3
Browne, Eyles Irwin Caulfield*, 3
Burgoyne, Thomas*, 7
Button, Henry, 3
Buzacott, Charles Hardie*, 3
Carey, John Randal, 7
Casey, James Joseph*, 3
Chataway, James Vincent*, 7
Chataway, Thomas Drinkwater*, 7
Clark, John Howard, 3
Clark, William Nairne, 1
Colebatch, Sir Harry Pateshall*, 8
Cowlishaw, James*, 3
Crisp, Christopher, 3
Davidson, James Edward, 8
Davies, Charles Ellis*, 8

Davies, John (1813-1872)*, 4
Davies, Sir John George*, 8
Dawson, Andrew*, 8
Demaine, William Halliwell*, 8
Denison, Sir Hugh Robert, 8
Derrington, Edwin Henry, 4
Dunn, Andrew (1854-1934)*, 8
Dunn, Andrew (1880-1956), 8
Dunn, William Herbert Alan, 8
Dunstan, Thomas*, 8
Eggers, Karl Friedrich Wilhelm, 4
Elliott, Robert Charles Dunlop*, 8
Fairfax, Sir James Oswald, 8
Fairfax, Sir James Reading, 8
Fairfax, John*, 4
Fawkner, John Pascoe*, 1
Fink, Theodore*, 8
Fisher, Joseph*, 4
Fitzpatrick, John Charles Lucas*, 8
Fletcher, James*, 4
Franklyn, Henry Mortimer, 4
Garrett, Thomas*, 4
Gill, Henry Horatio*, 4
Gillies, John*, 9
Gocher, William Henry, 9
Graham, Charles James*, 4
Groom, Henry Littleton*, 9
Groom, William Henry*, 4
Halfey, John*, 4
Harper, Charles*, 4
Harrison, James*, 1
Heydon, Jabez King, 1
Hocking, Sidney Edwin, 9
Holder, Sir Frederick William*, 9
Hoolan, John*, 9
Hunt, Thomas*, 4
Jones, Auber George*, 4
Jones, Richard (1816-1892)*, 2
Lake, George Hingston*, 9
Lansell, Sir George Victor*, 9
Laurie, Henry, 10
Lawson, Louisa, 10
Lewis, Charles Ferris, 5
Lockwood, Alfred Wright, 10
Longman, Albert Heber, 10
McCourt, William Joseph*, 10
Macdougall, John Campbell, 2
McGarvie, William, 2
McIntosh, Hugh Donald*, 10
Mackay, Angus*, 5
McKinley, Alexander*, 5
Mackinnon, Lauchlan, 10
Mackinnon, Lauchlan*, 5
Mackinnon, Sir Lauchlan Charles, 10
Macleod, William, 10
Macrossan, John Murtagh*, 5
Melville, Henry, 2
Mennell, Philip Dearman, 10
Miller, Gustave Thomas Carlisle*, 10
Morgan, Sir Arthur*, 10
Morgan, James*, 5
Mott, George Henry, 10
Mott, Hamilton Charnock, 10
Murdoch, Sir Keith Arthur, 10

Nichols, George Robert*, 5
Nobbs, John (1845-1921)*, 11
O'Connor, Joseph Graham*, 5
O'Loghlin, James Vincent*, 11
Osburne, Richard, 5
O'Sullivan, Richard, 5
Packer, Robert Clyde, 11
Parker, Frank Critchley, 11
Powell, James Alexander, 11
Reilly, Joseph Thomas, 11
Rolph, Sir Gordon Burns, 11
Rolph, William Robert, 11
Shakespeare, Arthur Thomas, 11
Shakespeare, Thomas Mitchell*, 11
Shenton, Arthur, 6
Sholl, Robert John, 6
Simons, John Joseph*, 11
Smith, Sir James John Joynton*, 11
Smith, James MacCallum*, 11
Sommerlad, Ernest Christian*, 12
Stephens, Alfred Ward, 2
Stephens, Edward James, 6
Stephens, Thomas Blacket*, 6
Stirling, Edmund, 6
Swan, James, 6
Syme, David, 6
Syme, Sir Geoffrey, 12
Tait, James McAlpine, 6
Taylor, Harry Samuel, 12
Thomas, Robert, 6
Thomas, Robert Kyffin, 6
Treflé, John Louis*, 12
Varley, George Henry Gisborne*, 12
Vincent, Roy Stanley*, 12
Vogt, George Leonard, 12
Ward, Ebenezer*, 6
Willis, William Nicholas*, 12
Wilson, Edward, 6
Winter, Joseph, 6
Winter, Samuel Vincent, 6
Wren, John, 12
Wynne, Watkin, 12
NOVELIST, see Writer
NURSE
Barron, Ellen, 7
Bean, Isabelle, 7
Bell, Jane, 7
Bidmead, Martha Sarah, 7
Booth, Doris Regina, 7
Cawood, Dorothy Gwendolen, 7
Chatfield, Florence, 7
Clarke, Margaret Turner, 3
Conyers, Evelyn Augusta, 8
Creal, Rose Ann, 8
Davidson, Ethel Sarah, 8
Finlay, Mary McKenzie, 8
Gould, Ellen Julia, 9
Graham, Margaret, 9
Gray, Ethel, 9
Hickson, Ella Violet, 9
Hill, Kate, 9
Holden, Frances Gillam, 9
Kellett, Adelaide Maud, 9
Kenny, Elizabeth, 9

Keys, Constance Mabel, 9
Kirkcaldie, Rosa Angela, 9
Kirkpatrick, Mary, 9
McCarthy, Dame Emma Maud, 10
Osburn, Lucy, 5
Parry, Annie Bertha, 11
Paten, Eunice Muriel Harriett Hunt, 11
Pidgeon, Elsie Clare, 11
Pocock, Mary Anne, 11
Pratt, Rachel, 11
Richardson, Ethel Tracy, 11
Ross-King, Alice, 11
Shaw, Edna Mary Anna Jane, 11
Skinner, Mary Louisa, 11
Sorensen, Christense, 12
Sutherland, Sulina Murray MacDonald, 6
Turriff, Haldane Colquhoun, 6
Walker, Jean Nellie Miles, 12
Wayn, Amelia Lucy, 12
Wheeler, Annie Margaret, 12
White, Jessie McHardy, 12
Wilson, Grace Margaret, 12
military
Barron, Ellen, 7
Bell, Jane, 7
Bidmead, Martha Sarah, 7
Cawood, Dorothy Gwendolen, 7
Conyers, Evelyn Augusta, 8
Creal, Rose Ann, 8
Davidson, Ethel Sarah, 8
Deacon, Clare, 8
Finlay, Mary McKenzie, 8
Gould, Ellen Julia, 9
Graham, Margaret, 9
Gray, Ethel, 9
Imlay, Ellen Jeanie, 9
Kellett, Adelaide Maud, 9
Kelly, Alicia Mary, 9
Kenny, Elizabeth, 9
Keys, Constance Mabel, 9
Kirkcaldie, Rosa Angela, 9
McCarthy, Dame Emma Maud, 10
Parry, Annie Bertha, 11
Paten, Eunice Muriel Harriett Hunt, 11
Pidgeon, Elsie Clare, 11
Pocock, Mary Anne, 11
Pratt, Rachel, 11
Richardson, Ethel Tracy, 11
Ross-King, Alice, 11
Sorensen, Christense, 12
Walker, Jean Nellie Miles, 12
White, Jessie McHardy, 12
Wilson, Grace Margaret, 12
OMNIBUS PROPRIETOR
Clapp, Francis Boardman, 3
Stewart, Sir Frederick Harold*, 12
OPHTHALMOLOGIST
Barrett, Sir James William, 7
Gibson, John Lockhart, 8
Rudall, James Thomas, 6
OPTICIAN
Baker, Henry Herbert, 7
Waterworth, John Newham, 12

ORCHARDIST
Arnot, Arthur James, 7
Bird, Bolton Stafford*, 3
Butler, William Frederick Dennis, 7
Campbell, Archibald George, 7
Carruthers, George Simpson*, 7
Chaffey, William Benjamin, 7
Cherry, Percy Herbert, 7
Edgell, Robert Gordon, 8
Fletcher, James Lionel, 8
Freame, Wykeham Henry Koba, 8
Harper, Charles Walter, 9
Heane, James, 9
Hely, Frederick Augustus, 1
Hill, Richard*, 4
Hunt, John Charles*, 9
Jasprizza, Nicholas, 4
Kingsford, Richard Ash*, 5
Laffer, George Richards*, 9
Lancaster, Samuel*, 9
McNeil, Neil, 5
Mathews, Gregory Macalister, 10
Murphy, Herbert Dyce, 10
Nobbs, John (1845-1921)*, 11
Nobelius, Carl Axel, 5
Playford, Thomas*, 11
Pye, James*, 5
Robinson, Gerald Henry, 11
Rowell, James*, 11
Scurry, William Charles, 11
Shoobridge, Louis Manton*, 11
Shoobridge, Robert Wilkins Giblin, 11
Shoobridge, William Ebenezer*, 11
Tate, Ralph, 6
Wanliss, Harold Boyd, 12
Wettenhall, Holford Highlord*, 6
Wettenhall, Marcus Edwy*, 12
Whittell, Hubert Massey, 12
Willmott, Francis Edward Sykes*, 12
Woods, James Park, 12
ORCHIDOLOGIST, *see* Botanist
ORGANBUILDER
Dodd, Josiah Eustace, 8
Fincham, George, 4
Richardson, Charles, 11
Whitehouse, Joseph Howell, 12
ORGANIST, *see* Musician
ORNITHOLOGIST
Broinowski, Gracius Joseph, 3
Campbell, Archibald George, 7
Campbell, Archibald James, 7
Carter, Thomas, 7
Cayley, Neville William, 7
Cotton, John, 1
Ewing, Thomas James, 1
Finsch, Otto, 4
Gould, John, 1
Hall, Robert, 9
Iredale, Tom, 9
Jackson, Sidney William, 9
Keartland, George Arthur, 9
Latham, John, 2
Le Souef, William Henry Dudley, 10
Littler, Frank Mervyn, 10

Mathews, Gregory Macalister, 10
Mattingley, Arthur Herbert Evelyn, 10
Ramsay, Edward Pierson, 6
White, Samuel, 6
White, Samuel Albert, 12
Whittell, Hubert Massey, 12
PACIFIST
Hills, John Francis, 9
John, Cecilia Annie, 9
Moore, Eleanor May, 10
Rivett, Albert, 11
PALAEONTOLOGIST
Anderson, Charles, 7
Chapman, Frederick, 7
Dun, William Sutherland, 8
Etheridge, Robert, 8
Hall, Thomas Sergeant, 9
McCoy, Sir Frederick, 5
Mitchell, John, 10
PASTORALIST
Angliss, Sir William Charles, 7
Fairbairn, Frederick William, 8
Fairbairn, Sir George*, 8
Kidman, Sir Sidney, 9
New South Wales
Aarons, Joseph, 3
Abbott, William Edward*, 7
Angel, Henry, 3
Armstrong, John (1837-1899), 3
Armstrong, Thomas, 3
Arnold, William Munnings*, 3
Austin, Albert, 3
Baillieu, Edward Lloyd, 7
Baldwin, Charles, 3
Barker, Thomas*, 1
Barnes, Henry, 3
Barton, Russell*, 3
Bayly, Nicholas Paget, 3
Bettington, James Brindley (1796-1857), 3
Bettington, James Brindley (1837-1915), 3
Blackwood, John Hutchison*, 3
Blaxland, Gregory, 1
Blaxland, John, 1
Bowman, George Pearce, 3
Bowman, James, 1
Boyd, Archibald, 1
Boyd, Benjamin, 1
Bradley, William, 3
Brodribb, William Adams (1809-1886)*, 3
Broughton, Thomas Stafford*, 3
Buchanan, William Frederick, 3
Buckland, Thomas, 3
Buckley, Henry*, 3
Burdekin, Sydney*, 3
Busby, William*, 3
Cameron, Donald, 7
Campbell, Charles, 1
Campbell, John Archibald, 7
Campbell, Robert (1769-1846), 1
Carington, Rupert Clement George, 7
Carson, Duncan, 7
Charlton, Andrew Murray, 7
Cope, William, 8
Cory, Edward Gostwyck, 1
Coward, Harry Keith, 8
Cox, Edward King*, 3
Cox, George Henry*, 3
Creswick, Alexander Thomson, 8
Crommelin, George Whiting, 3
Crowther, Henry Arnold, 8
Cudmore, Daniel Henry, 8
Dalton, James, 4
Dangar, Albert Augustus, 4
Dangar, Henry, 1
Dangar, Thomas Gordon Gibbons*, 4
Dangar, William John, 4
Darley, Benjamin, 4
Davis, William Walter*, 8
Dawson, Robert, 1
Dawson, Robert Barrington, 4
Day, George*, 4
Desailly, Francis William Wisdom, 4
Desailly, George Peter, 4
De Salis, Leopold Fabius Dietegan Fane*, 4
Dickson, John, 1
Dobie, John, 1
Docker, Joseph*, 4
Donaldson, Sir Stuart Alexander (1812-1867)*, 4
Dowling, Vincent James, 4
Doyle, Cyrus Matthew, 1
Drysdale, George Russell, 4
Dulhunty, Robert Venour, 1
Dun, Percy Muir, 8
Dutton, William Hampden, 1
Eales, John, 1
Ebden, Charles Hotson*, 1
Everett, Edwin, 4
Everett, George, 4
Everett, John, 4
Eyre, Edward John, 1
Faithfull, William Pitt*, 4
Falkiner, Franc Sadlier, 4
Fitzgerald, Nicholas*, 4
Fitzgerald, Robert*, 4
Flood, Edward*, 4
Forster, Thomas Richmond, 8
Forster, William*, 4
Garland, James*, 4
Godfrey, Frederick Race*, 4
Gordon, Samuel Deane*, 4
Gormly, James*, 4
Graves, James Abraham Howlin*, 4
Greene, George Henry*, 9
Hall, Arthur Charles, 9
Hall, Edward Smith, 1
Hall, Thomas Simpson, 4
Halliday, William*, 4
Hamilton, Edward William Terrick, 4
Hardy, John Richard, 4
Hay, Sir John*, 4
Higgins, Patrick*, 4
Hill, Richard*, 4
Hobler, George, 1
Hopkins, Francis Rawdon Chesney, 4

Hovell, William Hilton, 1
Hughes, Fred William, 9
Hungerford, Thomas*, 4
Hunt, Alfred Edgar*, 9
Hurley, John (1796-1882)*, 4
Imlay, George, 2
Imlay, Peter, 2
Innes, Archibald Clunes, 2
Irving, Clark*, 4
Jardine, John, 4
Jennings, Sir Patrick Alfred*, 4
Jones, Auber George*, 4
Jones, Richard (1786-1852), 2
Kater, Henry Edward, 5
Kater, Sir Norman William*, 9
Kelly, John Edward*, 5
King, Philip Gidley*, 5
Lackey, Sir John*, 5
Lamb, Walter, 5
Lang, Gideon Scott*, 2
Lawson, William, 2
Lee, Benjamin*, 5
Lee, George, 5
Lee, William*, 2
Litchfield, James, 5
Lloyd, Charles William, 5
Lord, George William*, 5
Loughlin, Peter Ffrench*, 10
Lowe, Robert, 2
Lyne, Sir William John*, 10
Macansh, John Donald*, 5
Macarthur, Elizabeth, 2
Macarthur, Hannibal Hawkins, 2
Macarthur, James, 2
Macarthur, John, 2
Macarthur, Sir William*, 5
Macarthur-Onslow, Francis Arthur, 10
Macarthur-Onslow, George Macleay, 10
Macarthur-Onslow, James William*, 10
Macartney, Henry Dundas Keith, 10
McCaughey, Sir Samuel*, 5
McCulloch, George, 5
McGarvie, William, 2
McIlrath, Sir Martin, 10
McIlrath, William, 10
Mackay, James Alexander Kenneth*, 10
Mackenzie, Sir Robert Ramsay*, 5
Mackinnon, James Curdie, 10
Macleay, Sir George*, 2
Macleay, Sir William John*, 5
McMaster, Sir Frederick Duncan, 10
McPherson, Sir Clive, 10
McPhillamy, John Smith*, 5
Main, Hugh*, 10
Mair, Alexander*, 10
Manning, James Alexander Louis, 5
Marsh, Matthew Henry*, 5
Mate, Thomas Hodges*, 5
Meredith, Charles*, 5
Mitchell, James, 5
Mocatta, George Gershon, 5
Montague, Alexander*, 5
Moore, Joshua John, 2
Morris, Augustus (1820?-1895)*, 5

Mosman, Archibald, 2
Munro, Hugh Robert, 10
Murray, Sir Terence Aubrey*, 2
Newland, Simpson*, 11
Niall, Kenneth Mansfield, 11
Oakes, George*, 5
O'Brien, Cornelius, 2
O'Brien, Henry, 2
Ogilvie, Edward David*, 5
Osborne, Henry*, 2
Osborne, Pat Hill*, 5
Patterson, Daniel Whittle Harvey, 11
Patterson, John Hunter (1841-1930), 11
Patterson, John Hunter (1882-1963), 11
Peppin, George Hall, 5
Peter, John, 5
Prell, Charles Ernest, 11
Ranken, George, 2
Reid, David, 2
Reid, John, 6
Riley, Alexander, 2
Riley, Edward, 2
Robertson, Alexander William, 6
Robertson, Sir John*, 6
Rotton, Henry*, 6
Rouse, Richard (1842-1903)*, 6
Rouse, Richard (1843-1906), 6
Rundle, Jeremiah Brice*, 6
Rusden, George William, 6
Rutherford, James, 6
Rutledge, Thomas Lloyd Forster*, 11
Ryan, James Tobias*, 6
Ryrie, Sir Granville de Laune*, 11
Sinclair, Sir Colin Archibald*, 11
Sloane, Thomas Gibson, 11
Sloman, Thomas Martin, 2
Stephens, Alfred Ward, 2
Strachan, Hugh Murray, 12
Suttor, Sir Francis Bathurst*, 6
Suttor, William Henry (1805-1877)*, 6
Suttor, William Henry (1834-1905)*, 6
Taylor, William (1818-1903)*, 6
Tindal, Charles Grant, 6
Tooth, Edwin, 6
Tooth, Robert*, 6
Tout, Sir Frederick Henry*, 12
Trethowan, Sir Arthur King*, 12
Triggs, Arthur Bryant, 12
Tyson, James*, 6
Waddell, Thomas*, 12
Wallace, Arthur Cooper, 12
Watt, Ernest Alexander Stuart, 12
Watt, Walter Oswald, 12
Wearne, Walter Ernest*, 12
Webster, Ellen*, 12
Webster, William Maule (McDowell), 12
Wenz, Paul, 12
White, Harold Fletcher*, 12
White, Henry Luke, 12
White, James (1828-1890)*, 6
White, James Cobb*, 12
Wilson, John Bowie*, 6
Wolseley, Frederick York, 6
Woore, Thomas, 6

Wyndham, George, 2
Zouch, Henry, 6
Northern Territory
Buchanan, William Frederick, 3
Buck, Robert Henry, 7
Chewings, Charles, 7
Lewis, John*, 10
Queensland
Allan, James Thomas, 3
Allan, William*, 3
Allingham, Christopher, 3
Aplin, William*, 3
Archer, Archibald*, 1
Archer, Charles, 1
Archer, Colin, 1
Archer, David, 1
Archer, Edward Walker*, 7
Archer, John, 1
Archer, Robert Stubbs, 7
Archer, Thomas (1823-1905), 1
Archer, William, 1
Atherton, John, 3
Bassett, William Augustus, 7
Beit, William, 3
Bell, Ernest Thomas*, 7
Bell, James Thomas Marsh, 7
Bell, Sir Joshua Peter*, 3
Bracker, Frederick John Henry, 3
Brookes, Herbert Robinson, 7
Buckland, Sir Thomas, 7
Cameron, John*, 7
Campbell, John (d.1876), 1
Carson, David, 3
Casey, Richard Gardiner*, 3
Christison, Robert, 3
Clark, Charles George Henry Carr*, 3
Clark, George John Edwin*, 3
Clark, James, 8
Clarke, Sir Rupert Turner Havelock, 8
Collier, Jenkin, 3
Collins, John William Fitzclarence, 8
Collins, Robert, 3
Collins, Robert Martin, 3
Costello, John, 3
Cotton, Alfred John, 8
Coxen, Charles*, 3
Coxen, Henry William, 3
Crombie, James*, 8
Cudmore, James Francis, 8
Cunningham, Arthur Henry Wickham, 8
Currie, John Lang, 3
Daintree, Richard, 4
Dalrymple, David Hay*, 8
Dalrymple, George Augustus Frederick
  Elphinstone*, 4
De Satgé, Oscar John*, 4
Deuchar, John, 4
Dodd, Arthur William, 8
Donaldson, John*, 4
Dorsey, William McTaggart, 4
Douglas, John*, 4
Dow, John Lamont*, 4
Dowling, Vincent James, 4
Durack, Patrick, 4

Dutton, Charles Boydell*, 4
Eales, John, 1
Eather, Richmond Cornwallis, 8
Edkins, Edward Rowland, 4
Edkins, Edward Rowland Huey, 8
Elder, David, 4
Elliott, Gilbert*, 4
Ewan, James, 4
Fairbairn, Stephen, 8
Fairfax, John Hubert Fraser, 8
Fanning, Frederick, 4
Fetherstonhaugh, Cuthbert, 4
Finch-Hatton, Harold Heneage, 4
Fisher, Charles Brown, 4
Fleming, Joseph*, 4
Fletcher, John William*, 8
Forbes, Frederick Augustus*, 4
Forrest, William*, 8
Forster, William*, 4
Forsyth, James*, 8
Gordon, Samuel Deane*, 4
Gore, St George Richard*, 4
Graham, Charles James*, 4
Grant, Alexander Charles, 9
Grant, William, 9
Gregson, Jesse, 4
Guthrie, Thomas, 4
Haly, Charles Robert*, 4
Hann, William, 4
Henry, Ernest, 4
Hill, Charles Lumley*, 4
Hodgson, Sir Arthur*, 4
Hungerford, Thomas*, 4
Ivory, James, 4
Jardine, Francis Lascelles, 4
Jowett, Edmund*, 9
Kennedy, Alexander, 5
Kerr, George*, 9
King, George (1814-1894)*, 5
Lamb, Edward William*, 5
Lamb, John de Villiers, 5
Lawless, Clement Francis, 2
Lawless, Paul, 2
Leslie, Patrick, 2
Love, James Simpson, 10
Macansh, John Donald*, 5
Macartney, John Arthur, 5
McConnel, David Cannon, 5
MacGregor, Duncan, 5
McIlwraith, Sir Thomas*, 5
McIntyre, Duncan, 5
Mackenzie, Sir Evan, 5
Mackenzie, Sir Robert Ramsay*, 5
McLean, John Donald*, 5
McMaster, Sir Fergus, 10
Marshall, Norman, 10
Miles, William*, 5
Moffatt, Thomas de Lacy*, 5
Morehead, Boyd Dunlop*, 5
Moreton, Berkeley Basil*, 5
Morgan, Godfrey*, 10
Morris, Augustus (1820?-1895)*, 5
Murray, Henry William, 10
Murray, John (1837-1917)*, 10

Murray-Prior, Thomas Lodge*, 5
Nelson, Sir Hugh Muir*, 10
Newton, Frank Graham, 11
Niall, James Mansfield, 11
Norton, Albert*, 5
Palmer, Sir Arthur Hunter*, 5
Parry-Okeden, David, 11
Pattison, James Grant, 11
Peppin, Frederick Loch, 5
Persse, De Burgh Fitzpatrick*, 5
Petrie, Thomas, 5
Prell, Charles Ernest, 11
Ramsay, Robert (1818-1910)*, 6
Ranken, George, 6
Ricardo, Percy Ralph, 11
Richardson, John*, 6
Russell, Henry Stuart, 2
Salisbury, Alfred George, 11
Scott, Walter Jervoise, 6
Sellheim, Philip Frederic, 6
Slade, William Ball, 11
Taylor, James*, 6
Thorn, George Henry*, 6
Tooth, Atticus, 6
Tooth, William Butler*, 6
Towner, Edgar Thomas, 12
Walker, Frederick, 6
Wallace, Donald Smith*, 6
Walsh, William Henry*, 6
White, James Charles, 6
White, William Duckett*, 6
Whittingham, Arthur Herbert*, 12
Wienholt, Arnold*, 6
Wienholt, Arnold, 12
Wienholt, Edward*, 6
Wilson, James Lockie, 12
Wright, Colin William, 12
Young, William John, 12
South Australia
Allen, William, 1
Angas, John Howard, 3
Bagot, Charles Hervey*, 1
Bagot, Edward Meade, 3
Baker, John*, 3
Boothby, Thomas Wilde*, 3
Browne, John Harris, 3
Browne, William James*, 3
Chambers, James, 3
Chambers, John, 3
Chapman, Edgar, 3
Cowan, Sir John*, 8
Cudmore, Daniel Michael Paul, 8
Cudmore, James Francis, 8
Davenport, Sir Samuel*, 4
Dean, Edwin Theyer, 8
Duffield, Walter*, 4
Duncan, Sir John James*, 4
Dutton, Frederick Hansborough,
   1
Elder, Sir Thomas*, 4
Finnis, John, 1
Fisher, Charles Brown, 4
Gilbert, Joseph, 4
Giles, Clement*, 9

Hack, Wilton, 4
Hagen, Jacob, 1
Hardy, Arthur*, 4
Hawker, Charles Allan Seymour*, 9
Hawker, Edward William*, 9
Hawker, George Charles*, 4
Hay, Alexander*, 1
Horn, William Austin*, 9
Hughes, John Bristow, 4
Hughes, Sir Walter Watson, 4
Hunter, James Arthur Carr, 1
Jenkins, Sir George Frederick*, 9
Magarey, Thomas*, 2
Maurice, Price, 5
Melrose, Sir John, 10
Moorhouse, Matthew, 5
Mortlock, William Ranson*, 5
Niall, James Mansfield, 11
Reynell, John, 6
Riddoch, George*, 11
Riddoch, John*, 11
Rounsevell, William Benjamin*, 11
Salter, William, 6
Smith, Richard, 6
Smith, Tom Elder Barr, 11
Stirling, Sir John Lancelot*, 6
Sturt, Evelyn Pitfield Shirley, 6
Tennant, Andrew*, 6
Waite, Peter, 6
Warnes, Mary Jane, 12
Wilson, Sir James Milne*, 6
Tasmania
Balfe, John Donnellan*, 3
Bell, Sir George John*, 7
Bell, John, 1
Best, Henry, 1
Bethune, Walter Angus, 1
Blacklow, Archibald Clifford*, 7
Brock, Harold James, 7
Brock, Henry Eric, 7
Brown, Nicholas John*, 3
Brumby, James, 1
Clark, George Carr, 1
Clarke, William John Turner, 1
Cox, James, 1
Darling, Joseph*, 8
Dodery, William*, 4
Dry, Richard, 1
Gibson, David, 1
Headlam, Charles, 4
Leake, John, 2
Learmonth, William, 5
Lord, Edward, 2
Murray, Hugh, 2
Page, Samuel, 2
Parsons, Charles Octavius, 2
Pillinger, Alfred Thomas, 5
Reid, Alexander, 2
Robertson, William (1798-1874), 6
Talbot, William, 2
Von Stieglitz, Frederick Lewis, 2
Weston, William Pritchard*, 2
Youl, Alfred, 12
Youl, Sir James Arndell, 6

Victoria

Armstrong, James, 3
Armstrong, Robert Grieve, 3
Armstrong, William, 3
Armytage, Charles Henry, 3
Armytage, Frederick William, 3
Armytage, George, 1
Arthur, Henry, 1
Atkinson, Evelyn John Rupert, 7
Austin, Albert*, 7
Austin, Edwin Henry*, 7
Austin, James (1810-1896), 1
Austin, Sidney*, 7
Austin, Thomas, 1
Balcombe, Alexander Beatson, 3
Barbour, Robert*, 3
Barker, Edward, 3
Barker, John, 3
Barker, William, 3
Beggs, Hugh Norman, 7
Beggs, Robert Gottlieb, 7
Beggs, Theodore*, 7
Belcher, George Frederick*, 3
Beveridge, Peter, 3
Black, George, 3
Black, Niel*, 3
Blackwood, Robert Officer, 7
Bon, Ann Fraser, 7
Bourchier, Sir Murray William James*, 7
Browne, Thomas Alexander, 3
Campbell, Alexander, 1
Campbell, Colin*, 3
Campbell, William*, 3
Carter, Charles, 3
Carter, Samuel, 3
Castella, Charles Hubert de, 3
Castella, Paul Frédéric de, 3
Chirnside, Andrew Spencer, 3
Chirnside, John Percy*, 7
Chirnside, Thomas, 3
Clarke, Sir Rupert Turner Havelock, 8
Clarke, William John Turner, 1
Clarke, William Lionel Russell*, 8
Cooke, Cecil Pybus, 3
Cooke, Samuel Winter*, 8
Cotton, John, 1
Crompton, Joseph, 3
Crooke, Edward, 3
Cumming, John (1830-1883)*, 3
Curr, Edward, 1
Curr, Edward Micklethwaite, 3
Currie, Sir (Henry) Alan, 8
Currie, John Lang (1818-1898), 3
Currie, John Lang (1856-1935), 8
Dawson, James, 4
Degraves, William*, 4
Dennis, Alexander, 4
Dowling, Thomas*, 4
Drysdale, Anne, 1
Ebden, Charles Hotson*, 1
Fairbairn, Charles, 8
Fairbairn, George*, 4
Fairbairn, James Valentine*, 8
Fisher, Charles Brown, 4

Fisken, Archibald, 4
Flower, Horace, 4
Forlonge, William*, 1
Foster, John*, 1
Foster, John Leslie Fitzgerald Vesey*, 4
Fraser, Sir Simon*, 4
Gardiner, John, 1
Glass, Hugh, 4
Godfrey, Frederick Race*, 4
Gotch, John Speechly, 4
Greaves, Edwin, 9
Greaves, William Clement, 9
Greene, Molesworth Richard, 4
Grice, Richard, 4
Griffith, Charles James*, 4
Guthrie, Thomas, 4
Hamilton, Thomas Ferrier, 4
Harrison, John, 4
Haverfield, Robert Ross, 4
Hawdon, Joseph, 1
Henty, Edward*, 1
Henty, Francis, 1
Henty, John, 1
Henty, Thomas (1775-1839), 1
Henty, Thomas (1836-1887)*, 4
Highett, John, 4
Hobson, Edward William, 1
Hood, Robert Alexander, 9
Hope, Robert Culbertson*, 4
Hopkins, John Rout*, 4
Horsfall, John Sutcliffe, 4
Hunter, Alexander Maclean, 1
Hunter, Andrew Francis, 1
Hunter, John (1820-1868), 1
Hunter, William Fergusson, 1
Jackson, Samuel, 2
Joyce, Alfred, 2
Kelly, Sir George Dalziel, 9
King, John (1820-1895)*, 5
King, William Essington, 5
Lascelles, Edward Harewood, 5
Learmonth, Peter, 5
Learmonth, Somerville, 2
Learmonth, Thomas (1818-1903), 2
Learmonth, William, 5
Ligar, Charles Whybrow, 5
McArthur, John Neil*, 10
Macartney, John Arthur, 5
McCulloch, William*, 5
McDougall, Archibald Campbell, 5
MacGregor, Duncan, 5
Mackay, Martin, 5
Mackinnon, Daniel, 5
Mackinnon, Lauchlan*, 5
Macknight, Charles Hamilton, 5
McLaurin, James, 5
McLeish, Duncan, 10
McLeod, John Norman*, 10
McMillan, Angus*, 2
MacPherson, John Alexander, 5
Manifold, Edward, 10
Manifold, John, 2
Manifold, Peter, 2
Manifold, Thomas, 2

Manifold, Sir Walter Synnot*, 10
Manifold, William Thomson, 10
Maygar, Leslie Cecil, 10
Mercer, George Duncan, 2
Mercer, John Henry, 2
Miller, Sir Edward*, 10
Mollison, Alexander Fullerton, 2
Mollison, William Thomas*, 2
Moore, James (1807-1895), 5
Morton, William Lockhart, 5
Murphy, Sir Francis*, 5
Murray, John (1851-1916)*, 10
Newcomb, Caroline Elizabeth, 1
Nicholson, Mark*, 5
Officer, Charles Myles*, 5
Officer, Sir Robert*, 2
Officer, Suetonius Henry, 5
Ormond, Francis (1829-1889)*, 5
Palmer, Sir James Frederick*, 5
Palmer, Thomas McLeod, 5
Pearson, William*, 5
Pennington, John Warburton*, 11
Pohlman, Robert Williams*, 5
Reid, David*, 6
Reid, Robert Dyce*, 6
Riddell, John Carre*, 6
Robertson, William (1798-1874), 6
Russell, George, 2
Russell, Philip (1796?-1844), 2
Russell, Philip (1822?-1892)*, 6
Russell, Thomas*, 6
Savage, Robert, 6
Shaw, Thomas, 6
Simson, Robert*, 6
Skene, Thomas*, 11
Sladen, Sir Charles*, 6
Snodgrass, Peter, 2
Strachan, James Ford*, 2
Street, Geoffrey Austin*, 12
Swanston, Charles, 2
Synnot, Monckton, 6
Taylor, William (1818-1903)*, 6
Thomson, Alexander*, 2
Treasure, Harry Louis, 12
Wallace, Donald Smith*, 6
Weatherly, Lionel James, 12
Weatherly, William, 12
Wettenhall, Holford Highlord*, 6
Whyte, James*, 6
Willis, Edward, 6
Wills, Horatio Spencer Howe*, 2
Wilson, Sir Samuel*, 6
Winter, James, 6
Winter, Samuel Pratt, 6
Winter-Irving, William Irving*, 6
Wynne, Agar*, 12
Wyselaskie, John Dickson, 6
Yuille, William Cross, 6
Western Australia
Broadhurst, Charles Edward, 3
Brockman, Edmund Ralph*, 3
Brockman, William Locke*, 1
Brown, Maitland*, 3
Buchanan, Nathaniel, 3

Burges, William, 1
Burt, Septimus*, 7
Bussell, Alfred Pickmore, 3
Carter, Thomas, 7
Crawford, Alexander, 8
Davies, Maurice Coleman, 4
Dempster, Andrew*, 4
Dempster, Charles Edward*, 4
Dempster, James McLean, 4
Durack, Michael Patrick*, 8
Durack, Patrick, 4
Emanuel, Isadore Samuel, 8
Hall, William Shakespeare, 4
Hann, Frank Hugh, 4
Harper, Charles*, 4
Hassell, Albert Young*, 4
Hassell, John Frederick Tasman*, 4
Hooley, Edward Timothy*, 4
Lee Steere, Sir Ernest Augustus, 10
Lefroy, Anthony O'Grady, 5
Lefroy, Sir Henry Bruce*, 10
MacDonald, Charles, 5
MacDonald, William Neil, 5
McLeod, Donald Norman*, 10
Male, Arthur*, 10
Marmion, William Edward*, 10
Martin, William Clarence, 10
Monger, Alexander Joseph, 10
Moore, George Fletcher, 2
Moore, William Dalgety*, 5
Murphy, Bennett Francis, 10
Padbury, Walter*, 5
Pearse, William Silas*, 5
Phillips, Samuel Pole*, 5
Prinsep, Henry Charles, 11
Richardson, Alexander Robert*, 11
Rose, Edwin*, 11
Rose, George Canler, 11
Rubin, Mark, 11
Sholl, Horatio William*, 11
Sholl, Robert Frederick*, 11
Steere, Sir James George Lee*, 12
Venn, Henry Whittall*, 12
Wittenoom, Sir Edward Charles*, 12
Wittenoom, Frederick Francis Burdett, 12
PATENT ATTORNEY
Griffith, Arthur Hill*, 9
Spruson, Wilfred Joseph*, 12
PATHOLOGIST
Allen, Sir Harry Brookes, 7
Anderson, Phyllis Margery, 7
Bryce, Lucy Meredith, 7
Cleland, Sir John Burton, 8
Cobb, Nathan Augustus, 8
Dalyell, Elsie Jean, 8
Duhig, James Vincent, 8
Mollison, Crawford Henry, 10
Neild, James Edward, 5
PATRON
Dyer, Louise Berta Mosson Hanson, 8
Hinton, Howard, 9
Stenhouse, Nicol Drysdale, 6
PEARLER
Broadhurst, Charles Edward, 3

Clark, James, 8
De Rougemont, Louis, 8
Hall, William Shakespeare, 4
Male, Arthur*, 10
Muramats, Jirō, 10
Rubin, Mark, 11
Satō, Torajirō, 11
Sholl, Horatio William*, 11
Sholl, Robert Frederick*, 11
Solomon, Vaiben Louis*, 12
Taylor, Henry Joseph Stirling, 12
Tyas, John Walter, 6
PENAL REFORMER
Maconochie, Alexander, 2
PHARMACIST
Bailey, Arthur Rudolph, 7
Blackett, Cuthbert Robert*, 3
Blacklow, Archibald Clifford*, 7
Bosisto, Joseph*, 3
Clements, Frederick Moore, 8
Dalrymple, David Hay*, 8
Embley, Edward Henry, 8
Faulding, Francis Hardey, 4
Gabriel, Charles John, 8
Green, William Herbert*, 9
Grimwade, Edward Norton, 9
Grimwade, Harold William, 9
Heron, Alexander Robert, 9
Kernot, Charles*, 5
McGirr, John Joseph Gregory*, 10
MacPherson, Margaret, 10
Neild, James Edward, 5
Nicholas, George Richard Rich, 11
Potts, Henry William, 11
Sargent, Oswald Hewlett, 11
Shenton, George, 2
Soul, Caleb, 6
Soul, Washington Handley, 6
Steele, Bertram Dillon, 12
Von Doussa, Heinrich Albert Alfred*, 12
Wheen, Harold, 12
PHILOLOGIST
Boyce, William Binnington, 3
Nicholson, George Gibb, 11
PHILOSOPHER
Alexander, Samuel, 7
Anderson, Sir Francis, 7
Anderson, John, 7
Brown, William Jethro, 7
Gibson, William Ralph Boyce, 8
PHOTOGRAPHER
Barnett, Henry Walter, 7
Beattie, John Watt, 7
Birtles, Francis Edwin, 7
Caire, Nicholas John, 3
Cazneaux, Harold Pierce, 7
Daintree, Richard, 4
Degotardi, John, 4
De Rougemont, Louis, 8
Docker, Ernest Brougham, 8
Duryea, Townsend, 4
Fauchery, Antoine Julien, 4
Freeman, James, 4
Freeman, William Glover Webb, 4

Gabriel, Charles Louis, 8
Glenny, Henry, 4
Hurley, James Francis, 9
Kauffmann, John, 9
Kerry, Charles Henry, 9
King, Henry, 9
Lindt, John William, 5
Mattingley, Arthur Herbert Evelyn, 10
Moore, Annie May, 10
Moore, Minnie Louise, 10
Nettleton, Charles, 5
Smith, Julian Augustus Romaine, 11
Smithies, Frederick, 11
Sweet, Samuel White, 6
Wilkins, Sir George Hubert, 12
PHYSICIAN, *see* Medical practitioner
PHYSICIST
Bernacchi, Louis Charles, 7
Bragg, Sir William Henry, 7
Bragg, William Lawrence, 7
Grant, Sir Kerr, 9
Laby, Thomas Howell, 9
Love, Ernest Frederick John, 10
Lyle, Sir Thomas Ranken, 10
McAulay, Alexander, 10
McAulay, Alexander Leicester, 10
Madsen, Sir John Percival Vaissing, 10
Martin, Florence, 10
Pollock, James Arthur, 11
Ross, Alexander David, 11
Slattery, Joseph Patrick, 11
Stone, William, 12
Sutherland, William, 12
Threlfall, Sir Richard, 12
Vonwiller, Oscar Ulrich, 12
PHYSIOLOGIST
Kellaway, Charles Halliley, 9
Martin, Sir Charles James, 10
PHYSIOTHERAPIST
Alexander, Frederick Matthias, 7
PIONEER SETTLER
Batman, John, 1
Bussell, Alfred Pickmore, 3
Dalrymple, Ernest George Beck
    Elphinstone, 1
Henty, Jane, 1
Hopwood, Henry, 4
Larnach, John, 2
Leslie, Patrick, 2
Litchfield, Jessie Sinclair, 10
Newland, Ridgway William, 2
Watson, Mary Beatrice Phillips, 6
PLANTER
Fitch, Algernon Sydney, 8
Michelides, Peter Spero, 10
Murray-Prior, Thomas Lodge*, 5
Nicolay, Charles Grenfell, 5
copra
Abel, Charles William, 7
McLaren, John, 10
Mouton, Jean Baptiste Octave, 10
Mullaly, John Charles, 10
sugar
Adams, Walter*, 3

Airey, Henry Parke, 7
Black, Maurice Hume*, 3
Buss, Frederic William, 7
Cowley, Sir Alfred Sandlings*, 3, 8
Cran, James, 8
Crawford, Thomas William*, 8
Davidson, John Ewen, 8
Draper, Alexander Frederick John, 8
Drysdale, George Russell, 4
Drysdale, John, 4
Fanning, Edward, 4
Fitzgerald, Thomas Henry*, 4
Gibson, Angus*, 4
Gyles, John, 1
Hope, Louis*, 4
Ingham, William Bairstow, 4
Ivory, James, 4
Johnson, George, 9
Johnstone, Robert Arthur, 4
Komine, Isokichi, 9
Leon, Andrew, 5
Macdonald, Alexander Rose, 5
Murray, John (1837-1917)*, 10
Perry, John*, 11
Raff, George*, 6
Rankin, Colin Dunlop Wilson*, 11
Scott, Thomas Alison, 2
Swallow, Thomas, 6
Swayne, Edward Bowdich*, 12
Whish, Claudius Buchanan*, 6

PLASTERER
Frost, Frederick Charlesworth, 8

PLUMBER
Duggan, William Joseph, 8
Gibb, William, 8
O'Keeffe, David Augustus, 11
West, John Edward*, 12

POET, *see* Writer

POLICE COMMISSIONER
Cahill, William Geoffrey, 7
Chomley, Hussey Malone, 3
Dashwood, George Frederick, 1
Henderson, Sir Edmund Yeamans Walcott, 4
Leane, Sir Raymond Lionel, 10
Lord, John Ernest Cecil, 10
MacKay, William John, 10
MacMahon, Sir Charles*, 5
Miles, William Augustus, 2
Mitchell, Sir William Henry Fancourt*, 5
O'Halloran, Thomas Shuldham*, 2
Parry-Okeden, William Edward, 11
Seymour, David Thompson, 6
Standish, Frederick Charles, 6
Stott, Robert, 12
Tolmer, Alexander, 6
Urquhart, Frederic Charles, 12
Warburton, Peter Egerton, 6

POLICE OFFICER
Armfield, Lillian May, 7
Armit, William Edington, 3
Barrington, George, 1
Brennan, Martin, 7
Bruce, George, 1

Burbury, Thomas, 1
Burgess, Francis*, 1
Burke, Robert O'Hara, 3
Chapman, Israel, 1
Christie, John Mitchell, 7
Climpson, Joseph, 8
Cocks, Fanny Kate Boadicea, 8
Dana, Henry Edward Pulteney, 1
Davies, John (1813-1872)*, 4
Day, Ernest Charles, 8
Douglas, Alexander Douglas, 4
Foelsche, Paul Heinrich Matthias, 4
Fosbery, Edmund Walcott, 4
French, Sir George Arthur, 8
Garland, James*, 4
Gates, William, 1
Gordon, Adam Lindsay*, 4
Griffin, Thomas John Augustus, 4
Hannell, James*, 4
Hardwicke, Charles Browne, 1
Harris, John (fl.1783-1803), 1
Hopwood, Henry, 4
Howe, John, 1
Hunter, Andrew Francis, 1
Johnstone, Robert Arthur, 4
Kable, Henry, 2
Knatchbull, John, 2
Kossak, Ladislaus Sylvester, 5
Laing, Henry, 2
Larkin, Edward Rennix*, 9
Maclanachan, James*, 5
McLerie, John, 5
Mair, William, 5
Massey, Thomas, 2
Middleton, John, 5
Minchin, William, 2
Moore, Nicholas, 10
Morrison, Edward Charles, 10
Oakes, Francis, 2
O'Callaghan, Thomas, 11
O'Donnell, David George, 11
Pitt, Richard, 2
Pope, Charles, 11
Pottinger, Sir Frederick William, 5
Robertson, Gilbert, 2
Rossi, Francis Nicholas, 2
Rule, James, 6
Simoi, 11
Spain, William*, 2
Spyer, Haden Daniel, 12
Sturt, Evelyn Pitfield Shirley, 6
Thompson, Andrew, 2
Timperley, William Henry, 6
Uhr, Wentworth D'Arcy, 6
Walker, Frederick, 6
Walsh, John Joseph, 12
Wild(e), Joseph, 2
Willshire, William Henry, 12
Windeyer, Charles, 2
Zouch, Henry, 6

POLITICAL ACTIVIST
Boote, Henry Ernest, 7
Campbell, Thomas Irving, 7
Coote, William, 3

Desmond, Arthur, 8
Dickinson, Edward Alexander, 8
Dowling, Edward, 8
Earsman, William Paisley, 8
Ferguson, William, 8
Fleming, John William, 8
Freeman, Paul, 8
George, Henry, 4
Gocher, William Henry, 9
Goddard, Benjamin, 9
Gresham, William Hutchison, 4
Harris, William, 9
Harrison, John, 4
Hughes, Agnes Eva, 9
Judkins, William Henry, 9
Leeper, Alexander, 10
Macdermott, Henry, 2
Meagher, Thomas Francis, 2
O'Connell, Cecily Maude Mary, 11
Patten, John Thomas, 11
Prichard, Katharine Susannah, 11
Redmond, John Edward, 6
Schiassi, Omero, 11
Sergeyev, Fedor Andreyevich, 11
Skurrie, Joseph, 11
Vaughan, Dorothy, 12
Voigt, Emil Robert, 12
Walpole, Herbert Reginald Robert
 Seymour, 12
Walsh, John Joseph, 6
Watriama, William Jacob, 12

POLITICAL PARTY ORGANIZER
Casey, Gilbert Stephen, 7
Collings, Joseph Silver*, 8
Daley, Jane, 8
Hall, John Joseph, 9
Hinchcliffe, Albert, 9
McDonald, Lewis, 10
McNamara, Daniel Laurence, 10
Merrett, Sir Charles Edward, 10
Munro, Edward Joy, 10
Parkhill, Sir Robert Archdale, 11
Stewart, Archibald, 12
Toomey, James Morton, 12
Ward, Frederick Furner, 12
Willis, Ernest Horatio, 12

POLITICIAN, *see also* Mayor; Premier;
Prime Minister
Lockwood, Joseph, 10
Britain
Bathurst, Henry, 1
Boyce, Sir Harold Leslie, 7
Camden, Earl, 1
Cardwell, Viscount Edward, 3
Carnarvon, Earl of, 3
Cecil, Robert Arthur Talbot Gascoyne, 3
Dilke, Sir Charles Wentworth, 4
Dundas, Henry, 1
Glenelg, Baron, 1
Goderich, Viscount, 1
Goulburn, Henry, 1
Grey, Henry George, 1
Heaton, Sir John Henniker, 4
Hobart, Robert, 1

Hogan, James Francis, 4
Horton, Sir Robert Wilmot, 1
Macqueen, Thomas Potter, 2
Marsh, Matthew Henry, 5
Murray, Sir George, 2
Newcastle-under-Lyme, Henry Pelham
 Fiennes Pelham Clinton, 5
Phillips, Marion, 11
Primrose, Archibald Philip, 5
Redmond, William Hoey Kearney, 6
Russell, Lord John, 2
Stanley, Edward George Geoffrey Smith, 2
Wilson, Sir Leslie Orme, 12
Commonwealth
Abbott, Percy Phipps, 7
Adamson, John, 7
Anstey, Francis George, 7
Archer, Edward Walker, 7
Archibald, William Oliver, 7
Arthur, John Andrew, 7
Baker, Sir Richard Chaffey, 7
Bamford, Frederick William, 7
Barker, Stephen, 7
Barnes, John, 7
Barrett, John George, 7
Batchelor, Egerton Lee, 7
Bell, Sir George John, 7
Best, Sir Robert Wallace, 7
Blackburn, Maurice McCrae, 7
Blacklow, Archibald Clifford, 7
Blakeley, Arthur, 7
Bolton, William Kinsey, 7
Bonython, Sir John Langdon, 7
Bowden, Eric Kendall, 7
Boyd, James Arthur, 7
Braddon, Sir Edward Nicholas Coventry, 7
Brand, Charles Henry, 7
Brennan, Francis, 7
Brennan, Thomas Cornelius, 7
Cameron, Cyril St Clair, 7
Cameron, Sir Donald Charles, 7
Cameron, Donald James, 7
Cann, George, 7
Catts, James Howard, 7
Chanter, John Moore, 7
Chapman, Sir Austin, 7
Charleston, David Morley, 7
Charlton, Matthew, 7
Chataway, Thomas Drinkwater, 7
Coleman, Percy Edmund Creed, 8
Collett, Herbert Brayley, 8
Considine, Michael Patrick, 8
Cook, James Newton Haxton Hume, 8
Cook, Robert, 8
Cooke, Samuel Winter, 8
Cox, Charles Frederick, 8
Crawford, Thomas William, 8
Crouch, Richard Armstrong, 8
Cunningham, James, 8
Cusack, John Joseph, 8
Daly, John Joseph, 8
Davies, William, 8
Dawson, Andrew, 8
De Largie, Hugh, 8

Dooley, John Braidwood, 8
Downer, Sir John William, 8
Drake, James George, 8
Drake-Brockman, Edmund Alfred, 8
Duncan, Walter Leslie, 8
Dunn, James Patrick Digger, 8
Elliott, Harold Edward, 8
Elliott, Robert Charles Dunlop, 8
Ewing, Sir Thomas Thomson, 8
Fairbairn, Sir George, 8
Fairbairn, James Valentine, 8
Falkiner, Franc Brereton Sadleir, 8
Fenton, James Edward, 8
Ferguson, John (1830-1906), 8
Findley, Edward, 8
Fleming, William Montgomerie, 8
Foster, Richard Witty, 8
Fowler, James Mackinnon, 8
Foxton, Justin Fox Greenlaw, 8
Frazer, Charles Edward, 8
Fuller, Sir George Warburton, 8
Fysh, Sir Philip Oakley, 8
Garden, John Smith, 8
Gardiner, Albert, 8
Gellibrand, Sir John, 8
Gibson, William Gerrand, 8
Givens, Thomas, 9
Glasgow, Sir Thomas William, 9
Glassey, Thomas, 9
Glynn, Patrick McMahon, 9
Gordon, Sir David John, 9
Gould, Sir Albert John, 9
Grant, Donald McLennan, 9
Green, Albert Ernest, 9
Gregory, Henry, 9
Groom, Arthur Champion, 9
Groom, Sir Littleton Ernest, 9
Groom, William Henry, 4
Gullett, Sir Henry Somer, 9
Guthrie, James Francis, 9
Guthrie, Robert Storrie, 9
Hall, David Robert, 9
Hannan, Joseph Francis, 9
Hardy, Charles Downey, 9
Harrison, Eric Fairweather, 9
Hawker, Charles Allan Seymour, 9
Higgins, Henry Bournes, 9
Higgs, William Guy, 9
Hill, William Caldwell, 9
Holder, Sir Frederick William, 9
Holland, Henry Edmund, 9
Howse, Sir Neville Reginald, 9
Hunter, James Aitchison Johnston, 9
Irvine, Hans William Henry, 9
Isaacs, Sir Isaac Alfred, 9
Johnson, Sir William Elliot, 9
Johnston, Edward Bertram, 9
Jolly, William Alfred, 9
Jowett, Edmund, 9
Keating, John Henry, 9
Kelly, William Henry, 9
Kennedy, Thomas James, 9
Kingston, Charles Cameron, 9
Kirwan, Sir John Waters, 9

Kneebone, Henry, 9
Knox, William, 9
Lacey, Andrew William, 9
Lambert, William Henry, 9
Lamond, Hector, 9
Lang, John Thomas, 9
Latham, Sir John Greig, 10
Lawson, Sir Harry Sutherland Wightman, 10
Leckie, John William, 10
Livingston, John, 10
Lynch, Patrick Joseph, 10
Lyne, Sir William John, 10
McCay, Sir James Whiteside, 10
McClelland, Hugh, 10
McColl, James Hiers, 10
McDonald, Charles, 10
McDougall, John Keith, 10
McEacharn, Sir Malcolm Donald, 10
McGrath, David Charles, 10
McGregor, Gregor, 10
Mackay, George Hugh Alexander, 10
McLachlan, Alexander John, 10
McLean, Allan, 10
McMillan, Sir William, 10
McNeill, John James, 10
McNicoll, Sir Walter Ramsay, 10
McWilliams, William James, 10
Mahon, Hugh, 10
Maloney, William Robert Nuttall, 10
Manifold, James Chester, 10
Mann, Edward Alexander, 10
Marks, Walter Moffitt, 10
Marr, Sir Charles William Clanan, 10
Massy-Greene, Sir Walter, 10
Matheson, Sir Alexander Perceval, 10
Mauger, Samuel, 10
Maxwell, George Arnot, 10
Millen, Edward Davis, 10
Millen, John Dunlop, 10
Moloney, Parker John, 10
Mullan, John, 10
Neild, John Cash, 10
Nelson, Harold George, 10
Newlands, Sir John, 11
Nock, Horace Keyworth, 11
O'Connor, Richard Edward, 11
Ogden, James Ernest, 11
O'Keefe, David John, 11
O'Malley, King, 11
Orchard, Richard Beaumont, 11
Parkhill, Sir Robert Archdale, 11
Paterson, Thomas, 11
Pearce, Sir George Foster, 11
Perkins, John Arthur, 11
Plain, William, 11
Playford, Thomas, 11
Poynton, Alexander, 11
Pratten, Herbert Edward, 11
Prowse, John Henry, 11
Quick, Sir John, 11
Rae, Arthur Edward George, 11
Reid, Robert, 11
Roberts, Ernest Alfred, 11

Robinson, Sir Arthur, 11
Rodgers, Arthur Stanislaus, 11
Rowell, James, 11
Russell, Edward John, 11
Ryan, Thomas Joseph, 11
Ryrie, Sir Granville de Laune, 11
St Ledger, Anthony James, 11
Salmon, Charles Carty, 11
Sampson, Burford, 11
Skene, Thomas, 11
Smith, Arthur Bruce, 11
Smith, Miles Staniforth Cater, 11
Smith, Sydney (1856-1934), 11
Smith, William Henry Laird, 11
Spence, William Guthrie, 6
Spooner, Eric Sydney, 12
Stewart, Sir Frederick Harold, 12
Stewart, Percy Gerald, 12
Street, Geoffrey Austin, 12
Symon, Sir Josiah Henry, 12
Theodore, Edward Granville, 12
Thomas, Josiah, 12
Thompson, Charles Victor, 12
Thompson, William George, 12
Thomson, Dugald, 12
Thorby, Harold Victor Campbell, 12
Turley, Joseph Henry Lewis, 12
Turner, Sir George, 12
Walker, James Thomas, 12
Watkins, David, 12
Watson, William, 12
Watt, William Alexander, 12
Webster, William, 12
West, John Edward, 12
Wienholt, Arnold, 12
Wilks, William Henry, 12
Willis, Henry, 12
Wilson, Sir Reginald Victor, 12
Wise, George Henry, 12
Wynne, Agar, 12
Zeal, Sir William Austin, 12
Japan
Satō, Torajirō, 11
New South Wales
Abbott, Joseph, 3
Abbott, Sir Joseph Palmer, 3
Abbott, Robert Palmer, 3
Abbott, William Edward, 7
Abigail, Francis, 3
Alderson, William Maddison, 3
Alexander, Maurice, 3
Allen, Alfred, 3
Allen, George, 1
Allen, Sir George Wigram, 3
Allen, William Bell, 3
Allen, William Johnston, 3
Ardill, George Edward (1889-1964), 7
Arnold, William Munnings, 3
Arthur, Richard, 7
Asher, Morris, 3
Ashton, James, 7
Baddeley, John Marcus, 7
Badgery, Henry Septimus, 3
Bailey, John, 7

Baker, Ezekiel Alexander, 3
Ball, Richard Thomas, 7
Barbour, Robert, 3
Barker, Thomas, 1
Barton, Sir Edmund, 7
Barton, Russell, 3
Bavister, Thomas, 7
Bayley, Sir Lyttleton Holyoake, 3
Beeby, Sir George Stephenson, 7
Bell, Archibald (1804-1883), 1
Berry, Alexander, 1
Bettington, James Brindley (1796-1857), 3
Black, George Mure, 7
Black, John, 3
Black, Reginald James, 7
Bland, William, 1
Booth, John, 3
Bowker, Richard Ryther Steer, 3
Bowman, Alexander, 3
Boyce, Francis Stewart, 7
Boyd, Benjamin, 1
Braddon, Sir Henry Yule, 7
Bradley, William, 3
Braund, George Frederick, 7
Broadhurst, Edward, 3
Brodribb, William Adams (1809-1886), 3
Brookfield, Percival Stanley, 7
Brooks, William, 7
Broughton, Thomas Stafford, 3
Brown, Alexander, 7
Brown, Stephen Campbell, 3
Brown, Thomas, 7
Browne, William Henry, 7
Brunker, James Nixon, 3
Bruntnell, Albert, 7
Bruxner, Sir Michael Frederick, 7
Buchanan, David, 3
Buckley, Henry, 3
Burdekin, Marshall, 3
Burdekin, Sydney, 3
Burns, John Fitzgerald, 3
Burton, Sir William Westbrooke, 1
Busby, William, 3
Butler, Edward, 3
Buttenshaw, Ernest Albert, 7
Byrnes, James (1806-1886), 3
Byrnes, William, 3
Cameron, Angus, 3
Campbell, Alexander, 3
Campbell, Charles, 1
Campbell, John (1802-1886), 1
Campbell, Robert (1769-1846), 1
Cann, George, 7
Cann, John Henry, 7
Carmichael, Ambrose Campbell, 7
Chaffey, Frank Augustus, 7
Chanter, John Moore, 7
Chapman, Sir Austin, 7
Charles, Samuel, 3
Charlton, Matthew, 7
Christie, William Harvie, 3
Clark, George Daniel, 8
Clarke, Henry, 3
Clarke, William, 3

Coates, Joseph Farrar, 8
Cocks, Sir Arthur Alfred Clement, 8
Cohen, Henry Emanuel, 3
Cohen, John Jacob, 8
Collins, Charles, 3
Colls, Thomas, 3
Colquhoun, Percy Brereton, 8
Combes, Edward, 3
Connell, Hugh John, 8
Cooper, Sir Daniel, 3
Cooper, Walter Hampson, 3
Copeland, Henry, 3
Cotton, Francis, 8
Cowper, Charles, 3
Cox, Sir Edward John Owen, 8
Cox, Edward King, 3
Cox, George Henry, 3
Crawford, Thomas Simpson, 8
Creed, John Mildred, 3
Crick, William Patrick, 8
Cullen, Sir William Portus, 8
Cunneen, James Augustine, 3
Curley, James, 3
Curr, Edward, 1
Currey, William Matthew, 8
Cusack, John Joseph, 8
Dacey, John Rowland, 8
Dalgleish, Daniel Cameron, 4
Dalley, William Bede, 4
Dangar, Henry Cary, 4
Dangar, Thomas Gordon Gibbons, 4
Darley, Sir Frederick Matthew, 4
Darvall, Sir John Bayley, 4
Davidson, (Charles) Mark Anthony, 8
Davies, John (1839-1896), 4
Davies, William, 4
Davies, William, 8
Davis, Thomas Martin, 8
Davis, William Walter, 8
Day, George, 4
Deniehy, Daniel Henry, 4
De Salis, Leopold Fabius Dietegan Fane, 4
Dickinson, Sir John Nodes, 4
Dickson, James, 4
Dobie, John, 1
Docker, Joseph, 4
Donaldson, Robert Thomas, 8
Douglas, John, 4
Douglass, Henry Grattan, 1
Driver, Richard, 4
Drummond, David Henry, 8
Dumaresq, William John, 1
Dunn, William Fraser, 8
Dunningham, Sir John Montgomery, 8
Durack, Ernest, 8
Eagar, Geoffrey, 4
Edden, Alfred, 8
Egan, Daniel, 4
Estell, John, 8
Ewing, Sir Thomas Thomson, 8
Fairfax, John, 4
Faithfull, William Pitt, 4
Fallon, Cyril Joseph, 8
Fallon, James Thomas, 4

Farleigh, John Gibson, 8
Farnell, Frank, 8
Farrar, Ernest Henry, 8
Fegan, John Lionel, 8
Fell, David, 8
Fell, William Scott, 8
Fitzgerald, John Daniel, 8
Fitzgerald, Robert, 4
Fitzpatrick, John Charles Lucas, 8
Fitzpatrick, Michael, 4
Fitzsimons, Herbert Paton, 8
Fitzsimons, William Robert, 8
Fleming, William Montgomerie, 8
Fletcher, James, 4
Flood, Edward, 4
Flowers, Fred, 8
Forlonge, William, 1
Forsyth, Archibald, 4
Foster, William John, 4
Fowler, Elizabeth Lilian Maud, 8
Fowler, Robert, 4
Frazer, John, 4
Gale, John, 4
Gardiner, Albert, 8
Garland, James, 4
Garland, John, 8
Garran, Andrew, 4
Garrard, Jacob, 4
Garrett, Thomas, 4
Garvan, James Patrick, 4
Gibbes, John George Nathaniel, 1
Gillies, John, 9
Godfrey, Frederick Race, 4
Goldfinch, Sir Philip Henry Macarthur, 9
Goodchap, Charles Augustus, 4
Goold, Stephen Styles, 4
Gordon, Samuel Deane, 4
Gormly, James, 4
Gould, Sir Albert John, 9
Graham, Sir James, 4
Grahame, William Calman, 9
Grant, Donald McLennan, 9
Graves, James Joseph, 9
Grayndler, Edward, 9
Greene, George Henry, 9
Greenwood, James, 4
Greville, Edward, 4
Griffith, Arthur Hill, 9
Gullett, Henry, 9
Hall, David Robert, 9
Halliday, William, 4
Hamilton, Edward William Terrick, 4
Hammond, Mark John, 4
Hankinson, Robert Henry, 9
Hannell, James, 4
Hargrave, John Fletcher, 4
Harpur, Joseph Jehoshaphat, 1
Harris, John (1838-1911), 4
Harris, Sir Matthew, 9
Hawkins, Herbert Middleton, 9
Hay, Sir John, 4
Haynes, John, 4
Hely, Hovenden, 4
Henley, Sir Thomas, 9

Heydon, Charles Gilbert, 9
Heydon, Louis Francis, 9
Hickey, Simon, 9
Higgins, Patrick, 4
Hill, George, 4
Hill, Richard, 4
Hogue, James Alexander, 9
Holden, George Kenyon, 4
Hollis, Robert, 9
Holroyd, Arthur Todd, 4
Holt, Thomas, 4
Holtermann, Bernhardt Otto, 4
Hoskins, James, 4
Houghton, Thomas John, 9
Howie, Sir Archibald, 9
Hughes, John Francis, 9
Hughes, Sir Thomas, 9
Humphery, Frederick Thomas, 4
Hungerford, Thomas, 4
Hunt, Alfred Edgar, 9
Hunt, John Charles, 9
Hurley, John (1796-1882), 4
Hurley, John (1844-1911), 4
Hutchinson, William Alston, 4
Hyam, Solomon Herbert, 4
Icely, Thomas, 2
Inglis, James, 4
Innes, Sir Joseph George Long, 4
Innes-Noad, Sidney Reginald, 9
Irving, Clark, 4
Isaacs, Robert Macintosh, 4
Jacob, Archibald Hamilton, 4
Jamison, Sir John, 2
Jeanneret, Charles Edward, 4
Jessep, Thomas, 9
Johnson, Robert Ebenezer, 4
Jones, Auber George, 4
Jones, Richard (1786-1852), 2
Jones, Richard (1816-1892), 2
Joseph, Samuel Aaron, 4
Josephson, Joshua Frey, 4
Kater, Sir Norman William, 9
Kavanagh, Edward John, 9
Kay, Alick Dudley, 9
Keegan, John Walter, 9
Keegan, Thomas Michael, 9
Kelly, John Edward, 5
Kemp, Charles, 2
Kethel, Alexander, 9
Kidd, John, 5
Kilburn, John George, 9
King, George (1814-1894), 5
King, Philip Gidley, 5
Kneeshaw, Frederick Percival, 9
Knox, Sir Adrian, 9
Knox, Sir Edward, 5
Lackey, Sir John, 5
Laidlaw, Thomas, 5
Lamaro, Joseph, 9
Lamb, John, 2
Lang, Gideon Scott, 2
Lang, John Dunmore, 2
Langwell, Hugh, 9
Larkin, Edward Rennix, 9

Latimer, Hugh, 10
Latimer, William Fleming, 10
Law, Sydney James, 10
Lazzarini, Carlo Camillo, 10
Leary, Joseph, 5
Lee, Benjamin, 5
Lee, Charles Alfred, 10
Lee, John Robert, 10
Lee, William, 2
Lees, Samuel Edward, 10
Levien, Robert Henry, 10
Levy, Sir Daniel, 10
Levy, Lewis Wolfe, 5
Ley, Thomas John, 10
Lloyd, George Alfred, 5
Long, William Alexander, 5
Lord, George William, 5
Loughlin, Peter Ffrench, 10
Lowe, Robert (1811-1892), 2
Lucas, John, 5
Lysaght, Andrew, 10
Lysaght, Andrew Augustus, 10
McArthur, Alexander, 5
Macarthur, Hannibal Hawkins, 2
Macarthur, James, 2
Macarthur, Sir William, 5
Macarthur-Onslow, James William, 10
McCaughey, Sir Samuel, 5
McCourt, William Joseph, 10
McDonald, George Roy William, 10
Macdonell, Donald, 10
McElhone, John, 5
McGirr, John Joseph Gregory, 10
McIntosh, Hugh Donald, 10
Macintosh, John, 5
Mackay, James Alexander Kenneth, 10
Mackellar, Sir Charles Kinnaird, 10
Mackinnon, Lauchlan, 5
MacLaurin, Sir Henry Normand, 10
Macleay, Sir George, 2
Macleay, Sir William John, 5
McMillan, Sir William, 10
McPhillamy, John Smith, 5
McRae, Christopher John, 10
Magrath, Edward Crawford, 10
Main, Hugh, 10
Manning, Sir Henry Edward, 10
Manning, Sir William Montagu, 5
Manning, Sir William Patrick, 10
Marks, Ernest Samuel, 10
Marks, John, 5
Marsh, Matthew Henry, 5
Martin, Lewis Ormsby, 10
Mate, Thomas Hodges, 5
Meagher, John, 10
Meagher, Richard Denis, 10
Meeks, Sir Alfred William, 10
Melville, Ninian, 5
Merewether, Francis Lewis Shaw, 5
Merriman, James, 5
Millen, Edward Davis, 10
Miller, Gustave Thomas Carlisle, 10
Minahan, Patrick Joseph, 10
Mitchell, Ernest Meyer, 10

Mitchell, James, 2
Mitchell, Joseph Earl Cherry, 5
Molesworth, Voltaire, 10
Montague, Alexander, 5
Montefiore, Jacob Levi, 5
Moore, Charles (1820-1895), 5
Moore, Samuel Wilkinson, 10
Moriarty, Abram Orpen, 5
Moriarty, Merion Marshall, 5
Morris, Augustus (1820?-1895), 5
Mullins, John Lane, 10
Murdoch, Sir James Anderson, 10
Murray, Sir Terence Aubrey, 2
Mutch, Thomas Davies, 10
Neild, John Cash, 10
Ness, John Thomas, 11
Nicholas, Harold Sprent, 11
Nichols, George Robert, 5
Nicholson, Sir Charles, 2
Nicholson, John Barnes, 11
Nicoll, Bruce Baird, 5
Nielsen, Niels Rasmus Wilson, 11
Nobbs, John (1845-1921), 11
Norton, James, 2
Norton, John, 11
Oakes, Charles William, 11
Oakes, George, 5
O'Connell, Sir Maurice Charles, 5
O'Connor, Daniel, 5
O'Connor, Joseph Graham, 5
O'Connor, Richard Edward, 11
O'Conor, Broughton Barnabas, 11
Ogilvie, Edward David, 5
Onslow, Arthur Alexander Walton, 5
Osborne, Henry, 2
Osborne, John Percy, 11
Osborne, Pat Hill, 5
O'Sullivan, Edward William, 11
Owen, Robert, 5
Parkes, Varney, 11
Peden, Sir John Beverley, 11
Perkins, John Arthur, 11
Perry, John, 11
Piddington, Albert Bathurst, 11
Piddington, William Henry Burgess, 11
Piddington, William Richman, 5
Pilcher, Charles Edward, 11
Playfair, (John) Thomas, 5
Playfair, Thomas Alfred (Creer) John, 11
Plunkett, John Hubert, 2
Preston Stanley, Millicent Fanny, 11
Primrose, Hubert Leslie, 11
Pulsford, Edward, 11
Pye, James, 5
Quinn, Patrick Edward, 11
Rae, Arthur Edward George, 11
Raphael, Joseph George, 6
Renwick, Sir Arthur, 6
Reymond, Joseph Bernard, 6
Richardson, John, 6
Riddell, Campbell Drummond, 2
Rigg, William, 11
Riley, Alban Joseph, 6
Ritchie, Robert Adam, 6

Roberts, Charles James, 6
Robey, Ralph Mayer, 6
Robinson, Joseph Phelps, 2
Robson, William, 11
Robson, William Elliot Veitch, 11
Roseby, John, 6
Rosenthal, Sir Charles, 11
Ross, Andrew Hendry, 6
Rotton, Henry, 6
Rouse, Richard (1842-1903), 6
Rundle, Jeremiah Brice, 6
Rutledge, Thomas Lloyd Forster, 11
Ryan, James, 11
Ryan, James Tobias, 6
Ryrie, Sir Granville de Laune, 11
Sadleir, Richard, 2
Salomons, Sir Julian Emanuel, 6
Samuel, Sir Saul, 6
Schey, William Francis, 11
Scott, Alexander Walker, 6
Shakespeare, Thomas Mitchell, 11
Simpson, Sir George Bowen, 6
Sinclair, Sir Colin Archibald, 11
Slattery, Thomas Michael, 11
Sleath, Richard, 11
Smart, Thomas Ware, 6
Smith, Arthur Bruce, 11
Smith, Henry Gilbert, 2
Smith, Sir James John Joynton, 11
Smith, John (1811-1895), 6
Smith, John (1821-1885), 6
Smith, Robert Burdett, 6
Smith, Sydney (1856-1934), 11
Smith, Thomas Whistler, 2
Snodgrass, Kenneth, 2
Sommerlad, Ernest Christian, 12
Spain, William, 2
Spence, William Guthrie, 6
Spooner, Eric Sydney, 12
Spring, Gerald, 6
Spruson, Wilfred Joseph, 12
Stephen, Sir Alfred, 6
Stephen, Sir Matthew Henry, 6
Stephen, Montagu Consett, 6
Stephen, Septimus Alfred, 6
Stewart, John (1810-1896), 6
Stopford, Robert, 12
Storey, Sir David, 12
Sutherland, John, 6
Suttor, Sir Francis Bathurst, 6
Suttor, William Henry (1805-1877), 6
Suttor, William Henry (1834-1905), 6
Taylor, Adolphus George, 6
Taylor, Sir Allen Arthur, 12
Taylor, Hugh, 6
Taylor, Patrick Thomson, 12
Terry, Samuel Henry, 6
Therry, Sir Roger, 2
Thomas, Josiah, 12
Thomson, Dugald, 12
Thomson, Sir Edward Deas, 2
Thorby, Harold Victor Campbell, 12
Thornton, George, 6
Thrower, Thomas Henry, 12

Tighe, Atkinson Alfred Patrick, 6
Toohey, James Matthew, 6
Toohey, John Thomas, 6
Tooth, Robert, 6
Tooth, Sir Robert Lucas Lucas-, 6
Tooth, William Butler, 6
Torpy, James, 6
Tout, Sir Frederick Henry, 12
Towns, Robert, 6
Traill, William Henry, 6
Treflé, John Louis, 12
Trethowan, Sir Arthur King, 12
Trickett, William Joseph, 6
Turner, William, 6
Tyrrell, Thomas James, 12
Varley, George Henry Gisborne, 12
Vaughn, Robert Matterson, 6
Vickery, Ebenezer, 6
Vincent, Roy Stanley, 12
Wade, Benjamin Martin, 12
Walder, Sir Samuel Robert, 12
Walker, Thomas, 6
Walker, Thomas (1804-1886), 2
Walker, William, 6
Walsh, William Henry, 6
Want, John Henry, 12
Want, Randolph John, 6
Ward, Sir Edward Wolstenholme, 6
Watkins, David, 12
Watson, James, 6
Watson, John Christian, 12
Watt, John Brown, 6
Wearne, Joseph (1832-1884), 6
Wearne, Walter Ernest, 12
Weaver, Reginald Walter Darcy, 12
Webb, Edmund, 6
Webster, Ellen, 12
Webster, William, 12
Weekes, Elias Carpenter, 6
Wentworth, William Charles, 2
Wetherspoon, John, 12
Wheeler, John, 12
Whiddon, Samuel Thomas, 12
White, Francis, 6
White, George Boyle, 6
White, Harold Fletcher, 12
White, James (1828-1890), 6
White, James Cobb, 12
White, Robert Hoddle Driberg, 6
Wilks, William Henry, 12
Willis, Albert Charles, 12
Willis, Henry, 12
Willis, William Nicholas, 12
Wilshire, James Robert, 6
Wilson, John Bowie, 6
Winchcombe, Frederick Earle, 12
Windeyer, Richard, 2
Windeyer, Sir William Charles, 6
Wisdom, Sir Robert, 6
Wise, Bernhard Ringrose, 12
Wise, Edward, 6
Wright, Francis Augustus, 6
Wright, John James, 6
Young, James Henry, 6

New Zealand
Savage, Michael Joseph, 11
Papua and/or New Guinea
Brennan, Edward Thomas, 7
Queensland
Adams, Walter, 3
Adamson, John, 7
Airey, Peter, 7
Allan, William, 3
Annand, James Douglas, 7
Aplin, William, 3
Appel, John George, 7
Archer, Archibald, 1
Archer, Edward Walker, 7
Archibald, John, 7
Atkin, Robert Travers, 3
Barlow, Andrew Henry, 7
Barnes, George Powell, 7
Barnes, Walter Henry, 7
Bedford, George Randolph, 7
Bell, Ernest Thomas, 7
Bell, Sir Joshua Peter, 3
Bell, Joshua Thomas, 7
Benson, John Robinson, 3
Beor, Henry Rogers, 3
Black, Maurice Hume, 3
Blair, Sir James William, 7
Blakeney, Charles William, 3
Bowman, David, 7
Bramston, Sir John, 3
Brennan, Frank Tennison, 7
Brentnall, Frederick Thomas, 3
Brookes, William, 3
Brooks, Samuel Wood, 3
Browne, Eyles Irwin Caulfield, 3
Buckley, Henry, 3
Bulcock, Robert, 3
Butler, Robert John Cuthbert, 7
Buzacott, Charles Hardie, 3
Cameron, John, 7
Campbell, John Dunmore, 7
Carroll, Robert Joseph, 7
Casey, Richard Gardiner, 3
Challinor, Henry, 3
Chataway, James Vincent, 7
Chubb, Charles Edward, 3
Clark, Charles George Henry Carr, 3
Clark, George John Edwin, 3
Collings, Joseph Silver, 8
Cooper, Sir Pope Alexander, 8
Corfield, William Henry, 3
Cowley, Sir Alfred Sandlings, 3, 8
Cowlishaw, James, 3
Coxen, Charles, 3
Coyne, John Harry, 8
Cribb, Benjamin, 3
Cribb, James Clarke, 8
Cribb, Robert, 3
Cribb, Thomas Bridson, 8
Crombie, James, 8
Curtis, George Silas, 8
Dalrymple, David Hay, 8
Dalrymple, George Augustus Frederick
  Elphinstone, 4

Dash, John, 8
Deane, John Horace, 8
Demaine, William Halliwell, 8
De Satgé, Oscar John, 4
Donaldson, John, 4
Drake, James George, 8
Dunn, Andrew (1854-1934), 8
Dunstan, Thomas, 8
Dunstan, William John, 8
Dutton, Charles Boydell, 4
Edmondstone, George, 4
Elliott, Gilbert, 4
Elphinstone, Augustus Cecil, 8
Ferguson, John (1830-1906), 8
Fihelly, John Arthur, 8
Finney, Thomas, 4
Fitzgerald, Thomas Henry, 4
Fleming, Joseph, 4
Fletcher, John William, 8
Forbes, Frederick Augustus, 4
Forrest, Edward Barrow, 8
Forrest, William, 8
Forsyth, James, 8
Fowles, Edwin Wesley Howard, 8
Foxton, Justin Fox Greenlaw, 8
Fraser, Simon, 4
Fryar, William, 4
Garrick, Sir James Francis, 4
Gibson, Angus, 4
Givens, Thomas, 9
Glassey, Thomas, 9
Gledson, David Alexander, 9
Gore, St George Richard, 4
Graham, Charles James, 4
Grant, Kenneth McDonald, 9
Gray, George Wilkie, 9
Green, William Herbert, 9
Groom, Henry Littleton, 9
Groom, William Henry, 4
Haly, Charles Robert, 4
Hamilton, John (1841-1916), 4
Hamilton, William, 9
Hanran, Patrick Francis, 9
Hardacre, Herbert Freemont, 9
Harris, George, 4
Hawthorn, Arthur George Clarence, 9
Hemmant, William, 4
Higgs, William Guy, 9
Hill, Charles Lumley, 4
Hodel, Joseph, 9
Hodgkinson, William Oswald, 4
Hodgson, Sir Arthur, 4
Hoolan, John, 9
Hope, Louis, 4
Hunter, John McEwan, 9
Hurley, John (1844-1911), 4
Huxham, John Saunders, 9
Hynes, Maurice Patrick, 9
Ivory, Francis Jeffrey, 4
Jones, Alfred James, 9
Jones, Rees Rutland, 9
Jordan, Henry, 4
Kates, Francis Benjamin, 5
Kerr, George, 9

King, Henry Edward, 5
King, Reginald Macdonnell, 9
Kingsford, Richard Ash, 5
Kirwan, Michael Joseph, 9
Lamb, Edward William, 5
Larcombe, James, 9
Leahy, John, 10
Lennon, William, 10
Lesina, Vincent Bernard, 10
Longman, Irene Maud, 10
Macansh, John Donald, 5
Macartney, Sir Edward Henry, 10
MacDevitt, Edward O'Donnell, 5
McDonald, Charles, 10
McDonnell, Francis, 10
Macgroarty, Neil Francis, 10
Mackay, George Hugh Alexander, 10
McLean, John Donald, 5
Macrossan, Hugh Denis, 10
Macrossan, John Murtagh, 5
Marks, Charles Ferdinand, 10
Mein, Charles Stuart, 5
Meston, Archibald, 5
Miles, William, 5
Moffatt, Thomas de Lacy, 5
Moreton, Berkeley Basil, 5
Morgan, Godfrey, 10
Morgan, James, 5
Mosman, Hugh, 5
Mullan, John, 10
Murphy, Peter, 10
Murray, John (1837-1917), 10
Murray-Prior, Thomas Lodge, 5
Newell, John, 5
Nicholson, Sir Charles, 2
Norton, Albert, 5
O'Connell, Sir Maurice Charles, 5
O'Doherty, Kevin Izod, 5
Ogden, Anthony, 11
O'Sullivan, Patrick, 5
O'Sullivan, Thomas, 11
Paget, Walter Trueman, 11
Pattison, William, 5
Pease, Percy, 11
Perkins, Patrick, 5
Persse, De Burgh Fitzpatrick, 5
Plant, Edmund Harris Thornburgh, 5
Powers, Sir Charles, 11
Pring, Ratcliffe, 5
Pugh, Theophilus Parsons, 5
Raff, George, 6
Ramsay, Robert (1818-1910), 6
Rankin, Colin Dunlop Wilson, 11
Reid, Matthew, 11
Roberts, James Henry Cecil, 11
Rutledge, Sir Arthur, 11
Sheridan, Richard Bingham, 6
Sizer, Hubert Ebenezer, 11
Stephens, Thomas Blacket, 6
Stodart, James, 12
Stopford, James, 12
Swayne, Edward Bowdich, 12
Taylor, James, 6
Thomas, Lewis, 6

Thompson, John Malbon, 6
Thorn, George, 6
Thynne, Andrew Joseph, 12
Tolmie, James, 12
Tozer, Sir Horace, 12
Turley, Joseph Henry Lewis, 12
Tyson, James, 6
Wallace, Donald Smith, 6
Walsh, William Henry, 6
Welsby, Thomas, 12
Whish, Claudius Buchanan, 6
White, John, 12
White, William Duckett, 6
Whittingham, Arthur Herbert, 12
Wienholt, Arnold, 6
Wienholt, Arnold, 12
Wienholt, Edward, 6
Wilson, Walter Horatio, 12
South Australia
Andrews, Richard Bullock, 3
Angas, George Fife, 1
Angas, John Howard, 3
Angus, William, 7
Anstey, Edward Alfred, 7
Archibald, William Oliver, 7
Ash, George, 7
Babbage, Benjamin Herschel, 3
Bagot, Charles Hervey, 1
Bagot, Edward Daniel Alexander, 7
Baker, Sir Richard Chaffey, 7
Bardolph, Douglas Henry, 7
Bardolph, Kenneth Edward Joseph, 7
Barrow, John Henry, 3
Basedow, Herbert, 7
Basedow, Martin Peter Friedrich, 7
Batchelor, Egerton Lee, 7
Bice, Sir John George, 7
Birrell, Frederick William, 7
Blundell, Reginald Pole, 7
Blyth, Neville, 3
Bonney, Charles, 3
Boothby, Thomas Wilde, 3
Brooker, Thomas Henry, 7
Brookman, Sir George, 7
Browne, William James, 3
Bruce, Theodore, 7
Bundey, Sir William Henry, 3
Burgoyne, Thomas, 7
Campbell, Allan, 7
Catt, Alfred, 3
Charleston, David Morley, 7
Cohen, Sir Lewis, 8
Coles, Sir Jenkin, 8
Coneybeer, Frederick William, 8
Cooke, Ebenezer, 3
Coombe, Ephraim Henry, 8
Copley, William, 8
Cotton, George Witherage, 3
Cowan, Sir John, 8
Craigie, Edward John, 8
Darling, John (1831-1905), 4
Darling, John (1852-1914), 4
Dashwood, Charles James, 8
Davenport, Sir Samuel, 4

Denny, William Joseph, 8
Duffield, Walter, 4
Duncan, Sir John James, 4
Dunn, John (1802-1894), 4
Dunn, John (1830-1902), 4
Edwards, Albert Augustine, 8
Elder, Sir Thomas, 4
Fisher, Sir James Hurtle, 1
Fisher, Joseph, 4
Forster, Anthony, 4
Foster, Richard Witty, 8
Fowler, George Swan, 4
Freeling, Sir Arthur Henry, 4
Giles, Clement, 9
Gillen, Peter Paul, 9
Glyde, Lavington, 4
Glynn, Patrick McMahon, 9
Goode, Sir Charles Henry, 4
Gordon, Adam Lindsay, 4
Gordon, Sir John Hannah, 9
Gordon, Sir Thomas Stewart, 9
Grainger, Henry William Allerdale, 9
Gwynne, Edward Castres, 4
Hagen, Jacob, 1
Hague, William, 9
Hannaford, Ernest Hayler, 9
Hardy, Arthur, 4
Hare, Charles Simeon, 4
Hawker, Edward William, 9
Hawker, George Charles, 4
Hay, Alexander, 1
Herbert, Charles Edward, 9
Holden, Sir Edward Wheewall, 9
Homburg, Hermann Robert, 9
Homburg, Robert, 9
Hooper, Richard, 9
Horn, William Austin, 9
Howe, James Henderson, 9
Hudd, Sir Herbert Sydney, 9
Hughes, John Bristow, 4
James, David, 9
Jenkins, Sir George Frederick, 9
Johnson, Joseph Colin Francis, 9
Kingston, Sir George Strickland, 2
Kirkpatrick, Andrew Alexander, 9
Kneebone, Henry, 9
Krichauff, Friedrich Eduard Heinrich
  Wulf, 5
Laffer, George Richards, 9
Lake, George Hingston, 9
Landseer, Albert Henry, 9
Lewis, John, 10
Livingston, John, 10
Lucas, Sir Edward, 10
Lyons, Herbert William, 10
McGregor, Gregor, 10
McPherson, John Abel, 10
Magarey, Thomas, 2
Martin, James, 5
Mills, William George James, 10
Mitchell, Samuel James, 10
Morphett, Sir John, 2
Mortlock, William Ranson, 5
Moulden, Beaumont Arnold, 10

Muecke, Hugo Carl Emil, 10
Murray, David, 5
Neales, John Bentham, 2
Newland, Simpson, 11
Newland, Victor Marra, 11
Newlands, Sir John, 11
O'Halloran, Thomas Shuldham, 2
O'Loghlin, James Vincent, 11
O'Loughlin, Laurence Theodore, 11
O'Malley, King, 11
Parkin, William, 5
Parsons, Sir Herbert Angas, 11
Parsons, John Langdon, 11
Pflaum, Friedrich Jacob Theodor, 11
Poynton, Alexander, 11
Price, John Lloyd, 11
Randell, William Richard, 6
Rees, Rowland, 6
Richards, Herbert Clarence, 11
Riddoch, George, 11
Riddoch, John, 11
Ritchie, Sir George, 11
Roberts, Ernest Alfred, 11
Ross, Sir Robert Dalrymple, 6
Rounsevell, John, 11
Rounsevell, William Benjamin, 11
Ryan, Thomas, 11
Sandford, Sir James Wallace, 11
Scherk, Theodor Johannes, 11
Sellar, James Zimri, 11
Simpson, Alfred Muller, 6
Smeaton, Thomas Hyland, 11
Smith, Sir Edwin Thomas, 6
Solomon, Emanuel, 6
Solomon, Judah Moss, 6
Stephens, Edward, 2
Stirling, Sir Edward Charles, 6
Stirling, Sir John Lancelot, 6
Stow, Augustine, 6
Stow, Randolph Isham, 6
Symon, Sir Josiah Henry, 12
Tennant, Andrew, 6
Tomkinson, Samuel, 6
Townsend, William, 6
Tucker, Charles, 12
Vardon, Edward Charles, 12
Vardon, Joseph, 12
Vaughan, John Howard, 12
Verran, John Stanley, 12
Von Doussa, Charles Louis, 12
Von Doussa, Heinrich Albert Alfred, 12
Wallis, Frederick Samuel, 12
Ward, Ebenezer, 6
Way, Sir Samuel James, 12
Whitford, Stanley R., 12
Young, Sir Frederick William, 12

Tasmania
Adams, Robert Patten, 3
Aikenhead, James, 1
Allison, William Race, 1
Anstey, Thomas, 1
Archer, Joseph, 1
Archer, William, 3
Balfe, John Donnellan, 3

Bedford, Edward Samuel Pickard, 3
Bethune, Walter Angus, 1
Bird, Bolton Stafford, 3
Bisdee, Edward, 1
Blacklow, Archibald Clifford, 7
Brown, Nicholas John, 3
Burgess, Francis, 1
Burgess, William Henry (1847-1917), 3
Butler, Henry, 3
Cameron, Donald (1814-1890), 3
Cameron, Donald Norman, 7
Carruthers, George Simpson, 7
Clark, Andrew Inglis, 3
Cleburne, Richard, 1
Collins, George Thomas, 8
Coote, Audley, 3
Crawford, Andrew, 3
Crookes, John, 1
Crosby, William (1832-1910), 3
Crowther, Edward Lodewyk, 3
Culley, Charles Ernest, 8
Darling, Joseph, 8
Davies, Charles Ellis, 8
Davies, John (1813-1872), 4
Davies, Sir John George, 8
Dobson, Alfred, 4
Dobson, Sir William Lambert, 4
Dodds, Sir John Stokell, 4
Dodery, William, 4
Dowling, Henry (1810-1885), 1
Driscoll, Cornelius, 1
Eady, Charles John, 8
Elliston, William Gore, 1
Evans, Alexander Arthur, 8
Fenton, Michael, 1
Fitzgerald, George Parker, 4
Forster, Matthew, 1
Foster, John, 1
Gant, Tetley, 8
Giblin, Lyndhurst Falkiner, 8
Gill, Henry Horatio, 4
Gleadow, John Ward, 1
Goodwin, William Lushington, 1
Grant, Charles Henry, 9
Grant, Charles William, 9
Gray, James, 4
Grubb, Frederick William, 4
Grubb, William Dawson, 4
Gunn, Ronald Campbell, 1
Hamilton, John (1834-1924), 4
Hart, William, 4
Henry, John, 9
Henty, Charles Shum, 1
James, Sir Claude Ernest Weymouth, 9
Jensen, Jens August, 9
Kermode, Robert Quayle, 2
Langdon, William, 2
Lawrence, William Effingham, 2
Lewis, Arndell Neil, 10
Lillico, Sir Alexander, 10
McCall, Sir John, 10
McGregor, Alexander, 5
Maclanachan, James, 5
McWilliams, William James, 10

Meredith, Charles, 5
Miles, Edward Thomas, 10
Miller, Maxwell, 5
Miller, Robert Byron, 5
Morrison, Askin, 5
Murdoch, Thomas (1868-1946), 10
Nairn, William Edward, 5
Nicholls, Sir Herbert, 11
Nichols, Hubert Allan, 11
Officer, Sir Robert, 2
Ogden, James Ernest, 11
O'Keefe, David John, 11
O'Reilly, Christopher, 5
Payne, Herbert James Mockford, 11
Pillinger, Alfred Thomas, 5
Rogers, John Warrington, 6
Sadler, Robert James, 11
Salier, George, 6
Scott, James Reid, 6
Shields, Tasman, 11
Shoobridge, Louis Manton, 11
Shoobridge, William Ebenezer, 11
Sleigh, William Campbell, 6
Smith, James (1827-1897), 6
Smith, James William Norton, 6
Soundy, Sir John, 12
Von Stieglitz, Frederick Lewis, 2
Walker, John, 2
Wardlaw, Alan Lindsay, 12
Wedge, John Helder, 2
Woods, Walter Alan, 12
Youl, Alfred, 12
United States
Hoover, Herbert Clark, 9
Victoria
Abbott, Joseph Henry, 3
à Beckett, Thomas Turner, 3
à Beckett, William Arthur Callander, 3
Adamson, Travers, 3
Anderson, Joseph, 1
Anderson, Robert Stirling Hore, 3
Anderson, William, 3
Anderson, William Acland Douglas, 3
Anstey, Francis George, 7
Ashworth, Thomas Ramsden, 7
Aspinall, Butler Cole, 3
Austin, Albert, 7
Austin, Edward Arthur, 7
Austin, Edwin Henry, 7
Austin, Sidney, 7
Bailey, Henry Stephen, 7
Baillieu, William Lawrence, 7
Baker, Thomas (1840-1923), 7
Balfour, James, 3
Barr, John Mitchell, 3
Barrett, John George, 7
Bayles, Norman, 7
Bayles, William, 3
Beaney, James George, 3
Beaurepaire, Sir Francis Joseph Edmund, 7
Beazley, William David, 7
Beckett, William James, 7
Beggs, Theodore, 7

Belcher, George Frederick, 3
Bell, James, 3
Bell, William Montgomerie, 1
Benjamin, Sir Benjamin, 3
Bennett, George Henry, 7
Bennett, Henry Gilbert, 7
Best, Sir Robert Wallace, 7
Billson, Alfred Arthur, 7
Billson, George, 7
Billson, John William, 7
Bindon, Samuel Henry, 3
Black, Niel, 3
Blackburn, Doris, 7
Blackburn, Maurice McCrae, 7
Blackett, Cuthbert Robert, 3
Blackwood, John Hutchison, 3
Blair, David, 3
Bosisto, Joseph, 3
Bourchier, Sir Murray William James, 7
Boyd, James Arthur, 7
Brodribb, William Adams (1809-1886), 3
Bromley, Frederick Hadkinson, 7
Brooke, John Henry, 3
Brophy, Daniel, 3
Brown, Frederick, 3
Brown, James Drysdale, 7
Brown, Joseph Tilley, 7
Brunton, Thomas, 3
Buchanan, James, 3
Bunny, Brice Frederick, 3
Burrowes, Robert, 3
Bussau, Sir Albert Louis, 7
Butters, James Stewart, 3
Cain, William, 3
Cameron, Ewen Hugh, 3
Cameron, James, 7
Campbell, Colin, 3
Campbell, Donald, 7
Campbell, Envidale Savage Norman, 3
Campbell, William, 3
Carter, Godfrey Downes, 3
Casey, James Joseph, 3
Cassell, James Horatio Nelson, 3
Chandler, Alfred Elliott, 7
Chapman, Henry Samuel, 3
Childers, Hugh Culling Eardley, 3
Chirnside, John Percy, 7
Clark, Alfred Thomas, 3
Clark, Robert, 3
Clarke, Sir Andrew, 3
Clarke, Sir Francis Grenville, 8
Clarke, Sir William John, 3
Clarke, William Lionel Russell, 8
Cohen, Edward, 3
Cohen, Harold Edward, 8
Cohen, Isaac Henry, 8
Cole, George Ward, 1
Cook, James Newton Haxton Hume, 8
Cooke, Samuel Winter, 8
Cooper, Thomas, 3
Coppin, George Selth, 3
Cowie, James, 3
Crews, John Branscombe, 3
Cumming, John (1830-1883), 3

Cumming, Thomas Forrest, 3
Cuthbert, Sir Henry, 3
Davies, David Mortimer, 4
Davies, Sir John Mark, 4
Davies, Sir Matthew Henry, 4
Deakin, Alfred, 8
Degraves, William, 4
Denovan, William Dixon Campbell, 4
Derham, Frederick Thomas, 4
Dobson, Frank Stanley, 4
Don, Charles Jardine, 4
Donaghy, John, 4
Dow, John Lamont, 4
Dowling, Thomas, 4
Duffy, John Gavan, 4
Ebden, Charles Hotson, 1
Eggleston, Sir Frederic William, 8
Embling, Thomas, 4
Evans, George Samuel, 4
Everard, John, 4
Fairbairn, Sir George, 8
Fairbairn, George, 4
Fairbairn, James Valentine, 8
Fawkner, John Pascoe, 1
Fellows, Thomas Howard, 4
Fetherston, Richard Herbert Joseph, 8
Findley, Edward, 8
Fink, Benjamin Josman, 4
Fink, Theodore, 8
Fitzgerald, Nicholas, 4
Forlonge, William, 1
Foster, John Leslie Fitzgerald Vesey, 4
Fraser, Alexander, 4
Fraser, Sir Simon, 4
Gaunson, David, 4
Gillott, Sir Samuel, 9
Goudie, Sir George Louis, 9
Graham, George, 9
Graham, James, 4
Grant, James Macpherson, 4
Graves, James Abraham Howlin, 4
Gray, Moses Wilson, 4
Greeves, Augustus Frederick Adolphus, 4
Griffith, Charles James, 4
Grimwade, Frederick Sheppard, 4
Groom, Arthur Champion, 9
Hagelthorn, Frederick William, 9
Halfey, John, 4
Hall, George Wilson, 4
Ham, Cornelius Job, 4
Hancock, John, 9
Harker, George, 4
Harper, Robert, 9
Harris, Sir John Richards, 9
Harrison, James, 1
Hearn, William Edward, 4
Henty, Edward, 1
Henty, Henry, 4
Henty, James, 1
Henty, Stephen George, 1
Henty, Thomas, 4
Higgins, Henry Bournes, 9
Highett, William, 4
Higinbotham, George, 4

Hirsch, Maximilian, 9
Holden, George Frederick, 9
Hope, Robert Culbertson, 4
Hopkins, John Rout, 4
Humffray, John Basson, 4
Hunt, Thomas, 4
Hutchinson, William, 9
Ievers, William (1839-1895), 4
Illingworth, Frederick, 9
Ireland, Richard Davies, 4
Isaacs, Sir Isaac Alfred, 9
James, Charles Henry, 4
Jenner, Caleb Joshua, 4
Johnston, James Stewart, 4
Jones, Charles Edwin, 4
Jones, John Percy, 9
Jones, Joseph, 4
Kennedy, Thomas James, 9
Kernot, Charles, 5
Kiernan, Esmond Laurence, 9
King, John (1820-1895), 5
King, John Charles, 2
Kirton, Joseph William, 9
Knox, Sir George Hodges, 9
Lalor, Peter, 5
Lancaster, Samuel, 9
Lang, Matthew, 5
Langdon, Thomas, 9
Langlands, Henry, 2
Langridge, George David, 5
Langton, Edward, 5
Lansell, Sir George Victor, 9
Laurens, John, 5
Lazarus, Daniel Barnet, 10
Lemmon, John, 10
Levey, George Collins, 5
Levi, Nathaniel, 5
Levien, Jonas Felix Australia, 5
Lind, Sir Albert Eli, 10
Linton, Sir Richard, 10
Livingston, Thomas, 10
Loader, Thomas, 5
Longmore, Francis, 5
Lorimer, Sir James, 5
Luxton, Sir Harold Daniel, 10
Luxton, Thomas, 5
Lyall, William, 5
Lyell, Andrew, 5
Macadam, John, 5
McArthur, John Neil, 10
MacBain, Sir James, 5
McBride, Sir Peter, 10
McBryde, Duncan Elphinstone, 10
McColl, Hugh, 5
McColl, James Hiers, 10
McCombie, Thomas, 5
McCulloch, William, 5
McCutcheon, Robert George, 10
McDougall, Robert, 5
McGrath, David Charles, 10
McGregor, Martin Robert, 10
McIntyre, Sir John, 5
Mackay, Angus, 5
McKenzie, Hugh, 10

Mackey, Sir John Emanuel, 10
McKinley, Alexander, 5
Mackinnon, Donald, 10
Mackinnon, Lauchlan, 5
Mackrell, Edwin Joseph, 10
McLellan, William, 5
McLeod, Donald, 10
McLeod, Donald Norman, 10
McLeod, John Norman, 10
MacMahon, Sir Charles, 5
McMillan, Angus, 2
McNamara, Daniel Laurence, 10
MacPherson, John Alexander, 5
McWhae, Sir John, 10
Madden, Sir Frank, 10
Madden, Sir John (1844-1918), 10
Madden, Walter, 10
Maloney, William Robert (Nuttall), 10
Manifold, Sir Walter Synnot, 10
Mason, Francis Conway, 5
Mauger, Samuel, 10
Mercer, John Henry, 2
Michie, Sir Archibald, 5
Miller, Sir Edward, 10
Miller, Henry, 5
Milne, Sir William, 5
Mirams, James, 5
Mitchell, Sir William Henry Fancourt, 5
Mollison, William Thomas, 2
Moor, Henry, 2
Moore, David, 5
Morey, Edward, 5
Murphy, Sir Francis, 5
Nicholson, Mark, 5
Nimmo, John, 5
Officer, Charles Myles, 5
O'Grady, Michael, 5
Old, Francis Edward, 11
Olney, Sir Herbert Horace, 11
Ormond, Francis (1829-1889), 5
Orr, William (1843-1929), 11
Outtrim, Alfred Richard, 11
Owens, John Downes, 5
Palmer, Sir James Frederick, 5
Pearson, Charles Henry, 5
Pearson, William, 5
Pennington, John Warburton, 11
Pinnock, James Denham, 2
Pitt, William (1855-1918), 11
Pittard, Alfred James, 11
Plain, William, 11
Pohlman, Robert Williams, 5
Pratt, Joseph Major, 11
Purves, James Liddell, 5
Pyke, Vincent, 5
Quick, Sir John, 11
Ramsay, Robert (1842-1882), 6
Reay, William Thomas, 11
Rees, John, 6
Reid, David, 6
Reid, Robert Dyce, 6
Richardson, Horace Frank, 11
Riddell, John Carre, 6
Robertson, William (1839-1892), 6

Robinson, Sir Arthur, 11
Rogers, John William Foster, 6
Russell, James, 6
Russell, Philip, 6
Russell, Thomas, 6
Ruthven, William, 11
Rutledge, William, 2
Ryan, Thomas, 11
Sachse, Arthur Otto, 11
Salmon, Charles Carty, 11
Saltau, Marcus, 11
Sargood, Sir Frederick Thomas, 6
Shackell, James, 6
Shields, Clive, 11
Simson, Robert, 6
Skinner, Henry Hawkins, 11
Smith, Alexander Kennedy, 6
Smith, Edmund Edmonds, 11
Smith, John Thomas, 6
Smith, Louis Lawrence, 6
Smith, Robert Murray, 6
Smith, William Collard, 6
Snodgrass, Peter, 2
Snowball, Oswald Robinson, 12
Snowden, Sir Arthur, 12
Solly, Robert Henry, 12
Stawell, Sir William Foster, 6
Steinfeld, Emanuel, 6
Stephen, George Milner, 2
Stephen, James Wilberforce, 6
Sternberg, Joseph, 12
Stewart, Percy Gerald, 12
Strachan, James Ford, 2
Stuart, Francis, 12
Styles, James, 12
Sullivan, James Forester, 6
Swinburne, George, 12
Syme, Ebenezer, 6
Taverner, Sir John William, 12
Taylor, William (1818-1903), 6
Thomson, Alexander, 2
Toutcher, Richard Frederick, 12
Trenwith, William Arthur, 12
Tucker, Albert Edwin Elworthy Lee, 6
Tudor, Francis Gwynne, 12
Tunnecliffe, Thomas, 12
Vale, Richard Tayler, 6
Vale, William Mountford Kinsey, 6
Verdon, Sir George Frederic, 6
Vogel, Sir Julius, 6
Wales, Sir Alexander George, 12
Wallace, Arthur Knight, 7
Wallace, Donald Smith, 6
Wallace, John Alston, 6
Webb, William Telford, 6
Weber, Ivy Lavinia, 12
Weedon, Sir Henry, 12
Were, Jonathon Binns, 2
Westgarth, William, 6
Wettenhall, Holford Highlord, 6
Wettenhall, Marcus Edwy, 12
Wilkie, David Elliot, 6
Williams, Edward David, 12
Williams, Henry Roberts, 12

Wills, Horatio Spencer Howe, 2
Wilson, Sir Samuel, 6
Winter, Joseph, 12
Winter-Irving, William Irving, 6
Wood, John Dennistoun, 6
Woods, John, 6
Wrixon, Sir Henry John, 6
Wynne, Agar, 12
Zeal, Sir William Austin, 12
Zox, Ephraim Laman, 6
Zwar, Albert Michael, 12
Zwar, Henry Peter, 12

Western Australia
Allen, Joseph Francis, 7
Angelo, Edward Houghton, 7
Angwin, William Charles, 7
Bath, Thomas Henry, 7
Boan, Henry, 7
Boyland, John, 7
Boyle, Ignatius George, 7
Briggs, Sir Henry, 7
Broadhurst, Charles Edward, 3
Brockman, Edmund Ralph, 3
Brockman, William Locke, 1
Brown, Maitland, 3
Burt, Septimus, 7
Bussell, John Garrett, 1
Clifton, Marshall Waller, 3
Cockburn-Campbell, Sir Thomas, 3
Connolly, Sir James Daniel, 8
Cowan, Edith Dircksey, 8
Crowder, Frederick Thomas, 8
Cunningham, James, 8
Davy, Thomas Arthur Lewis, 8
De Hamel, Lancel Victor, 8
Dempster, Andrew, 4
Dempster, Charles Edward, 4
Denton, James Samuel, 8
Draper, Thomas Percy, 8
Drew, John Michael, 8
Durack, Michael Patrick, 8
Dwyer, Sir Walter, 8
Ellis, Henry Augustus, 8
Ewing, John, 8
Forrest, Alexander, 8
Fraser, Sir Malcolm, 4
Gardiner, James, 8
George, William James, 8
Green, Albert Ernest, 9
Gregory, Henry, 9
Hackett, Sir John Winthrop, 9
Harper, Charles, 4
Harper, Nathaniel White, 9
Hassell, Albert Young, 4
Hassell, John Frederick Tasman, 4
Haynes, Richard Septimus, 9
Hayward, Thomas, 4
Hensman, Alfred Peach, 4
Holman, Mary Alice, 9
Hooley, Edward Timothy, 4
Illingworth, Frederick, 9
Johnson, William Dartnell, 9
Johnston, Edward Bertram, 9
Keane, Edward Vivien Harvey, 5

Keenan, Sir Norbert Michael, 9
Kenneally, James Joseph, 9
Kingsmill, Sir Walter, 9
Kirwan, Sir John Waters, 9
Lane, Zebina Bartholomew, 9
Latham, Sir Charles George, 10
Leake, George, 2
Leake, George Walpole, 5
Leake, Sir Luke Samuel, 5
Loton, Sir William Thorley, 10
Lynch, Patrick Joseph, 10
Lynn, Robert John, 10
McCallum, Alexander, 10
Mackie, William Henry, 2
Male, Arthur, 10
Marmion, William Edward, 10
Matheson, Sir Alexander Perceval, 10
Molloy, Thomas George Anstruther, 10
Monger, Frederick Charles, 10
Monger, John Henry, 5
Moore, William Dalgety, 5
Moran, Charles John, 10
Nanson, John Leighton, 10
Nathan, Sir Charles Samuel, 10
Nelson, Wallace Alexander, 10
North, Charles Frederic, 11
Padbury, Walter, 5
Parker, Hubert Stanley Wyborn, 11
Parker, Sir Stephen Henry, 11
Paterson, William, 11
Pearse, William Silas, 5
Phillips, Samuel Pole, 5
Piesse, Frederick Henry, 11
Randell, George, 6
Richardson, Alexander Robert, 11
Robinson, Robert Thomson, 11
Rose, Edwin, 11
Sanderson, Archibald, 11
Shenton, George, 6
Sholl, Horatio William, 11
Sholl, Robert Frederick, 11
Simons, John Joseph, 11
Smith, Henry Teesdale, 11
Smith, James MacCallum, 11
Speight, Richard, 6
Steere, Sir James George Lee, 12
Stuart, John Alexander Salmon, 12
Taylor, George, 12
Venn, Henry Whittall, 12
Vosper, Frederick Charles Burleigh, 12
Walker, Thomas, 6
Willmott, Francis Edward Sykes, 12
Wisdom, Evan Alexander, 12
Wittenoom, Sir Edward Charles, 12
Wright, John Arthur, 12
Yelverton, Henry John, 6

POTTER
Boyd, William Merric, 7
Reynell, Gladys, 11

PREACHER, *see also* Missionary
Ardill, George Edward (1857-1945), 7
Field, Edward Percy, 8
Fisher, James Cowley Morgan, 4
Hassall, Rowland, 1

Hussey, Henry, 4
Innes, Frederick Maitland*, 4
Judkins, William Henry, 9
Parker, Edward Stone, 5
Pidgeon, Nathaniel, 2
Reed, Henry, 2
Ridley, John, 2
Short, Benjamin, 6
Spence, Catherine Helen, 6
Taylor, William (1821-1902), 6
Tom, William, 2
Torr, William George, 12
Trigg, Henry, 2
Turner, Martha, 6
Unaipon, David, 12
Virgo, John James, 12
Walch, Charles Edward, 6
White, Ellen Gould, 12
Wroe, John, 2

PREMIER

New South Wales

Bavin, Sir Thomas Rainsford, 7
Carruthers, Sir Joseph Hector McNeil, 7
Cowper, Sir Charles, 3
Dibbs, Sir George Richard, 4
Donaldson, Sir Stuart Alexander
(1812-1867), 4
Dooley, James Thomas, 8
Farnell, James Squire, 4
Forster, William, 4
Fuller, Sir George Warburton, 8
Holman, William Arthur, 9
Jennings, Sir Patrick Alfred, 4
Lang, John Thomas, 9
Lyne, Sir William John, 10
McGowen, James Sinclair Taylor, 10
Mair, Alexander, 10
Martin, Sir James, 5
Parker, Sir Henry Watson, 5
Parkes, Sir Henry, 5
Reid, Sir George Houstoun, 11
Robertson, Sir John, 6
See, Sir John, 11
Stevens, Sir Bertram Sydney Barnsdale,
12
Storey, John, 12
Stuart, Sir Alexander, 6
Waddell, Thomas, 12
Wade, Sir Charles Gregory, 12

Queensland

Byrnes, Thomas Joseph, 7
Dawson, Andrew, 8
Denham, Digby Frank, 8
Dickson, Sir James Robert, 8
Douglas, John, 4
Gillies, William Neil, 9
Griffith, Sir Samuel Walker, 9
Herbert, Sir Robert George Wyndham, 4
Kidston, William, 9
Lilley, Sir Charles, 5
Macalister, Arthur, 5
McCormack, William, 10
McIlwraith, Sir Thomas, 5
Mackenzie, Sir Robert Ramsay, 5

Moore, Arthur Edward, 10
Morehead, Boyd Dunlop, 5
Morgan, Sir Arthur, 10
Nelson, Sir Hugh Muir, 10
Palmer, Sir Arthur Hunter, 5
Philp, Sir Robert, 11
Ryan, Thomas Joseph, 11
Smith, William Forgan, 11
Theodore, Edward Granville, 12
Thorn, George Henry, 6

South Australia

Ayers, Sir Henry, 3
Baker, John, 3
Barwell, Sir Henry Newman, 7
Blyth, Sir Arthur, 3
Boucaut, Sir James Penn, 3
Bray, Sir John Cox, 3
Butler, Sir Richard, 7
Butler, Sir Richard Layton, 7
Cockburn, Sir John Alexander, 8
Colton, Sir John, 3
Downer, Sir John William, 8
Dutton, Francis Stacker, 1
Finniss, Boyle Travers, 1
Gunn, John, 9
Hanson, Sir Richard Davies, 4
Hart, John, 4
Hill, Lionel Laughton, 9
Holder, Sir Frederick William, 9
Jenkins, John Greeley, 9
Kingston, Charles Cameron, 9
Morgan, Sir William, 5
Peake, Archibald Henry, 11
Playford, Thomas, 11
Price, Thomas, 11
Reynolds, Thomas, 6
Richards, Robert Stanley, 11
Solomon, Vaiben Louis, 12
Strangways, Henry Bull Templar, 6
Torrens, Sir Robert Richard, 6
Vaughan, Crawford, 12
Verran, John, 12
Waterhouse, George Marsden, 6

Tasmania

Agnew, Sir James Willson, 3
Braddon, Sir Edward Nicholas Coventry, 7
Champ, William Thomas Napier, 3
Chapman, Thomas Daniel, 3
Crowther, William Lodewyk, 3
Dobson, Henry, 8
Douglas, Sir Adye, 4
Dry, Sir Richard, 1
Dwyer-Gray, Edmund John Chisholm, 8
Earle, John, 8
Evans, Sir John William, 8
Fysh, Sir Philip Oakley, 8
Giblin, William Robert, 4
Gregson, Thomas George, 1
Hayes, John Blyth, 9
Innes, Frederick Maitland, 4
Kennerley, Alfred, 5
Lee, Sir Walter Henry, 10
Lewis, Sir Neil Elliott, 10
Lyons, Joseph Aloysius, 10

252

McPhee, Sir John Cameron, 10
Ogilvie, Albert George, 11
Propsting, William Bispham, 11
Reibey, Thomas, 6
Smith, Sir Francis Villeneuve, 6
Solomon, Albert Edgar, 12
Weston, William Pritchard, 2
Whyte, James, 6
Wilson, Sir James Milne, 6
Victoria
Allan, John, 7
Argyle, Sir Stanley Seymour, 7
Bent, Sir Thomas, 3
Berry, Sir Graham, 3
Bowser, Sir John, 7
Duffy, Sir Charles Gavan, 4
Dunstan, Sir Albert Arthur, 8
Elmslie, George Alexander, 8
Francis, James Goodall, 4
Gillies, Duncan, 4
Haines, William Clark, 4
Heales, Richard, 4
Hogan, Edmond John, 9
Irvine, Sir William Hill, 9
Kerferd, George Briscoe, 5
Lawson, Sir Harry Sutherland Wightman, 10
McCulloch, Sir James, 5
McLean, Allan, 10
McPherson, Sir William Murray, 10
Munro, James, 5
Murray, John (1851-1916), 10
Nicholson, William, 5
O'Loghlen, Sir Bryan, 5
O'Shanassy, Sir John, 5
Patterson, Sir James Brown, 5
Peacock, Sir Alexander James, 11
Prendergast, George Michael, 11
Service, James, 6
Shiels, William, 11
Sladen, Sir Charles, 6
Turner, Sir George, 12
Watt, William Alexander, 12
Western Australia
Colebatch, Sir Harry Pateshall, 8
Collier, Phillip, 8
Daglish, Henry, 8
Forrest, Sir John, 8
James, Sir Walter Hartwell, 9
Leake, George, 10
Lefroy, Sir Henry Bruce, 10
Mitchell, Sir James, 10
Moore, Sir Newton James, 10
Morgans, Alfred Edward, 10
Rason, Sir Cornthwaite Hector William James, 11
Scaddan, John, 11
Throssell, George, 12
Willcock, John Collings, 12
Wilson, Frank, 12
PRIME MINISTER
Barton, Sir Edmund, 7
Bruce, Stanley Melbourne, 7
Cook, Sir Joseph, 8

Deakin, Alfred, 8
Fisher, Andrew, 8
Hughes, William Morris, 9
Lyons, Joseph Aloysius, 10
Page, Sir Earle Christmas Grafton, 11
Reid, Sir George Houstoun, 11
Scullin, James Henry, 11
Watson, John Christian, 12
PRINTER
Barnard, James, 1
Bennett, Samuel, 3
Bent, Andrew, 1
Best, Charles, 1
Best, Henry, 1
Brooks, William*, 7
Cavenagh, George, 1
Degotardi, John, 4
Eggers, Karl Friedrich Wilhelm, 4
Fenton, James Edward*, 8
Ferres, John, 4
Findley, Edward*, 8
Green, Percy Gordon, 9
Hassell, George Frederick, 9
Higgs, William Guy*, 9
Hinchcliffe, Albert, 9
Houghton, Thomas John*, 9
Howe, George, 1
Hughes, George, 1
Hussey, Henry, 4
Kernot, Charles*, 5
Khull, Edward, 5
Kirkpatrick, Andrew Alexander*, 9
Lane, Frederick Claude Vivian, 9
Lees, Samuel Edward*, 10
Lithgow, Alexander Frame, 10
McCarron, John Francis, 5
McCutcheon, Robert George*, 10
McDonald, Lewis, 10
Macdougall, John Campbell, 2
McPherson, John Abel*, 10
Massina, Alfred Henry, 5
Molineux, Albert, 5
O'Connor, Joseph Graham*, 5
Penfold, William Clark, 11
Prendergast, George Michael*, 11
Pugh, Theophilus Parsons*, 5
Richards, Thomas, 6
Ross, James, 2
Sands, John, 6
Shea, Ernest Herbert, 11
Sligo, Archibald Douglas, 11
Stephens, Alfred Ward, 2
Stirling, Edmund, 6
Thomas, William Kyffin, 6
Troedel, Johannes Theodor Charles, 6
Vardon, Joseph*, 12
Wallis, Frederick Samuel*, 12
Wills, Horatio Spencer Howe*, 2
Winter, Joseph*, 12
PRISON ADMINISTRATOR
Bisdee, John, 1
Bowden, Edmund, 1
Conder, Walter Tasman, 8
Mullen, Leslie Miltiades, 10

Murphy, George Francis, 10
Neitenstein, Frederick William, 10
Paton, John, 5
Scanlan, John Joseph, 11
Timperley, William Henry, 6
PROFESSOR
Agriculture
Angus, William*, 7
Cherry, Thomas, 7
Custance, John Daniel, 3
Lowrie, William, 10
Paterson, John Waugh, 11
Perkins, Arthur James, 11
Richardson, Arnold Edwin Victor, 11
Waterhouse, Walter Lawry, 12
Watt, Sir Robert Dickie, 12
Anatomy
Berry, Richard James Arthur, 7
Halford, George Britton, 4
Hunter, John Irvine, 9
Jones, Frederic Wood, 9
Smith, Sir Grafton Elliot, 11
Watson, Archibald, 12
Anthropology
Davidson, Daniel Sutherland, 8
Radcliffe-Brown, Alfred Reginald, 11
Archaeology
Childe, Vere Gordon, 7
Architecture
Wilkinson, Leslie, 12
Astronomy
Cooke, William Ernest, 8
Biochemistry
Martin, Sir Charles James, 10
Priestley, Henry, 11
Young, William John, 12
Biology
Cobb, Nathan Augustus, 8
Dakin, William John, 8
Dendy, Arthur, 8
Flynn, Theodore Thomson, 8
Goddard, Ernest James, 9
Haswell, William Aitcheson, 9
Johnston, Thomas Harvey, 9
Spencer, Sir Walter Baldwin, 12
Botany
Ewart, Alfred James, 8
Lawson, Abercrombie Anstruther, 10
Osborn, Theodore George Bentley, 11
Chemistry
Fawsitt, Charles Edward, 8
Masson, Sir David Orme, 10
Masson, Sir James Irvine Orme, 10
Rennie, Edward Henry, 11
Rivett, Sir Albert Cherbury David, 11
Smith, John (1821-1885)*, 6
Steele, Bertram Dillon, 12
Wilsmore, Norman Thomas Mortimer, 12
Classics
Badham, Charles (1813-1884), 3
Dettmann, Herbert Stanley, 8
Dunbabin, Robert Leslie, 8
Irving, Martin Howy, 4
Kelly, David Frederick, 5

Michie, John Lundie, 10
Naylor, Henry Darnley, 10
Read, Henry, 6
Scott, Walter, 11
Williams, William Henry, 12
Woodhouse, William John, 12
Woolley, John, 6
Economics
Brigden, James Bristock, 7
Giblin, Lyndhurst Falkiner*, 8
Irvine, Robert Francis, 9
Mills, Richard Charles, 10
Education
Mackie, Alexander, 10
Smyth, John, 12
Wrigley, Leslie James, 12
Embryology
Hill, James Peter, 9
Engineering
Barraclough, Sir Samuel Henry Egerton, 7
Blakey, Othman Frank, 7
Burn, Alan, 7
Chapman, Sir Robert William, 7
Gibson, Alexander James, 8
Hawken, Roger William Hercules, 9
Kernot, Wilfred Noyce, 9
Kernot, William Charles, 5
Madsen, Sir John Percival Vaissing, 10
Payne, Henry, 11
Warren, William Henry, 6
English
Allen, Leslie Holdsworth, 7
Boulger, Edward Vaughan, 3
Brereton, John Le Gay, 7
Gosman, Alexander, 4
Holme, Ernest Rudolph, 9
Jacobs, Joseph, 9
Morris, Edward Ellis, 5
Murdoch, Sir Walter Logie Forbes, 10
Sinclaire, Frederick, 11
Stable, Jeremiah Joseph, 12
Strong, Sir Archibald Thomas, 12
Wallace, Sir Robert Strachan, 12
Entomology
Davidson, James, 8
Forestry
Jolly, Norman William, 9
Geology
Cotton, Leo Arthur, 8
David, Sir Tannatt William Edgeworth, 8
Gregory, John Walter, 9
Krausé, Ferdinand Moritz, 5
Liversidge, Archibald, 5
Richards, Henry Caselli, 11
Skeats, Ernest Willington, 11
Thomson, Alexander Morrison, 6
Woolnough, Walter George, 12
History
Elkington, John Simeon, 8
Hearn, William Edward*, 4
Heaton, Herbert, 9
Henderson, George Cockburn, 9
Scott, Sir Ernest, 11
Shann, Edward Owen Giblin, 11

Wood, George Arnold, 12
Language
Butler, Thomas John, 7
Cosh, James, 3
Harper, Andrew, 9
MacCallum, Sir Mungo William, 10
Murray, George Gilbert Aimé, 10
Nicholson, George Gibb, 11
O'Neill, George, 11
Smith, Thomas Jollie, 11
Todd, Frederick Augustus, 12
Waterhouse, Eben Gowrie, 12
Law
Allen, Sir Carleton Kemp, 7
Brown, William Jethro, 7
Charteris, Archibald Hamilton, 7
Cobbett, William Pitt, 8
Cumbrae-Stewart, Francis William Sutton, 8
Jenks, Edward, 9
McDougall, Dugald Gordon, 10
Moore, Sir William Harrison, 10
Peden, Sir John Beverley*, 11
Salmond, Sir John William, 11
Mathematics
Bragg, Sir William Henry, 7
Carslaw, Horatio Scott, 7
Gurney, Theodore Thomas, 4
Lamb, Sir Horace, 5
McAulay, Alexander, 10
Michell, John Henry, 10
Nanson, Edward John, 10
Pell, Morris Birkbeck, 5
Priestley, Henry James, 11
Weatherburn, Charles Ernest, 12
Wilson, William Parkinson, 6
Wilton, John Raymond, 12
Medicine
Allan, Robert Marshall, 7
Cairns, Sir Hugh William Bell, 7
Lambie, Charles George, 9
Mills, Arthur Edward, 10
Sandes, Francis Percival, 11
Sutton, Harvey, 12
Wilson, James Thomas, 12
Windeyer, John Cadell, 12
Woollard, Herbert Henry, 12
Mining
Whitfeld, Hubert Edwin, 12
Music
Benjamin, Arthur Leslie, 7
Bradley, Joseph, 7
Davies, Edward Harold, 8
Hart, Fritz Bennicke, 9
Hutchens, Francis, 9
Ives, Joshua, 9
Laver, William Adolphus, 10
Marshall-Hall, George William Louis, 10
Peterson, Franklin Sievright, 11
Natural History
Stephens, William John, 6
Natural Science
McCoy, Sir Frederick, 5
Tate, Ralph, 6

Oriental Studies
Sadler, Arthur Lindsay, 11
Pathology
Allen, Sir Harry Brookes, 7
Cleland, Sir John Burton, 8
Welsh, David Arthur, 12
Philology
Scutt, Cecil Allison, 11
Strong, Herbert Augustus, 6
Tucker, Thomas George, 12
Philosophy
Alexander, Samuel, 7
Anderson, Sir Francis, 7
Anderson, John, 7
Andrew, Henry Martyn, 3
Gibson, William Ralph Boyce, 8
Laurie, Henry, 10
Lyle, Sir Thomas Ranken, 10
Mayo, George Elton, 10
Mitchell, Sir William, 10
Muscio, Bernard, 10
Quaife, Barzillai, 2
Stewart, John McKellar, 12
Physics
Bragg, William Lawrence, 7
Duffield, Walter Geoffrey, 8
Grant, Sir Kerr, 9
Laby, Thomas Howell, 9
McAulay, Alexander Leicester, 10
Ross, Alexander David, 11
Threlfall, Sir Richard, 12
Vonwiller, Oscar Ulrich, 12
Physiology
Chapman, Henry George, 7
Cotton, Frank Stanley, 8
Osborne, William Alexander, 11
Robertson, Thorburn Brailsford, 11
Stirling, Sir Edward Charles*, 6
Stuart, Sir Thomas Peter Anderson, 12
Psychology
Lovell, Henry Tasman, 10
Miller, Edmund Morris, 10
Theology
Adam, David Stow, 7
Albiston, Arthur Edward, 7
Angus, Samuel, 7
Veterinary Science
Stewart, James Douglas, 12
Woodruff, Harold Addison, 12
Zoology
Agar, Wilfred Eade, 7
Dakin, William John, 8
PROSPECTOR
Bayley, Arthur Wellesley, 7
Buchanan, William Frederick, 3
Carr-Boyd, William Henry, 3
Crotty, James, 8
Crowther, Edward Lodewyk*, 3
Esmond, James William, 4
Frencham, Henry, 4
Gill, Henry Horatio*, 4
Hannan, Patrick, 9
Hargraves, Edward Hammond, 4
Lasseter, Lewis Hubert, 9

Leahy, Michael James, 10
Michel, Louis John, 5
Miles, John Campbell, 10
Moore, Thomas Bather, 10
Mulligan, James Venture, 5
Nash, James, 5
Newell, John*, 5
Palmerston, Christie, 5
Pearce, Samuel William, 11
Rasp, Charles, 6
Syme, David, 6
Uhr, Wentworth D'Arcy, 6
PROSTITUTE
Devine, Matilda, 8
Leigh, Kathleen Mary Josephine, 10
PROTECTOR OF ABORIGINES
Bland, Rivett Henry, 3
Bleakley, John William, 7
Cahill, Patrick, 7
Cahill, William Geoffrey, 7
Dawson, James, 4
Donaldson, Robert Thomas*, 8
Handt, Johann Christian Simon, 1
Meston, Archibald*, 5
Milligan, Joseph, 2
Moorhouse, Matthew, 5
Neville, Auber Octavius, 11
Parker, Edward Stone, 5
Parry-Okeden, William Edward, 11
Robinson, George Augustus, 2
Roth, Walter Edmund, 11
Thomas, William, 2
Thornton, George*, 6
Vickers, Allan Robert Stanley, 12
Wyatt, William, 2
PSYCHIATRIST
Downey, Michael Henry, 8
Jones, William Ernest, 9
Montgomery, Sydney Hamilton Rowan, 10
Nowland, Horace Henry, 11
Ross, Chisholm, 11
Sinclair, Eric, 11
Smith, William Beattie, 11
Winn, Roy Coupland, 12
PSYCHICAL RESEARCHER
Hodgson, Richard, 4
PSYCHOLOGIST
Davey, Constance Muriel, 8
Ellis, Henry Havelock, 4
Fowler, Hugh Lionel, 8
Lovell, Henry Tasman, 10
Mayo, George Elton, 10
Muscio, Bernard, 10
Parker, Henry Thomas, 11
Porteus, Stanley David, 11
Rivett, Doris Mary, 11
Stoneman, Ethel Turner, 12
PUBLIC SERVANT, *see also* Civil official
Britain
Belstead, Charles Torrens, 3
Elliot, Thomas Frederick, 1
Gairdner, Gordon, 1
Hamilton, Sir Robert George Crookshank,
  4

Hay, Robert William, 1
Herbert, Sir Robert George Wyndham*, 4
Trollope, Anthony, 6
Yencken, Arthur Ferdinand, 12
Commonwealth
Ainsworth, George Frederick, 7
Allen, George Thomas, 7
Beeby, Doris Isabel, 7
Bracegirdle, Sir Leighton Seymour, 7
Brigden, James Bristock, 7
Broinowski, Robert Arthur, 7
Brown, Sir Harry Percy, 7
Campbell, Archibald James, 7
Clemens, Sir William James, 8
Collins, James Richard, 8
Collins, Sir Robert Henry Muirhead, 8
Crommelin, Minard Fannie, 8
Daly, Charles Studdy, 8
Deane, Percival Edgar, 8
Dowse, Richard, 8
Duffy, Charles Gavan, 8
Edwards, William Burton, 8
Ewing, Robert, 8
Fuhrman, Osmond Charles William, 8
Gale, Walter Augustus, 8
Garran, Sir Robert Randolph, 8
Gepp, Sir Herbert William, 8
Heathershaw, James Thomas, 9
Hillary, Michael James, 9
Houghton, Sydney Robert, 9
Hunt, Atlee Arthur, 9
Israel, John William, 9
Jarvis, Eric Roy, 9
Jones, Harold Edward, 9
Kavanagh, Edward John*, 9
Knowles, Sir George Shaw, 9
Kraegen, Edward Charles, 9
Lightfoot, Gerald, 10
Lockyer, Sir Nicholas Colston, 10
Macandie, George Lionel, 10
McDougall, Frank Lidgett, 10
McGlinn, John Patrick, 10
Macgregor, Lewis Richard, 10
McLachlan, Duncan Clark, 10
McLaren, Sir John Gilbert, 10
Marr, Sir Charles William Clanan*, 10
Mehaffey, Maurice William, 10
Miller, David, 10
Mills, Stephen, 10
Mulvany, Edward Joseph, 10
Murdoch, John Smith, 10
Oakley, Robert McKeeman, 11
O'Reilly, Dowell Philip, 11
Oxenham, Justinian, 11
Percival, Arthur, 11
Pethebridge, Sir Samuel Augustus, 11
Robertson, William Apperley Norton, 11
Sadlier, Clifford William King, 11
Scott, Sir Robert Townley, 11
Sharwood, William Henry, 11
Sheehan, Sir Henry John, 11
Shepherd, Malcolm Lindsay, 11
Sholl, Richard Adolphus, 11
Smith, Issy, 11

Starling, John Henry, 12
Steward, Sir George Charles Thomas, 12
Templeton, Henry Barkley, 12
Thomas, William Charles, 12
Treloar, John Linton, 12
Trumble, Thomas, 12
Wales, Sir Alexander George*, 12
Walters, Henry Latimer, 12
Watson, Charles Vincent, 12
Williams, George Davies, 12
Wollaston, Sir Harry Newton Phillips, 12

India
Braddon, Sir Edward Nicholas Coventry*, 7

New South Wales
Anderson, Henry Charles Lennox, 7
Armstrong, Richard Ramsay, 3
Arnold, Richard Aldous, 7
Balcombe, Alexander Beatson, 3
Barling, Joseph, 3
Barney, George, 1
Beardsmore, Robert Henry, 7
Beuzeville, James, 3
Bingle, Walter David, 7
Bowen, George Meares Countess, 1
Bridges, Sir William Throsby, 7
Brown, Walter Ernest, 7
Brownlow, Frederick Hugh Cust, 7
Bruce, Alexander, 3
Byrnes, James (1806-1886)*, 3
Calvert, John Jackson, 3
Campbell, Walter Scott, 7
Carron, William, 3
Chapman, William Neate, 1
Christie, William Harvie, 3
Combes, Edward*, 3
Cracknell, Edward Charles, 3
Cropper, Charles William, 8
Dawson, Robert Barrington, 4
De La Condamine, Thomas, 1
Dowling, Edward, 8
Du Faur, Frederick Eccleston, 4
Dumaresq, Henry, 1
Duncan, William Augustine, 1
Eagar, Geoffrey*, 4
Egan, Daniel*, 4
Elliott, Gilbert*, 4
Elyard, Samuel, 4
Elyard, William (1804-1865), 4
Fitz, Robert, 1
Fitzgerald, Richard, 1
Fitzpatrick, Michael*, 4
Fraser, Archibald Colquhoun, 4
Garling, Frederick (1806-1873), 1
Gibbes, John George Nathaniel, 1
Gisborne, Henry Fyshe, 1
Golding, Isabella Theresa, 9
Gregory, David William, 4
Halloran, Henry, 4
Harington, Thomas Cudbert, 1
Harper, George, 1
Hay, Clifford Henderson, 9
Hayes-Williams, William Gordon, 9
Hixson, Francis, 4

Holdsworth, Philip Joseph, 4
Holme, John Barton, 9
Holmes, William, 9
Horniman, Vicary, 9
Houston, William, 4
Hull, Arthur Francis Basset, 9
Hume, Andrew Hamilton, 1
Jacob, Archibald Hamilton*, 4
Jamieson, John, 2
Jaques, Theodore James, 4
Jevons, William Stanley, 4
Kendall, Thomas Henry, 5
Lee, Benjamin*, 5
Leibius, Charles Adolph, 5
Lewis, George, 10
Lithgow, William, 2
Lockyer, Sir Nicholas Colston, 10
Lyne, Charles Emanuel, 10
McDonald, George Roy William*, 10
Mackaness, John, 2
McLachlan, Duncan Clark, 10
Maclean, Harold, 5
Maitland, Edward, 5
Mann, David Dickenson, 2
Manning, John Edye, 2
Marin la Meslée, Edmond Marie, 5
Mathews, Hamilton Bartlett, 10
Matthews, Susan May, 10
Maxted, Sydney, 10
Mayne, William Colburn, 5
Merewether, Edward Christopher, 5
Merewether, Francis Lewis Shaw*, 5
Mills, Stephen, 10
Moore, Joshua John, 2
Moriarty, Abram Orpen*, 5
Nichols, Isaac, 2
O'Brien, John Patrick, 11
O'Connell, Sir Maurice Charles*, 5
O'Connor, Richard, 5
Oliver, Alexander, 5
Oliver, Charles Nicholson Jewel, 11
O'Reilly, Walter Cresswell, 11
Parker, Sir Henry Watson*, 5
Pearce, Simeon Henry, 5
Poate, Frederick, 11
Rae, John, 6
Robinson, Michael Massey, 2
Rolleston, Christopher, 6
Roper, John, 6
Rose, David, 2
Sceusa, Francesco, 11
Scott, Thomas Alison, 2
Shepherd, Malcolm Lindsay, 11
Slattery, Thomas Michael*, 11
Smith, Stephen Henry, 11
Smith, Sydney (1880-1972), 11
Spence, John, 12
Spring, Gerald*, 6
Spruson, Joseph John, 12
Stephen, George Milner*, 2
Stephen, William Wilberforce, 6
Stevens, Sir Bertram Sydney Barnsdale*, 12
Suttor, John Bligh, 6

Templeton, Henry Barkley, 12
Tompson, Charles (1807-1883), 2
Trumper, Victor Thomas, 12
Turner, Alfred Allatson, 6
Tye, Cyrus Willmot Oberon, 12
Walker, Richard Cornelius Critchett, 6
Walker, Robert Cooper, 6
Walters, Henry Latimer, 12
Webb, Frederick William, 12
Wentworth, D'Arcy, 2
Whiddon, William Henry, 12
Wood, Harrie, 6
Northern Territory
Knight, John George, 5
McMinn, Gilbert Rotherdale, 5
Papua and/or New Guinea
Armit, William Edington, 3
Champion, Herbert William, 7
Chinnery, Ernest William Pearson, 7
Hides, Jack Gordon, 9
Hunter, George, 4
Hunter, Robert, 4
Imlay, Norman George, 9
Page, Harold Hillis, 11
Queensland
Anderson, John Gerard, 3
Appel, George, 3
Beal, George Lansley, 7
Bernays, Charles Arrowsmith, 3
Bernays, Lewis Adolphus, 3
Birkbeck, Gilbert Samuel Colin Latona, 7
Bleakley, John William, 7
Bourne, Joseph Orton, 3
Broadbent, Joseph Edward, 7
Buckley, Henry*, 3
Chester, Henry Marjoribanks, 3
Connah, Thomas William, 8
Dalrymple, George Augustus Frederick
  Elphinstone*, 4
Drury, Albert Victor, 4
Eden, Charles Henry, 4
Evans, George Essex, 8
Ferry, Thomas Arthur, 8
Fihelly, John Arthur*, 8
Gall, William, 8
Gordon, Patrick Robertson, 4
Gore, St George Ralph, 4
Graham, Arthur Ernest James Charles
  King, 9
Grano, Paul Langton, 9
Heath, George Poynter, 4
Ivory, Francis Jeffrey*, 4
Jordan, Henry*, 4
King, Henry Edward*, 5
Knowles, Sir George Shaw, 9
Lamb, Edward William*, 5
Landsborough, William, 5
Lyster, John Sanderson, 10
McCawley, Thomas William, 10
Macdonald, Alexander Rose, 5
Macgregor, Lewis Richard, 10
Mullan, John*, 10
Parry-Okeden, William Edward, 11
Payne, Sir William Labatte Ryall, 11

Pethebridge, Sir Samuel Augustus, 11
Scott, Sir Robert Townley, 11
Sheridan, Richard Bingham*, 6
Stephens, James Brunton, 6
Story, John Douglas, 12
Toft, John Percy Gilbert, 12
Traill, William Henry*, 6
Whish, Claudius Buchanan*, 6
South Australia
Blackmore, Edwin Gordon, 3
Bonney, Charles*, 3
Boothby, Josiah, 3
Boothby, William Robinson, 3
Cooke, Ebenezer*, 3
Douglas, William Bloomfield, 4
Finniss, Boyle Travers*, 1
Gill, Thomas, 9
Gillen, Francis James, 9
Goyder, George Woodroffe, 4
Halcomb, Frederick, 9
Jackson, John Alexander, 2
McCann, Sir Charles Francis Gerald, 10
Minchin, Richard Ernest, 5
O'Halloran, William Littlejohn, 2
Russell, James George, 11
Searcy, Alfred, 11
Smyth, Charles Edward Owen, 12
Stow, Augustine*, 6
Torrens, Sir Robert Richard*, 6
Wainwright, John William, 12
Weir, Stanley Price, 12
Tasmania
Arthur, Henry, 1
Balfe, John Donnellan*, 3
Bartley, Theodore Bryant, 1
Boothman, John Broadhurst, 1
Buckley, William, 1
Champ, William Thomas Napier*, 3
Clarke, Sir Andrew*, 3
Counsel, Edward Albert, 8
Crouch, Thomas James, 3
Driscoll, Cornelius, 1
Dry, Richard, 1
Dumaresq, Edward, 1
Emmett, Henry James, 1
Falconer, William Rose, 4
Gellibrand, Sir John*, 8
Gray, James*, 4
Gunn, Ronald Campbell*, 1
Hamilton, William Henry, 1
Henslowe, Francis Hartwell, 1
Hill, Samuel Prout, 1
Hull, Hugh Munro, 4
Johnston(e), Robert Mackenzie, 9
Kay, William Porden, 2
Lakeland, John, 2
Lascelles, Thomas Allen, 2
Mault, Alfred, 5
Mitchell, Sir William Henry Fancourt*, 5
Morgan, John, 2
Mulgrave, Peter Archer, 2
Mullen, Leslie Miltiades, 10
Murdoch, Peter, 2
Nairn, William Edward*, 5

O'Connor, Roderic, 2
Ogilvy, Arthur James, 5
Packer, Frederick Augustus Gow, 5
Parramore, William Thomas, 2
Salisbury, William Robert Peel, 11
Sorell, William (1800-1860), 2
Steward, Sir George Charles Thomas, 12
Turnbull, Adam (1803-1891), 2
Whyte, James*, 6
Victoria
Andrews, John Arthur, 7
Archer, William Henry, 3
Archibald, Jules François, 3
Barker, John, 3
Belcher, George Frederick*, 3
Campbell, Envidale Savage Norman, 3
Carlile, Sir Edward, 7
Cassell, James Horatio Nelson, 3
Champ, William Thomas Napier*, 3
Childers, Hugh Culling Eardley*, 3
Collins, Sir Robert Henry Muirhead, 8
Croll, Robert Henderson, 8
Crowe, Robert, 8
Cuthbertson, Margaret Gardiner, 8
Davidson, William, 8
De Satgé, Oscar John*, 4
Douglass, Benjamin, 4
Duffy, Charles Gavan, 8
Finn, Edmund, 1
Foster, John Leslie Fitzgerald Vesey*, 4
Fullarton, Robert Russell, 4
Gaunt, William Henry*, 4
Giles, Ernest, 4
Harriman, Benjamin Cosway, 4
Harrison, Henry Colden Antill, 4
Hobbs, James, 1
Hodgkinson, Clement, 4
Howitt, Alfred William, 4
Irving, Martin Howy, 4
Kay, Joseph Henry, 2
Kenyon, Alfred Stephen, 9
Le Souef, Albert Alexander Cochrane, 5
Levey, James Alfred, 10
Lewis, Fred, 10
McCrae, George Gordon, 5
McGowan, Samuel Walker, 5
McVilly, Cecil Leventhorpe, 10
Martin, Arthur Patchett, 5
Martin, David, 10
Minogue, Michael Andrew, 10
Moore, Henry Byron, 5
Moriarty, Daniel, 10
Mulvany, Edward Joseph, 10
Murphy, George Read, 10
O'Dowd, Bernard Patrick, 11
Osborne, John Walter, 5
Outtrim, Frank Leon, 11
Pitt, Henry Arthur, 11
Read, Charles Rudston, 6
Ritchie, Edgar Gowar, 11
Robertson, William Apperley Norton, 11
Rusden, George William, 6
Rusden, Henry Keylock, 6
Shaw, Ebenezer, 11

Shillinglaw, John Joseph, 6
Smyth, Robert Brough, 6
Stewart, James Campbell, 12
Templeton, William, 6
Thwaites, William, 12
Topp, Charles Alfred, 6
Toutcher, Richard Frederick*, 12
Trumble, Thomas, 12
Wardell, William Wilkinson, 6
Webb, George Henry Frederick, 6
Wekey, Sigismund, 6
Wilks, William Henry*, 12
Wollaston, Sir Harry Newton Phillips, 12
Wright, William Henry, 6
Yuill, William John, 12
Western Australia
Bland, Revett Henry, 3
Burt, Octavius, 7
Clay, Henry Ebenezer, 3
Daglish, Henry*, 8
Gale, Charles Frederick, 8
Gale, Walter Augustus, 8
Gibbs, Herbert William, 8
James, John Charles Horsey, 4
Jewell, Richard Roach, 4
Johnston, Harry Frederick, 9
Jull, Martin Edward, 9
Lefroy, Anthony O'Grady, 5
Martin, Edward Fowell, 10
Meares, Richard Goldsmith, 2
Neville, Auber Octavius, 11
North, Frederic Dudley, 11
Prinsep, Henry Charles, 11
Shapcott, Louis Edward, 11
Sholl, Richard Adolphus, 11
Sholl, Robert John, 6
Taylor, Henry Joseph Stirling, 12
Timperley, William Henry, 6
Trethowan, Hubert Charles, 12
Truscott, William John, 12
Tuckett, Francis John, 12
Tuckett, Lewis, 12
Walter, William Ardagh Gardner, 12
PUBLICAN, *see* Hotelkeeper
PUBLISHER, *see also* Music publisher
Broadbent, George Robert, 7
Catts, Dorothy Marguerite, 7
Catts, James Howard*, 7
Cole, Edward William, 3
Dowling, Henry (1810-1885)*, 1
Dwight, Henry Tolman, 4
Greville, Edward*, 4
Ham, Theophilus Job, 4
Ham, Thomas, 4
Howe, George, 1
Howe, George Terry, 1
Kelly, John Edward*, 5
Lothian, Thomas Carlyle, 10
McCarron, John Francis, 5
Melville, Henry, 2
Miles, William John, 10
Moffitt, William, 2
Molineux, Albert, 5
Parker, Frank Critchley, 11

Pearson, Joseph, 11
Preece, Frederick William, 11
Preece, John Lloyd, 11
Püttmann, Hermann, 5
Robertson, George, 6
Robertson, George, 11
Robinson, Herbert Edward Cooper, 11
Rowlandson, Alfred Cecil, 11
Smith, Sydney George Ure, 11
Stephens, Alfred George, 12
Stephens, John, 2
Stephensen, Percy Reginald, 12
Taylor, Florence Mary, 12
Taylor, George Augustine, 12
Tegg, James, 2
Tegg, Samuel Augustus, 2
Vidler, Edward Alexander, 12
Wilmot, Frank Leslie Thompson, 12

RABBI
Abrahams, Joseph, 7
Boas, Abraham Tobias, 7
Cohen, Francis Lyon, 8
Danglow, Jacob, 8
Davis, Alexander Barnard, 4
Falk, Leib Aisack, 8
Freedman, David Isaac, 8
Rintel, Moses, 6

RABBITER
Corey, Ernest Albert, 8
Gascoigne, Stephen Harold, 8

RACEHORSE TRAINER
Blacklock, Walter, 7
Bowman, Alexander*, 3
Cawker, Thomas, 3
Connolly, Eric Alfred, 8
Corrigan, Tom, 3
De Mestre, Etienne Livingstone, 4
Donohoe, James Joseph (c.1860-1925), 8
Holt, Michael, 9
McNamara, David John, 10
Murphy, Bennett Francis, 10
Payten, Bayly William Renwick, 11
Payten, Thomas, 11
Price, George Richard, 11
Scobie, James, 11
Tait, John, 6
Watson, George John, 6

RADIO BROADCASTER
Bennett, Alfred Edward, 7
Conder, Walter Tasman, 8
Doyle, Stuart Frank, 8
Edwards, George, 8
Ferry, Michael Augustus, 8
Fisk, Sir Ernest Thomas, 8
Lawrence, Charles Edward, 10
Leckie, Hattie Martha, 10
Littlejohn, Emma Linda Palmer, 10
Lumsdaine, John Sinclair, 10
McCann, Edward John, 10
McDowall, Valentine, 10
Mann, Edward Alexander*, 10
Maxwell-Mahon, William Ion, 10
Ordell, Talone, 11
Ross, John Howlett, 11

Saunders, Ambrose George Thomas, 11
Vaude, Charlie, 12
Voigt, Emil Robert, 12
Welch, Eric Wilfred, 12
Williams, Harold Parkyn, 12

RADIOLOGIST
Argyle, Sir Stanley Seymour*, 7
Clendinnen, Frederick John, 8
Clendinnen, Leslie John, 8
Hancock, William John, 9
Harris, Lawrence Herschel Levi, 9
Hewlett, Herbert Maunsell, 9
McDowall, Valentine, 10

RAILWAY WORKER
Boswell, William Walter, 7
Carroll, John, 7
Davey, Phillip, 8
Harrison, John, 4
McCash, John McDonald, 10
Miller, William, 5
Milne, Edmund Osborn, 10
Newlands, Sir John*, 11
Picton, Edward Benjamin, 11
Saunders, John Victor, 11
Sixsmith, William, 6
Smith, Sydney (1856-1934)*, 11
Stansfield, William, 12
Stevens, Arthur Borlase, 12
Whitford, Stanley R.*, 12
Willcock, John Collings*, 12
Young, William Ramsay, 11

RAILWAYS COMMISSIONER
Cann, John Henry*, 7
Clapp, Sir Harold Winthrop, 8
Cleary, William James, 8
Eddy, Edward Miller Gard, 8
Fehon, William Meeke, 8
Ford, Richard, 4
Goodchap, Charles Augustus*, 4
Hill, Henry John, 4
Kirkcaldie, David, 9
Martindale, Ben Hay, 5
Moncrieff, Alexander Bain, 10
Oliver, Charles Nicholson Jewel, 11
Pope, Harold, 11
Speight, Richard*, 6
Tait, Sir Thomas James, 12
Webb, William Alfred, 12
Wright, John Arthur*, 12

REFINER
Buhôt, John, 3
Kemble, Francis, 2
Knox, Sir Edward*, 5

RELIGIOUS BROTHER
Joyce, Edmund Michael, 9
Keaney, Paul Francis, 9
Laboureyas, Pierre, 5
O'Driscoll, Charles Xavier, 11
Purton, David Gabriel, 11
Treacy, Patrick Ambrose, 6

RELIGIOUS SISTER
Anglican
Clutterbuck, Katherine Mary, 8
Crawford, Emma, 8

Silcock, Emma Caroline, 11
Stevens, Jemima Elizabeth Mary, 12
Catholic
Abbott, Gertrude, 7
Barron, Johanna, 7
Barry, Mary Gonzaga, 3
Benson, Louisa, 7
Brennan, Sarah Octavia, 7
Bruton, Dorothy Josephine, 7
Bruton, Mary Catherine, 7
Daly, Anne, 8
Desmond, Anna Maria, 8
Forbes, Catherine Ellen, 8
Frayne, Ursula, 4
Gibbons, Geraldine Scholastica, 4
Leehy, Mary Agnes, 10
Lynch, Annie, 10
McGuigan, Brigid, 10
McKillop, Mary Helen, 5
McLaughlin, Clara Jane, 10
MacRory, Margaret, 10
Mulquin, Katherine, 10
Noblet, Marie Therese Augustine, 11
O'Brien, Catherine Cecily, 11
O'Connell, Cecily Maude Mary, 11
O'Connor, Eily Rosaline, 11
Partridge, Bridget, 11
Potter, Norah Mary, 11
Rowland, Caroline Ann, 11
Synan, Mary, 12
Whitty, Ellen, 6
RESTAURATEUR, *see also* Caterer
Bright, Charles, 3
Fauchery, Antoine Julien, 4
Lucas, Antony John Jereos, 10
Mei Quong Tart, 5
Romano, Azzalin Orlando, 11
Triaca, Camillo, 12
Vigano, Mario Antonio Francesco Battista
   Virginio, 12
RETAILER, *see also* Storekeeper
Ahern, Thomas, 7
Alexander, Maurice*, 3
Annand, James Douglas*, 7
Baird, Adam, 7
Barnes, Walter Henry*, 7
Beirne, Thomas Charles, 7
Benjamin, David Samuel, 7
Boan, Henry*, 7
Buss, Frederic William, 7
Christmas, Harold Percival, 7
Clark, Sir Reginald Marcus, 8
Davis, James, 1
Edments, Alfred, 8
Fairley, Sir Andrew Walker, 8
Farmer, Sir William, 4
Fink, Benjamin Josman*, 4
Finney, Thomas*, 4
Fitzgerald, George Parker*, 4
Foy, Francis, 8
Foy, Mark, 8
Gibson, William, 8
Gilpin, Oliver, 9
Grace, Joseph Neal, 9

Hitchcock, George Michelmore, 4
Hordern, Anthony (1842-1886), 4
Hordern, Sir Samuel, 9
Hordern, Samuel, 4
Jones, Sir Charles Lloyd, 9
Kiernan, Esmond Laurence*, 9
Kippax, Alan Falconer, 9
Leslie, William Durham, 10
McBride, Sir Peter*, 10
McCathie, Harriette Adelaide, 10
McLean, William, 5
Mather, Joseph Francis, 10
Mather, Robert, 2
Miller, Alexander, 10
Monger, John Henry*, 5
Murdoch, Sir James Anderson*, 10
Myer, Simcha Baevski, 10
Nock, Thomas, 11
Rogers, Charles, 6
Snow, Sir Sydney, 12
Solomon, Isaac, 2
Solomon, Joseph, 2
Stanford, Thomas Welton, 12
Symonds, Saul, 12
Watson, James Henry, 12
Zimpel, William James, 12
ROWER
Beach, William, 3
Fairbairn, Stephen, 8
Horniman, Vicary, 9
Kelly, Frederick Septimus, 9
McVilly, Cecil Leventhorpe, 10
Pearce, Henry John, 5
Pearce, Henry Robert, 11
Rogers, George Edgar, 11
Searle, Henry Ernest, 6
Stanbury, James, 12
Trickett, Edward, 6
Tulloch, Eric William, 12
RURAL WORKER, *see also* Drover;
Shearer
Allum, Mahomet, 7
Aslatt, Harold Francis, 7
Barry, John Arthur, 7
Bishop, Charles George, 7
Blackman, Meredith George, 7
Boake, Barcroft Henry Thomas, 3
Boucaut, Sir James Penn*, 3
Buck, Robert Henry, 7
Clarke, John (1846?-1867), 3
Clarke, Thomas, 3
Cole, George Henry, 8
Corfield, William Henry*, 3
Coyne, John Harry*, 8
Crommelin, George Whiting, 3
Farber, Henry Christian, 8
Fatnowna, John Kwailiu Abelfai, 8
Forbes, William Anderson, 4
Fraser, Simon Alexander, 8
Johns, Joseph Bolitho, 4
Kenniff, James, 9
Kenniff, Patrick, 9
Knight, Albert, 9
Lihou, James Victor, 10

Loveless, George, 2
McPherson, (James) Alpin, 5
Martin, William Clarence, 10
Morant, Harry Harbord, 10
Mullagh, Johnny, 5
Neilson, John Shaw, 10
Nielsen, Niels Rasmus Wilson*, 11
Ogden, James Ernest*, 11
Ogilvie, William Henry, 11
O'Meara, Martin, 11
Orton, Arthur, 5
Pitt, Marie Elizabeth Josephine, 11
Pumpkin, 5
Rogers, William Richard, 11
Savage, Michael Joseph, 11
Skuthorp(e), Lancelot Albert, 11
Tjangamarra, 12
Upfield, Arthur William, 12
Wallis, William Dane, 12
Wilson, Mark, 12

SADDLER
Colton, Sir John*, 3
Cowie, James*, 3
Forster, William Mark, 4
Holden, Henry James, 9

SALVATIONIST
Booth, Herbert Henry, 7
Bruntnell, Albert*, 7
Gore, John, 4
Hay, James, 9
McKenzie, William, 10
Perry, Joseph Henry, 11
Whatmore, Hugh Edward, 12

SCHOLAR
Badham, Charles (1813-1884), 3
MacCallum, Sir Mungo William, 10
Macleay, William Sharp, 2
Serle, Percival, 11
Stawell, Florence Melian, 12
Strong, Sir Archibald Thomas, 12
Tucker, Thomas George, 12
Woodward, Frank Lee, 12

SCHOOL PRINCIPAL
Adamson, Lawrence Arthur, 7
Anderson, Peter Corsar, 7
Andrew, Henry Martyn, 3
Archer, Francis Henry Joseph, 7
Armitage, Frederick, 3
Aspinall, Arthur Ashworth, 7
Badham, Edith Annesley, 7
Bailey, Margaret Ann Montgomery, 7
Barbour, George Pitty, 7
Bean, Edwin, 3
Bee, James, 7
Best, Amy Jane, 3
Bethune, John Walter, 7
Bickersteth, Kenneth Julian Faithfull, 7
Blanch, George Ernest, 7
Board, Peter, 7
Boyd, William Alexander Jenyns, 7
Braim, Thomas Henry, 3
Briggs, Sir Henry*, 7
Bromby, John Edward, 3
Brooks, George Vickery, 7

Brown, Francis Ernest, 7
Bruton, Dorothy Josephine, 7
Buckland, John Richard, 3
Buckland, John Vansittart, 3
Cameron, Donald (1838-1916), 3
Cape, William Timothy, 1
Carter, Herbert James, 7
Chandler, Thomas Charles, 7
Chapple, Frederic, 7
Clarke, Marian, 8
Clemes, Samuel, 8
Coates, Joseph, 3
Cohen, Fanny, 8
Crowther, Henry Arnold, 8
Dettmann, Herbert Stanley, 8
Dixon, Horace Henry, 8
Druitt, Thomas, 4
Dumolo, Nona, 8
Farr, George Henry, 4
Fewings, Eliza Ann, 8
Fidler, Mabel Maude, 8
Forrest, Robert, 1
Franklin, Richard Penrose, 8
Garvin, Lucy Arabella Stocks, 8
George, Madeline Rees, 8
Girdlestone, Henry, 9
Graebner, Carl Friedrich, 9
Gratton, Norman Murray Gladstone, 9
Green, Florence Emily, 9
Hamilton, Alexander Greenlaw, 9
Harker, Constance Elizabeth, 9
Harper, Andrew, 9
Harris, Richard Deodatus Poulett, 4
Henn, Percy Umfreville, 9
Humble, George Bland, 4
Irving, Martin Howy, 4
Jacob, Caroline, 9
Jobson, Nancy, 9
Jones, Kathleen Annie Gilman, 9
Kane, Henry Plow, 2
Kellow, Henry Arthur, 9
Kerr, James Semple, 9
Kilgour, Alexander James, 9
Krome, Otto Georg Hermann Dittmar, 9
Langham, Frederick, 5
Langley, George Furner, 9
Le Couteur, Philip Ridgeway, 10
Lilley, Kathleen Mitford, 10
Littlejohn, William Still, 10
Lucas, Arthur Henry Shakespeare, 10
Macarthur, George Fairfowl, 5
McBurney, Samuel, 5
McComas, Jane Isabella, 10
Mackness, Constance, 10
MacNeil, Neil Harcourt, 10
McNicoll, Sir Walter Ramsay*, 10
Marden, John, 10
Matthews, William, 5
Montgomery, Christina Smith, 10
Moore, Joseph Sheridan, 5
Morres, Elsie Frances, 10
Morris, Edward Ellis, 5
Morrison, Alexander, 5
Morrison, Charles Norman, 10

Morrison, George, 5
Neighbour, George Henry, 10
Palmer, Thomas, 11
Parkinson, Charles Tasman, 11
Parsons, Joseph, 11
Perkins, Frederick Thomas, 11
Prescott, Charles John, 11
Purton, David Gabriel, 11
Robertson, Margery Fraser, 11
Robson, Ernest Iliff, 11
Rolland, Sir Francis William, 11
Rowland, Percy Fritz, 11
Shann, Frank, 11
Sharman, Matthew Stanton, 11
Shepherdson, John Banks, 2
Sly, Joseph David, 6
Soubeiran, Augustine, 12
Spielvogel, Nathan Frederick, 12
Stephens, William John, 6
Sutherland, Alexander, 6
Thornber, Catherine Maria (1837-1924), 12
Tildesley, Evelyn Mary, 12
Tisdall, Alice Constance, 12
Torr, William George, 12
Unwin, Ernest Ewart, 12
Vance, George Oakley, 6
Ward, John Frederick, 12
Way, Arthur Sanders, 6
Weatherly, May Isabella, 12
Weigall, Albert Bythesea, 6
Wheatley, Frederick William, 12
Whyte, Patrick, 6
Wilkinson, Dorothy Irene, 12
Williams, William Henry, 12
Wilson, John Bracebridge, 6
Wilson, John Purves, 12
Zercho, Charles Henry, 12
Zercho, Frederick William, 12

SCHOOL PROPRIETOR
Benham, Ellen Ida, 7
Best, Amy Jane, 3
Boehm, Traugott Wilhelm, 7
Brown, Margaret Hamilton, 7
Buntine, Walter Murray, 7
Card, Mary, 7
Cole, Joseph Stear Carlyon, 8
Crowther, George Henry, 8
Elliston, William Gore*, 1
Evans, Matilda Jane, 4
Halloran, Laurence Hynes, 1
Henderson, Isabella Thomson, 9
Lawton, John Thomas, 10
Muirden, William, 10
Newton, Frederick Robert, 5
O'Hara, John Bernard, 11
Plume, Henry, 11
Rendall, Charles Henry, 11
Stephens, Arthur Augustus, 12
Thornber, Catherine Maria (1812?-1894), 12
Watson, Mary Beatrice Phillips, 6
Whinham, John, 6
Young, John Lorenzo, 6

SCIENTIST, see also Astronomer;
Bacteriologist; Biochemist; Biologist;
Botanist; Chemist; Entomologist;
Epidemiologist; Geologist; Mineralogist;
Naturalist; Ornithologist; Palaeontologist;
Physicist; Physiologist; Seismologist;
Wheat-breeder; Zoologist
Babbage, Benjamin Herschel*, 3
Dawes, William, 1
Kay, Joseph Henry, 2
McAlpine, Daniel, 10
McGowan, Samuel Walker, 5
Macnamara, Dame Annie Jean, 10
Neumayer, Georg Balthasar von, 5
Townson, Robert, 2
SCULLER, see Rower
SCULPTOR
Ball, Percival, 7
Baskerville, Margaret Francis Ellen, 7
Bowes, William Leslie, 7
Cohn, Carola, 8
Cowan, Theodora Esther, 8
Gilbert, Charles Marsh Web, 9
Hoff, George Rayner, 9
Illingworth, Nelson William, 9
Mackennal, Sir Edgar Bertram, 10
Montford, Paul Raphael, 10
Parker, Harold, 11
Porcelli, Pietro Giacomo, 11
Richardson, Charles Douglas, 11
Sani, Tomaso, 6
Sheppard, Benjamin, 11
Simonetti, Achille, 6
Stanford, William Walter Tyrell, 6
Summers, Charles, 6
Thomas, Margaret, 6
Triaca, Camillo, 12
White, James, 12
Woolner, Thomas, 6
SEALER
Kable, Henry, 2
Kelly, James, 2
Lord, Simeon, 2
Underwood, James, 2
Underwood, Joseph, 2
SECULARIST
Symes, Joseph, 6
SEISMOLOGIST
Pigot, Edward Francis, 11
SELECTOR
Morrow, James, 5
Neilson, John, 10
Sorenson, Edward Sylvester, 12
Sternberg, Joseph*, 12
Stewart, Percy Gerald*, 12
Trethowan, Sir Arthur King*, 12
Tritton, Harold Percy Croydon, 12
SERICULTURIST
Beuzeville, James, 3
Coote, William, 3
SHEARER
Cooper, William, 8
Davidson, James, 8

Ferguson, William, 8
Howe, John Robert, 9
Macdonell, Donald*, 10
Milerum, 10
Tritton, Harold Percy Croydon, 12
Tuckett, Francis Curtis, 12
SHEEP-BREEDER
Aitken, John, 1
Bayly, Nicholas Paget, 3
Body, Eliel Edmund Irving, 7
Cumming, Thomas Forrest*, 3
Falkiner, Franc Brereton Sadleir*, 8
Falkiner, Otway Rothwell, 8
Guthrie, James Francis*, 9
Hood, Robert, 9
Keynes, Joseph, 9
Keynes, Richard Robinson, 9
Litchfield, James, 5
Marina, Carlo, 5
Merriman, George, 10
Merriman, Sir Walter Thomas, 10
Mills, Charles, 5
Mills, William George James*, 10
Peppin, Frederick Loch, 5
Peppin, George, 5
Peppin, George Hall, 5
Richmond, James, 6
Rouse, Richard (1843-1906), 6
Smith, John (1811-1895)*, 6
Wells, Thomas, 2
SHIP CHANDLER
Gresham, William Hutchison, 4
Kopsen, William, 9
Salting, Severin Kanute, 2
Verdon, Sir George Frederic*, 6
SHIP-OWNER
Appleton, William Thomas, 7
Bingle, John, 1
Blackwood, John Hutchison*, 3
Boyd, Benjamin, 1
Brown, John, 7
Burke, John, 7
Burke, John Edward, 7
Burns, Sir James, 7
Cadell, Francis, 3
Campbell, James, 7
Campbell, William Douglas, 1
Carey, John Randal, 7
Currie, Archibald, 3
Curtis, Anthony, 1
Dacre, Ranulph, 1
Dangar, Frederick Holkham, 4
Darley, Benjamin, 4
Enderby, Samuel, 1
Facy, Peter (1822-1890), 4
Fanning, William, 4
Fitch, Algernon Sydney, 8
Foster, John*, 1
Griffiths, John, 1
Griffiths, Jonathon, 1
Grose, Joseph Hickey, 1
Harrap, Alfred, 4
Hinton, Howard, 9
Hogan, Michael, 1

Holyman, James, 9
Holyman, William, 4
Holyman, William, 9
Huddart, James, 4
Ingle, John, 2
Jeanneret, Charles Edward, 4
Langdon, William*, 2
Lee, Benjamin*, 5
Lilly, James, 5
Lynn, Robert John*, 10
McEacharn, Sir Malcolm Donald*, 10
McGregor, Alexander*, 5
McIlwraith, Andrew, 10
McIlwraith, John, 5
McMeckan, James, 5
Manning, Edye, 2
Merriman, James*, 5
Miles, Edward Thomas*, 10
Miller, Robert William, 10
Mitchell, Joseph Earl Cherry*, 5
Murnin, Michael Egan, 5
Nichols, Isaac, 2
Nicoll, Bruce Baird*, 5
Padbury, Walter*, 5
Paterson, James, 5
Perdriau, Henry Carter, 11
Philp, Sir Robert*, 11
Randell, William Richard*, 6
Reed, Henry, 2
Rigg, William*, 11
Ritchie, Thomas, 2
Robinson, Sir Thomas Bilbe, 11
Seal, Charles, 2
Sleigh, Harold Crofton, 11
Smith, Edmund Edmonds*, 11
Smith, William Howard, 6
Syme, David York, 12
Taylor, Sir Allen Arthur*, 12
Towns, Robert*, 6
Watt, Ernest Alexander Stuart, 12
Winder, Thomas White Melville, 2
Yabsley, William, 6
SHIPBUILDER
Booth, John*, 3
Cook, Solomon, 3
Cuthbert, John, 3
Degraves, Peter, 1
Franki, James Peter, 8
Griffiths, Jonathon, 1
Kennedy, Colin, 9
Kennedy, John, 9
Kennedy, Malcolm, 9
Komine, Isokichi, 9
Korff, John, 5
Lowe, William, 2
McGregor, John Gibson, 5
Moore, Thomas, 2
Palmer, Thomas Fyshe, 2
Ransom, Thomas, 2
Reeks, Walter, 11
Rowntree, Thomas Stephenson, 6
Underwood, James, 2
Yabsley, William, 6

SHIPPING AGENT
Black, John*, 3
Hassell, John Frederick Tasman*, 4
Macdonald, Benjamin Wickham, 10
Tucker, Charles*, 12
SILVERSMITH
Linton, James Alexander, 10
Wendt, Joachim Matthias, 12
SINGER
Austral, Florence Mary, 7
Beatty, Raymond Wesley, 7
Beaumont, Edward Armes, 3
Bracy, Henry, 7
Brownlee, John Donald Mackenzie, 7
Carandini, Marie, 3
Castles, Amy Eliza, 7
Collier, Frederick Redmond, 8
Crossley, Ada Jemima, 8
Dawson, Peter Smith, 8
Gordon, Margaret Jane, 9
Griffen Foley, James Joseph, 9
Hayes, Catherine, 4
John, Cecilia Annie, 9
Lawrence, Marjorie Florence, 10
Loitte, Lavinia Florence de, 12
McEachern, Walter Malcolm Neil, 10
Melba, Dame Nellie, 10
Moncrieff, Gladys Lillian, 10
Mummery, Joseph Browning, 10
Palmer, Rosina Martha Hosanah, 5
Sherwin, Frances Amy Lillian, 6
Stevens, Horace Ernest, 12
Stralia, Elsa, 12
Tritton, Harold Percy Croydon, 12
Vernon, Howard, 12
Wiedermann, Elise, 11
Williams, Harold John, 12
Young, Florence Maude, 12
SOCIALIST
Ahern, Elizabeth, 7
Bennett, Henry Gilbert*, 7
Champion, Henry Hyde, 7
Laidler, Thomas Percival, 9
Lane, William, 9
Locke, Lilian Sophia, 10
McNamara, Matilda Emilie Bertha, 10
McNamara, William Henry Thomas, 10
Mann, Thomas, 10
Matthias, Elizabeth, 10
Rosa, Samuel Albert, 11
Sceusa, Francesco, 11
Winspear, William Robert, 12
SOCIOLOGIST
Collier, James, 8
Pavy, Emily Dorothea, 11
SOLDIER, *see also* Marine
Alderman, Walter William, 7
Birdwood, William Riddell, 7
Bridges, Sir William Throsby, 7
Campbell, Gerald Ross, 7
Chauvel, Sir Henry George, 7
Chirnside, John Percy*, 7
Chumleigh, Harold Vere, 7
Costello, James Jasper, 8

Easterbrook, Claude Cadman, 8
Edwards, John Harold McKenzie, 8
Finn, Henry, 8
Foott, Cecil Henry, 8
Forsyth, John Keatly, 8
Foster, Hubert John, 8
Foster, William James, 8
French, Sir George Arthur, 8
Gwynn, Sir Charles William, 9
Hutton, Sir Edward Thomas Henry, 9
James, Tristram Bernard Wordsworth, 9
Jess, Sir Carl Herman, 9
Lee, George Leonard, 10
Legge, James Gordon, 10
Levien, Cecil John, 10
Lyster, John Sanderson, 10
Newland, James Ernest, 11
Parnell, John William, 11
Peck, John Henry, 11
Phillips, Owen Forbes, 11
Ramaciotti, Gustave Mario, 11
Sandford, Augustus Henry, 11
White, Sir Cyril Brudenell Bingham, 12
White, Dudley Persse, 12
Whitham, John Lawrence, 12
Wieck, George Frederick Gardells, 12
British
Abbott, Edward, 1
Allman, Francis, 1
Alt, Augustus Theodore Henry, 1
Anderson, Joseph, 1
Anderson, William Acland Douglas, 3
Antill, Henry Colden, 1
Balfour, William, 1
Barker, Collet, 1
Barney, George, 1
Bayly, Nicholas, 1
Bell, Archibald (1773-1837), 1
Bell, Thomas, 1
Bellasis, George Bridges, 1
Bishop, Peter, 1
Brabyn, John, 1
Bridges, Sir (George) Tom Molesworth, 7
Bruce, John, 3
Brumby, James, 1
Bull, John Edward Newell, 3
Bunbury, Henry William St Pierre, 1
Butler, James, 1
Cameron, Charles, 1
Carey, George Jackson, 3
Champ, William Thomas Napier*, 3
Christie, William Harvie, 3
Chute, Sir Trevor, 3
Cimitiere, Gilbert, 1
Clarke, Sir Andrew*, 3
Clogstoun, Henry Oliver, 8
Cotton, Sir Sidney John, 1
Cox, William, 1
Crummer, James Henry, 1
Cuthbertson, John, 1
Darling, Sir Charles Henry, 4
De La Condamine, Thomas, 1
Druitt, George, 1
Edge, Fane, 1

Edwards, Sir James Bevan, 4
Elliott, Gilbert Charles Edward, 8
Erskine, James, 1
Faithful, William, 1
Fanning, Frederick, 4
Faunce, Alured Tasker, 1
Foveaux, Joseph, 1
Fyans, Foster, 1
Geils, Andrew, 1
Gibbes, John George Nathaniel, 1
Grose, Francis, 1
Gunning, George Weston, 1
Gunter, Howel, 9
Henderson, Sir Edmund Yeamans Walcott, 4
Holden, John Rose, 1
Huon de Kerilleau, Gabriel Louis Marie, 1
Innes, Archibald Clunes, 2
Irwin, Frederick Chidley, 2
Kelsall, Roger, 2
Kemp, Anthony Fenn, 2
Kempt, John Francis, 5
Lawson, William, 2
Laycock, Thomas (1756?-1809), 2
Laycock, Thomas (1786?-1823), 2
Light, William, 2
Lindesay, Sir Patrick, 2
Lockyer, Edmund, 2
Logan, Patrick, 2
Lonsdale, William, 2
Lyttleton, William Thomas, 2
Macarthur, Sir Edward, 5
Macarthur, John (1767-1834), 2
McDonald, Hugh, 2
MacKellar, Neil, 2
Mair, William, 5
Meares, Richard Goldsmith, 2
Minchin, William, 2
Molle, George James, 2
Montagu, John, 2
Mundy, Godfrey Charles, 2
Nairn, William, 2
Nepean, Nicholas, 2
Nickle, Sir Robert, 5
O'Connell, Sir Maurice Charles*, 5
O'Connell, Sir Maurice Charles Philip, 2
O'Hea, Timothy, 5
Ovens, John, 2
Palmer, George Thomas, 2
Pasley, Charles, 5
Paterson, William, 2
Paton, John, 5
Piper, John, 2
Pratt, Sir Thomas Simson, 5
Rose, David, 2
Ross, Sir Robert Dalrymple*, 6
Rossi, Francis Nicholas, 2
Rowley, Thomas, 2
Ryan, Thomas, 2
Schaw, Charles, 2
Scratchley, Sir Peter Henry, 6
Seymour, David Thompson, 6
Shadforth, Thomas, 2
Sinclair-Maclagan, Ewen George, 11

Slade, Ernest Augustus, 2
Snodgrass, Kenneth, 2
Squires, Ernest Ker, 12
Stewart, William, 2
Strickland, Sir Edward, 6
Sturt, Charles, 2
Thorn, George*, 6
Tims, Martin, 2
Townson, John, 2
Victor, James Conway, 2
Wallis, James, 2
Ward, Sir Edward Wolstenholme*, 6
Wylly, Guy George Egerton, 12
Wynyard, Edward Buckley, 2
Yencken, Arthur Ferdinand, 12

colonial

Anderson, William Acland Douglas, 3
Bartlett, Charles Henry Falkner Hope, 7
Byron, John Joseph, 7
Dibdin, Edward John, 8
Disney, Thomas Robert, 4
Downes, Major Francis, 4
Gunter, Howel, 9
Legge, William Vincent, 5
Murray, Pembroke Lathrop, 10
Price, Thomas Caradoc Rose, 11
Richardson, John Soame, 6
Roberts, Charles Fyshe, 6

Maori Wars

McLerie, John, 5
Pratt, Sir Thomas Simson, 5
Richardson, John Soame, 6
Ross, Sir Robert Dalrymple*, 6
Strickland, Sir Edward, 6

South African War

Abbott, John Henry (Macartney), 7
Airey, Henry Parke, 7
Antill, John Macquarie, 7
Bailey, Henry Stephen*, 7
Bell, Frederick William, 7
Bell, Sir George John*, 7
Belt, Francis Walter, 7
Bennett, Alfred Joshua, 7
Bessell-Browne, Alfred Joseph, 7
Bisdee, John Hutton, 7
Brand, Charles Henry*, 7
Browne, Reginald Spencer, 7
Bruche, Sir Julius Henry, 7
Burley, Johnston, 7
Burnage, Granville John, 7
Butler, Charles Philip, 7
Byron, John Joseph, 7
Cameron, Cyril St Clair*, 7
Cameron, Donald, 7
Cameron, Sir Donald Charles*, 7
Cameron, Donald James*, 7
Carington, Rupert Clement George, 7
Carter, Hubert Reginald, 7
Cass, Walter Edmund Hutchinson, 7
Chalmers, Frederick Royden, 7
Christian, Sydney Ernest, 7
Cope, William, 8
Cox, Charles Frederick*, 8
Dartnell, William Thomas, 8

Dodds, Thomas Henry, 8
Dove, Frederick Allan, 8
Dowse, Richard, 8
Edwards, Percy Malcolm, 8
Elliott, Harold Edward*, 8
Evans, Alexander Arthur*, 8
Forbes, Arthur Edward, 8
Forth, Nowell Barnard de Lancey, 8
Fraser, John Edward, 8
Gaunt, Cecil Robert, 8
Glasfurd, Duncan John, 9
Glasgow, Sir Thomas William*, 9
Goold-Adams, Sir Hamilton, 9
Gordon, Grosvenor George Stuart, 9
Gordon, Joseph Maria, 9
Granville, Cecil Horace Plantagenet, 9
Handcock, Peter Joseph, 9
Hawker, James Clarence, 9
Heritage, Francis Bede, 9
Hoad, Sir John Charles, 9
Holdsworth, Albert Armytage, 9
Holman, Richard Charles Frederick, 9
Holmes, William, 9
Irving, Godfrey George Howy, 9
Johnston, George Jameson, 9
Kelly, Robert Hume Vandeleur, 9
Kendall, Ernest Arthur, 9
Kyngdon, Leslie Herbert, 9
Lasseter, Henry Beauchamp, 5
Leane, Edwin Thomas, 10
Lee, John Henry Alexander, 10
Legge, James Gordon, 10
Lenehan, Robert William, 10
Livingstone-Learmonth, Frederick Valiant
  Cotton, 10
Longstaff, William Frederick, 10
Loynes, James, 10
Lynch, Thomas (Joseph), 10
McArthur, John (1875-1947), 10
Macarthur-Onslow, Francis Arthur, 10
Macarthur-Onslow, James William*, 10
McGlinn, John Patrick, 10
McIntosh, Harold, 10
Mackay, James Alexander Kenneth*, 10
McLeish, Duncan, 10
Mann, Sir Frederick Wollaston, 10
Maygar, Leslie Cecil, 10
Meredith, John Baldwin Hoystead, 10
Miller, David, 10
Morant, Harry Harbord, 10
Mullen, Leslie Miltiades, 10
Newland, Victor Marra*, 11
Newton, Frank Graham, 11
Owen, Percy Thomas, 11
Owen, Robert Haylock, 11
Parrott, Thomas Samuel, 11
Price, Thomas Caradoc Rose, 11
Rankin, Colin Dunlop Wilson*, 11
Ricardo, Percy Ralph, 11
Roberts, Ernest Alfred*, 11
Rogers, James, 11
Rowell, James*, 11
Royston, John Robinson, 11
Rudduck, Harold Sugden, 11

Ryrie, Sir Granville de Laune*, 11
Sellheim, Victor Conradsdorf Morisset, 11
Shields, Sir Douglas Andrew, 11
Smyth, Sir Nevill Maskelyne, 12
Stevenson, George Ingram, 12
Stodart, Robert Mackay, 12
Tivey, Edwin, 12
Toll, Frederick William, 12
Trevascus, William Charles, 12
Tunbridge, Walter Howard, 12
Vernon, Hugh Venables, 12
Waite, William Charles Nightingale, 12
Walker, James, 12
Wallis, William Dane, 12
Watriama, William Jacob, 12
Watson, William Walker Russell, 12
White, Samuel Albert, 12
Whittle, John Woods, 12
Wienholt, Arnold*, 12
Wilson, James Lockie, 12
Wilson, Lachlan Chisholm, 12
Wylly, Guy George Egerton, 12

Sudan War
Airey, Henry Parke, 7
Bartlett, Charles Henry Falkner Hope, 7
Bennett, Alfred Joshua, 7
Brownlow, Frederick Hugh Cust, 7
Cope, William, 8
Finn, Henry, 8
Kyngdon, Leslie Herbert, 9
Lynch, Thomas (Joseph), 10
Parrott, Thomas Samuel, 11
Richardson, John Soame, 6

World War I
Abbott, Percy Phipps*, 7
Anderson, Sir Robert Murray McCheyne,
  7
Annand, Frederick William Gadsby, 7
Anthon, Daniel Herbert, 7
Antill, John Macquarie, 7
Arnold, Thomas Francis, 7
Aslatt, Harold Francis, 7
Bagot, Edward Daniel Alexander*, 7
Baker, Thomas Charles Richmond, 7
Ball, George, 7
Barnett, Charles Leslie, 7
Beardsmore, Robert Henry, 7
Beatham, Robert Matthew, 7
Bell, Sir George John*, 7
Bennett, Alfred Joshua, 7
Bessell-Browne, Alfred Joseph, 7
Bethune, Frank Pogson, 7
Betts, Selwyn Frederic, 7
Birkbeck, Gilbert Samuel Colin Latona, 7
Birks, Frederick, 7
Bisdee, John Hutton, 7
Bishop, Charles George, 7
Black, Percy Charles Herbert, 7
Blackburn, Arthur Seaforth, 7
Blackman, Meredith George, 7
Bolton, William Kinsey, 7
Borella, Albert Chalmers, 7
Boswell, William Walter, 7
Bourchier, Sir Murray William James*, 7

Bourne, George Herbert, 7
Boxer, Walter Henry, 7
Boyce, Sir Harold Leslie, 7
Boyd, Theodore Penleigh, 7
Brand, Charles Henry*, 7
Braund, George Frederick*, 7
Brazenor, William, 7
Brennan, Edward Thomas*, 7
Bridges, Sir William Throsby, 7
Brigden, James Bristock, 7
Brinsmead, Horace Clowes, 7
Brown, Herbert Basil, 7
Brown, Walter Ernest, 7
Browne, Reginald Spencer, 7
Bruche, Sir Julius Henry, 7
Bruxner, Sir Michael Frederick*, 7
Buckley, Alexander Henry, 7
Buckley, Maurice Vincent, 7
Bugden, Patrick Joseph, 7
Burdett, Basil, 7
Burley, Johnston, 7
Burnage, Granville John, 7
Burston, James, 7
Burton, Alexander Stewart, 7
Butler, Charles Philip, 7
Cameron, Cyril St Clair*, 7
Cameron, Donald, 7
Cameron, Sir Donald Charles*, 7
Campbell, Edward (1883-1944), 7
Campion, Sir William Robert, 7
Cann, George*, 7
Carmichael, Ambrose Campbell*, 7
Carne, Walter Mervyn, 7
Carroll, John, 7
Carter, Herbert Gordon, 7
Carter, Hubert Reginald, 7
Cass, Walter Edmund Hutchinson, 7
Castleton, Claud Charles, 7
Chaffey, Frank Augustus*, 7
Chalmers, Frederick Royden, 7
Cheeseman, William Joseph Robert, 7
Cherry, Percy Herbert, 7
Chisholm, Alexander, 7
Christian, Sydney Ernest, 7
Christie, Robert, 7
Clark, James Purcell, 8
Clark, James William, 8
Clarke, Charles James, 8
Clarke, William Lionel Russell*, 8
Climpson, Joseph, 8
Clogstoun, Henry Oliver, 8
Cohen, Harold Edward*, 8
Collett, Herbert Brayley*, 8
Collins, Herbert Leslie, 8
Conder, Walter Tasman, 8
Connell, Hugh John*, 8
Cooke, Thomas, 8
Corey, Ernest Albert, 8
Corlette, James Montagu Christian, 8
Cotter, Albert, 8
Coward, Harry Keith, 8
Cox, Charles Frederick*, 8
Coxen, Walter Adams, 8
Coyne, David Emmet, 8

Crouch, Richard Armstrong*, 8
Crowther, Henry Arnold, 8
Currey, William Matthew*, 8
Currie, Patrick, 8
Dadson, Leslie, 8
Dalley, John Bede, 8
Dalley-Scarlett, Robert, 8
Daly, Clarence Wells, 8
Dalziel, Henry, 8
Dartnell, William Thomas, 8
Davey, Phillip, 8
Davidson, William St John Stevens, 8
Davis, Charles Herbert, 8
Day, Robert Alexander, 8
Dean, Edwin Theyer, 8
Dean, George Henry, 8
Deane, Percival Edgar, 8
Denehy, Charles Aloysius, 8
Denham, Howard Kynaston, 8
Denny, William Joseph*, 8
Denton, James Samuel*, 8
Dibdin, Edward John, 8
Dodd, Arthur William, 8
Dodds, Thomas Henry, 8
Donnelly, John Francis, 8
Douglas, Roger, 8
Dowse, Richard, 8
Drake-Brockman, Edmund Alfred*, 8
Duffy, Sir Charles Leonard Gavan, 8
Duggan, Bernard Oscar Charles, 8
Dun, Percy Muir, 8
Duncan, Walter John Clare, 8
Dunn, William Fraser, 8
Dunstan, William, 8
Dyett, Sir Gilbert Joseph Cullen, 8
East, Hubert Fraser, 8
Eather, Richmond Cornwallis, 8
Edgerton, Eric Henry Drummond, 8
Edwards, Percy Malcolm, 8
Elliott, Charles Hazell, 8
Elliott, Gilbert Charles Edward, 8
Elliott, Harold Edward*, 8
Evans, Alexander Arthur*, 8
Evans, Daniel Edward, 8
Ewen, John Carr, 8
Farrell, John, 8
Fizelle, Reginald Cecil Grahame, 8
Fletcher, James Lionel, 8
Follett, Frank William, 8
Forth, Nowell Barnard de Lancey, 8
Fowler, Hugh Lionel, 8
Fowles, Herbert James, 8
Franklin, Richard Penrose, 8
Fraser, John Edward, 8
Freame, Wykeham Henry Koba, 8
Frost, Frederick Charlesworth, 8
Fuhrman, Osmond Charles William, 8
Fuller, Colin Dunmore, 8
Fysh, Sir Wilmot Hudson, 8
Gaby, Alfred Edward, 8
Garratt, Charles Clement, 8
Gaunt, Cecil Robert, 8
Geake, William Henry Gregory, 8
Gellibrand, Sir John*, 8

Gerard, Edwin Field, 8
Gibb, William, 8
Giblin, Lyndhurst Falkiner*, 8
Glasfurd, Duncan John, 9
Glasgow, Sir Thomas William*, 9
Goddard, Henry Arthur, 9
Gordon, Bernard Sidney, 9
Gordon, Grosvenor George Stuart, 9
Grant, Douglas, 9
Grant, William, 9
Granville, Cecil Horace Plantagenet, 9
Gregory, Jack Morrison, 9
Grieve, Robert Cuthbert, 9
Griffiths, Thomas, 9
Grimwade, Harold William, 9
Gwynn, Sir Charles William, 9
Hall, Arthur Charles, 9
Hallahan, Walter Rewi, 9
Ham, Wilbur Lincoln, 9
Hamilton, John, 9
Hammond, George Meysey, 9
Hardie, John Jackson, 9
Hardie, John Leslie, 9
Harper, Robert Rainy, 9
Harrison, Eric Fairweather*, 9
Harry, Gilbert, 9
Hawker, Charles Allan Seymour*, 9
Healy, Cecil Patrick, 9
Heane, James, 9
Henley, Frank Le Leu, 9
Heritage, Francis Bede, 9
Heron, Alexander Robert, 9
Herring, Sydney Charles Edgar, 9
Hillary, Michael James, 9
Hoad, Oswald Vick, 9
Hobbs, Sir Joseph John Talbot, 9
Hodgson, William Roy, 9
Hogue, Oliver, 9
Holdsworth, Albert Armytage, 9
Holmes, William, 9
Houghton, Sydney Robert, 9
Howell, George Julian, 9
Howell-Price, Frederick Phillimore, 9
Howell-Price, Owen Glendower, 9
Howell-Price, Philip Llewellyn, 9
Howell-Price, Richmond Gordon, 9
Howie, Laurence Hotham, 9
Hudd, Sir Herbert Sydney*, 9
Hughes, Francis Augustus, 9
Hughes, Frederic Godfrey, 9
Hurst, John Herbert, 9
Hyman, Arthur Wellesley, 9
Idriess, Ion Llewellyn, 9
Imlay, Alexander Peter, 9
Imlay, Norman George, 9
Ingram, George Mawby, 9
Inwood, Reginald Roy, 9
Irving, Godfrey George Howy, 9
Jacka, Albert, 9
Jackson, John William Alexander, 9
James, William Edward, 9
Jarvis, Eric Roy, 9
Jeffries, Clarence Smith, 9
Jensen, Joergen Christian, 9

Jobson, Alexander, 9
Johnston, Charles Melbourne, 9
Johnston, George Jameson, 9
Johnstone, John Lorimer Gibson, 9
Kaeppel, Carl Henry, 9
Keatinge, Maurice Barber Bevan, 9
Kendall, Ernest Arthur, 9
Kennedy, Thomas, 9
Kenny, Thomas James Bede, 9
Keysor, Leonard Maurice, 9
Kirkpatrick, John Simpson, 9
Kneeshaw, Frederick Percival*, 9
Knight, Albert, 9
Knox, Sir George Hodges*, 9
Lahey, Romeo Watkins, 9
Lalor, Vivian William, 9
Langley, George Furner, 9
Langley, Hudson John Watson, 9
Lansell, Sir George Victor*, 9
Larkin, Edward Rennix*, 9
Laseron, Charles Francis, 9
Lawlor, Adrian, 10
Lawrence, Gordon Ord, 10
Lawson, James, 10
Lay, Percy, 10
Layh, Herbert Thomas Christoph, 10
Leak, John, 10
Leane, Allan William, 10
Leane, Edwin Thomas, 10
Leane, Sir Raymond Lionel, 10
Lee, John Robert*, 10
Lewis, Arndell Neil*, 10
Lihou, James Victor, 10
Lind, Edmund Frank, 10
Littler, Charles Augustus Murray, 10
Loftus-Hills, Clive, 10
Longstaff, William Frederick, 10
Longworth, William (1892-1969), 10
Lord, John Ernest Cecil, 10
Lording, Rowland Edward, 10
Lowerson, Albert David, 10
Loynes, James, 10
Luxton, Sir Harold Daniel*, 10
Lynas, William James Dalton, 10
Lynch, Thomas (Joseph), 10
McArthur, John (1875-1947), 10
Macarthur-Onslow, George Macleay, 10
Macartney, Henry Dundas Keith, 10
McCann, William Francis James, 10
McCarthy, Lawrence Dominic, 10
McCash, John McDonald, 10
McCay, Sir James Whiteside*, 10
McCormack, William Thomas
  Bartholomew, 10
MacDonald, James Stuart, 10
McDougall, Frank Lidgett, 10
McDougall, Stanley Robert, 10
McGee, Lewis, 10
McGlinn, John Patrick, 10
McIntosh, Harold, 10
Mackenzie, Roderick, 10
Mackenzie, William Kenneth Seaforth, 10
Macnaghten, Charles Melville, 10
MacNeil, Neil Harcourt, 10

McNicoll, Sir Walter Ramsay*, 10
McSharry Terence Patrick, 10
Mactier, Robert, 10
McVilly, Cecil Leventhorpe, 10
Maguire, James Bernard, 10
Main, Hugh, 10
March, Frederick Hamilton, 10
Margolin, Eliezer, 10
Marks, Douglas Gray, 10
Marr, Sir Charles William Clanan*, 10
Marshall, Norman, 10
Martin, Edward Fowell, 10
Martin, William Clarence, 10
Martyn, Athelstan Markham, 10
Massie, Robert John Allwright, 10
Mathias, Louis John, 10
Matthews, Harley, 10
Maxwell, Joseph, 10
Maxwell-Mahon, William Ion, 10
Maygar, Leslie Cecil, 10
Melbourne, Alexander Clifford Vernon, 10
Meredith, John Baldwin Hoystead, 10
Milligan, Stanley Lyndall, 10
Mills, Arthur James, 10
Mills, Charles, 10
Mills, Richard Charles, 10
Milne, Edmund Osborn, 10
Milne, John Alexander, 10
Monash, Sir John, 10
Moore, Donald Ticehurst, 10
Moore, James Lorenzo, 10
Moore, John Charles, 10
Morrison, Edward Charles, 10
Mullaly, John Charles, 10
Mullen, Leslie Miltiades, 10
Munro, Edward Joy, 10
Murdoch, Thomas (1876-1961), 10
Murphy, Bennett Francis, 10
Murphy, George Francis, 10
Murray, Henry William, 10
Mustar, Ernest Andrew, 10
Neville, Dalton Thomas Walker, 11
Newland, Victor Marra*, 11
Newton, Frank Graham, 11
Nicholson, Edmund James Houghton, 11
O'Brien, John Patrick, 11
O'Keeffe, David Augustus, 11
Olden, Arthur Charles Niquet, 11
Oldfield, William Albert Stanley, 11
Oliver, Donald Percy, 11
O'Meara, Martin, 11
O'Reilly, Walter Cresswell, 11
Owen, Robert Haylock, 11
Page, Harold Hillis, 11
Parker, Hubert Stanley Wyborn*, 11
Partridge, Eric Honeywood, 11
Paterson, Alexander Thomas, 11
Paterson, Andrew Barton, 11
Paton, John, 11
Pearse, Samuel George, 11
Peeler, Walter, 11
Perry, Stanley Llewellyn, 11
Phillips, Herbert Peter, 11
Picton, Edward Benjamin, 11

Playfair, Thomas Alfred (Creer) John*, 11
Poole, Daniel, 11
Pope, Charles, 11
Pope, Harold, 11
Pye, Cecil Robert Arthur, 11
Quinn, Hugh, 11
Rankin, Colin Dunlop Wilson*, 11
Rawlings, William Reginald, 11
Reynell, Carew, 11
Robertson, James Campbell, 11
Rogers, James, 11
Rogers, William Richard, 11
Rosenthal, Sir Charles*, 11
Royston, John Robinson, 11
Ruthven, William*, 11
Rutledge, Thomas Lloyd Forster*, 11
Ryan, Edward John Francis, 11
Ryrie, Sir Granville de Laune*, 11
Sadlier, Clifford William King, 11
St Clair, William Howard, 11
Salisbury, Alfred George, 11
Sampson, Burford*, 11
Sargent, Foster Henry Hartley, 11
Scanlan, John Joseph, 11
Schwarz, Walter Leslie, 11
Scott, Allan Humphrey, 11
Scott, William Henry, 11
Scott, William John Rendell, 11
Scurry, William Charles, 11
Sellheim, Victor Conradsdorf Morisset, 11
Shang, Caleb James, 11
Shout, Alfred John, 11
Silas, Ellis Luciano, 11
Sinclair, William, 11
Sizer, Hubert Ebenezer*, 11
Skeyhill, Thomas John, 11
Smith, Issy, 11
Smith, Miles Staniforth Cater*, 11
Smith, Robert, 11
Smith, Sir Ross Macpherson, 11
Smyth, Sir Nevill Maskelyne, 12
Somerville, George Cattell, 12
Spain, Alfred, 12
Spedding, Quentin Shaddock, 12
Stace, Arthur Malcolm, 12
Stacy, Bertie Vandeleur, 12
Stansfield, William, 12
Stapleton, Claude Augustine, 12
Statton, Percy Clyde, 12
Steele, Alexander, 12
Stephenson, Sir Arthur George, 12
Stevens, Arthur Borlase, 12
Stevenson, George Ingram, 12
Stewart, James Campbell, 12
Stodart, Robert Mackay, 12
Stokes, Edward Sutherland, 12
Storkey, Percy Valentine, 12
Street, Geoffrey Austin*, 12
Sullivan, Arthur Percy, 12
Swadling, William Thomas, 12
Symons, William John, 12
Thomas, William Charles, 12
Thompson, Duncan Fulton, 12
Thompson, William George*, 12

Thorpe, Harry, 12
Throssell, Hugo Vivian Hope, 12
Thurston, Frederick Arthur, 12
Timms, Edward Vivian, 12
Tivey, Edwin, 12
Toft, John Percy Gilbert, 12
Toll, Frederick William, 12
Tomholt, Sydney John, 12
Towner, Edgar Thomas, 12
Townsend, Alfred Richard, 12
Townsend, George Wilfred Lambert, 12
Traill, John Charles Merriman, 12
Treloar, George Devine, 12
Treloar, John Linton, 12
Trevascus, William Charles, 12
Tubb, Frederick Harold, 12
Tuckett, Francis Curtis, 12
Tuckett, Francis John, 12
Tuckett, Joseph Helton, 12
Tuckett, Lewis, 12
Tuckett, Philip Samuel, 12
Tulloch, Eric William, 12
Tunbridge, Walter Howard, 12
Tunn, John Patrick, 12
Turnbull, Ernest, 12
Ulm, Charles Thomas Philippe, 12
Ulrich, Theodore Friederick, 12
Upfield, Arthur William, 12
Vaughan, John Howard*, 12
Vennard, Alexander Vindex, 12
Vernon, Geoffrey Hampden, 12
Vernon, Hugh Venables, 12
Vickers, William, 12
Vincent, James, 12
Vincent, Roy Stanley*, 12
Viner, William Samuel, 12
Viney, Horace George, 12
Waite, William Charles Nightingale, 12
Walker, Sir Harold Bridgwood, 12
Walker, Hurtle Frank, 12
Walker, James, 12
Waller, Mervyn Napier, 12
Wallis, William Dane, 12
Wanliss, Cecil, 12
Wanliss, David Sydney, 12
Wanliss, Harold Boyd, 12
Wardlaw, Alan Lindsay*, 12
Wark, Blair Anderson, 12
Waterhouse, Walter Lawry, 12
Watriama, William Jacob, 12
Watson, Charles Vincent, 12
Watson, Stanley Holm, 12
Watson, William Thornton, 12
Watson, William Walker Russell, 12
Weathers, Lawrence Carthage, 12
Welch, Eric Wilfred, 12
Wheen, Arthur Wesley, 12
White, Alexander Henry, 12
White, Harold Fletcher*, 12
Whittell, Hubert Massey, 12
Whittle, John Woods, 12
Wilder-Neligan, Maurice, 12
Williams, Francis Edgar, 12
Williams, Harold John, 12

Williams, Robert Ernest, 12
Wilson, Gordon Campbell, 12
Wilson, Herbert Ward, 12
Wilson, James Alexander Campbell, 12
Wilson, James Lockie, 12
Wilson, Lachlan Chisholm, 12
Wiltshire, Aubrey Roy Liddon, 12
Winter, Anthony William, 12
Wisdom, Evan Alexander*, 12
Wolfe, Herbert Austin, 12
Woodruff, Harold Addison, 12
Woods, James Park, 12
Woods, Percy William, 12
Woodward, Oliver Holmes, 12
Young, William Ramsay, 12
World War II
O'Reilly, Alfonso Bernard, 11
Patten, John Thomas, 11
Peeler, Walter, 11
St Clair, William Howard, 11
Scanlan, John Joseph, 11
Scott, William John Rendell, 11
Squires, Ernest Ker, 12
Vernon, Geoffrey Hampden, 12
Waite, William Charles Nightingale, 12
Walker, Allan Seymour, 12
Watson, William Thornton, 12
SOLICITOR *see* Lawyer
SPELAEOLOGIST
Trickett, Oliver, 12
SPIRITUALIST
Browne, Hugh Junor, 3
Stanford, Thomas Welton, 12
Terry, William Henry, 6
SPORTS ADMINISTRATOR, *see also*
Football administrator
Clibborn, Thomas Strettel, 3
Coombes, Richard, 8
Creswell, John, 8
Cropper, Charles William, 8
Donohoe, William Patrick, 8
Ransford, Vernon Seymour, 11
Smith, Sydney (1880–1972), 11
Trumble, Hugh, 12
Virgo, John James, 12
Wardill, Benjamin Johnston, 6
SPORTS INSTRUCTOR
Bjelke-Petersen, Hans Christian, 7
Weber, Clarence Alfred, 12
Weber, Ivy Lavinia*, 12
STATISTICIAN
Archer, William Henry, 3
Coghlan, Sir Timothy Augustine, 8
Hayter, Henry Heylyn, 4
Johnston(e), Robert Mackenzie, 9
Knibbs, Sir George Handley, 9
Wickens, Charles Henry, 12
STENOGRAPHER
Moore, Eleanor May, 10
STOCK AND STATION AGENT
Allan, William*, 3
Angelo, Edward Houghton*, 7
Badgery, Henry Septimus*, 3
Bagot, Edward Meade, 3

Boothby, Thomas Wilde*, 3
Brewster, John Gray, 3
Brown, Joseph Tilley*, 7
Brunker, James Nixon*, 3
Bruxner, Sir Michael Frederick*, 7
Campbell, Thomas Irving, 7
Coles, Sir Jenkin*, 8
Connor, Daniel, 8
Dean, George Henry, 8
Dennys, Charles John, 4
Forsyth, George, 4
Fraser, Simon*, 4
Garland, James*, 4
Gibson, Robert, 8
Groom, Arthur Champion*, 9
Guthrie, Thomas, 4
Hagelthorn, Frederick William*, 9
King, Arthur Septimus, 5
King, William Essington, 5
Lawson, James, 10
Lewis, John*, 10
McKenzie, Hugh*, 10
McLean, Allan*, 10
Morehead, Boyd Dunlop*, 5
Peck, Harry Huntington, 11
Peck, John Murray, 5
Pitt, George Matcham, 5
Quinn, John, 11
Ranken, George, 6
Reynell, Walter, 6
Rodgers, Arthur Stanislaus*, 11
Rowley, Stanley Rupert, 11
Sternberg, Joseph*, 12
Taverner, Sir John William*, 12
Walsh, James Morgan, 12
Weaver, Reginald Walter Darcy*, 12
Webster, William Maule (McDowell), 12
Wittenoom, Sir Edward Charles*, 12

STOCK-BREEDER, *see also*
Dog-breeder; Sheep-breeder
Barnes, Henry, 3
Bolden, Armyne, 1
Bolden, John Satterthwaite, 1
Bolden, Lemuel, 1
Bolden, Sandford George, 1
Brisbane, William Peter, 7
Clarke, Sir William John*, 3
Dawson, Robert Barrington, 4
De Mestre, Etienne Livingstone, 4
Deuchar, John, 4
Dowling, Vincent James, 4
Hordern, Anthony, 9
Hordern, Sir Samuel, 9
Icely, Thomas*, 2
McDougall, Charles Edward, 10
McDougall, Robert*, 5
Slade, William Ball, 11
Tanner, Alfred John, 12
Thompson, John Low, 6
Town, Andrew, 6
Wilson, James Lockie, 12
Wright, Colin William, 12

STOCKBROKER
Baillieu, Edward Lloyd, 7

Black, Reginald James*, 7
Brookman, Sir George*, 7
Burns, John Fitzgerald, 3
Butters, James Stewart*, 3
Claxton, Norman, 8
Cran, Robert (1856-1940), 8
Crowder, Frederick Thomas*, 8
Denovan, William Dixon Campbell*, 4
Dyason, Edward Clarence Evelyn, 8
Everard, John*, 4
Glover, Charles Richmond John, 9
Khull, Edward, 5
Luxton, Thomas*, 5
Lyons, Thomas, 10
McWhae, Sir John*, 10
Meudell, George Dick, 10
Monger, Frederick Charles*, 10
Newland, Victor Marra*, 11
North, John Britty, 5
Palmer, Joseph, 11
Pitt, Henry Arthur, 11
Roberts, William Joshua, 11
Robertson, James Campbell, 11
Robinson, Lionel George, 11
Sadler, Robert James*, 11
Tivey, Edwin, 12
Wallen, Robert Elias, 6
Were, Jonathon Binns*, 2
Westgarth, William*, 6

STOREKEEPER
Aarons, Joseph, 3
Abbott, Joseph Henry*, 3
Adcock, William Eddrup, 7
Aplin, William*, 3
Asher, Morris*, 3
Bagot, Edward Meade, 3
Bassett, Samuel Symons, 7
Bell, James*, 3
Berry, Sir Graham*, 3
Berry, William, 7
Boucher, Frederick, 1
Buring, Theodor Gustav Hermann, 3
Burke, Thomas Michael, 7
Burns, Sir James, 7
Catt, Alfred*, 3
Cheeseman, William Joseph Robert, 7
Chin Kaw, 7
Cohen, Henry Emanuel*, 3
Collins, Charles*, 3
Coppleson, Albert Abram, 8
Corfield, William Henry*, 3
Cotton, George Witherage*, 3
Cowie, James*, 3
Cowper, Charles*, 3
Davies, William*, 4
Dean, Horace, 4
Dempster, Charles Edward*, 4
Derrington, Edwin Henry, 4
Dickson, James*, 4
Durack, Ernest*, 8
Falkiner, Franc Sadlier, 4
Fallon, James Thomas*, 4
Fleming, Joseph*, 4
Forbes, Frederick Augustus*, 4

Forsyth, George, 4
Foster, Richard Witty*, 8
Gardiner, John, 1
Gibson, William Gerrand*, 8
Gillen, Peter Paul*, 9
Glenny, Henry, 4
Goddard, Benjamin, 9
Goldstein, Jacob Robert Yannasch, 9
Goudie, Sir George Louis*, 9
Gray, Isabel, 9
Groom, William Henry*, 4
Grose, Joseph Hickey, 1
Hague, William*, 9
Hankinson, Robert Henry*, 9
Hanran, Patrick Francis*, 9
Hassall, Rowland, 1
Henry, Frederick Ormiston, 9
Horrocks, Joseph Lucas, 4
Houlding, John Richard, 4
Hutchinson, William Alston*, 4
Jennings, Sir Patrick Alfred*, 4
Joubert, Jules François de Sales, 4
Kashiwagi, Taira, 9
Kidd, John*, 5
Laidlaw, Thomas*, 5
Langlands, George, 5
Laycock, Thomas (1786?-1823), 2
Lee, Charles Alfred*, 10
Leon, Andrew, 5
Levy, Lewis Wolfe*, 5
Lockwood, Joseph, 10
Lyons, Samuel, 2
McGrath, David Charles*, 10
McRae, Christopher John*, 10
Mate, Thomas Hodges*, 5
Matthews, Daniel, 5
Meagher, John*, 10
Monger, Alexander Joseph, 10
Montague, Alexander*, 5
Muramats, Jirō, 10
Newell, John*, 5
Oddie, James, 5
Osburne, Richard, 5
O'Sullivan, Patrick*, 5
Pennington, John Warburton*, 11
Perry, John*, 11
Piesse, Frederick Henry*, 11
Pyke, Vincent*, 5
Rason, Sir Cornthwaite Hector William
    James*, 11
Richardson, John*, 6
Rossi, Maffio, 11
See Poy, Tom, 11
Serisier, Jean Emile, 6
Shelley, William, 2
Strachan, James Ford*, 2
Sullivan, James Forester*, 6
Tewksbury, William Pearson, 12
Thompson, Andrew, 2
Wade, John, 12
Wallace, John Alston*, 6
Williams, Edward David*, 12
Willis, William Nicholas*, 12
Wisdom, Evan Alexander*, 12

Wright, John James*, 6
Young, James Henry*, 6
SUFFRAGIST
Lawson, Louisa, 10
Lee, Mary, 10
Locke, Helena Sumner, 10
Matters, Muriel Lilah, 10
Montefiore, Dorothy Frances, 10
Ogg, Margaret Ann, 11
Pankhurst, Adela Constantia Mary, 12
Smyth, Bridgetena, 12
Windeyer, Mary Elizabeth, 12
SURFER
Gocher, William Henry, 9
SURGEON, *see* Medical practitioner
SURVEYOR
Adams, Philip Francis, 3
Ainsworth, Alfred Bower, 7
Alt, Augustus Theodore Henry, 1
Baragwanath, William, 7
Bennett, William Christopher, 3
Black, Alexander, 3
Boake, Barcroft Henry Thomas, 3
Boothby, Benjamin, 3
Boyd, Edward, 1
Bracewell, David, 1
Brooks, Joseph, 7
Burnett, James Charles, 3
Calder, James Erskine, 1
Cambage, Richard Hind, 7
Campbell, John Fauna, 7
Canning, Alfred Wernam, 7
Clarke, Sir Andrew*, 3
Coane, John Montgomery, 8
Conder, Charles Edward, 3
Coote, William, 3
Cotton, Hugh Calveley, 1
Counsel, Edward Albert, 8
Dangar, Henry, 1
Darke, John Charles, 1
Day, Theodore Ernest, 8
Derry, John Dickson, 4
Dixon, Robert, 1
Drake-Brockman, Frederick Slade, 8
Dumaresq, Edward, 1
Evans, George William, 1
Ewing, John*, 8
Ewing, Sir Thomas Thomson*, 8
Feez, Adolph Frederick Milford, 8
Finniss, Boyle Travers*, 1
Fitzgerald, Robert David, 4
Fitzgerald, Thomas Henry*, 4
Fletcher, Charles Brunsdon, 8
Florance, Thomas, 1
Forrest, Sir John*, 8
Fossey, Joseph, 1
Fox, Henry Thomas, 4
Frankland, George, 1
Fraser, Sir Malcolm*, 4
Freeling, Sir Arthur Henry*, 4
Freycinet, Louis-Claude Desaulses de, 1
Frome, Edward Charles, 1
Fryar, William*, 4
Furber, Thomas Frederick, 8

Giblin, Ronald Worthy, 8
Gosse, William Christie, 4
Gould, Charles, 4
Govett, William Romaine, 1
Goyder, George Woodroffe, 4
Gregory, Sir Augustus Charles, 4
Gregory, Francis Thomas, 4
Grimes, Charles, 1
Hallen, Ambrose, 1
Hallen, Edward, 1
Harris, George Prideaux Robert, 1
Hellyer, Henry, 1
Hoddle, Robert, 1
Hodgkinson, Clement, 4
Hunt, Charles Cooke, 4
Jamieson, William, 9
Johnston, Harry Frederick, 9
Kentish, Nathaniel Lipscomb, 2
King, Philip Gidley*, 5
Kingston, Sir George Strickland*, 2
Laing, Charles, 2
Lardner, John, 5
Lee, John Henry Alexander, 10
Lewis, Mortimer William, 2
Ligar, Charles Whybrow, 5
Light, William, 2
Lindsay, David, 10
Macdonald, Alexander Cameron, 5
McDowall, Archibald, 10
McLean, Alexander Grant, 5
McMinn, Gilbert Rotherdale, 5
McMinn, William, 5
Madden, Walter*, 10
Mann, John Frederick, 5
Mathews, Hamilton Bartlett, 10
Mathews, Robert Hamilton, 5
Meehan, James, 2
Milligan, Stanley Lyndall, 10
Mills, Peter, 2
Mitchell, Sir Thomas Livingstone, 2
Moore, Henry Byron, 5
Moriarty, Edward Orpen, 5
Oxley, John Joseph William Molesworth, 2
Percival, Arthur, 11
Perdriau, Stephen Edward, 11
Perry, Samuel Augustus, 2
Poate, Frederick, 11
Power, Robert, 2
Ranken, George, 6
Roe, John Septimus, 2
Russell, Robert, 2
Scott, James (1810-1884), 2
Scott, Thomas, 2
Scrivener, Charles Robert, 11
Sellheim, Victor Conradsdorf Morisset, 11
Sharland, William Stanley, 2
Skene, Alexander John, 6
Sprent, James, 2
Stanley, Owen, 2
Stapylton, Granville William Chetwynd, 2
Sweet, Samuel White, 6
Tarrant, Harley, 12
Thomson, James Park, 12
Tietkens, William Harry, 6

Trickett, Oliver, 12
Tully, William Alcock, 6
Tyers, Charles James, 2
Wark, Blair Anderson, 12
Wedge, John Helder*, 2
Weingarth, John Leopold, 12
Wells, Lawrence Allen, 12
White, George Boyle*, 6
Whyte, Patrick, 6
Wollaston, Tullie Cornthwaite, 12
Woore, Thomas, 6
SWIMMER
Baker, William Harold, 7
Beaurepaire, Sir Francis Joseph Edmund*, 7
Cavill, Frederick, 7
Cavill, Richmond Theophilus, 7
Charlton, Andrew Murray, 7
Durack, Sarah, 8
Healy, Cecil Patrick, 9
Kellermann, Annette Marie Sarah, 9
Kieran, Bernard Bede, 9
Lane, Frederick Claude Vivian, 9
Longworth, William (1892-1969), 10
Matson, Phillip Henry, 10
TAILOR
Broughton, Thomas Stafford*, 3
Dooley, James Thomas*, 8
Jones, Charles Edwin*, 4
Jones, John Percy*, 9
TANNER
Alderson, William Maddison*, 3
Farleigh, John Gibson*, 8
Michaelis, Moritz, 5
Willis, Henry*, 12
Wilshire, James, 2
Wilshire, James Robert*, 6
Zwar, Albert Michael*, 12
Zwar, Henry Peter*, 12
TAXI PROPRIETOR
Tewksbury, William Pearson, 12
TAXIDERMIST
Whitfield, George, 6
TEACHER, *see also* Art teacher; Dance teacher; Educationist; Music teacher; School principal; Technical educator; University teacher
New South Wales
Alanson, Alfred Godwin, 7
Anderson, John, 1
Anderson, Maybanke Susannah, 7
Bennett, Alfred Joshua, 7
Beuzeville, James, 3
Bourke, John Philip, 7
Bowden, Thomas, 1
Callaghan, James Joseph, 7
Cape, William, 1
Cary, Henry, 3
Crook, William Pascoe, 1
Dove, Frederick Allan, 8
Dumolo, Elsie, 8
Duncan, William Augustine, 1
Dwyer, Catherine Winifred, 8
Ellis, Henry Havelock, 4

Eyre, John (1768-1854), 1
Fizelle, Reginald Cecil Grahame, 8
Gardner, William, 1
Gilmore, Dame Mary Jean, 9
Golding, Annie Mackenzie, 9
Griffith, Arthur Hill*, 9
Harris, John (1754-1819), 1
King, William Francis, 5
Loughlin, Peter French*, 10
McCormick, Peter Dodds, 10
McGuinness, Arthur, 10
Mackenzie, David, 2
Makinson, Thomas Cooper, 2
Mitchell, John, 10
Murphy, George Francis, 10
Muscio, Florence Mildred, 10
O'Brien, Catherine Cecily, 11
Reid, Jane Sinclair, 11
Rowe, Richard, 6
Sadleir, Richard*, 2
Sconce, Robert Knox, 2
Selle, Walter Albert, 11
Skerst, Arnold Oscar Hermann Gregory von, 11
Skillen, Elizabeth, 11
Stone, Louis, 12
Taber, Thomas, 2
Tildesley, Beatrice Maude, 12
Tilly, William Henry, 12
Wade, Robert Thompson, 12
White, William Duckett*, 6
Williamson, Francis Samuel, 12
Woodcock, Lucy Godiva, 12
Woolls, William, 6
Young, William Blamire, 12
Norfolk Island
Nobbs, George Hunn, 2
Queensland
Airey, Peter*, 7
Buchanan, Florence Griffiths, 7
Bulcock, Emily Hemans, 7
Currie, Patrick, 8
Edwards, Lewis David, 8
Farrell, John, 8
Fletcher, James Lionel, 8
Nicholson, John Henry, 5
Ryan, Thomas Joseph*, 11
Stephens, James Brunton, 6
Tolmie, James*, 12
South Australia
Basedow, Martin Peter Friedrich*, 7
Brown, Mary Home, 7
Hills, John Francis, 9
Hübbe, Ulrich, 4
Rechner, Gustav Julius, 6
Roach, Bertie Smith, 11
Scherk, Theodor Johannes*, 11
Standley, Ida, 12
Taplin, George, 6
Thornber, Ellen, 12
Thornber, Rachel Ann, 12
Tasmania
Bjelke-Petersen, Hans Christian, 7
Bonwick, James, 3

Buckland, William Harvey, 3
Cairnduff, Alexander, 1
Conder, Walter Tasman, 8
Frost, John, 1
Hebblethwaite, James, 9
Joyce, Edmund Michael, 9
Lyons, Joseph Aloysius*, 10
Propsting, William Bispham*, 11
Ross, James, 2
Smith, Ivy Blanche Irene, 11
Stevens, Jemima Elizabeth Mary, 12
Torres Strait
Zahel, Ethel May Eliza, 12
Victoria
à Beckett, Ada Mary, 7
Aston, Matilda Ann, 7
Baker, Catherine, 7
Barron, Johanna, 7
Bonwick, James, 3
Buchanan, Gwynneth Vaughan, 7
Cass, Walter Edmund Hutchinson, 7
Cuthbertson, James Lister, 3
Denehy, Charles Aloysius, 8
Foott, Mary Hannay, 4
Foran, Martin Henry, 8
Greig, Clara Puella, 9
Guerin, Julia Margaret, 9
Hackett, William Philip, 9
Hansen, Martin Peter, 9
Hart, Alfred, 9
Hart, Thomas Stephen, 9
Heagney, Muriel Agnes, 9
Hoad, Sir John Charles, 9
Hogan, James Francis, 4
Jess, Sir Carl Herman, 9
Johnson, Florence Ethel, 9
Kaeppel, Carl Henry, 9
Leach, John Albert, 10
McCay, Sir James Whiteside*, 10
McNamara, Frank (Francis) Hubert, 10
Moloney, Parker John*, 10
Pescott, Edward Edgar, 11
Porteus, Stanley David, 11
Pye, Hugh, 11
Rentoul, Annie Rattray, 11
Tisdall, Henry Thomas, 12
West, John, 12
Williams, Robert Ernest, 12
Williams, Susannah Jane, 12
Williamson, Francis Samuel, 12
Woodfull, William Maldon, 12
Western Australia
Bennett, Mary Montgomerie, 7
kindergarten
Banks, Elizabeth Lindsay, 3
Benjamin, Sophia, 7
De Lissa, Lillian Daphne, 8
Dumolo, Harriet Alice, 8
Longman, Irene Maud*, 10
Morice, Louise, 10
Pye, Emmeline, 11
Simpson, Martha Margaret Mildred, 11
TECHNICAL EDUCATOR
Bassett, William Frederick, 3

Bayldon, Francis Joseph, 7
Bruce, John Leck, 7
Campbell, Frederick Alexander, 7
Clark, Donald, 8
Clunies Ross, William John, 8
Eade, Joel, 4
Fenner, Charles Albert Edward, 8
Hoadley, Charles Archibald Brookes, 9
King, George Raymond, 9
Nangle, James, 10
Potts, Henry William, 11
Roberts, Mary Ellen, 11
Schauer, Amy, 11
Selfe, Norman, 6
Shea, Ernest Herbert, 11
Sterne, Elizabeth Anne Valentine, 12
Story, Ann Fawcett, 12
Süssmilch, Adolph Carl von de Heyde, 12
Swain, Herbert John, 12
Zercho, Frederick William, 12

TELEGRAPHIST
Grant, Kenneth McDonald*, 9

TEMPERANCE ADVOCATE
Bowes, Euphemia Bridges, 7
Bulcock, Robert*, 3
Dalgarno, Isabella, 4
Facy, Peter (1822-1890), 4
Heales, Richard*, 4
Kirby, Joseph Coles, 5
Kirk, Maria Elizabeth, 9
Lee, Betsy, 10
McCorkindale, Isabella, 10
McLean, Margaret, 10
Munro, James*, 5
Nicholls, Elizabeth Webb, 11
Nolan, Sara Susan, 11

TENNIS PLAYER
Akhurst, Daphne Jessie, 7
Brookes, Sir Norman Everard, 7
O'Hara Wood, Hector, 11
Patterson, Gerald Leighton, 11
Poidevin, Leslie Oswald Sheridan, 11
Sharp, Granville Gilbert, 11

THEATRE PROPRIETOR
Chapman, Edgar, 3
Sidaway, Robert, 2
Wyatt, Joseph, 2

THEATRICAL MANAGER
Atkins, John Ringrose, 3
Boucicault, Dionysius George, 3
Bracy, Henry, 7
Brough, Lionel Robert, 3
Dampier, Alfred, 4
Darrell, George Frederick Price, 4
Kean, Charles John, 5
Knowles, Conrad Theodore, 2
Lazar, John, 2
Levey, Barnett, 2
Rickards, Harry, 11
Simmons, Joseph, 2
Thatcher, Richmond, 6
Westmacott, Charles Babington, 12
Wilkie, Allan, 12
Williamson, James Cassius, 6

THEATRICAL PRODUCER
Holt, Joseph Thomas, 4
McMahon, Gregan, 10
Musgrove, George, 5
Ribush, Dolia, 11
Wilton, Olive Dorothea Graeme, 12

THEOLOGIAN
Adam, David Stow, 7
Angus, Samuel, 7
Boyce, William Binnington, 3
Cairns, Adam, 3
Campbell, Alexander James, 3
Gosman, Alexander, 4

THEOSOPHIST
Arundel, George Sydney, 7
Bean, Isabelle, 7
Bennett, Alfred Edward, 7
Leadbeater, Charles Webster, 10

TINSMITH
Barrett, John George*, 7
Simpson, Alfred, 6

TOWN CLERK
Annand, Frederick William Gadsby, 7
Bold, William Ernest, 7
Dowse, Thomas, 4
FitzGibbon, Edmund Gerald, 4
Humble, George Bland, 4
Kerr, William, 2
King, John Charles*, 2
Laurie, Henry, 10
McLeod, Donald*, 10
Marshall, William Henry George, 5
Nesbitt, Thomas Huggins, 11
Rae, John, 6
Williams, Robert Ernest, 12
Worsnop, Thomas, 6

TOWN PLANNER
Reade, Charles Compton, 11
Stapley, Frank, 12

TRADE UNIONIST
Bailey, John*, 7
Barker, Tom, 7
Barnes, John*, 7
Bennet, David, 3
Blakeley, Arthur*, 7
Blundell, Reginald Pole*, 7
Bowman, David*, 7
Brennan, Peter Joseph, 3
Bromley, Frederick Hadkinson*, 7
Cameron, Angus*, 3
Carroll, Robert Joseph*, 7
Casey, Gilbert Stephen, 7
Cohen, Laurence, 8
Crampton, Walter Russell, 8
Crofts, Charles Alfred, 8
Culley, Charles Ernest*, 8
Dash, John, 8
De Largie, Hugh*, 8
Demaine, William Halliwell*, 8
Dixon, Francis Burdett, 4
Don, Charles Jardine*, 4
Douglass, Benjamin, 4
Duffy, Maurice Boyce, 8
Dunstan, William John*, 8

Elmslie, George Alexander*, 8
Farrar, Ernest Henry*, 8
Flowers, Fred*, 8
Garrard, Jacob*, 4
Graves, James Joseph*, 9
Greville, Henrietta, 9
Gunn, John*, 9
Hall, George Wilson*, 4
Hannan, Joseph Francis*, 9
Heagney, Muriel Agnes, 9
Hogan, Edmond John*, 9
Hollis, Robert*, 9
Hynes, Maurice Patrick*, 9
Lacey, Andrew William*, 9
Lane, Ernest Henry, 9
Lane, William, 9
McCallum, Alexander, 10
McClintock, Albert Scott, 10
McCormack, William*, 10
McGowen, James Sinclair Taylor*, 10
Mann, Thomas, 10
Miller, Emma, 10
Miller, Montague David, 10
Mullan, John*, 10
Murphy, William Emmett, 5
Nelson, Harold George*, 10
Ogden, Anthony*, 11
O'Neill, John Henry, 11
Osborne, John, 5
Osborne, John Percy*, 11
Price, John Lloyd*, 11
Ross, Robert Samuel, 11
Ryan, Thomas*, 11
Somerville, William, 12
Stewart, Archibald, 12
Stopford, James*, 12
Stuart, John Alexander Salmon*, 12
Swadling, William Thomas, 12
Talbot, John Richard, 6
Taylor, George*, 12
Theodore, Edward Granville*, 12
Thrower, Thomas Henry, 12
Toomey, James Morton, 12
Tudor, Francis Gwynne*, 12
Tunnecliffe, Thomas*, 12
Turley, Joseph Henry Lewis*, 12
Tyrrell, Thomas James*, 12
Watson, Phebe Naomi, 12
Zadow, Christiane Susanne Augustine, 12
bootmakers
Billson, John William, 7
Solly, Robert Henry*, 12
Trenwith, William Arthur*, 12
bricklayers
Bavister, Thomas*, 7
Kilburn, John George*, 9
clerks
Coleman, Percy Edmund Creed*, 8
Verran, John Stanley*, 12
clothing trades
Lazzarini, Carlo Camillo*, 10
Lemmon, John*, 10
Swanton, Mary Hynes, 12
Wallis, Alfred Russell, 12

masons
Smith, Thomas (1823-1900), 6
Stephens, James, 6
miners
Baddeley, John Marcus*, 7
Bowling, Peter, 7
Boyland, John*, 7
Brookfield, Percival Stanley*, 7
Charlton, Matthew*, 7
Clark, Robert*, 3
Considine, Michael Patrick*, 8
Curley, James*, 3
Earle, John*, 8
Gledson, David Alexander*, 9
Hooper, Richard*, 9
McVicars, John, 10
Nelson, Charles, 10
Nicholson, John Barnes*, 11
Orr, William (1900-1954), 11
Powell, James Alexander, 11
Sleath, Richard*, 11
Spence, William Guthrie*, 6
Thomas, Josiah*, 12
Verran, John*, 12
Watkins, David*, 12
Willis, Albert Charles*, 12
plumbers
Cameron, Donald James*, 7
Duggan, William Joseph, 8
West, John Edward*, 12
pressers
Barker, Stephen*, 7
Kavanagh, Edward John*, 9
railway workers
Catts, James Howard*, 7
Dooley, John Braidwood*, 8
Hyett, Francis William, 9
Moroney, Timothy, 10
Schey, William Francis*, 11
seamen
Davis, Thomas Martin*, 8
Guthrie, Robert Storrie*, 9
Seymour, Charles, 11
Walsh, Thomas, 12
shearers
Grayndler, Edward*, 9
Hamilton, William*, 9
Lambert, William Henry*, 9
Lundie, Francis Walter, 10
Macdonell, Donald*, 10
McNeill, John James*, 10
Rae, Arthur Edward George*, 11
Spence, William Guthrie*, 6
Temple, David, 12
Woods, Walter Alan*, 12
teachers
Alanson, Alfred Godwin, 7
Johnson, Florence Ethel, 9
McGuinness, Arthur, 10
Matthews, William, 5
St Ledger, Anthony James*, 11
Woodcock, Lucy Godiva, 12
telegraphists
Dunkley, Louisa Margaret, 8

Kraegen, Edward Charles, 9
typographers
Birrell, Frederick William*, 7
Hancock, John*, 9
Hinchcliffe, Albert, 9
Magrath, Edward Crawford*, 10
Wallis, Frederick Samuel*, 12
Watson, John Christian*, 12
TRADER
Bishop, Charles, 1
Cadell, Francis, 3
Campbell, William Douglas, 1
Dillon, Peter, 1
Goldie, Andrew, 4
Hayes, William Henry, 4
Hernsheim, Eduard, 4
Hunter, George, 4
Hunter, Robert, 4
Ingham, William Bairstow, 4
Ledger, Charles, 5
Lucas, Walter Henry, 10
Mouton, Jean Baptiste Octave, 10
Pearce, Henry John, 5
Ritchie, Sir George*, 11
Rubin, Mark, 11
Seymour-Symers, Thomas Lyell, 2
Shelley, William, 2
Tishler, Joseph, 12
Williams, John (1797?-1872), 2
TRANSPORTEE
Abbott, Francis, 3
Angel, Henry, 3
Arscott, John, 1
Austin, James (1776-1831), 1
Barrington, George, 1
Baughan, John, 1
Belbin, James, 1
Bellasis, George Bridges, 1
Bent, Andrew, 1
Blackburn, James, 1
Bland, William*, 1
Bock, Thomas, 1
Boothman, John Broadhurst, 1
Bracewell, David, 1
Brady, Matthew, 1
Bruce, George, 1
Bryant, Mary, 1
Buckley, William, 1
Burbury, Thomas, 1
Cadman, John, 1
Cash, Martin, 1
Catchpole, Margaret, 1
Chapman, Israel, 1
Chartres, George, 1
Collits, Pierce, 1
Cooper, Daniel, 1
Cooper, Robert, 1
Crossley, George, 1
Crowder, Thomas Ristol, 1
Davies, John (1813-1872)*, 4
Davis, Edward, 1
Davis, James, 1
Donohoe, John, 1
Dowse, Thomas, 4

Eagar, Edward, 1
Elliott, (William) Edward, 1
Everingham, Matthew James, 1
Eyre, John (b.1771), 1
Fitzgerald, Richard, 1
Gannon, Michael, 4
Gatehouse, George, 1
Gibson, David, 1
Gould, William Buelow, 1
Graham, John, 1
Grant, John, 1
Greenway, Francis, 1
Griffiths, Jonathon, 1
Groom, William Henry, 4
Grove, James, 1
Guest, George, 1
Halloran, Laurence Hynes, 1
Harris, John (fl.1783-1803), 1
Hayes, Sir Henry Browne, 1
Hopwood, Henry, 4
Horrocks, Joseph Lucas, 4
Howe, Michael, 1
Hurley, John (1796-1882), 4
Hutchinson, William, 1
Irving, John, 2
Johns, Joseph Bolitho, 4
Johnston, Esther, 2
Jorgenson, Jorgen, 2
Kable, Henry, 2
Knatchbull, John, 2
Laing, Henry, 2
Larra, James, 2
Levey, Solomon, 2
Lord, Simeon, 2
Loveless, George, 2
Lucas, Nathaniel, 2
Lycett, Joseph, 2
Lyons, Samuel, 2
McCarty, Denis, 2
McEvilly, Walter O'Malley, 5
McKay, Alexander, 2
Mann, David Dickenson, 2
Massey, Thomas, 2
Meehan, James, 2
Melville, Francis, 5
Mitchel, John, 2
Moffitt, William, 2
Morgan, Molly, 2
Murray, Robert William Felton Lathrop, 2
Nash, Robert, 2
Nichols, Isaac, 2
Oatley, James, 2
O'Doherty, Kevin Izod, 5
O'Shaughnessy, Edward, 2
O'Sullivan, Patrick, 5
Packer, Charles (Stuart Shipley) Sandys, 5
Pamphlett, Thomas, 2
Petchy, John, 2
Power, Henry, 5
Ransom, Thomas, 2
Redfern, William, 2
Redmond, Edward, 2
Reibey, Mary, 2
Richardson, John Matthew, 2

Robinson, Michael Massey, 2
Rodius, Charles, 2
Rose, Thomas (d.1837), 2
Ruse, James, 2
Savery, Henry, 2
Sidaway, Robert, 2
Solomon, Emanuel, 6
Solomon, Isaac, 2
Squire, James, 2
Strange, Frederick, 2
Suffolk, Owen Hargraves, 6
Terry, Samuel, 2
Thompson, Andrew, 2
Thompson, Richard, 2
Thomson, James Alexander, 2
Tucker, James, 2
Underwood, James, 2
Vaux, James Hardy, 2
Wainewright, Thomas Griffiths, 2
Warby, John, 2
Watling, Thomas, 2
Wells, Thomas, 2
Whyte, Thomas, 2
Wild(e), Joseph, 2
Wilkes, William Charles, 6
Wilson, John, 2
Wiseman, Solomon, 2
political
Anderson, John, 1
Dry, Richard, 1
Frost, John, 1
Fulton, Henry, 1
Gates, William, 1
Gerrald, Joseph, 1
Hayes, Michael, 1
Holt, Joseph, 1
Lynch, John, 2
Margarot, Maurice, 2
Maum, William James, 2
Meagher, Thomas Francis, 2
Mealmaker, George, 2
Mitchel, John, 2
Muir, Thomas, 2
O'Brien, William Smith, 2
O'Reilly, John Boyle, 5
Palmer, Thomas Fyshe, 2
Prieur, François Xavier, 2
Skirving, William, 2
Williams, Zephaniah, 2
TREPANGER
Using Daeng Rangka, 6
TROTTING OFFICIAL
Hungerford, Richard Colin Campbell, 9
TROTTING TRAINER
Moulds, Constance, 10
UNDERTAKER
Chipper, Donald John, 7
Fitzpatrick, Columbus, 4
Melville, Ninian*, 5
Weathers, Lawrence Carthage, 12
UNIVERSITY ADMINISTRATOR
Barff, Henry Ebenezer, 7
Barlow, William, 7
Blackburn, Sir Charles Bickerton, 7

Brownless, Sir Anthony Colling, 3
Clarke, George (1823-1913), 3
Cumbrae-Stewart, Francis William Sutton, 8
Hodge, Charles Reynolds, 9
Kennedy, Hugh, 5
MacCallum, Sir Mungo William, 10
MacFarland, Sir John Henry, 10
MacLaurin, Sir Henry Normand*, 10
Merewether, Francis Lewis Shaw*, 5
Mitchell, Sir William, 10
Murdoch, Sir Walter Logie Forbes, 10
Priestley, Sir Raymond Edward, 11
Selle, Walter Albert, 11
Serle, Percival, 11
Spencer, Sir Walter Baldwin, 12
Stewart, John McKellar, 12
Story, John Douglas, 12
Sutherland, Alexander, 6
Tyas, John Walter, 6
Wallace, Sir Robert Strachan, 12
Whitfeld, Hubert Edwin, 12
UNIVERSITY TEACHER, *see also*
Professor
à Beckett, Ada Mary, 7
Adam, George Rothwell Wilson, 7
Adamson, Lawrence Arthur, 7
Allen, Horace William, 7
Ampt, Gustav Adolph, 7
Anderson, Phyllis Margery, 7
Anderson, Valentine George, 7
Armstrong, William George, 7
Atkinson, Meredith, 7
Bage, Anna Frederika, 7
Barff, Henry Ebenezer, 7
Barker, Edward, 3
Barrett, Sir James William, 7
Barton, George Burnett, 3
Bavin, Sir Thomas Rainsford*, 7
Beg, Wazir, 3
Behan, Sir John Clifford Valentine, 7
Benham, Ellen Ida, 7
Benham, Frederic Charles Courtenay, 7
Bird, Frederic Dougan, 7
Blackburn, Sir Charles Bickerton, 7
Blackmore, Edwin Gordon, 3
Boas, Isaac Herbert, 7
Borthwick, Thomas, 7
Brennan, Christopher John, 7
Brereton, Ernest Le Gay, 7
Buchanan, Gwynneth Vaughan, 7
Cameron, Samuel Sherwen, 7
Chambers, Thomas, 3
Champion de Crespigny, Sir Constantine
  Trent, 7
Chapman, Frederick, 7
Chapman, Henry Samuel*, 3
Cleary, William James, 8
Cohen, Fanny, 8
Cole, Percival Richard, 8
Cox, James Charles, 3
Craig, Robert Gordon, 8
Dale, John, 8
Daneš, Jiří Václav, 8

D'Arcy, Dame Constance Elizabeth, 8
Davey, Constance Muriel, 8
Derham, Enid, 8
Dixson, Thomas Storie, 8
Dobson, Frank Stanley*, 4
Downes, Rupert Major, 8
Downey, Michael Henry, 8
Dun, William Sutherland, 8
Edwards, Lewis David, 8
Edye, Sir Benjamin Thomas, 8
Ellis, Constance, 8
Ferguson, Sir David Gilbert, 8
Fidler, Isabel Margaret, 8
FitzGerald, Sir Thomas Naghten, 4
Fowler, Hugh Lionel, 8
Furber, Thomas Frederick, 8
Hall, Thomas Sergeant, 9
Hamlyn-Harris, Ronald, 9
Hargrave, John Fletcher*, 4
Hentze, Margaret Edith, 9
Hone, Frank Sandland, 9
Howchin, Walter, 9
Jauncey, Leslie Cyril, 9
Johnson, John Andrew, 9
Jose, Arthur Wilberforce, 9
Knibbs, Sir George Handley, 9
Knight, John George, 5
Krome, Otto Georg Hermann Dittmar, 9
Latham, Richard Thomas Edwin, 10
Le Couteur, Philip Ridgeway, 10
Le Souef, Ernest Albert, 10
Leverrier, Francis Hewitt, 10
Lewis, Arndell Neil*, 10
Lightfoot, Gerald, 10
Lodewyckx, Augustin, 10
Love, Ernest Frederick John, 10
McBurney, Mona Margaret, 10
MacCormick, Sir Alexander, 10
Mackay, John Hilton, 10
Mackey, Sir John Emanuel*, 10
Madigan, Sir Cecil Thomas, 10
Marks, Gladys Hope, 10
Martin, Sir Charles James, 10
Maudsley, Sir Henry Carr, 10
Mawson, Sir Douglas, 10
Melbourne, Alexander Clifford Vernon, 10
Mitchell, Ernest Meyer*, 10
Moloney, Patrick, 5
Murphy, Jeremiah Matthias, 10
Neild, James Edward, 5
Oliphant, Ernest Henry Clark, 11
Osborne, George Davenport, 11
Partridge, Eric Honeywood, 11
Pearson, Charles Henry*, 5
Piper, Arthur William, 11
Pittman, Edward Fisher, 11
Pollock, James Arthur, 11
Poole, Thomas Slaney, 11
Portus, Garnet Vere, 11
Pritchard, George Baxter, 11
Purton, David Gabriel, 11
Rivett, Doris Mary, 11
Robertson, William Apperley Norton, 11
Robinson, Frederick Walter, 11

Rodway, Leonard, 11
Ross, Chisholm, 11
Ross, Euphemia Welch, 11
Schiassi, Omero, 11
Sewell, Sir Sidney Valentine, 11
Skillen, Elizabeth, 11
Sladen, Douglas Brooke Wheelton, 6
Smith, Alfred Mica, 6
Stillwell, Frank Leslie, 12
Sutherland, William, 12
Sweet, Georgina, 12
Taylor, Thomas Griffith, 12
Teece, Richard Clive, 12
Tracy, Richard Thomas, 6
Tuckfield, William John, 12
Webb, Jessie Stobo Watson, 12
Wellish, Edward Montague, 12
Williams, Susannah Jane, 12
Wilson, Herbert Ward, 12
Windeyer, Richard, 12
Zelman, Samuel Victor Albert, 12

VETERINARY INSPECTOR
Bruce, Alexander, 3
Curr, Edward Micklethwaite, 3
Gordon, Patrick Robertson, 4
Robertson, William Apperley Norton, 11

VETERINARY SURGEON
Cameron, Samuel Sherwen, 7
Gilruth, John Anderson, 9
Irving, James, 9
Irving, James Washington, 9
Kendall, Ernest Arthur, 9
Kendall, Hector, 9
Kendall, William Tyson, 9
Pottie, John, 5
Quinn, John, 11
Rudduck, Harold Sugden, 11
Stewart, James Douglas, 12
Stewart, John (1810-1896)*, 6
Stewart, John (1832-1904), 6

VIGNERON
Adams, Philip Francis, 3
Angus, James, 7
Angus, John Henry Smith, 7
Auld, Patrick, 3
Bassett, Samuel Symons, 7
Bassett, William Augustus, 7
Bernacchi, Angelo Giulio Diego, 7
Best, Henry, 3
Best, Joseph (1830-1887), 3
Buring, Hermann Paul Leopold, 3
Buring, Theodor Gustav Hermann, 3
Busby, James, 1
Carmichael, Henry, 1
Castella, Charles Hubert de, 3
Castella, Paul Frédéric de, 3
Cleland, George Fullerton, 3
Crompton, Joseph, 3
De Pury, Frédéric Guillaume, 4
Donovan, Thomas Joseph, 8
Fallon, James Thomas*, 4
Ferguson, Charles William, 4
Gilbert, Joseph, 4
Gramp, Gustav, 4

Gramp, Johann, 4
Gramp, Louis Hugo, 4
Hamilton, Frank, 9
Hamilton, Henry, 9
Hardy, Thomas, 4
Harris, Sir John Richards*, 9
Irvine, Hans William Henry*, 9
Johnston, James Stewart*, 4
King, James (1800-1857), 2
Laver, Alfred Edmund, 10
Lindeman, Henry John, 5
McWilliam, John James, 10
Marina, Carlo, 5
Matthews, Harley, 10
Morris, George Francis, 5
Murray, Andrew, 5
Panton, Joseph Anderson, 5
Penfold, Christopher Rawson, 5
Reid, Curtis Alexander, 6
Reymond, Joseph Bernard*, 6
Reynell, Carew, 11
Reynell, John, 6
Reynell, Walter, 6
Roth, Adam, 11
Rowan, Andrew, 6
Salter, Edward, 6
Salter, William, 6
Seppelt, Joseph Ernest, 6
Seppelt, Oscar Benno Pedro, 6
Serisier, Jean Emile, 6
Smith, Louis Lawrence*, 6
Smith, Samuel, 6
Smith, Sidney, 6
Tardent, Henry Alexis, 12
Walker, Hurtle Frank, 12
Waylen, Alfred Robert, 6
Wilkinson, Audrey Harold, 12
Windeyer, Archibald, 2
Windeyer, Richard, 2
Woods, James Park, 12
Wyndham, George, 2

VIOLINIST, see Musician
VIOLIN-MAKER
Smith, Arthur Edward, 11
VISITOR
Edinburgh, Alfred Ernest Albert,
  Duke of, 4
WALKER
King, William Francis, 5
WATCHMAKER
Abbott, Francis, 3
Albert, Jacques, 7
McDonald, Charles*, 10
Oatley, James, 2
WEAVER
Mealmaker, George, 2
WELFARE WORKER
Ardill, George Edward (1857-1945), 7
Barnett, Frederick Oswald, 7
Bates, Daisy May, 7
Beadle, Jane, 7
Bennett, Mary Montgomerie, 7
Board, Ruby Willmet, 7
Bon, Ann Fraser, 7

Booth, Mary, 7
Carson, Alfred, 7
Chase, Muriel Jean Eliot, 7
Chisholm, Caroline, 1
Clark, Caroline Emily, 3
Clarke, Margaret Turner, 3
Cocks, Fanny Kate Boadicea, 8
Cowan, Edith Dircksey*, 8
Dobson, Emily, 8
Drummond, Stanley Gillick, 8
Fairbridge, Kingsley Ogilvie, 8
Farrelly, Mary Martha, 8
Forster, William Mark, 4
Gerard, Alfred Edward, 8
Goldstein, Jacob Robert Yannasch, 9
Hammond, Robert Brodribb Stewart, 9
Haugh, Denis Robert, 9
Henderson, Jessie Isabel, 9
Hinder, Eleanor Mary, 9
Hopkins, Felicia, 9
Judkins, George Alfred, 9
Longman, Irene Maud*, 10
Matthews, Susan May, 10
Matthias, Elizabeth, 10
Maxted, Edward, 10
Maxted, Sydney, 10
Olney, Sir Herbert Horace*, 11
Onians, Edith Charlotte, 11
Rivett, Elsie Grace, 11
Seager, Alexandrine, 11
Sutherland, Sulina Murray MacDonald, 6
Waterworth, Edith Alice, 12
Wheeler, Annie Margaret, 12
WHALER
Birch, Thomas William, 1
Birnie, James, 1
Boyd, Benjamin, 1
Bunker, Eber, 1
Campbell, Alexander, 1
Collins, William, 1
Curtis, Anthony, 1
Dutton, William, 1
Enderby, Samuel, 1
Finnis, John, 1
Griffiths, John, 1
Hart, John*, 4
Henty, Stephen George*, 1
Imlay, Alexander, 2
Imlay, George, 2
Imlay, Peter, 2
Jones, Richard (1786-1852), 2
Jorgenson, Jorgen, 2
Mills, Charles Frederick, 2
Mills, John Brabyn, 2
Mosman, Archibald, 2
Murphy, Herbert Dyce, 10
Petchy, John, 2
Raine, Thomas, 2
Samson, Lionel, 2
Seal, Charles, 2
WHEAT-BREEDER
Farrer, William James, 8
Pridham, John Theodore, 11
Pye, Hugh, 11

Soutter, Richard Ernest, 12
Sutton, George Lowe, 12
Waterhouse, Walter Lawry, 12
WHEELWRIGHT
Lee, Sir Walter Henry, 10
WOMEN'S RIGHTS ACTIVIST, *see also*
Suffragist
Anderson, Maybanke Susannah, 7
Baines, Sarah Jane, 7
Beadle, Jane, 7
Bear, Annette Ellen, 7
Bromham, Ada, 7
Clisby, Harriet Jemima Winifred, 3
Dexter, Caroline, 4
Dugdale, Henrietta Augusta, 4
Dwyer, Catherine Winifred, 8
Geach, Portia Swanston, 8
Glencross, Eleanor, 9
Golding, Annie Mackenzie, 9
Goldstein, Vida Jane Mary, 9
Goode, Agnes Knight, 9
Guerin, Julia Margaret, 9
Hain, Gladys Adeline, 9
Halley, Ida Gertrude Margaret, 9
Heagney, Muriel Agnes, 9
Henry, Alice, 9
Holden, Frances Gillam, 9
Littlejohn, Emma Linda Palmer, 10
Luffman, Lauretta Caroline Maria, 10
McAulay, Ida Mary, 10
McLean, Margaret, 10
McNamara, Matilda Emilie Bertha, 10
Miller, Emma, 10
Morice, Louise, 10
Moss, Alice Frances Mabel, 10
Murdoch, Lesley Elizabeth, 10
Muscio, Florence Mildred, 10
Pankhurst, Adela Constantia Mary, 12
Parkes, Hilma Olivia Edla Johanna, 11
Rischbieth, Bessie Mabel, 11
Scott, Rose, 11
Spence, Catherine Helen, 6
Taylor, Irene Frances, 12
Windeyer, Margaret, 12
WOODCARVER
Harvey, Lewis Jarvis, 9
Howitt, William, 9
Payne, Ellen Nora, 11
Prenzel, Robert Wilhelm, 11
WOOLBROKER, *see also* Merchant, wool
Abbott, Joseph*, 3
Aitken, George Lewis, 7
Carson, Duncan, 7
Cuningham, Hastings, 3
Dennys, Charles John, 4
Ebsworth, Frederick Louis, 4
Ebsworth, Octavius Bayliffe, 4
Goldsbrough, Richard, 4
Guthrie, James Francis*, 9
Guthrie, Thomas, 4
Horsfall, John Sutcliffe, 4
Josephson, Joshua Frey*, 4
Kelly, Thomas Hussey, 5
Lascelles, Edward Harewood, 5

McComas, Robert Bond Wesley, 10
Macredie, William, 5
Mort, Thomas Sutcliffe, 5
Renard, Jules, 6
Roberts, Gerald Alleyne, 11
Stephens, Thomas Blacket*, 6
Strachan, Hugh Murray, 12
Synnot, Monckton, 6
Vicars, Sir John, 12
Whitton, Ivo Harrington, 12
Winchcombe, Frederick Earle*, 12
Young, Sir Walter James, 12
WRITER, *see also* Biographer; Critic
Abbott, John Henry (Macartney), 7
à Beckett, Sir William, 3
Adams, Agnes Eliza Fraser, 10
Adams, Arthur Henry, 7
Adams, Francis William Lauderdale, 3
Airey, Peter*, 7
Alanson, Alfred Godwin, 7
Arden, George, 1
Astley, William, 3
Aston, Matilda Ann, 7
Atkinson, Caroline Louisa Waring, 3
Atkinson, Evelyn John Rupert, 7
Atkinson, James, 1
Backhouse, James, 1
Bailey, Albert Edward, 7
Banfield, Edmund James, 7
Barnett, Percy Neville, 7
Barry, John Arthur, 7
Bayldon, Arthur Albert Dawson, 7
Baylebridge, William, 7
Baynton, Barbara Jane, 7
Becke, George Louis, 7
Beeby, Sir George Stephenson*, 7
Bevan, Theodore Francis, 3
Bjelke-Petersen, Marie Caroline, 7
Blacket, Wilfred, 7
Blackmore, Edwin Gordon, 3
Boake, Barcroft Henry Thomas, 3
Boote, Henry Ernest, 7
Boothby, Guy Newell, 7
Boreham, Frank William, 7
Bourke, John Philip, 7
Boyd, Archibald, 1
Boyd, Edith Susan, 7
Brady, Edwin James, 7
Brennan, Christopher John, 7
Brereton, John Le Gay, 3
Brereton, John Le Gay, 7
Bridges, Hilda Maggie, 7
Bridges, Royal Tasman, 7
Broinowski, Robert Arthur, 7
Broome, Mary Anne, 3
Browne, Thomas Alexander, 3
Bruce, Minnie Grant, 7
Bulcock, Emily Hemans, 7
Burn, David, 1
Button, Henry, 3
Caffyn, Stephen Mannington, 3
Cambridge, Ada, 3
Carboni, Raffaello, 3
Catts, Dorothy Marguerite, 7

Chabrillan, Céleste de, 3
Chambers, Charles Haddon Spurgeon, 7
Chomley, Charles Henry, 7
Clarke, Marcus Andrew Hislop, 3
Clay, Henry Ebenezer, 3
Cobb, Chester Francis, 8
Cockerill, George, 8
Collier, James, 8
Collins, Cuthbert Quinlan Dale, 8
Cooper, Walter Hampson*, 3
Cottrell, Ida Dorothy Ottley, 8
Couvreur, Jessie Catherine, 3
Cox, Erle, 8
Croll, Robert Henderson, 8
Cronin, Bernard Charles, 8
Cross, Zora Bernice May, 8
Cunningham, Peter Miller, 1
Curlewis, Ethel Jean Sophia, 12
Curr, Edward Micklethwaite, 3
Cuthbertson, James Lister, 3
Daley, Victor James William Patrick, 8
Dalley, John Bede, 8
Darrell, George Frederick Price, 4
Davis, Arthur Hoey, 8
Deamer, Mary Elizabeth Kathleen Dulcie, 8
Deniehy, Daniel Henry*, 4
Dennis, Clarence Michael James, 8
Derham, Enid, 8
De Rougemont, Louis, 8
Desmond, Arthur, 8
Devanny, Jane, 8
Dexter, Caroline, 4
Dickens, Charles, 4
Dilke, Sir Charles Wentworth, 4
Doorly, James Gerald Stokely, 8
Dorrington, Albert, 8
Duggan, Edmund, 8
Dunlop, Eliza Hamilton, 1
Dwyer, James Francis, 8
Dyson, Edward George, 8
Eden, Charles Henry, 4
Ellis, Henry Havelock, 4
Emmett, Evelyn Temple, 8
Eredia, Manuel Godinho de, 1
Esson, Thomas Louis Buvelot, 8
Evans, George Essex, 8
Evans, Matilda Jane, 4
Farrell, John, 4
Fauchery, Antoine Julien, 4
Finn, Edmund, 1
Fisher, Mary Lucy, 8
Fitchett, William Henry, 8
Fleming, William Montgomerie*, 8
Foott, Mary Hannay, 4
Forbes, William Anderson, 4
Forster, Johann Georg Adam, 1
Forster, William*, 4
Foster, John Leslie Fitzgerald Vesey*, 4
Fowler, Francis Edmund Town, 4
Fowler, James Mackinnon*, 8
Franklin, Stella Maria(n) Sarah Miles, 8
Fullerton, Mary Eliza, 8
Furphy, Joseph, 8

Gardner, William, 1
Gaunt, Mary Eliza Bakewell, 8
Gay, William (1865-1897), 8
Gerard, Edwin Field, 8
Gerstaecker, Friedrich, 4
Gibbs, Cecilia May, 8
Gilmore, Dame Mary Jean, 9
Glenny, Henry, 4
Goldhar, Pinchas, 9
Gordon, Adam Lindsay*, 4
Gould, Nathaniel, 9
Grano, Paul Langton, 9
Grant, John, 1
Grimshaw, Beatrice Ethel, 9
Groom, Arthur, 9
Gunn, Jeannie, 9
Gye, Harold Frederick Neville, 9
Hales, Alfred Arthur Greenwood, 9
Halloran, Henry, 4
Hanson, Sir Richard Davies*, 4
Hardie, John Jackson, 9
Harding, George Rogers, 4
Harford, Lesbia Venner, 9
Harpur, Charles, 1
Harris, Alexander, 1
Hartigan, Patrick Joseph, 9
Hatfield, William, 9
Hay, William Gosse, 9
Haydon, George Henry, 4
Hayward, Charles Wiltens Andrée, 9
Hebblethwaite, James, 9
Heney, Thomas William, 9
Henning, Rachel Biddulph, 4
Hervey, Grant (Madison), 9
Hill, Samuel Prout, 1
Hodgson, Christopher Pemberton, 4
Hogan, James Francis, 4
Hooley, Edward Timothy*, 4
Hopkins, Francis Rawdon Chesney, 4
Horne, Richard Henry, 4
Hornung, Ernest William, 9
Houlding, John Richard, 4
Howitt, Richard, 4
Howitt, William, 4
Hume, Fergusson Wright, 4
Idriess, Ion Llewellyn, 9
Inglis, James*, 4
James, John Stanley, 4
James, Winifred Llewellyn, 9
Jeffery, Walter James, 9
Jeffreys, Charles, 2
Jephcott, Sydney Wheeler, 9
Jones, Doris Egerton, 9
Kelly, Ethel Knight, 9
Kelly, William (1813?-1872), 5
Kendall, Thomas Henry, 5
Kentish, Nathaniel Lipscomb, 2
Kingsley, Henry, 5
Kirkland, Katherine, 2
Knowles, Marion, 9
Labilliere, Francis Peter, 5
Landor, Edward Willson, 2
Lang, John, 5
Lavater, Louis Isidore, 10

Lawlor, Adrian, 10
Lawson, Henry, 10
Lawson, William, 10
Leakey, Caroline Woolmer, 5
Lindsay, Norman Alfred Williams, 10
Lindsay, Philip, 10
Litchfield, Jessie Sinclair, 10
Lloyd, Jessie Georgina, 5
Locke, Helena Sumner, 10
Long, Richard Hooppell, 10
Lorimer, Philip Durham, 5
Lower, Leonard Waldemere, 10
Loyau, George Ettienne, 5
Luffman, Lauretta Caroline Maria, 10
Luffman(n), Charles (Bogue), 10
Lynch, Arthur Alfred, 10
McCrae, George Gordon, 5
McCrae, Hugh Raymond, 10
McDougall, John Keith*, 10
McFarland, Alfred, 5
Mack, Amy Eleanor, 10
Mack, Marie Louise Hamilton, 10
Mackaness, George, 10
Mackellar, Isobel Marion Dorothea, 10
McKellar, John Alexander Ross, 10
Mackenzie, David, 2
Mackness, Constance, 10
McLaren, John, 10
McMillan, Robert, 10
Maitland, Edward, 5
Manning, Emily Matilda, 5
Manning, Frederic, 10
Martin, Arthur Patchett, 5
Martin, Catherine Edith Macauley, 10
Melville, Henry, 2
Meredith, Louisa Ann, 5
Michael, James Lionel, 5
Mitchell, Isabel Mary, 10
Moloney, Patrick, 5
Moore, Joseph Sheridan, 5
Mordaunt, Evelyn May, 10
Morris, Myra Evelyn, 10
Morton, Frank, 10
Mudie, James, 2
Mundy, Godfrey Charles, 2
Murdoch, Madoline, 10
Murdoch, Sir Walter Logie Forbes, 10
Murdoch, William David, 10
Murphy, George Read, 10
Muskett, Alice Jane, 10
Neilson, John Shaw, 10
Newland, Simpson*, 11
Nicholas, John Liddiard, 2
Nicholson, John Henry, 5
Nisbet, James Hume, 11
O'Dowd, Bernard Patrick, 11
Ogilvie, William Henry, 11
Ogilvy, Arthur James, 5
O'Hara, John Bernard, 11
Oliphant, Ernest Henry Clark, 11
O'Neill, George, 11
O'Reilly, Alfonso Bernard, 11
O'Reilly, Dowell Philip, 11
Osborne, William Alexander, 11

O'Shaughnessy, Edward, 2
Owen, Albert John (Harrison), 11
Palmer, Edward Vivian, 11
Palmer, Janet Gertrude, 11
Parkes, Sir Henry*, 5
Paterson, Andrew Barton, 11
Pedley, Ethel Charlotte, 11
Phillips, Rebecca, 11
Pitt, Marie Elizabeth Josephine, 11
Power, Marguerite Helen, 11
Praed, Rosa Caroline, 11
Pratt, Ambrose Goddard Hesketh, 11
Prichard, Katharine Susannah, 11
Prieur, François Xavier, 2
Pulsford, Edward*, 11
Püttmann, Hermann, 5
Püttmann, Hermann Wilhelm, 5
Pyke, Vincent*, 5
Quinn, Patrick Edward*, 11
Quinn, Roderic Joseph, 11
Rae, John, 6
Rawson, Wilhelmina Frances, 11
Rentoul, Annie Rattray, 11
Rhodes, Fred, 11
Richardson, Ethel Florence Lindesay, 11
Roach, Bertie Smith, 11
Robinson, Michael Massey, 2
Rogers, John William Foster*, 6
Romilly, Hugh Hastings, 6
Rosman, Alice (Grant) Trevenen, 11
Rowcroft, Charles, 2
Salvado, Rosendo, 2
Sandes, John, 11
Savage, John, 2
Savery, Henry, 2
Searcy, Alfred, 11
Sidney, Samuel, 2
Simpson, Helen de Guerry, 11
Skeyhill, Thomas John, 11
Skinner, Mary Louisa, 11
Sladen, Douglas Brooke Wheelton, 6
Sorenson, Edward Sylvester, 12
Souter, Charles Henry, 12
Souter, David Henry, 12
Spence, Catherine Helen, 6
Spencer, Thomas Edward, 12
Spielvogel, Nathan Frederick, 12
Stephens, James Brunton, 6
Stephensen, Percy Reginald, 12
Stone, Louis, 12
Stonehouse, Ethel Nhill Victoria, 12
Stow, Catherine Eliza Somerville, 12
Suffolk, Owen Hargraves, 6
Sulman, Florence, 12
Supple, Gerald Henry, 6
Taylor, Sir Patrick Gordon, 12
Tench, Watkin, 2
Thirkell, Angela Margaret, 12
Thomas, Margaret, 6
Threlkeld, Lancelot Edward, 2
Thwaites, Frederick Joseph, 12
Tildesley, Beatrice Maude, 12
Tildesley, Evelyn Mary, 12
Timms, Edward Vivian, 12

Tishler, Joseph, 12
Tomholt, Sydney John, 12
Tompson, Charles (1807-1883), 2
Trollope, Anthony, 6
Tucker, James, 2
Turnbull, Gilbert Munro, 12
Turner, Ethel Mary, 12
Turner, Lilian Wattnall, 12
Turner, Walter James Redfern, 12
Twopeny, Richard Ernest Nowell, 6
Unaipon, David, 12
Upfield, Arthur William, 12
Vidal, Mary Theresa, 2
Wainewright, Thomas Griffiths, 2
Walch, Garnet, 6
Wall, Dorothy, 12
Walsh, James Morgan, 12
Watson, Elliot Lovegood Grant, 12
Watt, Ernest Alexander Stuart, 12
Wawn, William Twizell, 6
Wekey, Sigismund, 6
Wells, Thomas, 2
Wentworth, William Charles*, 2
Wenz, Paul, 12
Wheelwright, Horace William, 6
White, Ellen Gould, 12
White, Gilbert, 12
White, Myrtle Rose, 12
Whitehead, Charles, 6
Whitworth, Robert Percy, 6
Whyte, William Farmer, 12
Wilcox, Mary Theodora Joyce, 10
Williamson, Francis Samuel, 12
Wilmot, Frank Leslie Thompson, 12
Wilson, Thomas, 2
Wilson, William Hardy, 12
Wood, Thomas, 12
Woolner, Thomas, 6
Worsnop, Thomas, 6
Wright, David McKee, 12

YACHTSMAN
Webb, Chris, 12

Webster, Edwin Herbert, 12

ZOO DIRECTOR
Le Souef, Albert Alexander Cochrane, 5
Le Souef, Albert Sherbourne, 10
Le Souef, Ernest Albert, 10
Le Souef, William Henry Dudley, 10
Minchin, Alfred Corker, 10
Minchin, Alfred Keith, 10
Minchin, Richard Ernest, 5
Minchin, Ronald Richard Luther, 10
Roberts, Mary Grant, 11

ZOOLOGIST, *see also* Entomologist;
Ornithologist
Agar, Wilfred Eade, 7
Bancroft, Thomas Lane, 7
Brazier, John William, 3
Buchanan, Gwynneth Vaughan, 7
Clark, Hubert Lyman, 8
Cox, James Charles, 3
Dakin, William John, 8
Dendy, Arthur, 8
De Vis, Charles Walter, 4
Flynn, Theodore Thomson, 8
Gabriel, Charles John, 8
Gatliff, John Henry, 8
Gray, John Edward, 1
Harrison, Launcelot, 9
Haswell, William Aitcheson, 9
Hill, James Peter, 9
Iredale, Tom, 9
Krefft, Johann Ludwig Gerard, 5
McCulloch, Allan Riverstone, 10
MacKenzie, Sir William Colin, 10
May, William Lewis, 10
Ogilby, James Douglas, 11
Shirley, John, 11
Sweet, Georgina, 12
Verco, Sir Joseph Cooke, 12
Wade, Robert Thompson, 12
Waite, Edgar Ravenswood, 12

CONSOLIDATED CORRIGENDA

compiled by DARRYL BENNET

Australian Dictionary of Biography

Volume   1 : 1788-1850 A-H

Volume   2 : 1788-1850 I-Z

Volume   3 : 1851-1890 A-C

Volume   4 : 1851-1890 D-J

Volume   5 : 1851-1890 K-Q

Volume   6 : 1851-1890 R-Z

Volume   7 : 1891-1939 A-Ch

Volume   8 : 1891-1939 Cl-Gib

Volume   9 : 1891-1939 Gil-Las

Volume 10 : 1891-1939 Lat-Ner

Volume 11 : 1891-1939 Nes-Smi

Volume 12 : 1891-1939 Smy-Z

'An error doesn't become a mistake until you refuse to correct it.'
                                        Orlando Battista

This list reprints, consolidates and, where necessary, amends corrigenda already published for Volumes 1 to 11. Amended corrigenda are identified by an asterisk. The omission of a previously published corrigendum indicates that it has been cancelled. New corrigenda for Volumes 1 to 12, correcting errors discovered since Volume 12 was published in 1990, are also included and are identified by two asterisks.

Only corrections are shown; additional information is not included; nor is any re-interpretation attempted. The sole exception to this procedure is when new details become available on parents, or about births, deaths and marriages.

Documented corrections are welcomed from readers. Additional information, with sources, is also invited and will be placed in the appropriate files for future use. Such material should be sent to:

The General Editor
Australian Dictionary of Biography
Research School of Social Sciences
The Australian National University
G.P.O. Box 4
CANBERRA ACT 2601

Volume 1: 1788-1850 A-H

v PREFACE
line 3 *for* , *read* .

vii ACKNOWLEDGMENTS
line 9 *for* H. *read* W.
line 36 *for* O'Keefe *read* O'Keeffe

xiiib AUTHORS
lines 12-14 *transpose* McLAREN *and* McLACHLAN (with subjects)

5b ALLAN, D.
line 24 *for* About *read* In

6a ALLEN
line 15 *delete* , Moore's successor
lines 39-40 *delete* the Auxiliary Bible Society,

6b line 30 *for* 1860 *read* 1866

7b ALLISON
line 44 *delete* [q.v.]

8a line 23 *for* September 1846 *read* August 1848

9b ALLPORT
line 28 *for* brother *read* son

11b ALT
line 13 *for* 1758 *read* 1757

14a ANDERSON, J.
line 12 *for* 1848 *read* 1841
line 13 *for* returned to England *read* had moved to India

27a ARMYTAGE
**line 14 *delete* , an army subaltern,

27b ARNDELL
lines 6-14 *for* He was a son . . . daughter who later *read* He was baptized on 4 May 1753 at Kington, Herefordshire, son of Anthony Arndell and his wife Elizabeth, née Harris. His son John, by his wife Susanna, was later a medical assistant at Norfolk Island and his natural daughter Esther

28a line 8 *after* wife *insert* (whom he married in 1807 at Windsor)

32a ARTHUR
line 2 *after* was *insert* born on 5 February 1808,
line 4 *for* 18 *read* 16
line 28 *for* next year *read* in 1836
line 29 *for* In *read* On 28 *and for* 1826 *read* 1836

32b ARTHUR, G.
lines 9-10 *delete* where . . . port
lines 19-20 *for* thanked . . . on *read* praised his gallantry in action.

33a lines 1-2 *for* his . . . and *read* On his return Arthur was given the freedom of the city of

line 46 *delete* improperly

33b line 8 *for* at the end of *read* in April

37a **line 56 *for* K.H. *read* K.C.H.

38b ARTHUR
line 34 *after* 1843 *insert* .
lines 34-44 *delete* and joined . . . was sold.

38b ATKINS (BOWYER)
line 2 *after* was *insert* born on 22 March 1745,
line 4 *delete* Lady

39a line 11 *for* 1791 *read* 1792

42b ATKINSON
lines 17-18 *for* died in infancy. *read* lived to a ripe old age at Orange.

47a BAGOT
line 1 *for* HARVEY *read* HERVEY

48a BAILEY
line 1 *for* 1873 *read* 1879
line 6 *for* LL.B. *read* LL.D.

50a BALL
line 1 *for* d. 1818 *read* 1756-1818
line 2 *after* naval officer, *insert* was baptized on 7 December 1756 at Woodchurch, Cheshire, son of George Ball, gentleman, and his wife Lucy. Henry

50b lines 37-40 *for* been . . . duty. *read* sufficiently recovered to return to duty in December 1792 and in 1795 was promoted captain.
lines 52-58 *for* Ball died . . . August 1789. *read* On 17 June 1802 in London Ball had married Charlotte Foster (d. 1803); on 19 July 1810 at Kingston-upon-Thames he married Anne Georgianna Henrietta Johnston. He died on 22 October 1818 at Mitcham, Surrey, survived by his wife and by his daughter Ann Maria (b. *c.*1797) whose mother was the convict Sarah Partridge.

51a BALLOW
line 1 *for* 1809 *read* 1804
line 9 *for* 1837 . . . government *read* 1838 after serving as assistant surgeon at the Sydney general
line 43 *for* Thomson *read* Thompson

56a BANNISTER
line 64 *delete* re-em-

56b line 1 *for* ployment by *read* compensation from

57a BARKER
line 1 *for* 1786 *read* 1784
line 2 *for* in January 1786 and *read* on 31 December 1784 at Hackney,

Middlesex, England, son of William Barker and his wife whose father was Samuel Collet. He
lines 8-9 *for* , whence . . . regiment *read* . He sailed
line 9 *for* 1827 *read* 1828
line 10 *for* February 1828 *read* July

57b   BARKER, T.
line 9 *for* November *read* October
58a   line 51 *for* Royal Exchange *read* Sydney Exchange Co.

59b   BARNES
line 16 *for* Patterson *read* Paterson
60a   line 1 *for* Selby *read* George Town

61b   BARRALLIER
line 6 *for* 1764-1832 *read* 1749-1809
line 7 *for* nephew *read* relative

63b   BARRINGTON
bibliog. line 2 *for* 1830 *read* 1930

64a   BARTLEY
line 25 *for* seven *read* nine

65a   BASS
line 1 *for* filled *read* fitted
65b   line 31 *delete* Hawaiian and
line 32 *after* Sandwich *insert* (Hawaiian)

66b   BATE
line 7 *for* His *read* A

67a   BATEMAN
line 7 *after* four *insert* surviving
line 8 *for* in 1851 *read* on 17 August 1850

70b   BATMAN
lines 40-41 *for* in . . . city. *read* held by the Museum of Australia.
lines 43-44 *for* possibly . . . bookshop. *read* is in the Mitchell Library.

71a   BAUDIN
line 1 *for* THOMAS NICHOLAS *read* NICOLAS THOMAS
line 3 *for* DESAULES *read* DESAULSES
73a   bibliog. line 3 *for* Nicholas *read* Nicolas

74a   BAUGHAN
line 5 *for* a pair of *read* five

79a   BELL
line 41 *delete* Royal

83a   BELLASIS
line 35 *for* [qq.v.] *read* [q.v.]

84a   BENJAMIN
lines 12-16 *for* The partnership . . . marriages. *read* On 15 April 1840 he married Julia, daughter of Abraham Moses.

87b   BENT, E.
lines 18-19 *for* Letters and Journal *read* letters and journal

92a   BERRY
line 3 *for* seven *read* nine
92b   line 37 *for* 21 *read* 22

99a   BIGGE
line 4 *for* second *read* third
line 14 *for* 1814 *read* 1813
line 47 *for* weaken- *read* weakening

102b   BIRABAN
line 7 *for* returned *read* was taken
103a   line 2 *for* Known . . . tribe *read* He returned to Lake Macquarie and
line 13 *for* 'Maggill' *read* 'Magill'

105a   BIRNIE
lines 42-43 *for* considered . . . Gipps *read* not confirmed until 1838
line 47 *delete* also

108a   BISHOP, C.
line 33 *for* Nothing . . . him. *read* He appears to have died in 1810.

109b   BLACKBURN
line 44 *for* where . . . 1846 *read* , which from 1843 became increasingly the main centre of his activities. From 1844 he
line 45 *for* as *read* was *and after* and *insert* later
line 49 *for* 20 *read* 16
110a   line 5 *after* the *insert* Fitzroy
line 22 *for* -43 *read* -41
line 23 *for* 1839 *read* 1840
line 44 *delete* and court-house
line 62 *for* - *read*)
line 63 *delete* 40)
110b   line 1 *for* Town. *read* Town,

111b   BLAIR
line 1 *for* 1889 *read* 1880
112a   lines 51-54 *for* In 1883 . . . 1889. *read* On 11 June 1880 he died at his home, Greenmount, Toorak.

118b   BLIGH
line 4 *for* customs officer. *read* boatman and land waiter in the customs service.
line 45 *for* 30 *read* 29

127b   BOSTON
bibliog. line 2 for *Surprize* read *Surprise*

127b   BOUCHER
line 1 *after* FREDERICK *insert* (1801-1873)
128b   lines 5-6 *delete* may . . . who
bibliog. line 4 for *South* read *Southern*

132a   BOURKE
line 18 *for* 2 *read* 4

line 26 *for* 4 *read* 7
132b line 63 *for* 1838 *read* 1837

138a BOWMAN
line 32 *for* Elizabeth *read* Mary

141b BOYD
line 21 *for* Governor-General *read* Sir Charles

144a BRABYN
line 6 *after* sailed *insert* with his Spanish wife Mary (d. 1796), son and daughter
line 28 *after* Denison, *insert* née Howard,
144b lines 15-20 *for* Although . . . position *read* In January 1812 he returned to Sydney in the *Guildford* with Lawson and Bell [qq.v.]
line 56 *for* a *read* the

145a BRADLEY
line 7 *for* Mitchell *read* Witchell

147b BRADY
bibliog. line 2 *for* 1896 *read* 1895

149a BRENAN
line 17 *for* refused confirmation. *read* had already appointed Francis Fisher.

150b BRIGSTOCKE
**line 3 *for* Llawhaddon *read* Llawhaden

153a BRISBANE
line 55 *for* Church *read* London
153b lines 10-13 *for* lifted . . . ending *read* did not apply any censorship when W. C. Wentworth's [q.v.] *Australian* began publication, and ended

155b BROMLEY
line 6 *for* surgeon-superintendent *read* surgeon in the *Calcutta*. He made another visit
line 9 *for* both *read* these latter

157a BROOKS
line 9 *for* had to row *read* sailed
157b line 5 *delete* Richard

158b BROUGHTON, W.
line 11 *for* three *read* four

168b BROWNE, W.
line 5 *for* Ballinvonear *read* Ballin-voher
169a line 54 *after* Willis *insert* [q.v.]

169b BROWNING
line 42 *for* Arthur *read* Franklin

172a BRUNY D'ENTRECASTEAUX
line 11 *for* Péron [q.v.] *read* Piron
172b bibliog. line 1 *for* M. *read* E. P. E.

176a BUNCE
line 5 *for* 1835 *read* 1833

176b lines 20-22 *for* voyaged down . . . boat. *read* followed the course of the Murray River to the sea.
177a bibliog. line 7 *for* Leichardt *read* Leichhardt

178a BUNKER
line 1 *for* 1762 *read* 1761
lines 2-5 *for* married . . . 1786. *read* was born on 7 March 1761 at Plymouth, Massachusetts, United States of America, son of James Bunker and his wife Hannah, née Shurtleff. On 16 November 1786 at St George-in-the-East, Middlesex, England, he married Margrett, daughter of Captain Henry Thompson, R.N., and his wife Isabella, née Collingwood, who was first cousin to Admiral Cuthbert Collingwood.

181b BURN
line 22 *for* Jermima *read* Jemima
182a line 5 *for* Castledown *read* Castle Town
line 33 *after* Fenton *insert* [q.v.]
line 43 *for* Jermima *read* Jemima

186a BURTON
line 20 *for* elected *read* appointed
line 21 *for* 23 March *read* 9 February

189a BUSBY
line 63 *for* -1886 *read* -1887

192a CADMAN
line 30 *after* with *insert* her *and after* daughters *insert* from a previous alliance

195b CALLAGHAN
line 2 *for* 1851 *read* 1815

197b CAMPBELL
line 2 *for* Sunipole *read* Sunipol

201b CAMPBELL, P.
line 1 *delete* (fl.
line 2 *for* 1826-1841) *read* (1809-1848) *and after* public servant, *insert* son of Ronald Campbell and his wife Charlotte, née Cloeté,
202b line 46 *after* Wales. *insert* He died in London on 4 October 1848.

207b CAMPBELL
line 8 *for* Ramsey *read* Ramsay [qq.v.]

215b CATCHPOLE
line 40 *after* died *insert* on 13 May 1819

221b CHISHOLM
lines 23-24 *delete* which . . . authoress,

223a CIMITIERE
line 18 *delete* [q.v.]

228b CLARKE, W.
line 2 *for* 1801? *read* 1805
line 3 *for* in London, *read* on 20 April
1805 in Somerset, England,
229a line 12 *for* Glenorchy *read* Campbell
Town
229b line 29 *for* 15 *read* 13

236b COLLINS
line 4 *for* of eight children *read*
child
line 7 *for* Harriet *read* Henrietta
Caroline
line 8 *for* Pack *read* Park
line 9 *for* 1690? *read* 1684
237a lines 8-9 *for* As . . . husbands, he *read*
He
238a line 2 *delete* [q.v.]

246a COOPER, D.
line 14 *for* predeceased him *read* had
died *and after* 1836 *insert* ; his third
wife Alice survived him

247a CORDEAUX
line 19 *for* Cars *read* Caro
lines 62-64 *delete* Thomas Moore . . .
England,
247b line 1 *delete* and

248a COTTER
line 3 *for* Banty *read* Bantry

251b COVER
line 29 *for* Hassell *read* Hassall

254b COWPER
line 53 *for* -29 *read* and 1829
255a line 30 *for* Frederick *read* Frederic

256b COX, J.
line 12 *for* five *read* three
257a line 1 *for* In *read* On 12
line 2 *for* Connell of Sydney. *read*
Connel at St John's Church, Parramatta.
line 50 *after* 1829-34 *insert* and
1851-54
lines 51-54 *delete* In 1856 . . . Tasmania.
line 60 *for* only one *read* seven

257b COX, J. E.
lines 3-5 *for* England . . . Suffolk *read*
Suffolk, England. On 19 January
1821 he married Mary Ann Halls at
St James's, Bristol,
258a line 38 *for* Elliot *read* Elliott

261a CROOKES
line 3 *for* Antrim *read* Tyrone
line 28 *for* 1865 *read* 1864

262a CROSS
lines 54-55 *for* a New Zealand
missionary. *read* sometime of the
London Missionary Society.

264a CROWDER
lines 23-24 *for* May 1793 *read*
January 1794

266a CUNNINGHAM
line 28 *for* 1829 *read* 1820

275a DACRE
line 19 *for* Bennett *read* Bennet

277a DAMPIER
line 1 *for* 1652 *read* 1651
lines 2-3 *for* 8 June 1652 *read* 5 September 1651
278a line 26 *after* work. *insert* He died in
London in 1715.
bibliog. line 5 *after* 1962) *insert*
; L. R. Marchant, 'William Dampier',
JRWAHS, 6 (1963).

279b DANA
line 6 *for* efforts *read* effects

280a DANGAR
line 46 *for* Darkbrook *read* Dart-
brook

282b DARLING
line 1 *for* 1775 *read* 1772
286a line 58 *after* by *insert* his wife,

288a DASHWOOD
line 6 *for* six *read* four
lines 8-9 *delete* until . . . granted

288b DAVEY
line 2 *for* soldier *read* royal marine
289a line 44 *for* 1814 *read* 1815
lines 52-58 *delete* , and in the mean-
time . . . six months

291a DAVIES
line 12 *for* George *read* Charles

291b DAVIES, R.
line 11 *for* IV *read* III

293b DAVIS, C.
line 4 *delete* [q.v.]

294a DAVIS
line 9 *for* Waters *read* Water

295a DAVY
line 5 *after* and *insert* was a house
surgeon at

297a DAWBIN
line 46 *after* farm *insert* and was
buried in Melbourne general cemetery

300a DAWSON
line 3 *delete* Belford,

300a DAY
line 2 *after* of *insert* John Day,
line 4 *after* Ireland *insert* , and his
wife Charlotte, née Denny
300b lines 19-21 *for* After . . . Maitland.
read As police magistrate again at

Maitland, he was also commissioner, Court of Requests, from 1841 and of insolvent estates from 1842.
lines 47-50 *for* he returned . . . 1850. *read* his estate was sequestrated in 1848. Next year he was appointed to Sydney and from 1 January 1851 was provincial inspector of police for the northern district.
line 55 *for* in *read* on 6
line 56 *for* at Campbelltown. *read* in the Anglican cemetery, East Maitland.

301a DEANE
line 62 *for* Rosa *read* Rosalie
line 64 *for* violoncello *read* violin
301b line 1 *for* Morris . . . violin. *read* Charles Muzio the violoncello.
line 3 *for* Paine *read* Smith

306a DE WESSELOW
line 1 *delete* hyphens *after* DE *and after* SIMPKINSON *and after* DE

306b DICKSON
line 25 *after* sale *insert* .
lines 25-26 *for* and . . . England. *read* He lost the case *Brown* v. *Dickson* and had to pay £333 in damages. He was also prosecuted for forgery and absconded to England while on bail.

315b DOUGLASS
line 57 *for* 73 *read* 75

316b DOWLING
line 39 *for* six *read* seven

317a DOWLING, J.
line 1 *after* (1787-1844), *insert* judge,

325b DRUMMOND
line 35 *for* [q.v.] *read* [qq.v.]

327a DRUMMOND, John
line 20 for *Marquess* read *Marquis*

328b DRY
lines 53-56 *delete* and would . . . of him

329b DRY
line 26 *delete* the transportationist *and after* Douglas *insert* [q.v.]

331b DULHUNTLY
lines 40-41 *for* St James's Church *read* St James's, Sydney,
332a line 41 *delete* [q.v.]

333b DUMARESQ, H.
lines 14-15 *for* 'Paul's Letters to his Kinsfolk'. *read* Paul's Letters to his Kinsfolk (1816).

338a DUNLOP, E.
bibliog. line 2 *for* Thelkeld *read* Threlkeld

338b DUNLOP
line 21 *for* life *read* list

343a EAGAR
line 15 *for* Richard *read* Robert

348a EARLE
line 12 *for* 1796, *read* 1796.

349b EASTY
line 3 *for* . *read* ,
line 9 *delete* [q.v.]

351a EDGE
line 1 *after* -marshal, *insert* enlisted in the New South Wales Corps on 6 March 1790 and embarked in April. He
line 3 *for* some . . . March *read* in February
line 5 *for* , *read* .
lines 6-10 *delete* and . . . corps.

356a ELLISTON
line 12 *for* an alderman *read* a commissioner
line 13 *for* 1854 *read* 1855

357b ENDERBY
line 39 *for* Gladwyn *read* Goodwyn

361a EWING
line 9 *for* the bishop of Tasmania *read* Bishop Broughton [q.v.]
line 17 *after* convicts. *insert* He was priested by Bishop Nixon [q.v.] on 21 September 1843.

367a FAITHFUL
line 24 *delete* née Pitt,
line 25 *for* Matcham *read* Pitt, née Matcham,

370a FAWKNER
line 51 *for* Dalhousie *read* Talbot

371a FENTON
line 35 *for* newly *read* new

378b FINNISS
lines 40-42 *for* became . . . 1881. *read* acted as auditor-general in 1876 and served on the Forest Board in 1875-81.

389b FLINDERS
lines 3-4 *for* parish . . . Grammar School *read* Grammar School and by the vicar of Horbling

395a FORBES
lines 9-15 *for* they were . . . Forbes, *read* , when bills to license auctioneers and places of public entertainment were submitted to Forbes, they were found by him to be open to the objection in law that had been fatal to the first six clauses of the Newspaper Regulating Act,
398b line 54 *after* Newtown, *insert* Sydney,

400a FORBES
line 46 *for* in August *read* on 15 April

407b FOSTER
line 32 *for* Gippsland *read* Hobart

413a FRANKLIN
line 24 *for* K.H. *read* K.C.H.
line 40 *for* February *read* January

419a FROST
line 3 *for* Wales *read* England
419b line 54 *for* Port *read* Point

422b FYANS
line 8 *for* 1810 *read* 1811
lines 11-12 *for* did . . . July *read* had returned to England by May
line 14 *for* The next month *read* On 3 February 1818
lines 21-22 *delete* after . . . war,
423a line 1 *for* some three *read* four
line 12 *after* Knatchbull *insert* [q.v.]
line 17 *for* sixty *read* fourteen

425b GARDINER
line 23 *for* busines *read* business

426a GARDNER
lines 3-4 for *County Durham* read *Countess of Durham*
line 8 *for* W. *read* the late H.
line 14 for *Country* read *County*

426b GARLING
line 31 *for* Next day *read* On 11 December
line 34 *for* November *read* December

434b GAWLER
line 24 *for* 15 *read* 10

437a GELLIBRAND
line 9 *for* Risby *read* Kerby
437b lines 44-47 *for* He was . . . Hesse. *read* He and his companion, G. B. L. Hesse, probably lost their horses and perished in the summer heat. The mystery was not solved.

442b GILCHRIST
lines 20-21 *for* Royal Exchange *read* Sydney Exchange Co.

446a GIPPS
**line 2 *for* Ringwold *read* Ringwould
453a bibliog. line 10 *for* moments *read* comments

453a GISBORNE
line 1 *after* FYSHE *insert* (FYSCHE)

454a GLEADOW
line 13 *for* Kearton *read* Keaston

456a GLOVER
line 24 *for* Mill's *read* Mills

line 27 *for* Westmore- *read* Westmor-

457b GOODWIN
line 34 *for* a £400 fine *read* damages of £400
458a bibliog. line 8 *for* 13, 662 *read* 13,662

464b GOULBURN, F.
line 36 *for* in May *read* on 10 February

468a GRAHAM
line 8 *after* Raine *insert* [q.v.]

469b GRANT, John
lines 21-23 *for* and . . . voyage *read* . With Hayes, who joined him briefly in exile on the island that year,

476a GREGSON
line 20 *for* 1846 *read* October 1845

485b GRIFFITHS, J.
line 1 *for* 1766?-1840? *read* 1773-1839
lines 3-4 *for* , reputedly . . . Walker. *read* in 1773, son of Thomas Griffiths and his wife Sarah, née Withers.
line 4 *for* 22 *read* 15
line 16 *for* 1802 *read* 1806
486b line 7 *for* about 1840. *read* in November.
line 8 *for* twelve *read* nine
line 9 *for* 1801? *read* 1801
line 10 *after* born *insert* on 23 August 1801

487b GRIMES
line 14 for *Buffalo* read *Cumberland*

490a GROSE
line 1 *for* 1784 *read* 1788?
line 2 *after* was *insert* baptized at Deptford, London, on 17 August 1788, son of Howell William Grose and his wife Sarah. He was
line 56 *after* Bathurst. *insert* He had married three times: Mary Ann Deaton (d. 1824) on 13 May 1822; Irene Deaton on 2 November 1829; and Elizabeth Slater on 30 May 1840. A son of his second marriage, and his third wife, their son and two daughters survived him.

492a GUNN
line 4 *for* youngest *read* fourth
line 21 *for* two children *read* child *and delete* and
line 22 *for* Francis were *read* was
493a line 24 *for* Five years later *read* On 18 December 1839
line 27 *for* five *read* nine
*line 37 *for* 23 *read* 13

497a HACK
line 3 *for* 18 *read* 2
line 9 *for* 1829 *read* 1827

498a HACKING
line 11 *after* European. *insert* In
1794 he was granted thirty acres at
Hunter's Hill.
lines 13-14 *delete* and . . . Hill

501b HALL
line 13 *for* George *read* William

502a HALL, E. Swarbreck
line 41 *delete* [q.v.]
line 45 *for* 1831 *read* 1851
502b line 55 *for* one year *read* shortly

505b HALLER
line 1 *for* b. 1808 *read* 1808-1886
lines 14-15 *for* Presbyterian *read*
Congregationalist
506a lines 24-25 *delete* is assumed to
have
line 26 *for* daughter. *read* two daughters; he died at East Melbourne on 29
March 1886.

506a HALLORAN
line 2 *after* (1765-1831), *insert*
bogus
lines 7-17 *for* Westminster . . . Aberdeen. *read* Christ's Hospital. He en-
tered the navy in 1781 but was gaoled
in 1783 for stabbing and killing a
fellow midshipman. Acquitted in
1784, he married Mary Boutcher and
ran a school at Exeter until 1788 and
then an academy at Alphington until
he became insolvent in 1796. He was
also charged with immorality. A pro-
fessed Roman Catholic, he recanted
in 1792 but never won the Anglican
ordination he wanted. In 1797-98 he
was in the navy posing as a chaplain.
In 1800 he was awarded a doctorate
in divinity at King's College, Aberdeen.
506b line 41 *after* his *insert* second
line 42 *after* and *insert* their un-
married mother, Lydia Anne (Anna)
Halloran, who may have been his own
niece. He
507a line 12 *delete* eldest
line 18 *after* son. *insert* The Colonial
Office advised Governor Darling of
Halloran's shady career and rejected
his appeal for a land grant for his
establishment.
line 59 *for* Halloran's first wife *read*
Anna
line 62 *delete* also
507b bibliog. line 10 *after* 1831 *insert*
; K. Grose, 'Dr. Halloran', *Aust J of
Education*, Oct 1970

509b HAMPTON
bibliog. line 9 *for* (JRWAHS) *read*
(RWAHS)

511a HARDWICKE
lines 15-16 *for* first . . . *Kangaroo.*
read master of the cutter *Elizabeth.*
line 19 *for* 1816 *read* 1819 it was
alleged that
line 21 *delete* , seemingly
line 36 *for* 100 *read* 500
line 39 *delete* in . . . *Elizabeth*

514b HARPUR
line 38 *after* Wills *insert* [q.v.]

520a HARRISON
line 2 *for* in *read* at Bonhill near
line 3 *for* near Ben Lomond *read* ,
Dunbartonshire,
line 7 *after* Anderson *insert* (Anderson's University)
line 8 *for* Mechanics' Institute *read*
Glasgow Mechanics' Institution
line 10 *for* about 1832 *read* in 1835
520b line 20 *after* represented *insert*
Geelong and
line 21 *for* -61 *read* -60
line 35 *for* Rodey *read* Rocky

523b HASSALL
line 45 *for* Quensland *read* Queensland

524a HAWDON
line 58 *for* After . . . he *read* She died
in 1854. In 1872 his son Arthur
Joseph
line 61 *for* at Christchurch. *read* in
Canterbury, New Zealand.

524b HAWKINS
line 36 *for* owned *read* leased
525a lines 12-14 *for* a . . . foundation. *read*
a founding trustee of All Saints' College, Bathurst.
lines 18-19 *for* and . . . [qq.v.] *read*
[q.v.]
bibliog. line 1 for *SMH* read *Sydney
Herald*

526b HAYES
lines 13-15 *for* defiant . . . and *read*
defiance of Governor King earned
Grant exile on Norfolk Island, Margarot and Hayes in

529b HELY
line 3 *for* at . . . Ulster *read* in County
Tyrone

534b HEYDON
line 40 *for* 1838 *read* 1839

538b HINDMARSH
line 23 *for* Gaieta *read* Gaeta

543a HOBLER
line 1 *for* 1801 *read* 1800
line 2 *for* probably . . . Devonshire.

read born on 6 September 1800 at Islington, London, son of Francis Helvetius Hobler and his wife Mary, née Furby.
line 5 *after* Hertfordshire. *insert* On 21 October 1822 at Cadbury, Devon, he married Ann Turner.
line 12 *delete* Ann, née Turner,
line 13 *for* six *read* nine

544a   line 5 *for* in 1881. *read* on 13 December 1882 and was buried at San Leander.

544b   HOBSON
lines 17-20 *delete* The . . . it.

545a   line 41 *for* In September *read* On 9 September
line 42 *after* Marie *insert* Anne Martha Celine Helena

549b   HOLDEN
line 5 *for* 7 *read* 8

555a   HOSKING
lines 25-27 *for* For a . . . with *read* His father was the London agent of Eagar [q.v.] & Forbes and John became the partner of
line 55 *for* most *read* some

556a   HOVELL
line 6 *for* Europe *read* London on 10 May 1810
line 8 *for* junior . . . Foscari *read* [q.v.]
556b   line 12 *for* Sydney *read* Gunning
557a   line 23 *after* Goulburn *insert* , survived by a natural son

558b   HOWE
lines 20-21 *for* as . . . Horatio, *read* a son, Horatio Spencer Wills [q.v.],

562b   HULL
line 1 *for* 1786 *read* 1787
lines 2-4 *for* 21 August . . . children *read* 13 August 1787 in the parish of Iwerne, Dorset, England, son
line 6 *for* Rose *read* Catherine, née Short
line 13 *for* Thomas *read* Mark
line 18 *after* England, *insert* and
line 20 *for* Captain *read* Lieutenant
line 21 *for* Coldstream *read* Scots *and* for , *read* .

563b   HUME
line 15 *for* Barker *read* Barber

564a   HUME, H.
lines 19-20 *delete* site . . . village of *and after* Bungonia *insert* district
*564b   line 60 *after* John *insert* and

566a   HUMPHREY
line 11 *for* dolorite *read* dolerite
566b   line 40 *delete* [q.v.]

572b   HUNTER, J. *et al*
lines 10-22 *for* Phillip with . . . Meanwhile *read* Phillip. An elder cousin John Hunter traded with James Watson in 1839-43.
*line 23 *for* had become *read* became

573a   HUON
line 1 *for* KERRILLEAU *read* KERILLEAU
573b   line 28 *for* Kerrilleau *read* Kerilleau
line 48 *for* His *read* At Parramatta on 16 March 1812 his
line 52 *for* 1815 *read* 1811
line 54 *for* Kerrilleau's *read* Kerilleau's

574a   HUTCHINS
line 49 *delete* [q.v.]

575a   HUTCHINSON
line 62 *after* Sutton *insert* Forest

577b   HUXLEY
line 10 *delete* (M.B. London, 1845)

Volume 2: 1788-1850 I-Z

2a   IMLAY
**line 1 *for* 1787- *read* 1797?-
*line 2 *for* 1795-1847 *read* 1794-1846 *and for* 1801- *read* 1800?-
**lines 4-5 *for* born . . . family. *read* baptized on 22 January 1797, 1 August 1794 and 30 March 1800 at Aberdeen, Scotland, sons of Alexander Imlay, farmer and merchant, and his wife Agnes, née Bron. Young
3a   line 4 *for* In . . . 1847 *read* On 26 December 1846
**line 12 *for* Peter . . . 1841, *read* On 23 February 1853 Peter married Jane Maguire with Presbyterian forms at St Andrew's Church, Sydney. He had
**lines 16-17 *for* in 1881 . . . daughters. *read* on 8 March 1881, survived by Jane and three of their daughters.

5a   IRWIN
line 17 *for* 13th *read* 63rd
line 31 *for* four . . . three *read* five sons and four
5b   line 49 *for* Sterling *read* Stirling

17a   JOHNSON
line 1 *for* 1753 *read* 1753?
line 11 *for* London *read* Oxford *and for* 1786 *read* 1784
19a   lines 38-40 *delete* Seven . . . Norfolk.

19b JOHNSTON
line 1 *for* 1771? *read* 1767
line 2 *for* about 15 *read* 20

24a JONES, D.
line 9 *for* -1893 *read* -1894

32b KANE
line 57 *after* where *insert* on 1 May
1883
line 58 *for* Lily *read* Alicia

35b KAY
line 45 *for* 33 *read* 34

36a KEARNEY
line 28 *after* Nash *insert* [q.v.]

36b KELLY
lines 2-3 *for* 29 November *read* 24
December
37b bibliog. line 8 *for* Mar *read* May

41a KEMP
line 47 *delete* in 1853
41b line 39 *for* 1856 *read* 1854

44a KENNEDY
bibliog. line 1 *before* E. Beale *insert*
W. Carron, *Narrative of an ex-
pedition . . . for the exploration of the
country lying between Rockingham
Bay and Cape York* (Syd, 1849);

46b KENT
line 28 *for* principle *read* chief

51a KERR
line 24 *for* Charles *read* William
line 25 *delete* [q.v.]

52a KINCHELA
line 9 *for* 1831 *read* 1832
52b **line 3 *for* James Butler *read* John

55a KING, J. C.
line 4 *after* King *insert* (d. 1840)
line 5 *for* farmer. *read* farmer, and his
wife Martha Jane, née Henry.

56a KING
line 32 *after* February *insert* 1788

61b KING, P. P.
line 43 *for* 83 *read* 84
63a line 42 *for* 1834 *read* 1839
63b line 59 *after* became *insert* stock
line 60 *for* 1854 *read* 1851
**line 62 *for* 1898 *read* 1897

72a LAKELAND
bibliog. line 2 *for* 1813 *read* 1818

73a LAMB
line 9 *for* Royal Exchange *read*
Sydney Exchange Co.
line 20 *delete* first

75b LANG
line 52 *for* Riverina *read* Riverine

81a LANG
line 27 *delete* In January 1859

84b LANGLANDS
lines 6-7 *for* on New Year's Day *read*
in early January
85a line 10 *for* 1849 *read* 1848
bibliog. line 5 *for* Nonformists *read*
Nonconformists

85b LA PEROUSE
line 7 *for* discovered *read* learned
line 43 *delete* [q.v.]

89a LA TROBE
line 3 *for* 30 *read* 20
91a line 16 *for* 1846 *read* 1846-47
92b line 24 *for* 1864 *read* 1865
line 25 *delete* , based . . . lieut-
governor

96a LAWSON
line 35 *for* next year *read* in January
1812
lines 36-37 *for* Admiral . . . place.
read Guildford.
96b line 22 *delete* [q.v.]
lines 33-34 *delete* In 1828 . . .
horses.

97a LAYCOCK
line 4 *delete* and . . . 1790
line 6 *for* 1791. *read* 1791 and arrived in Sydney in H.M.S. *Gorgon* in
September.

97b LAYCOCK, T. (1786?-1823)
*line 6 *delete* and was . . . when he

101b LEE
line 16 *delete* [q.v.]
102a line 51 *for* -58 *read* -59

108a LESLIE
line 50 *for* George *read* John
Clements

108b LEVEY
line 1 *after* BARNETT *insert*
(BERNARD)

114a LHOTSKY
line 1 *for* (b. 1800) *read* (1795?-
1866?)
line 2 *for* on . . . 1800 *read* probably
in 1795
114b line 25 *for* The last *read* A late
line 29 *after* gold. *insert* He died
probably on 23 November 1866
in the Dalston German Hospital,
London.

116a LIGHT
line 28 *after* November *insert* 1806

119a LILLIE
bibliog. lines 6-7 for *Evening* . . . 3
read *Lyttelton Times,* 4

121a LOANE
line 60 *for* Macquarie *read* Davey
line 63 *for* Mrs Hotson *read* Madame
D'Hotman

123a LOCKYER
line 3 *for* at Wembury *read* in St Andrew's Parish, Plymouth,
lines 4-5 *for* Edmund . . . Joan. *read* Thomas Lockyer, sailmaker, and his wife Ann, née Grose.
*line 9 *after* August. *insert* At Galle, Ceylon (Sri Lanka), on 12 August 1806 he married a widow Dorothea Agatha Young, née de Ly. She died in Ceylon on 13 September 1816; on 6 October Lockyer married Sarah Morris.
line 11 *for* Most of his *read* His
line 12 *before* India *insert* England, Ireland,
*lines 15-16 *for* Sarah . . . their *read* and ten
123b lines 61-62 *for* His first wife *read* Sarah
124a lines 1-2 *for* eight . . . second. *read* a son of his first marriage, nine children of his second and three of his third.

124a LOGAN
line 44 *for* Alan *read* Allan
line 46 *for* 5700 *read* 4449

124b LONSDALE
line 1 *for* 1800? *read* 1799
line 2 *after* administrator, *insert* was born on 2 October 1799,

143b LYTTLETON
line 22 *for* Lyttelton *read* Lyttleton

144b MACARTHUR, A.
line 19 *for* , and . . . Jones *read* Jones and his wife Fanny Edith

144b MACARTHUR, E.
line 1 *for* 1767? *read* 1766
lines 2-3 *for* née . . . farmers *read* was born on 14 August 1766 in Devon, England, daughter of Richard Veale, farmer, and his wife Grace, who were

149b MACARTHUR, J.
line 2 *after* born *insert* on 15 December 1798
line 3 *delete* the . . . and
lines 9-10 *for* in Hereford *read* at Hackney, London,
151b line 57 *for* in *read* from
line 58 *for* licences *read* an annual licence
152a line 13 *delete* Bland,

153b MACARTHUR, John
line 1 *after* 1767 *insert* ?
line 5 *after* second *insert* surviving
line 8 *for* Katharine *read* Catherine
157b line 35 *for* 150,000 *read* 15,000

160b McCRAE
**line 24 *for* in 1890. *read* on 24 May 1890 at Hawthorn.

**line 25 *for* eight *read* seven surviving

163b MACDOUGALL
line 60 *for* John *read* James

171a MacKELLAR
**line 42 *for* son, *read* son was
**line 43 *for* 1795), *read* 1796).
**lines 43-46 *delete* came . . . St Vincent.

172a McKENZIE
line 2 *for* 1768 *read* 1769
line 3 *for* probably in Scotland. *read* on 4 September 1769 at Hammersmith, London, son of Alexander Mackenzie, of the Stamp Office, and his wife Mary, née Price. He married Elizabeth Punnett (d. 1795) on 30 June 1792 at St Vincent, West Indies.
line 6 *for* sister *read* cousin
172b lines 5-6 *delete* and . . . Australia

180b McLEAY
line 7 *for* Christina *read* Christiana
line 8 *for* Colonel *read* Captain

190b MACQUARIE
line 15 *for* along *read* among
194a line 26 *for* elegaic *read* elegiac

196a MACQUEEN
line 34 *for* debtors *read* creditors

198a MAKINSON
line 12 *for* Bird *read* Sumner

206a MARGAROT
line 1 *after* MARGAROT *insert* ,

207a MARRIOTT
line 10 *for* 1829 *read* 1833
line 11 *for* 1835 *read* 1836
207b line 14 *for* In December 1859 *read* On 28 January 1860

207b MARSDEN
lines 1 and 3 *for* 1764 *read* 1765

213a MARTENS
line 43 *for* Church *read* cemetery

213b MASON
line 1 *delete* (d. 1821)
214a line 4 *after* Mary *insert* , but went ashore at Portsmouth and disappeared

218a MEAGHER
lines 8-9 for *News,* read *News. and delete* which . . . cause.
line 11 *for* Confederate *read* Union

220a MEEHAN
line 24 *for* laid out *read* surveyed

226a MIDDLETON
lines 7-8 *for* his wife's death *read* the death of his wife Mary Ann, née Hull,

226b line 62 *for* Richard *read* Robert

231a MILLS
line 1 *for* 1808 *read* 1810
231b line 25 *for* H *read* N
line 35 *for* 1849 *read* 1852

233a MINCHIN
line 3 *after* Tipperary *insert* , son of George Minchin
233b lines 36-37 *delete* when MacKellar . . . sea
line 54 *for* George *read* John

234b MITCHEL
line 51 *for* O'Dogherty *read* Izod O'Doherty [q.v.]
235a line 15 *for* O'Dogherty *read* O'Doherty
line 58 *for* two *read* three

235b MITCHELL
lines 7-8 *for* three years later *read* in April 1812
lines 18-24 *delete* He had . . . *Neptune.*

243b MOLLISON
lines 3-4 *for* overlanders . . . parliament *read* overlanders and pastoralists

244a line 28 *for* 1856 *read* 1858

246a MONDS
line 48 *for* 1885 *read* 1888

251a MONTEFIORE
lines 27-30 *for* Early . . . London. *read* After the depression the Montefiore firm in Sydney went bankrupt. The London firm had suspended payment in 1841 and Montefiore had returned to England.

254a MOORE, J.
line 1 *for* d. *read* 1790-
line 39 *after* snr' *insert* [q.v.]

254b MOORE, T.
line 30 *for* named *read* at

264b MOUNTGARRETT
line 4 *after* Ensign *insert* Hugh

268a MUNDY
line 1 *delete* ?
line 2 *after* was *insert* born on 10 March 1804,
line 24 *after* 1860 *insert* survived by his wife Louisa Katrina Herbert, whom he had married in Sydney on 6 June 1848, and by their son
line 36 *after* accompanied *insert* his cousin

269a MURDOCH, P.
line 1 *delete* ?
lines 2-6 *for* descended . . . Wallaces *read* born on 15 January 1795, son of James Murdoch and his wife Frances, daughter of John Wallace,
269b lines 21-24 *delete* in December . . . He
line 32 *delete* whose Christian names were
line 33 *after* Brown, *insert* whom he had married on 5 February 1830 at Capelrig,
line 34 *after* later *insert* , survived by four children

272a MURRAY, J.
line 41 *for* 1801 *read* 1802
line 46 *delete* [q.v.]

274b MURRAY
line 41 *for* 1840, *read* 1834,

278a NAIRN
lines 47-48 *delete* , where . . . 1829

280a NATHAN
line 25 *for* 1890 *read* 1898

280a NEALES
lines 4-5 *for* a sister of Jeremy *read* née

283b NICHOLSON
lines 6-7 *delete* and . . . Egremont

285a line 57 *for* He had two *read* Of his three *and for* Archibald, *read* Archibald was
line 59 *after* Sydney *delete* ,

285b NIXON
line 30 *for* 1848 *read* 1847

288b NOBBS
lines 47-48 *delete* as a priest

290b OAKDEN
lines 3-4 *delete* (where . . . discoverer)
line 31 *for* Georgiana *read* Georgina

294a O'BRIEN
line 48 *for* 1848 *read* 1849

295b O'CONNELL
line 14 *for* 1834 *read* 1835

297a OFFICER
line 12 *for* Jamima *read* Jemima
298a line 19 *delete* from parliament

298b O'FLAHERTY
lines 60-63 *for* played . . . York. *read* appeared at theatres in New York, Philadelphia and other cities.
299a bibliog. insert *Bow Bells,* 21 Dec 1864.

311a PALMER, P.
line 18 for *William Bryan* read *Warrior*

321b PEEL
line 3 *for* many *read* four
lines 4-5 *delete* , and . . . longer

325b PETRIE
line 3 *after* Scotland, *insert* son of Walter Petrie and Margaret, née Hutchinson,
326a line 47 *after* fied. *insert* At Edinburgh in 1821 he had married Mary Cuthbertson; they had nine sons and a daughter.
line 49 *delete* lord

335b PIPER
line 56 *for* illusion *read* allusion

337a PLATT
**line 3 *for* Bashford *read* Basford

337b PLUNKETT
line 4 *for* Ireland. *read* Ireland, son of George Plunkett and his wife Eileen, née O'Kelly.
line 11 *for* 1824 *read* 1823
338a line 2 *for* , *read* .
lines 2-6 *delete* beginning . . . lash.
339a line 64 *for* reformed *read* Executive

348a POWELL
lines 21-22 *for* administered . . . 1818. *read* died in August 1836, having married James Moore in June 1829.

348a POWER
line 21 *for* Margaret Ellen *read* Agnes, née Brooke,

349a POWLETT
line 4 *for* a *read* Rev. Charles Powlett, sometime
line 11 *for* two *read* three
line 12 *for* first recorded *read* foundation
line 49 *for* In 1850 *read* On 23 April 1851

355a PUGH
line 2 *after* practitioner, *insert* son of William Bowdler Pugh,
355b line 10 *after* first *insert* by a medical practitioner
line 34 *after* 1874. *insert* On 27 April 1876 at Hurstpierpoint, Sussex, he married Sarah Ann Webb.
line 35 *for* Their *read* The *and after* child *insert* of his first marriage

360b RAINE
line 46 *for* 30 March *read* 6 April

364b RAVEN
line 54 *for* Squires *read* Squire [q.v.]

367a READ
line 34 *for* no relation *read* his son

367a READ (REID)
lines 1-2 *for* (b. 1796?) *read* (c.1796-1862)

367b line 6 *after* Pitt Street *delete* . and *insert* ; but his death certificate was to name his father as Richard Read, artist.
lines 52-56 *delete* The absence . . . New South Wales.
line 61 *after* advertisements. *insert* Read died on 16 January 1862 in East Melbourne and was buried in Melbourne general cemetery.

373a REED
line 25 *after* from *insert* the bankrupt estate of

375b REID, A.
line 34 *for* 1836 *read* 1834

376a REID, D.
line 2 *for* 1856 *read* 1826

378b RIDDELL
line 46 *for* January *read* February

382b RITCHIE
line 24 *after* her *insert* at Launceston

392a ROEMER
line 1 *for* (b. 1799) *read* (1799-1874)
lines 2-3 *for* was . . . Germany. *read* was baptized at Leipzig, Saxony, on 11 May 1799, the son of Carl Wilhelm Maximilian vön Römer, an officer in the Royal Saxon Regiment, and his wife Justine Dorothee, née Frohlich.
392b lines 8-9 *for* None . . . traced. *read* In 1852 at Lambeth he had married Clementina Levett who bore him a son and daughter. Roemer died in Stuttgart, Germany, on 26 July 1874 and was survived by his wife and two children.

392b ROGERS
line 4 *for* After admission *read* He went
line 5 *for* , *read* .
lines 5-8 *delete* he . . . 1844.

399a ROSS
bibliog. line 7 *after* Lamb *insert* -Smith

403a ROWLEY
line 13 *for* Piper *read* Townson

404a RUMKER
lines 27-28 *delete* , through . . . Brisbane,

407a RUSSELL
line 22 *for* was *read* continued to be

408b RUSSELL, P.
line 1 *for* 1796? *read* 1796
line 12 *after* Russell *insert* , born on 30 June 1796,

411a RUTLEDGE
line 5 *for* Langford *read* Longford
412a line 17 *for* 1858 *read* 1852
412b bibliog. line 3 *for* Osborne *read* Osburne

417b SAMSON
line 37 *after* 1878. *insert* He was a nominee in the Western Australian Legislative Council in 1849-56 and 1859-68.

419a SAVAGE
line 34 *for* John *read* Thomas

430b SCOTT, T. A.
line 25 *after* Williams *insert* [q.v.]

431b SCOTT, T. H.
line 3 *for* baptized on 24 *read* born on 17
line 17 *for* was . . . been *read* went bankrupt as
line 21 *delete* his brother-in-law
lines 30-31 *for* advanced . . . priesthood *read* became a priest the same year, and
line 31 *for* and *read* was
line 39 *for* accepted appointment as *read* was appointed
432b line 10 *delete* a Tory and
line 11 *for* progressives of *read* friends of Governor Brisbane in
line 63 *for* However, he did *read* His resignation was accepted on 14 November
433a line 1 *for* not . . . until *read* and on *and* delete , when

436a SHARLAND
line 3 *delete* surgeon, *and* Mary
lines 3-4 *delete* , née Culley
line 14 *for* Frederick *read* Frederic
lines 18-19 *delete* 1829 . . . and in
line 19 *after* 1835 *insert* he
lines 21-22 *delete* from practice,
lines 46-47 *delete* after . . . Frankland [q.v.]
436b line 26 *for* 1849 *read* September 1848
lines 28-30 *delete* was . . . then
line 32 *for* Sara *read* Sarah
line 35 *for* Nodd *read* Nod, Surrey
line 40 *for* Frederick *read* Frederic

444a SIDAWAY
line 1 *for* 1757? *read* 1758
line 2 *after* was *insert* born on 14 January 1758 and baptized on 5 February at St Leonards, Shoreditch, London, son of John Sidaway of Horse Shoe Alley, and his wife Elizabeth. Robert was
line 4 *for* housebreaking *read* stealing
line 33 *delete* aged 52,

444b SIDDINS
line 2 *for* between *read* to
lines 3-4 *delete*, calling periodically at Port Jackson
line 4 *for* arrived *read* was in Port Jackson
line 30 *for* Siddons *read* Siddins
line 31 *after* Powell *insert* [q.v.]
line 32 *for* at Parramatta *read* on the Parramatta Road
*line 37 *after* master *insert* and part owner *and for* 1819 *read* 1818 *and delete* July
lines 38-39 *for* he returned from Macquarie Island. *read* it was sold.

445b SIMMONS
line 1 *for* 1880? *read* 1893
446b line 14 *after* portraiture'. *insert* He died in Sydney on 9 August 1893.

448a SIMPSON
line 1 *for* 1792? *read* 1793
line 2 *for* born *read* baptized on 29 July 1793
*line 23 *for* a woman *read* in 1838 Sophia Anne Simpson, a relation
*lines 58-61 *for* About 1846 . . . standing, *read* By 1845 he had built a cottage in Goodna, which

453a SMITH, T.
line 28 *for* the *read* an
line 34 *for* 1857-58 *read* 1857-59
lines 34-35 *for* Royal Exchange *read* Sydney Exchange Co.

465b SPENCER
**line 15 *for* K.H. *read* K.C.H.

466a SPODE
line 26 *for* 1828 *read* 1827
line 28 *for* 1829 *read* 1828
line 29 *for* 1832 *read* 1831

467a SPRENT
line 49 *after* Oakes *insert* [q.v.]

467b SQUIRE
line 3 *after* convicted *insert* for highway robbery
468b lines 10-11 *delete* who also . . . Fleet and

471a STANLEY
line 49 *for* Harvey's *read* Hervey

479a STEPHENS
line 63 *for* five *read* three

480b STEPHENS, E.
bibliog. line 1 *for* F *read* J

482a STEVENSON
line 14 *delete* , née Hutton,
line 17 *for* widow *read* daughter
482b line 20 *for* 18 *read* 19

482b STEWART
**line 17 *delete* by purchase

489a STOKES
line 16 *for* October *read* December

495a STRZELECKI
bibliog. line 12 *for* Harvard *read*
Havard

495a STURT
line 5 *for* Napier Lennox *read* Lenox
Napier

495b lines 19-20 *after* appointed *delete* ,
possibly . . . Governor Darling,

498b bibliog. line 4 *for* 6 *read* 5

501b SWANSTON
line 21 *for* largely . . . for *read* an early
subscriber to

505b TEGG
line 15 *for* W. *read* Gideon
line 16 *delete* Wilson

506b TENCH
line 11 *for* 1792 *read* 1791

528a THOMSON
line 61 *after* tions), *insert* and
lines 62-64 *delete* and . . . spire),

531a THROSBY
lines 57-59 *for* and . . . and *read* arrived in the *Mangles* in August 1820
and at Liverpool in 1824 married Bet-
sey, daughter of William Broughton
[q.v.];

535a TORRENS
line 24 *for* Associaiton *read* Association

546b UNDERWOOD
lines 1-15 *for* (1776?-1844) . . . Kable
[q.v.]. *read* (1771-1844), shipbuilder,
distiller and merchant, was born on 4
September 1771 at Bermondsey,
London, son of Thomas Underwood
and his wife Mary, née Forster. Although he is traditionally supposed to
have come to New South Wales with
the First Fleet, he was sentenced to
seven years transportation at Maidstone in 1790 and arrived in Sydney
in the *Admiral Barrington* in October 1791. He learned the trade of
boatbuilder, probably briefly under
Stephen Todd, formerly a carpenter
in the *Barwell*, who was engaged to
build a 34-ton sloop for the Hawkesbury River trade in 1797; he built the
Diana in 1798-99 which later became the property of Underwood and
his partner Henry Kable [q.v.].

547a line 55 *for* £1700 *read* £6200
547b line 3 *for* three- *read* two-
line 18 *for* Soon . . . 1842 *read* In
March 1840
lines 19-20 *delete* , aged 67,
lines 22-23 *delete* Underwood . . .
Kendall.

line 27 *for* 1811 *read* 1810
lines 32-33 *for* Shurwell *read*
Sherwell
lines 33-34 *for* but . . . marriage. *read*
who bore him a son William.

548b UNDERWOOD
line 14 *for* Surgeon *read* the emanci-
pist
lines 25-26 *for* three . . . Frederick,
read four daughters and two sons.
The elder, Frederick, was
line 27 *for* who *read* and

549a UTHER
line 12 *for* -1844 *read* -1848

550a VALE
line 8 *for* 1811 *read* 1812
line 11 *for* London *read* Ely
550b line 12 *for* -39 *read* -31

555b VIDAL
lines 1-2 *for* 1869 *read* 1873 *and*
before née *insert* author,
line 2 *for* born *read* baptized
line 4 *delete* child and only
line 7 *after* Reynolds *insert* .
line 8 *delete* and also related to
line 11 *after* Ionica *insert* , were
young Mary's brothers
line 20 *delete* Furse

556a line 21 for *Geoffrey* read *Geoffry*
line 43 *for* in England in 1869. *read* at
Sutton, Suffolk, England, on 19 November 1873.
line 44 *for* the first *read* an early

556b VLAMINGH
line 51 *after* Australia *insert* , although Willem Janssen [q.v.] had
been an earlier visitor

557a VON STIEGLITZ
line 29 *for* 1851 *read* 1856
line 31 *for* council *read* assembly
557b line 19 *for* 1884 *read* 1889
line 28 *for* died in *read* died on 14
April
line 34 *after* Portland *insert* Bay District

558a WAINEWRIGHT
line 36 *for* In 1821 *read* On 13 November 1817

565b WALKER
lines 23-24 *for* In 1860 . . . Ann, *read*
On 25 July 1860 at Holy Trinity
Church, Sydney, he had married with
Anglican rites Jane,

569a WALSH
line 3 *for* 12 *read* 10
569b line 6 *after* Ireland *insert* Treherne
570a line 32 *for* March *read* February

575a WATLING
bibliog. line 8 *for* N *read* M

576a WEDGE
lines 30-31 *for* by . . . government
read as a Tasmanian parliamentary
paper
line 51 *after* 1857 *insert* , as member
for North Esk,

577b WELSH
lines 23-24 *delete* his wife . . . , and

580a WENTWORTH
line 57 *delete* Though unpaid,
582a lines 14-15 *for* was . . . midshipman
read died at sea as a petty officer

585b WENTWORTH
lines 42-45 *for* the . . . Wales. *read*
civilian juries were allowed in civil
cases on the application of both parties and the approval of the Supreme
Court.

590a WERE
lines 13-19 *for* Despite . . . Nicholas.
read In February 1841 Were had become an agent for Henry Dendy.
Were's subsequent business failure
and bankruptcy in 1843 forced Dendy
into insolvency; both their interests
in the Brighton Estate were acquired
eventually by Were's eldest brother
Nicholas who lived in England.

597a WICKHAM
line 3 *for* December *read* November
line 4 *for* Captain *read* Lieutenant
line 5 *after* R.N. *insert* and his wife
Ellen Susannah, née Naylor.
line 18 *for* a *read* on 27 October 1842
Anna,
lines 36-37 *delete* in 1857

606a WILLS
line 5 *for* 2 *read* 4

608b WILSHIRE
line 38 *for* for *read* 'for

613a WILTON
line 3 *after* born *insert* on 24 October
1795
line 48 *for* B *read* K

613b WINDER
line 18 *for* Laverton *read* Leverton

618a WITTENOOM
line 1 *for* 1789 *read* 1788
line 2 *after* born *insert* on 24 October
1788

623a WOOLLEY
line 28 *delete* first

631a WYNYARD
line 29 *for* Cowe *read* Lowe

633b YOUNG
line 51 *for* [q.v.] *read* junior

Volume 3: 1851-1890 A-C

8a à BECKETT
line 27 *for* that year *read* 1863
*line 56 *for* In December *read* On 28
December

10a à BECKETT, T.
line 11 *after* 1892. *insert* He left
his estate to his surviving children
and his second wife Laura Jane, née
Stuckey.
bibliog. line 8 *for* 1860-80 *read* 1859-
69

15a ADAMS, F.
bibliog. line 5 *for* Gavan *read*
Gavah

18a ADAMSON
line 1 *for* 1828 *read* 1827
line 3 *after* born *insert* on 6 August
1827
line 49 *after* Stevenson. *insert* She
died in 1864 and on 26 August 1873
at Geelong he married Catherine
Synnot.

18b AGNEW
line 1 *for* WILSON *read* WILLSON

19b AH MOUY
line 37 *for* Cheok Hong Cheong *read*
Cheong Cheok Hong

20b ALDERSON
line 37 *for* Milford *read* Mitford

21b ALLAN
line 47 *delete* [q.v.]
22a line 40 *for* His son George *read* He

24a ALLAN, W.
bibliog. line 3 *for* 1897 *read* 1891

27a ALLEYNE
lines 24-25 *for* also . . . administer
read administered

31a ANDERSON, R.
line 32 *for* Crocker *read* Croker

31b ANDERSON
lines 53-54 *for* by a radical candidate
read and 1894
line 59 *for* Michael *read* Matthew

32a ANDERSON, W. A.
line 4 *after* only *insert* surviving

37a ANGAS
line 38 *for* 1871 *read* 1876

39b APLIN
line 3 *for* Cowl, *read* Combe
line 7 *for* Burton *read* Bourton

41a ARCHER
line 23 *for* elected *read* the member
line 24 *for* to *read* in *and for* 1855
read 1851-55

line 27 *for* Deloraine *read* again
line 31 *for* resigned *read* was absent
line 34 *for* 1866, however, *read* 1856
line 36 *after* October *insert* 1866

43b ARCHIBALD
line 38 *for* 'ease' *read* 'case'

46b line 30 *for* Australia's *read* New South Wales's

49a ARMITAGE
line 14 *delete* at Madras
line 17 *for* In July 1855 *read* That year
line 19 *after* Wales. *insert* He arrived in Sydney in January 1855.

50a ARMSTRONG
line 3 *for* on Jersey *read* at St Peter, Jersey,
line 4 *after* Islands *insert* , sixth son of Francis Wheeler Armstrong and his wife Esther Françoise, née Quett(e)ville *and for* 1848 *read* 1847
line 11 *after* Turkey. *insert* On 20 August 1857 at St Helier, Jersey, he married Eliza Susannah Mallet. *and for* 1870 *read* 1871

50b line 29 *for* 25 *read* 26 *and after* 1910. *insert* He was survived by two sons and a daughter.

51a ARMSTRONG
line 40 *for* Rupert *read* Robert
line 53 *after* 1871 *insert* -72
line 58 *for* née Elliott, *read* Elliot, née Armstrong,

52a ARMYTAGE
line 47 *for* Geelong *read* the Diocesan
line 48 *after* was *insert* part of

56a ASTLEY
line 6 *for* 1855 *read* 1859

57a ATHERTON
lines 7-8 *for* steamship *Great Britain.* *read* brig *Briton.*

58b ATKIN
line 9 *for* Staffordshire *read* Shropshire
line 39 *for* March *read* January
line 41 *for* On 26 April *read* In

63a AUSTRALIE
line 2 *for* EMILIE *read* EMILY MATILDA

63a AYERS
line 12 *for* 1841 *read* 1840

67b BADGERY
line 5 *for* seventh *read* fourth
line 6 *after* his *insert* second

70b BADHAM
line 28 for *Minemosyne* read *Mnemosyne*

71a lines 17-18 *for* the ... Union *read* are the Badham Building, the Badham room in the union,

71b BAGOT, R.
line 2 *for* in *read* at Fontstown,

72a line 3 *for* Edward *read* Edwards
lines 3-4 *for* Australia as a youth *read* Sydney in 1849

72b lines 29-30 *for* Gregor ... him. *read* Gregory.
line 32 *for* nineties *read* eighties

74a BAILEY
bibliog. line 3 *for* 27 *read* 28

75a BAKER
line 25 *for* Salamons *read* Salomons

76b BAKER, J.
line 43 *for* eight *read* twelve

78b BALCOMBE
line 24 *for* Juanna *read* Juana
line 30 *for* He *read* In 1846 he
lines 31-34 *for* which . . . variants, *read* Chen Chen Gurruck, or Tichingorourke, changing the name

80a BALFE
line 29 *for* -81 *read* -80
line 59 *for* four *read* three

81a BALFOUR
line 39 *for* south *read* north

93a BARKER
line 38 *for* 1868 *read* 1867

95a BARKLY
line 42 *for* 'Left' . . . Conservatives *read* radicals and ministerialists
lines 48-49 *for* was . . . in *read* died on 17

109b BARRY
lines 33-34 *delete* and . . . off

111b BARRY, Z.
line 2 *after* born *insert* on 1 February 1827
line 25 *for* 1862 *read* 1861

116a BASSETT
*line 35 *for* About 1853 *read* In 1854

116b lines 60-61 *for* London ... 1890) *read* Edinburgh (M.R.C.S.; M.D., 1880)

120b BAYLIS
line 6 *for* 21 June 1831 *read* 27 June 1832
line 7 for *Edinburgh Castle* read *City of Edinburgh*

122a BAYLY
line 16 *for* objected to *read* disliked *and for* shows. *read* shows;

lines 17-18 *for* His . . . reflect *read* but he won several prizes, reflecting

123b BEAN
lines 24-25 *delete* the . . . [q.v.],

124a line 41 *for* John *read* Evelyn

124b line 2 *for* He was the *read* With J. L. Cuthbertson [q.v.] he was a

137b BELMORE
line 8 *for* Scone *read* Muswellbrook

139b BENJAMIN
lines 12-15 *for* officially . . . [q.v.] *read* was present at the formal opening of Princes Bridge

147b BEOR
line 59 *for* July *read* June

150b BERRY
line 8 *delete* [q.v.]

152b BERRY
line 10 *for* 12 *read* 2

157a BEST, J.
line 7 for *Vibilier* read *Vibilia*

157b line 51 *for* Adrian's *read* Aidan's

165b BIRD
line 46 *for* 1897 *read* December 1896

177b BLACKMORE
bibliog. line 1 *before* Early *insert* M.E.P. Sharp et al,

181b BLAND
line 1 *for* RIVETT *read* REVETT (RIVETT)
line 5 *for* Mary *read* Emma
line 6 *for* Rivett *read* Revett

182a line 6 *for* opthalmia *read* ophthalmia

190b BONWICK
line 4 *for* child *read* son

195a BOOTHBY
line 49 *for* 121 *read* 84

197a BOOTHBY
line 20 *for* Boothy *read* Boothby

197b line 32 *for* 1864 *read* 1861
line 47 *for* 1866 *read* 1864

203a BOWEN
line 21 *for* 1856 *read* 1854 *and delete* Roma

206b lines 31-32 *for* four . . . daughter *read* one son and four daughters

207a bibliog. line 3 *for* Carnavon *read* Carnarvon

208b BOWMAN
line 15 *for* Carey's *read* Cary's [q.v.]

218b BRAIM
line 47 *for* 1867 *read* 1866

line 49 *for* Islington *read* Ilsington
line 53 *for* September *read* November

221b BRAZIER
line 3 *delete* McMillan
line 5 *for* Eliza, née Warren *read* Mary, née McMillan

239a BRODRIBB
line 8 *for* -96 *read* -95 *and for* rector *read* vicar

240b BROMBY
line 61 *for* 1863 *read* 1864

244a BROOKE
lines 44-45 *for* E. *read* C. *and for* (later Vezin [q.v.]) *read* [q.v. Charles Young]

245a BROOKE, J.
line 4 *for* and . . . Brooke. *read* Brooke and his wife May Ann, née Wright.
line 16 *for* In . . . Victoria *read* Brooke arrived in Melbourne in April 1853

245b line 39 *after* 1902. *insert* In 1849 he had married Harriet Williamson; they had three sons and three daughters.

253a BROUGH
line 25 *for* (b. 1848) *read* [q.v.]

254b BROUGHTON
line 19 *for* Murrumbidgee *read* Lachlan

263b BROWN, N.
line 4 *for* second *read* eldest
line 5 *after* Brown *insert* , cooper, *and for* 1829 *read* 1833
lines 6-7 *for* keeper . . . store *read* a storekeeper
lines 11-12 *delete* where . . . migrated,
line 40 *for* the . . . November *read* a poll on 19 December

264a line 35 *for* 1902 *read* 1900-03

273a BROWNRIGG
line 27 *for* In that year *read* On 11 October 1862
line 28 *for* Georgina *read* Georgiana Eliza

277a BRUCE, J. M.
lines 19-20 *for* Presbyterian *read* Baptist
line 22 *for* four *read* three

280a BRUNTON
line 44 *for* 1860 *read* 1868

282a BUCHANAN
line 26 *for* Schools *read* School

283b BUCHANAN
line 24 *for* South Eastern *read* Southern

284a BUCHANAN, N.
line 28 *for* Thompson *read* Thomson

284b line 11 *for* 1865 *read* 1864

288a BUCKLAND, J.
line 16 *for* Frederick *read* Frederic
line 18 *for* 13 *read* 3

296a BUNCLE
bibliog. line 2 *for* 2 *read* 27

297b BUNNY
line 29 *for* linguistic *read* linguist

299b BURGESS
line 6 *for* civil *read* civic

301b BURKE
lines 10-12 *for* When it . . . he held *read* Discharged at his own request in June 1848, he took up

308b BURT
bibliog. line 1 *for* McClemens *read* McClemans

310b BUSSELL
line 4 *for* fifth *read* sixth

311a lines 33-34 *for* St Mary's . . . 1834. *read* Wonnerup on 22 August 1850.
line 37 *for* soon *read* later
line 52 *delete* at Bunker Bay

311b line 40 *for* 2 December 1875 *read* 1 December 1876
lines 42 and 48 *for* Isaac *read* Isaacs
line 54 *for* On . . . he *read* He
line 55 *for* 1882. *read* 1882, at Brookhampton farm, near Bridgetown.

314b BUTLER
line 7 *for* 1822 *read* 1821
line 36 *for* In 1878 *read* On 29 October 1877

315b BUTLER
line 3 *delete* surgeon
line 7 *for* four *read* five

316a line 42 *for* 1884 *read* 1885

320b BUZACOTT
line 3 *for* July *read* August

323a BYRNES
line 27 *after* Taylor *insert* [q.v.]

336a CAMERON
line 2 *for* 1874 *read* 1875

338b CAMERON, E.
line 13 *for* 1863 *read* 1860

341a CAMPBELL
lines 28-29 *for* by 1850 *read* in 1843
line 48 *after* the *insert* Sydney branch of the

347a CAMPBELL, W.
line 3 *for* in *read* on 17 July 1810 at

347b lines 9-10 *for* Macarthur's . . . Mountains *read* Macarthurs' Richlands station near Goulburn

348b line 11 *after* died *insert* in London

348b CANI
line 8 *for* Ferreti *read* Ferretti

351a CANTERBURY
line 11 *for* 23 *read* 24
line 12 *for* Thomson *read* Tomson

351a CARANDINI
line 10 *after* Jerome *insert* Carandini
lines 10-11 *delete* di Carandini
line 11 *for* 1814? *read* 1803

352a *before* CARBONI *insert* Cross Reference CARANDINI, ROSINA; *see* PALMER, ROSINA

352a CARBONI
line 1 *for* 1820 *read* 1817
line 3 *for* 24 June 1820 *read* 15 December 1817

357a CARR-BOYD
line 4 *delete* Dr
line 7 *for* There *read* At Campbell Town

363a CARTER, G.
line 1 *for* 1831 *read* 1830

363b line 36 *delete* aged 71

364a CARY
line 39 *for* 1839 *read* 1838

365a CASEY
line 21 *for* Mandurang *read* Sandhurst
line 23 *delete* He . . . and
line 24 *for* in *read* In *and after* -80 *insert* he

366a CASEY, R.
line 39 *for* Terrick *read* Terrick Terrick
line 47 *for* 1892 *read* 1893

366b lines 15-16 *delete* remained . . . he
line 17 *for* sons *read* children

367b CASSELL
line 23 *for* Bereford *read* Bruford

370b CATHCART
lines 21-22 *for* Edward Price George Darrell *read* George Frederick Price Darrell

373b CHALLINOR
line 1 *delete* ?
line 2 *after* born *insert* on 22 June 1814
lines 6-7 *for* With . . . he *read* He
lines 11-12 *for* the Limestone area (later Ipswich) *read* Ipswich
line 17 *for* After . . . he *read* He

375b CHALMERS
line 59 *for* 1886 *read* 1885

376b CHALMERS
lines 2-3 *for* February *read* September

380b CHAPMAN, H.
line 3 *after* born *insert* on 21 July 1803
382a line 8 *for* 1867 *read* 1868

384a CHARLES
line 33 *for* about 1853 *read* on 30 May 1855

391b CHIRNSIDE
line 3 *for* Berwickshire *read* Cockburnspath, East Lothian,
line 5 *for* Fairs *read* Fair
line 37 *before* building *insert* later
lines 38-39 *delete* in the 1850s
line 42 *for* and *read* ; his son later acquired
392b line 8 *for* Bigbie *read* Begbie

393a CHOMLEY, A.
line 20 *for* infancy. *read* infancy, and five daughters.

394a CHRISTIE
**lines 54-56 *for* 1844 . . . secretary. *read* 1841-42 was secretary-treasurer of the Australian Club.

395b CHRISTISON
line 25 *for* Tovey *read* Lovey
line 28 *for* 1884 *read* 1880 in London *and after* Mary *insert* Godsall

398b CLARK
line 44 *for* 1875 *read* 1874
399a line 21 *for* Alexandra *read* Alexandrina
line 22 *for* née Dickson, *read* Dickson, née McGregor, whom he had married on 1 July 1874,

399b CLARK
line 30 *after* and *insert* South Hobart in
400b line 7 *for* Edmond *read* Edmund

403a CLARK
line 1 *after* London *insert* , son of Daniel Clark and his wife Susanna, née Strudwicke

404a CLARK
line 44 *for* 3 *read* 30 *and for* 1876 *read* 1877
line 49 *for* 15 *read* 16

407b CLARK, R.
line 17 *delete* after two years
lines 18-19 *for* In 1863 . . . Kernighan, *read* There, on 26 June 1862 at the Wesleyan parsonage he married Sarah Jane Kernaghan,

409a CLARKE
line 15 *after* Royal *insert* Military

412b CLARKE, G.
line 19 *after* Martha *insert* Clarke

414b CLARKE, J.
lines 18-19 *for* provided illustrations for *read* published
415a line 8 *for* Waterloo *read* Woolloomooloo
line 13 *after* Jones, *insert* née Gater, *and for* about *read* on 10 April
line 14 *for* three *read* four
line 15 *for* three *read* two

415b CLARKE
lines 13-18 *for* In 1900 . . . president *read* In 1898-99 she was a member of the Women's Hospital Committee and in 1900 president of the Alliance Française,
line 19 *after* Children, *insert* and

417b CLARKE
lines 48-50 *for* none . . . traced. *read* at least two married in Victoria and survived him.

419b CLARKE, W.
line 1 *for* b. 1843 *read* 1843-1903
420a line 60 *after* 1886. *insert* He died at Cape Town on 9 March 1903 and in the same week his only son William Mortimer was killed in a riot.

420b CLARKE, W. B.
line 35 for *Exequaile* read *Exequiale*

423a CLARKE
line 50 *for* Cobram *read* Cobran

426b CLIBBORN
line 46 *for* cousin *read* witness at the marriage

430a CLISBY
line 28 *after* borgian). *insert* She married Henry Edward Walker at Trinity Church, Adelaide, on 25 February 1848.

436b COHEN
line 7 *for* five *read* four *and for* three *read* four

439a COLE
lines 53-54 *for* Jordan . . . Hobart *read* Jorden, of Lauderdale, New Town, Tasmania

443a COLLINS
line 42 *for* Gwendolyne *read* Gwendoline
443b line 17 *for* Robert was *read* Robert and William were
lines 18-19 *for* He was *read* They were
line 21 *for* He was *read* They were

line 22 *for* his *read* the
bibliog. line 2 *for* 1934 *read* 1923

452a COOPER
line 40 *for* 1855 *read* 1855-56

465a CORRIGAN
lines 22-23 *for* smooothly . . . division.
read smoothly.

468b COTTEE
line 60 *for* civil *read* civic
469a **line 2 *for* him *read* the trade
bibliog. line 1 for *One* read *A*

471a COUVREUR
lines 5-6 *for* two . . . daughters *read*
her sisters

473b COWIE
line 26 *for* on 9 June *read* in August

478b COWPER
lines 13-14 *for* and . . . quarrel *read* .
He had already quarrelled
line 19 *for* 1859 *read* 1858

482b COX
line 42 *for* Soarr *read* Scarr
483a lines 23-24 *for* the first *read* an early

486b COX
line 9 *for* education *read* Church
schools

489b CRACKNELL
line 3 *for* Salamons *read* Salomons

493b CREWS
bibliog. line 9 *for* 1860-80 *read* 1859-
69

495b CRISP
line 48 *delete* 8
bibliog. lines 4-5 *for* 4 June . . . 1916
read 7 Dec 1889, 8 May 1897,
4 June, 23 July 1898, 5 Nov 1963,
7 July 1966

498b CROSBY
line 33 *for* In 1859 *read* On 14 February 1857

503a CROWTHER
line 33 *for* opthalmology *read* oph-
thalmology
line 48 *for* Rosa *read* Elizabeth Rosaline

503b line 22 *for* 1878-84 *read* 1878-86 and
1897-1909
line 23 *for* 1886-1909 *read* 1886-
97
line 42 *for* 1881 *read* 1882

506a CUNINGHAM
line 53 *delete* less
506b line 1 *delete* successful as
lines 4-5 *for* concluded . . . premature.
read was associated with the 1879-80
Strathleven shipment.
line 7 *for* daughter *read* sister

509a CURRAN
line 1 *for* Julian *read* J. E. Tenison-
509b line 23 *for* Julian *read* Tenison-

509b CURRIE
lines 14-19 *for* he . . . Melbourne.
read , with W. A. Boyd and Thomas
Elder Boyd, junior, he bought the
Elizabeth and from January 1855,
with T. E. Boyd only, traded in coas-
tal, New Zealand and Chinese waters.
The partners established a shipping
company in Melbourne and in the
1860s bought at least nine vessels.

511b CURRIE
line 18 *for* built *read* leased

512b CUSTANCE
line 57 *for* Lawrie *read* Lowrie

514a CUTHBERT, J.
line 8 *for* 19 *read* 29
514b bibliog. line 3 *for* 9 *read* 10

Volume 4: 1851-1890 D-J

2a D'ALBERTIS
line 12 *for* 1876 *read* 1872
line 22 *for* April *read* November
line 30 *after* November *insert* 1875
and after Somerset *insert* , Queensland,

9b DALLEY
bibliog. line 14 *for* Angus *read* Augustus

23b DARVALL
line 45 *for* 1850- *read* 1851-

27b DAVIES
line 20 *for* Melbourne *read* Sydney
lines 21-24 *for* Hebrew . . . months.
read police force. In November 1840
he was appointed chief constable at
Penrith and on 16 December married
Elizabeth Ellis. He resigned his post
next March when his foster-brother
Edward [q.v.1 Davis] was hanged as a
bushranger.
line 40 *delete* married . . . and
line 55 *delete* George
line 56 *after* Auber *insert* George

29b DAVIES
line 3 *for* Tetfield *read* Tetbury
lines 25-27 *for* most . . . second. *read*
four of six sons and two of six daughters of his first marriage, and one of
four sons and the one daughter of his
second marriage.
line 39 *for* five *read* eight
lines 59-64 *for* London . . . Jessie *read*
Bank of Australasia. He moved to
Melbourne, joined the London Char-
tered Bank of Australia and later the
Australian Deposit and Mortgage

Bank Ltd, becoming manager in 1883. He had married Sarah Ann Staples in 1877 but she died in 1879, survived by their infant son; in 1887 he married Jessie

30a line 1 *for* MacMurtrie *read* McMurtrie

lines 2-3 *delete* became . . . He

30b line 50 *for* second . . . Boyle *read* wife

line 51 *for* two *read* three

line 62 *for* two *read* three *and for* seven *read* six

31a line 8 *for* his . . . Malvern *read* Windaree, Williams Road, Toorak,

line 49 *for* three *read* four

line 50 *for* thirteen *read* fourteen

38b DE BOOS
line 21 *for* -73 *read* -71

43a DE MESTRE
line 59 *after* George *insert* T. *and after* Rowe *delete* [q.v.]

44b DENIEHY
line 32 *for* 1844 *read* 1845

45a line 19 *for* world *read* word

46a line 3 *for* Jamieson *read* Jameson

46b bibliog. lines 11-12 delete *Bathurst* . . . 1865;

57a DERHAM
line 23 *for* 1856 *read* 1854

64b DEXTER
line 18 *for* 1857 *read* 1858

67b DIBBS
line 16 *for* February *read* January

79a DOBSON
line 21 *for* March *read* December

line 26 *for* 1877 *read* 1887

80a DODDS
line 22 *for* 1878-87 *read* 1878-86 *and after* Hobart *insert* , and in 1886-87 South Hobart,

81b DODERY
line 48 *for* Westmorland *read* Longford (Westmorland)

line 63 *for* elder *read* younger

line 64 *for* younger *read* elder

83a DONAGHY
line 3 *for* After *read* Before

lines 4-5 *delete* John . . . John

line 6 *for* were *read* had been

line 15 *for* 1868 *read* 1886

87b DOUGLAS
line 20 *for* (1840-1927) *read* (1839-1926)

88a line 17 *for* -70 *read* -71

line 18 *for* 1870-71 *read* 1871-72

89b DOUGLAS
line 18 *for* nominated *read* elected

line 21 *for* held the seat *read* sat in the reconstituted council

line 34 *for* October *read* December

93a DOUGLASS
line 17 *for* March *read* April

95b DOWIE
line 23 *after* Walker *insert* [q.v.]

106b DU CANE
lines 25-26 *delete* He . . . Domain.

108b DU FAUR
line 2 *for* Tonkin *read* Donkin

113a DUFFY
line 49 *for* Of *read* Duffy's eldest son was John Gavan [q.v.]; of

115b DUNCAN, J.
line 11 *for* o *read* to

116b DUNN
line 7 *for* Taunton *read* Tawton

line 21 *for* Anne, *read* Ann, née Rowe (d. 1870), whom he had married in 1828,

117a line 20 *for* mill *read* office

line 23 *for* in 1870 *read* on 27 February 1872

line 64 *for* enlarged *read* rebuilt

119a DURACK
**line 3 *after* eldest *insert* son

123a DYMOCK
lines 9-10 *delete* a councillor . . . University

127a EBSWORTH
line 4 *after* his *insert* second

lines 10-24 *for* Frederick . . . company. *read* Frederick reached Sydney in the *Hashemy* on 25 January 1839 and in October set up as a woolbroker in Pitt Street. He also acted as agent for the Australian Agricultural Co. which his father had helped to promote; his half-brother Henry Thomas Ebsworth was secretary of the company in England and his cousins James Edward and Thomas Lindsey Ebsworth were respectively its assistant commissioner and accountant in New South Wales.

line 33 *for* Royal Exchange *read* Sydney Exchange Co.

line 39 *for* 18 *read* 19

132a EGGLESTON
line 2 *for* in *read* on 2

132b line 14 *for* three *read* two *and for* one daughter *read* two daughters

136b ELLERY
line 7 *for* 1873 *read* 1870 as a captain

line 8 *for* Corps *read* and Signal Corps;

lines 8-9 *delete* (Submarine . . . until
line 10 *for* 1889 *read* December 1888

137a ELLIOTT
line 12 *for* Westrip *read* Neestrip

149b FALCONER
**line 2 *after* was *insert* born on 27 November 1818 at Muirkirk, Ayrshire, Scotland,
**line 3 *after* Falconer, *insert* ironworks manager, and his wife Helen, née Gillies. William senior was a
**lines 4-5 *delete* of Ayrshire, Scotland

150a **line 44 *delete* St John's Church,
**line 51 *after* Church *insert* , New Town,

150b FALKINER
**line 3 *after* Beechwood, *insert* Nenagh,

154b FARNELL
line 25 *for* January *read* February

155a bibliog. line 13 *for* 1893 *read* 1883

155b FARR
line 40 *for* -95 *read* -96

157b FAUCETT
line 28 *for* November *read* October
line 34 *for* 10 *read* 20

159b FAULDING
line 31 *delete* [q.v.]

176a FITZGERALD
line 12 *for* Lane *read* Love

182a FITZHARDINGE
line 11 *delete* erroneously

186b FLEMING
line 18 *delete* [q.v.]

187b FLEMING
line 58 *for* 1872 *read* 1870

193a FOLEY
line 51 *for* House *read* Horse

199a FORSTER, W.
line 6 *for* 1816. *read* 1817,

207b FOSTER
bibliog. line 14 *for* 1893 *read* 1883

216b FRASER, Sir Simon
line 46 *for* Anne *read* Anna
line 51 *for* 1897 *read* 1885

229b GARDINER
line 18 *for* after . . . leave *read* skipped bail

232a GARLICK
line 19 *for* 1874- *read* 1832?-

233b GARRAN
line 45 *for* point *read* extent

234b GARRARD
line 37 *delete* in 1895-98
line 38 *after* and *insert* from 1895

235a GARRETT
line 32 *for* 1864- *read* 1865-

235b line 37 for Craigon read Creagan, whom he had married on 30 September 1856,

237b GARVAN
line 58 *for* 1898 *read* 1908

239b GAUNT
line 4 *for* a daughter *read* two daughters
line 5 *for* Arthur *read* Archer

240b GEOGHEGAN
line 10 *for* Easter . . . 1835 *read* 21 February 1830

241b GEORGE
line 44 *for* May *read* March

243b GIBLIN
line 13 *for* John *read* Henry
line 38 *delete* for nine months *and for* 1870 *read* 1870-72

245a GILBERT
line 20 *for* Mann *read* Manns

245b line 14 *for* Wowingragang *read* Wowingragong
line 16 *delete* who . . . them

246a GILES
line 5 *after* Hospital *insert* (where he was admitted as William Ernest Powell Giles)

246b line 39 *for* Egerton *read* Warburton

248b GILL
line 27 *delete* John *and after* Appel *insert* [q.v.]

250b GILLBEE
line 17 *for* Philip *read* Phillips

253b GLADMAN
line 35 *for* 1882 *read* 1886

260a GOLDIE
line 4 *delete* Sir

264a GOODLET
line 28 *for* 1903 *read* 1913
line 36 *for* Boys' School *read* Academy

267a GOOLD
line 38 *for* editior *read* editor

267b GORDON
lines 23-24 after November insert 1853

269a GORDON, A.
line 2 *after* born *insert* on 14 October 1815

272a GORE
line 6 *for* 1879 *read* 1878

274a GORMLY
line 13 *for* In *read* On 28 December
line 14 *for* Mary *read* Margaret

278b GOYDER
line 1 *for* WOODROOFE *read* WOODROFFE

279b line 3 *for* prevailed *read* prevails

282b GRAHAM
lines 42-43 *for* a founding *read* an early

286b GRAY
lines 5-6 *for* by . . . migrated *read* in 1843 was transported *and after* Town *insert* for subornation
line 57 *for* his wife died, *read* the death of his wife Mary, née Newton, whom he had married in April 1848,

290b GREENUP
line 15 *after* April *insert* 1850

294a GREGORY
line 13 *for* Charles *read* Henry

294b lines 2-3 *for* 1863 . . . 1879. *read* 1863, on 12 March 1875 was replaced as surveyor-general by W. A. Tully [q.v.], and became geological surveyor.

295a **line 18 *for* Rainsworth *read* Rainworth
line 39 *for* Cantini *read* Catani
line 55 *for* Gascoigne *read* Gascoyne

295b line 17 *for* four *read* five
lines 23-24 *for* 21 August *read* 23 October

299a GRIBBLE
line 7 *for* at 20 *read* on 4 February 1868

303a GRIMWADE
line 16 *for* 1888- *read* 1889-

305a GROOM
line 62 *for* 1859- *read* 1860-

305b GRUBB
line 3 *after* London *insert* , son of William Grubb and his wife Hannah, née Rockliff

306b GUERARD
line 39 *for* Wetterboro *read* Wetterbord

307a bibliog. line 11 *for* ML *read* Dixson Lib

308b GUNTHER
line 3 *for* 28 *read* 25
line 21 *for* 1867- *read* 1868-

311a GUTHRIE
line 6 *for* bought *read* leased

313a HACK
lines 7-8 *delete* by . . . overland

318b HALE
line 47 *for* resigned *read* went to England

319a HALES
line 10 *for* Rocke *read* Roche

327a HALLORAN
line 4 *for* his . . . (Laura) *read* Lydia
line 5 *after* Hall *insert* (?)

329a HAM
line 18 *for* 10 March *read* 8 March

333a HAMMOND
line 29 *for* 1876 *read* 1878

347a HARGRAVES
bibliog. line 8 *for* 10 *read* 38

355b HART
lines 46-47 *delete* where . . . acres

356b HART
line 6 *after* November *insert* 1902
line 9 *for* 17 *read* 7
line 15 *for* twelve *read* eleven
line 17 *after* married *insert* a widow *and after* Noble *insert* , née Keam

358b HASSELL
line 6 *delete* [q.v.]

359b line 25 *for* Ethyl *read* Ethel

360b HAWKER
line 20 *for* 1811- *read* 1821-

362a HAY
line 4 *after* runs *insert* .
lines 5-6 *delete* and as . . . district.

365a HAYNES
line 15 *for* W. T. *read* W. H.

385a HERLITZ
**line 3 *for* Niese, Saxony, Germany *read* Neisse, Silesia, Prussia

386b HERZ
line 2 *delete* the first committee of
line 3 *for* Musical Association *read* Association of Professional Musicians,
lines 6-8 *for* the twenty-five . . . founding of *read* twelve who founded

389b HIGGINS
line 8 *for* Victorian *read* Victoria

390b HIGHETT
lines 4-5 *for* Thomas Austin [q.v.] *read* William Harding
line 17 *for* four *read* five *and for* two daughters. *read* one daughter.
line 45 *for* near Benalla. *read* , Maindample.

406b HODGSON, C.
lines 11-12 *for* died . . . Hakodate *read*

died at Pau *and after* 1865 *insert* , leaving a wife and daughter

408b HOFFNUNG
line 29 *for* 1857 *read* 1858

414a HOLT, T.
line 8 *for* 1822-32 *read* 1832-42

416a HOLYMAN
line 37 *for* 1883 *read* 1882

417b HOOLEY
line 3 *for* 3 October *read* 30 September
418a line 46 *for* May 1869 *read* April 1868
418b line 32 *after* wife, *insert* one of his

423b HORDERN
line 38 *for* Milton *read* Wilton
line 39 *for* and *read* , Picton, and in 1887 to build

424b HORNE, T.
lines 2-3 *for* in London . . . Horne; *read* on 8 June 1800 at Chiswick, Middlesex, England, eldest son of Rev. Thomas Horne and his wife Cecilia Clementina Eliza, née Zoffany;
line 10 *delete* attorney-general,
line 12 *after* Maria *insert* née Hyriott, whom he had married in 1826,

427a HORSFALL
line 18 *for* Carrington *read* Carington
line 43 *for* 300 *read* 200

428a HOSE
line 2 *after* born *insert* on 24 September 1826
line 3 *delete* Rev.
line 16 *for* 1854 *read* 1855

429b HOSKINS
bibliog. line 9 *for* -1893 *read* -1883

443a HUMBLE, W.
line 3 *for* Whitby *read* Thornton Steward
443b line 31 *for* Mary *read* Emma
line 32 *for* in 1861 *read* on 22 July 1865

447b HUNT, J.
bibliog. line 2 *for* 1971 *read* 1970

449a HUNTER
lines 13-14 *for* but . . .raise *read* and raised

456b INGHAM
*line 42 *for* deputy- *read* judicial

458b INNES
line 52 *for* Campbell Town *read* South Esk

459a line 16 *for* 1878 *read* 1880

460b IRELAND
line 1 *for* 1816 *read* 1815
line 2 *after* born *insert* on 27 October 1815
line 12 *for* 1852 *read* 1853

466b JACK
lines 25-26 *for* Simpson, née Love *read* Love, née Simpson

471a JARDINE
lines 18-19 *for* government resident *read* police magistrate
line 20 *for* resident *read* magistrate
line 27 *for* Sydney Grammar *read* The King's
lines 45-48 *for* acted . . . available. *read* was appointed police magistrate in 1868.
471b line 8 *for* November *read* October

472b JEANNERET
lines 49-50 *for* 1887-94 *read* 1887-89 and 1891-94

486a JOHNSTON, J. S.
line 24 *for* Busten *read* Austen

492a JOSEPH
lines 7-8 *for* native languages *read* the Maori language

Volume 5: 1851-1890 K-Q

xiiia AUTHORS
after KEITH, B. H.: *Morrison, G. in-sert* KEMPE, H.: *Mortlock.*
xiiib line 16 for *Loder* read *Loader*
xva line 25 *for* RODGERS *read* ROGERS

17b KERFERD
lines 4-6 *for* member of . . . and Mexico, *read* book-keeper,
lines 7-9 *delete* Although . . . Collegiate
18a lines 1-5 *for* Institute . . . Victoria. *read* Unhappily married, Joseph took a position in a merchant house at Zacatecas, Mexico, in 1843 and began trading on his own account. After being employed as a boilermaker and in two Liverpool merchants' offices, George migrated to Victoria.
lines 7-12 *delete* Most accounts . . . parent company.

20b KERNOT
lines 20-21 *delete* and the . . . chair there

24b KIDD
line 10 *for* June *read* August

25a KIMPTON
line 28 *after* Charles *insert* Leslie

29b KING, P.
line 8 for *Adventurer* read *Adventure*

34b KINTORE
line 1 for SIR read EARL OF,
line 11 for earl read duke

41b KRANEWITTER
**line 55 for 15 read 25

58a LANDSBOROUGH
line 8 for magisrate read magistrate

60a LANGHAM
line 33 for Cakubau's read Cakobau's

61b LANGRIDGE
line 3 for William read John

68a LASSETTER
line 32 for 1894 read 1895
line 46 for in read on 19 August

68a LATHAM
line 2 after born insert on 20 July 1839

68b line 60 after cemetery. insert He was survived by his daughter Bertha Martha and a son, Lambert, of his second marriage.

70a LAWES
lines 50-51 for seven sons read six children

76a LEE, D.
author for THERESA read THERESE

83a LEVIEN
line 8 for a . . . Geelong read Geelong Grammar School

83b line 38 for James read John

94b LIVERSIDGE
bibliog. line 4 for 1961 read 1968

99b LOFTUS
line 14 for a peer read 'a peer'

100a bibliog. line 1 for governors read governor

100a LONG
line 17 for built read later bought

102b LORIMER
line 14 for Swyre read Swire and for Son read Sons

105a LOUREIRO
line 6 for a Belgian girl related to read the sister of
line 53 for Uffizzi read Uffizi

107b LUCAS
line 26 for first cousin read family connexion

113a LUXTON
line 20 for In read On 3 September

117b LYSTER
author for THERESA read THERESE

121a MACANSH
line 11 for in 1843 read about 1846
line 14 delete , in 1845
line 24 delete and Albilah, *and after* 1875 insert and Albilbah in 1880

124b MACARTHUR, W.
line 14 for wool read sheep

127a MACBAIN
line 19 delete [q.v.]

132b MCCOMBIE
line 6 for March read April

133b MCCONNEL
line 45 for John read James

134a MCCOY
line 50 for Airey read Airy

136a MCCRACKEN
line 1 for 1815 read c.1813

136b line 39 for 70 read 72
line 46 for sons, read son
line 47 for Collier, read nephew Coiler

142b MCCULLOCH
line 28 for Wright read [F.A.] Wright [q.v.]

143a MCCULLOCH, W.
line 38 for Wright read [F.A.] Wright [q.v.]

147a MACDONALD
bibliog. line 1 for McAlister read MacAlister

153b MACFARLANE
line 40 for and four sons read , four sons and a daughter

161a MCILRAITH, T.
line 46 for in read at Maxwelltown, Dumfriesshire,

168b MACKAY
line 16 for In . . . Melbourne read Describing himself as widowed, on 30 November 1861 at Fitzroy
line 17 for O'Shannasy read O'Shannassy

169a line 32 delete first
lines 33-34 for two sons and three daughters read three sons and two daughters

170b MACKENZIE
line 14 for 1842 read 1841
line 17 for 1844 read 1843
line 22 for 2 November 1844 read 1 August (with Catholic rites) and 1 September (with Presbyterian forms) 1845

171a lines 5-6 delete sold . . . and
lines 23-24 delete but . . . made

172b MACKIE
line 50 *after* Horsham *delete* where
and insert .
line 51 *for* in December 1860 *read*
In September 1861
line 52 *after* Lyon *insert* Williamson
at Geelong

174b MCKINLAY
line 2 *for* 16 *read* 26
line 5 *for* Mary *read* Catherine

175a lines 8-9 *for* reached . . . Buchanan.
read established a depot at Lake
Buchanan in mid-October.
line 11 *for* William *read* Charles
line 19 *after* December *insert* at
Cooper's Creek
lines 22-24 *for* to the Gulf . . . *Victoria. read* back to his depot, then
northward.
lines 25-27 *for* returned . . . Eyre.
read had been instructed to explore
north and west of Lake Eyre.
line 29 *for* turned north. *read* made
for the Gulf of Carpentaria in hope of
meeting H.M.V.S. *Victoria.*

175b line 2 *for* 22 *read* 17
lines 31-34 *for* favoured . . . Rivers.
read found patches of good country
south-east of the Adelaide River.
line 39 *for* July *read* August
line 40 for *Pioneer* read *Beatrice*
line 41 *after* Australia *insert* , reporting favourably on Port Darwin and
Anson Bay
line 51 *for* 17 January *read* 31 December

180a MCLACHLAN
line 2 *for* Mary, née Bruce. *read*
Marion, née McDugald.

181a line 4 *after* his *insert* second *and for*
Smith *read* Bruce, late Smith, whom
he had married on 12 March 1858 at
St Kilda,

181b MACLANACHAN
line 10 *for* -83 *read* -84

182a MCLAURIN
line 3 *for* 2 *read* 20

189a MACMAHON
line 11 *for* Royal Irish Constabulary in
1851. *read* Dublin County Militia
Regiment.
lines 14-15 *for* in October *read* on
18 November

192a MCNAB
line 10 *for* admitted *read* ordained

193b MCNEIL
line 1 *for* 1857 *read* 1855
line 3 *for* 1857 *read* 1855 *and for*
Dingwell *read* Dingwall
line 4 *for* Inverness-shire *read* Rossshire

line 5 *for* McNeil *read* MacNeil

196b MCPHILLAMY
line 12 *for* 1828. *read* 1838.

201a MAIS
line 30 *for* Institute *read* Institution

206b MANNING
**line 36 *for* Wanagabra *read* Warragaburra

208b MANNING
line 1 *for* August *read* March

211b MARKS
line 1 *for* 1827 *read* 1826
line 3 *for* 1827 *read* 1826
line 4 *for* eldest *read* second

212a MARSDEN
line 3 *for* at O'Connell Plains, *read*
and baptized at St John's Church,
Parramatta, on 9 March,

216a MARTIN
line 28 for *Literature* read *The beginnings of an Australian literature*
(London, 1898)
line 48 *for* Harriete *read* Harriette

227b MAT(T)HEWS
lines 8-10 *for* under . . . Edinburgh.
read for her farewell Australian season.

236a MELVILLE
line 5 *for* Judiciary *read* Justiciary

236b line 29 *for* 1852 *read* 1853

237a MELVILLE, N.
line 7 *for* Judiciary *read* Justiciary

238b MENDES DA COSTA
lines 26-31 *for* In the 1850s . . .
to Adelaide *read* With his sister, on
4 February 1848

239a MENKENS
**line 2 *for* Varelin *read* Varel

239b bibliog. line 2 *for* 1971 *read* 1970

240a MEREDITH
line 10 *for* September 1860 when
read June 1861 although *and after*
leave *insert* from September 1860
line 13 *for* -70 *read* -71
line 14 *for* -75 *read* -76
lines 21-23 *for* Innes . . . [q.v.]. *read*
Innes [q.v.], and under Reiby [q.v.]
was colonial treasurer from 20 July
1876 to 9 August 1877, and minister
for lands and works from 21 July to 21
August 1876.
line 40 *for* 1832 *read* 1835

241a MEREWETHER
line 34 *for* In *read* On 11 April

243a MESTON
lines 5-7 *delete* ; his . . . Castle

248b MIKLUHO-MAKLAI
line 1 *after* MIKLUHO-MAKLAI,
insert NICHOLAI
250a line 29 *for* favourably *read* unfavour-
ably

252b MILLER
line 41 *for* District *read* Province
line 42 *for* March *read* April *and for*
District *read* Province
line 43 *for* January 1867 *read* 1866

260b MITCHELL
line 63 *for* James *read* Edward
Christopher *and after* Merewether
insert [q.v.]

263a MOCATTA
line 32 *delete* on the Darling Downs
263b lines 10-11 *for* in 1857 *read* on 4
March 1858 *and for* Harriet *read*
Harries Hankin, née

267b MONGER
line 18 *for* He *read* On 21 July 1857
at St James's Church, Westminster,
London, he

269b MONTEFIORE
line 10 *for* 1849 *read* 1853
line 13 *for* Australian *read* Australasian

270a MONTEFIORE
line 5 *after* Hannah *insert* , née Montefiore
270b line 26 *for* B. *read* R.

279a MOORE, M.
lines 3-4 *for* of Irish parents *read*
daughter of James Edward Sullivan
and his wife Bridget Mary, née
Whelan,
279b line 13 *delete* [q.v.]

282a MOORHOUSE
line 12 *for* 1897 *read* 1879

285a MORESBY
line 4 *for* Captain *read* Admiral

287b MORGAN
line 45 *after* D'Arcy *insert* [q.v.]
line 56 *for* 1863 *read* 1883

294a MORRIS
lines 57-58 for *Australasians* read
Australasia

302a MORTLOCK
author *after* bibliography *insert* H.
KEMPE

306b MUELLER
line 4 *for* Schleswig-Holstein *read*
Mecklenburg-Schwerin
308b line 19 *for* 1861 *read* 1871
line 21 *for* 1868 *read* 1869
line 22 *for* 1869 *read* 1879

309b MULLEN
line 9 *for* Jun. & *read* jun. and

310b MULLIGAN
**line 3 *for* Dumgoodland *read*
Drumgooland

315b MURNIN
line 21 *for* Royal Exchange *read*
Sydney Exchange Co.
316a line 1 *for* first *read* second *and after*
Arnold, *insert* née Thomson, whom
he had married on 10 March 1860,
line 5 *for* second *read* first *and after*
Grace *insert* née *and after* Abbott
insert (d. 1856)

316b MURPHY, D.
lines 16-17 *for* the . . . archbishopric
read was granted the title of archbishop *honoris causa*

318a MURPHY, F.
lines 1-2 *delete* Herbert . . . 1912,

330a NEUMAYER
line 2 *for* Kirchenbolanden *read*
Kircheimbolanden

342a NICOLLE
**line 7 *after* in 1853. *insert* On 27
July 1848 at St James's Church,
Westminster, London, he had married Catherine Henrietta Jacobine
Schick (d. 1862).
*lines 8-9 *for* in New . . . 1859; *read*
married a widow Jane Williamson,
née Shearman, on 5 April 1862;
line 10 *delete* two years later
342b lines 38-39 *delete* and remarried

349a OAKDEN
bibliog. line 4 *for* Soc *read* Inst

349b OAKES
line 3 *delete* Rev. *and for* , Wesleyan
read [q.v.]
line 4 *delete* missionary,
lines 43-47 *for* By 1854 . . . 4000
sheep. *read* In the 1850s he had four
runs in the Wellington District
amounting to some 132 400 acres
and capable of carrying 3560 cattle.

353a O'CONNOR, M.
line 25 for *liminem* read *limina*

355a ODDIE
bibliog. line 2 *for* 1885 *read* 1855

361b O'HEA
line 7 *for* 19 *read* 9
lines 21-22 *delete* and . . . to
362a line 30 *for* commander *read* colonel
bibliog. line 3 *for* 'The V.C. of
Timothy O'Hea' *read* Strange new
world, 2nd ed (Syd

366b O'MAHONY
line 44 *after* Quinn *insert* [q.v.]

372a O'REILLY, T.
line 3 *after* Man, *insert* and baptized
on 11 December 1819,

372b ORMOND
line 6 *for* Essen *read* Esson

373a lines 28-30 *for* the . . . 1861 *read*
sections of Bangal station across the
river from Borriyaloak
line 37 *for* Ann *read* Mary

377a OSBORNE
line 23 *for* Bunbery *read* Bunbury
line 26 *for* Jefferies *read* Jeffries

377a OSBURN
line 11 *for* Kaiserwerth *read* Kaiserswerth

385a OWEN
line 27 *delete* chairman of committees
and

393a PALMER
line 10 *for* Sydney *read* Melbourne
line 12 *for* 1842 . . . Melbourne *read*
1842,

393b PALMER, R.
lines 4-5 *for* the Marchese . . . Sazano
read Jerome Carandini, Marquis of
Sarzano,

394b PALMER, T.
line 25 *for* Kalakua *read* Kalakaua

395a PALMERSTON
line 2 *for* was baptized *read* claimed
to have been baptized
line 4 *for* probably *read* and to be
the

395b lines 3-5 *delete* ; more likely . . .
1870
lines 33-34 *delete* by not . . . women
and
line 47 *for* a publican's *read* an architect's

397b PARKER, H.
line 20 *for* built *read* bought and improved

410b PASLEY
line 63 *for* 1800- *read* 1880-

412b PATERSON
line 9 *for* Dabies *read* Dobies
bibliog. line 9 *for* 17 Apr *read* 16
Apr

415b PATTERSON
lines 10-11 *for* outspoken . . . unremarkable, his *read* his administration
was unremarkable, his outspoken and
uncompromising support for

417b PATTISON
line 33 *for* 1866 *read* 1886

428b PELL
line 6 *for* 1783- *read* 1764-

440b PETRIE, T.
line 6 *for* March *read* October

446b PITT
line 6 *for* Eliza *read* Elizabeth *and*
after Laycock *insert* [q.v.]

449b POHLMAN
lines 8-15 *for* and Henry Phillips . . .
10 000 sheep. *read* bought several
thousand sheep and part of Darlington station, near Kyneton, in 1841;
this became Glenhope station. In January 1851 Robert's share of the run
was transferred to Frederick, who
held it until 1857.

465b QUINN
line 9 *for* Pius IX *read* Gregory XVI
line 10 *for* 1847 *read* 1846

467a QUINN
line 17 *for* Cathedral *read* Pro-
Cathedral

Volume 6: 1851-1890 R-Z

4a RAMSAY
line 42 *for* lithology *read* ichthyology

26a RICHARDSON
line 10 *for* 1837 *read* 1838 *and for*
Caroline read *Fergusson*

48b ROBINSON
line 4 *for* gaity *read* gaiety

57a ROPER
line 1 *after* 1822 *insert* ?
line 2 *for* born *read* brought up
line 3 *for* Edward *read* Thomas
line 4 *for* Elizabeth, née Flower *read*
Frances, née Nurse

59a ROSEBY
line 59 *for* -83 *read* -82

59b ROSS
line 1 *after* ANDREW *insert*
HENDRY
line 2 *after* born *insert* on 1 August
1829

65a ROUSE
line 18 *for* runs *read* properties

66a ROWAN
lines 27-28 *for* District . . . Downs.
read District.

69a ROWE
bibliog. line 2 *for* 1971 *read* 1970

73b RUSDEN, H.
line 6 *for* Townshend *read*
Townsend

74a lines 51-52 *for* first . . . Victoria in
read Victorian Cremation Act,

75a RUSSELL
line 39 *for* Three *read* Four

78a RUTHERFORD
line 3 *for* Amhurst *read* Amherst

84a SAMUEL
line 14 *for* store *read* branch
84b line 42 *for* exploiting *read* attempting
to exploit

86a SANDS
lines 24, 29, 62, 63 *for* MacDougall
read McDougall

96b SCOTT, H.
lines 9-10 *for* churchyard . . . Church.
read Church of England cemetery
with Presbyterian forms.

101b SELLHEIM
lines 17-18 *for* Morrisset *read*
Morisset
line 22 *for* Rachael *read* Rachel

115b SHEARER
line 4 *for* Beaufort *read* Stirling

126a SIMPSON
line 4 *for* Wesleyan . . . clergyman
read gentleman,

127a SIMPSON, G.
line 44 *for* 1888- *read* 1889-

136a SLY
line 7 *for* about 1839 *read* on 7 May
1834

138a SMART, T. W.
line 27 *for* Queensland *read* the
Moreton Bay District

149b SMITH
line 62 *for* pthisis *read* phthisis

152a SMITH
line 56 *for* five *read* four
line 57 *for* 1885- *read* 1884-

161a SMITH, W. H.
lines 42-43 *for* in 1884 . . . decade
read afterwards and
161b line 10 *for* 1888 *read* 1884 *and for*
son *read* sons Walter S. and
line 11 *after* him. *insert* He continued
as chairman until 1887.

166a SPEIGHT
line 8 *for* at 19 *read* on 1 May
1860

170a SPENCE
lines 20-21 *for* International *read*
Industrial

174a STANTON
line 16 *for* St Giles . . . Fields. *read*
Lincoln's Inn Fields.
174b bibliog. line 6 *for* 1971 *read* 1970

178b STEINFELD
**line 3 *for* Oberglogan *read* Ober
Glogau

182a STEPHEN
line 56 for *Briellat* read *Breillat*
184b line 20 *for* Thakombau *read* Cakobau
185a line 1 *for* mischievious *read* mischiev-
ous

197a STEPHENS, W.
line 3 *for* Levans *read* Levens
197b line 1 *for* John *read* William
line 2 *for* Levans *read* Levens

204b STRANGWAYS
lines 15-17 *for* Supporting . . . River.
read He supported exploration and
development.

205a STRELE
**lines 2-3 *for* Nassereit *read* Nas-
sereith

205b STREMPEL
line 14 *for* Phillip Jacoq *read* Philipp
Jacob

217a STUTCHBURY
lines 25-26 *for* About . . . son. *read* On
2 August 1820 at St Giles, Cripple-
gate, he had married Hannah Louisa
Barnard who bore him a daughter
Louisa Mary.

219b SUMMERS
line 1 *for* 1827 *read* 1825
line 2 *for* 1827 *read* 1825
line 3 *after* Charlton *insert* Mackrell
220a line 2 *for* 1852 *read* 1854

220b SUMMERS, J.
line 2 *after* Charlton *insert* Mackrell

223a SUTHERLAND, G.
line 33 *for* 1879 *read* 1877

229a SUTTOR
line 19 *for* 1859-64 *read* 1859 and
1860-64
229b line 36 *for* Julia Nina Frances *read*
Julia Frances Nina

255a TENISON-WOODS
**lines 44-46 *delete* and the paper . . .
Australia'

263a THOMAS, Mesac
bibliog. line 2 *for* 1864 *read* 1964

265a THOMPSON
line 7 *for* McCoombie *read* McCombie

266b THOMPSON
lines 2-5 *for* London . . . for *read*
London, son of Samuel Solomon,
tobacco manufacturer, and his wife
Jessie, née Levi. He used the sur-
name
*267a lines 20-25 *for* a widow . . . infant.

read his wife Rose Maria, née Barnett, whom he had married at Fitzroy on 12 February 1868, three daughters and a son John.
bibliog. line 1 *for* Top *read* Tony

270a THOMSON
lines 56-57 *after* was *insert* secretary and *and for* Sydney branch. *read* association.
270b line 14 *for* admission *read* re-admission

273a THORN
lines 13-14 *after* Uniacke *delete* , Oxley's [q.v.] companion

276a TIGHE
line 3 *after* born *insert* on 3 March 1827
line 5 *for* 17th *read* 28th *and after* Regiment *insert* , and his wife Sarah, née McNamara
lines 5-8 *for* probably . . . 28th Regiment; *read* , with his family and some of his regiment, reached Sydney on 4 February 1836 in the *Susan* and was stationed at Parramatta;

279a TINLINE
line 8 *after* Murray *insert* , in memory of his mother's family name,

280a TODD
line 4 *for* eldest *read* second
281b lines 45-46 *for* were the . . . show *read* consistently showed
line 47 *after* -general *insert* (retired June 1905)
lines 48-50 *for* although . . . 1905. *read* despite the Public Officers Retirement Act (1903), he did not leave the State public service until 1907.

284a TOOHEY
line 58 *for* colony. *read* colony'.

287b TOOTH, W.
line 16 *delete* , Queensland,

298a TRAILL
line 7 *delete* and London
line 11 *delete* (Westeve)
line 13 *for* 1790- *read* 1793-
298b line 15 *for* New Year's *read* Boxing
line 52 *for* 6d. *read* 6d.,

305b TRUGERNANNER
line 32 *for* -51 *read* -47

311b TURNER, C.
bibliog. line 6 for *Wisden's* read *Wisden*

320a TYSON
line 23 *for* £1000 *read* £2000 for two years

332b VERJUS
line 21 *for* Issoudoun, France, *read* Oleggio, Piedmont,

344b WALKER
line 20 *for* (1906) *read* (1890)

356b WARREN
line 9 *for* Wolverhampton *read* Wolverton

365a WATT
line 30 *for* 1863 *read* 1866

369b WEARNE
line 1 *for* St Levan *read* Ponsanooth

375a WEEKES
line 36 *for* -57 *read* -53

379b WESTGARTH
line 14 *for* 11 *read* 23
380a line 40 *for* mid- *read* November

389a WHITE, J. C.
line 12 *for* and *read* but
line 13 *for* stock *read* works
389b line 2 *for* about 1850 *read* in June 1854

400a WILKIE
line 43 *delete* and later . . . Club

407a WILLIAMSON
lines 59-64 *for* That . . . Ltd; *read* In 1910 a proprietary company J. C. Williamson Ltd was formed with Ramaciotti as managing director; next year the company absorbed (Sir Rupert) Clarke and (Clyde) Meynell Pty Ltd;

409b WILLOUGHBY
bibliog. line 2 *for* Mercer *read* Nurser

409b WILLS
line 3 *for* August *read* December
410a line 1 *after* Melbourne *insert* Cricket

412a WILSHIRE
bibliog. line 7 *for* 1950 *read* 1850

418b WILSON, S.
*line 46 *for* Yanco on the Murrumbidgee River *read* Yanko on the Yanko Creek

425b WINTER, S. P.
line 20 *after* eldest *insert* surviving

428b WISE
line 49 *for* Jefferies *read* Jeffreys

429a WISE, G.
line 12 *for* Muswellbrook *read* Scone

433b WOOD
line 39 *for* -08 *read* -09

441b WRIGHT
line 12 *for* At 9 *read* In boyhood

454a YOUNG
line 7 *for* 1890- *read* 1880-

Volume 7: 1891-1939 A-Ch

xiiib AUTHORS
line 59 *for* GUNSON, Neil *read* GUNSON, Niel

xiva line 59 *for* HOWARD, M. G. *read* HOWARD, M. J.

2b ABBOTT, P.
lines 5-6 *delete* , and grandson of Edward Abbott [q.v.1]

3a lines 14-16 *for* That year . . . later *read* He was appointed to command the 63rd Battalion, but it was disbanded before seeing action, and he served in France

7a ABIGAIL
lines 6-7 *delete* As 'Zero' . . . (1901).

27b ALBERT
line 6 *for* Maria *read* Mary
line 7 *for* Allen *read* Allan

37b ALLAN, R.
lines 6-9 *for* the Brisbane . . . matriculated *read* Scots College, Sydney, and Brisbane Grammar School, matriculating

40a ALLARD
line 12 *for* Conves *read* Couves

59b ANDERSON, J.
line 18 *for* omittted *read* omitted

64a ANDERSON
line 18 *for* Welch *read* Walsh

65a ANDRADE
line 50 *for* cemetary *read* cemetery

66b ANDREWS, C.
line 1 *for* PATON *read* PAYTON

94a ARGYLE
line 31 *after* Montford *insert* [q.v.]

99b ARNOLD, R.
line 7 *for* 187178 *read* 1871-78

102a ARTEM (Cross Reference)
line 1 *for* SERGEEV *read* SERGEYEV

114a ASHTON, J. R.
line 5 *delete* Florentine
line 6 *after* Count *insert* Carlo *and after* Rossi *insert* , a Sardinian diplomat

115a line 34 *for* Kensingto *read* Kensington

117a ASPINALL
line 5 *delete* an Australian-born

122a ATKINSON
bibliog. line 5 *for* formal *read* Formal

123a AUSTIN
line 58 *for* 1913- *read* 1910-

134a BAILEY
lines 1-3 *for* About 1879 . . . founded *read* By 1871 he was in Sydney with his mother; she remarried in 1879 and about 1886 founded what became

138b BAILLIEU
line 7 *for* England *read* Wales

141a line 54 *for* 1906 *read* 1905

148a BAINTON
line 23 *for* Sawell *read* Saywell

167b BARACCHI
line 10 *for* conferred upon *read* appointed *and after* him *insert* a commander of
line 11 *delete* of Knight Commander

176b BARLOW
line 19 *delete* successfully
line 20 *for* incomes *read* accounts

181a BARNES
line 39 *for* J. *read* A. N.

184a BARR SMITH (Cross Reference)
**line 1 *delete* SIR
**line 2 *delete* SIR

189a BARRETT, J. W.
line 25 *for* cemetary *read* cemetery

198b BARTON
line 8 *for* (Earl) *read* (Sir John)

199b line 2 *after* pay *insert* 3 per cent annually on

208a BATES
line 16 *after* [q.v.]. *insert* On 13 March 1884, at Charters Towers, Daisy May O'Dwyer married Edwin Henry Murrant. It is almost certain that this was Harry Harbord Morant [q.v.]. Shortly afterwards, he and Daisy separated.

212b BATTYE
line 16 *delete* (Earl)

216a BAVIN
line 6 *for* 1934-41 *read* 1936-40

220a BAYLES
line 50 *for* 82 640 *read* £82 640

222b BAYNTON
line 20 *for* 'Scrammy' *read* 'Scrammy 'and'
line 55 *for* Cinese *read* Chinese

228a BEAN
line 40 *for* 1942 *read* 1943

230b BEAR (BEAR-CRAWFORD)
line 41 *after* Suffrage *insert* (Franchise)

232b BEARDSMORE
    bibliog. line 2 *for* 1938 *read* 1968

238b BECKE
    line 60 *for* bankruptm *read* bank-
    rupt.

239a bibliog. line 9 *for* A. G. *read* B.
    bibliog. line 10 *for* Stephens *read*
    Stevens

240a BECKETT
    lines 52-54 *for* held . . . Works *read*
    was honorary minister

240b BEDFORD
    line 13 *for* Surrey *read* Suffolk

245b BEEBY
    line 59 *for* 2 August *read* 21 July
246b bibliog. line 8 *for* (1962) *read*
    (1953)

254a BELL
    lines 22 and 57 *for* McNab *read*
    Macnab

271a BENNETT
    line 6 *for* R. M. Schenk *read* R. S.
    Schenk [q.v.]

274b BERNACCHI
    line 1 *for* GUILIO *read* GIULIO

275b BERNACCHI, L.
    line 4 *for* Guilio *read* Giulio

283a BETTS
    line 6 *before* grandson *insert* great-

313b BLACKET
    line 57 *for* wisdon *read* wisdom

315b BLACKLOW
    line 42 *for* a. *read* and

318b BLAIR
    line 34 *for* MacLeod *read* Macleod
    [q.v.]
    line 38 *for* MacLeod *read* Macleod

334b BOISMENU
    line 7 *after* Congregation *insert* of the
    Missionaries

340b BONYTHON
    line 10 *delete* (Earl)

342a BONYTHON
    line 57 *for* Kim *read* Kym

352a BOSCH
    line 44 *for* 1927 *read* 1928
    line 45 *for* chairs *read* a chair

363a BOWLES
    line 41 *for* Canberra *read* Aus-
    tralian
    line 44 *for* Memories *read* Memory
363b line 3 *for* Memories *read* Memory
    line 12 *for* 1935 *read* 1937

369b BOYCE, F.
    line 37 *for* 1940 *read* 1934

375a BOYD
    **line 2 *for* A widower . . . years, *read*
    His wife died in 1916 and

409a BRIDGES
    line 45 *delete* (Earl)

428a BROOKES
    line 24 *delete* first

430b BROOKMAN
    line 1 *after* Pearce *insert* [q.v.]
    line 49 *delete* (Earl)

439a BROWN, H. P.
    author *for* M. G. HOWARD *read* M. J.
    HOWARD

444b BROWN, M.
    lines 29-30 *for* Maria Montessori
    read Friedrich Froebel

468a BRUXNER
    lines 33-36 *for* 5th Australian . . .
    (New England) and *read* 6th Aus-
    tralian (New England) Light Horse
    redesignated the 5th the following
    year, he
    line 38 *for* his regiment *read* the 6th
    L.H.R., Australian Imperial Force,

484a BURGOYNE
    line 10 *for* Jervis *read* Lewis
    line 27 *for* His . . . died *read* He was
    divorced in 1871
    line 28 *delete* 1871
484b line 46 *for* three *read* eleven *and for*
    five *read* four

490a BURNS
    line 1 *for* Navigation *read* Shipping
491a line 43 *delete* south . . . Equator

509a BUTLER
    lines 16-18 *for* Failing . . . resigned
    read He resigned from the museum

522b CAHILL, P.
    bibliog. line 1 *for* 1979 *read* 1985

524b CAIRNS
    line 14 *for* 1925-26 *read* 1926-27

551a CAMPBELL
    lines 47-48 *for* Campbell . . . Hill *read*
    Campbell's wife took up shares in a
    company formed
    line 50 *for* his wife's *read* her
    line 51 *for* he *read* Campbell
    line 56 *for* Wingarra *read* Winga-
    rara
551b line 40 *for* 1915 *read* 1916
    line 46 *delete* winning

555b CANN
    line 33 *for* -1912 *read* -1913

561a CARINGTON
    line 20 *for* Brigade *read* Regiment

562a CARLTON
line 36 *for* 1930 *read* 1931
line 38 *for* 9.2 *read* 9.4

562b CARMICHAEL
line 4 *after* Carmichael, *insert* native-born
line 6 *delete* , both Scottish-born

567a CARNEGIE
line 13 *for* (Earl) *read* (Sir)

571a CARR
line 11 *delete* lieutenant

575a CARRUTHERS
line 50 *for* National Australasian *read* Australasian Federal
line 51 *for* March 1891 *read* September 1897

580a CARSON, D.
line 20 *for* Rompacy *read* Rompaey

586a CASE
line 24 *for* paler *read* paper

588b CASTLES
line 37 *for* Chapell *read* Chappell

606a CHAMPION DE CRESPIGNY
line 6 *for* Francis *read* Frances
line 7 *for* Chauncey *read* Chauncy

609a CHANTER
line 36 *delete* and agriculture

611a CHAPMAN, E.
line 15 *for* 1887 *read* 1884

Volume 8: 1891-1939 Cl-Gib

x COMMITTEES
line 9 *for* O'Hagen *read* O'Hagan

12b CLARK
lines 13-14 *delete* and . . . stamp

28a CLENDINNEN
lines 40-44 *delete* Both . . . Paris.

32b CLUNE
line 6 *for* 1897 *read* 1879

49b COGHLAN
line 47 *for* December 1905 *read* February 1906

70b COLLIER
lines 39-40 *for* December . . . referendum, *read* March 1918
line 42 *after* utterances *insert* during the second conscription referendum

73a COLLINGRIDGE DE TOURCEY
line 45 *after* founded *insert* one of
line 46 *for* Club *read* clubs

105a COOPER
line 3 *for* Luton *read* Chatham

120a COTTON
line 1 *for* At the 1894 *read* Defeated in 1894, at the 1895
line 4 *delete* from 1895

129b COX, E.
**line 3 *for* Langharne *read* Laugharne

135a CRAIGIE
bibliog. line 1 *delete* NSW Public Service Board, *and after* Progress *insert* (Melb)

140b CRAWFORD, T.
line 5 *for* eldest *read* youngest *and for* fifth *read* ninth

145a CRESWELL
line 31 *for* Cresswell *read* Creswell
145b line 53 *for* Cresswell *read* Creswell

159b CROSSLEY
line 42 *for* 1907-08 *read* 1908-09

161a CROUCH
line 6 *after* youngest *insert* government

168b CULLEN
line 26 *for* the McGowen [q.v.] government's *read* acting Premier W. A. Holman's [q.v.]
line 28 *for* dissolved *read* prorogued

185a CUSSEN
lines 29-30 *delete*, S. H. Z. Woinarski and G. Piggott

196a DALLAS
line 35 *for* 279 cm *read* 188 cm

199b DALRYMPLE
line 6 *for* predeceased *read* survived

203b DANEŠ
line 22 *for* 1910 *read* 1909

207a DARCY
line 16 *for* cognescenti *read* cognoscenti

212a DARLING
line 5 *after* retiring *insert* (temporarily)
line 33 *for* Assembly *read* Council

220b DAVID
line 2 *for* -26 *read* -27

223b DAVIDSON, C.
**line 4 *after* second *insert* surviving

229b DAVIDSON, W.
line 29 *for* 180 *read* 183

256b DEAMER
**line 5 *for* 1906 *read* 1907
**lines 15-16 *for* 8 August 1907 *read* 26 August 1908

line 21 *for* Macintosh *read* McIntosh

265a DE BERNALES
line 17 *for* Hill *read* Bill

270b DE GARIS
line 32 *for*, and next year established *read*. From 1883 he had been prominent in

302b DICKINSON, S.
line 4 *for* H. W. *read* Kirk White
line 7 *after* degree. *insert* On 5 September 1876 at Northampton, Massachusetts, Sidney married Minnie Stockwell (d. 1877); on 1 October 1879 he married Marion Miller.

303a lines 45-46 *for* It is . . . America, but *read* The Dickinsons left Melbourne in March 1893, returning to Philadelphia where
line 51 *for* son. *read* daughter.

316a DODS
line 11 *for* 1880 *read* 1879

317a line 17 *after* Spain *insert* [q.v.]

324b DOOLEY
line 56 *for* 21 December *read* 20 December
line 63 *for* Ligouri *read* Liguori

330b DOWNER
line 5 *for* J. & G. *read* G. & J.

340b DRAKE-BROCKMAN, F.
line 21 *for* 1875 *read* 1876

374b DUNN
line 48 *for* August *read* July

380a DUNSTAN, E.
**line 3 *for* Kirkhampton *read* Kilkhampton

388b DWYER
line 21 *for* Ligouri *read* Liguori
line 58 *for* Ligouri *read* Liguori

393b DYER
line 16 *for* 1933 *read* 1932
line 23 *for* taught at *read* attended

398b DYSON
line 37 *for* -1953 *read* -1952

402a EARLE
lines 12-13 *for* Waratah *read* Franklin

402a EARP
line 5 *for* Shetton *read* Shelton

418b EDWARDS, L.
line 46 *for* 10 *read* 17

441b ESTELL
line 1 *for* 1938 *read* 1928

456a FAHEY
line 3 *for* Rossmore *read* Glenough

457a FAIRBAIRN
line 49 *delete* 1890 and

468a FARNELL
line 20 *for* 1891 *read* 1894

484b FERGUSON, D.
line 2 *for* 1926 *read* 1921
line 3 *for* Ligouri *read* Liguori
line 4 *for* Brigid *read* Bridget

489b FETHERSTON
line 47 *after* retired *insert* after defeat

491a FIASCHI
line 39 *for* commander *read* officer

507a FISHER
line 56 *for* 30 *read* 27

509b FISK
line 13 *for* Engineersn *read* Engineers,
line 15 *for* 1951m In 1o23 *read* 1951. In 1923
line 21 *for* 192on *read* 1929,

523a FLETCHER
line 1 *for* BRUNSDEN *read* BRUNSDON

528a FLIERL
lines 3-4 *for* Wilhelm Kelhofer. *read* Georg Pilhofer.

530a FLOWERS
line 5 *for* 70 *read* 54

531a FLOYD
line 3 *for* choral *read* carol

536a FOLEY (Cross Reference)
**line 1 *for* GRIFFEN-FOLEY *read* GRIFFEN FOLEY

545b FORREST
lines 33-34 *for* They . . . flourish *read* While they live they flourish

554b FORSYTH
line 49 *for* 1918 *read* 1922

573b FRANKLIN
line 8 *for* Karl *read* Carl

574b FRANKLIN
line 33 *for* Adams's *read* Addams's

594b FULLER, B.
**line 9 *for* Garnet- *read* Garnet

595b FULLER, G.
line 13 *for* many *read* some
line 17 *for* never *read* rarely

596a line 20 *for* September *read* October
lines 55-56 *after* October *insert* 1921
line 57 *delete* Liberal

596b line 34 *for* 1924 *read* 1925

598b FULLWOOD
line 9 *for* 1881 *read* 1883

600b FURPHY
line 50 *for* father . . . family *read* brother John in his

601a line 20 *delete* in Shepparton

601b line 42 *for* 1912 *read* 1905-06

622b GARRAN
lines 29-32 *delete* He . . . matters'.

640b GEPP
line 17 *for* nights *read* mornings
line 23 *for* 1896 *read* 1898

654a GIBSON
author *for* ATCHINSON *read* ATCHISON

660b GIBSON
lines 11-12 *for* began the teaching *read* became the first full-time teacher

Volume 9: 1891-1939 Gil-Las

x COMMITTEES
line 9 *for* O'Hagen *read* O'Hagan

xvb AUTHORS
after line 22 *insert* McGILL, Mary-anne: *Laffer.*

13a GILLOTT
line 18 *for* Crocker *read* Croker

31a GLYNN
lines 34-35 *delete* —the first . . . suffrage

34a GOBLE
line 50 *for* 1926 *read* 1925

53a GORDON, J.
line 14 *for* fop *read* for

59b GOULD, A.
lines 16-17 *for* 1876, he . . . fortune. *read* 1894, he made his fortune from copper.

70a GRAINGER
lines 59-60 *for* , but . . . known. *read* with Georg Widmann.

71a lines 18-19 *for* in February *read* on 7 January

87b GRAYSON
**line 53 *for* French *read* Pomeranian

107a GRIFFEN FOLEY
**line 17 *delete* [q.v.]

142b GUNN
bibliog. line 10 *for* Univ Adel *read* Flinders Univ

149a HACKETT
line 7 *for* 1878 *read* 1876

153a HACKETT, W.
line 8 *for* 1689 *read* 1690

153b line 21 *for* John's *read* Joan's

183b HANCOCK
line 12 *for* 1885 *read* 1886
line 26 *for* 1920 *read* 1922
line 33 *after* August *insert* 1896

184a line 6 *for* 1925 *read* 1924
line 9 *for* 1918 *read* 1917

212a HARRIS, L.
lines 10-12 *delete* His . . . Paris.

212b HARRIS, M.
line 32 *for* Mary *read* Nancy

224a HARVEY
line 27 *after* Rich *insert* [q.v.]
line 28 *delete* [qq.v.]

234b HAWKER, H.
lines 17-18 *for* as . . . reach *read* at over

254a HENDERSON
line 12 *delete* ; M.A., 1901
line 24 *after* 1898 *insert* ; M.A., 1901
line 64 *delete* the

254b lines 1-2 *for* Murray . . . Tinline [q.v.6], *read* (Sir) George Murray [q.v.] to establish the Tinline scholarship to commemorate his mother's family name,

255a line 18 *for* Port *read* Lake

262b HENNESSY, A.
line 9 *for* 1969 *read* 1959

283b HIGGINS
line 17 *for* Later that year *read* In late 1905
**line 18 *for* Cozens *read* Cosens

306b HINKLER
line 60 *for* Maud *read* Maude

323b HOGAN
line 1 *for* EDMUND *read* EDMOND
line 6 *for* Edmund *read* Edmond
line 9 *for* Edmund *read* Edmond

344b HOLMAN
line 18 *for* 12 appointments in 1911-12 *read* 11 appointments in 1912
line 19 *for* 70 *read* 59

345b line 23 *for* be *read* he

363a HOPETOUN
line 61 *delete* of state

367b HORN
line 4 *for* eldest *read* second

371b HOSKINS
line 44 *for* Esbank *read* Eskbank

392b HUGHES
line 34 *for* and Waddell [qq.v.] *read* , Carruthers and Wade [qq.v.11,7,12]

396a HUGHES
line 54 *for* W. M. *read* W. F.

398a line 2 *for* president *read* premier
399b line 49 for *Politicians* read *Policies*
412b HURLEY
      line 4 *for* on the *read* at
      line 5 *for* plateau *read* Plateau
420a HYDE
      line 3 *for* Southampton *read* Portsmouth
439a IRVINE, R.
      lines 13-14 *for* and three sons *read* , two sons and a daughter
459b JACKSON
      line 10 for *zoological* read *oological*
481b JENSEN, H.
      line 6 *for* accidental electrocution *read* sustaining burns in a grass fire
491a JOHN
      **line 3 *for* Hirwaun *read* Hirwain
545a KEENAN
      lines 33-34 *for* was . . . landslide *read* did not contest the election
552a KELLY, A. E. B.
      line 28 *after* Weatherly *insert* [q.v. Lionel Weatherly]
574b KERNOT
      line 35 *for* -1963 *read* -1958
595b KING, G. (Cross Reference)
      lines 1-2 *delete in toto*
595b KING, H.
      line 7 *delete* [q.v.]
642a LACEY
      line 18 *for* Premier's *read* Premiers'
652b LAMBIE
      lines 45-46 *for* Greek into English *read* English into Greek
655a LANCASTER, G. B. (Cross Reference)
      lines 1-2 *delete in toto*
658b LANE
      lines 40-43 *delete* founded . . . and
663a LANG
      lines 29-31 *delete* , after . . . leadership
      line 53 *for* January *read* February
671a LANGWELL
      bibliog. line 6 *for* Mrs W. J. *read* Mr W. J.

Volume 10: 1891-1939 Lat-Ner

ix   COMMITTEES
      line 16 *for* O'Hagen *read* O'Hagan
3b   LATHAM
      **lines 42-43 *delete* Pankhurst
4b   line 56 *for* introduced *read* was responsible for

line 57 *for* Financial Agreement Enforcement Act *read* Financial Agreements Enforcement Acts
      line 57-58 *for* in 1931 *read* of 1932
81a   LEVERRIER
      lines 55-56 *delete* , the day France fell,
100a LIGUORI (Cross Reference)
      line 2 *for* BRIGID MARY *read* BRIDGET
106a LINDSAY
      line 15 *for* Next year *read* In 1885-86
      lines 55-58 *for* he dismissed . . . officers. *read* four of his party resigned.
106b lines 2-4 *delete* In 1892 . . . society.
      line 38 *delete* two of
      bibliog. line 9 for *New York* read *NT*
137b LONGFORD
      line 28 *for* Cozens *read* Cosens
165a LUCAS, W.
      line 7 *for* Australian Union Steamship *read* Australasian United Steam
      line 11 *for* Australian *read* Australasian
      line 16 *for* When *read* Before
      line 17 *after* was *insert* formally
      line 18 *after* Ltd *insert* , and after 1896 *delete* ,
165b line 27 *for* When *read* With
      lines 27-28 *for* succeeded in gaining *read* seeking
177b LYNCH
      lines 28-29 *delete* to Prime Minister Bruce [q.v.7]
205a McBEATH
      line 40 *delete* Pankhurst
211b MacCALLUM
      line 26 *for* the first such *read* an early
248b McDONALD
      line 58 *for* 1913 *read* 1914
252b McDONALD
      line 1 *delete* RICHARD
289b MACKAY
      line 19 *for* the Whites *read* Frank
302b MACKENNAL
      bibliog. line 2 for *techniques* read *tendencies*
311a MACKIE
      line 31 *for* Anne *read* Annie
321a McLACHLAN, D.
      **line 3 *for* probably in *read* on 24 April

359a MacPherson
line 30 *for* af *read* of

394a Mann, F.
bibliog. line 1 *for* F. H. *read* F. M.

401a Mannix
line 13 *for* soldier *read* sailor

419a Marriott (Cross Reference)
**line 1 *for* LOUISE *read* LOUISA

442b Mathews, H.
line 45 *for* inver *read* invar

470a Meagher, R.
lines 44-45 *for* an 1890 *read* a

473b Meares
line 38 *for* William *read* Thomas

483a Melrose
line 14 *for* 1892 *read* 1894

483b Melvin
line 36 *for* Sydney *read* Melbourne

498b Milerum
line 20 *for* on *read* an

532b Mitchell
**line 3 *for* Ballieston *read* Baillieston

552a Moncrieff
line 53 for *Collitt's* read *Collits'*
line 54 for *Collitt's* read *Collits'*

556a Monk
line 27 for *Collitt's* read *Collits'*

558b Montgomery, H.
line 1 *delete* Sir

562b Moore, C.
line 8 *for* 14 *read* 13
line 11 *for* 1896 *read* 1895

579a Moran
lines 53-54 *for* Sherwin *read* Sheerin

581b Morant
line 8 *for* He . . . when *read* When
line 9 *for* and enlisted *read* he enlisted in Adelaide

590b Morres
line 8 *for* Highton *read* Newtown
lines 52-53 *for* The Hermitage *read* Geelong Grammar School, Highton

657b Myer
**line 3 *for* Kritchev *read* Krichev
**line 4 *for* Moghilev *read* Mogilev
**line 10 *for* Mogilso *read* Krichev
**line 11 *for* Kritchev *read* Krichev
660b line 3 *for* Brighton *read* Melbourne general

665a Nanya
line 13 *for* Don *read* Dan

Volume 11: 1891-1939 Nes-Smi

45b Oakes, C.
line 18 *for* 1921 *read* 1920
line 19 *for* next year *read* in 1922

54b O'Connor, C.
author *after* Tauman *insert* *

70a Ogilvie, W.
line 21 *for* 1899 *read* 1889

78b Oldfield
line 48 *for* 1934 *read* 1933

84b O'Malley
line 60 *after* the *insert* former

115a Owen
line 22 *for* 1898 *read* 1899

122b Page, E.
line 28 *for* K.C.M.G. *read* G.C.M.G.

127b Palmer
lines 56-57 *for* permaent *read* permanent

140b Parkes
**line 3 *for* Skövda *read* Skövde

151a Partridge
line 18 *for* Ligouri *read* Liguori
line 27 *for* Ligouri *read* Liguori
151b line 31 *for* 31 June *read* 30 June
line 54 *for* Ligouri *read* Liguori

152b Partridge
line 39 *for* three novels *read* a collection of short stories
line 40 *after* Denison' *insert* and at least one novel

155a Paterson
line 12 *for* Hugh Salway *read* Herbert Salwey

163a Patten
line 14 *after* [q.v.], *insert* later

187a Pearson, A.
author *after* Jewell *insert* *

188a Pearson
line 24 *delete* Solvol

225 Running Head
for Picton *read* Piddington

226 Running Head
for Picton *read* Piddington

243b Plain
line 26 *for* Fienne *read* Feinne

324a Rae
**lines 16-17 *for* Masters' and Servants' Act (1856) *read* Masters and Servants Act (1857)

352b Reid
line 31 *for* by adopting a *read* . He had previously attacked Labor's

364b RENTOUL
line 31 *for* 1912. *read* 1920.

365b RESCH
**lines 6-7 *delete* Dortmund-

370a RIBUSH
line 11 *delete* , about Eureka,

403b RIX NICHOLAS (Cross Reference)
**line 2 *delete* RIX

428b ROBINSON, W.
line 4 *for* BENNET *read* BENNETT

463b ROTH
lines 51-52 for *Melbidis* read *Melbidir*

474b RUBIN
**line 4 *for* Salant *read* Salantai

512b SALMOND
line 1 *for* 1855 *read* 1876
lines 2-3 *for* of philosophy . . . University of *read* at the Theological Hall,

515b SANDERSON
line 13 *for Christchurch read* Christchurch
line 18 *for Christchurch read* Christchurch

525b SAVAGE
line 2 *for* Labor *read* Labour

549b SCOTT, W. H.
line 3 *for* Omaru *read* Oamaru

555a SCULLIN
lines 17-18 *for* abolition *read* suspension

580a SHARP
line 28 *for* two operettas *read* an operetta
line 29 *for* texts *read* a text
lines 30-31 *delete* , and *The* . . . Next year
line 31 *before* he *insert* . In 1892

649b SMITH, I.
line 16 *for* Department *read* Board

649b SMITH, I. B.
line 30 *after* poverty- *insert* stricken children. After further mothers'

655b SMITH
line 30 *for* a.m. *read* p.m.

Volume 12: 1891-1939 Smy-Z

5a SMYTHE
**line 37 *for* Halle *read* Hallé

6a SNOOK
**line 31 *for* -commander *read* -commodore

21a SOUTER, C.
**lines 35-36 *delete* and the . . . Authors,

22a SOUTHERN
**line 24 *for* Grosvernor *read* Grosvenor

26b SPAULL
**line 15 *for* anomolies *read* anomalies

78b STEVENS, E.
**line 20 *for* Athanaeum *read* Athenaeum

88a STEWART
**line 55 *for* Roseveare *read* Rosevear

99a STONE
**line 24 *after* Singleton's *insert* [q.v.6]

100a STONE, L.
**lines 24-25 *for* Marshall *read* Marshal

112b STORY
**line 5 *after* Jones *insert* [q.v.9]

127b STUART, F.
**line 28 *after* Glass *insert* [q.v.9]

130b STUART
**line 18 *delete* from 1891

134a SUGDEN
**line 46 *for* nonconformist *read* Nonconformist
**line 49 *for* Peoples' *read* People's

143b SUTTON, H.
**line 1 *delete* VINCENT

155a SYME, Geoffrey
**line 6 *for* K.C.M.G. *read* K.B.E.

156a SYMON
**line 54 *for* league *read* League

167b TARCZYNSKI
**line 38 *for* is *read* was

189a TAZEWELL
**line 3 *for* Newtown *read* New Town

222a THRING, W.
**line 34 *for* stragegy *read* strategy

230b TILDESLEY
**line 6 for *Beckitt's* read *Beckett's*

231a **bibliog. line 17 *for* Kensington *read* South Yarra

235b TISHLER
**line 41 *for* Fitzhenry *read* Fitz Henry

237a TIVEY
**bibliog. line 1 *for* A. E. *read* A. D.

259a TRENWITH
**line 26 *for* Workingman's *read* Working Men's
259b **line 62 *for* expulson *read* expulsion

287a TURNBULL, E.
**line 27 *for* 70 000 *read* thousands of

289b TURNER
**line 4 *for* Newtown *read* New Town

297b TURNER
**line 8 *for* School of Mines *read* Working Men's College

299a TWEDDLE
**bibliog. line 1 *for* G. A. L. *read* J. A. L.

317b VERBRUGGHEN
**line 20 *after* Cowen *insert* [q.v.3]

344b WADE
**lines 30-31 *for* palaeicthyologist *read* palaeichthyologist
**line 39 *for* Challows *read* Challoner's
**line 40 *for* Vallance *read* Valence

348b WAINWRIGHT
**line 39 *for* Australia *read* Australian

353b WALES
**lines 36-37 *for* nominated *read* elected

354b WALEY
**line 38 *for* Miner's *read* Miners'

358a WALKER
**line 19 *for* E. V. *read* (Sir) Edwin

363b WALL
**line 3 *for* Kilburnie *read* Kilbirnie

383b WARD
**line 58 *for* Mackay *read* McKay

417b WATTERSTON
**bibliog. line 4 *for* (Perth) *read* (Syd)

426b WEBB
**line 48 *for* aquaintance *read* acquaintance

439b WELLISH
**line 14 *for* Thompson's *read* Thomson's
**lines 18-19 *for* Thompson *read* Thomson

472a WHITE, M.
**line 11 *for* 1idwife *read* midwife

506a WILLIAMS, S.
**line 5 *after* Williams *insert* [q.v.]

519b WILSON
**line 21 *after* Crawford *insert* [q.v.8]

520a WILSON, D. L.
**line 40 *for* des la Société *read* de la Société
**line 51 *for* Branton *read* Brunton [q.v.7]

543b WINTER
**line 5 *for* 1899 *read* 1889

555a WOLFE
**line 12 *for* wonder fully *read* wonderfully

561b WOODHOUSE
**line 36 *for* Hasting's *read* Hastings's

563b WOODRUFF
**bibliog. line 8 *for* Engles *read* Engel

579a WREFORD
**line 18 *for* dynamnic *read* dynamic

588b WUNDERLICH
**line 19 *for* Barotra *read* Borotra

592b WYNNE, W.
**lines 31-32 *for* fundamentallly *read* fundamentally

599b YOUNG, W. B.
**line 35 *after* Fawkner's *insert* [q.v.1]

605b ZEAL
**line 48 *for* coined *read* used